Justice for Victims of Crime

Albin Dearing

Justice for Victims of Crime

Human Dignity as the Foundation of Criminal Justice in Europe

Springer

Albin Dearing
Freedom and Justice Department
European Union Agency for Fundamental Rights
Vienna, Austria

ISBN 978-3-319-45046-9 ISBN 978-3-319-45048-3 (eBook)
DOI 10.1007/978-3-319-45048-3

Library of Congress Control Number: 2016952526

Printed on acid-free paper

This Springer imprint is published by Springer Nature
The registered company is Springer International Publishing AG
The registered company address is: Gewerbestrasse 11, 6330 Cham, Switzerland

Für Helene, Johannes und Mateo

Preface

What this Book is About?

In a sense, this book suggests a redefinition of the term 'crime'. Currently, 'crime' denotes a violation of criminal law provisions. This book claims that 'crime' should be understood as the violation of the human rights of an individual (or of individuals) and that the responses to criminal offences should reflect this understanding.

To give an example, if a person threatens another with a gun demanding that she hand over her money, this would commonly be seen as a violation of a criminal code's legal provision prohibiting armed robbery. However, it is suggested here that this incident should primarily be interpreted as a violation of an individual's rights not to be threatened with violence and to the respect of her property, as well as a behaviour that is disrespectful to this individual as a person. Hence, what this book maintains is that the crime of armed robbery should not be reduced to the violation of a (nation) state's laws, but should appreciate what it means to the victim as a person and member of the human family—the violation of her dignity and rights.

Based on a sketch of a human-rights based criminal justice system previously published by the author (2003), this book makes an effort to elaborate this redefinition of 'crime'—as a rights violation beyond a law violation—because unless 'crime' is defined in a manner relating it to the rights and personhood of an individual (or individuals), courts will fail to deliver justice to victims, and the rights of victims will not fully materialise. Only once we acknowledge what the criminal offence means to the victim as a person holding rights and that the victim, for what the offence means to her, is entitled to the solidarity of her legal community, will rights of victims become a significant part of the everyday reality of criminal justice in Europe.

Hence, this book is about victims of crime and victims of severe human rights violations and about how these two categories can be inextricably linked to one another by a re-conceptualisation of 'crime'. Any effective system of human rights, so it is maintained, is dependent on criminal law protection. However, to effectively protect human rights, mere legal provisions are not enough. If the police, public prosecutors' offices and criminal courts fail to bring offenders to justice, if, in other words, *impunity* of severe human rights violations prevails, then, consequently, the human rights of individuals to life, physical integrity, autonomy, and property erode and lose their value, credibility and practical meaning. What then is at stake and what criminal justice defends is the authority and effectiveness of a system of human rights. Criminal justice is an indispensable means of avoiding a situation where those responsible for severe human rights violations are not held to account, victims are not recognised and redressed and human rights are not defended and preserved.

The reverse dependency of criminal law and criminal justice on human rights is of a different nature. While human rights cannot be *effective* without criminal justice, criminal justice—so it will be argued—cannot be *justified* in a convincing manner except as a means of protecting human dignity and human rights. In a society committed to human dignity as its moral and political basis, the only convincing justification of criminal justice rests in its contribution to the protection of human dignity and human rights.

In short, what should be recognised as the legitimate objective of criminal justice is human rights protection, because criminal justice is, on the one hand, indispensable in this role and, on the other, without any legitimation to exist beyond this function. As will be seen, this human rights protection centres on human dignity, in which the victim and the offender share. Therefore, in the following chapters much revolves around the concepts of punishment and human dignity and how these two concepts interlink in a proper concept of 'crime'.

The Traditional View and a Fresh Start

Many academics and practitioners working in the field of criminal justice do not support this interpretation of criminal law. In their opinion, it is not the victim of a severe human rights violation, but the state that is entitled to the punishment of the offender; the reason being that the offence is viewed as essentially not an infringement of human rights, but a violation of a state's criminal law provisions protecting public order and public interests.

However, according to consistent case-law of the European Court of Human Rights in Strasbourg (ECtHR) the right to an effective remedy under Article 13 of the European Convention on Human Rights (ECHR) grants certain rights to victims of serious human rights violations (see FRA 2014, pp. 25–28). In addition to the payment of compensation where appropriate, this comprises a right to "a thorough and effective investigation capable of leading to the identification and punishment of those responsible," including effective access for the victim to the procedure (*CLR*, para. 149). Unfortunately, the police and prosecutors are not always in a position to establish the evidence required to bring offenders to justice, but in any case authorities must observe due diligence (*Virabyan*, para. 178). In the words of the ECtHR (*Mustafa Tunç*, para. 173), the "obligation to conduct an effective investigation is an obligation not of result but of means: the authorities must take the reasonable measures available to them to secure evidence concerning the incident at issue."

Hence, what is referred to in the title of this book as justice for victims of crime has a firm basis in the right of a victim of a severe human rights violation to the competent authorities' best efforts to ensure that offenders are identified, prosecuted, convicted and, in appropriate cases, also punished. This book does not ask primarily whether victims of severe human rights violations are entitled to the identification, prosecution and punishment of offenders, as abundant case-law of the ECtHR provides sufficient evidence in this respect already. Instead, it enquires into the rationale of these rights and how this rationale relates these rights to the tasks of criminal justice. In the traditional perspective, the core task of criminal justice is the preservation of a state's criminal law provisions, challenged by criminal offences. If that is followed, then paying attention to the rights of victims, at best, complements, and is incidental to, the task of criminal justice, which however is primarily about convicting and sentencing offenders in the public interest represented by the state. If, on the other hand, a crime is a violation of the rights of an individual, who for that reason is acknowledged as the victim of that crime, then the victim and her rights to the identification, conviction and, in appropriate cases, also punishment of offenders move from the sidelines to the centre stage. As will be seen, it is exactly because the offender violated fundamental rights of the victim that the offender deserves to be convicted and punished. In any case, all depends on how one conceptualises the notion of a 'crime'.

In legal terms, victims' rights are, first, a matter of substantive, not of procedural law, a matter, that is, of what constitutes a crime and which rights result from the fact that a crime has been committed. The ECtHR insists that victims should have effective access to the investigation procedure. However, it is hardly promising to introduce the victim to criminal proceedings if these proceedings, in the understanding of the acting professionals, are not about the rights of individuals, but about public interests. On the other hand, if the proceedings are about the violation of the victim's rights and status as a person, victims' procedural rights would merely reflect this fact.

In other words, contradictory answers to the question of the appropriate role of victims in criminal proceedings originate from a deeper disagreement over the subject matter of criminal justice, of what, that is, constitutes a crime. In the traditional perspective, criminal offences are violations of a state's criminal law provisions, and consequently criminal justice is fundamentally a matter between the offender and the state. Criminal justice, in this perspective, does not concern the victim as an individual rights-holder, but at best as a witness and bystander. Hence, there is little to be gained in implanting the victim in the traditional system of criminal justice.

Victims' rights are not merely about painting the victim into the old scenery of criminal justice, but about reconstructing criminal justice on a new basis. What hence can explain criminal lawyers' reluctance to reorient criminal justice towards the objective of protecting human rights is the fact that, to affiliate the criminal justice system to a new objective, a few superficial corrections of criminal procedural law are indeed not sufficient. What is required is a new conceptualisation of criminal justice from scratch on an entirely different foundation: from criminal justice protecting the law and public interests of a society to criminal justice protecting the dignity and rights of individuals.

This book aims to begin work on this fundamental reconstruction and to help pave the way to a criminal justice system based on a concept of human dignity and human rights. For this purpose, the relevant human rights of individuals are analysed. The right, that is, of a crime victim to the conviction and, in appropriate cases, also punishment of the offender, the right of an offender to, by being punished, take responsibility and on this basis come to terms with her society, as well as the legitimate interest of all other members of the legal community to trust in the effective protection of their rights, equal to the rights of victims and offenders. Taking all these rights seriously in rebuilding criminal justice requires the readiness to question many traits of the existing system, including those that today appear as unquestionable and a matter of course. It requires the willingness, that is, to give up cherished assumptions and concepts.

To this end, a broader concept of criminal justice is endorsed, which advocates that consideration should be given not only to the legal issue of a criminal law infringement, but also to those individuals of flesh and blood whose rights have been violated. To this, traditionalist opponents answer that victims indeed deserve to be supported and compensated, but that neither of these tasks would necessarily be dealt with by the criminal justice system. Support is primarily a matter of establishing appropriate victim support services and offering therapies, and compensation of damages relating to civil rather than criminal law and justice.

However, what the approach presented in the following chapters highlights as the central focus, is not the damage or harm suffered by the victim, but the *wrong* that constitutes both a severe human rights violation and a criminal offence. This wrong done against the victim, unlike 'damage' and 'harm', is a thoroughly normative, not an empirical or descriptive, category. What constitutes the wrong suffered by the victim is the violation of her rights.

The wrong done against the victim is thus on the one hand a normative category, but on the other it is situated at the level of real normative interaction and communication. The wrong is what the offence *means* to the victim and what must not pass *uncontradicted*. Wronging, charging, prosecuting, defending, convicting, sentencing and punishing are all meaningful acts embedded in flows of real life communication and overall in the normative 'language game' of criminal justice (Dearing 2003).

Traditionally, the first question in criminal law theory asks why the state has the right to punish its citizens. However, from a human rights point of view this is the wrong question to ask. The state has only an instrumental status as a means of protecting the human rights of its citizens, where the term 'citizens' roughly refers to all the individuals who live on a state's territory under a legal order, including many who pay taxes to fund state institutions. A state does not hold rights against its citizens. From a human rights perspective, the question should be whether some individuals have a right to the conviction and, in appropriate cases, also punishment of others. Unless individuals have such rights, they cannot task the state with effecting them. Thus, a human rights-based approach to criminal justice is premised on the existence of rights of individuals, rather than states, to the punishment of offenders. The crucial question relates to the moral and political basis of such rights, and in particular to the foundation of a right of the victim to the conviction and punishment of the offender. Any reconstruction of criminal justice based on human dignity is necessarily premised on such rights.

Criminal justice can be conceived and legitimised as an institution protecting human rights against severe violations. After all, the entire normative order of the European Union is founded on human dignity and human rights. Criminal justice should not remain an exemption. Hence, the task is to construct a theory of criminal justice that comprehensively founds the rights of victims, offenders and all others on the same core principles of human dignity and human rights.

A Brief Overview

This book is organised in five chapters, where the first chapter formulates two questions—how to define 'crime' and how to justify punishment. The two core concepts needed to provide the answers, namely 'punishment' and 'human dignity', are clarified in the second and third chapter while the fourth chapter sets out to answer these questions. The fifth chapter reflects on the consequences of adopting the human rights-based approach put forward in this book.

The **first chapter** critically assesses the traditional paradigm of criminal justice and presents promising developments since the 1980s towards a human rights paradigm of criminal justice. In particular, the important developments originating from the ECtHR and other human rights actors are highlighted.

However, it shows that the initiatives of these human rights actors are not always based on a fully convincing theory of criminal justice. Whilst the ECtHR often stresses deterrence as the objective of criminal justice, it is questionable whether such an objective of punishment fits a human rights-based approach. Among theorists of criminal law there is a fairly wide-spread consensus that consequentialist theories of punishment—justifying criminal law and criminal justice by their beneficial consequences—are not able to demonstrate why punishment is not only useful but also just. In the history of criminal law theory this standard criticism has repeatedly been levelled against all utilitarian approaches, including, long ago, by Kant and Hegel as well as—much later—by Hart (1968) and many since.

Hence, what is an issue is the lack of a convincing theory of criminal justice that would conclusively integrate the victim and her rights in a comprehensive concept of criminal justice and punishment. What is needed is an explanation of why human dignity and human rights justify and even require convicting and punishing citizens; and when it comes to searching for a point of departure, the wrong done to the victim is a promising candidate.

Therefore, the following chapters compile and assemble components of a theory of criminal justice based on human dignity in general and on the victim's right to the conviction and, in appropriate cases, also punishment of the offender in particular.

The **second chapter** is inspired by the observation that punishment is a human universal, meaning that it exists, and has existed, in one form or another, in all known human societies as a mechanism aimed at preserving social norms by sanctioning infringements. Chapter 2 reflects on this universality and enquires into the basic mechanism underlying all punishment. One element is that only a mechanism ensuring that norm violations are sanctioned enables human societies to develop stable social norms of cooperation, including among strangers. Hence, societies are premised on their members' propensity to punish those who disregard social norms of fair cooperation.

This leads on to the question of how this general inclination to punish offenders can be explained. The answer is that individuals are motivated by powerful punitive sentiments, such as feelings of anger and resentment towards the offender. The wrong done to the victim establishes the crucial link between the offence as a norm violation and the punitive sentiments of the community, which ensure that the victim is supported in seeking redress for the wrong suffered.

However, an understanding of the social functions of punishment is not tantamount to its justification. What remains to be answered is the crucial question of which—if any—social norms are significant enough—and for what reason—to legitimise the punishment of infringements. Yet this question can only be asked meaningfully relative to a certain normative order. The function of punishment is to secure a society's normative basis, which obviously changes over time. This is the reason why making fun of the king means something different in times of an absolutist monarch and in a modern society, and burning the national flag is perceived differently in a closed state based on national pride compared to a liberal pluralist society. Therefore, the **third chapter** clarifies the characteristics of a society committed to the values of human dignity and human rights.

This commences with an appreciation of Kant's view that what lies at the heart of human dignity is individual autonomy, but proceeds to reject the Kantian notion of autonomy as a capability inherent in all human beings. Instead Fichte's view is adopted in assuming that human beings are born without the ability to master normative categories and in fact without the language-based ability of agency altogether. Only by being called on by their society—based on its normative order—do humans develop as persons in a world of normative and cultural categories. It follows that all social institutions, including the criminal justice system, are tied to the normative framework of their societies and their evolution. Punishment develops in relation to the normative order it preserves and has to be analysed strictly as a function of a wider normative framework. As concerns contemporary societies, it is suggested to denote as 'humanist' a society that is strictly based on human dignity and constructed to foster the development of human beings as respected, autonomous and accountable persons. Within the framework of a humanist society the notion of 'crime' is to be defined in relation to human dignity and human rights.

From this, the **fourth chapter** presents an updated definition of 'crime' and spells out a justification of punishment within the normative order of a decent - humanist - society, a society, that is, which is oriented towards progressively making human dignity and human rights a reality. It shows that such a normative order is confronted with the particular challenge of what is coined 'Kant's principle' and considers how to justify punishment in relation to an offender who is entitled to autonomy, to be treated, that is, by her own laws. From this challenge results a sharp limitation of the legitimacy of criminal justice, namely its restriction to only preserve those preconditions on which human dignity is premised.

What, at this stage of a society's normative development forms the core element of any justification of punishment, is the right of the victim of a human rights violation to an effective remedy, ensuring that the offender is required to right the wrong done to the victim and to also make amends to all other members of the legal community. However, it will be maintained that the victim's rights alone do not justify the conviction and punishment of offenders. What is decisive is the offender's own right to be treated as an accountable person. The victim's right to justice and the offender's right to be respected as an accountable person are intrinsically interrelated and mutually reinforcing. However, they both flow from the same principle of human dignity.

The **fifth chapter** concludes this book by summarising its line of argument and by highlighting some significant characteristics of a human rights-based approach to criminal justice as compared to traditional views. It insists that more room should be left for the participation of the victim and the offender, to whom the offence 'belongs' as a significant element of their biography.

The Political Dimension

Could this book have been written 60 years ago? Probably not. The human rights perspective on criminal justice has become possible—and necessary—because of a fundamental change of the socio-political environment in which the institutions of criminal justice are embedded. Conceptualising criminal justice as an indispensable means of human rights protection suggests itself because of the recent success of human dignity and human rights as a moral and political founding concept apt to serve as the basis for constructing a global humanist society that overcomes its historical predecessors—the authoritarian and the liberal, value-neutral nation state. The rise of human rights after the 1960s coincided with the decline of the post-Second World War global order that was based mainly on the relations between sovereign nation states and their loyal citizens, in any case on a nation state-centred political system.

As a response to Nazism and Auschwitz, the concepts of human dignity and human rights elaborating on human dignity have been in the air since 1945 and the basis of the moral consensus defined in the Universal Declaration of Human Rights (UDHR), which was the immediate answer to fascism and the Shoah (Mosink 1999 provides a detailed analysis of how the UDHR reacts to Nazi totalitarianism). But it was only two decades later that, in a situation of socio-political unrest and turmoil, these concepts emerged as the only remaining credible ideology that is apt to serve as a basis for constructing a peaceful global order (Moyn 2012, 2014, 2015, pp. 172–174).

Until then, it had been assumed that liberal democratic nation states would, as a matter of course, respect and promote human rights. Yet the relationship between the liberal nation state and human rights over the 1960s evolved into an issue. Young people's refusal to support the US in waging an imperialist war in Vietnam became emblematic of their scepticism of state authorities and of an emerging globalised and cosmopolitan perspective and conscience. In America and Europe, a generation of young adults cared for civilians dying in Vietnam or suppressed in Latin-America by authoritarian regimes and started to ask questions about the military and political involvement of 'their' countries.

As a consequence of this nation state scepticism and cosmopolitism, human dignity developed from a sophisticated philosophical concept into a primarily political—and later also legal—category, which served—and still serves—as a basis for challenging the performance of state authorities and for creating, as an alternative to the nation state, the vision of a global humanist society that pursues the objective of equally supporting all human beings in developing as respected, autonomous and accountable persons. Over the last three decades, individuals lodging complaints against 'their own' states with regional or international tribunals, as well as treaty bodies assessing the human rights performance of governments, emerged as expressions of the new state-critical orientation of human rights. If anything, the concept of human dignity has the potential to serve as the basis for constructing a global cosmopolitan order. Capitalizing on this potential, the concept of a humanist society is apt to generate a counter-narrative in opposition to the nationalism and racism inherent in a political order established by nation states claiming sovereignty and rights to exclude. While the nation state concept stresses the dividing lines separating peoples and countries from one another, the vision of a global humanist society builds on the unity of all members of the human family sharing in one human dignity.

By its conversion from a state-centred to a rights-based institution, the criminal justice system follows this route. The question is no longer to what extent the state feels inclined to punish its citizens, but how effectively state authorities meet their obligations to respect human dignity and to reinforce the human rights of individuals by means of criminal justice.

The European Union, like any political structure, requires a normative basis. This basis is essentially the concept of human dignity highlighted by Article 2 of the Treaty of the European Union and fleshed out by the EU Charter of Fundamental Rights. If this basis is not to remain theoretical, but to become practically effective, human dignity and human rights must be effeectively supported and protected against acts that call them into question. However, when it comes to severe violations of human dignity, the only appropriate means of expressing censure, of redressing victims, and of holding offenders to account is a criminal justice response.

This book emphasises the historical and political significance of human dignity and human rights as core elements of a humanist society that is aware of the necessity to protect its own normative preconditions; and it stresses that the criminal justice system is a crucially important component of any normative order. Therefore, the question of how the criminal justice system can be conceived and established to serve the principle of human dignity and the establishment of a humanist society is of concern not only to legal experts, but to the entire polity.

It is in this situation that the crime victim returns as a main actor to the stage of criminal justice. This had been her stage over a long period in history, when formally conducting feuds against the offender and her family—first independent of state institutions, later in front of the bars of a court—had been the main mechanism of law enforcement. It is the underlying normative order that has changed since these times. Today the victim can claim her rights and her share in human dignity. The return of the victim marks the transformation of criminal justice from an institution serving the nation state, to an institution enforcing the human rights and dignity of individuals as members of the human family.

Vienna, Austria Albin Dearing

References

Dearing, A. (2003). Strafjustiz als Integration: Elemente einer an den Menschenrechten orientierten, opfergerechten Strafjustiz. In W. Stangl & G. Hanak (Eds.), *Innere Sicherheiten* (pp. 165–192). Baden-Baden, Germany: Nomos.

FRA. (2014). *Victims of crime in the EU: The extent and nature of support for victims*. Luxembourg: Publications Office of the European Union.

Hart, H. L. A. (1968). *Punishment and responsibility: Essays in the philosophy of law* (revised edition). Oxford University Press.

Moyn, S. (2012). *The last Utopia: Human rights in history*. Cambridge, MA: Harvard University Press.

Moyn, S. (2014). *Human rights and the uses of history*. London: Verso.

Moyn, S. (2015). *Christian human rights*. Philadelphia, PA: University of Pennsylvania Press.

Acknowledgments

I am forever indebted and grateful to Cerys Gibson for her help and insightful comments. Fortunately, only she knows what this book would look like without her support.

The views expressed in this book are solely those of the author and its content does not necessarily represent the views or position of the European Union Agency for Fundamental Rights.

This book I dedicate to my children Helene, Johannes and Mateo.

Contents

List of Abbreviations

CAT	Committee Against Torture (United Nations)
CJEU	Court of Justice of the European Union
ECHR	European Convention on Human Rights (Council of Europe Convention for the Protection of Human Rights and Fundamental Freedoms, signed in Rome on 4 November 1950)
ECtHR	European Court of Human Rights (Council of Europe)
FRA	European Union Agency for Fundamental Rights
GCC	Gene-culture coevolution
UDHR	Universal Declaration of Human Rights (adopted by the UN General Assembly on 10 December 1948)
VRD	Victims' Rights Directive (Directive 2012/29/EU of the European Parliament and of the Council of 25 October 2012 establishing minimum standards on the rights, support and protection of victims of crime)

Chapter 1
Criminal Justice in Need of a Paradigm Shift

1.1 The Current Situation of Victims' Rights in Europe: Common Rights Without a Common Rationale

This Chapter sets out the current justification for punishment in Western societies and highlights a fundamental inconsistency between the traditional understanding of criminal justice and the developing rights of crime victims to play a significant role in criminal proceedings.

Over the last four decades, victims' rights rapidly emerged in criminal proceedings across Europe. Since the late 1970s, the Council of Europe has been the main actor driving this development by drawing up a mounting body of standards. Among them feature most prominently Resolution (77) 27 on the Compensation of Victims of Crime, adopted by the Committee of Ministers in September 1977, the European Convention on the Compensation of Victims of Violent Crime (ETS No. 116, 1983), Recommendation No. R (85) 11 on the position of the victim in the framework of criminal law and procedure of June 1985 and by Recommendation No. R (87) 21 on the assistance to victims and the prevention of victimisation. Such standards serve to ensure that the victim is given more procedural rights in the criminal justice system.

In the 1970s and 1980s, the main emphasis was placed on limiting the harm done to victims. This was ensured through victim support services, by making sure that the victim was compensated, by protecting the victim against repeat victimisation—in particular in the context of domestic violence and sexual abuse—and overall by ensuring that the harm done by the offender was not augmented and exacerbated by a criminal justice system operating over the head of the victim and without much consideration of the trauma suffered by the victim.

With the new millennium, the European Union took over the role of trendsetter. On 15 March 2001, the Council Framework Decision on the standing of victims in criminal proceedings was adopted, which marks a turning point as through the steering of the European Union, the focus of policies moved from protection to

A. Dearing, *Justice for Victims of Crime*, DOI 10.1007/978-3-319-45048-3_1

empowerment and victims' access to justice. Under the heading "Respect and recognition", Article 2 of the Framework Decision defines its objective as: "Each Member State shall ensure that victims have a real and appropriate role in its criminal legal system."

In its *Katz* judgment, the CJEU in 2008 underlined this objective and emphasised that victims have a right to give testimony in the course of the criminal proceedings which can be taken into account as evidence (CJEU, *Katz*, para. 47). In its ruling in the joined cases of *Gueye and Salmerón Sánchez*, the CJEU (in para. 59 of the judgment) stressed that

> to guarantee that the victim can effectively and adequately take part in the criminal proceedings, his or her right to be heard must permit not only the possibility of objectively describing what happened, but also the opportunity to express his or her opinion.

This comes close to stating that the victim must not be reduced to the role of a witness but allowed to act as a party to the proceedings. Hence, the Framework Decision had a potential to herald the end of an era of side-lining victims in Europe. However, to date, it has not, arguably with a few exceptions.

This is not to say that the development concerning legal regulations did not continue. Rather, when on 16 November 2015 the deadline for the transposition of the Victims' Rights Directive (Directive 2012/29/EU of the European Parliament and of the Council of 25 October 2012 establishing minimum standards on the rights, support and protection of victims of crime, henceforth VRD) passed, the development of victims' rights in the European Union had arrived at its next level. This is with the exception of Denmark, which is not obliged by the Directive, but remains bound by the provisions of the older Framework Decision (for a comprehensive presentation of the VRD refer to Berger 2013, pp. 364–370; Rafaraci 2015).

Again, the main purpose of the Directive, as defined in the first sentence of Article 1, is "to ensure that victims of crime receive appropriate information, support and protection and are able to participate in criminal proceedings." This objective follows from the novel understanding, expressed in Recital 9 of the VRD, which clearly states:

> Crime is a wrong against society as well as a violation of the individual rights of victims. As such, victims of crime should be recognised and treated in a respectful, sensitive and professional manner without discrimination of any kind based on any ground such as [. . .].

The first sentence can be taken to indicate that a crime is, firstly, the violation of the rights of an individual, who because of this violation is referred to as the 'victim'; and that the crime also concerns, secondly, all other individuals living in a society, as their equal rights too are indirectly called into question by the offender. The second sentence quoted above can be read as suggesting that victims, *because* crimes violate their rights, should be recognised and respected throughout criminal proceedings as the persons primarily and immediately affected by the offences. Thus the VRD makes a strong case for allowing the victim to play an important role in criminal proceedings. It has been claimed that 'this change in perspective constitutes a cultural revolution that introduces into the balancing act between the needs of the authority and individual freedoms the need to respect the rights of the victim, as a 'co-protagonist' in the proceedings and no longer as a person with extremely limited procedural rights' (Alvaro and D'Andrea 2015, p. 316).

However, traditionally, a crime is conceived as a violation of a criminal code protecting public interests; and as long as this traditional understanding is not profoundly challenged, as long as the new legislative approach to victims' rights is not translated into new basic concepts of crime and criminal justice, the likelihood is that the impact of new legislation will remain modest. As long as we lack a succinct narrative of criminal justice protecting the rights of individuals, victims' rights are unlikely to make their way into the minds of lawyers and other practitioners populating the institutions of the criminal justice system.

This has not been a well-developed doctrine. It requires a theoretical framework that provides a conceptual and argumentative basis underpinning the emerging rights of victims and integrating the victim, her role and her rights convincingly in the rationale and framework of criminal justice. Victims' rights have scarcely been incorporated into the theory of punishment and criminal justice and therefore—even where they gradually make their way into procedural law—they find themselves in a delicate and exposed position because of the complexities and inconsistencies within the theory and practice of criminal justice.

The present book advocates the view that a fully satisfactory integration of victims' rights in criminal law and criminal justice cannot be achieved without a shift of paradigm from a state-centred to human-rights based approach to criminal law and criminal justice. Rejecting the assumption that states—or countries or societies—are as collectivities and in their own right legitimised to punish, the following chapters investigate the alternative explanation, namely that states are tasked to punish by the individual human beings forming a legal community. What hence is analysed is the rights of individuals to the prosecution, conviction and, in appropriate cases, also punishment of offenders.

To make this argument clearer, this introductory chapter lays out some differences between the traditional view and human-rights based concept of criminal justice.

1.2 A State-Centred Versus a Human-Rights Based Approach

The most basic difference between a state-centred and a human-rights based approach to criminal law and criminal justice concerns the very concept of what forms a criminal offence. In the traditional view, a criminal offence is a violation of a public interest vindicated by the state, whilst in a human-rights based approach it is a violation of at least one individual's human rights. Hence, in the traditional view, criminal law protects public interests, whilst in a human-rights based understanding, criminal law protects a system of human rights. This crucial and profound difference naturally affects virtually all aspects of criminal justice, many of which will be highlighted throughout the following chapters.

Famously, a victim before the U.S. Presidential Committee enquiring into the situation of victims expressed his sentiments by crying: "Why didn't anyone consult me? I was the one who was kidnapped, not the state of Virginia" (Richards 2009, p. 303). However, the traditional view depicts criminal justice as a matter between the state and the offender, where the state is represented by the police, public prosecutors and courts. As Rook (2002, p. 37) has formulated this crucial point:

> Members of the legal profession have come to regard criminal cases as contests between the state as prosecutor and the defendant. [. . .] Criminal offences are offences against the state, and should be prosecuted when it is in the public interest to do so. The sentence is passed in the public interest.

In general, the term 'public' can mean two things: it can refer, as a shorthand, either to all individuals living at a certain place or to the people as a whole. Public transportation and the town library are open to the public in the sense that anyone can use their services. However, saying that criminal justice is a matter of public concern or that a court acts in the public interest refers not to every individual viewed in isolation, but to a roughly organised and integrated community as an entirety and its collective interests. It is in this sense that, in the traditional perspective, criminal law belongs entirely to a polity's public sphere, represented and enacted by state institutions.

Criminal justice, in this view, does not take place among individual citizens within a community, but as a matter of the legal community, represented by the state, against individual offenders. This view places the latter outside and in opposition to her community. It is about a case of a state against an individual defendant or several defendants.

A telling expression of the state-centred paradigm concerns the many cases where public prosecutors waive the state's right to the punishment of offenders. This demonstrates their belief that it is up to state representatives to refrain from prosecuting and punishing offenders when it suits state policies. Under so-called opportunity principles, public prosecutors are vested with various discretionary powers to drop proceedings.

If a defendant is charged with a number of offences, some offences may not be investigated if the prosecutor believes that they would, in case of a conviction, not affect the sentence. The sentence is seen as quantifying the amount of punishment to which the state is entitled and hence, in the end, the only relevant result with no consideration given to the victims of the offences.

In other instances, prosecution is discontinued based on out-of-court settlements, such as the offender paying an amount of money to the state or a charity. Occasionally, tight statutory periods of limitation result in prosecutors closing files before the case has even started. Amnesties, rights of pardon and immunities all allow offenders to enjoy impunity for various reasons. All these examples have one feature in common. They allow the state to dispose of criminal cases with little regard to the rights of victims to access justice, or to the legitimate interest of all individuals living on a state's territory to see that offenders are indiscriminately held to account for their criminal actions to ensure the effective protection of the population's human rights. Thus, the primary function of criminal justice to consistently and reliably defend human rights against severe violations can be compromised through state-enacted legislation.

The victim—the one who was injured, or robbed—is, in this perspective, no more than a prerequisite of the situation in which the crime occurred. As much as drug trafficking involves drugs and armed robbery some weapon, assault, rape and murder require that someone is there to be assaulted, raped, or killed. For certain crimes, a victim is part of the scenery in which the offence is committed, but is no more than that. The victim shrinks to an element of the crime. Michael Thompson, in answering the question "What is it to Wrong Someone?" (2004, p. 344), explains this view in the following terms:

> The verdict of the jury, 'Guilty!', expresses a property of one agent, not a relation of agents. If another agent comes into the matter – if there is, as we say, a 'victim' – it is, so to speak, as raw material in respect of which one might do wrong. The position occupied by other agents in the associated legal facts might equally be held by rare birds or old buildings.

In marked contrast, the view advocated here perceives the victim as the person whose human rights have been violated by the offender, a position that cannot also be occupied by rare birds or old buildings. In this view, the offence is an action that involves more than one individual: at least one person, that is, whose human rights have been violated, and at least one person, who is held to account for that human rights violation. It is, in this view, the victim who has been wronged, not the state, and it is therefore the victim who can legitimately take issue with the offender's behaviour and expect that justice is done, not the state representing the people, or the public.

This is not meant to say that *only* the victim is affected. As human rights are attributed to individuals because they are human beings and hence define the legal status of any person—a status that is equal to all human beings—all other individuals are affected indirectly and hence concerned. What the offender calls into question is the respect and rights owed to persons for the sole reason of their status as persons. All individuals are interested in the vindication of the victim's human rights as they flow from human dignity as the common denominator of the status of all persons and from legal norms equally protecting the dignity and the rights of all. Crimes concern 'the public' not as a collective entity distinct from individuals, but as an expression that captures all individuals, united by laws that treat them on an equal footing.

Antony Duff highlights this point when explaining what it means to consider crimes 'public wrongs' (2009, p. 52):

> Now it might be tempting to suppose that a public wrong 'affects the community' only if it somehow harms or injures [...] 'the community' as a whole. [...] But this is not how we should understand the idea of a public wrong since [...] to portray the criminal wrongfulness of such victimising crimes as murder, rape, wounding and fraud as consisting in the harm that they do to 'the public' is to distort the matter: they are wrongs because of what they do to their direct victims, and they are crimes or public wrongs, not because of some further injury that they do to 'the public', but because they are wrongs that properly concern

> 'the public', i.e. wrongs that properly concern us all as citizens. What the offender is called to answer for in such cases, what he is condemned for, should [. . .] be [. . .] the wrong that he did to his victim.

Hence, a crime is a wrong done to the victim, but it is a 'public wrong' because it violates the victim's human rights and therefore calls into question a crucially important status that the victim shares with all others. This is the difference between human rights and, for instance, contractual entitlements. If an individual has bought a table and hence owes the furniture store or carpentry the price of the table, her eventual failing to pay her debt in no way impacts on the rights of all. The store's contractual rights are of a merely private nature in the sense that they do not represent rights common to all human beings. Contractual rights are not part of what it means to be a person. Human rights are.

However, in the traditional perspective, the rationale of criminal justice is to effectively assert a state's substantive criminal law, which is depicted as protecting—not the rights of individuals, but—public interests or common goods or some similar collective asset. The relevant German term is '*Rechtsgut*', which denotes virtually any interest protected by a criminal law provision. If an interest is protected by criminal law, it is thereby acknowledged as a public interest. By threatening criminal sanctions, the law demonstrates its authority and upholds public trust in its rule and its ability to protect and defend public or common interests (or *Rechtsgüter*).

In this perspective, the state creates criminal laws, identifies, prosecutes and condemns infringements of these laws, and enforces the punishment of the offender to which the state is entitled by virtue of the violation of its laws. In a grand, somewhat insular monologue, the state creates criminal law provisions, determines violations and enforces criminal law, thus demonstrating the state's and the law's authority.

What happens in the course of criminal proceedings, matters to the extent that it enables state authorities to identify a violation of criminal law and to convict and punish those responsible. In the traditional perspective, the offender is the state's opponent, whose possible resistance must be overcome. Criminal justice is directed against the offender. This places the offender outside and in opposition to criminal justice. This is even true when criminal justice claims to be beneficial to offenders. It is then still up to the state to decide what is in the offender's best interest. Offenders, defence lawyers and witnesses stand "outside the mainstream flow of cases through the system from police to sentence" and "tend to be viewed as problems to be managed, rather than as integral parts of justice" (Shapland 2000, p. 148). The core function of criminal justice is the production of convictions and sentences in which the state is triumphant and demonstrates the law's superiority over the offender's wrongful conduct. From the law's perspective, the offence is a disturbance that needs to be corrected, trouble that needs to be fixed. In short: criminal justice is the institution of the law's self-assertion against an offender whose conduct has a potential to question the rule of (criminal) law.

In this setting, the victim is not a main figure, if a figure at all. The offence is not perceived as a violation of an individual's rights but as an infringement of a state's laws. Strictly speaking, the state, is the real victim and therefore entitled to the punishment of the offender. In German legal language the state's right to the punishment of the offender is called '*staatlicher Strafanspruch*' and denotes precisely what, in this system, criminal proceedings are mainly about. The offender has violated the laws of the state; hence the state is entitled to the punishment of the offender ('Aus der Verübung einer mit Strafe bedrohten Handlung erwächst dem Staat […] ein Anspruch auf Bestrafung des Schuldigen', Malaniuk 1947, p. 1).

In European criminal courts, individual victims have for a long time been—and in many countries still are—denied a significant role in criminal proceedings and often only make a short appearance when called upon as witnesses to fulfil their duties in supporting law enforcement, i.e. the conviction of offenders to which the state—on behalf of 'society'—is entitled. In his seminal article on "Conflicts as Property" Christie sketched the basic problem in the following terms (1977, p. 3):

> The key element in a criminal proceeding is that the proceeding is converted from something between the concrete parties into a conflict between one of the parties and the state. So, in a modern criminal trial, two important things have happened. First, the parties are being *represented*. Secondly, the one party that is represented by the state, namely the victim, is so thoroughly represented that she or he for most of the proceedings is pushed completely out of the arena, reduced to the triggerer-off of the whole thing. She or he is a sort of double loser, first, *vis-à-vis* the offender, but secondly and often in a more crippling manner by being denied rights to full participation in what might have been one of the more important ritual encounters in life. The victim has lost the case to the state.

By the state's gradual usurpation of the 'ownership' of a crime committed, "any 'rights' victims have to 'own' their own experience of victimization and its aftermath have been eroded over time" (Goodey 2005, p. 126).

The core concern of the present book is to argue this final point, and explain why states should return the case to the victim and on what handover conditions, e.g. concerning the rights of others, including prominently the offender/defendant. The offence is a real-life, normative conflict between the victim and the offender occurring within a community of law, rights and obligations. It has far-reaching consequences for the rights and the social status of victims and offenders.

Many will not agree with this analysis because they do not view a criminal offence as a conflict between the victim and the offender but as a violation by the perpetrator of a state's criminal law. They believe that a crime is a public issue and therefore should be conceptualised without recourse to the rights of the individuals affected. Arguably, when it comes to advocating victims' rights, the most crucial point is our understanding of what constitutes a criminal offence. The very concept of a state holding rights against its citizens is questionable and can be criticised as reflecting an outdated view of states as polities and their citizens as opposed to one another with competing interests, the state pursuing public, individuals their private interests. This view characterises the ideas of liberal constitutionalism, dating back to times when citizens advocated fundamental rights as limiting the divine rights of monarchs or the legitimate powers of nation states. However, this model is obsolete because of profound historical and political developments. In a democracy, the institutions making up a state are of a purely instrumental status as a means of promoting the rights and legitimate interests of individuals and cannot claim their own rights on a par with or above the rights of individuals. As will be laid out in Chap. 3, in a societal and legal order based on the concepts of human dignity and human rights, only the rights of individuals can legitimise the conviction and, in appropriate cases, also punishment of offenders. Unless a state is seen as a natural entity, inherently valuable, or as instituted by a divine will, it derives legitimacy solely from its ability to put human rights into practice.

In this vein, Tugendhat (2007, p. 136) insists that human rights are the only remaining basis of legitimacy of a modern as opposed to a traditional, authoritarian state:

> Die Menschenrechte sind der wesentliche Bestandteil der Legitimität *jedes* Staates, *sofern* und *wann immer* man den Glauben an eine traditionalistische und d.h. autoritäre Legitimität verworfen hat.

It follows that construing offending as an issue that the state has with the offender and consequently founding criminal justice on the state's entitlement to the punishment of the offender raises questions as to the foundation and legitimacy of such an entitlement.

Many other areas of public administration have adopted a service orientation by placing the rights and interests of citizens as their customers—and taxpayers—onto centre stage, and hence accept that their performance will be assessed against how well they meet the legitimate expectations of their customers. Yet the idea that the institutions forming the criminal justice system should be assessed on a similar basis against how they meet the rights and legitimate expectations of individuals concerned—of victims, offenders, witnesses, their families and others—has hardly emerged. The reason is that criminal justice has traditionally not been understood as an institution tasked with safeguarding the rights and legitimate interests of individuals but rather as a system where the state is concerned with its own rights.

Hence it has been claimed that criminal justice, instead of speaking 'only to itself in its own courtroom' should develop into a public service that acknowledges its responsibilities to various parties, including victims, offenders and wider communities, and allows citizens to see that it relates to their concerns (Shapland 2000, pp. 159–160). 'The courts would be there for the people, rather than the people being there for the courts' (Shapland 2000, p. 161).

Currently the view that the victim should have a role to play and rights allowing her to participate in criminal proceedings is gaining ground. It is increasingly felt that victims of crime can legitimately expect some reaction demonstrating that the community of which offenders and victims are part, distances itself from the offender's conduct and sides with the victim. This tendency finds its most powerful expression in the European Union's VRD.

However, criminal proceedings serve to realise and enact substantive criminal law and hence cannot develop detached from this basis. If a crime is essentially a violation of public interests vindicated by state authorities, it is indeed not clear why the victim should be involved in proceedings. If on the other hand a crime is a violation of human rights, it follows that the individual whose rights have been infringed should be allowed to perform and be supported in performing a very essential role in proceedings; and the tasks and roles of public actors involved would need to be adapted accordingly. The more the traditional system of criminal justice comes under pressure to acknowledge rights of victims to have a say in proceedings, the more it becomes evident that such a role of the victim is not compatible with the traditional paradigm of criminal law that conceives a criminal offence as a matter between the state and the offender.

1.3 Conceptualising the Victim

Obviously, the terms 'crime', 'victim' and 'offender' are intricately intertwined and therefore can only be analysed together. Any reconceptualisation of 'crime' affects the concept of a 'crime victim'. However, the opposite holds as well: any concept of 'victim' relates to a concept of 'crime', and hence the 'victim' cannot be reconceptualised without considering the consequences concerning the concept of what is referred to as 'crime'.

To date no consensus exists as to what defines a victim. Rather, in this respect four paradigms can be distinguished, which will be referred to as 'witness', 'damage', 'harm', and 'rights' paradigm (FRA 2014, pp. 28–32).

1.3.1 The Witness Paradigm

In the traditional paradigm, the victim serves as a source of information as to the circumstantiality of her victimisation, which is understood as an instance of disregard of a state's criminal laws. Hence, there is no profound difference between the victim and other persons who have witnessed the offence. The victim's obligation to support the administration of criminal justice as a witness is the clearest expression of the traditional, state-centred understanding of criminal justice and, at the same time, a systematic violation of the human rights of victims.

In the traditional paradigm, criminal justice is conceived as a matter between the state and the offender; hence, the offence is understood as a violation of the provisions of a criminal code, but not as directed against an individual's rights. Hence, the victim is not an essential actor in the criminal justice system. What remains it that the person commonly referred to as victim will, subject to the circumstances of the case, often be in a position to support the administration of justice as a witness and is primarily thought of in that role. If the victim is required to act as a witness, she does not necessarily differ in that role from other witnesses who are not also victims.

Therefore, in the settings of criminal courts in Europe, individual victims have for a long time been—and in some countries still are—denied a significant role in criminal proceedings and often only appear in court when called upon as witnesses to fulfil their duties in supporting law enforcement, i.e. the conviction and, in appropriate cases, also punishment of offenders to which the state—on behalf of 'society'—is entitled.

The traditional paradigm reduces the victim to the function of delivering evidence in favour of a state's efforts to investigate and prosecute an offender and negates that the victim has suffered wrong, a violation, that is, of her rights. In traditional criminal justice systems, the position of the victim was and very often still is that of a witness obliged to support public interests by delivering their statement to the police and evidence in court. Reducing the role of the victim to the obligation to support the administration of criminal justice as a witness is the clearest expression of the traditional, state-centred understanding of criminal justice and shows disrespect of the victim as a rights-holder.

In the United Kingdom, the Code of Practice for Victims of Crime informs the victim in subsection 3.4 as follows:

> If you are not a witness in the case you are entitled to observe court proceedings from the public gallery.

Next to attending trial as a witness, the victim has no role to perform in the trial phase of proceedings in British courts that would distinguish her from the public, watching the proceedings from the gallery. "In court, victims have no status save as 'givers of evidence'" (Rook 2002, p. 37).

As a witness, the victim is often not even heard if the prosecutor believes that the victim's testimony is not needed for the case, which is a case of the state against the defendant. The contrast between a witness who is required to deliver evidence if needed by the state on the one hand and the role of a party to the proceedings whose most fundamental right is to be heard in court—and to be taken seriously—on the other succinctly reveals the difference between the traditional state-centred and a human rights-based approach.

Many victims who report to the police still experience the "disillusionment of being a witness rather than a client – that is, they will be treated as a disenfranchised bystander to their own experience" (Waller 2011, p. 1), which leaves a lot of victims indignant and angry. Richards (2009, p. 303) comments that collections of crime victims' stories "contain numerous examples of victims of serious offences who have been outraged at the lack of opportunity for victims to participate in the criminal justice system." He quotes a crime victim expressing his feelings about his role in proceedings:

> The charges were pressed in the name of the Queen, her Crown and dignity, and I was just a witness. I didn't like that bullshit – this happened to me. It didn't happen to the [. . .] Queen! I was always a bit pissed off about that.

The understanding that criminal justice protects, not the rights of individuals, but abstract goods, public interests, *Rechtsgüter,* has two fundamental consequences. Firstly, the individual victim of flesh and blood is reduced to the role of one potential witness among others. Secondly, by ignoring the status of the victim as the holder of the right that was violated by the offender and by attributing to the victim the supporting role of a witness, the state avoids acknowledging its own responsibility for not effectively protecting the rights of an individual and for allowing victimisations to happen. In the *Cowan* case, Advocate General Lenz commented on this relation between the state and the victim as follows (CJEU 1988, para. 52):

> In enacting legislation for the compensation of victims of crime it takes a position analogous to that of a guarantor with regard to compensation for harm which could not otherwise be redressed, harm arising from the infringement of rights which it was the State's duty to protect but which it was not able to guarantee.

This perspective can be extended to how the victim should be conceived in general: the state should treat the victim as the individual whose rights the state had a duty to protect but failed to do so effectively. It follows that the state is obliged to do what is in its power to do to limit the negative consequences on the victim and her rights of the state's failure to prevent the offence from occurring. Restoring and reinforcing the victim's status as a respected rights-holder is what the state owes to the victim in reaction to the offence, which the state failed to prevent.

In contrast, by treating the victim instrumentally as a means to the state's ends, the victim is depersonalised, not only by the offender, but also by the state. By denying the plain fact that the offence essentially concerns the victim and her rights and that therefore the victim's position is crucially different to the position of any other person in the proceedings, the criminal justice system denies the significance of the victim's rights and in this important respect sides with the offender. As long as a criminal justice system conceives of victims "as witnesses, as evidence, as objects to be used by the system" (Waller 2011, p. 7) and thus denies the particular status of the victim as the individual whose rights have been violated, it fails to acknowledge the victim's dignity and status as a person.

The right to equal treatment—Article 20 of the EU Fundamental Rights Charter—is violated not only by differentiations that have no sound basis but also by regulations that ignore significant differences. Treating victims and witnesses on an equal footing and thus ignoring that the victim is the very individual whose rights were infringed and who therefore is personally and immediately concerned to a degree that crucially differs from the experience of an average witness violates the victim's right to equal treatment under the Charter.

No one would consider treating the defendant as a witness. The reason is that a witness is, in principle, under an obligation to tell the truth and expected to endeavour to deliver an unbiased, sufficiently reliable account of what she observed. This is a reasonable demand as long as a person is essentially unconcerned by the offence and the outcome of criminal proceedings and hence is positioned at a certain distance from the case. Accordingly, the defendant is not under an obligation to deliver testimony as it is understood that for her too much is at stake so that a general duty imposed on her to testify objectively and truthfully would be unfair and in contradiction to her position as a party to the proceedings.

It is true that the victim is not at risk of being punished. However, what is at stake for her is nevertheless very substantial. The proceedings concern a severe violation of her rights. For her it is about whether the court attests that her rights have been violated, finds that the offender is responsible for this wrong and requests the offender to right this wrong by making appropriate amends for her wrongful behaviour and its consequences. Often for the victim, the answers to these questions decide whether she is able to overcome the experience of victimisation and move on in her life or whether this experience continues to weigh heavily on and, to a certain extent, impregnate her future. The performance of criminal justice often decides whether an individual who has suffered a severe violation of her human rights continues to remain a victim or leaves victimhood behind. However, it should be made clear here that the victim is entitled to have access to justice and to participate in proceedings due solely to the fact that her human rights have been severely violated, not premised on any descriptive categories such as the harm or trauma suffered or her real needs or interests.

This is the point where the main inconsistency shows. If we believe that criminal proceedings fundamentally concern the victim and the recognition of her rights then we cannot, at the same time, place her in the group of witnesses who are in principle unconcerned by the offence. Like the offender, the victim should be free to present her views on the facts of the case. Like defendants, victims will often choose to do so if they feel that it is in their best interest or simply the right thing to do and if the institutions and procedures forming the criminal justice system are designed to meet the victim's rights and needs in a victim-friendly manner. However, as is the case with defendants, the victim's statement is the statement of an interested party to the proceedings and not the—in principle—unbiased testimony of a casual bystander.

Treating a victim as a witness is profoundly disrespectful of the victim as a rights-holder and a person. By denying the plain fact that the offence is essentially a violation of the rights of the victim and that therefore the victim's position is fundamentally different to the position of witnesses or any other person, the criminal justice system negates the significance of the victim's rights and in this important respect sides with the offender. Instead of firmly rebutting the insinuation inherent in the offence that the rights of the victim are of minor relevance, the state, by not paying attention to the rights of the victim, aligns itself with the offender's views. Treating the victim instrumentally as a means to the state's ends is a second abuse amounting to a secondary victimisation and stands in contrast to respecting the victim as a person and human dignity as represented by the victim and her rights. As long as a criminal justice system conceives of the victim as a witness and thus denies the particular status of the victim as the person whose rights have been violated, criminal justice is in a marked opposition to and irreconcilable with a system based on human dignity and human rights.

Even in those systems where the victim is now increasingly enabled to participate in the proceedings she is often at the same time still treated as a witness. However, if one believes that criminal proceedings fundamentally concern the victim then one cannot, at the same time, place the victim in the category of witnesses who are in principle unconcerned by the offence. Like the offender, the victim should be free to present her views on the facts of the case. Like offenders, victims will often choose to do so if they feel that it is in their best interest or simply the right thing to do. However, as is the case with offenders, this would then be the statement of an interested party to the proceedings, in marked distinction from the unbiased testimony of a casual bystander.

Criminal justice protecting public interests and criminal justice protecting the rights of individuals are two fundamentally different concepts and orientations. While in the first paradigm it may be acceptable to oblige the victim to support the state in accomplishing its tasks, in the second it is the state's obligation to serve the interests of victims as individual rights-holders. In the first paradigm, treating the victim only as a witness may be appropriate, in the second it is not.

1.3.2 The Economic Model: The Damaged Victim as Civil Party

Another means of protecting the criminal justice system against victims and their ambitious claims is to offer second-best solutions pretending that they would be the best for the victim. These solutions have in common that they attempt to reconcile the interests of the victim with the criminal justice system without touching on the latter's underlying state-centred and collectivist rationale. The victim is declared 'the most important secondary matter'.

What characterises the damage paradigm is that the criminal justice system integrates the function of dealing with civil law based claims of individuals who, because of a criminal offence, have suffered damage and in this sense figure as an injured party. Accepting the victim as a civil party to the criminal proceedings enables the victim to participate and play an active role in the criminal proceedings. However, in a case dealing with murder, rape, deprivation of liberty or grave insult, the damage caused is not what is important. Hence, even when criminal courts concern themselves with civil law claims, this necessarily remains a side-event of criminal proceedings.

Where the victim is granted a substantive role in criminal courts, this move so far only takes the form of essentially appending the victim's participation in proceedings as an *additional* function or side track to the criminal justice system as it existed previously. In some systems, the victim, if she, because of the offence, suffered harm or traumatisation, is recognised as deserving of help, care and protection against 'secondary victimisation'. However, this does not touch on her basic position as a witness. In fact, many practitioners believe that supporting the victim, next to meeting legitimate interests of the victim, serves the purpose of fostering the victim's capability to give testimony and hence is a matter of public interests. Criminal justice is then still tasked mainly with enforcing the right of the state—or of society—to the punishment of the offender and with redressing the harm or damage incurred by the victim only as an auxiliary function.

As a result, tensions and ambivalences persist, which are caused by a basic and unresolved inconsistency between the rights of the victim—albeit now often acknowledged half-heartedly—on the one hand and the fundamental orientation and genuine logic of the criminal justice system on the other. On first sight, it seems that the traditional concept of the state's right to the punishment of the offender and the new vision of a victim's right to justice widely overlap. They both claim that the offender deserves to be punished for the wrong she has committed. However, the rationale and reasoning behind these claims differs widely, depending on whether the wrong is conceptualised as a violation of the state's criminal law or of the rights of an individual protected by criminal law. In the first case, the state, in the second case, the victim is entitled to redress.

The strategy underlying the—originally French—system of the victim as *partie civile* is to introduce the victim in the criminal justice system but to place her on a civil-law side-track. The wrong suffered by the victim is downgraded from a criminal matter to damage and to an issue of civil law and an ancillary matter of criminal justice. The victim is, in a sense, a party to the civil law proceedings that are conducted simultaneously in the same court room and within the wider framework of criminal proceedings.

As a result, the glass is both half full and half empty. While the victim, on the one hand, is tolerated in a criminal court and allowed to actively participate in criminal proceedings and authentically voice her concerns, she acts, on the other hand, only in a supporting role. The victim has rights to intervene as if she was a party to the genuine criminal proceedings, which she is not. The mimicry is so effective that it can easily be overlooked that the victim owes her rights as *partie civile* to some damage suffered as a *consequence* of the offence and thus to a civil-law claim and not to being *directly* wronged *by* the criminal offence.

The system of civil party fails to acknowledge the victim as a person wronged by a violation of her human rights, which is not premised or linked to the causation of damage. In fact, the system of the civil party only works as long as the victim can claim some sort of material or immaterial damage. This can be seen most clearly in cases of attempted offences, where the offender's action does not necessarily affect the situation of the victim, and so the victim will only have recourse to minimal civil damages, if any.

1.3.3 The Harm Paradigm: The Harmed and Vulnerable Victim in Need and Deserving of Support, Protection and State Compensation

The harm paradigm adheres to the general assumption that society should help those in need, at least, if they are not to blame for being in such a situation. An individual who suffers harm from a criminal offence is acknowledged as, to a certain extent, deserving of support and concern and of financial reparation

With regard to the situation in England and Wales and the 1996 Victim's Charter, Jo Goodey has observed that victims are seen as "a group to which the criminal justice system, from the police through to probation, owes some services" (2005, p. 128) adding:

> However, these services are not a right that victims can demand. Instead, victims might receive an apology or compensation if they complain of inadequate service provision. What the Victim's Charter does is indicate standards of service provision that victims can expect to receive. This position reflects the history of victim-centred criminal justice developments in England and Wales, a history that has been characterised as needs-based, and as stemming from a welfare tradition marked by volunteerism [...]. This 'needs-based' approach to victim services is highly discretionary as it distinguishes between those victims who are eligible for special service provision and those who are not, both overtly and covertly basing need on the idea of the deserving victim.

According to Goodey, the conceptualisation of "the victim" is "restricted by social constructions of appropriate victimhood rather than the actual needs of victims" (2005, p. 124):

> In other words, 'who' can be a victim is formulated around the idea of the 'innocent' and 'deserving' victim. Victims whose character, past conduct, or actions can be considered as undesirable, or as somehow contributing to their victimisation, are unlikely to be responded to sympathetically by the criminal justice system as deserving victims with particular needs to be met. In this atmosphere, girls and women who step outside the boundaries of respectable female behaviour, such as prostitutes and heavy drinkers [...], and men with criminal convictions [...] or associations with 'lawless' communities [...] are not generally considered as deserving and innocent victims.

Hence, in the needs paradigm, the focus is on the needs and vulnerability resulting from the harm suffered by the victim and on alleviating that harm. The focus is therefore on victim support, on protecting the victim against repeat victimisation and against further harm caused by an abusive, manipulative and objectifying criminal justice system—so-called secondary victimisation—as well as on state compensation as a means to relieve the victim of the economic consequences of the offence.

The common law countries never adopted the French system of *partie civile*. Hence, when in the wake of human rights in the late 1960s and the 1970s the victim and her legitimate interests were 'discovered', the need was particularly pressing to find a role for the victim that acknowledges the victim as personally affected by the offence and at the same time does not require a fundamental change of the criminal justice system. This resulted in the emergence of the 'harm/needs-paradigm'.

This paradigm finds a pure expression in the "Declaration of Basic Principles of Justice for Victims of Crime and Abuse of Power", adopted by the UN General Assembly in November 1985. The Declaration defines "victims" as meaning

> persons who, individually or collectively, have suffered harm, including physical or mental injury, emotional suffering, economic loss or substantial impairment of their fundamental rights, through acts or omissions that are in violation of criminal laws operative within Member States, including those laws proscribing criminal abuse of power.

Building on this approach, the harm/needs-paradigm has been developed to perfection by the International Criminal Court, or rather it has been pushed to its limits and to the point where victims' participation in criminal proceedings leads to tensions within a fundamentally adversarial system.

In the end, however, defining the victim in terms of harm caused by the offence does not work for two reasons, namely that such a definition is sometimes too broad and sometimes not broad enough. If one, for example, imagines a traffic accident caused by drunk driving that brings about the death of a person involved in the accident, it is not only the person killed who suffers harm and hence is a victim according to this definition. Her husband, so it can be assumed, suffers emotionally. Other persons experiencing shock and distress may include bystanders, the intervening professionals—the ambulance driver, police officers—and family members who later learn about the accident. In addition, the children of the woman killed will, next to emotional suffering, often incur economic losses, and the same may hold for her parents who she was supporting financially.

Not only does an offence often harm a long list of persons, often the victim is not harmed, as is the case with many forms of attempted offences (Hampton 2007, p. 110). It is easy to imagine a situation where a driver attempts to run over another individual with her car, fails to do so, but careers off the road and ends up being the only 'victim' of her offending.

However, the problem is not only that the harm/needs-approach misses the point of what constitutes criminal victimisation in contrast to natural disasters or severe misfortune. It also prompts the wrong consequences as it treats the harmed victim as a vulnerable human being in need of support and reparations and not as a person whose rights have been called into question and who therefore can legitimately expect to be confirmed by the legal community in her status as a person entitled to respect. Under the heading "Access to justice and fair treatment" the UN Declaration postulates that victims "should be treated with compassion and respect for their dignity" and that they "are entitled to access to the mechanisms of justice and to prompt redress, as provided for by national legislation, for the harm that they have suffered". But the "harm suffered" easily translates into terms of material and immaterial damage and can be dealt with in civil or adhesive proceedings, within or outside of the framework of criminal justice. Whether the criminal offence is conceptualised as a violation of the state's laws or as a violation of the rights of an individual, in either case the "harm suffered" does not touch on the normative essence of what constitutes crime (Hampton 2007, pp. 110–115).

This reductionist approach, which leaves out the normative aspects of the crime committed against the victim, implicates that the victim is treated on account of her physical, mental and emotional suffering and vulnerability, but not respected as a rights-holder. The primary measure to meet the needs of the harmed victim is the provision of support services, if appropriate in addition to the compensation of her damages. Neither of these functions is necessarily integrated in the system of criminal justice. Eliminating the element of the violation of her rights as the normative core of the concept of a crime victim makes it possible to separate the victim from criminal proceedings and to deal with her as merely a matter of psychosocial support and therapy.

Instead of acknowledging the victim as the individual who has been wronged and can legitimately expect that the offender makes amends for her wrongdoing to the victim, the latter is redefined as suffering, vulnerable and in need of care and protection. The reinterpretation of wrong as merely natural harm invites manipulative interventions. As Christie (1977, p. 4) has observed, a "non-conflict perspective is a precondition for defining crime as a legitimate target for treatment." The vague concept of harm functions to draw attention to those aspects "which the healer is particularly trained to handle" (Christie 1977, p. 5). This naturalist approach fits what on a critical note has been coined "The Age of Disabling Professions", when "the new dominant professions claim control over human needs" (Illich 1977, pp. 11, 13, 16). The disrespect of the victim as a person, participating in dignity and holding rights, comes with a risk that the criminal justice system, complemented by victim support services, develops into a "disabling service delivery system", where "social services create helplessness and legal agencies injustice" (Illich 1977, p. 28). The only way to avoid this risk is to, in all instances, treat the victim as wronged and as entitled to amends that restore her as a rights-holder.

After translating victimisation from a wrong—a 'moral injury' (Hampton 2007, p. 120)—into a naturalist notion of 'harm', and 'harm' into need, and need into a defect, the remaining defect can be decontextualised from the criminal offence and firmly linked to the victim by a formalised individual assessment of the victim, her personal vulnerability and her needs in terms of care, treatment and protection. Because services are "usually limited to individualized interaction, the interpretation of the need necessarily becomes individualized. The tool defines the problem rather than the problem defining the tool" (McKnight 1977, p. 79). The formal and standardised individual assessment of the victim's needs creates the basis for a reorientation of interventions from amending the wrong committed against the victim to healing and protecting the victim.

In the history of criminal justice, a strikingly similar tendency to decontextualise and personalise the issue occurred—and in some instances still occurs—in relation to offenders. Instead of acknowledging the offender as a person capable of realising that her action was wrong and of taking responsibility for it, it is 'discovered' that the real problem is not the offence but the essentially dangerous offender who because of her deficient personality is in need of reformatory treatment and correctional services. Ever since Wahlberg published his seminal book on the principle of individualisation in criminal justice (Wahlberg 1868), the idea had its supporters to focus the attention of criminal justice not on the offence but on the deficient personality of the individual offender and in particular, in the words of Christie (1977, p. 5), on

> those attributes in the criminal's background which the healer is particularly trained to handle. Biological defects are perfect. So also are personality defects when they are established far back in time – far away from the recent conflict.

This too risks a change of the criminal justice system from an enabling to a disabling and manipulative institution. Conceptualising the offence as an indication of the offender's need of curative treatment runs in parallel to conceiving of the offence as an indication that the victim may be harmed and in need of support and remedial interventions.

The fundamental problem created by the harm approach is that the wrong done to the victim is faded out. The term 'harm' does not indicate the responsibility of the offender. Hence, what remains as the rationale of punishment is only the abstract, impersonal and anaemic notion of the offence as a violation of criminal law. Treating the victim not as wronged but as harmed impairs the functioning of criminal justice. While there cannot be any objection to taking all aspects of the harm suffered by the victim seriously, this must not blur the fact that the offence is primarily a wrong done by the offender to the victim requiring essentially that the offender make amends for this wrong. While harm occurs in various contexts, the wrong done to the victim is what is specific about and what defines criminal victimisation.

From a political perspective, the harm/needs-paradigm fits into the world of a social welfarist nation state. In a rights-based approach, criminal justice reacts to the fact of a violation of an individual's rights and therefore somewhat schematically aims at determining and redressing the rights violation, as well as preventing its continuation or repetition. The rights-based approach conceptualises the victim as an empowered citizen and rights-holder within a democratic polity. While in this paradigm the victim's right to justice simply reflects the fact that the rights of the victim have been infringed and that the victim is entitled to be acknowledged as a rights-holder, in a harm-based approach any intervention is premised on real needs and hence on an individual assessment of the victim's actual needs and vulnerability caused by the harm suffered because of the criminal offence. This model tends to focus on and highlight the victim's trauma and frailty.

At this point, it should be acknowledged and stressed that, because of the efforts and success of those advocating a harm approach, in recent decades much has been achieved in terms of victim support, state compensation and the victim's protection against secondary victimisation. From the point of view of victims' legitimate interests, these achievements are important. However, on the other side of the coin there exists in harm-based approaches firstly a tendency to focus on the suffering and vulnerability of the victim, and secondly a risk that the baby is thrown out with the bathwater by protecting victims against, instead of within, the criminal justice system. Loyal to the hypotheses on which the paradigm is founded, the point of departure is the assumption that criminal justice has essentially nothing to do with the victim; next to the system's claims on the victim's cooperation and support as a witness providing evidence that serves the state's purpose of prosecuting offenders. Hence, the basic orientation is to restrict these claims on victims by stressing their vulnerability and the risks and challenges stemming from any involvement of the victim in criminal proceedings. As a result, protecting the victim is, within this paradigm, often understood as avoiding secondary victimisation by protecting the victim from falling into the hands of the criminal justice system.

In the witness paradigm there is, strictly speaking, no relation between the victim and the criminal justice system. In the damage paradigm, the interests of the state and the civil party are viewed as, to a certain extent, running in parallel and potentially reinforcing one another. However, the needs paradigm highlights the antagonism between the victim's personal interests and the criminal justice system and hence the need to limit the 'collateral damage' done by criminal proceedings to the victim and to support the victim in coping, not only with her victimisation, but also with criminal proceedings. Hence, the harm/needs-paradigm draws a clear demarcation line between criminal justice as a matter of *public* interest and the *personal* interests of the victim to be recognised as having suffered because of the offence, to be supported in overcoming these consequences, to receive reparation and to be protected against secondary or repeat victimisation.

There was—and still is—very reasonable scepticism of the practice of highlighting the risks of secondary victimisation inherent in criminal justice systems today. This is because, rather than insisting that the victim should be at the heart of the criminal justice system and that overcoming the risks of secondary victimisation is a prerequisite of any such inclusion, the harm-based approach historically rather added to victims' mistrust of and alienation from the criminal justice system. Instead of challenging the inbuilt abusive tendencies of the witness-paradigm and of criticising the attitudes of practitioners indifferent to the rights of victims, the harm/needs-model tended—and tends—to accept the antagonism of criminal justice and victims as a natural given. This position overlooks the fact that criminal justice, for most of its history, was an institution used by victims and their families in seeking justice and that an effective system of human rights cannot do without the criminal justice system protecting the rights of individuals against severe violations.

The crux of the matter is that 'harm', like 'injury' or 'damage', is a descriptive term that does not imply any normative judgment. An earthquake or an accident can cause harm without being a wrong. The harm suffered calls for medical treatment, a psycho-social intervention or state compensation of damages, but does not necessitate a normative or legal remedy restoring the victim as a person entitled to the respect of her rights. The term 'harm' obscures the crucial fact that a criminal offence, when directed against an individual, violates that person's rights and hence raises questions as to the community's reaction in terms of acknowledging the victim as a person and of holding offenders to account. Thus, the focus on the harm suffered by the victim diverts attention away from granting the victim access to justice. The harm suffered by the victim can be addressed to some extent outside the criminal justice system, including through social, health, and victim support services. Thus the harm-based approach leaves the concept of the victim as—at best—a witness in place and systematically denies victims access to criminal justice by concealing the fact that a criminal offence from the victim's perspective, denotes an infringement of her rights and disrespect of the victim as a person.

Treating the victim based on the actual harm suffered and her concrete needs has convincingly been compared to the rehabilitation model of dealing with offenders according to their needs and in an allegedly beneficial manner. Sebba (2000, p. 64) characterised the rehabilitation orientation in the following terms:

> Under the rehabilitation model, the victim (as previously was the case with the offender) is an object of policies implemented by professionals or bureaucrats who make determinations as to his or her best interests. This was the connotation of individualization when positivist criminology held sway.

To this, Sebba adds the remark that 'the second half of the twentieth century saw an increasing sensitivity to human rights, with the autonomy of the individual as one of its key concepts [. . .]; autonomy imports such rights as participation, self-expression and representation' (Sebba 2000, p. 64). In contrast, in the rehabilitation model it is not the victim's autonomous decision but the helper's diagnosis that decides on the appropriate intervention. Thus the rehabilitation model, which grounds the victim's claims in the state's duty of care, shares with all welfare policies the inbuilt risk of a paternalistic attitude, which can be overcome solely by assigning rights to the victim and allowing her to reach her own autonomous decisions, from sufficient resources made available to her including targeted support services, legal advice and legal aid if needed (Hörnle 2014).

One expression of the harm-based model is allowing victims to input into sentencing by describing the effect of the offence on themselves and their lives in the form of victim impact statements. In substance, by delivering such a statement, the victim provides evidence of certain aspects of the offence, which fits the victim's role as a witness. An assessment of the effects of victim impact statements in the UK has found that, "contrary to arguments that victim input leads to punitiveness and sentence harshness", such statements in fact "enhance proportionality and accuracy in sentencing" (Erez 2000, p. 173). While the victim as a witness remains obliged to deliver evidence, it is now added emphatically that the victim is also entitled to do so.

By defining the effect of the offence in terms of the suffering and harm inflicted on the victim and not in categories of an individual's rights being violated, victim impact statements foster the harm-based model. Consequentially Erez found that allowing victims in the UK to provide impact statements has "not affected fundamental principles underlying the adversarial legal system", nor "transformed victims into parties to proceedings" (2000, p. 173).

Neither the damage, nor the harm paradigm, challenges the basic assumption that criminal justice is, at its core, a matter between the state and the offender. In the damage paradigm, the civil party is a possible ally, but still maintains an external position from the perspective of the criminal justice system, while the public prosecutor and the defendant—or her counsel—take centre stage. Similarly, in the harm paradigm, the victim is protected from further harm resulting from her involvement in the criminal justice process, which revolves around the state and the offender. Hence in the damage and the harm paradigm the victim remains, from the perspective of the criminal justice system and its perceived objectives, either as a witness or irrelevant. Therefore, the damage and the harm/needs paradigm are complementary to the witness paradigm, as they do not challenge its premises.

1.3.4 Private Accusation and the Victim's Right to Enforce Public Prosecution

Private accusation instituted by the victim and prosecution on her request are relics of an era before monarchs, striving for absolutist powers of legislation in the seventeenth and eighteenth century, claimed criminal justice as a means of demonstrating that the law was an expression of their will and that hence any criminal offence was a matter of insubordination and a personal insult to the monarch. Even then criminal offences that related to particularly private matters—like trespassing in a private domicile, violation of secrecy of letters, violations of honour, adultery and sexual offences, minor forms of bodily injury or offences committed within a family—seemed both intimate and insignificant enough to be left to victims. The result was of a somewhat odd and hybrid nature. While state doctrine claimed that all powers were united and personified by the monarch and that hence the monarch was the incarnation of the state's laws and eventually offended by a criminal offence disobeying her laws, criminal proceedings were, for certain—'private'—offences, nevertheless initiated by private persons enabling them to pursue private interests supported by the powers of public authorities. Criminal justice was viewed as helping the victim in seeking redress and satisfaction for the criminal wrong incurred as a private person. Hence, the right to claim the punishment of the offender rested with the victim (Malaniuk 1947, p. 74).

It is worth noticing that even at times of monarchs' absolutist rule and nation states' unchallenged dominance victims were never entirely deprived of their right to claim redress in a criminal court for the wrong suffered, even if this right was increasingly restricted to exceptional cases. At all times, private accusation formed part of the criminal justice system, and indeed a part that cannot be explained unless one acknowledges the right of the victim to amends being made by the offender—and it is striking how this fact is systematically overlooked by the traditional narrative, which insists in a dogmatic manner that the victim cannot have a right to the prosecution, conviction or punishment of the offender (this inconsistency has rightly been observed by Holz 2007, p. 139).

In light of the following, another observation is appropriate at this point. Supporting the view that the victim is entitled to the conviction—and in some instances even to the punishment—of the offender does not necessarily imply that the victim should be burdened with the procedural task of charging the offender. A right of the victim to the conviction of the offender neither implicates that prosecuting the offender is exclusively of concern to the victim, nor that the victim's right to justice is her private matter and of no interest to her legal community. Leaving whether the offender is held to account or not to the private motion of the victim whether the offender is held to account or not can easily be understood as signalling that the primary rights of victims abused by the offender are of little significance. In particular, in cases of partner or ex-partner violence against women, private accusation amounts to a 'mechanism of discouragement' of victims and to an improper signal that the state attaches only subordinate importance to violence against women or considers 'domestic' violence a family matter (Spronz 2011).

What is more appropriate than private accusation is a mechanism allowing the victim to challenge decisions made by the public prosecutor not to prosecute or to discontinue proceedings. Several European legal orders grant the victim such a procedural right to judicial review of prosecutors' decisions, including the Klagserzwingungsverfahren under German Law and the victim's right to claim that the prosecutor continue prosecution—Fortsetzungsantrag—in Austrian proceedings. And, again, it is difficult to justify in a plausible manner why the victim and only the victim has such a procedural right without acknowledging a victim's legitimate interest in the prosecution, conviction and, in appropriate cases, also punishment of the offender (Holz 2007, pp. 138–141). This marks another blind spot in the traditional view of criminal justice.

1.3.5 *The Rights Paradigm*

The rights paradigm questions the basic premise of the witness paradigm, namely that the offence is directed against the state and not against the rights of the victim. The fundamental concern of the rights paradigm has been expressed, in clear terms, by Brienen and Hoegen (2000, pp. 30–31) as a conclusion of a comparative analysis of the position of victims in 22 European criminal justice systems:

> A crime is, first and foremost, to be regarded as a violation of the individual rights of the victim. No longer should a crime be seen only as an intrusion on public order, nor should the state be the sole agent seeking redress for the act committed. The change in criminal justice concepts in perceiving crime as a hostile act by one citizen against another, demands that the latter individual, i.e., the victim, also play a part in the aftermath of the crime.

Hence, in the rights paradigm the victim is conceived as the person whose rights—to life, to physical and sexual integrity, to property etc.—are protected by criminal law provisions and who is therefore directly concerned when an offence is committed. The rights paradigm turns the witness paradigm upside down: it is not the victim obliged by the state to support public interests as a witness; to the contrary, the state is taken by the victim to task for not effectively protecting her rights.

The rights model amounts to a veritable and fundamental change of paradigm. The wrong done to the victim is the very foundation of the entire system of criminal justice. It is not the state but the victim who is entitled to the conviction of the offender and hence to state authorities doing their best to identify, convict, and, in appropriate cases, even punish offenders.

The traditional paradigm recognises two actors, namely the state and the offender. The rights paradigm takes the shape of a triangular pyramid. The base area is triangular, as it has three parties at its corners, the victim, the offender, and the public prosecutor representing the rights of all members of the legal community. In this model, the court is located at the top of the pyramid. It is confronted with various claims of the parties, which all have their basis in human rights.

1.3.6 Victims' Primary, Secondary and Tertiary Rights

As a matter of terminology, primary, secondary and tertiary rights of victims will be distinguished.

The term 'primary rights' denotes an individual's rights the violation of which constitutes the criminal offence, while the term 'secondary rights' refers to the rights the victim has because of the violation of her primary rights. Hence, this book analyses the victim's secondary rights as consequential to the violation, by the offender, of the victim's primary rights.

It will be maintained that a victim of crime holds three secondary rights, namely to justice, to non-recurrence (protection against repeat victimisation) and to respectful treatment (protection against 'secondary victimisation', as will be explained in Chap. 4). The victim holds these three rights, because she is a victim, the person, that is, whose primary rights have been violated by the criminal offender. The right to justice encompasses several elements, including the right to know the truth, the right to the conviction and, in appropriate cases, also punishment of the offender as well as, again, in appropriate cases, the right to compensation. In legal terminology, a victim's secondary rights concern substantive, not procedural, law. They define what is owed to the victim, not how it is provided.

Tertiary rights are rights of victim's serving to implement their secondary rights, in particular within the framework of criminal proceedings. Because, for instance, the victim has a secondary right to justice, she has a tertiary right to challenge a prosecutor's decision to discontinue proceedings. Because the victim has a secondary right to be treated with care and respect and to be spared from secondary victimisation, the victim has, under certain conditions, a tertiary right to be protected against confrontation with the offender. However, there is not necessarily a one-to-one correspondence between secondary and tertiary rights. A victim's tertiary right to have access to a support service is not consequential to one particular secondary right but fosters the realisation of all three secondary rights of victims.

This book focuses on primary and secondary, not on tertiary rights of crime victims. It explores what it is that the victim can legitimately expect from criminal justice, not the procedural rights enabling victims to initiate and participate in proceedings. However, one main message is that tertiary—including procedural—rights must have a basis in secondary rights. Unless victims have a right to justice, it is unclear what place and role they have in criminal proceedings.

1.4 The Emerging Paradigm: States' Duty to Combat Impunity

1.4.1 In Need of a Paradigm Shift

The more the position of the victim develops in criminal proceedings, the more tensions and inconsistencies arise between criminal justice conceived as enforcement of criminal law in the public interest on the one hand and as protecting the rights of individuals on the other. This tension is seen most clearly when legislators must decide on the role of the victim, who is treated as a witness in the traditional system, but is necessarily admitted as a party to the proceedings if criminal justice is mainly about the violation of her rights.

Because of the unbroken dominance of the traditional, state-centred paradigm, there is a risk that new elements, which are introduced to inspire a new spirit and awareness of the rights of victims, are assimilated into the conventional logic and converted to work towards meeting the traditional ends of bringing an offender to justice (Reeves and Mulley 2000, p. 136). Reeves and Mully expressed their concern that 'when it comes to implementation, victims' interests become hijacked by the traditional criminal justice agenda' (2000, p. 142).

1.4.2 The Fundamental Inconsistency Between the Traditional Paradigm and Victims' Rights

Indeed, criminal justice protecting public interests and criminal justice protecting the rights of individuals are two fundamentally different concepts and orientations. While in the first paradigm, it seems appropriate to oblige victims to support the state in accomplishing the punishment of the offender, within a human rights paradigm exactly the opposite is true, that the state is obliged to serve the interests of individual rights-holders and to pay attention to all human rights at stake. Unless the fundamental difference of the two approaches is taken seriously, implanting victims' rights in traditional criminal justice systems with their state-centred orientation remains like grafting a green branch of victims' rights onto an old stock of a considerably more étatist and collectivist nature. This comes with a risk that the branch will not prosper and that the abuse of victims will prevail. Even in those systems where the victim is gradually recognised as a party to the proceedings, she is at the same time also treated as a witness. As a result, the system remains inconsistent, precarious and unstable (an analysis of these complexities provides Lüderssen 2002).

The thesis that is posited and explored holds that in criminal justice systems, complexities arise from a profound incompatibility between the tasks of protecting public interests and goods, defined by criminal law, on the one hand and protecting the rights of individuals on the other. As long as victims' rights are inserted into a framework that serves the state's entitlement to the punishment of the offender, they will continue to cause inconsistencies and frictions and to lose out whenever they interfere with 'public interests'.

Criminal justice could easily absorb and integrate victims' rights if it was largely founded on the rights of individuals. Yet to date it is not. The traditional view conceives of criminal justice not as an instrument of human rights protection, but a system that pursues a clearly more collectivist and étatist orientation, which runs counter to the strictly individualist approach of human dignity and human rights. The traditional criminal justice system has an instrumental view of the victim as primarily serving as a witness and tasked with delivering evidence in the public interest.

It is no coincidence that, to a certain extent, similar complexities arise in conceptualising offenders. Again, state-centred criminal law tends to view the offender as an object, as a means to public ends, serving the purpose of criminal justice to deter offences. This becomes evident when the offender is dealt with as a risk factor, a security issue or an enemy but is not respected and treated as a responsible actor and citizen capable of accounting for her actions, of making amends for the wrong she has done and of providing redress to victims. Instead of acknowledging and empowering the victim and the offender and of supporting them in overcoming their—inherently transitional—statuses, the traditional state-centred approach tends to reduce victims and offenders to objects of a state's manipulation in supposed and vague public interests. The traditional system relegates victims and offenders 'to the status of information providers for decisions, rather than people in whom the criminal justice system should be interested in their own right'(Shapland 2000, p. 157). Hence there is 'little idea' that 'justice incorporates both victims and offenders' (Shapland 2000, p. 148).

Therefore, the opposing orientations of the traditional state-centred concept of criminal justice as a means of enforcing criminal law and safeguarding public interests on the one hand, and of criminal justice as a system protecting the rights of individuals on the other, collide. The criminal justice system's difficulties in integrating victims' rights points to the necessity of leaving the state-centred paradigm behind, and of profoundly reconstructing criminal justice based on human dignity and human rights.

Victims' secondary rights to the conviction and, in appropriate cases, also punishment of offenders have the potential to serve as the very foundation and rationale of criminal law and criminal justice. What becomes visible on the horizon is a complete shift of paradigm of the criminal justice system, a metamorphosis from an étatist to human-rights based institution, which no longer contends itself with upholding an abstract rule of criminal law but progresses to the protection of concrete human rights of individuals. For this shift to come about, criminal law must be designed to protect human rights; and the entire criminal procedure needs to reflect the fact that the violation of an individual's rights, protected by criminal law, forms the very substance of the offence, which is the subject matter of the proceedings. Hence, the victim should, in the same way as the defendant, be acknowledged as a main stakeholder in, and party to, these proceedings.

As the criminal justice system currently stands, it is not sufficient to simply implant the victim as a new figure in proceedings. The necessary changes to the system concern not only the number of actors admitted on the stages of the criminal courts, but the very plot and style of the play performed. If we accept that one main objective of criminal proceedings is to acknowledge the victim as the person whose rights have been violated, and who for that reason can legitimately expect that the wrong is righted by amends made by the offender, then proceedings need to be carefully reconstructed to meet this aim. In relation to the common law countries, Jo Goodey has emphasised this point in the following terms (2005, p. 127):

> When and if victims' needs should be redefined as victims' rights is a debate that touches on underlying principles of justice. To put the victim at the heart of the criminal justice system is to reinterpret centuries of practice where the role between State and offender has been central to the resolution of crime and the administration of justice in common law systems, and the victim has been relegated to the role of witness.

1.4.3 The Necessity to Depart from Substantive Criminal Law

The objective of proceedings is not defined by procedural law, but by substantive criminal law (Schmidt 2015). Proceedings implement substantive criminal law; and it is substantive criminal law, which by defining what constitutes a 'crime' lays the basis for constructing appropriate reactions, aimed to remedy the commission of a crime. If substantive criminal law defines 'crime' as a violation of the laws of a state and, from this, grants the state a right to the punishment of the offender, then it is the task of criminal proceedings—governed by procedural law—to set out a procedure apt to ensure that the state's right to the punishment of the offender is effectively realised.

If, on the other hand, substantive criminal law defined 'crime' as the violation of the rights of an individual and, accordingly, granted this individual—the victim—a right to the identification and conviction of the offender, then criminal proceedings would be tasked with staging the implementation of this right of the victim. In any case, it is substantive criminal law, which by defining what constitutes a 'crime' predetermines what can be considered an appropriate reaction to crime; and it is then the criminal proceedings that enforce this reaction.

Very precisely, Tatjana Hörnle diagnosed the crux of the matter highlighting the absence of the victim in theories of crime and punishment and a general consensus among German lawyers that the state punishes offenders in the public interest of society as a collectivity and not in the interest of individual victims (2011, p. 29):

> Die nach wie vor herrschende Ansicht in der deutschen Strafrechtswissenschaft weist bei allen Unterschieden eine Gemeinsamkeit auf: die konsequent kollektivistische Auffassung. Ob es um die Bestätigung von Normen oder um die Verhinderung von zukünftigen Delikten geht: Die Bestrafung erfolgt nach gängiger Auffassung sowohl bei Taten gegen Kollektivrechtsgüter als auch bei Taten gegen Individualrechtsgüter ausschließlich im Interesse der Allgemeinheit. Damit wird ausgeblendet, dass bei schweren Straftaten gegen ein individuelles Opfer dessen allgemeines Persönlichkeitsrecht verletzt würde, wenn der Staat sich weigern würde, ein glaubhaftes Unwerturteil zu fällen.

Therefore, if victims' rights are to become effective, it is not sufficient to consider them only in the context of a procedure that is not designed to make victims' rights a reality, but is directed at achieving the aim of ensuring that the state's right to the punishment of the offender is met. Already in 1995 this has been pointed out by George Fletcher who observed (1995, p. 201):

> One lesson to be drawn from these disputes about the victim's role at various phases of the trial is that so much turns on our rationale for punishment. If we think of punishment primarily as a social measure, inflicted by the People for the future security of the people, then the public prosecutor emerges as the primary player in the trial. The people are represented in the prosecutor's office. The victim is left on the margins of the trial. If we think of punishment as a form of compensation for the wrong done, then the person to whom the compensation is owed, namely the victim, comes center stage.

Fletcher's own view on the matter is that neither of these approaches is correct, because punishment "is neither a means of engineering public safety nor a mode of compensation" (1995, p. 201); rather criminal justice is, in Fletcher's view, about restoring the victim "as a self-respecting, functioning member of society" (1995, p. 257). In any case, Fletcher makes his point that criminal proceedings implement substantive criminal law. If crime is essentially a wrong done to the victim, and if punishment is about redressing this wrong, then victims have an important role to perform in criminal proceedings.

It is exactly this paradigm shift that this book is about; and it is assumed here that the development of criminal justice from an institution enforcing rights of the state to an institution implementing rights of individuals, including the victim, is to be contextualised within the wider political framework of European polities moving beyond the historical phase of nation states towards a global polity based on the principles of human dignity and human rights.

The remainder of this chapter will set out the historical development of victims' rights and contextualise this development within the framework of international law progressively outlawing the impunity of grave human rights violations. The chapter will then examine the ECtHR's approach to protecting victim's rights through criminal law before concluding on the pitfalls of basing punishment on deterrence, and the advantages of instead using human dignity as a justification and basis for convicting and, in appropriate cases, punishing offenders.

1.5 First Seismic Activity

In the late 1960s until the mid-1990s, two pivotal developments occurred. Firstly, a human rights movement, relying on a cosmopolitan concept of human dignity, gained momentum. Secondly, the idea that the state is obliged to protect human rights by means of criminal law and criminal justice made significant headway. Jointly, these two developments have a potential to change profoundly the face of the criminal justice system.

In this regard, the battered-women's movements in the USA, in Britain and in other European countries were of crucial importance. They challenged the readiness of the police and criminal justice systems to evenly and consistently fulfil the core function of a state—to protect individuals' rights to dignity and physical integrity against violence. As a consequence, laws, policies and attitudes gradually improved in many countries, and the right of women to be effectively protected against violence, including by means of criminal justice, achieved international recognition at the UN World Conference on Human Rights in Vienna (June 1993) and at the Fourth UN World Conference on Women in Beijing (September 1995; Brückner 1998; Dobash and Dobash 1992; Klein et al. 1997). These movements represent paradigmatically the evolving claim of individuals to the protection of their dignity and human rights and, at the same time, challenge the patriarchal, authoritarian and discriminatory order inherent in nation states.

1.5.1 A Notable Root-Cause: Anti-Authoritarian Scepticism

Why did the position of the victim change, and why can this result in the reconstruction of criminal justice? To answer these questions, it is crucial not to overlook the tectonic shifts in the global social, moral and political landscape that occurred mainly within the two and a half decades between 1965 and 1990. This period saw many changes, including the crisis of the super-powers and the rise of the New Left and its anti-authoritarian and cosmopolitan values of individual freedom, peace, diversity, and the introduction of civil society's global responsibility.

During this period, the political and cultural landscape changed fundamentally in many Western societies. This affected the understanding of the relationship between states and their legitimate claims on the one hand, and individuals and their rights on the other. Before the 1960s, individuals were seen as deriving their fundamental status as citizens from their affiliation to, and birthright as, members of a nation-state—their 'home country.' However, during this period the state lost much of its reputation and appeal as an object of identification and source of pride as many individuals started to sceptically distance themselves from their state and its society.

In their relations to state authorities—including prominently the police and the institutions of criminal justice—individuals became more critical and more demanding. Until then, the supremacy and sovereignty of nation-states were solely premised on the states' readiness to allow for certain individual freedoms and to strike a balance between the rights and legitimate interests of individuals as citizens on the one hand, and public or national interests represented by the state, on the other. Yet from the late 1960s, the prestige of the nation-state as inherently and indisputably valuable in itself eroded, and began to be replaced by a more nuanced understanding of public authorities.

In a way, this resulted in a reversal of the relationship of states and individuals. Prior to this change, individuals were regarded and appreciated as useful members of their country, but now the instrumental function of state authorities as serving the rights of individuals is emphasised. In other words, the direction of functionality has changed: Instead of individuals deriving their status from their affiliation to and usefulness for their country, the state's legitimacy is viewed as premised on the rights of individuals, and the ability of state authorities to meet these rights. The state is seen as having only an instrumental status and legitimacy as a means to enable individuals to cooperate and live together peacefully in a territory.

Consequently, a consensus gradually emerged in the legal world that it is not sufficient for states to respect human rights as restrictions on, and limitations of, their own actions. If—or in historical terms once, citizens question why the police and criminal courts are needed (and financed by taxpayers), the fact that they do not interfere with the rights of individuals is not a convincing response. Such a result could be achieved more safely (and cheaply) by abandoning the police and courts altogether. Although this 'negative' function of the state is vital in securing to individuals a sphere of autonomy, this task alone is not exhaustive, as limitations on a state's actions do not prevent others from interfering with the rights of individuals. For example, an individual's right to physical integrity requires protection not only—and not even primarily—against state authorities but also against other 'non-state'—or 'private'—actors. Hence, comprehensive human rights protection is premised on a state taking effective action to discourage and prevent 'private' individuals from inflicting violence on one another.

In terms of the human rights doctrine, states have obligations not only to *respect*—refrain from interfering with—but also to *protect* human rights against violations from non-state actors. In Europe, this distinction was made by the ECtHR in its judgment in the case of *Ireland v the United Kingdom* in 1978. The case paved the way for the Court's *X and Y v the Netherlands* judgment of 1985, in which a state's obligation to protect the rights of individuals against interferences of other private—non-state—actors by means of criminal law provisions was spelled out for the first time. In Europe, the *X and Y* judgment lays the foundation for a victim's right to justice (the German term is '*Justizgewährungsanspruch*'; see Holz 2007; Schmidt 2015, p. 183).

In the 1980s, the regional human rights courts in Europe and America, which were among the main forces driving reform, made it clear that the objective of criminal law is human rights protection. Hence, the individual, whose rights the state failed to protect, can legitimately claim for the wrong to be righted and for state authorities to do everything reasonable to restore respect for her rights and to bring those responsible to justice. Not only are victims entitled to a thorough and effective investigation and prosecution, leading to the identification and punishment of offenders, they are also entitled to have access to criminal proceedings and to perform a substantial role within these proceedings (Holz 2007; FRA 2014, pp. 25-28).

1.5.2 First Indications of a Paradigm Shift at the International Level

Regional and international human rights actors gave the main impulses for the development of human-rights based approach to criminal justice. This approach first emerged over the 70s and 80s of the previous century when the issue of impunity surfaced as an endemic phenomenon in countries lacking efficient institutions of criminal justice and a strong rule of law. On an international scale, this development reflected the unbearable situation of human rights in many regions of the globe.

What figures prominently in the case-law of the court in Strasbourg are proceedings concerning the situation of the Kurdish minority at times of the Turkish 'deep state', when the Kurdish population living in the eastern provinces of Turkey faced severe forms of oppression from the hands of state agents and collaborators. The Turkish authorities were evidently reluctant to seriously investigate violent incidents (in which they were involved), which resulted in the widespread impunity of offences committed by state officials and their accomplices. These events demonstrated in a telling manner the precarious situation of human rights in conditions of a state—for political motives—systematically negating the rights of a segment of society or of political opponents or both. The situation of human rights in many countries was dictated by a similar political situation. On a global scale, these severe deficiencies made it difficult or impossible to further ignore the crucial functions of criminal justice in protecting human rights. Without functioning mechanisms of criminal justice, the human rights of individuals are, to a vast extent, left without effective protection.

A human rights approach to criminal justice does not depart from the question of whether a state is entitled to punish offenders. Instead, it asks in which circumstances, and to what extent, individuals are entitled to the protection of their rights by means of criminal law and criminal justice. Criminal justice—all of criminal justice—can be seen as answering this question. The obligation of states to punish reflects the entitlement of individuals to the punishment of offenders as a means of effective protection of their human rights. The emerging new paradigm hence departs from the old paradigm, assuming instead that, whenever fundamental aspects of human rights are at stake, states are not only entitled, but likewise obliged to provide effective protection of human rights by criminal law, investigations and proceedings. Hence, the emergence of victims' rights indicates a shift of paradigm, in the course of which the criminal justice system develops from institutions that are about *entitlements of the state* to the punishment of offenders to institutions that are *obliged* and consequently designed to meet human rights *claims of individuals* to criminal justice.

Another important incentive stems from the UN Convention against Torture and Other Cruel, Inhuman or Degrading Treatment or Punishment (CAT), which was adopted in 1984. Article 12 of the CAT states that a state party 'shall ensure that its competent authorities proceed to a prompt and impartial investigation, wherever there is reasonable ground to believe that an act of torture has been committed in any territory under its jurisdiction.' It is worth mentioning that the judgments passed under this provision relate not only to countries lacking a democratic political system but also to European states. For example, the UN Committee against Torture in 1993 ruled on a case of police violence in Vienna in 1988. It found that 15 months had passed before investigations were instituted against police officers who had been interrogated by an investigative judge for the abuse of detainees. The Committee found that this delay was irreconcilable with the state's obligation to promptly investigate suspicions of torture or inhuman treatment (CAT, *Halimi-Nedzibi v. Austria*).

If one had to decide on the year in which victims' rights finally entered the international stage of policy making and legislation, the year 1985 would be a strong candidate. In this year, the UN General Assembly adopted the Declaration of Basic Principles of Justice for Victims of Crime and Abuse of Power affirming 'the necessity of adopting national and international measures in order to secure the universal and effective recognition of, and respect for, the rights of victims of crime and of abuse of power'. In the same year, Recommendation No. R(85)11 on the Position of the Victim in the Framework of Criminal Law and Procedure was adopted by the Council of Europe's Committee of Ministers. Again in the same year, the ECtHR in Strasbourg reached its landmark decision on the rights of victims in the case of *X and Y v the Netherlands*, which will be explained in detail below.

The UN Declaration and the Council of Europe's Recommendation are clear expressions of the harm/needs paradigm in that they revolve around the harm suffered by the victim and the problems and needs resulting from that harm. Their general orientation is spelled out by the Recommendation's opening statement:

> [. . .] Considering that the objectives of the criminal justice system have traditionally been expressed in terms which primarily concern the relationship between the state and the offender;
>
> Considering that consequently the operation of this system has sometimes tended to add to rather than to diminish the problems of the victim;
>
> Considering that it must be a fundamental function of criminal justice to meet the needs and to safeguard the interests of the victim [. . .].

By referring to the 'problems', 'needs' and 'interests' of the victim, the Recommendation adopts an approach to criminal justice that focuses on the harm done to individuals and consequently on the deserving victim and her needs. The underlying premise is that a person who finds herself in a situation of distress is deserving of the compassion and support of her community. In a way, this harm-based approach corresponds with the concept of the social welfare state, which emphasises the community's solidarity with those in need. Thus, from the first conception of victim's rights at a regional and international level, the needs paradigm was adopted to compensate the victim for harm caused. This position is very different from the rights-based approach, the development of which will be explored later in this chapter.

1.5.3 The Inter-American Court of Human Rights (IACtHR)

Before analysing in some detail the ECtHR's case-law on the matter, it is worth mentioning that the Court in Strasbourg did not come up with its new approach in isolation, but acted in line with a current trend in legal development. As a point in case, it may be recalled that in 1988, the Inter-American Court of Human Rights (IACtHR) made a ground-breaking judgment in the case of *Velásquez-Rodríguez against Honduras*. The Court referred to Article 1 (1) of the American Convention on Human Rights which provides that the States Parties to the convention ensure to all persons subject to their jurisdiction the free and full exercise of the rights recognised by the convention. To show the subsequent line of argument pursued by the court the decisive paragraphs are quoted below:

> 174. The State has a legal duty to take reasonable steps to prevent human rights violations and to use the means at its disposal to carry out a serious investigation of violations committed within its jurisdiction, to identify those responsible, to impose the appropriate punishment and to ensure the victim adequate compensation.
>
> 175. This duty to prevent includes all those means of a legal, political, administrative and cultural nature that promote the protection of human rights and ensure that any violations are considered and treated as illegal acts, which, as such, may lead to the punishment of those responsible and the obligation to indemnify the victims for damages [...]
>
> 176. The State is obligated to investigate every situation involving a violation of the rights protected by the Convention. If the State apparatus acts in such a way that the violation goes unpunished and the victim's full enjoyment of such rights is not restored as soon as possible, the State has failed to comply with its duty to ensure the free and full exercise of those rights to the persons within its jurisdiction. The same is true when the State allows private persons or groups to act freely and with impunity to the detriment of the rights recognized by the Convention.

The first two paragraphs (paras. 174–175) highlight the victim's right to the prosecution of offenders as a matter of the preventive function of criminal law. As a means of preventing severe human rights violations, State Parties are under an obligation to criminalise and prosecute such violations. This obligation forms the cornerstone of the emerging new paradigm of criminal justice as a means of human rights protection. The third paragraph (para. 176) highlights the restorative function of criminal justice. By punishing human rights violations, the criminal court 'restores' the victim's full 'enjoyment' and 'exercise' of her human rights. This alludes to the function of rehabilitating the rights of the victim, thereby curtailing the negative effect of the offence on the victim's rights in real social life, as highlighted by the ECtHR's case-law under Article 13 ECHR.

The key innovation of the case lies in constructing the functions of criminal justice from the perspective of individuals' human rights, replacing an approach that departs from the interests of the state or the public or society as a whole. The *Velásquez-Rodríguez* judgment is one of the first signs of the shift of paradigm in the understanding of criminal justice not as reinforcing state's authority, but as confirming human dignity and the rights of victims.

In the following decades, victim's right of access to justice in the IACtHR's case-law emerged as combining the right to an effective remedy (Article 25 ACHR) with fair-trial rights (Article 8 ACHR). In its judgment of November 14, 2014 in the case of *Rodríguez Vera et al. (the Disappeared from the Palace of Justice) v. Colombia* the IACtHR summarised its case-law observing:

> 435. The Court recalls that, based on the protection granted by Articles 8 and 25 of the Convention, States are obliged to provide effective judicial remedies to the victims of human rights violations, which must be made available in accordance with the rules of due process of law.[...] The Court has also indicated that the right of access to justice must ensure, within a reasonable time, the right of the presumed victims or their next of kin that everything necessary is done to discover the truth of what happened and to investigate, prosecute and duly punish those eventually found responsible. [...]
>
> 436. The obligation to investigate human rights violations is one of the positive measures that States must take to ensure the rights recognized in the Convention. [...] Thus, starting with its first judgment, this Court has stressed the importance of the State's duty to investigate and punish violations of human rights, [...] and this is particularly important in view of the severity of the offenses committed and the nature of the rights harmed.

1.5.4 The European Court of Human Rights on States' Obligations to Protect Rights

During the 1970s, the ECtHR extended the significance of the rights guaranteed by the ECHR to imply that states are obliged to take action to effectively protect individuals' human rights. There is by now a clear understanding that states are obliged not only to *respect* human rights in the vertical relationship between the state's own actors and an individual subject, and to refrain from human rights violations committed by state actors (a 'negative obligation'), but also to take action aimed at *protecting* the rights of the individual (a 'positive obligation').

These obligations require states to act against infringements from the part of another private individual—or non-state actor. This assumption leads directly to the question of by which means a state can achieve a satisfactory level of protection.

The answer given by current human rights doctrine is that criminal sanctions are indispensable to *dissuade* serious human rights violations and to assure individuals of a sufficient level of protection of their rights (FRA 2012, p. 21). Hence, soon after the ECtHR recognised the positive obligation of states to protect human rights against the risk of victimisation by another private (non-state) actor, it then went on to accept that states cannot fulfil their obligations without enacting criminal law provisions. Thus, in the 1980s, the Court posited that effective protection against severe violations of human rights cannot be achieved by other means than by sufficiently *deterrent* criminalisation (where the difference between 'dissuasion' and 'deterrence' should not be overlooked).

Crucial steps were taken by the Court in the case of *Ireland v UK*, which was decided by the Court in plenary session in January 1978. This case dealt with systematic mistreatment by British security forces of persons suspected of having been involved in terrorist acts. In paragraph 239 of its judgment the ECtHR stated:

> By substituting the words 'shall secure' for the words 'undertake to secure' in the text of Article 1 [...], the drafters of the Convention also intended to make it clear that the rights and freedoms set out in Section I would be directly secured to anyone within the jurisdiction of the Contracting States [...]. That intention finds a particularly faithful reflection in those instances where the Convention has been incorporated into domestic law [...]. The Convention does not merely oblige the higher authorities of the Contracting States to respect for their own part the rights and freedoms it embodies; as is shown by Article 14 [...] and the English text of Article 1 [...] ('shall secure'), the Convention also has the consequence that, in order to secure the enjoyment of those rights and freedoms, those authorities must prevent or remedy any breach at subordinate levels.

The English text of Article 14 ECHR—the prohibition of discrimination—starts with the words 'The enjoyment of the rights and freedoms set forth in this Convention shall be secured without discrimination ...' According to the Court, to secure the rights embodied in the Convention state authorities 'must prevent or remedy any breach', a formula indicating that obligations to protect comprise these two components of preventing or remedying breaches.

This new approach was echoed by the Commission's decision of July 1978 (7154/75, *Association of Parents*, p. 32), where the Commission held: 'The concept that everyone's life shall be protected by law enjoins the State not only to refrain from taking life intentionally but, further, to take appropriate steps to safeguard life.' The following year, the Court in the case of *Marckx v. Belgium* introduced the terminology distinguishing between a state's positive and negative obligations. It held that a state is not merely compelled to abstain from an interference with the exercise of family life; 'in addition to this primarily negative undertaking, there may be positive obligations inherent in an effective 'respect' for family life' (ECtHR, 6833/74, *Marckx*, para. 31).

Some months later, this distinction was confirmed in the *Airey* case (ECtHR, 6289/73), which concerned a situation of domestic violence. Mrs. Johanna Airey, living in Cork, was frequently threatened with, and occasionally subjected to, physical violence by her husband. Her main complaint was that the state—Ireland—had failed to protect her against physical and mental cruelty from her violent husband. The Commission accepted the application in so far as Mrs. Airey's complaint that the prohibitive cost of proceedings amounted to a total inaccessibility and exclusiveness of the remedy of a judicial separation in the High Court. Accepting this argument, the Court found that Mrs. Airey did not enjoy an effective right of access to the High Court for the purpose of petitioning for a decree of judicial separation and that there has accordingly been a breach of Article 6 para. 1 ECHR. In addition, the applicant claimed that the absence of a modern, effective and accessible remedy for marriage breakdown under Irish law constituted a failure to respect her family life under Article 8 of the Convention. To this, the Court responded (paras. 32–33 of the judgment):

> The Court does not consider that Ireland can be said to have "interfered" with Mrs. Airey's private or family life: the substance of her complaint is not that the State has acted but that it has failed to act. However, although the object of Article 8 [...] is essentially that of protecting the individual against arbitrary interference by the public authorities, it does not merely compel the State to abstain from such interference: in addition to this primarily negative undertaking, there may be positive obligations inherent in an effective respect for private or family life. [...] the protection of their private or family life may sometimes necessitate their being relieved from the duty to live together. Effective respect for private or family life obliges Ireland to make this means of protection effectively accessible, when appropriate, to anyone who may wish to have recourse thereto. However, it was not effectively accessible to the applicant: not having been put in a position in which she could apply to the High Court [...], she was unable to seek recognition in law of her de facto separation from her husband. She has therefore been the victim of a violation of Article 8.

1.5.5 States' Obligations to Protect by Means of Enacting and Enforcing Criminal Law Provisions

The judgments presented above did not answer the question as to the means by which a state should fulfil its obligations of human rights protection, and in particular, to what extent such protection could require the adoption of criminal law provisions. This crucial question was decided in March 1985. Given the fundamental significance and innovation of the Court's judgment in the case of *X and Y v the Netherlands* (ECtHR, 8978/80), the relevant passages are of a striking and compelling simplicity.

The circumstances of the case pertained to a young woman who lived in a privately-run home for mentally disabled children and was sexually harassed by the son-in-law of the directress. When her father reported this to the police, the question arose of whether the victim or her father should sign the complaint that was required under Dutch law. While the police decided that the father should file the charges, a court later held that because of a gap in the law neither the victim nor her father was entitled to lodge the complaint.

The ECtHR, referring to the *Airey* judgment, started out from the assumption that an effective respect for private or family life may imply positive obligations, i.e. 'the adoption of measures designed to secure respect for private life even in the sphere of the relations of individuals between themselves' (ECtHR, 8978/80, *X and Y*, para. 23). Remarkably, the inconspicuous last phrase, assuming the relevance of the right under Article 8 ECHR to 'relations of individuals between themselves'—a dimension which lawyers refer to as the horizontal effects of human rights—occurs here for the first time in the Court's case law.

What then follows is a—telling—heading 'Necessity for criminal-law provisions' and four momentous paragraphs without a single reference to previous case law. The Court first admits that the choice of means adopted to secure compliance with Article 8 'in the sphere of the relations of individuals between themselves' is in principle a matter that falls within a states' margin of appreciation and goes on to state (8978/80, *X and Y*, para. 24):

> In this connection, there are different ways of ensuring 'respect for private life', and the nature of the State's obligation will depend on the particular aspect of private life that is at issue. Recourse to the criminal law is not necessarily the only answer.

However, supporting the view of the Commission's delegate that civil law lacked the deterrent effect inherent only in criminal law, the Court concluded (para. 27):

> The Court finds that the protection afforded by the civil law in the case of wrongdoing of the kind inflicted on Miss Y is insufficient. This is a case where fundamental values and essential aspects of private life are at stake. Effective deterrence is indispensable in this area and it can be achieved only by criminal-law provisions.

In the circumstances of the case, the Dutch criminal code did not provide Y 'with practical and effective protection'. Because of this lack of comprehensive protection, the Court found that the Netherlands violated the victim's rights under Article 8 ECHR (para. 30).

This case should be read in light of the Court's previous finding that the concept of private life 'covers the physical and moral integrity of the person, including his or her sexual life' (para. 22). It follows that according to the *X and Y* judgment, member states of the Council of Europe are obliged to protect individuals in their territories by means of comprehensive criminal law provisions against acts of physical, psychological and sexual violence, whenever 'fundamental values and essential aspects of private life are at stake'.

As quoted above, the court assumes that civil law cannot be tasked with functions of protection against violence. Indeed, civil law provisions traditionally lack not only sufficiently harsh sanctions, but also the connotations of censure and reprimand that are inherent and strong in criminal law sanctions.

In the following years, the new position adopted in the *X and Y* judgment only very gradually found its way into the Court's case-law. The judgment is first mentioned in the Commission's decision of October 1985 in the case of *Plattform 'Ärzte für das Leben'* (10126/82), where it is referenced as indicating that a state's positive obligations 'may involve the adoption of measures even in the sphere of the relations of individuals between themselves'. The same aspect of necessary horizontal protection measures is highlighted in a decision of the Commission (*N.*, 11366/85) of October 1986, as well as in the Court's judgment of June 1988 again in the case of *Plattform 'Ärzte für das Leben*. The Commission also refers to the same aspect of a state's obligation to protection measures in the horizontal relations of non-state actors between themselves in its Report in the *Costello-Roberts* case. However, none of these cases touches on matters of protection by means of criminal law.

The line of argument adopted in the *X and Y* judgment received its first comprehensive confirmation only in October 1996 by the Court's judgment in the case of *Stubbing et al. v. the United Kingdom* (22083/93). The subject matter of the procedure were time barred damage claims in four cases of sexual child abuse. In addressing the question of whether English laws deprived the victims of their right under Article 6 (1) of the Convention of access to a court, the Court consistently followed the line of argument from its *X and Y* judgment and found:

> 61. The Court observes, first, that Article 8 [...] is clearly applicable to these complaints, which concern a matter of 'private life', a concept which covers the physical and moral integrity of the person (see the X and Y v. the Netherlands judgment of 26 March 1985, Series A no. 91, p. 11, para. 22).
>
> 62. It is to be recalled that although the object of Article 8 [...] is essentially that of protecting the individual against arbitrary interference by the public authorities, it does not merely compel the State to abstain from such interference: there may, in addition to this primary negative undertaking, be positive obligations inherent in an effective respect for private or family life. These obligations may involve the adoption of measures designed to secure respect for private life even in the sphere of the relations of individuals between themselves (ibid. para. 23). [...]
>
> 64. Sexual abuse is unquestionably an abhorrent type of wrongdoing, with debilitating effects on its victims. Children and other vulnerable individuals are entitled to State protection, in the form of effective deterrence, from such grave types of interference with essential aspects of their private lives (see, mutatis mutandis, the above-mentioned X and Y judgment, p. 13, para. 27).
>
> 65. In the instant case, however, such protection was afforded. The abuse of which the applicants complained is regarded most seriously by the English criminal law and subject to severe maximum penalties [...].

Thus, the United Kingdom was found to be under an obligation to effectively protect the physical and moral integrity of individuals and, moreover, to have complied with this obligation by means of sufficiently dissuasive criminal law provisions.

In contrast, the case of *A. v. the United Kingdom* (25599/94, judgment from September 1998) disclosed a failure of English criminal law to effectively protect children against domestic violence. The applicant had been severely beaten by his stepfather with a garden cane 'which had been applied with considerable force on more than one occasion'. The Court resorted to its position, maintained in the judgments *X and Y* as well as *Stubbings*, that children are entitled to State protection in the form of effective deterrence, against 'such serious breaches of personal integrity'. Despite the fact that the applicant had been subjected to treatment severe enough to fall, according to the Court's assessment, within the scope of Article 3 of the Convention (the prohibition of torture or inhuman or degrading treatment or punishment), a jury had acquitted the applicant's stepfather assuming that the treatment in question amounted to 'reasonable chastisement'. Hence the English criminal law's failure to provide adequate protection constituted, in the view of the Court, a violation of Article 3 ECHR, a view, in fact, shared by the British government, which admitted to the need for legislative amendments.

Meanwhile, this line of case-law is fully established and has been reinforced by numerous judgments. The Court now consistently holds that whenever an individual makes a credible assertion that her rights have been severely violated, the Convention requires that there should be an effective official investigation, which should be capable of leading to the identification and punishment of those responsible, as otherwise the Convention would be ineffective in practice (*Adnaralov*, para. 48).

While under normal conditions protection by effective criminal law provisions is sufficient, it is not when there exist concrete indications pointing to an imminent risk of a rights violation. Already in 1998, a Grand Chamber passed a judgment in the landmark case of *Osman v. the United Kingdom* (No. 23452/94). This judgment is remarkable for the fact that it introduces two levels of risk to which two levels of necessary protection measures correspond. Under conditions of an increased level of risk, authorities may not rely on the general level of protection provided by criminal law provisions, but are obliged to adopt targeted protection measures. The relevant paragraphs of the judgment read as follows:

> 115. The Court notes that the first sentence of Article 2 § 1 enjoins the State not only to refrain from the intentional and unlawful taking of life, but also to take appropriate steps to safeguard the lives of those within its jurisdiction (see the L.C.B. v. the United Kingdom judgment [...]). It is common ground that the State's obligation in this respect extends beyond its primary duty to secure the right to life by putting in place effective criminal-law provisions to deter the commission of offences against the person backed up by law-enforcement machinery for the prevention, suppression and sanctioning of breaches of such provisions. It is thus accepted by those appearing before the Court that Article 2 of the Convention may also imply in certain well-defined circumstances a positive obligation on the authorities to take preventive operational measures to protect an individual whose life is at risk from the criminal acts of another individual. The scope of this obligation is a matter of dispute between the parties.
>
> 116. For the Court, and bearing in mind the difficulties involved in policing modern societies, the unpredictability of human conduct and the operational choices which must be made in terms of priorities and resources, such an obligation must be interpreted in a way which does not impose an impossible or disproportionate burden on the authorities. Accordingly, not every claimed risk to life can entail for the authorities a Convention requirement to take operational measures to prevent that risk from materialising. [...] In the opinion of the Court where there is an allegation that the authorities have violated their positive obligation to protect the right to life in the context of their above-mentioned duty to prevent and suppress offences against the person (see paragraph 115 above), it must be established to its satisfaction that the authorities knew or ought to have known at the time of the existence of a real and immediate risk to the life of an identified individual or individuals from the criminal acts of a third party and that they failed to take measures within the scope of their powers which, judged reasonably, might have been expected to avoid that risk.

In sum, duties of states to protect life are twofold. They, firstly, imply "putting in place effective criminal-law provisions to deter the commission of offences against the person backed up by law-enforcement machinery for the prevention, suppression and sanctioning of breaches of such provisions". Secondly, in situations where the "authorities knew or ought to have known at the time of the existence of a real and immediate risk to the life of an identified individual or individuals from the criminal acts of a third party", Article 2 ECHR obliges authorities to do what can be reasonably expected of them to address the risk.

The Court's requirement that criminal law provisions must be backed up by law-enforcement machinery for the prevention and suppression, but also for the sanctioning of criminal offences, which forms part of the basis of a victim's right to a thorough and effective investigation, will be dealt with later.

The ECtHR's case-law concerning states' obligations to criminalise severe human rights violations is fully developed in the Court's judgment of December 2003 in the case of *M.C. v. Bulgaria* (39272/98). The proceedings concerned a case of a young woman who had been raped twice within one night. Prosecution had failed because the competent authority had held that the offenders' conviction for rape was premised on establishing that the victim had offered resistance. The gap in the protection of sexual autonomy revealed by this case was assessed by the Court as a failure of the state concerned to comply with its obligations under Articles 3 and 8 of the Convention to *comprehensively* protect individuals against sexual violence by means of criminal law provisions. The Court, in defining its general approach, considered (in para. 150):

> Positive obligations on the State are inherent in the right to effective respect for private life under Article 8; [. . .]. While the choice of the means to secure compliance with Article 8 in the sphere of protection against acts of individuals is in principle within the State's margin of appreciation, effective deterrence against grave acts such as rape, where fundamental values and essential aspects of private life are at stake, requires efficient criminal-law provisions.

Therefore, 'States have a positive obligation inherent in Articles 3 and 8 of the Convention to enact criminal-law provisions effectively punishing rape' (para. 153). The Court considers that 'any rigid approach to the prosecution of sexual offences, such as requiring proof of physical resistance in all circumstances, risks leaving certain types of rape unpunished and thus jeopardising the effective protection of the individual's sexual autonomy' (para. 166; recently the Court has reinforced its stance in its *I.C. v. Romania* judgment, paras. 51-52).

The question is how far the limits of a state's obligation to criminalise extend. In this regard, a telling example is the *K.U.* case (judgment of December 2008). The facts of the case are given by the Court as follows:

> 7. On 15 March 1999 an unidentified person or persons placed an advertisement on an Internet dating site in the name of the applicant, who was 12 years old at the time, without his knowledge. The advertisement mentioned his age and year of birth, gave a detailed description of his physical characteristics, a link to the web page he had at the time, which showed his picture, as well as his telephone number, which was accurate save for one digit. In the advertisement, it was claimed that he was looking for an intimate relationship with a boy of his age or older "to show him the way".

> 8. The applicant became aware of the advertisement on the Internet when he received an e-mail from a man, offering to meet him and "then to see what you want".
>
> 9. The applicant's father requested the police to identify the person who had placed the advertisement in order to bring charges against that person. The service provider, however, refused to divulge the identity of the holder of the so-called dynamic Internet Protocol (IP) address in question, regarding itself bound by the confidentiality of telecommunications as defined by law.
>
> 10. The police then asked the Helsinki District Court (käräjäoikeus, tingsrätten) to oblige the service provider to divulge the said information pursuant to section 28 of the Criminal Investigations Act [...].
>
> 11. In a decision issued on 19 January 2001, the District Court refused since there was no explicit legal provision authorizing it to order the service provider to disclose telecommunications identification data in breach of professional secrecy. The court noted that by virtue of [...] the Coercive Measures Act [...] the police had the right to obtain telecommunications identification data in cases concerning certain offences, notwithstanding the obligation to observe secrecy. However, malicious misrepresentation was not such an offence.

The victim lodged a complaint that his right to respect for his private life had been violated (Article 8 ECHR) and that no effective remedy existed to reveal the identity of the person who had put a defamatory advertisement on the Internet in his name. After recalling its previous case-law—in particular the judgments in the cases *X and Y* as well as *M.C.*—the Court noted:

> 45. The Court considers that, while this case might not attain the seriousness of *X and Y v. the Netherlands*, where a breach of Article 8 arose from the lack of an effective criminal sanction for the rape of a girl with disabilities, it cannot be treated as trivial. The act was criminal, involved a minor and made him a target for approaches by paedophiles [...].
>
> 46. The Government conceded that, at the time, the operator of the Internet server could not be ordered to provide information identifying the offender. They argued that protection was provided by the mere existence of the criminal offence of malicious misrepresentation [...]. [...] the Court notes that the existence of an offence has limited deterrent effects if there is no means to identify the actual offender and to bring him to justice. [...]. For the Court, States have a positive obligation inherent in Article 8 of the Convention to criminalise offences against the person, including attempted offences, and to reinforce the deterrent effect of criminalisation by applying criminal-law provisions in practice through effective investigation and prosecution [...]. Where the physical and moral welfare of a child is threatened, such injunction assumes even greater importance. The Court notes in this connection that sexual abuse is unquestionably an abhorrent type of wrongdoing, with debilitating effects on its victims. Children and other vulnerable individuals are entitled to State protection, in the form of effective deterrence, from such grave types of interference with essential aspects of their private lives [...].

1.5.6 The ECtHR's Two Approaches to Criminal Law

So far, it has been demonstrated that states' obligations to enact effective criminal law provisions emerge in the case-law of the ECtHR because of states' duty to protect human rights by deterring the commission of offences that consist in serious human rights violations. This concept of protection by deterrence is at the forefront of the Court's argument. In the same vein, the Court has identified states' obligations to criminalise severe human rights violations under Articles 2 (right to life), 3 (prohibition of torture and inhuman or degrading treatment or punishment), 4 (prohibition of forced labour and slavery), 5 (1) (right to liberty and security) and 8 (right to respect for private and family life) of the Convention.

However, on closer inspection it appears that other parts of the Court's case-law imply a different purpose of criminal law and criminal justice (see FRA 2014, p. 26). In numerous cases the ECtHR has held that, where an individual has an arguable claim that she has suffered a grave violation of her human rights,

> Article 13 requires, in addition to the payment of compensation where appropriate, a thorough and effective investigation capable of leading to the identification and punishment of those responsible [...] and including effective access for the complainant to the investigation procedure (*Tanlı*, § 171).

In this context, the Court highlights the role of criminal justice in allowing a court to "deal with the substance of the relevant Convention complaint and to grant appropriate relief" (*Husayn*, para. 540). In cases where an individual has an arguable claim that she has suffered a severe human rights violation, the notion of an "effective remedy" is understood by the Court to entail "a thorough and effective investigation capable of leading to the identification and punishment of those responsible" (*Husayn*, para. 541). In other words, in the context of Article 13 ECHR, criminal proceedings are viewed as a means of bringing to the fore the wrong suffered by the victim and to grant the victim 'appropriate relief'.

In this perspective, criminal law is not only a means of preventing harm, but reflects, at a normative level, what is owed to the victims of severe human rights violations, in terms of recognising and righting the wrong they have suffered. Criminalising severe abuses, such as those denying sexual autonomy, allows the authorities to react to such abuses by acknowledging human rights violations, by holding offenders to account and by respecting victims as the persons whose rights have been violated and hence await vindication.

Victims of serious human rights violations under Article 13 ECHR are thus entitled to proceedings capable of leading to the identification and punishment of those accountable. This should be taken in combination with the *nullum crimen* principle of Article 7 of the Convention. According to this principle, no one shall be held to account for a criminal offence unless the act in question constituted a criminal offence *at the time when it was committed*. These two Articles add up to the duty of a state to, as a precautionary measure, criminalise all human rights violations which are severe enough to trigger a victim's right to the conviction and punishment of offenders under Article 13 ECHR. How else would a state comply with its obligations under the Convention, which obliges the state to carry out an investigation and to institute criminal proceedings in case of an arguable claim that a severe human rights violation has been committed, but also insists that no one can be prosecuted based on a retroactive criminal law provision? It follows that if a state fails to criminalise a certain serious human rights abuse, it can, in case of such an abuse, only choose between two violations of the Convention. Either the state grants the victim an effective remedy according to Article 13 ECHR and violates the *nullum crimen* principle, or it respects an individual's right under Article 7 ECHR, not to be convicted and punished based on retroactive laws but denies the victim an effective remedy. Only by comprehensively criminalising serious human rights violations is a state prepared to, in cases of (arguable claims of) such violations, fulfil its obligations under Article 13 ECHR to grant victims appropriate relief, while at the same time respecting the *nullum crimen* principle, under Article 7 ECHR.

It follows that if a certain conduct constitutes a severe violation of an individual's human rights—severe enough to justify its punishment—then its criminalisation is owed to the victims as a recognition of the wrong done to them. For instance, legislation penalising marital rape not only alerts husbands to what may happen to them if they abuse their spouses, but also and primarily acknowledges the right of women not to be raped by their husbands; and the penalty expresses that society takes this right seriously. Criminal codes are to be read not as an anthology of human rights violations, but as an expression of the significance of the rights at stake, which weighs heavily enough to justify severe penalties.

In other words, under Article 13 ECHR individuals are entitled to criminal law provisions incriminating grave interferences with essential aspects of their human rights for two reasons: Firstly, criminal law provisions acknowledge emphatically the wrong done to victims and indirectly acknowledge as significant the protected rights of individuals. Secondly, criminal law provisions provide the basis for granting victims access to justice in compliance with Article 7 ECHR and the corresponding right under Article 49 of the Charter. Therefore, victims 'have a right to access justice under Article 13 of the European Convention on Human Rights and, where applicable, under Article 47 of the Charter of Fundamental Rights of the European Union' (FRA 2016, p. 13; see also FRA 2012, p. 21, 2014, pp. 25–27).

1.5.7 Relations Between the Procedural Aspects and Article 13 ECHR

The Court has consistently found that a state's obligations under Article 13 ECHR are wider than its obligations under the procedural limbs of substantive articles. However, if one looks out for elements covered by Article 13 ECHR, but not also by the procedural aspects of substantive articles - such as Articles 2, 3 and 8 ECHR -, the only element that is mentioned exclusively under Article 13 is a victim's right to receive compensation, where appropriate. Hence, the obvious difference concerns the victim's civil law claims.

In the case of *I.P. versus the Republic of Moldova*, the Court found a procedural violation of Article 3 ECHR because the investigation "fell short of the requirements inherent in the State's positive obligations to effectively investigate and punish rape and sexual abuse" (para. 36). Proceeding to an examination under Article 13, the Court found that no separate issue arises under this provision concerning the victim's complaint about the ineffectiveness of the criminal investigation, but that there has been a violation of Article 13 concerning the lack of effective civil law remedies.

In a historical perspective, the Court first relied on Article 13, namely in the cases *Aksoy* (judgement of 18 December 1996), *Aydın* (judgement of a Grand Chamber of 25 September 1997), and *Menteş* (judgement of a Grand Chamber of 28 November 1997). However, in the first two cases, the Court had sufficient evidence in front of it allowing it to conclude that Article 3 ECHR had been violated in its substantive aspect. The *Menteş* case concerned the destruction of the victims' homes by Turkish security forces and the victims' expulsion from their village. Again, the Court was able to establish that Article 8 of the Convention had indeed been violated. Hence, in all three cases, the Court finds, in addition to an infringement of a substantive Article, that Article 13 also has been violated because the Turkish authorities failed to carry out an effective investigation.

What marks the decisive step towards the parallel systems of victims' rights to an effective investigation is the Court's judgment—of February 1998—in the *Kaya* case. Here the Court, in examining whether Turkey violated Article 2 ECHR, notices that "there is an insufficient factual and evidentiary basis on which to conclude that the applicant's brother was, beyond reasonable doubt, intentionally killed by the security forces in the circumstances alleged by the applicant" (para. 78). Still under the heading of Article 2, the Court then turns to examine the alleged inadequacy of the investigation. This finding is followed, in paragraph 86 of the judgment, by sentences that the Court has later on used verbatim in a plethora of rulings:

> The Court recalls at the outset that the general legal prohibition on arbitrary killing by agents of the State contained in Article 2 of the Convention would be ineffective, in practice, if there existed no procedure for reviewing the lawfulness of the use of lethal force by State authorities. The obligation to protect the right to life under Article 2, read in conjunction with the State's general duty under Article 1 of the Convention to "secure to everyone within their jurisdiction the rights and freedoms in [the] Convention", requires by implication that there should be some form of effective official investigation when individuals have been killed as a result of the use of force by, *inter alios*, agents of the State.

These sentences are followed by a reference to the *McCann* judgement, which indeed contains practically identical text. However, in the *McCann* ruling these sentences are immediately preceded by the Court's assessment that "it is unnecessary to decide in the present case whether a right of access to court to bring civil proceedings in connection with deprivation of life can be inferred from Article 2 para. 1 (art. 2-1) since this is an issue which would be more appropriately considered under Articles 6 and 13 (art. 6, art. 13) of the Convention—provisions (art. 6, art. 13) that have not been invoked by the applicants". Hence, the move to found the victim's right to an investigation on a procedural component of a substantive article—instead of or next to Article 13—does not have a source in the *McCann* case, but constitutes a genuine extension brought about by the *Kaya* judgment. In this judgment, the Court finds both an infringement of Article 2 in its procedural aspect, as well as a violation of Article 13. In respect of the latter, the Court, in addition to repeating its arguments from the *Aksoy* and the *Aydın* case, for the first time has reason to comment on the relationship between the new procedural aspects of substantive articles and Article 13. To that end, the Court only notes that "the requirements of Article 13 are broader than a Contracting State's procedural obligation under Article 2 to conduct an effective investigation". If one compares the contents of rights under both Articles, it is likely that what the Court has in mind here is the victim's right to have "effective access" to the investigation procedure.

On first sight, it is indeed in the context of the procedural aspects of substantive articles less obvious why the necessity to demonstrate the authorities' resolve to render criminal law provisions practically effective by carrying out investigations would also require that the victim should have access to these proceedings. However, in later judgments the Court has found various ways to replicate this element as well, e.g. by premising the credibility of criminal investigations on a sufficient element of their external control. Thus, the Court has held that

> [...] the investigation must afford a sufficient element of public scrutiny to secure accountability. Whilst the degree of public scrutiny required may vary, the complainant must be afforded effective access to the investigatory procedure in all cases (*Habimi et al.*, para. 75).

Lately the Court adds to the principles by which the procedural aspect of substantive articles is assessed the sentence that "the victim should be able to participate effectively in the investigation in one form or another" (*Husayn*, para. 480).

In any case, there is no explanation as to why the *Kaya* judgment introduced the procedural aspects instead of dealing with the effectiveness of review procedures exclusively under Article 13. One possible explanation would be that the right to an effective remedy under Article 13 of the Convention requires that the victim takes the initiative. It could seem to somewhat stretch the text of Article 13 to assume that the right of a victim to an effective remedy would include that the authorities have to take action of their own motion. The duty to carry out an investigation ex officio is easier to place under a substantive article. In fact, in the context of procedural limbs, the Court always stresses the obligation to carry out an effective *official* investigation, a term which does not appear in judgments under Article 13. On the other hand, in the *İlhan* case, the Court deals with the deficiencies of the proceedings under Article 13, although the victim had not turned to the authorities. The Court notes (in paragraph 63 of the judgment)

> that the Mardin public prosecutor had been informed that Abdüllatif had suffered serious injuries when he was apprehended by the gendarmes at his village. He was accordingly under the duty, imposed by Article 153 of the Code of Criminal Procedure, to investigate

> whether an offence had been committed. The Court is satisfied in these circumstances that the matter was sufficiently drawn to the attention of the relevant domestic authority. Given that Abdüllatif İlhan's circumstances would have caused him to feel vulnerable, powerless and apprehensive of the representatives of the State, he could legitimately have expected that the necessary investigation would have been conducted without a specific, formal complaint from himself or his family. The public prosecutor chose, however, not to inquire into the circumstances in which those injuries were caused.

However, because of this perfect parallelism it is unpredictable whether shortcomings of the investigation or prosecution are dealt with, by the Court, as a procedural aspect of the material right, or under Article 13, or both. In the *Ilhan* case, a Grand Chamber found that the victim had suffered torture and went on, without an explanation, to state that his "complaints concerning the lack of any effective investigation by the authorities into the cause of his injuries fall to be dealt with under Article 13 of the Convention" (para. 93). In other cases, the Court assesses the effectiveness of the investigation as a procedural aspect of a material article and concludes that no additional issue arises under Article 13. In a third group of cases the Court deals with the effectiveness of proceedings under both the material article and Article 13, usually pointing out that the requirements under Article 13 are broader (e.g. *Husayn*).

Hence, all that can be concluded is that the ECtHR's case-law recognises two sources of states' obligations to conduct an effective investigation and to institute criminal proceedings and thus rests on two pillars. What in the end is arguably the deeper reason of this close to perfect parallelism is the duality of the Court's approaches to criminal law and criminal justice as a means of deterring potential offenders on the one hand and as redressing the wrong suffered by victims on the other. If substantive articles necessitate the criminalisation of severe abuses as a means of deterring potential offenders, then it is indeed plausible that such deterrence remains effective only as long as, in case an offence is committed, the authorities demonstrate their resolve to fit their action of an investigation and proceedings to the word of the criminal code.

If one, on the other hand, shares the scepticism of many concerning deterrence as a justification of criminal law and criminal justice, then it is plausible to deal with a lack of an effective investigation and deficiencies of criminal proceedings exclusively under the heading of Article 13 ECHR and abandon altogether the concept of procedural aspects of substantive Convention articles.

1.5.8 Criminal Justice Serving to Eradicate Impunity of Grave Human Rights Violations

On 30 March 2011, the Council of Europe's Committee of Ministers adopted guidelines and reference texts entitled 'Eradicating impunity for serious human rights violations'. These documents can be read as recapping and concluding a development that started with the above-mentioned Recommendation adopted by the same

Committee in 1985, which was driven by the diagnosis of criminal justice systems' inability to appropriately consider the legitimate interests of victims.

The Guidelines' preamble commences as follows:

> The Committee of Ministers,
>
> Recalling that those responsible for acts amounting to serious human rights violations must be held to account for their actions;
>
> Considering that a lack of accountability encourages repetition of crimes, as perpetrators and others feel free to commit further offences without fear of punishment;
>
> Recalling that impunity for those responsible for acts amounting to serious human rights violations inflicts additional suffering on victims;
>
> Considering that impunity must be fought as a matter of justice for the victims, as a deterrent to prevent new violations, and to uphold the rule of law and public trust in the justice system, including where there is a legacy of serious human rights violations; [...]

What is remarkable is how the text blends human rights language with criminal justice terms, and flows seamlessly from evoking serious human rights violations and those responsible, to addressing crimes and perpetrators. The notion that does not require translation between the two is the term 'victim', which indiscriminately refers to the victim of a serious human rights violation and the victim of crime. This is because in this document, crime is, without hesitation, conceptualised as a serious human rights violation. Thus, the victim is considered as both a victim of a human rights violation and a victim of crime. This perspective is premised on the assumption that the state is obliged to criminalise severe human rights violations and thereby to ensure the consonance of human rights and criminal law.

While the following chapters share this basic approach of the Guidelines, they attempt to avoid a certain pitfall contained within them, which concerns the fact that the Guidelines, in defining the term 'victim', relapses into the old notion of 'a natural person who has suffered harm'. This approach is not consistent with the impunity-concept. If, in the case of the killing of an individual, a state is to be criticised for allowing such killing to go unpunished, then the basis of such criticism is a state's obligation to protect an individual's right to life and to grant an effective remedy in case of an arguable claim of a violation of that right. The victim's right to the identification and punishment of the offenders flows from her right to life under Article 2 ECHR and is not premised on any harm suffered. If the victim is shot at from a distance and missed and does not even notice that she has been attacked, she has clearly not suffered any harm but is still a victim of attempted murder because of the violation of her right to life under Article 2 of the Convention (Jesionek 2004, pp. 256-257). She is still entitled to the identification and punishment of the offender.

Thus, it can be seen that although the Guidelines have a clear, core message that serious human rights violations must 'as a matter of justice for the victims' not go unpunished, the Guidelines follows the old model of a harm-based definition of the victim, rather than departing from the primary rights of the victimised individual. This suggests that the new paradigm is only hatching and has not yet left all the fragmented eggshells of the harm-based approach entirely behind.

1.5.9 The Rome Statute of the International Criminal Court

This account of the evolution of the principle that impunity of severe human rights violations is unacceptable and that states therefore have a duty to criminalise, prosecute and punish severe human rights violations would be grossly incomplete without mentioning the Rome Statute of the International Criminal Court, which entered into force on 1 July 2002. To truthfully and accurately reflect the narrative underlying the Court, the initial paragraphs of the Preamble of the Rome Statute shall be quoted:

> The States Parties to this Statute,
>
> Conscious that all peoples are united by common bonds, their cultures pieced together in a shared heritage, and concerned that this delicate mosaic may be shattered at any time,
>
> Mindful that during this century millions of children, women and men have been victims of unimaginable atrocities that deeply shock the conscience of humanity,
>
> Recognizing that such grave crimes threaten the peace, security and well-being of the world,
>
> Affirming that the most serious crimes of concern to the international community as a whole must not go unpunished and that their effective prosecution must be ensured by taking measures at the national level and by enhancing international cooperation,
>
> Determined to put an end to impunity for the perpetrators of these crimes and thus to contribute to the prevention of such crimes,
>
> Recalling that it is the duty of every State to exercise its criminal jurisdiction over those responsible for international crimes, [...]

While this document sends a clear message to states that they should end the impunity of severe human rights violations by prosecuting and punishing offenders, it is fair to say that the text of the Preamble leans towards a preventive reasoning of criminal justice rather than stressing that justice is owed to victims. This attitude is also reflected by the fact that victims' rights to participation in proceedings before the Court are limited. In the pre-trial phase, victims may, under Article 15 of the Statute, make representations to the Pre-Trial Chamber. In disputes concerning the Court's jurisdiction, victims may submit observations to the Court. The prosecutor has to consider the interests of victims when deciding on whether to initiate an investigation. According to Article 64 of the Statute, the Trial Chamber must ensure that "a trial is fair and expeditious and is conducted with full respect for the rights of the accused and due regard for the protection of victims and witnesses". Again, while rights of the accused are recognised, similar procedural rights of victims are not. The same focus on protection, typical of the harm/needs paradigm, is shown in Article 68 of the Statute, which provides that the "Court shall take appropriate measures to protect the safety, physical and psychological well-being, dignity and privacy of victims and witnesses." The lumping together of victims and witnesses is, once more, evocative of a fairly traditional understanding of criminal justice.

As with the case-law of the ECtHR, the Rome Statute, on the one hand, emphasises the need to prosecute, convict, and punish those responsible for severe human rights violations, while, on the other hand, fails to provide a fully consistent rationale of criminal justice that would convincingly reason the punishment of offenders as a necessary and appropriate response to the wrong - rather than harm - done to their victims.

1.5.10 Recent Developments at State Level

An overview of relevant developments at state level cannot be offered here. Still, some examples serve to show how courts representing state parties to the ECHR have started to react to the ECtHR's case-law.

Particularly impressive are recent judgments taken by the German Constitutional Court, to be precise, one decision in 2010—in the case "*Polit-Sekte*"—two decisions in 2014—in the cases "*Tennessee Eisenberg*" and "*Gorch Fock*"—and two decisions in 2015—cases "*Blocksperre*" and "*Kunduz*" (on this case law see Sachs 2015; Schmidt 2015, pp. 195-196). In the *Kunduz* Decision the Constitutional Court summarised the law by positing, that, while the *Grundgesetz* in general does not grant individuals a right to the punishment of others, such rights can exist in three situations. These are firstly, in cases of significant violent crimes or comparable offences; secondly, when the victim is in a situation of state custody; and, thirdly, as regards offences committed by a state actor. In fact, the second and the third category can be merged as they both relate to forms of state involvement, either by positive action or by the omission of a state actor. Hence, the first group concerns a state's due diligence obligation to protect against non-State actors, while the other categories relate to a state's duty to respect fundamental rights of individuals and adopt measures accordingly.

Because of the fundamental importance of this line of decisions, the crucial paragraphs of the *Kunduz* decision shall be quoted in close to full length:

> Das Grundgesetz vermittelt grundsätzlich keinen Anspruch auf Strafverfolgung Dritter (a). Ein solcher Anspruch kann jedoch bei erheblichen Straftaten gegen das Leben, die körperliche Unversehrtheit, die sexuelle Selbstbestimmung und die Freiheit der Person, bei Straftaten gegen Opfer, die sich in einem besonderen Obhutsverhältnis zur öffentlichen Hand befinden sowie bei Delikten von Amtsträgern [...] in Betracht kommen (b). [...].

a) Art. 2 Abs. 2 Sätze 1 und 2 in Verbindung mit Art. 1 Abs. 1 Satz 2 GG verpflichten den Staat, sich dort schützend und fördernd vor das Leben, die körperliche Unversehrtheit, die Freiheit und die sexuelle Selbstbestimmung des Einzelnen zu stellen und sie vor rechtswidrigen Eingriffen von Seiten Dritter zu bewahren [. . .], wo die Grundrechtsberechtigten selbst nicht dazu in der Lage sind. Ein Anspruch auf bestimmte, vom Einzelnen einklagbare Maßnahmen ergibt sich daraus jedoch grundsätzlich nicht. Insbesondere kennt die Rechtsordnung in der Regel keinen grundrechtlich radizierten Anspruch auf eine Strafverfolgung Dritter [. . .].

b) Allerdings stellt die wirksame Verfolgung von Gewaltverbrechen und vergleichbaren Straftaten eine Konkretisierung der staatlichen Schutzpflicht aus Art. 2 Abs. 2 Sätze 1 und 2 in Verbindung mit Art. 1 Abs. 1 Satz 2 GG dar [. . .]. Diese kann Grundlage subjektiver öffentlicher Rechte sein.

aa) Insoweit besteht ein Anspruch auf eine effektive Strafverfolgung dort, wo der Einzelne nicht in der Lage ist, erhebliche Straftaten gegen seine höchstpersönlichen Rechtsgüter – Leben, körperliche Unversehrtheit, sexuelle Selbstbestimmung und Freiheit der Person – abzuwehren und ein Verzicht auf die effektive Verfolgung solcher Taten zu einer Erschütterung des Vertrauens in das Gewaltmonopol des Staates und einem allgemeinen Klima der Rechtsunsicherheit und Gewalt führen kann. In solchen Fällen kann, gestützt auf Art. 2 Abs. 2 Sätze 1 und 2 in Verbindung mit Art. 1 Abs. 1 Satz 2 GG, ein Tätigwerden des Staates und seiner Organe auch mit den Mitteln des Strafrechts verlangt werden [. . .]. Bei Kapitaldelikten kann ein solcher Anspruch auf der Grundlage von Art. 6 Abs. 1 und Abs. 2 Satz 1 GG in Verbindung mit Art. 2 Abs. 2 Satz 1 und Art. 1 Abs. 1 GG auch nahen Angehörigen zustehen.

bb) Ein Anspruch auf effektive Strafverfolgung kann sich auch aus einer spezifischen Fürsorge- und Obhutspflicht des Staates gegenüber Personen ergeben, die ihm anvertraut sind. Vor allem in strukturell asymmetrischen Rechtsverhältnissen, die den Verletzten nur eingeschränkte Möglichkeiten lassen, sich gegen strafrechtlich relevante Übergriffe in ihre Rechtsgüter aus Art. 2 Abs. 2 GG zu wehren (z.B. im Maßregel- oder Strafvollzug), obliegt den Strafverfolgungsbehörden eine besondere Sorgfaltspflicht bei der Durchführung von Ermittlungen und der Bewertung der gefundenen Ergebnisse.

cc) Ein Anspruch auf effektive Strafverfolgung kommt ferner in Fällen in Betracht, in denen der Vorwurf im Raum steht, dass Amtsträger bei Wahrnehmung hoheitlicher Aufgaben Straftaten begangen haben. Ein Verzicht auf eine effektive Verfolgung solcher Taten kann zu einer Erschütterung des Vertrauens in die Integrität staatlichen Handelns führen. Daher muss bereits der Anschein vermieden werden, dass gegen Amtswalter des Staates weniger effektiv ermittelt wird oder dass insoweit erhöhte Anforderungen an eine Anklageerhebung gestellt werden.

dd) Die (verfassungsrechtliche) Verpflichtung zu effektiver Strafverfolgung bezieht sich auf das Tätigwerden aller Strafverfolgungsorgane. Ihr Ziel ist es, eine wirksame Anwendung der zum Schutz des Lebens, der körperlichen Integrität, der sexuellen Selbstbestimmung und der Freiheit der Person erlassenen Strafvorschriften sicherzustellen. Es muss insoweit gewährleistet werden, dass Straftäter für von ihnen verschuldete Verletzungen dieser Rechtsgüter auch tatsächlich zur Verantwortung gezogen werden [. . .].

In principle, the Constitutional Court's decisions extend the settled case law of the Court in Strasbourg to a slightly wider range of situations than dealt with, to date, by the ECtHR.

What makes a crucial difference, though, is that the German court, by founding a state's obligations to investigate, prosecute, convict and punish on human dignity, as proclaimed and protected by Article 1 section 1 of the Grundgesetz, confers on these duties the particular status of obligations that are, because they flow from human dignity, out of reach of a parliament or a supranational organisation. Thus obligations to criminalise and to implement effectively criminal law provisions are elevated to the level of right that is not subject to the disposition of legislators or public authorities.

However, one particular aspect of the Constitutional Court's case-law provokes questions. In cases where an individual's personal interests (*höchstpersönliche Rechtsgüter*) have been violated, the victim's right to effective prosecution is, according to the Court, conditional on the individual's incapability to defend herself. This suggests that the victim has no right to investigations and prosecution if the authorities find that the victim would have been in a position to fend off the offender. It could follow that a victim of sexual harassment is entitled to an effective investigation, unless it is established that she would have been able to repel the aggressor herself, and a victim of burglary has a right to the prosecution of offenders except when it is established that she could have protected herself, e.g. by shooting at the offenders. However, this argument turns things upside down. There is a right, but not an obligation to defend oneself. The legal order, aimed at promoting peace, should by no means encourage individuals to take their rights in their own hands, nor sanction those who refrain from doing so and rely on the criminal justice system. It can only be hoped that the Constitutional Court clarifies or drops this restriction at the next occasion.

As far as can be seen, courts in the United Kingdom acknowledge a right of the victim to the investigation and prosecution of offenders neither under common law nor under the Human Rights Act 1998. However, this is with at least one notable exception, as seen in the Court of Appeal (Civil Division) judgment of 30 June 2015 in the cases of *Commissioner of Police of the Metropolis v. DSD and NBV and Alio Koraou v. Chief Constable of Greater Manchester Police*. In this judgment, Laws LJ, exploring the significance of Article 3 ECHR in light of the case-law of the ECtHR, acknowledged the principle "that serious violent crime by non-State agents generally requires a proper criminal investigation by the State". Laws elaborates this principle as follows:

> There is perhaps a sliding scale: from deliberate torture by State officials to the consequences of negligence by non-State agents. The energy required of the State to combat or redress these ills is no doubt variable, but the same protective principle is always at the root of it. The margin of appreciation enjoyed by the State as to the means of compliance with Article 3 widens at the bottom of the scale but narrows at the top. At what may, without belittling the victim, be called the lower end of the scale where injury happens through the negligence of non-State agents, the State's provision of a judicial system of civil remedies will often suffice: the individual State's legal traditions will govern the means of compliance in the particular case. Serious violent crime by non-State agents is of a different order: higher up the scale. In these cases, which certainly include DSD/NBV, a proper criminal investigation by the State is required.

In light of these slowly developing lines of case-law, it is fair to say that the emerging paradigm, based on the concept of victims' rights to investigations and the prosecution and conviction of offenders, which first developed as an element of international human rights law and has been consistently upheld by the ECtHR for more than three decades, is finally touching base at the level of states' courts.

1.6 Affirmative Versus Critical Criminal Law Doctrine

According to the ECtHR's case-law, as summarised in the preceding section, to argue for the punishment of the offender on behalf of the victim's rights can *per se* mean two things.

Firstly, that the offender must be punished to deter further offending and thus to *protect* the victim against repeat victimisation, either by the same offender or by someone else. In the ECtHR's case-law, this is what the procedural limb of substantive articles captures: rights cannot be effectively protected without deterrent criminal law provisions that are rigorously executed. However, while this is plausible in itself, the question remains, whether deterrence alone is a sufficient justification of punishment. It could be objected that the mechanism of deterrence does not show that the offender *deserves* to be deterred or to be used as a means of deterring others. This argument will be returned to below.

Secondly, the assumption that the victim is entitled to the punishment of the offender could mean that the offender must be punished to *respect* the victim and her primary rights. The offender must be punished, in this perspective, because she has disregarded rights of an individual and hence deserves to be punished as a means of vindicating the victim's primary rights. In this case, punishing the offender is viewed as an effective remedy against the rights violation—the wrong—suffered by the victim and answered for by the offender. In the case-law of the ECtHR, this is reflected by Article 13 ECHR, which is not about prevention but about doing justice, about what is owed to the individual, whose rights have been violated. This is the reason why the Court, in the context of Article 13 ECHR, also mentions compensation but never does so when dealing with the procedural aspects of substantive articles. Compensation is not a means of deterrence, but it is part of what is owed to the victim. It is a means of restoring the rights of the victim by 'rendering unto the victim that which is the victim's due.'

In the end, the question is: which of the two justifications—if any—can really carry the burden of legitimising the punishment of the offender. Does it matter? It certainly does. If deterrence was the proper rationale, it would be difficult to refute the consequence that sanctions are the more impressive the more severe they are. The aspect of doing justice to the rights of the victim, in contrast, sets an inherent limitation: the amount of punishment would need to reflect the seriousness of the violation of the primary rights of the victimised individual and to not deviate significantly from that measure. Other reasons for not using deterrence as the justification for punishment are laid out below. These include the disregard it shows to the victim and the offender, and its incongruity with human dignity.

1.6.1 Deterrent Punishment Disregards the Victim

There is a general argument against using deterrence as a justification for punishing in the name of the rights of the victim. As deterrence looks solely into the future, it disregards the concrete victim in the case by dissociating the sanction from the actual offence that has been committed. If punishment aims to deter future offending, then it answers to the exigencies of the rights of all individuals as potential future victims, but it denies the identifiable victim any privileged position. A deterrent punishment has nothing to do *specifically* with the victim's experience of a severe violation of her rights. If the purpose of punishment is—future-oriented—crime prevention, then punishment is not a means of—in any sense of the word—redressing the wrong done to the actual victim.

This, however, misses the reality of the criminal offence as the violation of the primary rights of the individual victim of flesh and blood. If the purpose of criminal justice was considered to be deterrence, then criminal proceedings would not concern victims any more than others. It could be left to the public prosecutor to represent the victim's rights, just as much as the public prosecutor represents the same rights of all others.

This is why the ECtHR's approach that takes Article 13 ECHR as the point of departure is indispensable. In what sense would punishment remedy the breach of the victim's primary rights if its objective was only to deter future offences and would not remedy the wrong suffered by the individual victim and vindicate the victim's primary rights and status as a rights-holder?

In the case of *Velásquez-Rodríguez against Honduras*, the Inter-American Court of Human Rights accurately stated that if the violation of the rights experienced by the victim:

> goes unpunished and the victim's full enjoyment of such rights is not restored as soon as possible, the State has failed to comply with its duty to ensure the free and full exercise of those rights to the persons within its jurisdiction.

If the punishment of the offender is to restore the rights of the victim—and the victim as a person—the conviction and punishment of the offender needs to maintain and demonstrate a clear and strong link with the concrete rights violation, that is, with the wrong done to the victim.

Therefore, punishment must answer to the individual offence and victimisation and not only relate to possible offences looming in the future. The victim and the public must be allowed to see that sanctions react to the rights violation suffered by the victim and redress this wrong.

Hence, at this stage the hypothesis is proposed that the aim of punishment is to allow the victim to maintain trust in the validity and authority of her rights, and of her status as a respected member of her community. If this hypothesis holds, punishing the offender would serve to reassure the victim that a violation of her rights will not go unpunished and that the offender will not 'get away with it' without making amends for disregarding the victim's rights. The objective of criminal justice is, then, not to deter offenders, but to grant relief to those seeking redress for an infringement of their primary rights. Hence, the basis of criminal justice is to be found in victims' rights under Article 13 ECHR and—correspondingly—under Article 47 of the Charter. This offers a concrete interpretation of what it could mean to avoid impunity of severe human rights violations.

1.6.2 Deterrent Punishment Disregards the Offender

In any case, deterrence alone is not adequate to justify punishment. It does not offer a sufficient basis for constructing a valid theory of punishment. While punishment will undoubtedly have some deterrent effect, it does not follow that the offender *deserves* to be punished in a deterrent manner, where the term 'deserves' implies that the offender is respected as a person and hence excludes any situation where the offender is objectified and used for the sake of others—be it 'the community' or other individuals. If criminal justice is to amount to more than a form of disciplining citizens in a style similar to animal training, what first has to be demonstrated is the legitimacy and moral imperative of punishment.

While deterrent effects of punishment exist, human dignity dictates that citizens must not be threatened with punishment unless it is fair; and in cases where punishment is fair, it should be administered on that basis and not for other reasons. Even if, for instance, it could be shown that imposing the death penalty had salient deterrent effects in certain cases, such evidence would not prove the death penalty to be fair and legitimate in relation to the offender. Similarly, even if it were demonstrated that considerable gains in deterrence could be achieved by handing down long-term prison sentences on pickpockets or on persons with mental disabilities or by punishing not only the offender but also her loved ones, such evidence would in no way convince us that such sentences are justifiable.

Another problem with deterrence is that it only sets limits in one direction. If deterrence necessitates and justifies punishing, one can never punish too much, as one can never prevent harm or protect goods too effectively. Hence, the aim of deterrence does not set an upper limit to punishment. Any restriction—such as proportionality—would have to originate from another consideration. It is difficult to argue that the severity of punishment should be proportional to, and thus reflect, the severity of the wrong done to the victim, unless one takes recourse to retribution as an objective of punishment. However, in such a case the objective of deterrence is rendered obsolete as while deterrence is in need of retribution operating as a limitation, retribution does not require deterrence as its complement. The appropriate, purposeful amount of punishment cannot be determined according to two profoundly different measures.

However, most importantly, deterring others by threatening them with punishment *per se* does not respect them as persons and citizens. Such an approach relies on the underlying assumption that the reason for not reoffending is not the offender's moral sense, but her fear of punishment, and that, as soon as this fear ceases, the person will 'feel free' to commit further offences. There are two principal objections to this approach. Firstly, it does not do justice to citizens as moral persons. Secondly, it is not realistic as to the possibility of establishing a social order by means of deterring citizens. An effective normative order is based upon the shared normative views of a community's members and not on the constantly terrorising threats of a powerful authority.

In other words, deterrence is a form of manipulation that creates heteronomy. For this reason, it is incompatible with the autonomy of an individual as a moral agent and stands in direct opposition to the concept of human dignity. In a humanist society, the law must respect and address individuals as moral persons, it must speak to the autonomous moral sense of citizens, not to their fear of harsh sanctions and suppression.

1.6.3 Kant's Principle

To argue that punishment is based on deterrence is incompatible with a proper understanding of what a system of human dignity and human rights requires. Threatening to punish citizens as a means of achieving their norm compliant behaviour is a violation of their autonomy as moral persons and therefore not a weapon available in the arsenal of a society committed to the values of human dignity and human rights.

The measure of any legitimate treatment of the offender is her dignity. Her status as a person protects the offender against being punished in the interest of others. The blame laid and the punishment inflicted on the offender have to stand the test of conforming to the offender's right to be treated with respect and in accordance with her autonomy. Famously, Kant (1797/1968, p. 331; 1996, p.105) claimed:

> Richterliche Strafe [. . .] kann niemals bloß als Mittel, ein anderes Gute zu befördern, für den Verbrecher selbst, oder für die bürgerliche Gesellschaft, sondern muß jederzeit nur darum wider ihn verhängt werden, weil er verbrochen hat; denn der Mensch kann nie bloß als Mittel zu den Absichten eines anderen gehandhabt und unter die Gegenstände des Sachenrechts gemengt werden, wowider ihn seine angeborne Persönlichkeit schützt [. . .]. Er muß vorher strafbar befunden sein, ehe noch daran gedacht wird, aus dieser Strafe einigen Nutzen für ihn selbst oder seine Mitbürger zu ziehen. Das Strafgesetz ist ein kategorischer Imperativ, und wehe dem! welcher die Schlangenwindungen der Glückseligkeitslehre durchkriecht, um etwas aufzufinden, was durch den Vorteil, den es verspricht, ihn von der Strafe, oder auch nur einem Grade derselben entbinde, nach dem pharisäischen Wahlspruch: 'es ist besser, daß ein Mensch sterbe, als daß das ganze Volk verderbe.'

> Punishment by a court [. . .] can never be inflicted merely as a means to promote some other good for the criminal himself or for civil society. It must always be inflicted upon him only because he has committed a crime. For a human being can never be treated merely as a means to the purposes of another or be put among the objects of rights to things: his innate personality protects him from this [. . .]. He must previously have been found punishable before any thought can be given to drawing from his punishment something of use for himself or his fellow citizens. The law of punishment is a categorical imperative, and woe to him who crawls through the windings of eudaemonism in order to discover something that releases the criminal from punishment or even reduces its amount by the advantage it promises, in accordance with the pharisaical saying, 'It is better for one man to die than for an entire people to perish.

As is often the case when reading Kant, the religious connotation showing in the last sentence must not be overlooked. What Kant hints at is his belief that any human being is created in God's image, represents potentially a moral universe—as did God's son—and for this quality deserves to be respected under all conditions (Hampton 2007, p. 122). The human face mirrors the image of God calling on the individual. Hence, nothing outweighs the dignity inherent in one individual human being. This unqualified and absolute respect for the individual person is the hub and pivot of Kantian ethics and rules out reducing one person to a means to the ends of others (Böckenförde 2014, p. 141; Hufen 2014, p. 152).

From what has just been said, the specific challenge faced by any attempt to justify punishment becomes evident. It can be referred to as Kant's principle, as it was Kant who first highlighted this particular aporia: if human dignity denotes a normative order that without any qualification—under all circumstances—respects individual autonomy, punishment, too, can only be justified if, and to the extent that, it respects the offender as an autonomous individual. It would have to be shown that punishment expresses, in Kant's terms, respect of humankind in the person of the offender (*'Achtung für die Menschheit, in der Person des Missetäters'*, Kant 1797/1982, p. 487). Only then can punishment be seen as compatible with human dignity and the autonomy of the offender as a person.

Human dignity is not a count noun. There is only one and the same human dignity, inherent in one person as much as in an entire people, and hence one life must not be sacrificed to the well-being of an entire people. The individual is protected by her dignity against being sacrificed to the rights or interests of others. Hence an offender may never be punished for the sake of others. In a normative order founded on the political ideal of human dignity the only reason justifying punishment is that punishment respects and does justice to the offender as a person and rights-holder. This axiom will be referred to as Kant's principle.

As will be discussed later, to Kant this principle is uncontroversial, as in his understanding, autonomy requires that a subject acts according to the categorical imperative and her conscience, which originates from a divine source and hence hardly ever fails. When committing a crime, an individual necessarily acts against her own better judgment—at least if it was a careful judgment—and hence does not deserve to be treated with much sympathy.

However, under the secular societal conditions of modern pluralism Kant's principle takes on a radically different relevance and significance. Under the conditions of moral relativism and pluralism autonomy entails, so it would seem, an individual's radical freedom to determine the laws by which she abides and from which alone her actions are to be judged. The individual can only be punished under laws to which she has given her consent as a law-giver. If one takes Kant at his word and adds the ingredients of a pluralist society the result makes it difficult to punish. If an unlimited principle of individual autonomy requires the state to accept a liberal, value-neutral position, it can be doubted that the state is, at the same time, in a position to punish offenders (Hampton 2007, pp. 149–150).

Hereinafter, an approach to criminal justice will be referred to as 'critical' if it respects the dignity and individual autonomy of the offender and accepts that criminal justice can be justified only if—and to the extent that—it is shown that the offender's dignity and autonomy are compatible with—or even premised on—these particular institutions and procedures of criminal justice. In contrast, all approaches justifying the offender's punishment by having recourse to the goods or interests of others or, in a paternalistic attitude, to the best interest of the offender, as defined by state authorities, will be called 'affirmative', as they accept and reinforce a state's power to subject individual citizens in the name of the people.

1.6.4 Affirmative Criminal Law Doctrine

The baseline reasoning of affirmative criminal law doctrine combines two assumptions: firstly, criminal law protects significant goods and interests. Secondly, it is the nation state, represented by parliament, that, by enacting criminal law provisions, defines what constitutes a significant good or interest. Criminal justice is viewed as necessary and legitimate as a means of—immediately—preserving criminal law (in German doctrine the pertinent notion would be '*Rechtsbewährung*') and—indirectly—protecting goods and interests (the German term would be '*Rechtsgüterschutz*'). This fundamental relation between criminal law and justice was already determined by Feuerbach in the formula that the law is sacred and the judge its servant (*"[...] das Gesetz ist heilig [...] Der Richter ist sein Diener*", quoted by Naucke 2007, p. 3).

Affirmative law doctrine operates within a nation state paradigm. It assumes as its point of departure that peoples organised in nation states are sovereigns and that their sovereignty is primarily expressed in terms of national legislation. Hence, criminal justice is legitimised by the fact that it is based on legislation, which it reinforces. By prosecuting, convicting and punishing offenders, criminal justice demonstrates the superior authority of criminal law as an enunciation of the nation state's sovereignty and deters offending by rendering it costly to do so. This is how criminal justice functions and preserves the laws inaugurated by the nation state. As the sovereignty of the people represented by the public institutions of a nation state is not questioned, criminal law and criminal justice are legitimised by the fact that the nation state firmly relies on them.

Punishment as the most severe sanction available to the legal order should be applied as a last resort. While many would agree with this statement, there is hardly a consensus as to the criteria that would qualify social norms as important enough to carry criminal sanctions. In practice, this lack of consented criteria justifying criminal law provisions and punishment comes with a risk of an inflationary use of criminal law. It enables, at times, the nearly all-purpose application of criminal justice as a means to counteract various sorts of societal nuisances, including minor forms of unpleasant, disorderly or undesirable conduct and occasionally results in criminal justice waging wars against illegally staying migrants, facemasks of demonstrators and head scarves of women. Arguably, the excessive use of criminal law as an almost catch-all 'solution' to various social and political problems endangers individual autonomy. This is possible as long as a sufficiently powerful, conclusive, and distinctive definition and restriction of the tasks and scope of criminal justice is not at hand.

The usual line of reasoning for justifying a public good or interest proceeds in two steps. The state—parliament—concludes that a certain type of conduct is unwelcome and compromises some public good; hence, it prohibits such conduct in the public interest. It is then found that this behavioural norm cannot be enforced without punishment, which is declared indispensable as a means of preserving the law. Punishment is announced as justified by its indispensability and the fact that it defends a norm declared by parliament as serving a common good or public welfare. This reasoning equates the function of criminal justice - defending legal norms - with its legitimacy.

This is not to say that criminal law is not a mechanism apt to preserve norms. To the contrary, this is exactly how criminal law and criminal justice operate. However, understanding how a tool works does not answer the question as to the conditions under which it is appropriate to apply that tool. Grasping the functions of punishment is one thing, justifying punishment quite another. What would need to be established is the particular quality distinguishing those norms of conduct that justify punishment as a means of their preservation. Only if law doctrine succeeds in working out convincing criteria that allow an assessment of norms as significant enough to justify a criminal law provision, can law doctrine start to function as a critical—'negative'—authority that provides a cogent explanation of criminal law and, at the same time, establishes a firm and powerful opposition to its current excessive use.

Affirmative criminal law doctrine sanctions criminal law as a means of preserving the rule of the nation state over the individuals living on its territory, but fails to restrict the power of parliament to legislate. It is left to parliament representing the sovereign people to decide who should be punished in the interest of the community and on what grounds.

In the perspective of affirmative criminal justice, the offender's punishment is justified simply by the fact that it is a necessary means of preserving the law and deterring future offences. Yet objectifying and using an individual as a means of serving the interests of others—namely future victims—violates human dignity. The very formula of deterrence runs counter to the concept of human dignity as it is commonly understood. This does not come as a surprise. By prioritising 'the people', organised within the political framework of a nation state, over the individual, the nation state paradigm tends to be inherently collectivist, authoritarian and in opposition to human dignity.

1.6.5 Human Dignity and Human Rights as Limitations of Criminal Law

The case-law of the Court in Strasbourg under Article 13 ECHR makes a crucial contribution to constructing criminal law and criminal justice as restricted by human dignity and human rights. According to this case-law, Article 13 ECHR grants the victim a right to the conviction and punishment of those responsible for severe human rights violations. This inspires the question of whether Article 13 ECHR can be read as not only founding, but also limiting the right to the punishment of offenders to severe human rights violations.

In reaction to a close to arbitrary use of criminal law, it has been suggested that criminal law and criminal justice have no legitimate basis unless matters of human rights protection are at stake. This is what Otfried Höffe assumes, who considers criminal law as a necessary element of any liberal social order based on human rights. Höffe sees human rights protection and criminal law as intrinsically linked to one another. Consequently, criminal law is illegitimate unless important aspects of human rights are at stake (Höffe 2008, p. 83).

> Dort, wo nicht Rechtsgüter menschenrechtlicher Dignität auf dem Spiel stehen, lässt sich die *ultima ratio* staatlichen Zwangs, das Strafrecht, schwerlich rechtfertigen.

Höffe claims that human rights stand out compared to any other value or political objective in such a privileged and exceptional manner that any other claim to criminal law protection is disqualified. Later, it will be argued that human dignity holds a privileged position compared to all other values and that position demarcates the domain of legitimate criminal law. The reasoning behind this assumption will be given in Chaps. 3 and 4, which analyse the concept of human dignity and how it provides a basis for criminal justice. At this point, it suffices to indicate that criminal justice preserves the norms on which the political system of a pluralist society is founded, in particular, on norms protecting autonomy by banning heteronomy, such as coercion or the violation of exclusive spheres of an individual's autonomy.

Hence human dignity is the crucial concept and main point of departure. It is viewed here not just as one value next to others, but as the moral basis of a modern, pluralist society. In line with significant human rights documents, it will be assumed that the concept of human dignity is the foundation for the entire construction of human rights, including the rights of victims of crime, and of all public institutions and administrative procedures aimed at implementing human rights standards.

Human dignity is right (*Recht*), not just law (*Gesetz*). Human dignity as a general normative principle founds the framework within which individuals claim and exercise political autonomy. However, human dignity, at the same time, sets limits to legislation and in particular to criminal law. Within a framework determined by human dignity, criminal law, like all law, is legitimate and authoritative to the extent that it acknowledges and respects every individual as a person. In the case of criminal law, this includes not only the victim, but also the offender. Thus, human dignity defines the basis, as well as the limits, of criminal law. This will be elaborated in Chaps. 3 and 4.

It is noteworthy that the Charter of Fundamental Rights of the European Union begins with human dignity. Article 1 of the Charter states: 'Human dignity is inviolable. It must be respected and protected.' In addition, human dignity is, according to Article 2 of the Treaty on European Union, a core value on which the Union is founded. Recently, the German Constitutional Court—in the case of *R.*—highlighted that the Union is *necessarily* founded based on human dignity, as those Member States, which are bound by the value of human dignity, cannot found and empower an organisation unless it operates in accordance with human dignity. This sets an inherent limit to the powers of the European Union and its institutions (the German keywords, operating as border signs, are *Solange* and *Identitätskontrolle*). Often the political dimension of the concept of human dignity is not fully understood or appreciated, in spite of the concept's obvious universalist and cosmopolitan connotations. In light of pending strategic political decisions whether to construct the European Union as a replica of the nation state at a larger scale or as a component within a peaceful global order, the full meaning of human dignity must be brought to bear. From an ethical point of view, the decisive category and point of reference is human dignity as the foundation of a humanist society, while the distinction between EU citizens and third country nationals is not a robust and 'resilient' normative construction. Therefore, the European Union should, in the author's view, primarily not be conceived of as a large-size edition of the nation state constituted by the borders of its territory, but as part of an emerging global order tasked with realizing human dignity. In the end, the vision of a humanist society demands that the separating effects of the Union's external borders should be gradually reduced and their permeability steadily increased with a view to, in the longer run, contribute to realizing, in an orderly and controlled manner, the right to free movement of all human beings at a global scale. And it is one and the same questionable right of the 'sovereign nation state' to define normative standards and to exclude from the status of (full) citizens those who fail to meet these standards that grounds the exclusion of foreigners and offenders.

The purpose of this book is to demonstrate how not only the rights of victims of crime, but the entire institution of criminal justice, can be conceived as flowing from the notion of human dignity and states' unconditional obligations to respect and protect human dignity and human rights. The objective is to show that the conviction and, in appropriate cases, also punishment of an offender expresses respect for the victim as a person and rights-holder but, equally importantly, also respects the offender as an accountable person responsible for her actions.

1.6.6 The Victim's Rights Alone Cannot Justify the Punishment of the Offender

Höffe emphasizes the rights of victims. According to Höffe, criminal law is a society's expression of its loyalty to human rights in general and victims' rights in particular. Criminal law protecting human rights only restricts the freedom of potential offenders to the extent necessary to preserve its citizens' confidence in the protection of their rights; it only takes the amount of freedom from offenders that they owe to their victims and to potential victims (Höffe 1999, p. 8):

> Das Strafrecht stellt das unverzichtbare Element einer menschenrechtsverpflichteten Selbstorganisation der Gesellschaft dar. Und nicht etwa schlechthin, wohl aber in dieser Funktion: als Schutzschild der Menschenrechte und Ausdruck der Verbundenheit der Gesellschaft mit den Opfern von Menschenrechtsverletzungen – was es den möglichen Tätern an Freiheit nimmt, gibt es den potentiellen Opfern an Vertrauen zurück – hat es Anspruch auf interkulturelle Gültigkeit.

However, the question remains whether punishment restoring the confidence of potential victims is justified. More precisely, the question is still whether a mechanism of punishment serving to redress the fragile balance of freedom upset by the offender comes down to just another form of instrumentalisation, only now not for the sake of the public, but for the sake of the victim and 'potential victims', which is a fairly broad category. Such an instrumentalisation would also show disrespect for the dignity of the offender, even if it were founded on the dignity of the victim.

More generally speaking, while the rights of victims are obviously an important aspect of criminal justice based on human dignity and human rights, what justifies the punishment of offenders cannot be rights of victims alone as it is not evident why satisfying the rights of victims would respect the dignity and autonomy of offenders. Any convincing justification of criminal justice necessarily departs from the individual autonomy of offenders and generates a theory of punishment from what is implied and inherent in the concept of human dignity, rather than positing rights of others in opposition to the offender's dignity and autonomy.

In other words, while it is true that victims are entitled to the conviction and, in appropriate cases, also punishment of offenders, this right is inherently premised on a justification of punishment that departs from the offender's perspective, dignity and rights and not from the situation and perspective of the victim. Such an approach would take Kant's principle seriously, that punishment cannot be justified as imposing hardship on one person for the sake of benefiting others, as such a 'justification' would objectify and reduce the human being to a mere instrumentality.

Chapter 3 will tackle this aporia by thoroughly investigating the concept of individual autonomy as a key element of human dignity. By sounding out the preconditions on which an individual's autonomy is premised, the precise scope of Kant's principle will be determined, assuming that Kant's principle does not inhibit normative claims on which individual autonomy itself is predicated.

1.6.7 Conclusion and Outlook

This introductory chapter set out to demonstrate that victims' rights in Europe have a basis in legally binding standards of European law, such as the European Convention on Human Rights and the European Union Charter of Fundamental Rights. However, on closer inspection this approach encounters complexities when it comes to the crucial question of how to legitimise the punishment of the offender in a manner that respects both the offender and the victim as persons. It appears that an approach that focuses mainly on the deterrent effects of punishment, as proposed by some of the ECtHR's case-law, loses sight of, and consequently entails a risk of disregarding, the concrete offender, the individual victim and their rights. Hence, this case-law alone does not readily or convincingly offer itself as a sound basis for the construction of a system of criminal justice reflecting the human dignity of victims and offenders.

This situation makes it necessary to dig deeper into the subject matter to arrive at a clearer understanding of punishment, human dignity and the rights of crime victims and offenders.

This further enquiry seriously considers the recently made distinction between the functionality of punishment and its justification. Chapter 2 analyses punishment as a mechanism capable of preserving social norms, but does not touch on the question of the legitimacy of criminal justice. The reason is that the latter question cannot be answered once and forever, but only in relation to a particular normative framework.

Hence, it is necessary to examine the normative framework of European societies. Chapter 3 assumes that the historic and political situation of these societies is marked by a current transition from nation states to a cosmopolitan normative order, based on the principles of human dignity and human rights. In this situation, it is important to understand the concept of human dignity and its impressive ability to answer to major challenges implied in this transition. One particularly important aspect relates to how a global political order is premised on the legitimacy provided by autonomous individuals.

From this preparatory work, Chap. 4 returns to the question of how prosecuting, convicting and punishing offenders can be justified within the framework set by the normative principle of human dignity, as well as to the question of how the rights of victims fit into this framework. The core element of a new paradigm of criminal justice is a revised concept of what constitutes a crime—not the violation of a law, but the violation of a system of human rights based on human dignity.

Punishment is viewed as a means, firstly, of restoring the victim as a person entitled to the respect of her rights, secondly, of restoring the offender as a person and a member of her community and, thirdly, of restoring, in a community of individuals, societal peace based on the rule of law and the confidence of all in the authority of their rights. It will be argued that the victim is entitled to the establishment of the truth, as well as to the conviction and, in appropriate cases, also punishment of the offender, because only such a reaction acknowledges the wrong encountered by the victim and restores the victim as a person entitled to respect. However it will not be argued that punishing the offender is justified by these rights of the victim. Rather, it will be argued that what justifies the punishment of the offender is the fact that human dignity dictates that the offender is to be treated as a person responsible for her action. Because of her participation in human dignity, the offender has a right to be held to account and, under certain conditions, even to be punished. This is the only possible justification of her punishment, as it respects Kant's principle, according to which convicting and punishing the offender have to be construed as means of respecting the offender as a person partaking in human dignity. The ultimate goal is to construct a truly critical theory of criminal law, a theory that brings to light the inherent limitations of criminal law's legitimacy.

Criminal justice systems oriented towards preserving the interests of a public conceived in terms of a nation state are gradually becoming an anachronism. Individuals are entitled to expect a criminal justice system to be concerned with the rights of individuals, not only with the laws of a nation state. In contemporary criminal courts, offenders and victims may experience that they are side-lined rather than taken seriously, manipulated rather than listened to, and discouraged rather than encouraged to act. Their discomfort may reflect a situation where their expectations are up to date, but the criminal justice system's ability to meet these expectations is not.

In this introductory chapter, it suffices to convey the basic message that criminal justice systems, if they are to overcome the orientation of protecting the interests of nation states and to adopt an approach founded on the normative principle of human dignity, will need to be reoriented towards respecting the victim and the offender as autonomous persons.

The following chapters argue that all human rights should be conceived as flowing from the one—strictly normative—concept of human dignity and that the purpose of criminal justice is to protect human dignity—personified by the victim, by the offender and by all other members of a legal community—and nothing else.

References

Alvaro, G., & D'Andrea, A. (2015). The impact of Directive 2012/29/EU on the Italian system for protecting victims of crime in criminal proceedings. In S. Ruggeri (Ed.), *Human rights in European criminal law: New developments in European legislation and case law after the Lisbon Treaty* (pp. 307–317). Cham, Switzerland: Springer.

Berger, M. (2013). *Organisation und Verfahren der ordentlichen Gerichtsbarkeit im Lichte der Rechtsprechung des Gerichtshofes der Europäischen Union*. Wien: MANZ Verlag.

Böckenförde, E.-W. (2014). Bleibt die Menschenwürde unantastbar? In B. Vogel (Ed.), *Umwertung der Menschenwürde: Kontroversen mit und nach Nietzsche* (pp. 127–143). Freiburg/München: Karl Alber.

Brienen, M. E. I., & Hoegen, E. H. (2000). *Victims of crime in 22 European criminal justice systems*. Nijmegen, The Netherlands: Wolf Legal Productions.

Brückner, M. (1998). *Wege aus der Gewalt gegen Frauen und Mädchen: Eine Einführung*. Frankfurt am Main, Germany: Fachhochschulverlag.

Christie, N. (1977). Conflicts as property. *British Journal of Criminology, 17*(1), 1–15.
Dobash, R. E., & Dobash, R. P. (1992). *Women, violence and social change*. New York: Routledge.
Duff, R. A. (2009). *Answering for crime: Responsibility and liability in the criminal law*. Oxford, England: Hart Publishing.
Erez, E. (2000). Integrating a victim perspective in criminal justice through victim impact statements. In A. Crawford & J. Goodey (Eds.), *Integrating a victim perspective within criminal justice* (pp. 165–184). Dartmouth, NH: Ashgate.
Fletcher, G. P. (1995). *With justice for some: Protecting victims' rights in criminal trials*. Reading, MA: Basic Books.
FRA. (2012). *Making hate crime visible in the European Union: Acknowledging victims' rights*. Luxembourg: Publications Office of the European Union.
FRA. (2014). *Victims of crime in the EU: The extent and nature of support for victims*. Luxembourg: Publications Office of the European Union.
FRA. (2016). *Ensuring justice for hate crime victims: Professional perspectives*. Luxembourg: Publications Office of the European Union.
Goodey, J. (2005). *Victims and victimology: Research, policy and practice* (1st ed.). Harlow, England: Longman.
Hampton, J. (2007). In D. Farnham (Ed.), *The intrinsic worth of persons: Contractarianism in moral and political philosophy*. Cambridge: Cambridge University Press.
Höffe, O. (1999). *Gibt es ein interkulturelles Strafrecht? Ein philosophischer Versuch*. Frankfurt am Main: Suhrkamp.
Höffe, O. (2008). *Kleine Geschichte der Philosophie* (2., durchgesehene Auflage.). München, Germany: C.H. Beck.
Hörnle, T. (2011). Gegenwärtige Strafbegründungstheorien: Die herkömmliche deutsche Diskussion. In A. von Hirsch, U. Neumann, & K. Seelmann (Eds.), *Strafe – Warum? Gegenwärtige Strafbegründungen im Lichte von Hegels Straftheorie* (pp. 11–30). Baden-Baden, Germany: Nomos.
Hörnle, T. (2014). Contribution to the discussion of the lecture of Matthias Jahn. In C. Prittwitz, M. Baurmann, K. Günther, M. Jahn, L. Kuhlen, & R. Merkel (Eds.), *Rationalität und Empathie: Kriminalwissenschaftliches Symposion für Klaus Lüderssen zum 80. Geburtstag* (pp. 166–167). Baden-Baden: Nomos.
Holz, W. (2007). *Justizgewähranspruch des Verbrechensopfers*. Berlin, Germany: Duncker & Humblot.
Hufen, F. (2014). Erosion der Menschenwürde? In B. Vogel (Ed.), *Umwertung der Menschenwürde: Kontroversen mit und nach Nietzsche* (pp. 144–162). Freiburg/München: Karl Alber.
Illich, I. (1977). Disabling professions. In I. Illich, I. K. Zola, J. McKnight, J. Caplan, & H. Shaiken (Eds.), *Disabling professions* (pp. 11–40). London: Marion Boyars.
Jesionek, U. (2004). Das Verbrechensopfer im künftigen österreichischen Strafprozessrecht. In C. Grafl & U. Medigovic (Eds.), *Festschrift für Manfred Burgstaller zum 65. Geburtstag* (pp. 253–265). Wien, Austria: Neuer Wissenschaftlicher Verlag.
Kant, I. (1797/1968). *Die Metaphysik der Sitten. Kants Werke. Akademie-Textausgabe Band VI* (pp. 203–494). Berlin, NY: Walter de Gruyter.
Kant, I. (1996). The metaphysics of morals. In M. J. Gregor (Ed.), *Cambridge texts in the history of philosophy*. Cambridge, England: Cambridge University Press.
Klein, E., Campbell, J., Soler, E., & Ghez, M. (1997). *Ending domestic violence: Changing public perceptions/halting the epidemic*. Thousand Oaks, CA: Sage.
Lüderssen, K. (2002). Historische Erkenntnisinteressen moderner Kriminalpolitik. In K. Lüderssen (Ed.), *Die Durchsetzung des öffentlichen Strafanspruchs* (pp. 21–37). Köln, Germany: Böhlau.
Malaniuk, W. (1947). *Lehrbuch des Strafrechtes: Erster Band*. Wien, Austria: Manzsche Verlagsbuchhandlung.

McKnight, J. (1977). Professionalized service and disabling help. In I. Illich, I. K. Zola, J. McKnight, J. Caplan, & H. Shaiken (Eds.), *Disabling professions* (pp. 69–91). London: Marion Boyars.
Naucke, W. (2007). Die zweckmäßige und die kritische Strafgesetzlichkeit, dargestellt an den Lehren J.P.A. Feuerbachs 1775–1833. In *Negatives Strafrecht: 4 Ansätze* (pp. 1–25). Berlin, Germany: LIT Verlag.
Rafaraci, T. (2015). New perspectives for the protection of the victims in the EU. In S. Ruggeri (Ed.), *Human rights in European criminal law: New developments in European legislation and case law after the Lisbon Treaty* (pp. 215–225). Cham, Switzerland: Springer.
Reeves, H., & Mulley, K. (2000). The new status of victims in the UK: Opportunities and threats. In A. Crawford & J. Goodey (Eds.), *Integrating a victim perspective within criminal justice* (pp. 125–145). Dartmouth, NH: Ashgate.
Richards, K. (2009). Taking victims seriously? The role of victims' rights movements in the emergence of restorative justice. *Current Issues in Criminal Justice, 21*(2), 302–320.
Rook, P. (2002). The standing of victims in the English criminal justice system. *ERA Forum, 3*(1), 37–39.
Sachs, M. (2015). Grundrechte: Anspruch des Opfers auf Strafverfolgung des Täters. *JuS, 2015*, 376–378.
Schmidt, A. (2015). Täter-Opfer-Staat: Zur Stellung des Opfers im Strafrecht. In M. Asholt et al. (Eds.), *Grundlagen und Grenzen des Strafrechts* (pp. 175–200). Baden-Baden: Nomos.
Sebba, L. (2000). The individualization of the victim: From positivism to postmodernism. In A. Crawford & J. Goodey (Eds.), *Integrating a victim perspective within criminal justice* (pp. 55–76). Dartmouth, NH: Ashgate.
Shapland, J. (2000). Victims and criminal justice: Creating responsible criminal justice agencies. In A. Crawford & J. Goodey (Eds.), *Integrating a victim perspective within criminal justice* (pp. 147–164). Dartmouth, NH: Ashgate.
Spronz, J. (2011). Caught up in Law. In J. Wirth (Ed.), *System failure: Male violence against women and children as treated by the legal system in Hungary today* (pp. 6–30). Budapest, Hungary: NANE Women's Rights Association & PATENT Association Against Patriarchy.
Thompson, M. (2004). What is it to wrong someone? A puzzle about justice. In R. J. Wallace, P. Pettit, S. Scheffler, & M. Smith (Eds.), *Reason and value: Themes form the moral philosophy of Joseph Raz* (pp. 333–384). Oxford, England: Clarendon Press.
Tugendhat, E. (2007). *Anthropologie statt Metaphysik*. München, Germany: C.H. Beck.
Wahlberg, W. E. (1868). *Das Princip der Individualisierung in der Strafrechtspflege*. C. Gerolds Sohn.
Waller, I. (2011). *Rights for victims of crime: Rebalancing justice*. Lanham, MD: Rowman & Littlefield Publishers.

Chapter 2
Punishment and Human Sociality

2.1 Why Punish? Three Questions to Explore

This chapter explores punishing 'in humans'. It seeks to answer the question why humans punish—and why they do so across cultures and times. If the phenomenon is universal in humans, there should also exist a universal explanation, a core function of punishment that makes it indispensable in all human societies. This would open up an anthropological dimension of punishing, presenting man as the animal that punishes.

To start with the notion of punishing in ordinary language, the Oxford English Dictionary defines the verb 'to punish' in the following terms: "Inflict a penalty or sanction on (someone) as retribution for an offence, especially a transgression of a legal or moral code", and offers the following example: "I have done wrong and I'm being punished for it." In this sentence, the 'and' and the 'for it' are the interesting elements. I am being punished for having done wrong. However, why—and in what sense—does the fact that I have done wrong provide a good reason for punishing me?

This chapter examines this crucial question from different perspectives. In doing so, the question, why humans punish wrongdoers, will be taken to mean three different things, namely reasons, proximate causes and ultimate causes. Before tackling the complex question of why it is that humans punish it may help to explain these terms in relation to a simpler question. For example, one can wonder why it is that children like to be close to their parents. To explore this phenomenon, one method could be to just ask children and to collect the reasons they explicitly give, such as daddy being a great cook or mummy being funny. However, some children would respond that it simply feels good to be with their parents. This points—beyond conscious reasons—to a potentially powerful motivation, namely to emotions fuelling the wish to be close to one's parents. Indeed, John Bowlby (1988) has collected abundant evidence demonstrating that children are genetically geared towards returning to their parents who provide a 'secure base' from which

A. Dearing, *Justice for Victims of Crime*, DOI 10.1007/978-3-319-45048-3_2

children depart when they explore their environment and to which they return in due course. This strong emotional attachment functions as a proximate cause that accounts for children's longing to be with their parents at intervals that increase with a child's development. However, if this attachment is encoded in the human genome, it must trigger behaviour that, at some point in the evolution of homo sapiens, conferred a crucial advantage on those who kept close to their parents. One obvious explanation is protection against predators, another that thus the little ones were not left behind when the band moved on. Hence, the ultimate causes of why children like to be close to their parents every now and then may date back to prehistoric times.

Similarly, the question can, firstly, be interpreted as asking why human societies punish. This question relates to the 'ultimate causation' of punishment. Asked differently, why, in the evolution of human polities, did punishment develop as a societal function? If humans punish—and they do, in one form or another, across all known societies—then one should expect some form of evolutionary explanation of this habit. This opens a study of the genealogy of punishment. In this regard, anthropological research provides a wealth of information, and game theoretical experiments contribute significant insights which will be explored later.

Secondly, in terms of 'proximate causes' or motivation, it can be asked what induces individuals to punish. We can explore the emotions and other 'irrational' forces driving punishment, of which individuals might not be aware. Thirdly, we can inquire into the reasons individuals give when asked explicitly why they punish or support punishing performed by others.

So far, we have examined why humans punish. What still remains is the issue of the justification of punishment. Why, and to what extent, would the fact that someone has done wrong legitimise her punishment? While this is the most complex question, it is in the end practically decisive and merits serious reflection. Despite all the evidence showing that humans are inclined to punish, one should still be ready to look out for an alternative to punishment in case no justification can be found for its use.

When it comes to justifying punishment, an important distinction should be made between absolutist and relativist ethics. If we consider the vast variety of forms of sanctioning that can be observed across cultures and times, we must ask ourselves whether we are looking for a general justification that holds across all ages and societies (absolutist); or if moral justifications—if at all—can be valid and convincing only in relation to a concrete society and its normative order at a given time (relativist)? Are we looking for one absolute justification of punishment, or for many relative justifications that are restricted to a specific societal context?

Here the view is held that some aspects of punishment are invariable while others change with their normative context. Punishment is a particular mechanism to shape and preserve social norms and a social order and is, in this function, corroborated and driven by powerful motives. These traits developed when human societies became sedentary, and have been hard-wired in these societies ever since. Briefly, punishment as a means of vindicating social norms is a human universal.

However, many other aspects are dependent on and relative to the historic normative context and hence variable over the centuries. This concerns, to some extent, the contents of the social norms protected by punishing, the basis of a social order's legitimation and the justification of punishment, the institutional framework of criminal justice, the roles performed by victims and offenders, as well as the many changing forms and levels of severity of punishment. While these changeable aspects will be dealt with later on in relation to contemporary European societies, the present chapter analyses the invariable, core elements of punishment—in a way the constant, unvarying semantics of punishment as a sign used in normative contexts.

2.2 The Ultrasociality Riddle

One of the striking features of humans is their ability to live together more or less—or even more and more—peacefully and to cooperate in ever larger numbers. This is made possible by one of the main inventions of *homo sapiens*, namely social norms created in prescriptive language, and expressed and reinforced by sanctions. Crudely speaking, social norms tell people how 'we do things'. In particular, social norms are passed on to children by teaching them how to perform various activities to become proper members of their society.

Anthropologists suggest that the crucial take-off of culture and normative language as human universals occurred in the Holocene when tribes settled in villages and engaged in long-term projects including breeding cattle, agriculture and the cultivation of land, as well as the construction of stable houses and irrigation systems.

However, that this happened—that this *could* happen—is puzzling. Looking at the mere size of human societies and their complex structures, researchers for some time found it difficult to explain the exceptional ability of humans to cooperate with genetically unrelated others, who they might not have seen before and often would not meet again. Anthropological studies and laboratory experiments suggest that neither selfish individuals nor selfish genes can account for the emergence of what was coined 'human ultrasociality' (Fehr and Gächter 2002; Turchin 2016). Traditional evolutionary approaches to cooperation based on conventional concepts such as kinship, reciprocity or reputation failed to explain large-scale human cooperation among hundreds and thousands of essentially unrelated persons. Hence, the issue of explaining *homo sapiens* as an essentially social animal and humans' refined abilities of social integration became a major issue of evolutionary and anthropologic debate.

Dawn broke when, in 1992, Boyd and Richerson published their seminal paper 'Punishment allows the evolution of cooperation (or anything else) in sizeable groups' (1992). By now a quite comprehensive and widely shared answer is available to the questions and riddles of human 'ultrasociality' (Boyd et al. 2003; Gintis 2008; Gintis et al. 2003; Jordan et al. 2013). Boyd and Richerson's publication also triggered an in-depth discussion of the fundamental importance of punishment to human sociality. (One remarkable aspect of this debate is that it was—and still is—conducted in the absence of criminal lawyers, who hardly took—or take—notice of this extensive and highly instructive discourse.)

On closer inspection, the ultrasociality riddle comprises two parts. The first questions *why* it is that humans gather in ever-larger groups, the second asks *how* they manage to do so.

Concerning the reasons *why* humans flock together, two issues are crucial. One relates to the effectiveness of joint efforts in achieving challenging tasks in relation to the group's environment, such as surviving inter-group warfare, hunting big animals, or building robust houses. The other is about internal differentiation, specialisation, and division of labour, which become possible only in sizeable groups, where at the same time some individuals collect water, some tend the fire, some look after infants, and still many others engage in hunting and fishing, and all these activities serve the interests of the community—'our' interests.

In particular, cooperation and specialisation in food production coupled with food sharing is highly beneficial to all members of a group. Illness or injuries can be fatal in the absence of others who are willing to share their prey. In humans, food sharing within the family and with those in need leads to a lowered mortality rate and enables a longer juvenile learning period (Mathew et al. 2013, pp. 47–49).

Given all these advantages, what is striking is not that cooperation developed among humans, but rather that it occurs only to a limited extent with other animals. The prospect that in numerous instances all would benefit from cooperation would hold for many animal societies just as well. Hence, one would expect cooperation to be widespread among—in particular—vertebrates. However, this is not the case. If sharing food with the sick or other family members is highly beneficial to all, it should be commonplace in a wide range of animal species. Yet, most mammals do not share their prey with others (Mathew et al. 2013, p. 47). Therefore, the question needs to be turned around to ask why cooperation is so rare in other animals. Animals do not cooperate on a large scale, while humans do. The question is what it is that enables humans to engage in joint activities that is not available to other species.

One answer is that other animals do not have a solution to what in game theory is called 'the n-person prisoners' dilemma' and means that for cooperation to develop, shirking duties must not pay.

The prisoner's dilemma (for a thorough analysis refer to Rapoport and Chammah 1970; Poundstone 1993; Ullmann-Margalit 1977) appears in the following situation: Two criminals, charged with having jointly committed a serious offence, are interviewed separately by the police. They have reason to believe that if neither confesses, both will be convicted only for a minor offence (say, prompting a sentence of about 6 months). However, each is told by the police that if one confesses and the other does not, the former will be rewarded by being released and the latter will be severely punished (by a prison term of about 3 years). On the other hand, if both confess, each will be punished, but less severely (say, 2 years' imprisonment). In this situation, prisoner A will consider that if B confesses, then A is better off if she confesses too (and consequently spends two instead of three years in prison). On the other hand, if prisoner B does not confess—thereby displaying an inclination to trust and cooperate—prisoner A is again better off if she confesses (no punishment compared to a sentence of 6 months). Hence A concludes that either way she is better off if she confesses. As the situation is exactly symmetrical from B's perspective, A has no reason to believe that B will hold her tongue. Hence, it is likely that in this situation both will confess and, consequently, spend 2 years in prison (together 4 years). This is remarkable, given that they would have both only spent 6 months in prison (together 1 year) had they both confided in one another, cooperated and kept silent. However, the problem is that from their *ex-ante* perspective the prisoners had no indication that the other would keep silent. On this basis, a norm of cooperation could not develop.

The same pattern—non-cooperation because of a strategic calculus—shows in situations involving more than two actors. One could imagine that a group cooperates in hunting buffalos and after many hours of hard and dangerous work returns to the camp with their prey. When it now comes to consuming the meat, those who have not participated in all the exhausting hunting and chasing are rested and easily defeat the fatigued hunters in struggling for the best and largest bits of meat. At the end of a long day, those who invested least are best off in terms of their 'enhanced fitness'. Consequently, the next morning, when it comes to deciding who goes hunting, many are reluctant. In the absence of norms effectively governing equal participation and investments in hunting and a fair sharing of the prey, those who cooperate lose out to shirkers and therefore, from an evolutionary point of view, the ability to cooperate cannot develop. Others would be inclined to follow the successful strategy of defecting. Hence shirking would rapidly emerge as the rule and not remain an exception. As a result, all will have less meat to consume. The failure of the group to cooperate negatively affects the fitness of its members. 'Ceteris paribus, having been a free-rider in past situations provides a healthy and financially well-equipped starting point for future actions. In the limit, past providers may not be able to contribute in the future due to excessive free-riding by others, while free-riders accumulate resources on their private accounts' (Gürerk et al. 2010, p. 2).

To sum up this section, while cooperation in large groups offers many benefits to group members—including avoidance of and protection from predators—'there are many potentially cooperative circumstances in which it is more advantageous for individuals to evade contributing to the collective and free riding on the contributions of others. This strategy will, unchecked, prove so successful that it will overrun an entire population, making group living an impossibility' (Shariff et al. 2011, p. 122).

2.3 Public Goods, Free Riding and Punishment in Game-Theory Experiments

Game theory has developed into a language shared among researchers across many disciplines, including economy, anthropology, psychology and political sciences. It has also been used successfully to simulate the interaction of a group of individuals jointly engaging in the production of public goods. Researchers have developed games to enable them to answer the question how in a group—interacting based on a few simple rules—cooperation can evolve. This issue has induced a vast array of results from many of these, slightly varying, experiments conducted as public goods games. Faintly resembling alchemists in search of the formula to produce gold, researchers have, for some time, repeated public goods games over and again, nuancing the rules, changing the number of participants and the number of rounds performed in a game, all the time hoping that someday an experiment would at last result in a group readily cooperating to the benefit of all,—and one eventually did (for a detailed account of the development of a theory of human sociality based on punishment see Gintis 2000).

Already in 1966, George Christopher Williams spotted the crucial problem with cooperation, namely the risk of free-riding and its detrimental effect on the group's morale and behaviour (1966). Even in a situation where cooperation would clearly be beneficial to all, it is likely not to come about, as long as those who cheat by parasitizing on the contributions of others are economically better off than those who invest in costly cooperation. In 1988, Harsanyi and Selten established the diagnosis that, even when players are allowed to negotiate, an agreement still has little chance of being kept, unless "the rules of the game make such agreement binding and enforceable" (1988, p. 3). Consequently, in 1992 Ostrom and others applied rules that combined 'covenants' with a 'sword', observing Hobbes' advice that "covenants, without the sword, are but words, and of no strength to secure a man at all" (Ostrom et al. 1992, p. 404; on Hobbes Ullmann-Margalit 1977, pp. 62–73). The authors arrived at the cautious but pioneering conclusion that possibly "some subjects can find yield-improving joint strategies, design a sanctioning mechanism, use the sanctioning mechanism, and achieve a high rate of conformance to their joint strategies" (Ostrom et al. 1992, p. 413).

The same year, Robert Boyd and Peter Richerson published their ground breaking article—titled "Punishment allows the evolution of cooperation (or anything else) in sizable groups"—which modelled the evolution of cooperation based on an opportunity of group members to punish those who deny fair contribution (1992).

2.3.1 In a Public Goods Game, Peer Punishment Enables a Group's Cooperation

Finally, in 2000, Fehr and Gächter convincingly demonstrated how punishment can work in laboratory conditions to sustain a social norm of cooperation (Fehr and Gächter 2000a, b, 2002; also Fischbacher et al. 2001).

Four group members are each handed 20 tokens worth some amount of real money. They then decide simultaneously how many tokens they want to keep for themselves—'consume privately'—and how much they contribute to a common pool (a 'joint project'). While making this decision, the participants are not able to see or communicate with other participants. To make cooperation awarding, for each token a participant invests in the project, *each* of the four players earns 0.4 tokens. Thus, the investor's personal return for investing one token in the project is 0.4, while the income *for the entire group* rises to 1.6 tokens. Because of this setting, *everyone benefits* from investments of any member in the joint project *independent of their own contributions*, which is why the project by definition involves a public good and why the issue of free-riding—the n-person prisoners' dilemma—arises. If all group members keep all their tokens for themselves, each participant ends up still with the 20 tokens she had from the beginning. In contrast, if all invest their total endowments in the joint project, each subject has an income of 32 tokens (or a profit of 12 tokens). After the game, participants are informed of the total amount of contributions to the project and hence can realise whether their own investment was higher or lower than the average contribution of others. The game is then repeated for another nine rounds.

But here is the dilemma: If one actor invests all her tokens in the project while the others keep their tokens for themselves, then she will end up with 8 tokens while all others will have 28 (their original 20 plus 8 tokens owing to the generous contributions of one participant). It is worth noting that such a participant who invests all she has in the public good, while no one else does, in the language of game theorists is tellingly referred to as 'S' for 'sucker' (e.g. Fehr and Gächter 1999).

Now the question is whether, under these conditions, participants are ready to contribute to the public good, trusting that others will do the same. Members of the group who fear that others will free ride on their contributions are likely to be discouraged from investing in the public good, which in turn may have a negative effect on the propensity of others to contribute.

The result is that in the described conditions the group is not able to maintain a sufficient level of stable cooperation, i.e. a high level of investments of participants in the joint project. While in the first round many participants display an impressive readiness to invest in the project—on average more than half of their endowment—cooperation spirals down over time and reaches very low levels in the last rounds.

However, now the experiment enters into a second stage of another ten periods, where each game is played in two steps. This second stage differs from the previous game only in that the participants are, after each game, informed of how much each of the other group members has contributed to the project. From this information, participants can reduce the income of another group member by assigning deduction points. These points are costly to the assigning participant with increasing marginal costs: assigning two deduction points, costs two tokens, but four deduction points cost six tokens and six points twelve. However, these points are also costly to the participant to whom they are attributed. For every point that a player is assigned, her income is reduced by 10 %. Thus if someone receives five points in total from other group members her income is reduced in this period of the game by half. Participants are then informed how many points they were assigned in total without learning which of the other players assigned deduction points or how many.

Fehr and Gächter (2000a) demonstrated that the introduction of this opportunity to 'punish' other group members very significantly improves the results of the game causing, over several periods, a considerable rise in contribution levels. While in the last (the tenth) period of the first stage—conducted without 'punishment' opportunity—investments are at the level of approximately one token, they immediately jump higher in period eleven, when the 'punishment' opportunity is introduced, to around eight tokens. In sharp contrast to the no-punishment condition, when the possibility to sanction others who fail to contribute their fair share to the joint project is provided, average contributions further increase up to a level of more than 90 % of endowments being invested in the joint project—to the benefit of all (for a discussion of the public goods game with third-party punishment see Gintis et al. 2005).

This indicates that the opportunity to sanction 'defectors' enables the group to immediately assume and to thereafter sustain stable cooperation at a fairly high and even mounting level of contributions to the public good. While in the absence of punishment, cooperation erodes and eventually collapses, the availability of a sanctioning mechanism fosters the emergence and maintenance of rules of fair cooperation. The punishment of shirkers enables a group's fair cooperation.

The interpretation of punishment as enabling cooperation is premised on the assumption that many participants are genuinely inclined to abide by standards of fair cooperation. In this regard the results from public-goods games coincide with findings from another game, fairly popular among game theorists, namely the ultimatum game. Two players are shown ten monetary units. One player, called the proposer, is told that she can offer any number of the ten units to the other player, called the responder. The proposer can make only one offer, which the responder can either accept or reject. If the responder accepts, the money is shared according to the offer. If the responder rejects, both players get nothing. Since the game is played only once and under conditions of strict anonymity, a self-regarding responder will accept any amount of money. Knowing this, a self-regarding proposer will offer the minimum of 1 unit. However, when the ultimatum game is actually played, only a minority of participants behave in such a selfish manner. Most proposers offer very substantial amounts, with half of the stake being the modal offer, and respondents routinely reject offers below 30 % (Gintis et al. 2005, pp. 11–13). These findings attest to the fact that subjects are intrinsically motivated to cooperate in a fair manner rendering each her due.

2.3.2 The Crucial Role of Third Parties: Punishment is Premised on an Emerging Normative Consensus

Fehr and Gächter have explained how cooperation can work based on the possibility of punishment. However, have they also demonstrated how cooperation in humans could have developed to start with? Not quite. Their results are not apt to account for punishment's evolutionary success. The reason is, that from a group perspective, punishing is obviously a very costly occupation. A punisher incurs costs with the sole aim of making the punished incur costs. Hence, while cooperation levels rise with punishment, so do expenses, because of necessary investments in punishing and the expenses incurred by the individuals who are punished. It has been demonstrated that, as a result, the group's net benefit from their improved cooperation is only marginal. Hence, a group that punishes in a Fehr/Gächter-style will cooperate, but at the end of the day still not fare much better than other groups who do not. While Fehr and Gächter powerfully demonstrated how punishment enables cooperation, they cannot also be praised for having convincingly solved the riddle of how large-scale cooperation could plausibly have developed in the evolution of *homo sapiens*.

In addition, the Fehr/Gächter experiment raises a theoretical question, namely, to what extent the attribution of deduction points *per se* resembles punishment in everyday life. The question is how to interpret an act of aggression if it is not backed by the normative views of the pertinent community. In such conditions the aggression can cause, not an improvement of a band's peaceful cooperation, but payback from the side of the aggressed group member. In other words, whether others interpret an aggression as legitimately responding to a norm violation or not is decisive for the perception of the aggressor as defending the group's rules or as only making trouble and consequently for the positive or adverse effects of the aggression on the group's cooperation.

In fact, the only difference between an aggression and punishment lies in their interpretation by the parties involved in the conflict and by observers. Harm deliberately inflicted on an individual constitutes mere violence, unless it is interpreted as acting within a normative order, as is the case with punishment, self-defence or law enforcement aiming to end a norm violation. Obviously, only humans can normatively contextualise the infliction of harm as an appropriate and fair reaction to a previous conduct that is assigned the particular meaning of violating a normative order. Such a sophisticated interpretation is premised on the capacity to command a normative language, a faculty that—maybe more than anything else—distinguishes humans from other animals.

Hence, if in the Fehr/Gächter-experiment, one participant sanctions another for not contributing sufficiently to the group's common project, this can be considered an instance of 'punishment' only under the condition that what the sanction aims to express is understood and backed by the normative views of others. As the participants in the game have no means of agreeing beforehand on what they consider an appropriate level of cooperation, there is a risk that a participant who is attributed deduction points retaliates because she, unlike the punisher, considers the level of her contributions as fair and appropriate. She perceives the deduction as an act of aggression rather than as a legitimate sanction.

In the setting created by Fehr and Gächter, a participant is informed only of the total amount of points assigned to her by the three other players and does not know which of the other participants assigned deduction points or how many. However, a participant who is sanctioned will suspect that those who contributed lavishly are also more motivated to invest in punishment and inclined to negatively judge the lower level of contributions displayed by others. This situation can lead to a situation where the generous cooperators are targeted for retaliation by those sanctioned in previous rounds, and consequently shy away from the high level of cooperation they would otherwise be willing to commit to. Hence, normative disagreement has a potential to undermine cooperation.

In this respect, an important contribution has been made by experiments published by Marco Casari and Luigi Luini in 2009, who in a public goods experiment found a significantly higher cooperation level under what they coined a "consensual punishment institution" compared to a protocol of peer punishment implemented by individuals in isolation. Under the consensual treatment, members could not on their own assign deduction points. They had to 'file a request' that another participant should be assigned a certain amount of such points. This suggestion was ignored unless at least one other participant also filed for the punishment of the subject in question. Hence punishment was carried out only when there was a coalition of two or more agents sharing the same normative assessment (Casari and Luini 2009, pp. 273–274). Such a rule premising peer punishment on the availability of a coalition significantly enhanced a group's performance. Consensual punishing generates what Casari and Luini call a "consensus dividend" (2009, p. 274). In the final period, the contributions under the protocol of consensual punishing rose to about nine tokens while they ended up around six tokens in the baseline treatment of individual punishing.

What is more remarkable, the consensual treatment achieved this high level of cooperation with a significantly smaller amount of punishment compared to the baseline treatment. Consensual punishing "generated punishment costs 10 percent lower than the Baseline rule and realized a contribution level 90 percent higher" (Casari and Luini 2009, p. 277). What Casari and Luini showed is that groups performing consensual punishment achieved a significant relative *payoff gain* of 13 %, while groups implementing the baseline treatment—punishing performed by individuals in isolation—suffered a relative *payoff loss*, which in the final period of the baseline treatment still amounted to 20 % (Casari and Luini 2009, p. 277). This suggests that in the consensual treatment—and only in this treatment—punishing is beneficial to the entire group to an extent that, under evolutionary conditions of competing communities, is capable of exerting selective pressure on groups who have not adopted such a punishing norm. This further indicates that punishment may not have evolved as a matter between an offender and a victim but necessarily involves third parties taking sides with the victim.

In other words, it is not sufficient that one individual feels that she has been treated in a disrespectful manner and therefore is inclined to retaliate. For a norm to develop, it is necessary that third parties sympathise with the victim and are ready to support her interpretation of the offender's behaviour as violating her *legitimate* interests and hence a social norm of fair cooperation.

In laboratory experiments, Fehr and Fischbacher (2004) explored the willingness of third parties to sanction defectors. They tested compliance with a norm of equal distribution conducting 'dictator games', where one participant (the 'dictator') receives an endowment while another obtains nothing. The dictator is then given the opportunity to transfer a share of his endowment to the other player (who is called the 'recipient'). Fehr and Fischbacher introduced a third party to the dictator game who could punish the dictator after observing her transfer to the recipient. The third party was able to attribute deduction points if she believed that the dictator had not passed on an appropriate share of his endowment to the recipient. Punishing was costly to this third party and to the dictator, as both parties had their payoff reduced by three points for each punishment point assigned. At the end of the experiment, points were transferred into real money.

The experiment aimed to see whether the third player would invest her endowment to punish the dictator for perceived violations of a norm of fair distribution although the third party was not affected by the dictator's behaviour. Fehr and Fischbacher found that most third parties punished dictators who transferred less than half of their endowment and that the severity of punishment was considerable. The authors concluded that "a large percentage of subjects are willing to enforce distribution and cooperation norms even though they incur costs and reap no economic benefit from their sanctions and even though they have not been directly harmed by the norm violation" (2004, p. 85).

These findings are corroborated by research showing that the pro-social function of third-party punishing is acknowledged and that subjects prefer to cooperate with partners who reliably punish defectors (dos Santos et al. 2013). Anthropological research has shown a strong positive relationship between third-party punishing and community size, such that individuals from larger communities are more willing to engage in third-party punishment (Ensminger and Henrich 2014, p. 8).

2.3.3 A Norm is a Public Good

A norm expresses emphatically how 'we do things' and hence creates an expectation that orients action (Jakobs 2008, p. 53). It is constituted of three elements. Firstly, the contents of a norm can be expressed in normative language, persuading people that they should behave in a certain manner, specified by the norm. Secondly, the norm exists in social reality to the extent that it actually guides actions; and it is a reliable source of expectations—and thus performs its beneficial functions—only to the extent that it effectively exists; and its effectiveness shows in situations where the norm is relevant and orients the behaviour of actors. To the extent that the norm is followed, it creates foreseeability and confidence and reduces contingency.

However, these two elements—normativity and regularity—are not enough. What is still missing becomes apparent if one compares a social norm to a commercial suggesting that consumers should buy a certain product. A commercial encourages consumers to behave in a certain manner; and whether it is effective or not can be measured by its effect on consumers' behaviour. However, a commercial's call is not authoritative. If a subject does not abide by the advice offered by the commercial, she is not met with her community's criticism, even if many others behave as advised by the commercial. In any case, consumers are free to follow the advice provided by commercials or not.

This is different in the case of a social norm. Not observing a social norm comes with a risk of being sanctioned. Hence, the third element constituting a social norm is how people react to deviation. A social norm can be conceived as an expectation that, when it is frustrated, triggers sanctioning the person who disappointed the expectation instead of leading to the conclusion that the expectation should be reviewed and potentially abandoned (Luhmann 2008). In the terminology suggested by Searle (2010, pp. 11–12), if we make a prediction of behaviour, we seek to fit the prediction to the world as we expect it to be, and if matters develop unexpectedly, we may, in the end, find that our prediction was wrong. However, with a *legitimate* expectation of a certain conduct, the action should comply with the expectation, and if in the end it does not, we will censure the action, not the expectation. A social norm implies a propensity of the members of a community to hold on to the expectation of norm-conformity, even when they experience that some do not abide by the norm. In other words, the notion of a social norm implies a community's readiness to take action to defend the norm against individuals calling it into question by their norm violating behaviour.

Any normative communication attempts to control another person's behaviour by relying on some sort of authority. If a police officer instructs a driver to stop her car, this instruction is an attempt to guide the driver's conduct; and this attempt is promising as the police officer can rely on her authority as a public official. The structure of this officer's order does not differ from the structure of a general law requiring that drivers put on a seat belt.

The next question is what creates and what undermines a norm's authority and reliability. Whether a social norm can be trusted and can perform its beneficial services is primarily a function of its observance. Whoever abides by the norm contributes to its standing and binding force, whoever flouts the norm undermines its credibility. Any action, which in a situation where the norm is relevant, adheres to the norm, is interpreted as a vote cast by the actor in favour of the norm's bindingness and suggesting to others that they should adopt the same stance. However, her contribution is premised on her autonomous agency, on her ability, that is, to express by her actions that she acknowledges and abides by or refutes normative claims on her behaviour. Her norm compliance supports the norm to the extent that her behaviour can be and actually is interpreted as an autonomous normative statement in favour of the norm and—importantly—an invitation to others to share the attitudes demonstrated by the agent (Stevenson 1963, p. 209).

This is the point where the crucial interdependence of individuals' agency and the normative order shows. A person, by observing a norm, at once recognises and produces the norm's authority. She thus actively contributes to interpreting the norm—the normative expectations of other members of her community—as binding, including on herself. Thus, her being bound by a norm is partly a repercussion of her own norm abiding behaviour; and a community's being bound by a norm is entirely the consequence of that community's adherence to the norm. This points to a fundamental recursiveness underlying any normative order. At large, norms are created by those who they bind. As a citizen, the individual participates in establishing the norms, by which she is bound as a subject (Günther 2005, p. 115).

A social norm is a public good. Thus Fehr and Gächter have argued that the analytical structure of a public-goods game is a good approximation to the question of how social norms are established and maintained (2000a). To the extent that social norms are coined in general and abstract terms, all benefit from the social norm and hence all can, as a matter of fair cooperation, be expected to contribute to the authority of the social norm by their norm-complying behaviour. However, those who do not contribute nevertheless draw advantage from the norm's existence and the foreseeability it produces. Thus, they exploit the contributions of others. Because of their abstract and general nature, social norms impact on the situation of all members of a society independently of whether they personally contribute to upholding the norm by abiding by it or not.

If a member does not abide by the law and share in the normative community's burden of norm-production, she can be seen as free-riding on the norm-compliance of others; and if she is not punished, the social norm in question is at risk of degenerating and disappearing. That is to say, if one individual benefits from others obeying the norm of not stealing from others, but engages in such activity herself and is not sanctioned, her example has a potential to frustrate, annoy and put off others, and hence the norm could, in the end, disappear.

The mode of a norm's existence is authority or bindingness. An instruction exists as a norm whenever it is invoked or acknowledged. Hence, both the single social norm and the entire normative order only become a reality when they recur in interactive processes of communication. They remain fluid and ephemeral (Berger 2009, p. 17), comparable to living organisms that only exist in the contingent biological processes of their continuous generation and reproduction.

One can distinguish between an order's legal validity and its social recognition and effectiveness (Holz 2015, pp. 44–45). In fact, this distinction has a long tradition (Kelsen 1979, p. 2; Stemmer 2008, p. 187). In the English speaking world, it is well known as the difference between law in the books and law in action, introduced by Roscoe Pound (1910). However, purely legal validity is only theoretical, whilst compliance is real. To observe that an instruction is legally valid as a legal norm means that it has been produced according to the relevant rules of a legal order. Its production can be considered a valid 'move' in a normative language game. But, this does not imply that the instruction is actually observed and practically relevant. In social reality, the norm only exists if individuals adhere to it, in situations where the norm is relevant, and through the sanctioning of defectors. A police officer issuing an order or a parliament passing legislation perform acts of communication that may have good prospects of being acknowledged by others as legally binding. Still, if one is interested in the reality of law and how it works, what alone is relevant is law in action. In fact, empirical research suggests that laws function less as causes of behaviour and more as predictors of behaviour: Subjects tend to abide by laws because—and as long as—they expect that others will do the same (Henrich and Ensminger 2014, p. 24). If a parliament is acknowledged as legitimate, subjects will tend to treat its laws as binding and expect others to abide by them. Still, from a theoretical point of view there is a difference between simply taking all legislation at face value and observing that at least certain laws are obeyed regularly, while others are not.

A norm's legal validity can only become practically relevant if people so decide. If a person wishes to abide—or to be seen as abiding—by the legal order as a matter of principle, she may adhere to a norm for the sole reason that she considers it legally valid. If a person values 'the rule of law', then she may take a norm's legal validity as an argument militating in favour of abiding by the norm, even in a situation where such compliance otherwise does not make much sense, like stopping and waiting in front of a red traffic light when, obviously, there is no one around to benefit from this behaviour. Still, such behaviour sends a signal that, in the view of its author, legal norms are to be observed even when this does not benefit anyone.

2.4 The Inherent Psychology of Punishment

Describing how group members should behave to allow the group to cooperate effectively is one thing; explaining why they would behave in this manner is quite another. People may or may not be aware of how their conduct affects the standards of cooperation of their communities; so we must explore the psychology of why individuals choose to punish others.

The question, why humans cooperate and punish shirkers, can be understood to mean different things. It may aim at the level of explicit *reasons* individuals give when asked why they abide by norms, punish offenders or approve punishing performed by others. However, one can also look at what people in situations of norm violations *actually do* with a view to identifying consistent patterns of behaviour, which possibly deviates from individuals' deliberate explanations.

What persons actually do is the result of various *motivational* factors, which include, but are not limited to, deliberate reasoning. Therefore, what is interesting at this point are the patterns of individuals' punishing behaviour and how they can be interpreted in a consistent manner, which may differ from the accounts individuals give deliberately when asked to explain their behaviour. For a moment, it is assumed that humans do not know exactly what they are doing when they punish.

2.4.1 Hypothesizing: Deterrent Punishing Versus Retribution

In criminal law theory, consequentialist (and more particularly utilitarian) approaches are usually distinguished from deontological theories. A consequentialist approach would assess an action based on its beneficial or detrimental—but in any case: empirical—consequences.

As an—admittedly somewhat outdated—example, the utilitarian views of Jeremy Bentham (1789) may serve to demonstrate the kind of approach typical for a consequentialist (and more particularly utilitarian) theory of punishment. Bentham presents the following "Principles of Punishment":

> Punishment, being primarily mischievous, is out of place when groundless, inefficacious, unprofitable, or needless. [. . .] Now, the aim of the legislator is (1) to prevent mischief altogether; (2) to minimise the inclination to do mischief; (3) to make the prevention cheap.
>
> Hence (1) the punishment must outweigh the profit of the offence to the doer; (2) the greater the mischief, the greater the expense worth incurring to prevent it; (3) alternative offences which are not equally mischievous, as robbery and robbery with murder, must not be equally punished; (4) the punishment must not be excessive, and therefore should take into account the circumstances influencing sensibility; (5) so also must the weakness of the punishment due to its remoteness, and the impelling force of habit.

This account is expressed through an arithmetical, economic logic. Punishment is described as a control tool which steers human behaviour, such as taxation or administrative fines imposed by the traffic police. The aim is to prevent mischief, and to do so cheaply. Complicated normative questions, including whether the offender deserves this kind of treatment, are not raised. If the ultimate objective is to maximise the wealth of a nation—irrespective of how this wealth and the costs incurred in its production are distributed—such an economic logic may be appropriate.

On the other hand, a deontological ethical theory evaluates an action independent of its future empirical consequences by focussing solely on its intrinsic quality. What justifies punishment is the fact that the offence is a wrong and hence the offender deserves to be punished. Such retributive theories of punishment aim to account for punishment solely by recourse to the fact that an offence has been committed and its gravity in terms of the wrong done.

The question here is whether the actual behaviour of people fits to any existing theory. In other words, whether a theory can be identified as underlying and explaining patterns of individuals' actual punishing behaviour.

One possible assumption would be that individuals punish when it is probable that it will, in the future, deter shirking behaviour. The setting of the public goods game, implemented by Fehr and Gächter, introduced the punishment option for rounds 11–20. Hence, shirkers in these rounds were aware of the risk they faced. Still some contributions were low enough to provoke deduction points. Thus, we must explore under which conditions participants made use of the option to punish other participants.

To suggest one explanation, if some group members, despite the punishment option introduced, still contribute significantly less than others, a subject may believe that, while the threat created by the punishment opportunity obviously did not prevent these shirkers from free-riding, experiencing real punishment will finally deter even the most hard-boiled defector from continuing to shirk. This explanatory model can be referred to as deterrent punishing. Punishment is applied to render effective a social norm that failed to be effective solely because of the punishment threat.

There still remain two sub-sets of explanations. Punishers may invest in the deterrence of free-riders because they hope for their *own* payoffs in later rounds. This motivation can be referred to as 'egotistic deterrence'. A second group of individuals would—consciously or unconsciously—invest in dissuading further shirking even if *only others* benefit from such an improvement, which could be considered 'altruistic deterrence'. Both of these motivations would render a practice of punishment instrumental, meaning that punishment is used to achieve a practical result, and thus fits within the consequentialist philosophy of punishment.

In contrast, if participants engage in costly punishment without seeking any future advantages or benefits for themselves or others, such a motivation would have to be seen as driven by the adherence to moral standards or by moral sentiments. Punishing is then executed as intrinsically valuable, as, that is to say, just the appropriate response to defecting, regardless of practical benefits. This fits within the deontological interpretation of punishment.

2.4.2 Deterrence Does Not Hold the Answer (I)

Whether the assumption of egotistic deterrence as punishment motivation holds as a valid explanation of real patterns of punishing behaviour can be examined when the prisoners'-dilemma game is repeated with changing participants. To achieve this effect, Fehr and Gächter (2000b) arranged what they called a 'perfect stranger'—as compared to a 'partner'—version of the game. In the perfect stranger setting, games were repeated for several rounds, but participants knew that they would not meet another player more than once. In contrast, in the partner version the same four members played over ten rounds.

If punishing is motivated by egotistic deterrence, participants will punish in the partner version but not in the perfect stranger treatment, as this setting rules out any possibility that the punisher herself would benefit from a deterrent effect of her investments in punishing. However, strikingly the pattern of punishment was almost identical in both versions. This clearly rules out egotistic deterrence as an explanation of punishment. The pattern of punishing behaviour displayed by participants cannot be accounted for as benefiting the punisher.

The *altruistic* version of deterrence—participants punishing defectors to incentivise them to cooperate, even if subsequently only other players benefit from such reform—is still a contender for a valid explanation for what motivates punishment. Indeed, Fehr and Gächter leaned towards such an interpretation of punishment as serving the interests of other players, assuming (2002, p. 139) that punishment provides "a material benefit for the future interaction partners of the punished subject but not for the punisher. Thus, the act of punishment, although costly for the punisher, provides a benefit to other members of the population by inducing potential non-cooperators to increase their investments. For this reason, the act of punishment is an altruistic act."

However, what did not fit this explanation was the fact that participants maintained their pattern of punishing behaviour even when the experiment was conducted as a one-shot game without any repetition and hence without the possibility of punishment serving *anybody* in later rounds. As Fehr and Gächter observed (2000a, p. 991): "A big question is however, why many subjects are willing to punish free riders in a one-shot context although this is costly." They concluded that "it seems quite likely that free riding causes strong negative emotions among the cooperators and that these emotions, in turn, trigger the willingness to punish free riders" (see also Fehr and Gächter 2002, p. 139; Gintis et al. 2005, pp. 171–175).

2.4.3 Betrayal Aversion and Conditional Cooperation

It is useful to change the perspective for a moment and consider why it is that individuals shirk. After all, what punishers—consciously or unconsciously—assume as the motives behind shirking may influence their punishing behaviour.

Again, two possible interpretations suggest themselves. The first explains defecting by the ruthless selfishness of shirkers, placing them in marked distance to the noble team spirit of those who invest in a joint project. An alternative explanation would premise the difference less on individuals' moral or immoral standards and attitudes and more on subjects' robust or feeble confidence in the norm compliance of others. After all, what needs to be explained is why in Fehr and Gächter's game without the punishment option, average contributions are around 60 % in the first round, but rapidly deteriorate in reaction to real or suspected freeriding of other participants. One explanation could assume that the real or perceived selfishness of shirkes has contagious effects on the morality of others. Another explanation would focus on participants' strong wish to avoid being exploited and 'looking stupid'. Already in 1999, Fehr and Gächter (1999, p. 9) theorised:

> We believe, in particular, that subjects strongly dislike being the 'sucker', i.e., being those who cooperate while other group members free ride. This aversion against being the 'sucker' might well trigger a willingness to punish free riders.

To capture this attitude, the term 'betrayal aversion' was coined (Kosfeld et al. 2005). A combination of a low level of confidence in the morals of others and a high level of betrayal aversion is apt to account for shirking just as well as crude and calculating egotism. Subjects with strong betrayal aversion act as 'conditional cooperators', who are willing to contribute to public goods if, and only as long as, they are confident that others will do the same and not abuse their trust. Hence, conditional cooperators should be in favour of introducing a punishment option, as it would allow them to trust that others have reason to cooperate.

However, from a conditional cooperator's perspective the introduction of a punishment threat, while being a step in the right direction, may *per se* still not provide sufficient guarantees, as the question remains whether others will actually incur the costs involved in punishing offenders. Here again, their betrayal aversion intervenes. If a conditional cooperator would find herself to be the only one shouldering the costs of punishing defectors, she would, again, experience the nagging feeling of paying to be a sucker. Hence, to some conditional cooperators, the introduction of the punishment option will provide sufficient reassurance, while others will remain sceptical. Only when they can see that third parties actually punish defectors, will these sceptics have confidence in the cooperation of others and overcome their betrayal aversion (Fehr and Fischbacher 2004). In a sense, what the punishment of defectors may mean to a conditional cooperator with a strong betrayal aversion is not that she is coerced, but rather that she is *enabled* to cooperate, in the sense that the punishment of shirkers allows her to overcome her betrayal aversion and to act freely on her genuine propensity to cooperate.

As far back as 1986, Yamagishi explored the inclination of participants in public goods games to invest in establishing a sanctioning system enabling them to punish the least cooperative group member(s) and thereby to stimulate other members' cooperation (Yamagishi 1986). Yamagishi distinguished 'high trusters' from 'low trusters'. As the first category of participants firmly believe in the cooperativeness of others, they display—at least in the first round of a public goods game—an unconditional inclination to cooperate, even in the absence of a sanctioning system, while 'low trusters' premise their willingness to cooperate on the existence of some form of effective sanctions. Consequently, when offered the opportunity to cooperate and invest in establishing and maintaining a sanctioning system, 'low trusters' readily invested more in this project than 'high trusters' (Yamagishi 1986, 1988).

Later, Yamagishi and Yamagishi suggested distinguishing 'trust' from 'assurance'. While trust is placed in another person's genuine goodwill and benign intent, assurance rests on the objective—and institutional—incentive structure that frames a relationship (Yamagishi and Yamagishi 1994). In this reading, punishing opportunities and, in particular, actual punishment do not foster trust but add to participants' assurance that others will cooperate.

On closer inspection, the assurance created by sanctions entails two aspects. The obvious one relies on the prospect that potential shirkers will seek to avoid the material and moral costs involved in being punished. However, also in another respect, punishment opportunities promise relief to conditional cooperators haunted by their betrayal aversion. If, despite of an essentially effective punishment threat, some dogged non-cooperator still shirks, the willing contributor will no longer feel that she is being taken for a fool. Once punishment opportunities are added to the game and implemented, the remaining risk of being tricked and of looking naïve, is balanced by the expectation that a free-rider will be punished and therefore will not be the 'one who laughs last'. Third parties punishing defectors sends a clear signal to betrayed victims that they were right to expect cooperation and that shirkers are prevented from profiting from their defecting, that, in short, shirking does not pay. Punishment prevents the shirker from benefiting from her shirking and thus eliminates an incentive to shirk (compare Weigend 2011, p. 36). As long as the community's commitment to punishing shirkers is strong, shirkers are effectively sanctioned and thus made to carry the costs of an investment in the norm's credibility and authority.

A credible punishment option changes the game's implicit power structure. Without punishment, participants are 'at the mercy' of others' cooperativeness. The sanctioning opportunity provides a remedy that, in case of offending, allows them to set things right by imposing costs on the defector who disappointed their legitimate expectations of fair cooperation and ignored a social norm of cooperation. Thus, punishment vindicates the norm and participants' legitimate expectations. Punishment is an investment in the validity, reliability and prestige of a social norm of cooperation; and it is the punished participant who, because she at first withheld her fair contribution, is now made to bear the larger part of the costs of this investment and thus to settle her debt to the social norm as a public good.

The character of punishment as an investment in the social norm becomes particularly clear, if not only the immediate victims of a norm violation, but also third parties, punish the defector. Punishment applied by third parties manifests the third parties' interest in the social norm and, in addition, sends a reassuring signal to victims asserting that they were right to expect and trust in the readiness of others to abide by the norms of fair cooperation. It also signals that they do not have reason to learn from the shirker and to adapt their behaviour to hers. It is then not the shirker who teaches an all too naïve and overly trusting cooperator a lesson about real life but the shirker who is being taught a lesson in fair cooperation.

What significantly differentiates the motive of 'norm vindication' from the incentive of 'risk reduction' is that making the shirker pay his debt to the social norm makes sense per se, irrespective of any future material benefits prompted by punishment.

Risk reduction as a strategy coincides with a deterrence model of punishing. In contrast, punishers' propensity to insist that the shirker too should settle her debt in terms of her fair share of investments in the standing and respect enjoyed by the social norm would figure as deontological in the sense that such a propensity leads to punishing defectors independent of any expected benefits. This punishment is owed to the social norm as a public good as well as to the victim who trusted in the binding nature of the social norm and in the willingness of others to, in case her legitimate expectations are disappointed, demonstrate solidarity with her. Punishment vindicates the social norm and makes the defector bear the larger part of the costs of this vindication. It subjects the defector to the norm and demonstrates that the defector too has to acknowledge and contribute to the authority of the norm. This sends a powerful message to conditional cooperators that they were right to rely on the norm and the punishment threat, to trust, that is, that participants either would cooperate or be sanctioned.

Casari and Luini found that participants observing that free-riders have actually been punished boosts cooperation. This seems to be the main positive effect of punishment on contributions (2009). Hence, the effectiveness of punishment in promoting cooperation is mainly premised not on how it affects the future conduct of the punished, but on how it reassures victims and others that they were right to confide in the authority of the social norm of cooperation, as well as in the readiness of third parties to defend the norm in the face of norm violations.

This sheds light on the interaction of cooperation and punishment. Punishment reacts to the plight of the victim. Hence, it would be premature to equate second-party and third-party punishment. In fact, in large-scale anthropological research, carried out by a research team around Jean Ensminger and Joseph Henrich, significant differences surfaced. In a cross-cultural perspective, these researchers explored fairness norms and punishment in 15—predominantly small-scale—societies by conducting three behavioural games across the societies researched, the dictator game (DG), the ultimatum game (UG)—a second-party punishment game—and the third-party punishment game (TPG). In the DG, two anonymous players are told that an amount of money is allotted to them as a pair. However, one player receives the total amount and has to decide how to divide the stake among them. As the second player cannot react in any way, the DG measures behavioural fairness in the absence of sanctions. The UG is a DG plus a victim-punishment option. Again, two players are informed that a stake has been allotted to them as a pair and that it is up to player 1 to offer a portion of the stake to player 2. But now player 2 can either accept or reject the offer. If she accepts, the stake is divided according to the offer. If she rejects, neither player receives anything. Thus player 2 is given an opportunity to protest against her unfair treatment. In the TPG—explained above— once again two players are allotted an amount of money. In addition, a third player gets one-half of this amount. As in the DG, one player passes on a portion of the stake to the other. However, if player 3 believes that player 1 failed to treat player 2 in a fair manner, she can fine player 1, by investing part of her endowment in punishing player 1. If player 3 pays 1 monetary unit, 3 units are deducted from what player 1 kept for herself.

What alone is interesting here is how the introduction of a punishment option affected the initial offer of player 1. The result was different from what the researchers expected. Introducing the 'threat' of second-party punishment—enabling the victim to punish player 1 in case of an offer perceived as unfair—leads to an increase of the amount offered to player 2. However, introducing the threat of third-party punishment—by allowing a third player to fine an unfair Dictator—leads to a decrease of the amounts offered by player 1. In the experiments carried out by Ensminger and colleagues, the mean offers were 37% of the stake in DGs, 39% in UGs, but only 32% in TPGs (Henrich et al. 2014, pp. 102–103). Henrich and Henrich repeated the experiments with undergraduate students in Arizona. Now the mean offers were 32% in DGs, 41% in UGs, and only 27% in TPGs (Henrich and Henrich 2014, p. 120). The pattern is similar. While enabling the victim of unfair treatment to protest her treatment increases the readiness to share the stake in a fair manner, third-party punishment leads to a deterioration of the offers made.

From these results it is obvious that subjects do not make fair offers because they fear punishment. If they did, mean offers would be low in DGs and high in TPGs. However, exactly the opposite is the case. Hence, the only plausible explanation is that people abide by norms of fairness, because they prefer to do so. Still, the challenge remains how to explain why victim punishing further encourages, while third-party punishing discourages, fairness in sharing the stake. As concerns third-party punishing, the authors offer the explanation that the introduction of a third-party punishment option causes a 'crowding-out effect', which means that the intrinsic motivation to act in a fair manner is impaired by the insinuation that individuals only cooperate because they fear punishment. If a third-party punishment risk exists, a fair offer can be interpreted as having been made only to avoid punishment and not as a voluntary commitment to fair cooperation. Thus the threat of punishment destroys 'the intrinsic pleasure or satisfaction' derived from treating others fairly (Henrich et al. 2014, p. 118).

Why then does the introduction of a second-party punishment option not destroy 'the intrinsic pleasure or satisfaction' of fairness? Enabling player 2 to react to unfair treatment does not necessarily imply that player 1 is suspected of being inclined to act in an unfair manner. It can also be interpreted as correcting the power balance, by no longer placing player 2 at the mercy of player 1. This accommodates the needs of conditional cooperators in reciprocal interactions. They will cooperate, firstly, because they want to and, secondly, because the punishment option allows them to keep their betrayal aversion in check.

Neurological research—exploring the effects of noninvasive stimulations of the right lateral prefontal cortex—suggests that the behaviour of player 1 can be explained as resulting from two opposite motives. While introducing a punishment threat weakens intrinsic—moral—motivation, it creates a contrary selfish motive to avoid punishment (Ruff et al. 2013). How the introduction of a punishment threat effects the behaviour of player 1 depends on the relative strength of these two effects working in opposite directions. If the result is different in the UG compared to the TPG, this means that either the crowding-out effect is weaker or the punishment threat is stronger—more credible—or both. If in prehistoric times punishment developed as the reaction of a victim to her unfair treatment, the introduction of punishment administered by the victim in response to such treatment may not run against our intrinsic moral intuitions, or at least less so than punishment enacted by a third party. In addition, under the same conditions, the expectation that the victim will punish in case of her unfair treatment may be stronger compared to the expectation of third-party punishment. This points to the potential significance of bringing the victim back into play. Punishment reacting to the wrong suffered by the victim may have different moral implications compared to punishment reacting to the violation of a nation state's norms.

What follows is, most of all, the necessity to draw a very clear distinction between intrinsic moral and extrinsic selfish motivation. Many complexities arise from the fact that punishment is both an expression of censure and harsh, unpleasant treatment, and it cannot reduce to only one of these functions.

A A punishment threat, on the one hand, expresses a social norm and, on the other, menaces harsh treatment and thus appeals to an individual's baser instincts of selfishness, not morality of selfishness, not morality. Threatening harsh treatment is not a moral argument, quite the contrary: it impairs—crowds out—morality. However, it indirectly serves morality by eliminating adverse extrinsic motives that otherwise could get in the way of morality, such as an individual's selfish longing to throw off the burden of normativity and to give herself fully to her personal desires and cravings. What the punishment threat asserts is that violating the norm is, from a moral point of view, wrong and, from a strategic perspective, unalluring. While a conditional cooperator, who has thoroughly internalised the norms of her society, truly prefers to cooperate, this does not mean that the frenzy of unrestrained passion and lust, lurking somewhere in the background of her mind, is unknown to her. It surfaces as suspicion that others could shirk and as the fear of being exploited. Harsh treatment is an investment in a norm of cooperation, but not because it morally convinces others, but because it eliminates or holds at bay the norm's most powerful adversary: an individual's desire to rid herself of the shackles of social norms. The promise that shirkers will be sanctioned allows conditional cooperators to cooperate voluntarily. Hart (1961, p. 193) expressed this view in admirably clear terms:

> No doubt the advantages of mutual forbearance are so palpable that the number and strength of those who would cooperate voluntarily in a coercive system will normally be greater than any likely combination of malefactors. Yet, except in very small closely-knit societies, submission to the system of restraints would be folly if there were no organization for the coercion of those who would then try to obtain the advantages of the system without submitting to its obligations. 'Sanctions' are therefore required not as the normal motive for obedience, but as a guarantee that those who would voluntarily obey shall not be sacrificed to those who would not. To obey, without this, would be to risk going to the wall. Giving this standing danger, what reason demands is *voluntary* cooperation in a *coercive* system.

2.4.4 Punishment is a Second-Order Public Good

If some invest in punishing defectors and others do not, all benefit equally from the maintenance of the social norm enforced, including those who have not contributed to punishing defectors. Those who did not contribute cannot be excluded from enjoying the added effectiveness of the social norm resulting from punishment implemented by others. If one assumes that the social norm enforced by punishment is beneficial to the group and hence a 'first-order public good' then punishment is a 'second-order public good' (Fehr and Gächter 2002, p. 137).

In a way, the results of the experiment conducted by Fehr and Gächter are more surprising than they may seem at first glance. The reason is that in the setting created by Fehr and Gächter, punishment is a public good just as much as the joint project. All benefit from the effects of punishment—from high levels of contributions to the public good—regardless of whether they have invested in punishing defectors or not. Therefore, it would appear that the same logic applies. While investing in punishment benefits the group, each participant will, viewed from an ex-ante perspective, conclude that, personally, she is better off if she refrains from incurring the costs of punishment. Hence, there is no reason to believe that others will punish norm violations. If others are not motivated to invest in the joint project—as shows over the first ten rounds—how can they be expected to invest in punishing?

All in all, Fehr and Gächter substituted one human cooperation riddle for another. They demonstrated impressively how humans cooperate based on a punishment option without providing a convincing explanation of why that is the case. What remains is the 'riddle of punishment', the question, that is, why humans punish.

As punishment is a—second-order—public good, the effectiveness of the norm requiring fair cooperation in punishing shirkers is premised on another punishment protocol threatening sanctions on those who do not contribute their fair share towards punishing. As such a protocol of 'meta-punishing' has, in the Fehr/

Gächter-setting, not been introduced in the public goods game, there is not more reason to believe that participants will be inclined to cooperate as was the case before the introduction of the punishment option (on second-level social dilemmas compare Ostrom 2005, pp. 256–259).

Actually, the 'meta-punishing' of those who shirked when it came to investing in the punishing of those who did not appropriately contribute to the joint project, would obviously represent a third-order public good. Hence, the whole concept of ensuring the provision of the first-order public good by introducing a punishment option as a second-order public good seemingly leads to an endless regress of public goods being safeguarded by other—higher-order—public goods. In short, the idea of reinforcing social norms of cooperation by introducing sanctions is, so it appears, illusory and doomed to fail (Kelsen 1979, p. 112).

However, public goods vary as to their incentive structures. The prisoner's dilemma-type of public good relies on the contributions of all and on the enforcement of a general spirit of abiding by the rules. The norms requiring all to pay taxes exemplifies this type of incentive structure. The more participants who adhere to the rule, the better for everyone—or at least that is the underlying assumption. However, there is also the 'volunteer's dilemma-type' of a public good, where someone has to do the job, but only one and not as many as possible. Game theorists have invented the Snowdrift game, where two cars are stuck behind a snowdrift. Someone has to shovel the snow, while the other can stay in the warm car. Each person would prefer to be the one staying in the car, but if one person refuses to shovel, the other will be ready to shoulder the effort.

It has been theorised that punishment has an incentive structure more like a volunteer's dilemma (Barclay and Kiyonari 2014, pp. 189–190). As long as one punishes, it is not necessary that others engage in punishing too. While this seems plausible, findings from research conducted by Casari and Luini (2009, 2012) indicate that this is not how punishment works in reality. Both the prisoner's and the volunteer's dilemma are premised on a *strategic* incentive structure and on a shared understanding that the public good is beneficial to all and that hence, in principle, sufficient numbers of subjects should be ready to contribute, if it becomes necessary. However, humans do not punish because it is necessary to achieve a certain goal, they punish because it feels good to right a wrong, and to ensure that the offender does not get away with it. It is not strategic reasoning, but a sense of fairness and powerful moral sentiments that motivate punishing.

2.4.5 Non-strategic, Expressive Punishment Driven by Strong Emotions

In 2005, Falk, Fehr and Fischbacher published a discussion paper that focused on the motivational driving forces behind sanctions in one-shot games (Falk et al. 2005). The authors tested various motives, including spite, inequality aversion and retaliation. They concluded that punishing is motivated by a strong inclination to retaliate, even when it is costly to the punisher. The researchers implemented two conditions with a high and a low level of sanction. In the high sanction condition, every money unit spent on punishment reduced the punished individual's payoff by 2.5 or 3 money units, while the same expenditure only caused a reduction of the punished individual's payoff by one money unit in the low sanction condition. Strikingly, "cooperators spend about 2.5 times *more* money on punishing defectors in the low than in the high sanction condition". This suggests that participants are willing to incur higher costs to achieve what they view as an appropriate sanctioning level. The authors conclude that these "results suggest that cooperators have a very strong motive for sanctioning" (p. 3).

On a closer inspection, two forms of retaliation can be distinguished. What is proportional to the wrong of the offender's action can either be the amount of punishment *enacted* by the punisher or *suffered* by the punished. Falk et al. (2005) summarise their findings, stating that "retaliation, i.e. the desire to harm those who committed unfair acts, seems to be the most important motive behind fairness-driven informal sanctions." This interprets punishing as centred on the pain *suffered* by the punished. Alternatively, what could be decisive for the punisher is more likely to be her action and what it expresses, and not so much its effect on the situation of the punished.

The difference is highly relevant in a setting where there is more than one potential punisher. In such a setting, the question arises whether one punisher adjusts her behaviour to the behaviour of others, taking the sanctions imposed by them into account. However, in the protocol chosen by Fehr and Gächter, all players punish simultaneously and hence do not know the amount of punishment inflicted by others. They thus cannot factor the punishment inflicted by others when deciding on their own sanctions.

Casari and Luini asked players to attribute deduction points, one player after another. They then compared the results of this sequential punishment protocol to simultaneous punishing. In a sequential setting, if what matters to punishers is the amount of punishment suffered by the punished then it is to be expected that punishers consider the sanctions already imposed by previous players (in the same round) and consequentially either refrain from attributing additional punishment points or at least reduce the amount of their punishment accordingly. Hence, the total amount of deduction points attributed in this setting should be considerably lower compared to simultaneous punishing. However, Casari and Luini found that this was not—or at least not to a significant extent—the case. Instead, they found that participants would punish the same amount, regardless of whether they had seen that the norm-breaker had already been punished by others.

This finding has far-reaching consequences. It is difficult to think of a more radical rebuttal of any sort of instrumental interpretation of punishment. Whatever effect a punisher would deliberately want to achieve—in terms of deterrence, rehabilitation, incapacitation etc.—the effect would depend on the punishment *sustained* by the offender and not on the individual contribution of one among several punishers. The only way to interpret such a behaviour is to perceive the action of punishing as expressing the indignation of the individual punisher. Punishment is an evaluation of the offence, and if in a sequential protocol, participants agree in their assessment of the wrong done by the offender this agreement is expressed in similar amounts of punishment imposed by the several participants. What matters to those who punish is the satisfaction they personally derive from their own activity of punishing the offender, because it feels right to punish shirkers who deserve to be punished. Therefore, Casari and Luini highlight the "expressive" and "emotional" function of punishing (2009, pp. 278–279).

The positive aspect of this behaviour is that it reliably avoids a 'snowdrift situation', where all rely on others to punish, which could undermine the credibility of the punishment threat. However, if this is how individuals punish, there is, on the negative side, a clear risk that a group oversteers the total amount of sanctions suffered by a defector, and that this effect is the stronger the larger the group. What hence becomes more imperative with mounting group size is the establishment of a procedural mechanism that brings about an agreement on the amount of punishment inflicted jointly on the offender, or tasks one participant with sanctioning the offender on behalf of the entire group.

2.5 Punitive Sentiments

In a powerful article—titled 'The Emotional Dog and Its Rational Tail: A Social Intuitionist Approach to Moral Judgment'—Jonathan Haidt (2001) suggested that, while subjects firmly believe that their decisions are based on sound reasoning, moral judgments in fact are generated by intuitions. Haidt believes that the role of reasoning, based on language and higher consciousness, is not so much to produce judgments but rather to, more or less successfully, provide *post hoc* constructions, rationalisations and justifications, explaining—to oneself and to others—why we adopt certain views and, sometimes, even convincing others that they should join us in these views (2001, p. 822, 2013, p. 52). Usually people are 'quite good at finding support for whatever they want to believe'—partly because they only look for confirming evidence (2001, p. 821, 2007, p. 998). However, sometimes they 'know' an action is wrong without being in a position to provide reasons that would account for their judgment, and sometimes their reasoning does not fit their intuitions, in which case they, when made aware of the discrepancy, rely on their intuitions and not on their reasoning. They are convinced that something is wrong, even when they have to admit that they cannot explain why. Reasoning is primarily a matter of communication to others and 'rarely used to question one's own attitudes and beliefs. It operates less like a truth-seeking philosopher and more like a lawyer defending a client' (2001, 2013, pp. 45–51).

Moral intuitions are powerful as they seem unquestionable to the subject who experiences them and are closely linked to the motivation of action. As much as persons believe that their perceptions simply represent the world surrounding them in a faithful, objective and accurate manner, and hence behave—in terms of epistemology—as naïve realists, they usually do not question their moral intuitions either. If they feel moral outrage over another person's conduct, they assume that the observed conduct is just essentially wrong. The moral evaluation is projected on to the conduct, as if its wrongfulness was part of its objective, 'natural' features (Carlsmith and Darley 2008). In other words, people feel that they *can see* that something is wrong by looking at it.

Haidt's model, to which he refers to as the 'social intuitionist model', highlights specific relations between moral emotions and moral judgments, which are caused by quick moral intuitions and followed, when needed, by slow, *ex post facto* moral reasoning (2001, p. 817). Moral intuitions are not only closely linked to moral judgments but also to action, which covaries with moral emotions more significantly than with moral reasoning (2001, p. 823). While immediate intuitive and emotional responses 'push' actors in a certain direction, they can be controlled and sometimes even overridden by either conflicting intuitions or conscious verbal reasoning, and both of these overriding forces often result from interactions with others (2007, 2013, p. 79).

In the following sections, it will be argued that punishing is motivated by the victim's feelings of insult, indignity, offence and indignation, as well as by others' anger and outrage caused by the wrong done to the victim. These sentiments correspond with the offender's feelings of guilt and shame. It is the powerful interaction of these complementary and mutually reinforcing emotions that drive punishment, and generate and sustain social norms as the foundation of human societies.

2.5.1 The Central Concern: the Wrong Suffered by the Victim

While it is plausible that sympathy for the victim mobilises support, it is so far not clear how punitive sentiments can help in preserving social norms. It is plausible that observing someone in distress causes feelings of sympathy and the wish to help. However, what remains to be explained is why these feelings turn against the offender or benefit social norms. It is not obvious why observing the victim's distress would trigger an inclination, not only to help the victim, but also to punish the offender. In fact, harm and suffering caused by an accident or a disease might also evoke, in observers, feelings of sympathy for the victim, but would not also lead to the specific sentiments of outrage and indignation.

What triggers these feelings, and what provides the necessary link between punitive sentiments on the one hand and a social norm on the other, is observers' sense that the victim has been not only harmed but *wronged*. The victim is perceived as being affected not by misfortune or disaster, but by *injustice*.

The term 'wrong' is normative. It implies that the victim experienced a violation of her *reasonable* expectation that others would respect her *legitimate* interests; and what makes her expectation reasonable is a social norm. The victim's interests are assessed by others in light of a social norm protecting them.

Because a social norm is necessarily abstract and covers not only the concrete instance of victimisation but all similar situations, it protects the interests of the victim as much as any equal interests of others. The social norm expresses that the legal community acknowledges and endorses the interests of the victim, protected by the norm. By disregarding the interests of the victim, as protected by the norm, the offender also disregards the norm and hence indirectly calls into question the equal interests of others. On the other hand, sanctioning the norm violation restores confidence in the authority of the social norm and hence benefits the victim, as well as indirectly benefitting others.

What the term 'wrong' then links together is the violation of a social norm and its immediate effect on the individual whose potential interests in a concrete situation, were protected by the norm and who relied on the norm compliance of others. The wrong is the norm violation viewed from the perspective of the individual whose legitimate interests, protected by the norm, were disregarded and infringed by the offender. The punishment of the offender restores and reinforces the norm's authority, its prescriptive and binding nature which serve all whose interests are protected by the norm. Thus, punitive sentiments driving punishment empower the victim and enable her to effectively demand that the offender be punished and the norm preserved.

The observers' perception and sense that the victim has been subjected to an act of injustice establishes the link between the offence and humans' punitive sentiments. The notion of the wrong done to the victim, which combines a normative and an emotional component, links the perceived violation of a social norm to the punitive sentiments of humans and thus triggers the emotions that, as an expression of solidarity with the victim, drive the punishment of the offender. Thus, the continued existence of the normative order is premised on punitive sentiments, which serve the interests of the victim, the preservation of the social norm endorsing the interests of the victim, as well as the entire normative order to which the norm belongs.

Moral theorists are often reluctant to pay attention to social emotions, such as the sentiments that were just discussed. What seems fundamentally problematic is the link between emotions and reason. In fact, emotions seem to be irrational almost by definition.

However, this is not necessarily true. What should not be overlooked is the practical and social function of moral sentiments. They can be translated into suggestions of action. Sympathy for the victim can be interpreted as encouraging support on the basis that the victim, because of the wrong done to her, is deserving of compassion, comfort and backing in claiming compensation from the offender. On the other hand, feelings of indignation towards the offender suggest that the offender has wronged the victim, compromised her society's normative order, and should be made to bear the consequences. This is why indignation turns against an offender, as much as sympathy for the victim forges an alliance in support of the victim. Because social sentiments easily translate into meaningful action, it is probable that social sentiments developed within normative interaction and represent the sediment of strategies that had proven successful over a long time period. In fact, if these emotions would not, under certain societal conditions, be beneficial in terms of fostering the coexistence of individuals in large communities, they could not have evolved at some stage in the history of humankind.

2.5.2 *Indignation and Just Desert*

Seeking to shed light on the question of proximate causation, Fehr and Gächter (2000b) explored the emotions involved in punishing. They conducted interviews which showed that free riding causes strong negative emotions such as indignation, anger or annoyance—in particular among those who contribute generously—and that these feelings trigger the willingness to punish free riders. In turn, to free riders, their punishment does not come as a surprise. Indeed, the negative emotions that they anticipate from other group members even exceed the actual adverse feelings of punishers. Thus, shirkers' awareness of the negative emotions which their conduct provokes ensures their ability to understand the reaction of punishers and accounts for the immediate group-beneficial effects of introducing a punishing opportunity.

The motivation driving punishment has been studied extensively, resulting in abundant and consistent evidence that punishment is motivated not by the wish to achieve practical results but by a strong aversion to inequity and selfishness (Cushman et al. 2009; Fehr and Schmidt 1999; Johnson et al. 2009; Raihani and McAuliffe 2012). Punishers aim at not allowing the shirker to get away with it, and making sure that shirking does not pay. Thus, the motivation behind punishing is to ensure that free-riding is not regarded as exemplary by others and prevent it gaining more popularity in the group.

Punishers' strong emotions account for their readiness to incur the costs of punishing and significantly increase the plausibility of the threat created by the punishment opportunity. It should be remembered that in the setting chosen by Fehr and Gächter by every point assigned to another participant her income was reduced by 10 %, yet participants still felt willing to punish perceived free riders. In another experiment (Falk et al. 2005), the benefits of punishing were considerably reduced. For each token invested by the punisher, the income of the punished participant was reduced by one token only, rather than 2.5 or 3 in the original experiment. Hence punishing did not change the payoff difference between the punisher and the punished. As a result, punishers were not only still willing to punish, but invested 2.5 times more in punishing defectors to achieve what they saw as appropriate sanctions—proportionate to the severity of the defection—even at considerably higher costs.

Psychological studies have directly contrasted preventive motives for punishment—such as incapacitation and deterrence—against a retributive orientation with findings consistently favouring the latter (Cushman 2013, pp. 346–347). As a result of a comprehensive review of the research conducted on the topic of citizens' intuitions on punishing, Carlsmith and Darley suggest a dual-process model of punishing reactions, where the first reaction to wrongdoing is intuitive, before, under certain circumstances, the reasoning system intervenes as a corrective. However, 'evidence suggests that both the intuitive and reasoning systems adhere to the principles of retribution' (Carlsmith and Darley 2008, p. 194) and are largely driven by moral outrage. Individuals' intuitions and their reasoning adhere to the principles of retribution and 'proportional just deserts', insisting on a moral proportionality between the blameworthiness of the offender, indexed by the offence's 'moral severity', and the degree of blame and censure, expressed by punishment (Carlsmith and Darley 2008, p. 233).

Carlsmith et al. argue that the chain of causation runs from moral outrage to blame and from blame to punishment. They maintain that a person who observes an intentional wrong, purposefully committed, 'experiences some degree of moral outrage, is able to assign a degree of blame for that act, and then generates a punishment commensurate with the blame' (Carlsmith et al. 2002, p. 296). Schnall and others have added to this that moral condemnation involves other feelings as well, including disgust and contempt (Schnall et al. 2008).

2.5.3 *The Inclination to Punish Defectors Bonds with Sympathy for Victims*

Fehr and Fischbacher (2004) introduced a third-party punishment option to a prisoners' dilemma game, which had two parts. In the first, two players were each endowed with 10 points. Each player could choose to keep her points or to transfer them to the other participant, in which case the experimenter tripled them. As they acted simultaneously, their decisions had no impact on the other participant's choices. If both transferred their endowments each earned 20 points. However, from a strictly egoistic perspective each player was, under all circumstances, better off if she kept her endowments for herself. A third player in stage one just observed the behaviour of the other two participants but in the second stage had the opportunity to intervene by assigning deduction points to uncooperative participants.

Fehr and Fischbacher found that 46 % of third players punished the defector if the other player cooperated. However, only 21 % of third parties punished if both players defected; and if they did, the level of punishment was very significantly lower. Overall, third-party punishment reduced the income of a player defecting on a cooperator by 10 points, while if both defected each would lose only 1.8 points.

The very significant difference in punishment levels is remarkable, given that the behaviour of the defecting participant and her deviation from the norm of cooperation is identical in both cases. Fehr and Fischbacher (2004, p. 73) assume that 'defection constitutes a less severe norm violation if the other player is also a defector'. However, this is not convincing in circumstances where a defector does not know in advance whether the other player will defect or not. (If she did, there would be no reason to punish at all.) Hence, the different severity of punishment cannot be related to the defector's behaviour.

Another possible explanation assumes that punishment demonstrates feelings of sympathy for, and solidarity with, victims. The readiness to engage—and invest—in vindicating the rights of a victim is considerably impaired if the victim displays exactly the same norm-violating behaviour as the offender. A third party is more likely to punish in favour of a victim who demonstrates that she is willing to invest in common tasks and trusts that the other player will be as well, thus displaying the attitude of public-spiritedness and loyal cooperation that deserves and evokes loyalty, including the punishment of the offender.

From a review of the body of research available in 2002, Carlsmith and colleagues have concluded that, in people's view, not only the public, but also the victim requires just deserts sanctioning of the offender. Unless punishment is imposed on the offender, "a real feeling of incompleteness lingers, and there is a sense that justice has not been done". Therefore, they conclude that "a just society is one that assigns just deserts punishments proportionate to the moral blameworthiness of the offense, and it must not fail to punish wrongdoing in these ways", to do justice to victims and preserve the law's moral authority and capacity to guide individuals' behaviour (Carlsmith et al. 2002, p. 297).

From this research it can be learned that, while punishment has developed as a mechanism to preserve social norms, what drives punishment is not individuals' platonic admiration for abstract norms but the concrete wrong suffered by the victim, by the individual, that is, whose legitimate interests, despite their protection by a social norm, have been infringed by the offender. Observers sense that the victim has been—not only disappointed or harmed but—wronged which triggers strong feelings of sympathy for the victim and of indignation towards the offender. These sentiments motivate bystanders' support for a retaliating victim or third-party punishing.

Researchers highlight the impact of empathy with and sympathy for victims of injustice, stressing that these emotions are powerful forces driving punishment. In particular, Hoffman has stressed that punishment is "influenced by the extent to which people empathize with victims and are empathically angry at perpetrators" (2001, p. 226). In Hoffman's understanding, empathy supports justice principles. Empathy's contribution is to transform moral principles into "hot cognitions – cognitive representations charged with empathic affect, thus giving them motive force" (2001, p. 239). On the other hand, justice principles give shape and moderate the empathic effect. In punitive justice, principles and laws of reciprocity and fairness act as a constraint on strong empathic bias against the offender. In short, empathy "supplies the prosocial motive force" while justice principles shape and control it (2001, p. 245).

Thus, empathic emotions can turn into strong feelings of injustice. Once charged with empathic emotion, the justice principle is activated whenever one learns of injustice done to a victim, even in the latter's absence, and operates as a strong motivation not only to comfort the victim, but also to rectify injustice. If a person, instead of cooperation, free rides on the other's contribution, we empathise with the victim's frustration and distress at being cheated. Because of the bonding of our empathic emotions with internalised norms of fair cooperation, our empathic distress is transformed into a sympathetic feeling of injustice suffered by the victim (Hoffman 2001, pp. 243–244).

Remarkably, Hoffman (2001, pp. 247–248) points out that when confronted with a moral dilemma, people look out for a victim for orientation. Even if explicit reasoning alludes to norms and social order, it is suspected that there may be a victim in the background. When confronted with a vignette of a man breaking into a store and stealing money, subjects base their disapproval on law and order but also readily imagine—or make up—that the store owner had worked hard for the money, of which he was in need and which he had saved for his family.

Hoffman refers to research conducted by William Damon (1990) according to which, when asked why stealing is wrong, half of the 4 to 8-year-old children and 80 % of the 9-year-olds gave empathic reasons—highlighting the harm done to the victim—rather than expressing fear of punishment. Hence, empathy with victims fuels disapproval of offenders and conformity with norms protecting individuals' interests, even where those interests are not obviously visible.

2.6 The Genetic and Neural Basis of Punishing

Generally speaking, acts of communication, occurring in the sphere of symbols and languages, are premised on activity, occurring in the world of biology and physiology. Therefore, if certain acts of communication fulfil a significant social function and hence are to be maintained, it is indispensable that at the level of physiology the desire is established to act with a view to expressing, at the level of meaning, whatever needs to be expressed. Emotions fulfil that function of driving acts of communication.

Abundant evidence exists which suggests that punishment is driven by strong emotions, which are so widespread that it is only plausible to consider a biological explanation. However, that punishment should be driven by emotions innate in humans, is, at first sight, not likely, at least for three reasons.

Firstly, if social emotions have a biological basis, the question arises of how grossly different, and sometimes rapidly changing, social orders can be reconciled with the assumption of a punishment mechanism that is driven by innate and hence inflexible forces.

Secondly, genes are a matter of individuals, whilst punishment is a matter of a society's normative order. It does not seem plausible that something that performs collective functions could have developed at the level of the genes of individual human beings.

Thirdly, there is no passage from genes to culture. If punishment has developed because of its social functions, how would the human genome know anything about it?

In order to clarify the concept of punitive sentiments these objections need to be explored in turn.

2.6.1 Flexible Social Norms and Persistent Punishing

Concerning the first objection, it should be remembered that first order behavioural rules and second order punishment rules rely on different incentive structures. Once a certain behaviour is criminalised, people often develop strong feelings about norm violations. Punishing is effective not because of second-order punishing, but because of people's inclination to punish those who do not abide by the rules and the satisfaction they derive from doing so. While, to be effective, behavioural rules rely on sanctions, norms of punishment do not, as they are underpinned by strong sentiments and not premised on another layer of third order punishment rules. Punishment emphatically asserts that a behavioural norm of cooperation should be considered and respected as a first-order public good, which everyone should support by contributing to its enforcement.

By their decisions to punish or to refrain from punishing, group members cast their votes in favour or against rules of behaviour, and in doing so they are motivated by, at times, complex normative assessments of the behaviour under consideration. There are limits to people's propensity to punish norm violations. Otherwise, processes of decriminalisation would be difficult to explain. However, decriminalisation results from a re-evaluation of behavioural norms, not from variations in subjects' propensity to punish. As long as a certain conduct is seen as wrong, subjects remain inclined to punish that behaviour, and the severity of the sanction will reflect the seriousness of the wrongdoing.

All in all, a social order serves to adapt a group's behaviour to a fluctuating natural environment only as long as it is sufficiently flexible and, at the same time, sufficiently reliable and stable. What allows for an effective equilibration of these conflicting orientations is the stratification of the normative order that combines rigorous punishing with more flexible behavioural norms. The interaction of variable behavioural norms on the one hand, and a resolute and unflinching propensity to punish offenders on the other, creates a mechanism that reconciles and balances flexibility and stability, both of which are preconditions of an effective social order. On the one hand, it was the flexibility of a social order—compared to inflexible, firmly wired genetic and instinctive determinants—and its adaptability to changing natural environments that provided the decisive advantage of humans as a social species compared to genetically hardwired animals (Shariff et al. 2011). On the other hand, social order can fulfil its functions only as long as social norms are adhered to, and that means are consistently enforced, despite the costs involved in such enforcement.

2.6.2 *Multilevel Selection*

Groups do not have genes. Only individuals do. This prompts the question, what then could ever relate the benefits reaped by a punishing society to the genetic development of its members? Multilevel selection holds the answer. Wilson (2014, p. 63) summarises the maxim that even if selfish members win within groups, still "groups of altruists best groups of selfish members."

Evidence indicates that the evolution of the normative code first developed at a small scale—at the level of band or tribal societies—integrating basic capacities of symbolic expression and mechanisms similar to punishment inherited from pre-human ape societies. This was possible in conditions of many small entities competing within a limited area. The decisive element allowing for such evolution is multilevel selection (Turchin 2016, pp. 81–94). Already Darwin (2004, p. 166) clearly formulated the crucial point:

> It must not be forgotten that although a high standard of morality gives but a slight or no advantage to each individual man and his children over the other men of the same tribe [. . .] an increase in the number of well-endowed men and an advancement in the standard of morality will certainly give an immense advantage to one tribe over another.

What Darwin suggests is that while genetic variation occurs—and can only occur—at the level of individuals, if individuals develop a sense of solidarity with and sympathy for individuals in distress—including victims of wrongs and injustices—then social norms intervene in the mechanism of selection in two respects. Firstly, selection at the individual level is impeded as those who are worse off genetically are supported socially. Secondly, selection can now function at the group level, favouring groups with higher moral standards, groups, that is, with more individuals displaying attitudes of group-solidarity, a sense of community and the readiness to invest in punishing shirkers to maintain social norms of cooperation and solidarity.

It should be noted that prosocial behaviour—as an investment in a public good—impacts negatively on the relative fitness of the individual displaying such behaviour who incurs the costs individually while the benefits are shared by all. If selection only operated at the individual level, evolution would eliminate social-minded individuals. Hence social norms can only develop when the positive effects of prosocial behaviour at group level (at the level of 'between-group selection') significantly outweigh the negative effects at the individual level (of 'within-group selection') (Wilson and Wilson 2007; Wilson 2013, pp. 52–56, 162–182, 2014, pp. 28–30, 178–179).

Groups that cooperate more effectively in hunting or warfare and care more about their members in need of support are overall more likely to survive. In other words, 'prosocial norms evolve not because they have superior fitness within groups, but because groups with prosocial norms outcompete groups that are deficient in this respect' (Gintis et al. 2005, p. 30). Hence, once moral norms start to develop, selective pressures favour communities with higher 'standards of morality' over those with a weaker sense of solidarity and belonging. In the end, the success of groups with higher moral standards has repercussions on the genetic evolution of humans, selecting for more social and cooperative individuals. Chudek et al. (2013, pp. 443–444) outline the interacting forces:

> Cultural group selection favours societies with cooperation-enhancing, often punishment-based norms. In such societies, individuals who recognize and emotionally internalize norms thrive. Eventually societies exist where most individuals genuinely *feel* that it's right to cooperate with others, even when a fully rational economic agent would know better. Norm psychology can turn *rationally* cooperative societies (where defection usually doesn't pay) into *highly* cooperative ones (where people cooperate even when defection does pay).

2.6.3 Gene-Culture Coevolution (GCC)

Indisputably, the body of normative information accumulates over generations forming a cultural heritage of increasing volume and complexity. However, the question arises of whether the history of humankind is a matter of culture alone. It was believed for some time that human development is driven by culture and that the factor of genetic evolution can be neglected. Thus, the palaeontologist Stephen Jay Gould expressed the view that "natural selection has almost become irrelevant in human evolution. There has been no biological change in humans in 40,000 or 50,000 years. Everything we call culture and civilization we've built with the same body and brain" (2002, pp. 27–28). However, today an impressive amount of evidence supports the opposite view. Not only did the evolution of the human genome not come to an end, it even considerably accelerated during the last 50,000 years (Haidt 2013, p. 250).

The vision of human culture rapidly developing according to its inherent dynamics and the human genome at the same time changing in conformity with the rules of biological evolution could seem a worrying suggestion. One is inclined to wonder about the various directions of these developments and the possible tensions and conflicts which arise. However, to this question the theory of gene-culture coevolution (GCC) provides a comforting answer: The developments of culture and the physical human evolution, while occurring in two distinct spheres, come with mechanisms that ensure a sufficient degree of coordination.

Although the concept of GCC was already suggested by Lumsden and Wilson in the early 80s (Alper and Lange 1981; Lumsden and Wilson 1980) it took about two decades until it found wider recognition (Chudek et al. 2013; Haidt 2013; Henrich and Henrich 2007; Kelly 2013). Through depicting human nature and human culture as two distinct, but interacting systems, GCC seeks to understand how genetic factors affect the evolution of culture, as well as the ways in which culture influences genetic evolution.

The answer is that culture and genes, while developing in accordance to their own set of rules, put selective pressure on one another, thereby relating and approximating their developmental paths to one another, *seemingly* creating a link. Both systems operate as constraints in the environment of the other system, thereby restricting the margins of its development. This does not suggest the existence of passages from one sphere to the other. Processes generating meaning in languages and physical processes occur in strictly distinct spheres—culture and living organisms—which have no common denominator or *passerelle* linking them to one another and therefore cannot possibly pass on and share information. However, as respective environments they mutually exert selective pressure and thereby *seemingly* form a unity and develop in a coordinated manner.

If siblings, brought up together, are made by their genes to find one another sexually unattractive, they will look out for other partners. Hence, it is genetic information that accounts for the highly significant cultural norms of incest avoidance and exogamy (Wilson 2013, p. 199). On the other hand, if, in an agricultural society, individuals who are able to digest milk are healthier than those who cannot, this puts selective pressure on the genome selecting for human organisms that have the necessary enzymes available to them. Originally, only babies produced lactase, the enzyme that converts lactose into digestible sugar. As soon as an infant was weaned from her mother's milk, her body stopped producing lactase. However, when herds of cows and goats were around, providing food all through the year, this factor operated a selection bias against shutting down lactase production and in favour of continuously extending its time-span. So far, four independent mutations have been discovered that prolong lactase production, one in Europe and three in Africa. This example of gene-culture coevolution is particularly well researched (Beja-Pereira et al. 2003).

In short, cultural developments operate constraints on genes by limiting their range of successful options, narrowing their margins of manoeuvre and creating conditions that favour some evolutionary paths over others. If groups who practice punishing score better in terms of the group's effective cooperation and peaceful existence, this advantage exerts selective pressure on the genetic development of humans, resulting in punitive sentiments.

Exactly the same happens in the opposite direction. Genetic factors favour some cultural developments over others. Wolf and Huang (1980) studied the histories of 14,200 Taiwanese women who were contracted as infants or small children for minor marriage. They were raised in intimate proximity with their future husbands. When these girls were adopted before 30 months of age, they later regularly resisted marriage with their social—although not physical—'brothers'. If marriages came about, they ended in divorce three times more often than others and produced 40 % fewer children. In short, to arrange social life in a manner that ignores genetic constraints produces stress and frustration. In light of this, humans may be well advised to consider their genetic features, including their moral sentiments, when considering their social behaviours.

If in the evolutionary history, or the phylogeny of humans, strong emotions have developed favouring the punishment of norm violators, a social order frustrating these emotions will come with a risk that individuals will vent their anger in an unforeseen and uncontrolled manner. Hence, arguably one function of the criminal justice system is to channel punitive sentiments into a procedure that offers a framework and a stage for the expression of anger, indignation, reproach and blame, as well as guilt and shame of offenders. The 1992 Los Angeles riots, following the acquittal of four police officers of the Los Angeles Police Department of the use of excessive force in the videotaped arrest and beating of Rodney King, serve as an example. Suspicion that the police are not held to account for their offending and hence that victims of police brutality are not acknowledged can trigger disturbances, as was the case in Husby in northern Stockholm in May 2013, or in Ferguson, Missouri, in August 2014.

Cultural innovations create new selective pressures that favour certain capacities, including those allowing individuals to easily access and use the normative information "stored in the cultural repository" (Kelly 2013, p. 506). GCC produces social instincts and intuitions that are sensitive to cultural information and facilitate a life in large, cooperative groups, including the capacity to cognise and internalise ethnic group boundaries and social norms. Human social intelligence rests on normative intuitions that work "quick, effortless, and (are) generally quite accurate" (Haidt 2001, p. 822).

If sanctioning norm violators is a crucial factor in the development of cooperation at group level, and if anger and indignation over the frustrated expectations of cooperative behaviour lead to a higher level of cooperation, then these combined factors are likely to select for groups with more individuals possessing a strong inclination to sanction shirkers. These mechanisms are apt to account for the evolution of punitive sentiments. Hence, once a social norm is learned, human instincts provide motivation to both comply with the norm and to punish those who violate it (Kelly 2013, p. 507), including such strong emotions as moral outrage and indignation in the face of norm-violations, as well as sympathy for victims.

Having dealt with the complexities involved in the explanation of how punishing can have a genetic basis, it should be added that it *obviously* does. There is firstly the fact that strong sentiments driving punishing can be observed in all, including blatantly different, human societies, premised only on a level of development beyond hunter-gatherer societies (which sometimes view punishment as a natural consequence of norm violations and hence do not perceive themselves as being in charge of enacting punishment). As emotions have physical and neural underpinnings, the ubiquity of punishment can hardly be explained without recourse to genetic factors.

There is secondly the fact that punishment has a normative meaning and hence is necessarily premised on a normative language, which exists only in human societies. Punishment—as a normative expression of censure—is unique in humans simply because normative language is. From these two facts it must be concluded that the sentiments driving punishing can have only evolved along with the cultural development of cooperation in human societies, including the ability to use normative languages.

2.6.4 Dual Inheritance Theory and the Normative Animal

The concept of Gene-culture coevolution (GCC) solves the riddle of human ultrasociality. Culture's repercussion on the genes of humans has an obvious potential to step up human cooperativeness and prosociality. In many ways, culture selects for sociable genes.

As early as in 1966, Geertz (1973, p. 46) called for "the discarding of a sequential view of the relations between the physical evolution and the cultural development of man in favour of an overlap or interactive view". Geertz (1973, p. 47) insisted that

> culture, rather than being added on, so to speak, to a finished or virtually finished animal, was ingredient, and centrally ingredient, in the production of that animal itself. The slow, steady, almost glacial growth of culture through the Ice Age altered the balance of selection pressures for the evolving *Homo* in such a way as to play a major directive in his evolution.

Later GCC was integrated as one element of a wider research paradigm, called Dual Inheritance Theory. Its foundations were laid by Robert Boyd and Peter Richerson in their publications, including *A dual inheritance model of the human evolutionary process* (1978), *Culture and the Evolutionary Process* (1985), and *Not by Genes alone* (2004). Recently, the theory has been brilliantly summarised and elaborated by Joseph Henrich (2015) and thoroughly discussed by Robert Paul (2015). In addition, basic assumptions of Dual Inheritance Theory are corroborated and complemented by research carried out by Michael Tomasello and his team—including Marco Schmidt and Hannes Rakoczy—who compare the behaviour of children to that of their nearest primate relatives, especially chimpanzees (Rakoczy and Schmidt 2013; Schmidt et al. 2011; Tomasello 2009, 2014).

In a nutshell, these anthropologists concur in Geertz' proposition that to understand human development we should pay close attention to how our genes and our culture interact. By mutually reinforcing their effects, genes and culture, in an upward spiralling manner, generate a unique species that is increasingly social and, from complex norms and their enforcement, progressively capable of coexisting peacefully and cooperating with others on ever larger scales. Their account of socio-cultural learning and how it affects our genetic disposition offers a powerful explanation of the development of human sociality and serves as a highly appropriate framework for investigating specific aspects of sociality, including sanctions in general and criminal justice in particular. At the macro-level, Dual Inheritance Theory stresses that any account of the development of humankind should consider two interacting forces, cultural evolution on the one hand and genetic evolution of cultural capacities on the other (Henrich and Henrich 2007). At the level of ontogeny, an individual's development is to be viewed as driven by two distinct sets of instructions, one genetic, and the other socio-cultural.

The need to figure out the local norms and comply with them has been with us from the beginning of human evolution. These conditions have selected for a "norm psychology: a suite of genetically evolved cognitive mechanisms for rapidly perceiving local norms and internalizing them" (Chudek et al. 2013, p. 443). As Joseph Henrich remarks, humans evolve as the species "designed for navigating a world with social rules and reputations, where learning and complying with these rules is paramount", combined with a strong inclination to detect and punish norm violators (2015, p. 316).

We internalize costly norms as goals in themselves, usually via cultural learning, and are particularly good at spotting norm violators, even when those violations have nothing to do with cooperation.

Evidence from developmental psychology—in particular from research conducted by Michael Tomasello and his collaborators—suggests that *homo sapiens* is the normative animal, the species that masters and applies normative language based on the general assumption that others act as they and we all should act. An impressive amount of research demonstrates that, from an early stage, children take a normative attitude toward others' conduct in social interactions (Keupp et al. 2013, 2016; Rakoczy and Schmidt 2013; Schmidt et al. 2011, 2012). They interpret acts performed by adults as governed by norms and hence as being performed either correctly or wrongly. Tomasello and his team found that 3-year-old children inferred normativity even when no normative or pedagogical language was used. The only cue the children were responsive to was whether their adult models performed an action as if they were just figuring it out on the spot or marking the action as familiar and well-known. In other words, children imitate because they feel that they should, because they believe that conduct displayed by competent others is conduct following rules that we all should follow, and children get mad when rules are violated (Henrich 2015, p. 189). Preschool children, on detecting the violation of a social norm, take action to enforce the norm on others, often even using generic normative language to do so (Schmidt and Tomasello 2012).

What distinguishes all human societies from the collective life of all other species is this innate sense of normativity, meaning the facts—highlighted by Henrich (2015, pp. 186–187)—that all humans live in worlds governed by social norms, care about these norms, in the sense that they "react negatively to violations" and assume that others, too, care about norms. At this point, the term 'culture' can be understood—in line with Hill (2007) and Gangestad (2011)—as denoting a system of acts of communication that generate norms, including essentially norms governing the use of symbols, norms banning violence and incest, norms regulating the creation and transmission of norms and culture and rituals that vindicate and reinforce symbolically norms and rights that have been infringed.

We are born to live a social life, a life in culture. It is because of our existence in culture and in biology as two distinct, but interacting spheres that we are clearly unique. We are genetically endowed with what Henrich and others (Chudek et al. 2013; Henrich 2015, p. 188; Rakoczy and Schmidt 2013) refer to as "norm psychology", comprising firstly the assumption that the social world is governed by norms and that the violation of these norms could and should have negative consequences for norm-violators, secondly the ability to rapidly internalise complex norms as goals in themselves, with the consequence that "our automatic and unreflective responses come to match the normatively required ones" (Henrich 2015, p. 189; Henrich and Ensminger 2014, pp. 22–24).

Cultural—societal—developments, in the end, select for genes matching these developments; and later these adapted genes, on a much shorter time scale, reinforce and drive cultural developments. That we are—also—a cultural species, means, according to Henrich (2015, p. 315),

> that, even in the short run (when genes don't have enough time to change), institutions, technologies, and languages are coevolving with psychological biases, cognitive abilities, emotional responses, and preferences. In the longer run, genes are evolving to adapt to these culturally constructed worlds, and this has been, and is now, the primary driver of human genetic evolution.

What Henrich refers to as norm-psychology is reminiscent of what in evolutionary epistemology is referred to as 'innate teachers' ('angeborene Lehrmeister'; Lorenz 1973; Riedl 1998). These 'innate teachers' operate as meta-instructions supporting the individual in learning and organising a social order. It can be conjectured that these 'innate teachers' include instructions such as 'If you detect regularities in the behaviour of your group's members, assume that they demonstrate how we do things and, hence, adopt the same behaviour!', or 'Don't allow others to violate our norms!', or 'As a default rule, assume that others are able to abide by our norms!'.

In any case, this approach differs from traditional views in that the latter consider cultural developments as following up on and continuing humans' genetic evolution, without, however, having any genetic consequences. Hence, it has been assumed that contemporary children start their socialisation exactly at the point from where their ancestors departed (Dux 2000, p. 61). However, apparently, that is not the case. Children today are born with a stronger social disposition, because "the central force driving human genetic evolution for hundreds of thousands of years, or longer, has been cultural evolution" (Henrich 2015, p. 316). Henrich (2015, p. 317) concludes:

> My point is that trying to understand the evolution of human anatomy, physiology, and psychology without considering culture-gene-coevolution would be like studying the evolution of fish while ignoring the fact that fish live, and evolved, underwater.

As Henrich points out (2015, p. 314), it would be wrong to view humans as a particularly bright, although less hairy kind of chimpanzee. Rather the appearance of homo sapiens marks what biologists refer to as a "major transition", an evolutionary step comparable to the "transition from independently replicating molecules to replicating packages called chromosomes".

> Our species' dependence on cumulative culture for survival, on living in cooperative groups, on alloparenting and a division of labor and information, and on our communicative repertoires mean that humans have begun to satisfy all the requirements for a major biological transition. Thus, we are literally the beginnings of a new kind of animal.

2.6.5 Ostracism

Across societies, what appears to be a common denominator of many forms of punishment can be reduced to the simple formula that, if an individual wants to be allowed to participate in and benefit from a group's cooperation, then she must abide by the group's rules. If she does not, she will eventually find herself excluded from the group's cooperation. An inclination to ban those who do not abide by common rules and ride free on the investments of others from a group's cooperation is deeply ingrained in human culture. Hence, an ultimate punishment of an individual who persistently violates the norms of her community is her exclusion. Ostracism terminates or suspends her membership in a normative community and her social status as a person. Because of her loss of this status, she is henceforth treated as an animal, not as a human being. In German, the term '*vogelfrei*' signifies that an ostracised individual is to be treated like a bird and not as a person.

Forms of ostracism, banishment, exile, excommunication or exclusion are pervasive across human societies. Ample evidence suggests that punishment is rooted in practices that cause not physical, but 'social pain': the experience of being excluded from one's community or of being restricted in participating in social life. Ostracism can occur as temporary or permanent exclusion from society. Locking offenders away in prisons constitutes a form of banishment from society, even if it is limited in time. The core element of these practices is not physical displacement, but social isolation—the fact that an individual is denied participation in the social life of a community. Instances where an individual is persistently ignored, shunned or not chosen as a cooperation partner resemble ostracism. (It may also be observed that many team sports know some sanction of—temporary or 'permanent'—banishment of players from the field that for the duration of the game signifies their social world.)

Recently, the mechanisms of how ostracism promotes cooperation, how reputational information is spread in groups, how this information—gossip—is used to select cooperation partners and to ostracise selfish individuals, and how ostracised subjects react by improving their level of cooperation have received ample attention by researchers (Beersma and Van Kleef 2011, 2012; Feinberg et al. 2014; Henrich and Henrich 2007; van Beest and Williams 2006; Wesselmann et al. 2012, 2014; Wilson 2014). Williams (2001) has contributed in-depth research on ostracism's impact on subjects. According to William, ostracism threatens four fundamental human needs: It deprives targets of their sense of belonging, it threatens targets' self-esteem, it undermines a subject's feeling of being in control of her social situation, and it demonstrates to the ostracised individual that life goes on without her and that her existence is not important.

In addition, research has revealed that there exists a powerful emotional side to ostracism. Wilson highlights as a "hereditary trait" of human behaviour "the overpowering instinctual urge to belong to groups. [...] To be kept forcibly in solitude is to be kept in pain, and put on the road to madness" (2014, p. 30).

Similarly, van Beest and Williams have pointed out that ostracism causes severe distress. They explain (2006, p. 918):

> Ostracism threatens the need for belonging because it divorces the individual from the group. It threatens self-esteem because individuals interpret their exclusion as a result of being unlikable. It threatens the need for control because unlike an argument or even a physical entanglement, ostracism is unilateral and unaffected by the individual's response. Finally, ostracism not only is a metaphor for death [. . .], threatening individuals' sense of existence and recognition, but also in extreme cases, leads to death in humans and animals.

The same authors conclude (2006, p. 918):

> Being ostracized – ignored and excluded – is painful and distressing. It severs our sense of belonging and feelings of connection with others; it makes us realize that others do not value us and consequently lowers our own self-esteem; it takes away any sense of control that we think we have in our social interaction with the others; and at perhaps a deeper level, it challenges our sense of existence.

Remarkably, the human brain displays similar reactions when experiencing physical pain and social exclusion, which indicates that it runs a common neural alarm system for physical and social stress (Eisenberger and Lieberman 2004, 2005; Ouwerkerk et al. 2005). Using functional magnetic resonance imaging to measure brain activity of participants in laboratory experiments, Eisenberger and Lieberman found that the anterior cingulate cortex plays a key role in the overlap of social and physical pain (2004; compare Dewall et al. 2010).

This evidences considerable overlap and a close relationship between physical and social pain in terms of the underlying neurobiological processes. These findings have been complemented by research showing how social and physical pain overlap in their psychological responses. *Both* social and physical pain thwart satisfaction on the four basic human needs of belonging, self-esteem, control, and meaningful existence. This can worsen the mood of the individual and—at least in certain circumstances—increase desire to aggress (Riva et al. 2011).

It appears that the human brain has developed a monitoring system that observes all indications of a risk of ostracism because of the severe impact of exclusion. Because ostracism threatens an individual's vital interests, individuals at the level of their brains' physiology—and hence as a result of their genetic evolution—"possess a system that both assesses their inclusion status and activates coping strategies when this status may fall short of a desired level" (Ouwerkerk et al. 2005, p. 322). Psychological research shows that in-group ostracism of children not only triggers strong feelings of stress, but also reactions of particular high-fidelity imitation and conformity as a means of reinclusion behaviour (Watson-Jones et al. 2014, 2016).

The existence of a regulatory inclusion monitoring system at the individual level has strong repercussions at the community level. The mere threat of ostracism provides social groups with a powerful means of suppressing behaviour that deviates from standards of cooperation, which protect the interests of the group's members (Ouwerkerk et al. 2005, p. 323). It functions in favour of the community's interests because individuals will seek to avoid what researchers coined the "social death penalty" (Ouwerkerk et al. 2005, p. 323).

Submission to a community's normative order is the price individuals pay for being admitted to the community as its member and for benefiting from its cooperation and protection; and exclusion is what the individual has to fear when she fails to properly perform her role as a member of her community. At early stages of normative development, forms of criticism appear which threaten exclusion before it is actually implemented against the recidivist. However, when a member of a group persistently violates the norms of fair cooperation she runs a risk of temporary or permanent ostracism, of losing, that is, her status as a member of a polity.

The currency, in which norm-compliance and norm-violations are calculated, is a person's social reputation. Social reputation means that an individual is acknowledged as abiding by the rules of a society and as thus cooperating in the generation of the normative order. A person who contributes her due to establishing and maintaining the social order deserves its protection and hence is to be respected. On the other hand, someone who consistently violates her society's norms is not deserving of their protection and may be harmed with impunity. In describing social life in the villages of Yasawa Island, Henrich (2015, p. 188) compares a subject's reputation to a shield that protects her from exploitation or harm by others.

> Violating norms, especially repeatedly, causes this reputational shield to drop and creates an opening for others to exploit the norm violator with relative impunity. Norm violators have their property (e.g., plates, matches, tools) stolen and destroyed while they are away fishing or visiting relatives in other villages; or they have their crops stolen and gardens burned at night. [...] Despite their selfish motivation, these actions sustain social norms, including cooperative ones, because – crucially – perpetrators can only get away with such actions when they target a norm violator, a person with his reputation shield down.

Many forms of punishment treat a person as having situated herself outside the normative order and, for that reason, as—to a certain extent—not being entitled to its protection. However, from the—'nosist'—perspective of the normative community this mechanism is functional only to the extent that such treatment is necessary as a means of sustaining social norms by making the norm violator remedy her wrongdoing. It is essential that the normative order defines how the offender's "reputation shield" can be reinstalled and the societal terms and conditions on which this reinstallation is premised.

2.6.6 Empathic Reactions of Newborns and Infants' Sympathy for Victims

The social judgments and reactions of adults are rooted in early developing pro-social emotions, including sympathy for victims of injustice and anger at subjects who behave in an uncooperative manner. Recent research conducted with children suggests that infants react empathically to the suffering of others, rapidly infer the existence of social norms, enforce prosocial norms on other children, react negatively to violations of rules and spontaneously sanction norm violators (Chudek et al. 2013, p. 444).

In the course of an extensive—although by now somewhat outdated—review of research of infant intersubjectivity, Trevarthen and Aitken have found that even newborn infants display an inclination "to communicate intricately with the expressive forms and rhythms of interest and feeling displayed by other humans" (2001, p. 3); "pride, jealousy, shame, resentment, rage, and the lasting evaluations and empathy of admiration, love, hate, and contempt" have "their foundations in dynamic reactions of even young infants to the feel of 'being present' with another" (2001, p. 20). The evolutionary products of group-selected behaviours are "idiosyncratic traits of our species", including an obsessive interest in others. Humans are "geniuses at reading the intentions of others, whereby they evaluate, proselytize, bond, cooperate, gossip, and control" (E. O. Wilson 2014, p. 30). Trevarthen has reduced the point in question to a succinct formula: "Infants, it appears, are born with motives and emotions for actions that sustain human intersubjectivity" (2011, p. 120).

It has long been known that newborns start to cry when they hear another infant crying. This phenomenon, called reactive cry, was studied by Simner (1971), who found it in 2 and 3 days old infants, as well as by Sagi and Hoffman (1976). What is even more remarkable is the fact that infants join in only to the crying of others. Martin and Clark (1982), testing earlier studies with the help of 70 newborn infants, discovered that their participants did not reactively cry when they listened to a recording of their own voice. Hence, the authors concluded that the responsive cry is an innate behaviour that specifically relates to peers. In line with these findings, Hoffman (1981) suggested that empathy is an evolutionary achievement of humans and has a neural base that may have been present early in human evolution. One feels better when one helps, while feelings of distress continue if one does not (2001, p. 31).

Early in the second year, children's empathic distress is transformed into a feeling of real compassion and concern for others in distress. From then on, children want to help not only to relieve their own distress but because they feel genuinely sorry for others and they begin making helpful advances. In other words, the self-other-differentiation 'produces a qualitative transformation of empathic into sympathetic distress' (Hoffman 2001, p. 88). In its more developed stages, empathy means not just the ability to feel what others feel but the ability to have feelings that are more congruent with and responsive to the *situation* of another than one's own, as when one feels anger on seeing someone being attacked even when the victim herself visibly feels sad or depressed rather than angry (Hoffman 2001, p. 30).

In addition, Vaish et al. (2009) explored whether 18–25 months old children sympathise with a person who has been harmed but expressed no emotion whatsoever. Even under these conditions, children showed more concern and supportive behaviour towards the victim than to a neutral person. The tested emotions and reactions were not triggered by emotional cues, but solely by the fact that a person had been harmed, and therefore instantiate sympathy for the victim.

The demonstration of harmful behaviour involved two experimenters, one playing the victim and one the perpetrator. The latter took the necklace of the 'victim', tore a picture that the victim had drawn etc. In a following scene, the children were handed balloons, as was the victim. When the latter 'accidentally' let go of her balloon, which floated to the ceiling, the reactions of the children were watched. Vaish and colleagues found, firstly, that children helped the victim significantly more than they helped another person in a control situation without prior victimisation, and, secondly, a high correlation between children's concerned looks when watching the victimisation and their subsequent readiness to help the victim, suggesting a link between victimisation and being helped. The authors suggest that the participating children already possess some affective perspective-taking skills enabling them to put themselves in the victim's situation (Vaish et al. 2009, p. 541). Tomasello (2009, p. 13) comments:

> This suggests that infants' naturally occurring empathetic or sympathetic responses to the victim's plight affected their tendency to help. It is this 'concern' then, we would argue, and not external rewards, that motivates young children's helping.

2.6.7 *Infants' Aversion Against Obstructive Behaviour and Appreciation of Punishment*

Research carried out by Rakoczy and his colleagues demonstrates that even toddlers infer social norms from observed behaviour and spontaneously sanction norm-violations. Three-year-olds reveal a clear awareness of the normative framework of games. When witnessing norm-violations, they display distinctively normative interventions. Two-year-olds show similar response patterns, though only in 'embyonic form' (Rakoczy et al. 2008, p. 879).

Other studies have demonstrated children's abilities to assess behaviour as cooperative or obstructive. Astonishingly, even infants display adverse reactions to those who, instead of helping and cooperating, obstruct the plans of others. Before infants have entered the world of social norms, they appreciate cooperation and have intuitions that correspond to adults' concepts of reward and punishment.

Hamlin et al. (2011) found that 8 months old infants prefer characters who they watched acting in a helpful and cooperative manner to individuals who impeded the endeavours of others. However, infants of about the same age favour those who react negatively towards others who previously displayed uncooperative behaviour over individuals who help obstructive others. In other words, they appreciate bad treatment directed towards uncooperative others. They thereby exhibit a more differential behaviour compared to infants of 5 months who, in an indiscriminative manner, prefer others who help, even if they help such persons who before obstructed the plans of others.

In the study, infants watched an animal hand puppet repeatedly and unsuccessfully trying to lift the lid of a box containing a rattle. The puppet was then either supported by another puppet who helped opening the box or was hindered by an 'antisocial puppet'. Judged by whom they chose to reach for, infants significantly more often preferred the cooperative puppet. They were then shown the antisocial puppet playing with a ball, which she dropped. On separate trials, the ball was given back to the unhelpful puppet by another puppet (a 'Giver') or taken away (by a 'Taker'). The young participants were then shown the Giver and the Taker and invited to take one of them. A significant majority of participants favoured the Taker, demonstrating that it is wrong of the Giver to cooperate with a puppet that is not cooperative. It is right to take the ball and thus sanction antisocial behaviour.

Thus by around 8 to 9 months of age, infants prefer individuals who support prosocial others, as well as subjects who sanction uncooperative ones. In contrast, 5 months old infants prefer the Giver to the Taker. This shows that they do not yet establish a contextual link between the taking of the ball and the previous uncooperative behaviour of the antisocial puppet (Hamlin et al. 2011). They do not have an issue with the Giver, as they do not yet sympathise with the victim or reproach the antisocial puppet.

Bloom (2013) reports an incident where a 1-year-old infant watched a puppet roll a ball to a second puppet, who passed the ball back. The first puppet then rolled the ball to a third puppet, who ran off with the ball. Next, the child had to choose between taking a treat away from the cooperative or from the antisocial puppet. Unsurprisingly, the infant took the treat from the latter, but apparently felt that this was not enough. 'The boy then leaned over and smacked this puppet on the head', Bloom recalls. In the infant's moral view, this was an instance where real punishment was called for.

These findings are highly relevant to a theory of punishment. Infants below 8 months of age are not capable of interpreting an aggressive act—taking the ball away—as a sanction, but children of 8 months or older are. The latter intuitively command the basic semantics of punishment. This divide coincides with the age when infants acquire what Stern calls a "sense of an intersubjective self" (2000) and Trevarthen and Aitken refer to as "secondary intersubjectivity" (2001, p. 5). At this age, the child acquires a sufficient 'working notion' of the inner mental and emotional states of others to imagine that the offender makes the victim feel bad, which enables the child to sympathise with the victim. Only because of this sympathy for the victim can the child develop negative emotions against the offender and, in the setting above, against the Giver. What this indicates is that the evolution of punitive sentiments is premised on and driven by a sense that the victim has been treated badly, resulting in sympathetic bonds being established with the victim. It is on this proto-normative, negative emotional evaluation of the offender's behaviour that later—around age 3 years—a verbal, in a sense fuller, normative assessment can be built.

2.6.8 'Inherent' and Conventional Wrong

From research carried out by Smetana, Nucci, Turiel and others originates another significant finding. At 3 years of age, children distinguish between two types of wrongs. They tell behaviour that immediately causes distress—such as destroying another child's balloon—from disappointing expectations resulting from an agreement—such as not abiding by the rules of a game. Harming others is perceived as inherently wrong, while not abiding by an agreed rule is viewed as a conventional wrong; and it is the presence or absence of a victim that distinguishes moral from conventional transgressions (Blair and Blair 2009; Nucci and Nucci 1982; Smetana 1981, 1985, 1989, 2006; Smetana, Killen and Turiel 1991). These domain distinctions are made my children across various cultures (Turiel 2008, p. 492).

Researchers make this distinction visible by introducing group affiliation, a difference, that is, between insiders—the members of a group who agree on rules of conduct—and outsiders who are not 'parties' to such agreements. While 3-year-old children enforced conventional game norms only for in-group members, they actively protested inherently distressing behaviour equally for in-group and out-group 'offenders' (Schmidt et al. 2012). Despite their in-group favouritism, young children nevertheless hold in-group members to standards whose violation they tolerate from outsiders.

2.6.9 The Neural Basis of Retributive Punishment

In addition to the anthropological and psychological research observing the behaviour and emotions of children referenced above, social neuroscience provides insight into the neural underpinnings of prosocial feelings like sympathy, betrayal aversion or the satisfaction of bringing justice to those who have been wronged. Applying, among others, the method of functional magnetic resonance imaging (fMRI), researchers have recently increased our knowledge of the neuronal basis of normative concepts—such as punishment and the violation of norms—at a breathtaking pace.

Researchers consistently identified the crucial role of certain brain areas, such as the anterior insular cortex, the amygdala and the ventral striatum, in producing social emotions (Lamm and Singer 2010). As Henrich observes (2015, p. 196):

> When people cooperate, give to charity, or punish norm violators in locally prescribed ways, the 'reward circuits' in their brains fire up. Some of these are the same circuits that fire when people are rewarded with money or food, yet in these costly social contexts, the circuits are firing despite the fact that individuals are actually losing money. [...] Neurologically speaking, people 'like' to comply with norms and punish norm violators.

Already in 2004, de Quervain and colleagues shed light on the neural basis of punishment. Using the method of positron emission tomography, they scanned the brains of subjects who participated in a game of loyal reciprocation, learned about a case of abuse of their trust and decided on the punishment of the defector. The authors found that punishment "activated the dorsal striatum, which has been implicated in the processing of rewards that accrue as a result of goal-directed actions". In addition, "subjects with stronger activations in the dorsal striatum were willing to incur greater costs in order to punish". The authors interpret their findings as supporting "the hypothesis that people derive satisfaction from punishing norm violations and that the activation in the dorsal striatum reflects the anticipated satisfaction from punishing defectors" (de Quervain et al. 2004, p. 1254). What motivates punishment is the expected satisfaction from its imposition (de Quervain et al. 2004, p. 1257). Research conducted more recently confirmed that punishing norm-violators activates cerebral reward circuits, and punishing by really hurting norm-violators (physically or monetarily) activates these rewards circuits more than punishing only symbolically (Henrich and Ensminger 2014, p. 26).

An fMRI investigation of the effects of belief in free will on third-party punishment, conducted by Krueger and other researchers, found that the belief in free will has a modest impact on the punishment of minor offences and no impact at all on sanctioning severe norm violations, including violent crime (Krueger et al. 2014). This underlines that what primarily drives punishment is the wrong suffered by the victim and not some abstract, anaemic concept of a norm violating behaviour.

However, while empathy plays an important role in establishing a normative order, recently Decety and Cowell (2014) have sounded a cautionary note highlighting the imprecision of the notion of empathy. The authors suggest distinguishing between three different aspects, namely emotional sharing (or emotional contagion), empathic concern and perspective taking. While there is no clear link between emotional sharing and morality, empathic concern leads to helping others in distress and is apt to drive moral behaviour. This is even more the case when individuals learn to consider the perspective of others. Neuroscience research demonstrates that when individuals adopt the perspective of another, neural circuits common to the ones underlying first-person experiences are activated. According to Decety and Cowell, this ability to effectively put oneself in another's shoes enables humans to expand empathic concern from the family and the tribe to humanity as a whole. Hence educational interventions should focus on the ability to adopt the perspective of others and on moral reasoning to elicit empathic concern for others, rather than emphasising emotional sharing (Decety and Yoder 2016).

Aydoğan and others (2014) found that the neuropeptide oxytocin enhances the inclination to punish free-riders, even in a situation where punishing does not come with the prospect of future material gains and is costly for the punisher. In addition, oxytocin increases the readiness to cooperate in a social dilemma game situation when a punishment option is available, but has no effect on cooperation in the absence of any sanctioning mechanism. The authors conclude that oxytocin enhances the level of confidence placed in a sanctioning mechanism. The enraging effects of free-riding and our desire to punish those who exploit our willingness to abide by norms and contribute to our community's cooperation in establishing a normative order are a corner-stone of criminal justice. Murphy (2011, p. 32) recalls the following episode, reported by the outstanding legal philosopher Herbert Morris, known for his awareness of the issues created by free riders:

> Morris once told me that he first got the idea for his theory on a Los Angeles freeway during a period of gridlock. All drivers were waiting in long lines for their turn to enter an exit lane when Morris saw a sports car speed along the shoulder, illegally pass a great many cars, and push itself into the exit lane in front of those who had been legally waiting their turn. He said he became absolutely furious at the arrogance and presumption of the driver of this sports car. His theory came to him as he asked himself the question 'Why does this make me so resentful?'

A fuller answer to Morris' question would need to take into account, firstly, the effects of oxytocin and, secondly, based on the model of GCC, an evolutionary explanation of the fact that unfair social behaviour triggers strong biological reactions.

2.7 The Mechanism of Punishment

2.7.1 The Semantics of Punishing: Punishment as Censure

One way of interpreting the results from the Fehr/Gächter-experiment is to assume that the game was, for the first ten rounds, played with a social norm of cooperation to which, starting from round 11, a punishment norm was added. But it would misinterpret a social norm to view it in isolation from its compliance *and* enforcement. Being abided by *and* being enforced is how a norm exists.

However, looking back at the first ten rounds conducted without the possibility of assigning deduction points, the gradual deterioration of contribution levels can be interpreted, in a sense, as a form of an imperfect sanctioning behaviour, given that the only possibility to 'punish' shirkers consists in withdrawing from the group's cooperation, thus expressing a form of protest. Withdrawing from cooperation may be appropriate in a dyadic relationship based on reciprocity. But in a situation where many individuals cooperate this form of 'sanctioning' harms all participants and not only defectors. While defectors may be ready to interpret the withdrawal of cooperation as sanctioning their shirking, others do not have reason to adopt such an interpretation with regard to their performance and may find it appropriate to 'retaliate' by retreating from cooperation as well. Hence such 'negative reciprocating' necessarily leads to a downward spiralling of contributions, whereas the targeted assignment of deduction points to a defector avoids these consequences. Thus, social norms of behaviour and targeted sanctions are interdependent and emerge together.

These observations allow for a clarification of the fundamental semantics of punishment. Punishment is hardship imposed on a person by an actor as a reaction to a norm violating behaviour of the punished subject. The hardship imposed on the wrongdoer as punishment serves two functions. As hardship it discourages shirkers and encourages conditional cooperators. As censure it signifies the social norm by rejecting its violation. People who understand normative language are able to interpret such an act, by which one actor imposes hardship on another, as induced by the wrongful conduct of the punished subject. Thus the punishment signifies both that a norm has been broken, and that such an act requires censure and hardship.

On closer inspection, punishment expresses two norms: a norm of fair cooperation and a norm about punishing shirkers (Holz 2015). Punishment signals that, firstly, it is wrong to act in such and such manner and that, secondly, those who do not abide by this norm *shall* be punished. In other terms, punishment—as an act of communication, a move in a normative language game—signifies that it is right to punish defectors, because they should not have wronged others. Thus punishing vindicates and reinforces both the first-order norm of cooperation and the second-order norm of punishing.

If one assumed that the behavioural norm comes first and is later enforced and maintained by a punishment mechanism, the question would arise how social norms develop and exist in the first place, prior to any enforcement. Fehr and Gächter have demonstrated that they do not, or at least not in a sustainable and robust manner. Punishing shirkers is a crucially important means of keeping a norm alive.

The sanction expresses the behavioural norm. The law book of the Saxons, which was written in Latin in 1221 and in German in 1224, stipulated basic norms of criminal law only by demanding the punishment of the offender in terms like the following:

> Den Dieb soll man hängen. [. . .] Alle Mörder und die den Pflug oder Mühlen oder Kirchen oder Kirchhöfe berauben und Mordbrenner [. . .] die soll man radebrechen. Die einen Mann erschlagen oder fangen oder berauben [. . .] und den Frieden brechen und beim Ehebruch ergriffen werden, denen soll man das Haupt abhauen [. . .] Welcher Christenmann ungläubig ist oder mit Zauberei umgeht oder mit Giftmischerei und des überführt wird, den soll man auf dem Scheiterhaufen verbrennen.

These various imaginative methods of executing death penalties signify different social norms, types of offences, and degrees of wrongdoing, and at the same time express distinct degrees of censure, indignation or disgust over the norms' violations. Thus, the sanction and the offence are symbolically tied together.

To give another example, when she lived with the Chewong of peninsular Malaysia, Signe Howell (1989, pp. 182–183) observed that

> Chewong language makes no distinction between what one may call the name of the rule, e.g., *talaiden*, the act that will lead to a punitive reaction, and the punitive act itself. [. . .] So the act and the consequences of committing them are united in the Chewong mind, and it is not possible to say which the word in specific cases actually is referring to.

Punishment emphatically disapproves behaviour as a wrong and thus, at once, expresses a behavioural norm. Stipulating that the behaviour is rejected because it is unnatural, immoral, illegal, unfair, or a sin, only specifies the normative context, but does not alter the essential function of punishment, which - besides imposing hardship - is to censure a certain behaviour as violating a social norm.

While in Chewong society all activities are covered with a thick layer of social norms, retribution for failing to abide by these norms is "in all cases supernatural, not human" (Howell 1989, p. 42). The Chewong have no "legal machinery" to cope with situations where individuals have stepped out of line (Howell 1989, p. 43). Thus, they avoid the risk of anti-social retaliation against punishers. The Chewong do gossip about each other's behaviour, but "this is chiefly in order to keep track of what is going on, not to pass moral judgment" (Howell 1989, p. 37). Hence, for instance rules of exogamy are expressed in terms of what happens to a person who violates them. Marriage between true siblings is "known as *jawad* and will result in the offenders being killed and eaten by a tiger". Marriage between parent and child "is *tanko*, after the superhuman being of that name who punishes the offenders by giving them stiff joints and, if the relations are not severed, by death" (Howell 1989, p. 26).

Whether an action violated social norms or not is seen in the outcome of the violation. Howell reports the story of a man of about 50 who lived with a prepubescent girl who, in addition to the inappropriate age difference, was his mother's brother's daughter's daughter, nor had the man notified the girl's older brother about his intentions, as he should have done. Not surprisingly, for the Chewong, the union was first considered to be *tanko*. However, it was later stated that it was not *tanko* after all, as they were both still alive. Again later, the girl died, and people "reverted to saying that the union was indeed *tanko*" (Howell 1989, p. 27). What can be learned is that punishment preserves norms by ensuring that norm violating behaviour is marked as such and sanctioned and hence neither morally, nor materially a successful or attractive strategy inviting followers; and it is, at this level of abstraction, not important whether punishment is effected by nature, the spirits of ancestors, policing gods, the victim's family or state institutions. What is decisive is that the offence prompts a sanction that expresses censure and discourages followers. Hence, everyone can see that a crime is a wrong that does not pay, even if the sanction occurs only many years after the offence (a phenomenon that is, by the way, not restricted to the world of the Chewong).

When in the initial phase the union was seen as *tanko*, the man was not censured for his behaviour, nor did others behave in any way differently towards him from what they had before. Still he knew that his behaviour was wrong. Hence, he took his wife and children from an earlier marriage and left the settlement and started to live with them at some distance from the group. As Howell comments, "[b]y removing himself physically, the man in question acknowledged that he had acted in such a way as to offend accepted ideas about good behaviour" (1989, p. 43). The man imposed punishment—in its classical form as ostracism—on himself as an expression of the norm violated, which he internalised and recognised. Paradoxically, by moving away he demonstrated that he was a Chewong. According to Howell, "[i]t is likely that the seriousness of the offence determines the distance a person moves. They said that if ever one member of the group were to kill another, he would move far away, being much too ashamed to continue living amongst friends and relatives" (1989, p. 43).

2.7.2 *Punishment as Hardship*

However, punishment is not only an expression of censure, but also real hardship. Therefore, two—crucially important—questions remain to be answered. The first asks why it is necessary that the offender should endure hardship, and the second enquires into the fairness of such treatment.

Punishment as a reaction to norm-violating conduct discourages potential imitators by demonstrating that violating the norm has adverse consequences, which make norm violations less attractive. It aims to demonstrate that shirking does not pay.

In addition, the punishment of the offender expresses the community's solidarity with the victim. It signals to the victim that the norm she trusted in is indeed valid, that she was right to expect norm-compliant behaviour, that hence the offender was wrong, and that the community will not allow the offender to get away with it, but make sure that her strategy is rid of any attractiveness. Hence, the hardship imposed on the offender reassures conditional cooperators that they can run the risk of being exploited by shirkers, as the latter will be made to pay for the unjust advantage gained by their shirking and therefore will not be the ones who laugh last.

In short, punishment prevents offenders from riding free on the norm compliant behaviour of others with impunity. Punishment is necessary as a means of protecting norms against shirkers. Similarly, Herbert Morris—first in 1965—put forward the following explanation (reprinted 1976, p. 24):

> At the core of any legal system is a set of rules, then, general compliance with which provides benefits for all persons. The benefits consist in one's having a sphere of interests immune from interference by others. There is good reason for believing that one has a moral obligation to obey such rules. This obligation derives from the fairness of one's assuming certain burdens that others have assumed and which make these benefits possible. Further, it is reasonable to support such kinds of rules with sanctions, for if there were no sanctions for noncompliance, those who voluntarily complied with the rules would have no protection against those prepared to accept the benefits of the system without assuming the burdens. But the burdens one morally assumes are merely those which are necessary for persons to assume if the benefits of the system are in fact to accrue.

What can be challenged is the assumption that complying with the norms of criminal law amounts to assuming a burden. In what sense is it burdensome to refrain from killing, raping and stealing? However, firstly, it is an obvious fact that some, in certain circumstances, are inclined and actually even give in to their inclinations to kill, rape or steal. Secondly, if many of us do not feel inclined to steal, murder, or rape (Hampton 2007, p. 109), this could, to a certain extent, be a consequence of processes of primary socialisation, in the course of which we have internalised a normative order that, however, is only maintained by censuring and punishing norm violations. In fact, everyone will experience situations, where she decides to abide by the rules, although she would feel tempted not to. Overall, anthropological research suggests that humans' 'selfish' nature and the motives provided by culture are to be seen as opposing forces. Culture modifies and conceals, but does not eradicate egoistic motives. According to Shariff, Norenzayan and Henrich, 'it is clear today that selfishness has been not wholly suppressed but ardently, adeptly, and adaptively hidden' (2011, p. 129). Thirdly, even if the offender's concrete conduct as such does not seem attractive to others, what can be tempting is the mere fact that the offender dispenses herself from the limitations and constraints imposed on her by the legal order. This aspect of her offending is most likely to entice followers, unless it is demonstrated that it has adverse consequences for the offender.

However, it is important not to confuse intrinsic normative motives with external incentives. After all, what can reinforce normative motives is not external incentives, but only normative communication and reasoning. Therefore, the function of punishment as hardship is, strictly speaking, not to create an external incentive—something like 'punishment avoidance'—but only to neutralise an external incentive by counterbalancing immoral temptations that can, in particular situations, override intrinsic morality. In addition to the moral superiority of law-abiding behaviour, which per se creates a strong intrinsic motive, punishment ensures that committing offences is not a rewarding strategy. Punishment thus prevents an external incentive from intervening, it makes sure that crime does not pay, at least not as a general strategy.

Committing a crime can have two meanings. It can, firstly, express the rejection of a norm of criminal law. It can, secondly, indicate that the offender, while in principle accepting this norm, due to the particular situation in which she acted, gave in to immoral temptations. In either case, punishment is an appropriate reaction as it, firstly, by censuring the offender's behaviour, expresses a community's resolve to maintain the norm in question and, secondly, counterbalances any rewarding consequences of the offence and thus discourages followers. Others will, in situations where they are tempted to shirk, remember that previous offenders were not allowed to get away with it. What at this point moves to the forefront is the importance of making the offender pay restitution to the victim and of confiscating proceeds of criminal activities. While these measures are not apt to express the condemnation inherent in convicting and punishing offenders and hence cannot replace criminal sanctions, they are capable of relieving the burden resting on the hardship function of punishment. They support punishment in its function of demonstrating that offending is not a materially successful strategy.

2.7.3 *Sharing in the Costs of a Norm: The 'Fairness' of Punishment*

Above it has been shown how punishing the shirker vindicates the social norm challenged by the defector's free-riding. Punishing the defector is a necessary means of demonstrating the binding character and authority of the social norm. What now needs to be added is that imposing hardship on the shirker can be fair.

The shirker, by disregarding a social norm, can be seen as incurring a debt to her community as she benefits from the norm without contributing to its validity and reliability. Quite the contrary, by shaking of the burdensome constraints of norm compliance and enjoying an undue amount of unrestrained freedom, the shirker calls the norm's authority into question and risks attracting followers. However, the unfair advantage achieved by shirking is countered by the defector's punishment, which imposes costs on her. Punishment is 'fair' because it defeats free-riding as a strategy to gain advantage from exploiting the cooperation of others.

In a just society, the burden of investments required to maintain social norms and the society's overall normative basis is fairly distributed among its members. There are three means of contributing to (the existence of) a norm and three forms of its impairment. Positive investments comprise of:

- norm-complying behaviour—expressing the reliability of a norm;
- the punishment of those who infringe the norm—demonstrating that shirking is not acceptable and does not pay; and
- support for punishing as enforcing a social norm—indicating that the norm is worth defending.

In contrast, negative investments—that curtail the norm's 'capital base'—entail:

- norm-violating behaviour—communicating that a norm can be ignored;
- failures to hold those to account who violate the norm—signalling that a norm can be ignored with impunity; and
- 'anti-social' retaliation against those who punish norm-violators, which discourages sanctioning defectors.

Punishment makes the defector bear the costs of a contribution to the credibility of the norm. What Fehr and Gächter demonstrated is that, while sanctions are costly, they are an effective investment in the reliability and authority of the behavioural norm that they enforce; and, what is more, it is the defector who is made to bear the larger share of the costs of this investment. Those who punish incur costs, which they are ready to bear as a means of defending the norm's existence against the threat created by the shirker's defecting. This cost can also be shared amongst the unified group of norm cooperators, whereas the cost of being punished tends to be on an individual basis. Thus punishing sends a strong signal of loyalty to the norm of proper social conduct. The norm's vindication is the immediate, intrinsic effect of sanctioning defectors.

Fehr and Gächter (2000a, b) also highlighted a significant correlation between the size of a participant's negative deviation from the mean level of contributions and the severity of punishment. The more severely a participant 'defects' compared to the average behaviour of other group members, the more others punish. To put it another way, the more important the infringed norm, the larger the debt incurred, the higher the compensation owed to the prestige of the social norm.

Above, the adjective 'fair' is placed in inverted commas. This is because here it describes a mechanism to sustain the existence of a norm by insisting on a fair distribution of the costs involved in preserving the norm. However, any substantive moral judgment is premised on an assessment of the contents of the norm in question. Some norms may be wrong and in this case *should* be undermined, e.g. criminal law provisions prohibiting homosexual intercourse or criminalizing migration. While it is true that an individual who disregards such prohibitions frustrates the efforts of those who abide by these norms and undermines the latter's authority, this may be precisely the right thing to do. If a norm is unjust, violating the norm, on first sight, denies loyal cooperation with those who abide by the norm, but, on second sight, is justified by the imperative to bring down an illegitimate norm.

In relation to the norm of cooperation, a defector can be seen as illegitimately appropriating an amount of freedom of choice. However, that is not the case, if the norm that is violated itself deprives the individual of autonomy which she can legitimately claim. Hence, there are two different points of view and two different levels of assessing a norm violation. From the internal—merely formal—perspective of those cooperating to maintain the norm, a defector rides free on the norm compliance of others and therefore acts in an 'unfair' manner. From an external—morally substantive—perspective, which also takes the legitimacy of the violated norm into consideration, defecting is not only *prima facie* 'unfair', but definitely unfair and morally wrong if, and only if, the norm is legitimate. Defecting is not objectionable if it can be interpreted as protesting an illegitimate norm. While this chapter only describes the mechanism—and semantics—of punishment as a tool used to defend a norm and does not include any assessment of the norm so defended, the next chapter will turn to the ensuing question, what legitimises criminal law provisions and justifies punishment.

2.7.4 Deterrence Does Not Hold the Answer (II)

Norm compliant behaviour can vindicate and sustain a norm as long as it is interpreted as actors' moral statements in favour of the norm. In contrast, if one assumes that the reason why people abide by a norm is not their deference—or at least consent—to the norm, but only their wish to avoid being punished, then their externally norm-compliant behaviour does not express any inner moral loyalty to the norm and hence cannot convince others to respect the norm, at least not for the reason that it *should* be respected.

Criminal law cannot, at the same time, treat individuals as amoral, cold and calculating egoists and as fair and conscientious cooperators. Threatening citizens with punishment frustrates the intentions of those who are willing to cooperate voluntarily and who by their behaviour want to demonstrate that they are fair moral agents. Threatening them with punishment suggests that they are—or at least may well be—crude, selfish utility-maximizers who abide by normative standards only to avoid sanctions. If, under the conditions created by the deterrent threat of punishment, a person abides by the norm, she can be interpreted as abiding by the norm for the sole reason of wanting to avoid being sanctioned. This is not an attractive option to a moral person.

The term, coined in experimental psychology to denote this issue, is 'crowding out'. External—unmoral, e.g. material—incentives crowd out intrinsic—moral—motives. Already in 1970, Titmuss described the basic pattern: Offering monetary compensation for donating blood reduces the number of donors. The reason is that people do not want to be seen as selling their blood as a means of gaining material benefits (Mellström and Johannesson 2008). Their intention to, by donating blood, show that they are good, loyal cooperators motivated by an exemplary community spirit is defeated by the existence of a material incentive. Titmuss analysed the disquieting effects of commercial blood programmes that drive out voluntary systems. As the result of his comprehensive research he concluded (1997, p. 314) that

> the commercialisation of blood and donor relationships represses the expression of altruism, erodes the sense of community, lowers scientific standards, limits both personal and professional freedoms, sanctions the making of profits in hospitals and clinical laboratories, legalises hostility between doctor and patient, subjects critical areas of medicine to the laws of the marketplace, places immense social costs on those least able to bear them - the poor, the sick and the inept - increases the danger of unethical behaviour in various sectors of medical science and practice, and results in situations in which proportionately more and more blood is supplied by the poor, the unskilled, the unemployed, Negroes and other low income groups and categories of exploited human populations of high blood yielders.

Similarly, the message sent by deterrent criminal law provisions that those who do not abide by the law will be punished appeals to individuals' self-interest and thus risks crowding out the intrinsic moral motives of those who reject being treated or seen as amoral risk factors. The threat of punishment is perceived as an 'unkind or hostile action', which 'destroys the cooperative nature of the task' (Gintis et al. 2005, p. 20). After all, autonomously abiding by the norms of her community more than anything else promotes 'an individual's sense of identity, participation and community' and, at the same time, discourages 'a sense of individual alienation' (Titmuss 1997, 290).

Günther Schulze and Björn Frank conducted experiments of corruption in two treatments, one with the possibility of detection and sanctions and one without (2003). It turned out that monitoring and deterrence destroyed participants'

> intrinsic motivation for honesty or low levels of corruption. People become dramatically less inclined to be honest when monitored! [...] In our case, surveillance increases overall corruptibility. [...] If surveillance crowds out intrinsic motivation in an experiment like ours it will certainly crowd out this motivation in real world situations.

Hence, there is a very crucial difference between the message sent by deterrence that 'Either you cooperate or you will be punished' and the baseline communication of retribution that 'We support you in cooperating by not allowing anyone to exploit your fair contributions'. Deterrence frustrates, while retribution fosters and protects intrinsic moral motives (Ostrom 2005). The point is that a system of criminal justice restricting itself to ensuring that shirkers are made to pay their fair due does not ex ante address anyone as a dangerous individual who cannot be trusted and will only conform to normative standards when threatened with punishment. In other words, in a retributive 'language game' criminal law provisions address all individuals respectfully as persons who are expected to abide by the law as long as their community assures them that they will not stand alone when others exploit their ethical conduct.

Ultimately, a criminal code's authority rests on the moral quality of the behavioural norm it stipulates and defends, not on its power to deter. Criminal law provisions are credible when they convince by their moral persuasiveness, not when they rely on the threat of punishment. Already in the 1980s, Tom Tyler conducted large-scale surveys in Chicago to assess individuals' motivation to obey the law and to cooperate. Already then, Tyler pitched instrumental against normative motives, highlighting that the instrumental perspective underlies deterrent punishing. He found that, in contrast to this instrumental approach, normative concerns are an important determinant of law-abiding behaviour, and the 'most important normative influence on compliance with the law is the person's assessment that following the law accords with his or her sense of right and wrong; a second factor is the person's feeling of obligation to obey the law and allegiance to legal authorities. [...] One important and striking finding of the study is the high level of normative commitment found among the public to abiding by the law' (2006, p. 64). The best strategy to maintain social order is to ensure that laws and public authorities have a basis in the normative consensus of the public. In any case, people's motivation to cooperate with the authorities 'is rooted in social relationships and ethical judgments, and does not primarily flow from the desire to avoid punishments or gain rewards' (Tyler 2006, p. 270; Tyler 2013).

In fact, if the mechanism of criminal law was based on deterrence, criminal justice would cease to be a matter of normativity altogether. It would shrink to the result of individuals' utility functions and strategies and treat individuals not as moral agents, united in a collective struggle and search for a just normative order, but like animals pursuing their selfish drives, needs and interests. Regarding the situation of criminal justice in the USA, there is abundant empirical evidence attesting to the negative effects of a policy based on deterrence. Such a policy is not only ineffective and costly, it also corrodes a society's normative foundation. Treating individuals as egoistic utility-maximizers teaches these individuals to act like and in the long run also to adopt the attitudes of selfish utility-maximizers. In the USA, a policy of drastically increased sentences has undermined citizens' confidence that the system is based on fairness. Consequently, their readiness to cooperate with and report to the police has declined. As a result, in order to implement their policies the law enforcement authorities were constrained to step up investments in surveillance. Tyler, who for many years researched the psychology of cooperation and its normative basis, summarizes the effects of this development (2013, p. 152):

> Research suggests that the increasing use of deterrence strategies and social control [...] has created an adversarial relationship between legal authorities and members of the communities they serve, especially with respect to racial and ethnic minority group members [...], leading the public to grow less compliant with the law and less willing to help the police to fight crime.

In other words, a strategy of deterrence is not only ineffective and highly costly, but it is also counterproductive. It destroys the very normative fabric that it intends to reinforce.

What defines a society and constitutes its identity is the shared beliefs of its members in a normative order based on fundamental values and norms, which are permanently enacted and reinforced by compliant interactions. From the perspective of social theory, action is not to be understood as an actor's following or breaking rules, but as expressing her normative views and personality and thus as engaging in the creation of a normative order (Joas 1996, 2001). However, such acts of normative communication are premised on a space of morality and hence on the absence of violence, threats, manipulation or other powerful external factors.

It follows that if criminal law 'is to address us as citizens (not as subjects), it must address us in terms of the values that supposedly structure our polity [...] we should refrain from murder, rape, theft and other such crimes not because the law prohibits them, but because they are wrongs' (Duff 2009, p. 86), and the primary reason for criminalising such wrongs is not to, by deterring potential offenders, prevent crimes, but to ensure that those who commit such crimes can be called to answer for them in criminal courts (Duff 2009, p. 84).

Hence, any sustainable normative order is premised on its members' conduct expressing their normative views and giving an example to others, thus investing in the norms they support and adhere to. Punishment as a mechanism to sustain norm-compliance does not function by general deterrence, but by assuring conditional cooperators that norms matter to their community and that hence they can trust that shirkers will not be allowed to get away with it with impunity. Punishment is essentially a normative statement that vindicates legitimate expectations and proves their frustration wrong.

2.7.5 For Comparison: Deterrent 'Punishing' in Animals

Aggression as a means of repudiating and deterring unwelcome behaviour is frequent in animals (Trivers 1971; Clutton-Brock and Parker 1995a; Silk 2005, pp. 61–62; Voland 2009, p. 80). Contexts in which such aggressions are applied include discouraging theft or parasites, disciplining offspring and establishing a position of dominance; in addition, males in a wide range of animal species coerce females to mate by sanctioning persistent refusal (Clutton-Brock and Parker 1995a, b).

From the aggressor's perspective, what must be considered is the fact that 'punishing' is costly for her as well and worthwhile only when it promises to effectively deter the other animal's unwelcome—fitness-reducing—behaviour rather than evoke retaliation. If the other animal is stronger, 'punishing' does not work. 'Punishing' in animals is therefore a means of exploiting and reinforcing power-imbalances.

As is the case with all patterns of animal behaviour—which cannot be selected for unless they ultimately benefit the organism performing them—'punishing' in animals is selfish, at least in the long run. It is an evolutionarily stable strategy as long as dominant individuals sanction subordinates to enforce their cooperation (Clutton-Brock and Parker 1995a). Sanctions demonstrate that the 'punisher' is not ready to put up with a subordinate's behaviour and therefore reacts aggressively. This renders the sanctioned behaviour costlier. It is in the subordinate animal's own best interest to refrain from behaviour that makes the dominant animal angry. In other words, by successfully punishing a behaviour, a pattern of conduct is established between the 'punisher' and the 'punished', in the sense that the 'punished' will refrain from such conduct and that the 'punisher' can, to a certain extent and for a certain time-period, rely on her subordinate not to repeat the 'punished' behaviour. If 'punishment' is executed with much ado—as is probable, for example, in apes—then bystanders who share the fate of being subordinates understand which sort of behaviour they should avoid to not provoke rage and unpleasant treatment.

According to Clutton-Brock and Parker, the intensity of sanctions is related to the significance of the issue from the 'punisher's' perspective (Clutton-Brock and Parker 1995a). In light of the economic logic of fitness enhancement, this seems plausible. The more important it is to prevent the recurrence of another animal's harmful conduct, the more should be invested in its prevention.

As this chapter deals with mechanisms of large-scale cooperation in humans it should be noted that one context where non-human animals commonly engage in punishing is the enforcement of cooperation. For example, chimpanzees form coalitions to gain access to resources and will on such occasions attack allies that fail to support them. In wasps, queens are aggressive to lazy workers, 'chasing, biting, grappling or bumping them' (Clutton-Brock and Parker 1995a, p. 214). Thus, in a way, 'punishment' is employed by non-human animals as a means of enforcing standards of cooperation.

Aureli and colleagues observed that punishment in social primates often involves kin of the principal protagonists. For example, macaques' attacks on a member of one matriline are often followed by retaliation against members of the aggressor's matriline by relatives of the victim (Aureli et al. 1992). In addition, Clutton-Brock and Parker (1995a) report that retaliation may involve unrelated 'friends' and allies on the side of the 'punisher' or the 'punished'. Instead of an isolated act of sanctioning what can develop amounts to a downright feud between two groups. Such a row can end with acts of appeasement and consolation. The risk of further retaliation can be minimised by ritualised reconciliation, involving 'affiliative behaviour or close physical contact shortly after an aggressive interaction' (Clutton-Brock and Parker 1995a). All these patterns of group behaviour exist in a similar nature amongst humans as well.

What motivates animals to sanction another individual's behaviour is frustration and anger. However, the same perception of another animal's behaviour infringing or threatening one's interests can lead to anger and aggression or to anxiety and avoidance depending on an assessment of the relative physical strength of the individuals involved. If in given circumstances sanctioning promises to achieve a deterrent effect, an angry reaction is plausible. If on the other hand aggression risks provoking further aggression from the side of the sanctioned, a fearful response is more likely. If the other's behaviour cannot be controlled, what remains is submission or withdrawal. In short, 'punishing' in animals is a *strategically* promising expression of anger in a situation marked by a power-imbalance to the advantage of the punisher, and the submission of the punished is then driven by fear of further sanctions.

What then is the difference between punishing in humans and in other animals? In both instances, punishment effects compliance. However, punishing in other animals aims at inducing compliance with the intentions of the punisher, while punishing in humans fosters compliance with a norm. Thus, humans are specific in that they seek to influence the conduct of others not by coercion, but by means of normative language, which draws its persuasive power from consented social norms.

Norms—ideally—do not pitch one individual against another or one fraction of a community against another. The 'other' of a norm is the unrestrained wants and desires of the individual. It posits the natural inclinations of one individual against the perspective and stance of 'the group', which—ideally—considers the legitimate interests of all members of the group. Punishment then serves to express the group's point of view and hence to vindicate a standard that the group endorses.

2.7.6 'Mutualism' and 'Nosism'

Recent decades have witnessed an important shift in the concept of human beings and their actions used in economics and neighbouring social sciences. As a result, the assumption of humans' fundamental egotism was replaced by a model that perceives subjects as genuinely and profoundly social and loyal to others and to their collectivities. This has been described by authors who have played a major role in this development in the following terms (Henrich et al. 2004, p. 8):

> In the past, the assumption that actors were rational was typically linked to what we call the *selfishness axiom* – the assumption that individuals seek to maximize their own material gains in these interactions and expect others to do the same. However, experimental economists and others have uncovered large and consistent deviations from the predictions of the textbook representation of *Homo economicus* [. . .]. Literally hundreds of experiments in dozens of countries using a variety of experimental protocols suggest that, in addition to their own material payoffs, people have social preferences: subjects care about fairness and reciprocity, are willing to change the distribution of material outcomes among others at a personal cost to themselves, and reward those who act in a pro-social manner while punishing those who do not, even when these actions are costly.

What defines the social then, is a—per se radically egalitarian—we-perspective that overcomes the fragmentation of a group and the 'egoism' of group members. It is a perspective based on the internalised norms of a community, which are interpreted as defining the shared intentionality of the community's members, in other words, as defining 'how we do things'. It is these shared normative views that motivate third-party punishing. According to Schmidt and Tomasello (2012, pp. 234–235), the experimental findings from analysing the behaviour of preschool children suggest an explanation like the following:

> When children begin to identify with their cultural group—which more and more research is showing happens at a very young age [. . .] —they understand that part of this group identification is that "we" do things in certain ways. Gilbert [. . .] argued that when someone wants to be a member of a group, they, in essence, jointly accept the social norms that the members of the group commit themselves to, which naturally includes upholding the norms when others in the group violate them [. . .]. And so, our proposal is that enforcing norms is

> an integral part of becoming a member of a cultural group, given individuals' evolved skills and motivations for shared intentionality and group identification [. . .]. Later in development, these same skills and motivations enable children to participate more fully in, and perhaps even contribute to, the institutional reality of their culture.

> The evolution of human cooperation has been made possible by people's tendency both to follow social norms and also to enforce them—and, indeed, to regulate individual behavior by internalizing group norms and applying them to the self in acts of guilt and shame [. . .]. People may follow social norms for external reasons [. . .], but people's enforcement of social norms suggests some kind of prosocial motivation toward, or identification with, their group and its lifeways, and a motivation to preserve them—a kind of group-mindedness. The fact that young children enforce social norms suggests that they are already participating in this collective intentionality.

Thus, it is the We that captures the moral point of view. As Fichte put it long ago, the unity of the I and the You constitutes the We of the moral world order (*"Die Einheit von Ich und Du ist das Wir der moralischen Weltordnung"*, quoted by Höffe 2008, p. 234). In fairly similar terms, Kant held:

> *Dem Egoism kann nur der* Pluralism *entgegengesetzt werden, d.i. die Denkungsart: sich nicht als die ganze Welt in seinem Selbst befassend, sondern als einen bloßen Weltbürger zu betrachten und zu verhalten* (1798a, p. 130 emphasis by Kant).

> The opposite of egoism can only be *pluralism*, that is, the way of thinking in which one is not concerned with oneself as the whole world, but rather regards and conducts oneself as a mere citizen of the world (1798b, p. 18).

For this perspective and attitude of collectiveness, here the term 'nosism' shall be suggested ('we' is in Latin '*nos*'). This concept complements the terms 'egotism' and 'altruism' and means an attitude of 'we-ness' that orients the action of group members towards common goals and norms. The individual experiences herself as a person—as a 'self'—'not directly, but only indirectly [...] from the generalized standpoint of the social group as a whole to which he belongs' (Mead 1934, p. 138). In George Herbert Mead's theory of ontogeny it is a crucially important point

> that the human self arises through its ability to take the attitude of the group to which he belongs - because he can talk to himself in terms of the community to which he belongs and lay upon himself the responsibilities that belong to the community; because he can recognize his own duties as over against others - that is what constitutes the self as such (Mead 1936, p. 375).

The individual internalises the norms of her group and the responsibilities attributed to her (see also Mead 1934, pp. 154–162).

According to Tomasello, the phase of a collective orientation is preceded by a stage of 'second-personal morality' shaping dyadic relationships based on the ethics of reciprocity (2016). However, while it is true that mutualism does not know the We of a group but only the We of the two of us, reciprocal relationships are premised on a general and abstract norm of reciprocity, just like a contract presupposes an abstract notion of a contract and otherwise could not be concluded. Hence, the social order emerges from a dense network of dyadic relationships based on general norms of reciprocity, the exchange of gifts and retaliation expressing disappointed expectations.

The point to make here is that normativity could not have developed from merely altruistic actions. Unless one interprets the gift as founding a relationship of trust and cooperation, normativity cannot evolve from dyadic relationships. What the individual learns, internalises and practices in such relationships is not the view of a generalised Other but the perspective of a generalised Us, even if it is only the two of us. Even dyadic relationships require a nosist interpretation.

Standards of behaviour adopted by the group are equally binding on all group members, independent of their physical strength. Social norms emerge from the cooperation of the members of a community, who jointly establish a force that is powerful enough to oppose and overcome the 'right of the mighty' that rules in non-human primate bands. The normative order results from the cooperation of a polity's members, who in their entirety control and restrain the conduct of even the strongest individuals.

Usually, the term 'nosism' denotes the habit of monarchs to refer to themselves as 'we' (the so-called *pluralis majestatis*), practices of authors who write 'we' when they want to politely include the reader (*pluralis modestiae*), or other specific uses of the word 'we'. This is not what is meant here. However, if one searches on the internet for the corresponding German term '*Nosismus*' one is, among other examples, informed of a campaign of the Lutheran Church in Hannover to promote community orientation and the readiness of members of their community to support one another. This sense of we-ness that motivates group members to pursue the common interests of the group is what the term 'nosism' refers to here, although without any religious connotations.

The term allows the clarification that any normative order is premised on nosism, on a sense of group solidarity and of members viewing themselves as belonging to a group. The moral point of view is not based on a one-sided ego or alter orientation towards promoting the interests of one person or certain persons, but on a *generalised* perspective that aims at preserving the preconditions on which the sustained existence of a group is premised.

The point of view of normativity is the perspective of the community's social order. If a victim 'punishes' an offender, she trusts that her action is interpreted by her legal community as appropriately reacting to the wrong suffered, and not as just an act of aggression. And it is by her community's normative order that the victim tells wrong from right.

Normativity is premised on and preserves a space for communication as an exchange of reasons and arguments, while coercion denies and destroys such communication. Recently, Charles Taylor has highlighted that 'the essential features of language which we have and our primate cousins lack' include 'our capacity for joint attention, or communion. I mean the capacity to bring out certain phenomena 'for us', in shared attention, as against their being just for me and for you, severally' (2016, p. 335). Thus languaging develops in a mode of nosism. The gradually emerging ban on violence opens the room for communicative interactions as a means of coordinating the actions of a group's members based on combined views and knowledge of the group's members. The prohibition of deception complements the ban on violence by ruling out another form of manipulation. Social values stressing the esteem and respect due to a reliable and effective cooperation partner encourage individuals to engage in cooperation. The preservation of any society is premised on maintaining this normative nucleus of individuals being initiated in a society as respected and responsible agents and members of a community, encouraged to participate in the group's cooperation.

Normative theorising remains relative to a We that is, more or less clearly, defined in time and space. As Antony Duff puts it (2009, p. 10):

> To deny the possibility of a priori normative theorising is not to deny the possibility of rational normative theorising: it is rather to insist that such theorising is possible only within some human practice. That practice, that 'form of life', provides the 'we' of and to whom we talk when we talk of what 'we' can or should say or think or do, and the language in which we can thus talk; but that 'we' can expand as we come to realise the porous character of the boundaries between different forms of life, and the possibilities of discussion between them. We need to recognise that any kind of normative theorising (indeed, any kind of theorising) constitutes not the detached and solitary contemplation of eternal truth to which Platonists might aspire, [...] but a conversation with an actual or imagined set of interlocutors that requires a shared background of understandings, values and expectations.

The development of a society's normative code advances to integrate ever larger communities in a nosism-based concept of normative cooperation, from bands to tribes, to sedentary settlements, to counties, principalities, empires or nation states, and finally to a global order of peaceful coexistence and cooperation. The categories and borders of earlier stages of a polity's development are not dissolved, but maintained as components and integrated in the organisation of the wider community, as are former nation states integrated as legal communities, defined by their criminal codes, within a global order based on the recognition of human dignity.

The We of human dignity is the human family. Although we delegate to states the tasks and powers of legislation and administration of criminal justice, courts convict offenders for violating the rights of members of the human family; and the international community must intervene if a state fails to ensure the rule of law and if impunity of human rights abuses prevails. In the words of Antony Duff, "what gives us standing to call criminal offenders to account is the fact that we are all members of the broad, indeed universal, community of moral agents" (2013, p. 133).

2.8 In Conclusion: Why Punish?

From all the preceding, what can be learned? If anything, then this: Criminal justice is not about crime prevention. It is about communicating norms, about insisting on these norms in the face of their violation, about limiting the damage done by offences and repairing what can be repaired of the community's normative fabric.

The way punishment functions resembles more a fire brigade than fire protection. Punishment is a 'fall-back position', a 'second-best solution', second to norm-abiding behaviour. However, if this 'plan B' would not be in place, the betrayal aversion of conditional cooperators would prevent them from cooperating and would destroy the normative order. It is the assurance that shirkers will be punished and fairness restored that allows conditional cooperators to cooperate. Normative language enables humans to live together peacefully and to cooperate effectively based on social norms, secured by punishment, envisaged and effected. The task of punishment, the only function it can fulfil, is to pronounce and defend social norms by countering their violations and by encouraging conditional cooperators.

The 'language game' of criminal justice comprises of such 'moves' as blaming, accusing, defending, arguing, taking sides, providing evidence, telling the truth, accepting responsibility, finding a judgment, and at least in some instances also sanctioning. It is, in one way or another, performed in all human societies; and all human beings who grasp the essentials of their society's normative code understand the basic semantics of blaming and sanctioning, which is premised on a shared symbolic code that allows the members of a community to interpret one act as answering to and censuring another. It works only because its meaning is commonly understood.

Hence, core elements can be distilled, which together define punishment. Punishment is privation or hardship, imposed on an individual by a legal community. It is understood that the imposition of privation has a particular normative meaning: it reacts to conduct of the punished individual by severely disapproving of this conduct as wronging another person and violating a social norm. Both the privation and the disapproval contribute, albeit in different ways, to the authority of the social norm violated and in cases where the norm protects legitimate interests of individuals, remedy the wrong suffered by the norm's presumed beneficiary. Thus convicting and punishing offenders reassures conditional cooperators and demonstrates that victims are not left alone.

Above, it was suggested that the question why humans punish could be understood as referring to three different issues, namely the reasons for and the proximate, and the ultimate causation of punishment. Some of these questions have been dealt with in this chapter and can be answered now.

Punishing developed as a practice performed across all known human societies as a means of preserving norms of fair cooperation. 'A key issue every society needs to resolve is how to move its members away from suboptimal selfish maximization of personal fitness toward the optimal overall fitness of the group as a whole'. The problem is solved by mutual monitoring and collective sanctioning (Chue et al. 2011, pp. 41–42).

Hence, punishment holds the answer to the puzzling question of how human ultra-sociality is possible. Jean Ensminger and Joseph Henrich summarize this answer (2014, p. 3):

> By contrast with other primates, how is it that human societies manage to solve problems collectively and entice individuals to operate against their own narrow, short-term, economic self-interest and instead engage in behavior that benefits the group as a whole, or

some significant subset? We argue that understanding the origins of such prosocial behavior, including the willingness to pay a price to punish those who violate such norms, is a necessary condition prior to the ability to live in large social groups with complex divisions of labor. Life in larger concentrations is in turn essential to economic growth and productivity, thus affording higher economic well-being.

The ultimate causes of punishment are necessarily a matter of beneficial consequences, as is all selection in evolution (Paul 2015, p. 62). Given the costliness of punishment, it is impossible to imagine how punishing, or the strong moral sentiments driving punishment, should have developed unless they provided to a community a very significant advantage in terms of the cooperating individuals' 'fitness'. However, what is beneficial to the community is not punishment as such, but the social norms punishment aims to preserve. What in the phylogeny of the human species selected for punishing, is its ability to shape and stabilise social norms that allow humans to live together peacefully and to cooperate effectively in large communities.

As to the forces driving the evolution of punishment, Gürerk, Irlenbusch and Rockenbach have highlighted one crucial factor—migration (Gürerk et al. 2006, 2014). In laboratory experiments they allowed participants to choose among two 'societies', one with, one without a punishment 'institution'. While many first preferred to play in the group without a punishment option, the experience of being exploited by free-riders made them soon change their mind and switch to the group with a punishment option. 'Voting with feet' is a powerful mechanism ensuring the spread of societies operating a punishment institution. Outside the laboratory, there are now several lines of empirical evidence supporting the importance of cultural group selection in prehistory, including competition among foragers (Henrich and Ensminger 2014, pp. 29–33).

The objective of punishment is norm preservation. Hence, punishment is beneficial precisely to the extent that the social norms it expresses and vindicates benefit a community. All punishment can do is preserve such norms by remedying norm violations.

Therefore, at the level of proximate causation—of what drives punishing in a particular instance of a norm violation—punishment is necessarily purely retributive. If it intended to reflect anything but the norm violation it expresses and reacts to, it would necessarily miss and defy its function of preserving a social norm.

Punishment achieves its objective of norm preservation by redressing the balance of a fair sharing of the burden of investments necessary to maintain a social norm. Because her offending potentially impaired the reliability of the norm, the offender incurs a debt to her community; she can be held to remedy this negative effect by making a positive contribution to the norm's authority. The social norm is a public good. Those who abide by the norm thereby invest in its standing, credibility, binding forces, in short: in preserving the social norm. On the other hand, those who flout the norm undermine its reliability. Having, by their norm-violating behaviour, potentially encouraged shirking and discouraged cooperation, offenders owe to the norm and to the victim compensation in terms of a contribution to the norm's authority, a contribution that acknowledges victims, demotivates shirkers and encourages cooperation. By sacrificing a good that is generally viewed as desirable, the offender demonstrates that offending has unpleasant consequences, which make it unattractive.

The punished offender's contribution to the norm demonstrates that not abiding by the norm is costly. This demonstration is apt to dissuade shirkers and to encourage conditional cooperators to trust that others have reason to abide by the norm and, if they ignore these reasons, will be held to pay their debt in a second round. Thus, punishment redresses the balance of fair contributions to the social norm that was upset by the shirker. It manifests that the social norm is generally binding and that everyone is expected to contribute to upholding the norm's credibility. Hence, the meaning of punishment is that an offender, for the sake of a victim and others, is held to settle her debt towards a social norm. In the interest of the victim and others, punishment makes the defector submit to the authority of the social norm she disregarded.

Punishment is costlier to the punished the more important the norm is to the victim and others and the more profoundly the offender has called the norm's authority into question, e.g. by infringing the norm more than once or with cold intent. The appropriate amount of punishment is hence a matter of an offender's fair contribution to the norm's authority and reliability.

Social norms, protecting legitimate interests, enable cooperation and peace in large communities; and punishment provides social norms with the binding forces and reliability on which their existence is premised. People do not have to look through this chain of functionalities to be able to appreciate and support an institution of criminal justice. To understand a concept means to know how it is used and does not imply the knowledge of how it works. People can use a computer without being able to construct one. Similarly, people learn the meaning of punishment in their childhood and later support punishment to maintain a social order, even if they do not exactly understand how the mechanism of criminal justice works. Everyone understands punishment as righting the wrong done to the victim or, more generally speaking, as defending a social order.

Hence, punishing is about doing justice for victims, but not only that. In addition, it is about safeguarding and maintaining a social norm as a public good. This is clear if one compares punishing to compensating the victim. Research conducted by Adams and Mullen (2014) demonstrates that people who are 'first asked how much to punish a perpetrator subsequently recommended less compensation for the victim relative to participants who were asked about compensation first'. Meaning: If the offender has been punished, something benefitting the victim has been done already, and hence less remains to be compensated. 'In contrast, participants punished perpetrators to the same degree regardless of whether they were first asked about compensation'. Beyond doing justice for the victim, the norm must be vindicated, and punishment expresses the severity of the offence, without pursuing any consequentialist objectives, as was highlighted above. What Fehr and Gächter have demonstrated is that, while sanctions are costly to the punisher and even more so to the individual punished, they are highly effective investments in the reliability of the—potentially beneficial—social norm which they enforce; and, what is more, it is the defectors who bear—not all, but—the larger share of the costs of these investments. While by defecting, a shirker first failed to contribute to the standing of the social norm and thus wronged those who rely on the authority of the norm, she is by her punishment forced to bear the costs of an investment in the authority of the norm. Thus the fair balance, requiring that all should contribute to the binding forces of the norm, is restored. The evidence referred to above consistently suggests a retributive and expressive modelling of punishment that considers the wrong suffered by the victim and the emotions it triggers.

What this body of research shows is merely that people act *as if* they were abiding by a retributivist ethical theory in the spirit of Kant or Hegel. What people actually do when they punish, fits a deontological, retributive logic. They react to perceived violations of norms of fair cooperation and to the wrong suffered by the victim by sanctioning the individual who did not abide by the norm, thus insisting that the offender too contributes her due to the norm as a public good. Retributivism spells out the universal function of punishment, of which those who punish are not necessarily aware.

Punishment works in one-shot games only because participants do not punish with the deliberate intention to deter or dissuade—in which case they would not punish in the last round of games. Instead, they demonstrate an unconditional resolve to punish for purely retributive reasons, thus forcing the offender to contribute their due to the norm's effectiveness. If individuals would punish on a consequentialist basis, this would undermine the credibility and preventive effectiveness of the penalty and hence of the social norm expressed by the sanction, as any offender could speculate that in her case the risk of reoffending would be assessed as low or the costs of punishment would be avoided. In other words, dissuasion is effective as the consequence of the effectiveness of a social norm, including all contributions deriving from the conviction and punishment of offenders. Dissuasion is *not* the motivation of punishers but only an *implicit* consequence of a sanctioning behaviour that is driven by an unflinching non-consequentialist, deontological motivation. What makes a punishment threat powerful is the determination of sufficiently many subjects to react to norm violations by punishing defectors, even in the absence of any foreseeable consequences rewarding them or others. Defectors are punished because participants *feel* that this is the right thing to do, as a means of asserting and defending a social norm of fair cooperation and of confirming the expectations of contributors who relied on the authority of the social norm and on the solidarity of others in coming to its defence.

When it comes to securing a society's normative basis, there is no alternative to sanctions, as we humans do not possess an alternative mechanism or set of emotions that would perform the same function of maintaining a social order. Rewards and praise cannot step in. A norm is a binary code distinguishing between norm abiding and norm violating behaviour. Norm abiding behaviour is dealt with as the rule, the normal case that can be expected and hence is by definition not remarkable. A third category—like 'abiding particularly well'—rarely exists. When it does, as is the case with medals for soldiers who follow commands even in situations when this is particularly dangerous, the distinction can only serve to highlight the difference between normal and exceptionally loyal behaviour, not between normal behaviour and norm violations. Hence, rewards can motivate loyal compliance, but cannot express or stabilise a norm (Popitz 2006, p. 142).

This chapter analysed punishment as a tool. It answered the question how punishment works as a mechanism and why, in light of its functionality, punishment plausibly evolved. However, this chapter did not touch on normative questions, such as under which conditions it may be justified to apply that tool, and if yes, what kind of punishment. Such normative questions can only be answered in relation to a concrete normative order and from its founding values and principles. It is obvious that the selection of social norms considered significant enough to require punitive sanctions differs among societies and changes over time to include or exclude such objectives as fighting witchcraft, heresy, vagabondage, lese-majesty, or adultery. It is likewise obvious that punishment takes very different shapes and expressions. While it is true that punishment in general can be used to preserve a normative order, this does not justify punishment in concrete Western democracies or indicate how the scope of criminal sanctions should be determined. These questions can only be answered within the complex normative framework of modern, democratic and pluralist societies.

Hence, before this task can be tackled (in Chap. 4), all depends on a thorough analysis and understanding of the normative basis of contemporary European societies, which is the objective of the following chapter; and if on anything, the moral and political order of post-war Europe is founded on the value and ideal of human dignity.

References

Adams, G. S., & Mullen, E. (2014). Punishing the perpetrator decreases compensation for victims. *Social Psychological and Personality Science*, 1–8. doi:10.1177/1948550614542346.

Alper, J. S., & Lange, R. V. (1981). Lumsden-Wilson theory of gene-culture coevolution. *Proceedings of the National Academy of Sciences of the United States of America, 78*(6), 3976–3979.

Aureli, F., Cozzolino, R., Cordischi, C., & Scucchi, S. (1992). Kin-oriented redirection among Japanese macaques: An expression of a revenge system? *Animal Behaviour, 44*(2), 283–291.

Aydoğan, G., Furtner, N., Kern, B., Jobst, A., Müller, N., & Kocher, M. (2014). *Oxytocin increases altruistic punishment among humans*. Presented at the NeuroPsychoEconomics Conference 2014 (p. 27), not published.

Barclay, P., & Kiyonari, T. (2014). Why sanction? Functional causes of punishment and reward. In P. A. M. Van Lange, B. Rockenbach, & T. Yamagishi (Eds.), *Reward and punishment in social dilemmas* (pp. 182–196). New York: Oxford University Press.

Beersma, B., & Van Kleef, G. A. (2011). How the grapevine keeps you in line gossip increases contributions to the group. *Social Psychological and Personality Science, 2*(6), 642–649. doi:10.1177/1948550611405073.

Beersma, B., & Van Kleef, G. A. (2012). Why people gossip: An empirical analysis of social motives, antecedents, and consequences. *Journal of Applied Social Psychology, 42*(11), 2640–2670. doi:10.1111/j.1559-1816.2012.00956.x.

Beja-Pereira, A., Luikart, G., England, P. R., Bradley, D. G., Jann, O. C., Bertorelle, G., et al. (2003). Gene-culture coevolution between cattle milk protein genes and human lactase genes. *Nature Genetics, 35*(4), 311–313. doi:10.1038/ng1263.

Bentham, J. (1789). *An introduction to the principles of morals and legislation.* CreateSpace Independent Publishing Platform.

Berger, W. (2009). *Macht.* Wien, Austria: facultas wuv.

Blair, R. J. R., & Blair, K. S. (2009). Empathy, morality, and social convention: Evidence from the study of psychopathy and other psychiatric disorders. In J. Decety & W. Ickes (Eds.), *The social neuroscience of empathy* (pp. 139–152). Cambridge, MA: The MIT Press.

Bloom, P. (2013). *Just babies: The origins of good and evil.* New York: Crown publishers.

Bowlby, J. (1988). *A secure base. Parent–child attachment and healthy human development.* New York: Basic Books.

Boyd, R., Gintis, H., Bowles, S., & Richerson, P. J. (2003). The evolution of altruistic punishment. *Proceedings of the National Academy of Sciences, 100*(6), 3531–3535. doi:10.1073/pnas.0630443100.

Boyd, R., & Richerson, P. J. (1985). *Culture and the evolutionary process.* Chicago: University of Chicago Press.

Boyd, R., & Richerson, P. J. (1992). Punishment allows the evolution of cooperation (or anything else) in sizable groups. *Ethology and Sociobiology, 13*(3), 171–195. doi:10.1016/0162-3095(92)90032-Y.

Carlsmith, K. M., & Darley, J. M. (2008). Psychological aspects of retributive justice. In *Advances in experimental social psychology* (Vol. 40, pp. 193–236). Elsevier. Retrieved March 5, 2016, from http://linkinghub.elsevier.com/retrieve/pii/S0065260107000044

Carlsmith, K. M., Darley, J. M., & Robinson, P. H. (2002). Why do we punish? Deterrence and just deserts as motives for punishment. *Journal of Personality and Social Psychology, 83*(2), 284–299.

Casari, M., & Luini, L. (2009). Cooperation under alternative punishment institutions: An experiment. *Journal of Economic Behavior & Organization, 71*(2), 273–282. doi:10.1016/j.jebo.2009.03.022.

Casari, M., & Luini, L. (2012). Peer punishment in teams: Expressive or instrumental choice? *Experimental Economics, 15*(2), 241–259. doi:10.1007/s10683-011-9292-6.

Chudek, M., Zhao, W., & Henrich, J. (2013). Culture-gene coevolution, large-scale cooperation, and the shaping of human social psychology. In K. Sterelny, R. Joyce, B. Calcott, & B. Fraser (Eds.), *Cooperation and its evolution* (p. 425). MIT Press.

Chue, C., Kim, Y., & Chaturvedi, A. (2011). Collective evolution: Revisiting Donald Campbell's legacy. In M. Schaller, A. Norenzayan, S. J. Heine, T. Yamagishi, & T. Kameda (Eds.), *Evolution, culture, and the human mind* (pp. 39–47). London: Routledge.

Clutton-Brock, T. H., & Parker, G. A. (1995a). Punishment in animal societies. *Nature, 373*, 209–216.

Clutton-Brock, T. H., & Parker, G. A. (1995b). Sexual coercion in animal societies. *Animal Behaviour, 49*(5), 1345–1365.

Cushman, F. (2013). The role of learning in punishment, prosociality, and human uniqueness. In K. Sterelny, R. Joyce, B. Calcott, & B. Fraser (Eds.), *Cooperation and its evolution* (pp. 333–372). MIT Press.

Cushman, F., Dreber, A., Wang, Y., & Costa, J. (2009). Accidental outcomes guide punishment in a "Trembling Hand" game. *PLoS One, 4*(8), e6699. doi:10.1371/journal.pone.0006699.

Damon, W. (1990). *Moral child: Nurturing children's natural moral growth.* New York: Free Press.

Darwin, C. (2004). *The descent of man, and selection in relation to sex* (Reprint.). London: Penguin.

de Quervain, D. J.-F., Fischbacher, U., Treyer, V., Schellhammer, M., Schnyder, U., Buck, A., et al. (2004). The neural basis of altruistic punishment. *Science 305*(5688), 1254–1258. doi:10.1126/science.1100735.

Decety, J., & Cowell, J. M. (2014). Friends or foes: Is empathy necessary for moral behavior? *Perspectives on Psychological Science, 2014*(9), 525–537.

Decety, J., & Yoder, K. J. (2016). Empathy and motivation for justice: Cognitive empathy and concern, but not emotional empathy, predict sensitivity to injustice for others. *Society of Neuroscience, 11*(1), 1–14.

Dewall, C. N., Macdonald, G., Webster, G. D., Masten, C. L., Baumeister, R. F., Powell, C., et al. (2010). Acetaminophen reduces social pain: Behavioral and neural evidence. *Psychological Science, 21*(7), 931–937. doi:10.1177/0956797610374741.

dos Santos, M., Rankin, D. J., & Wedekind, C. (2013). Human cooperation based on punishment reputation. *Evolution, 67*(8), 2446–2450. doi:10.1111/evo.12108.

Duff, R. A. (2007). *Answering for crime: Responsibility and liability in the criminal law*. Oxford, England: Hart Publishing.

Duff, R. A. (2013). Responsibility, citizenship, and criminal law. In R. A. Duff & S. P. Green (Eds.), *Philosophical foundations of criminal law* (pp. 125–148). Oxford, England: Oxford University Press.

Dux, G. (2000). *Historisch-genetische Theorie der Kultur: Instabile Welten. Zur prozessualen Logik im kulturellen Wandel*. Weilerswist, Germany: Velbrück Wissenschaft.

Eisenberger, N. I., & Lieberman, M. D. (2004). Why rejection hurts: A common neural alarm system for physical and social pain. *Trends in Cognitive Sciences, 8*(7), 294–300.

Eisenberger, N. I., & Lieberman, M. D. (2005). Why it hurts to be left out: The neurocognitive overlap between physical and social pain. In K. D. Williams, J. P. Forgas, & W. von Hippel (Eds.), *The social outcast: Ostracism, social exclusion, rejection, and bullying* (pp. 109–127). New York and Hove: Psychology Press.

Ensminger, J., & Henrich, J. (2014). Introduction, project history, and guide to the volume. In J. Ensminger & J. Henrich (Eds.), *Experimenting with social norms: Fairness and punishment in cross-cultural perspective* (pp. 3–18). New York: Russell Sage Foundation.

Falk, A., Fehr, E., & Fischbacher, U. (2005). Driving forces behind informal sanctions. *Econometrica, 73*(6), 2017–2030.

Fehr, E., & Fischbacher, U. (2004). Third-party punishment and social norms. *Evolution and Human Behavior, 25*(2), 63–87. doi:10.1016/S1090-5138(04)00005-4.

Fehr, E., & Gächter, S. (1999). *Cooperation and punishment in public goods experiments* (CESifo Working Paper Series No. 183). CESifo Group Munich. Retrieved April 26, 2015, from https://ideas.repec.org/p/ces/ceswps/_183.html

Fehr, E., & Gächter, S. (2000a). Cooperation and punishment in public goods experiments. *American Economic Review, 90*(4), 980–994.

Fehr, E., & Gächter, S. (2000b). Fairness and retaliation: The economics of reciprocity. *Journal of Economic Perspectives, 14*(3), 159–181.

Fehr, E., & Gächter, S. (2002). Altruistic punishment in humans. *Nature, 415*(6868), 137–140. doi:10.1038/415137a.

Fehr, E., & Schmidt, K. M. (1999). A theory of fairness, competition, and cooperation. *Quarterly Journal of Economics, 114*(3), 817–868. doi:10.1162/003355399556151.

Feinberg, M., Willer, R., & Schultz, M. (2014). Gossip and ostracism promote cooperation in groups. *Psychological Science, 25*(3), 656–664. doi:10.1177/0956797613510184.

Fischbacher, U., Gächter, S., & Fehr, E. (2001). Are people conditionally cooperative? Evidence from a public goods experiment. *Economics Letters, 71*(3), 397–404.

Freud, S. (1930). Das Unbehagen in der Kultur (1930). In A. Mitscherlich, A. Richards, & J. Strachey (Eds.), *Fragen der Gesellschaft, Ursprünge der Religion* (10th ed., Vol. IX, pp. 191–270). Frankfurt am Main, Germany: S. Fischer Verlag.

Gangestad, S. W. (2011). Exploring the evolutionary foundations of culture. In M. Schaller, A. Norenzayan, S. J. Heine, T. Yamagishi, & T. Kameda (Eds.), *Evolution, culture, and the human mind* (pp. 83–98). London: Routledge.

Geertz, C. (1973). The impact of the concept of culture on the concept of man. In *The interpretation of cultures* (pp. 33–54). New York: Basic Books.

Gintis, H. (2000). Strong reciprocity and human sociality. *Journal of Theoretical Biology, 206*(2), 169–179. doi:10.1006/jtbi.2000.2111.
Gintis, H. (2008). Punishment and cooperation. *Science, 319*(5868), 1345–1346. doi:10.1126/science.1155333.
Gintis, H., Bowles, S., Boyd, R., & Fehr, E. (2003). Explaining altruistic behavior in humans. *Evolution and Human Behavior, 24*(3), 153–172. doi:10.1016/S1090-5138(02)00157-5.
Gintis, H., Bowles, S., Boyd, R., & Fehr, E. (2005). Moral sentiments and material interests: Origins, evidence, and consequences. In H. Gintis, S. Bowles, R. Boyd, & E. Fehr (Eds.), *Moral sentiments and material interests: The foundations of cooperation in economic life* (pp. 3–39). Cambridge, MA/London: The MIT Press.
Gould, S. J. (2002). The spice of life. In *On creativity innovation and renewal: A leader to leader guide* (pp. 19–28).
Günther, K. (2005). *Schuld und kommunikative Freiheit. Studien zur personellen Zurechnung strafbaren Unrechts im demokratischen Rechtsstaat* (1st ed.). Frankfurt am Main, Germany: Klostermann, Vittorio.
Gürerk, Ö., Irlenbusch, B., & Rockenbach, B. (2006). The competitive advantage of sanctioning institutions. *Science, 312*(5770), 108–111.
Gürerk, Ö., Rockenbach, B., & Wolff, I. (2010). The effects of punishment in dynamic public-good games. Available at SSRN 1589362.
Gürerk, Ö., Irlenbusch, B., & Rockenbach, B. (2014). On cooperation in open communities. *Journal of Public Economics, 120*, 220–230.
Haidt, J. (2001). The emotional dog and its rational tail: A social intuitionist approach to moral judgment. *Psychological Review, 108*(4), 814–834.
Haidt, J. (2007). The new synthesis in moral psychology. *Science, 316*(5827), 998–1002. doi:10.1126/science.1137651.
Haidt, J. (2013). *The righteous mind: Why good people are divided by politics and religion*. London: Penguin.
Hamlin, J. K., Wynn, K., Bloom, P., & Mahajan, N. (2011). How infants and toddlers react to antisocial others. *Psychological and Cognitive Sciences, 108*(50), 19931–19936.
Hampton, J. (2007). In D. Farnham (Ed.), *The intrinsic worth of persons: Contractarianism in moral and political philosophy*. Cambridge: Cambridge University Press.
Harsanyi, J. C., & Selten, R. (1988). *A general theory of equilibrium selection in games* (Revised.). Cambridge, MA: MIT Press.
Hart, H. L. A. (1961). *The concept of law*. New York: Oxford University Press.
Henrich, J. (2015). *Secret of our success: How culture is driving human evolution, domesticating our species, and making us smarter*. Princeton: Princeton University Press.
Henrich, J., Boyd, R., Bowles, S., Camerer, C. F., Fehr, E., Gintis, H., et al. (2004). Overview and synthesis. In J. Henrich, R. Boyd, S. Bowles, C. F. Camerer, E. Fehr, & H. Gintis (Eds.), *Foundations of human sociality: Economic experiments and ethnographic evidence from fifteen small-scale societies* (pp. 8–54). Oxford, England: Oxford University Press.
Henrich, J., & Ensminger, J. (2014). Theoretical foundations: The coevolution of social norms, intrinsic motivation, markets, and the institutions of complex societies. In J. Ensminger & J. Henrich (Eds.), *Experimenting with social norms: Fairness and punishment in cross-cultural perspective* (pp. 19–44). New York: Russell Sage Foundation.
Henrich, J., Ensminger, J., Barr, A., & McElreath, R. (2014). Major empirical results: Markets, religion, community size, and the evolution of fairness and punishment. In J. Ensminger & J. Henrich (Eds.), *Experimenting with social norms: Fairness and punishment in cross-cultural perspective* (pp. 89–148). New York: Russell Sage Foundation.
Henrich, J., & Henrich, N. (2007). *Why humans cooperate: A cultural and evolutionary explanation*. Oxford, England: Oxford University Press.
Henrich, J., & Henrich, N. (2014). Fairness without punishment: Behavioral experiments in the Yasawa Islands, Fiji. In J. Ensminger & J. Henrich (Eds.), *Experimenting with social norms:*

Fairness and punishment in cross-cultural perspective (pp. 225–258). New York: Russell Sage Foundation.

Hill, K. (2007). Evolutionary biology, cognitive adaptations, and human culture. In S. W. Gangestad & J. A. Simpson (Eds.), *The evolution of mind: Fundamental questions and controversies* (pp. 348–356). New York: Guilford.

Höffe, O. (2008). *Kleine Geschichte der Philosophie* (2., durchgesehene Auflage.). München, Germany: C.H. Beck.

Hoffman, M. L. (1981). Is altruism part of human nature? *Journal of Personality and Social Psychology, 40*(1), 121–137.

Hoffman, M. L. (2001). *Empathy and moral development: Implications for caring and justice.* Cambridge University Press.

Holz, W. (2015). *Justizgewähranspruch des Verbrechensopfers.* Berlin, Germany: Duncker & Humblot.

Howell, S. (1989). *Society and Cosmos: Chewong of Peninsular Malaysia* (Reprint.). Chicago: University of Chicago Press.

Jakobs, G. (2008). *Norm, Person, Gesellschaft.: Vorüberlegungen zu einer Rechtsphilosophie.* (3., erhebl. veränd. Aufl.). Duncker & Humblot.

Joas, H. (1996). *Creativity of action.* Cambridge: Polity.

Joas, H. (2001). *The genesis of values.* Chicago: University of Chicago Press.

Johnson, T., Dawes, C. T., Fowler, J. H., McElreath, R., & Smirnov, O. (2009). The role of egalitarian motives in altruistic punishment. *Economics Letters, 102*(3), 192–194. doi:10.1016/j.econlet.2009.01.003.

Jordan, F. M., van Schaik, C., Francois, P., Gintis, H., Haun, D., Hruschka, D. J., et al. (2013). Cultural evolution of the structure of human groups. In P. J. Richerson & M. H. Christiansen (Eds.), *Cultural evolution: Society, technology, language, and religion* (pp. 87–116). MIT Press. http://mitpress.mit.edu/books/cultural-evolution.

Kant, I. (1798a). *Der Streit der Fakultäten. Anthropologie in pragmatischer Hinsicht. Band VII. Kants Werke Akademie Textausgabe.* Berlin, Germany: Walter de Gruyter & Co.

Kant, I. (1798b). *Anthropology from a pragmatic point of view.* (R. B. Louden, Ed.). Cambridge University Press.

Kelly, D. R. (2013). Moral disgust and the tribal instincts hypothesis. In K. Sterelny, R. Joyce, B. Calcott, & B. Fraser (Eds.), *Cooperation and its evolution.* Cambridge, MA: MIT Press.

Kelsen, H. (1979). *Allgemeine Theorie der Normen: Im Auftrag des Hans Kelsen Instituts aus dem Nachlass. Mit Beilage "Lippold, Sach- und Personenregister."* MANZ Verlag Wien.

Keupp, S., Bancken, C., Schillmöller, J., Rakoczy, H., & Behne, T. (2016). Rational over-imitation: Preschoolers consider material costs and copy causally irrelevant actions selectively. *Cognition, 147*, 85–92.

Keupp, S., Behne, T., & Rakoczy, H. (2013). Why do children overimitate? Normativity is crucial. *Journal of Experimental Child Psychology, 116*(2), 392–406.

Kosfeld, M., Heinrichs, M., Zak, P. J., Fischbacher, U., & Fehr, E. (2005). Oxytocin increases trust in humans. *Nature, 435*(7042), 673–676. doi:10.1038/nature03701.

Krueger, F., Hoffman, M., Walter, H., & Grafman, J. (2014). An fMRI investigation of the effects of belief in free will on third-party punishment. *Social Cognitive and Affective Neuroscience, 9* (8), 1143–1149. doi:10.1093/scan/nst092.

Lamm, C., & Singer, T. (2010). The role of anterior insular cortex in social emotions. *Brain Structure & Function, 214*(5–6), 579–591. doi:10.1007/s00429-010-0251-3.

Lorenz, K. (1973). *Die Rückseite des Spiegels. Versuch einer Naturgeschichte menschlichen Erkennens.* München, Germany: Piper.

Luhmann, N. (2008). *Rechtssoziologie* (4.). Wiesbaden, Germany: VS Verlag für Sozialwissenschaften.

Lumsden, C. J., & Wilson, E. O. (1980). Translation of epigenetic rules of individual behavior into ethnographic patterns. *Proceedings of the National Academy of Sciences of the United States of America, 77*(7), 4382–4386.

Martin, G. B., & Clark, R. D. (1982). Distress crying in neonates: Species and peer specificity. *Developmental Psychology, 18*(1), 3–9.

Mathew, S., Boyd, R., & van Veelen, M. (2013). Human cooperation among kin and close associates may require enforcement of norms by third parties. In P. J. Richerson & M. H. Christiansen (Eds.), *Cultural evolution. Society, technology, language, and religion* (pp. 45–60). Cambridge, MA: MIT Press.

Mead, G. H. (1934). *Mind, self, and society: From the standpoint of a social behaviorist.* Chicago: University of Chicago Press.

Mead, G. H. (1936). *Movements of thought in the nineteenth century.* Chicago: University of Chicago Press.

Mellström, C., & Johannesson, M. (2008). Crowding out in blood donation: Was Titmuss right? *Journal of the European Economic Association, 6*, 845–863. doi:10.1162/JEEA.2008.6.4.845.

Morris, H. (1976). Punishment for thoughts. In *On guilt and innocence: Essays in legal philosophy and moral psychology* (pp. 1–29). University of California Press.

Murphy, J. G. (2011). Repentance, mercy, and communicative punishment. In R. Cruft, M. H. Kramer, & M. R. Reiff (Eds.), *Crime, punishment, and responsibility: The Jurisprudence of Antony Duff* (pp. 27–36). New York: Oxford University Press.

Nucci, L. P., & Nucci, M. S. (1982). Children's responses to moral and social conventional transgressions in free-play settings. *Child Development, 53*(5), 1337–1342.

Ostrom, E. (2005). Policies that crowd out reciprocity and collective action. In H. Gintis, S. Bowles, R. Boyd, & E. Fehr (Eds.), *Moral sentiments and material interests: The foundations of cooperation in economic life* (pp. 253–275). Cambridge, MA/London: The MIT Press.

Ostrom, E., Walker, J., & Gardner, R. (1992). Covenants with and without a sword: Self-governance is possible. *The American Political Science Review, 86*(2), 404–417. doi:10.2307/1964229.

Ouwerkerk, J. W., Kerr, N. L., Gallucci, M., & Van Lange, P. A. M. (2005). Avoiding the social death penalty: Ostracism and cooperation in social dilemmas. In K. D. Williams, J. P. Forgas, & W. von Hippel (Eds.), *The social outcast: Ostracism, social exclusion, rejection, and bullying* (pp. 321–332). New York: Psychology Press.

Paul, R. A. (2015). *Mixed messages: Cultural and genetic inheritance in the constitution of human society.* Chicago: University of Chicago Press.

Popitz, H. (2006). *Soziale Normen.* Frankfurt am Main, Germany: Suhrkamp.

Pound, R. (1910). Law in books and law in action. *American Law Review, 44*, 12–36.

Poundstone, W. (1993). *Prisoner's dilemma* (Reprint edition.). New York: Anchor.

Raihani, N. J., & McAuliffe, K. (2012). Does inequity aversion motivate punishment? Cleaner fish as a model system. *Social Justice Research, 25*(2), 213–231. doi:10.1007/s11211-012-0157-8.

Rakoczy, H., & Schmidt, M. F. H. (2013). The early ontogeny of social norms. *Child Development Perspectives, 7*(1), 17–21.

Rakoczy, H., Warneken, F., & Tomasello, M. (2008). The sources of normativity: Young children's awareness of the normative structure of games. *Developmental Psychology, 44*(3), 875–881.

Rapoport, A., & Chammah, A. M. (1970). *Prisoner's dilemma.* Ann Arbor, MI: University of Michigan Press.

Richerson, P. J., & Boyd, R. (1978). A dual inheritance model of the human evolutionary process I: Basic postulates and a simple model. *Journal of Social and Behavioral Structures, 1*(2), 127–154.

Richerson, P. J., & Boyd, R. (2004). *Not by genes alone: How culture transformed human evolution.* Chicago: University of Chicago Press.

Riedl, R. (1998). *Die Ordnung des Lebendigen. Systembedingungen der Evolution.* Berlin, Germany: Parey.

Riva, P., Wirth, J. H., & Williams, K. D. (2011). The consequences of pain: The social and physical pain overlap on psychological responses. *European Journal of Social Psychology, 41*(6), 681–687. doi:10.1002/ejsp.837.

Ruff, C. C., Ugazio, G., & Fehr, E. (2013). Changing social norm compliance with noninvasive brain stimulation. *Science, 342*(6157), 482–484.

Sagi, A., & Hofmann, M. L. (1976). Empathic distress in the newborn. *Developmental Psychology, 12*(2), 175–176.

Schulze, G. G., & Frank, B. (2003). Deterrence versus intrinsic motivation: Experimental evidence on the determinants of corruptibility. *Economics of Governance, 4*, 143–160.

Schmidt, M. F. H., Rakoczy, H., & Tomasello, M. (2011). Young children attribute normativity to novel actions without pedagogy or normative language. *Developmental Science, 14*(3), 530–539.

Schmidt, M. F. H., Rakoczy, H., & Tomasello, M. (2012). Young children enforce social norms selectively depending on the violator's group affiliation. *Cognition, 124*(3), 325–333.

Schmidt, M. F. H., & Tomasello, M. (2012). Young children enforce social norms. *Current Directions in Psychological Science, 21*(4), 232–236.

Schnall, S., Haidt, J., Clore, G. L., & Jordan, A. H. (2008). Disgust as embodied moral judgment. *Personality & Social Psychology Bulletin, 34*(8), 1096–1109. doi:10.1177/0146167208317771.

Searle, J. (2010). *Making the social world. The structure of human civilization*. Oxford, England: Oxford University Press.

Shariff, A. F., Norenzayan, A., & Henrich, J. (2011). The birth of high gods: How the cultural evolution of supernatural policing influenced the emergence of complex, cooperative human societies, paving the way for civilization. In M. Schaller, A. Norenzayan, S. J. Heine, T. Yamagishi, & T. Kameda (Eds.), *Evolution, culture, and the human mind* (pp. 119–136). London: Routledge.

Silk, J. B. (2005). The evolution of cooperation in primate groups. In H. Gintis, S. Bowles, R. Boyd, & E. Fehr (Eds.), *Moral sentiments and material interests: The foundations of cooperation in economic life* (pp. 43–73). Cambridge, MA/London: The MIT Press.

Simner, M. L. (1971). Newborn's response to the cry of another infant. *Developmental Psychology, 5*(1), 136–150.

Smetana, J. G. (1981). Preschool children's conceptions of moral and social rules. *Child Development, 52*, 1333–1336.

Smetana, J. G. (1985). Preschool children's conceptions of transgressions: Effects of varying moral and conventional domain-related attributes. *Developmental Psychology, 21*(1), 18–29.

Smetana, J. G. (1989). Toddlers' social interactions in the context of moral and conventional transgressions in the home. *Developmental Psychology, 25*(4), 499–508.

Smetana, J. G. (2006). Social-cognitive domain theory: Consistencies and variations in children's moral and social judgments. In M. Killen & J. Smetana (Eds.), *Handbook of moral development* (pp. 119–153). New York: Psychology Press.

Smetana, J. G., Killen, M., & Turiel, E. (1991). Children's reasoning about interpersonal and moral conflicts. *Child Development, 62*(3), 629–644.

Stemmer, P. (2008). *Normativität: Eine ontologische Untersuchung*. Berlin, Germany: de Gruyter.

Stern, D. N. (2000). *The interpersonal world of the infant: A view from psychoanalysis and development psychology* (1st ed.). New York: Basic Books.

Stevenson, C. L. (1963). *Facts and values: Studies in ethical analysis*. Westport, CT: Greenwood Press.

Taylor, C. (2016). *The language animal: The full shape of the human linguistic capacity*. Cambridge, MA/London: The Belknap Press of Harvard University Press.

Titmuss, R. M. (1997). In A. Oakley & J. Ashton (Eds.) *The gift relationship: From human blood to social policy* (expanded and updated ed.). New York: The New Press.

Tomasello, M. (2009). *Why we cooperate*. Cambridge, MA: MIT Press.

Tomasello, M. (2014). *A natural history of human thinking*. Harvard University Press.

Tomasello, M. (2016). *A natural history of human morality*. Cambridge, MA: Harvard University Press.

Trevarthen, C. (2011). What is it like to be a person who knows nothing? Defining the active intersubjective mind of a newborn human being. *Infant and Child Development, 20*(1), 119–135. doi:10.1002/icd.689.
Trevarthen, C., & Aitken, K. J. (2001). Infant intersubjectivity: Research, theory, and clinical applications. *Journal of Child Psychology and Psychiatry, and Allied Disciplines, 42*(1), 3–48.
Trivers, R. L. (1971). The evolution of reciprocal altruism. *The Quarterly Review of Biology, 46* (1), 35–57.
Turchin, P. (2016). *Ultrasociety: How 10,000 years of war made humans the greatest cooperators on earth*. Beresta Books.
Turiel, E. (2008). The development of morality. In W. Damon & R. M. Lerner (Eds.), *Child and adolescent development: An advanced course* (pp. 473–514). Hoboken, NJ: Wiley.
Tyler, T. R. (2006). *Why people obey the law*. Princeton/Oxford: Princeton University Press.
Tyler, T. R. (2013). *Why people cooperate: The role of social motivations*. Princeton/Oxford: Princeton University Press.
Ullmann-Margalit, E. (1977). *The emergence of norms*. Oxford: Oxford University Press.
Vaish, A., Carpenter, M., & Tomasello, M. (2009). Sympathy through affective perspective taking and its relation to prosocial behavior in toddlers. *Developmental Psychology, 45*(2), 534–543.
van Beest, I., & Williams, K. D. (2006). When inclusion costs and ostracism pays, ostracism still hurts. *Journal of Personality and Social Psychology, 91*(5), 918–928. doi:10.1037/0022-3514.91.5.918.
Voland, E. (2009). *Soziobiologie. Die evolution von Kooperation und Konkurrenz* (3rd ed.). Heidelberg: Spektrum Akademischer Verlag.
Watson-Jones, R. E., Legare, C. H., Whitehouse, H., & Clegg, J. M. (2014). Task-specific effects of ostracism on imitative fidelity in early childhood. *Evolution and Human Behavior, 35*(3), 204–210.
Watson-Jones, R. E., Whitehouse, H., & Legare, C. H. (2016). In-group ostracism increases high-fidelity imitation in early childhood. *Psychological Science, 27*(1), 34–42.
Weigend, T. (2011). Kommentar zu Tatjana Hörnle, Gegenwärtige Strafbegründungstheorien. In A. von Hirsch, U. Neumann, & K. Seelmann (Eds.), *Strafe – Warum? Gegenwärtige Strafbegründungen im Lichte von Hegels Straftheorie* (pp. 31–41). Baden-Baden, Germany: Nomos.
Wesselmann, E. D., Nairne, J. S., & Williams, K. D. (2012). An evolutionary social psychological approach to studying the effects of ostracism. *Journal of Social, Evolutionary, and Cultural Psychology, 2012, 6*(3), 309–328.
Wesselmann, E. D., Williams, K. D., & Wirth, J. H. (2014). Ostracizing group members who can (or cannot) control being burdensome. *Human Ethology Bulletin, 29*(2), 82–103.
Williams, G. C. (1966). *Adaption and natural selection* (Second Printing.). Princeton, NJ: Princeton University Press.
Williams, K. P. (2001). *Ostracism. The power of silence*. New York: The Guilford Press.
Wilson, E. O. (2013). *The social conquest of earth* (Reprint edition.). New York: Liveright.
Wilson, D. S., & Wilson, E. O. (2007). Rethinking the theoretical foundation of sociobiology. *Quarterly Review of Biology, 82*(4), 327–348.
Wilson, E. O. (2014). *The meaning of human existence*. New York: Norton & Company.
Wolf, A. P., & Huang, C. (1980). *Marriage and adoption in China, 1845–1945*. Stanford, CA: Stanford University Press.
Yamagishi, T. (1986). The provision of a sanctioning system as a public good. *Journal of Personality and Social Psychology, 51*(1), 110–116.
Yamagishi, T. (1988). The provision of a sanctioning system in the United States and Japan. *Social Psychology Quarterly, 51*(3), 265–271.
Yamagishi, T., & Yamagishi, M. (1994). Trust and commitment in the United States and Japan. *Motivation and Emotion, 18*(2), 129–166.

Chapter 3
Human Dignity: The Right to be a Person

3.1 What this Chapter is About: Human Dignity and its Development

This chapter explores the concept of human dignity. As a first approximation, one can depart, again, from ordinary language noting that the Online Oxford English Dictionary explains the main meaning of the term 'dignity' as the "state or quality of being worthy of honour or respect". While there is no specific entry for 'human dignity', the notion 'human right' is defined as a "right which is believed to belong to every person". Assuming that 'human' in 'human dignity' means something similar to 'human' in 'human rights', it is maybe not too far-fetched to infer that 'human dignity' denotes the state or quality of being worthy of honour or respect, a state or quality that is believed to belong to every person. As a shorthand that does not leave out too much of the meaning, one can thus take the term 'human dignity' as referring to the respect to which every person is entitled.

As a next step, certain aspects of this concept can be tentatively extracted and highlighted, such as its individualism, universality and an emphasis on self-determination and self-definition.

'Individualism' means that the notion of human dignity emphatically values and appreciates the individual person and demands that the individual should be treated by others—and society—with respect. To be precise, the individual is appreciated *as an individual*, not only as belonging to a collective as its member. Thus, the concept of human dignity runs counter to collectivist and organicist ethics, which share the approach of valuing the individual primarily or exclusively as an element of a group, institution or community and often only in accordance with her contributions to the flourishing and welfare of this collective.

'Universality' stresses that the appreciation of the individual and the corresponding claim of respect owed to the person extend *indiscriminately to all human beings*. Hence, the concept of human dignity has, at first sight, an eminent egalitarian and global orientation. It suggests that all individuals, because of their

A. Dearing, *Justice for Victims of Crime*, DOI 10.1007/978-3-319-45048-3_3

status as human beings, meet on an equal footing and at eye level as entitled to respect. Hence the notion of human dignity rejects all forms of particularism, which stress distinctions between categories of human beings—such as nationalities, races or classes—and rank one over another. In a sense, the concept of human dignity already 'raises its eyebrows', when such a categorisation is made, even before it has been used to the detriment of one category of subjects, as all categorisations have the potential to undermine the basic equality of humans. The concept of universal human dignity has an inbuilt tendency to challenge, deconstruct and dissolve distinctions that serve to construct significant differences and to organise societal hierarchies in terms of an unequal distribution of powers and rights, such as nobility, racial or national supremacy, or gender hegemony.

It should be noted that the term 'human dignity' is used in the singular. To explain this metaphorically, human dignity does not work like billions of little spotlights, one per human being, but like one huge floodlight brightly illuminating all human beings. Switching off the light shed on one human being plunges all into darkness. Hence there cannot be something like a conflict between 'the human dignity of person A' and 'the human dignity of person B', as A and B share in only one and the same human dignity. Recognising human dignity in one person means looking at the person in the particular light of human dignity.

In a way and prima facie, the third element—of 'self-determination'—is consequential to the first two. If human beings relate to one another as peers, no one can claim a right to decide for another. This is the social and political side of the coin 'equality': No one can arrogate for herself the right to tell others what to do and, consequently, all have to decide for themselves. Peers accept one another as pursuing their personal objectives and moral concepts.

A fourth element—'self-definition'—flows from the third, again as a preliminary assumption. Because humans decide themselves how to act, they have to find out and decide for themselves which maxims to follow. Humans are all equal in rights and regard, but, in a sense, all different concerning the rules and normative principles by which they abide. The latter element links to the first component of 'individualism'. If the human being was viewed as bound by her instincts and blind determination, any particular respect would lack a basis. It is by how the individual abides by her laws and leads her unique life that she - according to our preliminary interpretation of human dignity - merits respect.

Hence, it appears that the concept of human dignity combines in a particular manner equality in status and diversity. Human conduct is fundamentally determined, not by nature, but by the human being herself. This idea of freedom, distinguishing humans from everything else, is again a core feature of the concept of human dignity. Humans define themselves. By any action they demonstrate who they are; and they permanently revise and update their self-concept.

This is, in fact, the element stressed in one of the first treatises on human dignity, the Renaissance philosopher Giovanni Pico della Mirandola's famous oration on the Dignity of Man (1486). Pico describes the creation of man in the following terms:

> Finally, the Great Artisan mandated that this creature who would receive nothing proper to himself shall have joint possession of whatever nature had been given to any other creature. He made man a creature of indeterminate and indifferent nature, and, placing him in the middle of the world, said to him 'Adam, we give you no fixed place to live, no form that is peculiar to you, nor any function that is yours alone. According to your desires and judgment, you will have and possess whatever place to live, whatever form, and whatever functions you yourself choose. All other things have a limited and fixed nature prescribed and bounded by our laws. You, with no limit or no bound, may choose for yourself the limits and bounds of your nature. We have placed you at the world's center so that you may survey everything else in the world. We have made you neither of heavenly nor of earthly stuff, neither mortal nor immortal, so that with free choice and dignity, you may fashion yourself into whatever form you choose. To you is granted the power of degrading yourself into the lower forms of life, the beasts, and to you is granted the power, contained in your intellect and judgment, to be reborn into the higher forms, the divine.'

Although based on relgious authority, this excerpt indicates that from the beginning, the concept of human dignity comes with the promise of "free choice". The individual may decide for herself who she wants to be; and, because what defines her is to a high degree her own actions, it entails a promise of autonomy. If others tell the individual who she is and force labels on her, this constitutes a violation of her dignity, which stands radically against all forms of—physical or symbolic—subjection, domination, heteronomy, paternalism and manipulation and it opens up the vista of the human individual as born free, not subjected to the will or concepts of another. However, the flipside of the coin is the challenging notion of a radically diverse society constituted by autonomous, self-defining individuals, a concept that raises questions as to the binding forces and means of integrating such a society.

The concept of human dignity is a late bloomer. Following some precursors in early Italian Renaissance—at the second half of the fifteenth century—it essentially stems from the late eighteenth century. However, it became politically momentous and powerful only another 150 years later, when after World War II it 'suddenly' made a breathtakingly successful appearance. What had been political and ethical theory before, emerged as an international human rights movement and rapidly increasing political and moral consensus after World War II (Hare 2009; Moyn 2012, 2014, 2015, pp. 172–174; Nickel 2007).

At the level of international human rights law, human dignity is acknowledged as the normative point of departure in the UN-Charter of 1945, in the Universal Declaration of Human Rights of 1948, and in the two UN human rights covenants of 1966, the preambles of which both start with the words:

> Considering that, in accordance with the principles proclaimed in the Charter of the United Nations, recognition of the inherent dignity and of the equal and inalienable rights of all members of the human family is the foundation of freedom, justice and peace in the world,
>
> Recognizing that these rights derive from the inherent dignity of the human person, [...]

Thus the "inherent dignity" of "all members of the human family" is not only chosen as the main reference point of the UN human rights covenants, but it is also acknowledged as the source of all human rights, which by that novel orientation are given a specific twist. If any concept, human dignity is the foundation stone, on which a conceptualization of the emerging global normative order can be based.

The significance of human dignity as a foundational and all-encompassing concept and as the cornerstone of the entire structure of human rights is shared by many international human rights documents. For instance, the European Committee on Social Rights, interpreting and applying the Revised European Social Charter, in 2004 stated (quoted by de Schutter 2014, p. 53):

> Human dignity is the fundamental value and indeed the core of positive European human rights law - whether under the European Social Charter or under the European Convention on Human Rights - and health care is a prerequisite for the preservation of human dignity.

In 1989, the International Law Institute adopted a Resolution that commences as follows (quoted by de Schutter 2014, p. 117):

> Article 1. Human rights are a direct expression of the dignity of the human person. The obligation of States to ensure their observance derives from the recognition of this dignity as proclaimed in the Charter of the United Nations and in the Universal Declaration of Human Rights.

In addition, human dignity is recognised in Europe at state level by several constitutions, including in Italy (1948), Germany (1955), and Sweden (1974) and at transnational levels.

Human dignity is also the normative concept—again, more than any other—on which the European Union is founded. This becomes most evident when looking at the Charter of Fundamental Rights of the European Union. The chapter heading of Title I of the Charter is "Dignity", and the heading of Article 1 is "Human dignity". The entire text of Article 1 consists only of two rather slim, but apodictic sentences:

> Human dignity is inviolable. It must be respected and protected.

The official "Explanations relating to the Charter of Fundamental Rights" contain, with reference to Article 1 of the Charter, only two paragraphs, which are, however, momentous and of great significance for the interpretation of the entire Charter and hence of all of the law of the Union.

> The dignity of the human person is not only a fundamental right in itself but constitutes the real basis of fundamental rights. The 1948 Universal Declaration of Human Rights enshrined human dignity in its preamble: 'Whereas recognition of the inherent dignity and of the equal and inalienable rights of all members of the human family is the foundation of freedom, justice and peace in the world.' In its judgment of 9 October 2001 in Case C-377/98 Netherlands v European Parliament and Council [2001] ECR I-7079, at grounds 70 — 77, the Court of Justice confirmed that a fundamental right to human dignity is part of Union law.

> It results that none of the rights laid down in this Charter may be used to harm the dignity of another person, and that the dignity of the human person is part of the substance of the rights laid down in this Charter. It must therefore be respected, even where a right is restricted.

Thus human dignity, in the architecture of the Charter, fulfils two normative functions. Firstly, it is a right next to other rights. Secondly, it is a founding principle and inherent in all rights, which substantiate, specify and highlight various aspects of the all-inclusive principle of human dignity. Human dignity provides the general orientation for all rights guaranteed by the Charter, which therefore have to be interpreted in light of the underlying concept of human dignity. Consequently, other rights cannot be in conflict with human dignity.

As to the Council of Europe, the concept of human dignity takes less centre stage in terms of the organisation's founding conventions. However, this appearance is misleading. As far as the ECHR is concerned, the ECtHR in 2002 highlighted the crucial significance of human dignity for the Convention in its judgment in the case of *Pretty v. the United Kingdom*. This was the case of a person suffering from motor neurone disease (MND), which is a progressive neuro degenerative disease of motor cells associated with progressive muscle weakness. Death usually occurs because of weakness of the breathing muscles, and no treatment can prevent the progression of the disease. In clarifying the relevant law, the Court postulated:

> 64. In the present case, although medical treatment is not an issue, the applicant is suffering from the devastating effects of a degenerative disease which will cause her condition to deteriorate further and increase her physical and mental suffering. She wishes to mitigate that suffering by exercising a choice to end her life with the assistance of her husband. As stated by Lord Hope, the way she chooses to pass the closing moments of her life is part of the act of living, and she has a right to ask that this too must be respected [...].
>
> 65. The very essence of the Convention is respect for human dignity and human freedom. Without in any way negating the principle of sanctity of life protected under the Convention, the Court considers that it is under Article 8 that notions of the quality of life take on significance. In an era of growing medical sophistication combined with longer life expectancies, many people are concerned that they should not be forced to linger on in old age or in states of advanced physical or mental decrepitude which conflict with strongly held ideas of self and personal identity.

Hence the ECtHR holds that Article 8 ECHR protects human dignity as an aspect of an individual's entitlement to the respect of her private life and the right to lead a self-determined life. Thus the notion of human dignity occupies a central position within the normative framework established by the ECHR. More recently, a Grand Chamber of the Court observed in its *Bouyid* judgment (para. 89):

> The word 'dignity' appears in many international and regional texts and instruments [...]. Although the Convention does not mention that concept – which nevertheless appears in the Preamble to Protocol No. 13 to the Convention, concerning the abolition of the death penalty in all circumstances – the Court has emphasised that respect for human dignity forms part of the very essence of the Convention [...], alongside human freedom [...].

Overall, the concept of human dignity cannot be denied a brilliance and charisma that qualifies the appearance of this notion as an event of world-historic significance with an indisputable impact on the international world order. With the Westphalian peace treaty, the vision of a European order of peacefully coexisting sovereign nation states emerged as the response to the deep crisis and catastrophe of the Thirty Years' War. Similarly, the vision of a normative order based on the inviolable sanctity of the human individual answered to the excesses of nationalism carried to the extreme of a fascist 'Führer state' and Stalinism in the first half of the twentieth century, heralding a paradigm shift in the global political order.

What then needs to be understood-and what is explored in this chapter-is how the concept of human dignity holds the answer to the specific burning issues that had surfaced during the 1930s, culminating in totalitarianism and the Second World War. The success of human dignity as a moral, political and legal concept cannot be explained by its sophistication and intellectual persuasiveness alone, but only in a historical and evolutionary perspective by the social and political functions this concept can perform. To that end, first the concept, then its political significance must be considered and appreciated.

3.2 Kant and the Concept of Innate Human Dignity

When it comes to exploring the concept of human dignity, one cannot but start with Kant. Kant's notion of human dignity based on autonomy had a powerful impact over centuries, and still has a strong influence on political and legal theory and practice—and justifiably so.

One aspect of Kant's significance relates to the fact that the authors of the German *Grundgesetz* drew inspiration from Kant (and Neo-Kantianism), in particular concerning the architecture of the *Grundgesetz*, which, in a monolithic structure, founds all rights on the notion of human dignity as stipulated and protected by Article 1 of the *Grundgesetz*, famously stating in its first paragraph:

> Die Würde des Menschen ist unantastbar. Sie zu achten und zu schützen ist Verpflichtung aller staatlichen Gewalt.

> Human dignity shall be inviolable. To respect and protect it shall be the duty of all state authority.

Kant's influence on the *Grundgesetz* and how it is interpreted by the German Constitutional Court, is widely acknowledged (Waldron 2015, p. 135). Bleckmann, for example, without further explanation, equates the concept of human dignity as autonomy, with the notion of human dignity as elaborated in Kant's Metaphysics of Ethics (Bleckmann 1988, p. 58).

The decision to found the normative basis of German society on the concept of human dignity inspired other constitutions and human rights documents, including the Charter of Fundamental Rights of the European Union, which in Article 1 echoes the *Grundgesetz*. Hence, there is a significant line of normative reasoning linking the Charter of Fundamental Rights to Kant's philosophy of dignity.

To fully appreciate Kant's theory of ethics, it would need to be contextualised in the rich and somewhat confusing intellectual landscape surrounding Kant in the 1760s. Kant's philosophy directly responds to the rationalism of Descartes, Leibniz and Wolff, to utilitarianism and sentimentalism of English and Scottish contemporary enlightenment philosophy—including Anthony Ashley Cooper, Third Earl of Shaftesbury, David Hume, and Francis Hutcheson—as well as to theosophy and mysticism as advocated by Emanuel Swedenborg and Friedrich Christoph Ötinger.

In addition, it strongly relates to—and turns against—the pantheism—or even atheism—of Radical Enlightenment as promoted by the Irish philosopher John

Toland, the Dutch jurist Jean Rousset de Missy, the French physician and philosopher Julien Offray de La Mettrie, the French philosophers and writers Pierre Bayle, Denis Diderot, Claude-Adrien Helvétius, Paul-Henry Thiry d'Holbach and the Marquis de Condorcet, and many others (over the last decade, Radical Enlightenment has attracted strong attention, see Israel 2011; Israel and Mulsow 2014; Jacob 2006; Mühlpfordt 2015).

However, most of all, Kant's philosophy reacts to the intellectual and political shockwaves caused by the revolutionary and strikingly successful rise of experimental physics and astronomy, suggesting itself as a basis for an entirely novel naturalistic and mechanistic interpretation of the cosmos and the human being. This new perspective is linked to names such as Newton, Kepler, Copernicus, and Giordano Bruno, who challenged the position of transcendental philosophy as the primordially relevant and valid interpretation of the world.

Against the rise of natural sciences and pantheistic worldviews, Kant insists that what makes humans unique is exactly the fact that they are not merely a matter of nature and causation, but primarily of moral autonomy. In fact, as practical reason maintains a position of supremacy in Kant's philosophy, it is the person's freedom from natural causation that defines what in Kant's view is genuinely human. By their autonomy, humans escape the determination of natural laws. Kant's concept of human dignity expresses an appreciation of an individual's freedom of action, which in Kant's perspective is the only possible starting point when it comes to constructing morality and a truly human polity. In Kant's perspective, the fact that humans are constituted not entirely in nature, but also in a cultural and normative sphere, releases them from the determining forces of their instincts and enables them to 'step back' from their action and to maintain a position of critical distance from their physical and emotional drives and urges. This distance and opposition opens a space for critical reflection, in which freedom and autonomy can develop, qualities on which any self-determined and idiosyncratic life is premised.

Kant's ethics represents deontology in its purest form, as he demands that we should not only comply with our moral duties and the law, but do so motivated precisely by the understanding and appreciation of these duties as the only available path to eternal happiness. What motivates morality is a sense of deep appreciation and respect for God's will. This is why Kant emphasises that moral perfection requires that one not only abides by the law but does so out of a sense of duty and respect of the law (1797/1968, p. 523).

What permeates the entirety of Kant's ethics is his deep protestant - pietistic - piety, which allows only for one supreme good, God's presence, that is, earned by respecting God's moral laws (1788/1968, p. 171). Kant refers to God as the holy legislator (*'der heilige Gesetzgeber'*) and extensively to the presence in God's kingdom as the supreme good (*'summum bonum'*, *'das höchste Gut'*). Kant concludes that by this notion of the supreme good as the final objective of all practical reason, the moral law leads to religion, to an understanding, that is, of all obligations as divine commands, emanating from the will of the morally perfect, supreme being (1788/2015, p. 104).

> In this way the moral law leads through the concept of the highest good, as the object and final end of pure practical reason, *to religion, that is, to the recognition of all duties as divine commands, not as sanctions – that is, chosen and in themselves contingent ordinances of another's will* – but as essential *laws* of every free will in itself, which must nevertheless be regarded as commands of the supreme being because only from a will that is morally perfect (holy and beneficent) and at the same time all-powerful, and so through harmony with this will, can we hope to attain the highest good, which the moral law makes it our duty to take as the object of our endeavours.

Kant continuously criticises what he calls the ethics of happiness ('*Glückseligkeitslehre*') and confronts it with the laws of morality, which are unimpressed by persons' needs and desires. After all, as Kant remarks (1797/1996, p. 95), in 'natural' conditions of anarchy or under a despotic rule, life may be more comfortable or pleasant than under conditions of autonomy. More precisely, Kant's point is not that happiness does not matter but rather that happiness is not an earthly category. Kant states clearly that morality is not about us leading a pleasant life in this world but about becoming *deserving* of (eternal) happiness (God's presence) in the next, which can only be achieved by abiding by the law for respect of the law (1788/2015, p. 104).

> [...] and although in the concept of the highest good [...] *my own happiness* is included, this is nevertheless not the determining ground of the will that is directed to promote the highest good; it is instead the moral law (which, on the contrary, limits by strict conditions my unbounded craving for happiness).

> For this reason, again, morals is not properly the doctrine of how we are to *make* ourselves happy but of how we are to become *worthy* of happiness. Only if religion is added to it does there also enter the hope of someday participating in happiness to the degree that we have been intent upon not being unworthy of it.

It should be noted that Kantian ethics is strictly deontological and hence stands in marked opposition to all consequential ethics that focus on promoting—not autonomy, but—happiness or wellbeing. A maxim of action cannot be accepted as a general law unless it respects all individuals' claims to autonomy.

Hence Kant insists on the primacy of normativity over any natural category and hence rejects both the rationalist concept of humans perfecting their nature and the consequentialist or utilitarian notion of the happiness of all as an ethic's foundation and point of departure. In the Groundwork, after notoriously claiming that the only thing that is conceivable as being unconditionally good is a good will, Kant (1785/1968, p. 395) adds that, had nature intended happiness to be the supreme good of humans, it would not have bothered to endow humans with practical reason. If this were the case, instincts would more reliably perform the function of selecting the proper objectives and means, thus orienting and guiding, in a reliable manner, humans' actions towards their happiness. The latter is a category of the sensual, not the intellectual world, and has nothing to do with morality.

Whenever Kant relates to the law, the splendour and grandeur of the divine is conspicuous, e.g. when he submits that the law is so sublime that one can hardly stand its sight, but can only note and conclude that the law—God's law—is present in all rational beings (1788/2015, p. 66):

> There is something so singular in the boundless esteem for the pure moral law stripped of all advantage – as practical reason, whose voice makes even the boldest evildoer tremble and forces him to hide from its sight, presents it to us for obedience – that one cannot wonder at finding this influence of a mere intellectual idea on feeling quite impenetrable for speculative reason and at having to be satisfied that one can yet see a priori as much: that such a feeling is inseparably connected with the representation of the moral law in every finite being.

Therefore, Kant's ethics is, on the one hand, still an inspiration to modern concepts of human dignity. What stands the test of time is Kant's intuition that human dignity is based on individual autonomy as the fact of not being subjected to the laws of nature - including one's own nature - and the right not to be subjected to another's will. Autonomy is the foundation of self-determination and self-constitution.

On the other hand, it is important to realise where an updated and fully secular interpretation of human dignity necessarily departs from Kant's assumptions. Certain elements of Kant's philosophy do not readily offer themselves as a basis of ethical or political theory in the twenty-first century. Kant's religious beliefs cannot found an ethical theory under the particular conditions of modern pluralist societies. Hence, the crucial question is what remains of Kant's ethics once its religious teleology and orientation towards achieving God's presence as the ultimate goal of all human existence is removed.

The answer is that, when it comes to founding ethics on human dignity, there is hardly an alternative to founding human dignity on autonomy, but that there is an alternative to founding autonomy on the calling of 'God'.

3.2.1 Human Beings Existing in Nature and Culture

One of the most prominent of Kant's many insights is the intuition that humans must be conceptualised as existing in two distinct spheres, one sensual or natural (*'Sinnenwelt'*) and one cultural or intellectual (*'Verstandeswelt'*). Hence Kant distinguishes the individual as a rational and moral being (*'Vernunftwesen', 'moralisches Wesen', 'homo noumenon'*) from the individual as a natural or physical being (*'Naturwesen', 'physisches Wesen', 'homo phaenomenon'*). It is only because of their existence in the moral sphere that subjects are able to overcome their natural predispositions and become free from their instincts, their sentiments, and from all other forms of physical causation (1797/1996, pp. 32, 177).

Humans have—and experience every day—the unique faculty of resisting their physical drives and inclinations. While animals are slaves of natural forces motivating their behaviour, humans are not, because they possess the ability to set themselves up in opposition to their needs, urges and desires. An autonomous act's radical independence of any natural motivation is premised on the existence of two strictly distinct spheres, one physical, and one moral, and on the existence of humans in both spheres. Without recourse to this moral sphere of autonomy and spirituality, human action would not be specifically human, but if it did not end in the natural sphere, it would not be action, impacting on an object world.

Hence the moral maxims which a person follows to be fully autonomous must not be caused—motivated—by anything that belongs to the person's physical sphere, but solely by moral reasoning (1785/2012, p. 70). Human dignity does not manifest itself when individuals allow themselves to indulge in their various natural pleasures, but when they free themselves from and 'rise above' the determining forces of their physical existence—their needs, lusts and whims.

3.2.2 Freedom, Autonomy and Dignity

To Kant, freedom is both an irrefutable fact and an incomprehensible property (1797/1996, pp. 173–174). Hence, for Kant the experience of freedom is the centre and pivot of his philosophy. No analysis reaches beyond the fact—obvious to Kant—that human beings experience a capacity to choose and to decide. It is, however, important to realise that 'freedom' in Kantian philosophy is not a political term referring to an individual's freedom from rule, but an anthropological category denoting the fact that a human being is free from her physiological instincts and drives, and hence exempt from 'natural causation'. Being free, to Kant, does not mean to be able to do as one pleases, but to be able not to do as one pleases.

The crucial term is 'autonomy', meaning the state of not being subjected to the rule of another person, but solely to one's own laws. Autonomy is premised on freedom. Only because the human individual is not blindly driven by natural forces but acquires—mysteriously, as Kant notes—freedom from 'natural laws', the question can arise as to which other laws she abides by; her own rules (autonomy) or the rules of another (heteronomy).

Different levels and qualities of agency can now be distinguished. Any social order is premised on subjects' moral decisions about whether to comply with a given normative order or not. Hence, any normativity is founded on choice. However, traditional societies restrict the normative issue to the question of how to correctly interpret—and conform to—the normative code of society. Only modern societies adopt a substantive notion of autonomy by calling on subjects to engage in moral legislation and the construction of a normative order. In this sense, traditional societies are defined by a 'closed', monist order whilst modern societies have an 'open', potentially pluralistic normative code that respects all individuals as lawgivers.

The choice to abide by a rule or not is inherent in any situation interpreted by an agent as governed by a normative claim on her action. Normativity is always and essentially a mechanism of communication that relies on decisions taken by a norm's addressee(s). However, Kant points out—and that is a crucial twist of his ethics—that choice necessarily comes with autonomy, the choice, that is, of the normative basis of one's decisions. From the very moment a person realises that it is up to her to decide on the course of her action, a rule, law or commandment can determine her action only if—and to the extent that—she so allows and thereby adopts the rule as her own. That is, from the moment she allows the rule to govern her decision and consequently her action. Although individuals are not necessarily—and in fact very often not—aware of this fact, they are compelled to—knowingly or unknowingly—act as their own 'legislators', and no person can avoid this responsibility.

Hence, there are two levels of choice: firstly, the decision on the course of one's action and, secondly, the choice of the maxims that one authorises to guide one's action; and in Kant's view these two levels of choice are tied together. The child knows no other law than the normative order she is taught by her parents. Yet once an adolescent discovers that there exists in her society more than one moral orientation she cannot escape the imperative of having to decide on—and adopt as hers—the norms that she acknowledges as legitimate and as apt to orient her action.

It should be stressed that autonomy to Kant is primarily not a moral or political claim, but - at a certain level of reflection - simply a fact. Because our actions are not a matter of blind causal determination, because we are able to reject the urges of our bodily inclinations and needs, as well as the normative impositions of powerful others, in whatever form or guise they confront us, it remains that whatever maxim we allow to determine our action is a maxim we have chosen. It is *analytically* true that the agency, which we experience in ourselves and observe in others every day, implies autonomy, our faculty to legislate and to act according to the laws that we embrace. If we understand ourselves as agents and not just—in a dark determinist perspective—as links in endless chains of blind causation, then we are compelled to realise that the only rules we are subjected to are the norms that we adopt for ourselves.

Whatever form of paternalism an individual may face, it is—at least theoretically—always up to her to revolt and to shake it off or not. In any case, the formula she adopts as the maxim guiding her action is *her* formula, *her* law, which results from many factors, including her temperament, her emotions, her normative experiences, and her life-story. An individual's moral personality shows and finds an authentic expression in the orientation she adopts for herself and in the relevant decisions she makes. Every single act is meaningful in signalling how its author, in a particular situation, acts on her autonomy and thus reveals her unique personality. By acting, we demonstrate who we are as moral persons. Practical reason—in combination with the courage to make use of it—form an undeniable and unshakable foundation of a subject's individual autonomy. In this crucial regard, all humans are equal.

In Kant's practical philosophy, autonomy and dignity coincide (von der Pfordten 2009, pp. 13–25, 2016, pp. 54–65). Kant defines dignity as (1785/1968, p. 434; 1785/2012, p. 46):

> die Würde eines vernünftigen Wesens, das keinem Gesetze gehorcht als dem, das es zugleich selbst gibt.

> the dignity of a rational being that obeys no law other than that which at the same time it itself gives.

Hence, it is autonomy that, in his view, accounts for human dignity (Kant 1785/1968, p. 436; 1785/2012, p. 48):

> *Autonomie* ist also der Grund der Würde der menschlichen und jeder vernünftigen Natur.
>
> *Autonomy* is thus the ground of the dignity of a human and of every rational nature.

In Kant's world, it is the capacity to autonomously legislate, and thereby to achieve a certain likeness to the divine lawgiver, that privileges and distinguishes humans from all other species. God's call on the individual human being to legislate in combination with an individual's unique conscience elevates the human individual as singular. Any being gifted with practical reason is a unique and valuable voice in the concert of moral lawgivers and hence deserving of our respect and highest esteem.

It should be noted briefly that Kant's notion of human dignity as reflecting the equal status of persons as autonomous lawgivers is broadly consistent with political views expressed much earlier, including prominently the English levellers—such as John Lilburne, Richard Overton, William Walwyn and Thomas Prince—who in the 1640s held—in the words of Lilburne—that initially men and women were 'by nature all equal and alike in power, dignity, authority and majesty'. Therefore, positions of authority require a basis in 'mutual agreement or consent' (quoted by Kloppenberg 2016, p. 108). Kant's particular contribution can be seen in providing a theoretical foundation for political views that had been 'in the air' for some time.

What violates Kantian dignity is all forms of heteronomy, any attempt, that is, to impose one's will on another person and to direct or manipulate her behaviour while bypassing or rendering irrelevant her autonomous decisions. A person who respects human dignity refrains from violence, threats, and deception, as well as from exploiting a situation of emergency or existential dependence. The only legitimate and respectful means of influencing the decisions of another person is moral reasoning and persuasion, whereby another person is led to adopt and incorporate a certain argument or aspect as part of the laws she gives herself.

What follows from Kant's concept of an autonomous person is responsibility. However, as humans are endowed by God with the capacity as legislators, for Kant, moral responsibility can exist only in relation to God. An individual may struggle to understand her mission and her unique part in the cooperation of lawgivers. In any case, she does not escape responsibility for how she made use of her gift of autonomy.

The somewhat peculiar mixture of radical equality of subjects on the one hand, and their radical uniqueness and idiosyncrasy on the other, that is characteristic for the concept of human dignity has, in Kantian philosophy, its reason in all individuals' direct normative communication with and accountability to God, which brings all individuals to the same level of God's immediate dialogue partners.

3.2.3 Legislation Based on Human Dignity

An individual cannot become aware of her autonomy as a human being without realising that all others are gifted with the same quality. Still continuing in a strictly analytical vein, Kant finds that individuals, while compelled to accept that they are free, cannot grasp the concept of their autonomy without acknowledging the same autonomy of any being that, like them, has a free will and commands practical reason. For Kant, this, again, is analytically true. If agency—the ability to decide on one's action—necessarily implies autonomy, then this holds for all agents.

Thus, humans inevitably come to understand their situation as the coexistence of equally autonomous subjects; and in this situation a rational being necessarily acknowledges the autonomy of all others. She would act against her better knowledge if she treated others as a means to her ends and not as called upon to follow their own laws, purposes and finality as much as she is called on to live in search of hers. Kant (1785/1968, p. 433; 1785/2012, p. 45) concludes that all reasonable beings inescapably respect others as ends in themselves:

> Denn vernünftige Wesen stehen alle unter dem *Gesetz*, daß jedes derselben sich selbst und alle anderen *niemals bloß als Mittel*, sondern jederzeit *zugleich als Zweck an sich selbst* behandeln solle.

> For all rational beings stand under the *law* that each of them is to treat itself and all others *never merely as a means*, but always *at the same time as an end in itself.*

Reasonable legislation takes human dignity as its point of departure, as well as the limitation that is inherent in the concept of equal human dignity and the coexistence of autonomous subjects.

Any reasonable person restricts her freedom to meet the conditions under which her freedom can coexist with the equal freedom of others. Notoriously, Kant (1797/1968, p. 230; 1797/1996, p. 24) submits:

> Das Recht ist also der Inbegriff der Bedingungen, unter denen die Willkür des einen mit der Willkür des andern nach einem allgemeinen Gesetze der Freiheit zusammen vereinigt werden kann.

> Right is therefore the sum of the conditions under which the choice of one can be united with the choice of another in accordance with a universal law of freedom.

Kant knows only one (human) right, namely the right to freedom defined as the right to act autonomously, according to one's moral laws, and not to be subjected to the coercion of another. Kant (1797/1968, p. 237; 1997/1996, p. 30) introduces the thesis by stating, in a heading, that there is only one innate right (*'Das angeborne Recht ist nur ein einziges'*) and continues to say (emphasis by Kant):

> *Freiheit* (Unabhängigkeit von eines anderen nötigender Willkür), sofern sie mit jedes anderen Freiheit nach einem allgemeinen Gesetz zusammen bestehen kann, ist dieses einzige, ursprüngliche, jedem Menschen, kraft seiner Menschheit, zustehende Recht.

> *Freedom* (independence from being constrained by another's choice), insofar as it can coexist with the freedom of every other in accordance with a universal law, is the only original right belonging to every man by virtue of his humanity.

Kant briefly mentions other rights, such as equality and freedom of expression, only to insist that they are merely aspects of the one general right to freedom of action.

However, Kant's position is premised on a refined understanding of the scope of the concept of autonomy. Certain spheres or domains would have to be determined and acknowledged as 'belonging to an individual' and hence protected against interference by others, as otherwise it is not clear what it means to impose one's will on another. The respect owed to my autonomy implies that others recognise that decisions, which substantially affect my protected spheres of interest, must not be made against my will. If I intrude into the apartment of another person in her absence and without her knowledge, it appears that I impinge on her privacy, which can be interpreted as a sphere that 'belongs to her'. Hence, respecting another's autonomy rules out invading such exclusive spheres of another person's autonomy.

In other words, an individual's autonomy covers spheres that are acknowledged as domains controlled by her. Private property is a case in point. Before someone takes or destroys my belongings, I should be asked. Before someone is subjected to medical treatment, she should be allowed to make an informed decision. The same holds with regard to an individual's right to control any intrusion into her body, her physical integrity, her health, her sphere of sexual intimacy, as well as her private or family life. All these domains constitute protected spheres of autonomy or-in Kant's view-aspects of a person's initial freedom.

The peaceful coexistence of autonomous persons is premised on a legal order that carefully and precisely stakes out territories of decision-making claims. Any assessment about whether an individual's decision disregards the autonomy of another presupposes a concept of domains, where a person reserves the right to exercise discretion and into which others may not interfere without the concerned person's consent. The concept of human dignity as self-determination under an individual's own laws takes shape when it is spelled out in terms of demarcated areas of an individual's affairs, into which others may not arbitrarily interfere. Laws in general, and criminal laws in particular, aim at preserving such spheres of individual autonomy.

Kant's notion of human dignity is still a valid definition of a minimal condition of any normative form of coexistence: that persons respect one another as persons, who are able to understand moral reasoning and to, from their normative assessment, make decisions concerning their affairs. It is only this renunciation of any attempt to impose one's decision on others that opens a space to normative communication. This reminds us of the initial purpose of normativity, which is to offer an alternative to a social structure defined by power and force. If an individual does not renounce violence, what follows is not another moral concept, but amorality, the natural condition of the stronger controlling, directing and abusing the weaker. Kant's freedom defines the baseline of any form of moral coexistence, of a moral *Lebensform*.

Hence the ultimate objective—or *telos*—of Kantian moral and legal theory is the peaceful, in a broader sense non-violent, coexistence of autonomous individuals, endowed with practical reason, under a general law that respects the autonomy of all persons. Respect of human dignity entails the obligation of an autonomous person to recognise others as persons endowed with equal autonomy. If a person proposes generally binding legislation, she must present morally convincing arguments that are apt to induce others to autonomously agree to this legislation, and thus to adopt it for themselves. Persuasive moral reasoning is the only means of exerting influence on the will of others that can do so without coercion ("*nötigende Willkür*").

A state's laws define and uphold the conditions of peacefully coexisting persons granting one another the widest range of autonomy compatible with the equal claims of others, and this is the ultimate purpose of laws. Kant's views in this regard (1797/1968, p. 355; 1797/1996, pp. 123–124) reads as follows:

> Man kann sagen, daß diese allgemeine und fortdauernde Friedensstiftung nicht bloß einen Teil, sondern den ganzen Endzweck der Rechtslehre innerhalb der Grenzen der bloßen Vernunft ausmache; denn der Friedenszustand ist allein der unter *Gesetzen* gesicherte Zustand des Mein und Dein in einer Menge einander benachbarter Menschen, mithin die in einer Verfassung zusammen sind [...] Denn was kann mehr metaphysisch sublimiert sein, als eben diese Idee, welche [...] in kontinuierlicher Annäherung zum höchsten politischen Gut, zum ewigen Frieden, hinleiten kann.

> It can be said that establishing universal and lasting peace constitutes not merely a part of the doctrine of right but rather the entire final end of the doctrine of right within the limits of reason alone; for the condition of peace is the only condition in which what is mine and what is yours are secured under *laws* for a multitude of human beings living in proximity to one another and therefore under a constitution. [...] For what can be more metaphysically sublimated than this very idea, which [...] can lead to continual approximation to the highest political good, perpetual peace.

Kant has no tolerance of violence or manipulation, and in particular, he insists that there is no excuse for lying. Deliberately misleading another person and thus depriving her of the possibility to make an informed decision negates her dignity. It seems that the mere imagination of a liar tricking another person evoked strong feelings of disgust in Kant. On one occasion, Kant even claims (1797/1968, p. 429; 1797/1996, p. 182, emphasis by Kant):

> Die größte Verletzung der Pflicht des Menschen gegen sich selbst, bloß als moralisches Wesen betrachtet (die Menschheit in seiner Person), ist das Widerspiel der Wahrhaftigkeit: die *Lüge* [...] Die Lüge ist Wegwerfung und gleichsam Vernichtung seiner Menschenwürde. Ein Mensch, der selbst nicht glaubt, was er einem anderen [...] sagt, hat einen noch geringeren Wert, als wenn er bloß Sache wäre [...].

> The greatest violation of a human being's duty to himself regarded merely as a moral being (the humanity in his own person) is the contrary to truthfulness, *lying*, [...] By a lie a human being throws away and, as it were, annihilates his dignity as a human being. A human being who does not himself believe what he tells another [...] has even less worth than if he were a mere thing [...].

3.2.4 God's Voice as Innate Conscience

For Kant, freedom and autonomy is what we experience in our daily lives, and it appears that all individuals have a natural command of moral categories. Therefore, to Kant it is obvious that "all moral concepts have their seat and origin completely a priori in reason, and indeed in the commonest human reason, just as in that which is speculative in the highest measure" (1785/2012, p. 25).

Yet how can this unique human capacity be explained? So far, two questions have not been touched on: How can the fact of practical reason in humans, which Kant treats as obvious, be accounted for; and why is reason motivationally strong enough to allow us to control our natural inclinations and to stand up against the powerful normative claims that we are exposed to in our daily lives? Kant's system is based on the fact of freedom, which he declares to be inexplicable, and on the assumption that morally sound action is motivated by the respect for the law. However, these answers do not silence the above questions as to the sources and the forces of morality.

Kant's concept of conscience is illuminating in answering these questions. When analysing the motivational forces driving our morality, Kant observes that "conscience is not something that can be acquired, [...] rather, every human being, as a moral being, *has* a conscience within him originally" (1797/1996, p. 160).

In the Doctrine of Virtue, there is a section titled "On a Human Being's Duty to Himself as His Own Innate Judge". Here Kant states that an individual's conscience is innate and inescapable; it is indelibly stamped on a human's mind. Kant believes that human beings exist, from birth, in both the physical and the moral sphere, and it is by their conscience that they are tied to the latter. In a manner bringing Freud and Kafka to mind, Kant vividly—and somewhat terrifyingly—describes conscience as a drama staged by a superior and potentially overwhelming force at an inner court, where a subject's thoughts are supervised, charged, reprimanded or excused, a court presided by a judge whose "horrible voice" cannot be quieted (1797/1968, p. 438; 1797/1996, p. 189).

> Das Bewußtsein eines *inneren Gerichtshofes* im Menschen ("vor welchem sich seine Gedanken einander verklagen oder entschuldigen") ist das Gewissen. Jeder Mensch hat *Gewissen* und findet sich durch einen inneren Richter beobachtet, bedroht und überhaupt im Respekt (mit Furcht verbundener Achtung) gehalten, und diese über die Gesetze in ihm wachende Gewalt ist nicht etwas, was er sich selbst (willkürlich) macht, sondern es ist seinem Wesen einverleibt. Es folgt ihm wie sein Schatten, wenn er zu entfliehen gedenkt. Er kann sich zwar durch Lüste und Zerstreuungen betäuben, oder in Schlaf bringen, aber nicht vermeiden, dann und wann zu sich selbst zu kommen, oder zu erwachen, wo er alsbald die furchtbare Stimme desselben vernimmt. Er kann es in seiner äußersten Verworfenheit allenfalls dahin bringen, sich daran gar nicht mehr zu kehren, aber sie zu *hören*, kann er doch nicht vermeiden.

> Consciousness of an *internal court* in man ('before which his thoughts accuse or excuse one another') is **conscience**.

> Every human being has a conscience and finds himself observed, threatened, and, in general, kept in awe (respect coupled with fear) by an internal judge; and this authority watching over the law in him is not something that he himself (voluntarily) *makes*, but something incorporated in his being. It follows him like his shadow when he plans to escape. He can indeed stun himself or put himself to sleep by pleasures and distractions, but he cannot help coming to himself or waking up from time to time; and when he does, he hears at once its fearful voice. He can at most, in extreme depravity, bring himself to *heed* it no longer, but he still cannot help *hearing* it.

Kant (1788/1968, p. 129; 1788/2015, p. 104) leaves no doubt that it is a divine authority that makes its voice heard and that all moral duties reflect divine commandments:

> Auf solche Weise führt das moralische Gesetz durch den Begriff des höchsten Guts, als das Objekt und den Endzweck der reinen praktischen Vernunft, zur Religion, d. i. zur Erkenntnis aller Pflichten als göttlicher Gebote, nicht als Sanktionen, d. i. willkürliche, für sich selbst zufällige Verordnungen eines fremden Willens, sondern als wesentlicher Gesetze eines jeden freien Willens für sich selbst, die aber dennoch als Gebote des höchsten Wesens angesehen werden müssen [. . .].

> In this way the moral law leads through the concept of the highest good, as the object and final end of pure practical reason, *to religion, that is, to the recognition of all duties as divine commands, not as sanctions—that is, chosen and in themselves contingent ordinances of another's will*—but as essential *laws* of every free will in itself, which must nevertheless be regarded as commands of the supreme being [. . .].

Kant's assumption that a multitude of autonomous individuals can live together under generally binding laws while, at the same time, everyone acts only according to her own laws, on first sight, seems to aspire to square the circle. However, on a closer inspection, there is reason to suspect that Kant trusted in the success of the exercise, because individuals, while listening carefully to their personal conscience, in fact, like an orchestra, all follow the same score. It is in the end one and the same divine voice to which all are listening. What enables the peaceful coexistence of autonomous subjects is their involvement in normative dialogues with God allowing them to understand the divine laws.

In Kant's (1800, pp. 316–317) view, the task of legislation is not to *invent* right and wrong but only to *administer* what individuals *intuitively* understand to be the moral facts. Sophisticated legal theory cannot reach beyond, and indeed, tends to spoil rather than foster common moral sense.

That humans legislate is a fact and a necessity. Yet it is also their mission. Otherwise, why would humans have been endowed by divine providence with freedom and autonomy? Humans are chosen to be free and thus rise above all other animals, they are called on to legislate and to, like apprentices of the 'holy legislator', strive to fulfil their mission by perfecting the legislation on which they base their actions and social life. When talking about morality, Kant often uses the image of an empire with one ruler ('*Oberhaupt*') and many citizens. Humans are, in Kant's view, obliged to live up to their crucially important mission as 'assistant' legislators. Kant states that everyone is not only able to, but also *obliged* to command metaphysics of ethics, enabling her to understand her duties, as otherwise she will not be in a position to perform her role as a legislator. In a somewhat circular line of reasoning, Kant (1797/1982, p. 321, AA VI 217) posits:

> [. . .] so wird eine praktische Philosophie [. . .] eine Metaphysik der Sitten voraussetzen und bedürfen: d.i. eine solche zu haben ist selbst *Pflicht*, und jeder Mensch hat sie auch, obzwar gemeiniglich nur auf dunkle Art in sich; denn wie könnte er, ohne Prinzipien a priori, eine allgemeine Gesetzgebung in sich zu haben glauben?

Kant does not doubt that everyone inherently commands a 'general legislation', albeit not as a matter of sophisticated theory but of common sense (*'gemeiner Menschenverstand', 'gemeine Menschenvernunft'*). In the preface to his *Groundwork* Kant explains that a Critique of practical reason is not needed so urgently because "human reason, even in the commonest understanding, can easily be brought to a high measure of correctness and accuracy in moral matters" (1785b, p. 7). Only philosophers meet difficulties over trying to define what is right or wrong, while ordinary people know this, according to Kant, without hesitation every day, just as much as they can tell their right from their left hand (1788/2011, p. 197, AA V 155). Kant (1785/2008, p. 31, AA IV 404) praises and admires everyone's faculty of practical reason.

The way Kant (1797/1982, p. 618) deals with matters of education bears witness to Kant's belief that children discover reason as a faculty that rests within them. They learn to reason as they learn to drink or to crawl: children bring along the predisposition that only needs to be aroused by a teacher. Moral concepts exist in a prefabricated format ready to be elicited and used:

> Der Lehrer leitet durch Fragen den Gedankengang seines Lehrjüngers dadurch, daß er die Anlage zu gewissen Begriffen in demselben durch vorgelegte Fälle bloß entwickelt (er ist die Hebamme seiner Gedanken) [. . .].

Kant's comparison of the teacher to a midwife who supports the careful delivery of a notion that exists already in a close to finished state in the child and only waits to be brought to light, is telling, as it suggests that the teacher has little or no influence on the content of her student's morality. Ernst Bloch commented ironically that in Kant's view a child's morality only waits to be unwrapped (Bloch 1985, pp. 191–192). The idea of practical reason innate in humans leaves little room for society to shape and determine normative concepts.

In light of all this, the two questions asked at the outset of this section can be answered clearly. What explains practical reason is the fact that humans are endowed by their creator with this unique faculty; and it is veneration for their creator that inspires humans' admiration and respect for his laws. In Kant's terms (1793/1968, pp. 6–7):

> Wenn die Moral an der Heiligkeit ihres Gesetzes einen Gegenstand der größten *Achtung* erkennt, so stellt sie auf der Stufe der Religion an der höchsten, jene Gesetze vollziehenden Ursache einen Gegenstand der *Anbetung* vor, und erscheint in ihrer Majestät.

Obviously, Kant's conviction that our practical reason is implanted in our hearts by a divine father accounts for his unlimited admiration of moral laws and obligations, which sometimes takes on an enthusiastic and submissive tone, e.g. when he exclaims, "*Pflicht! Du erhabener, großer Name*" (1788/2011, p. 113), or when he repeatedly and emphatically characterises the moral law as holy ("*Das moralische Gesetz ist heilig* (*unverletzlich*)", 1788/2011, p. 114; similar 108, 165). Another time (1796/2013, p. 13) he refers to the law as the most holy thing and the apple of God's eye (suggesting that God is watching us through his own law).

Because of this adoration, Kant's application of the law is rigorous, inflexible and occasionally, when Kant resorts to radical examples, assumes even a slavish character, e.g. when he insists that one must not lie to a killer asking the way to his next victim (1797/1982a).

In conclusion, Kant's ethics is premised on a religious supplement, which Kant (1793/1968, p. 6) also considers *inevitable*, a conclusion that is synthetic, but still follows *a priori*:

> Moral also führt unumgänglich zur Religion, wodurch sie sich zur Idee eines machthabenden moralischen Gesetzgebers außer dem Menschen erweitert, in dessen Willen dasjenige Endzweck (der Weltschöpfung) ist, was zugleich der Endzweck des Menschen sein kann und soll.

3.2.5 Political Implications

This chapter started with a riddle. The concept of human dignity—subsequent to forerunners in Italian Renaissance—results from the political and ethical discourses of the late eighteenth century. Still, the concept became influential only after the Second World War. This prompts the question how to explain this delay.

It must be observed that the Kantian notion of human dignity, for several reasons, was not apt to perform the political function that the concept of human dignity is capable of fulfilling today. The first reason is that Kant's philosophy is based on a certain—protestant—religion and indeed, on a particular view of the relationship between God and individuals, which is not apt to serve as the foundation of ethics in a secular and pluralist society. The second reason is that because Kant's dignity is premised on autonomy, it is difficult to see how small children or persons with mental disabilities preventing them from understanding normative concepts would share in human dignity. Kant's notion of autonomy is challenging and even elitist; after all, how many people live up to the ideal of acting only on maxims that they have critically reviewed and deliberately adopted for themselves? Indeed, according to Kant, a person partakes in human dignity only to the extent that she takes autonomous decisions, decisions, that is, which respect the laws of practical reason and morality (Schüttauf 2012, p. 31).

Hence, the third and most fundamental objection to Kant's concept of dignity is that what Kant values is not so much the human individual, but the laws of morality. Kant appreciates the human individual only to the extent that the individual submits to the laws of morality and thus sets a good example to others. Kant's dignity is nothing but the dignity of a righteous person or rather the dignity of a person's righteousness. Kant puts forward (1785/1968, p. 401):

> Alle Achtung für eine Person ist eigentlich nur Achtung fürs Gesetz (der Rechtschaffenheit sc.), wovon jene uns das Beispiel gibt. [. . .] Alles moralische so genannte Interesse besteht lediglich in der Achtung fürs Gesetz.

Thus human dignity, as conceived by Kant, is not a quality that all humans possess indiscriminately and unconditionally, but rather a distinction that some, by submitting to the law, become deserving of to a certain extent for a certain while.

Humans partake in the exquisite sphere of dignity to the degree that and as long as they acquire and act on the ability to make autonomous decisions, decisions, that is, that abide by the laws of reason.

These attitudes—reverence for 'law and order' rather than for the human individual—explain Kant's political conservativism. Kant does not advocate democracy, thereby following Rousseau, whose argument that democracy is most prone to civil war impressed Kant, to whom peace and societal stability were so dear. Therefore, Kant also fiercely condemned any government's violent overthrow. Kant insists on the separation of legislative and executive power and submits that such a separation is not possible in a democracy, which is, in Kant's view, a majority's despotism. Even the idea of a constitution limiting the powers of the monarch, seems absurd to Kant (*'ein Unding'*, 1797/1968, p. 439).

Much of Kant's practical philosophy can be read as demonstrating the necessity of—and providing a justification for—governmental powers and the unconditional rule of law. Kant argues that there is no alternative to a state vested with the sanctioning powers of criminal justice and that individuals not only want to, but also are obliged to, submit to state power, allowing everyone to escape the threats of natural conditions so vividly and gloomily pictured by Kant. The social contract expresses the legitimacy and reasonableness of a government in general and of criminal justice in particular, which Kant (1797/1982, p. 430) takes pain to present as a strictly logical consequence of all subjects' practical reason.

In Kant's view, others pose a risk to us by their very nature, and it is hence not prudent to wait until they have acted on their attitudes (1797/1982, pp. 424–425). Occasionally, Kant maintains that in the initial situation, before a state is founded, we have a right to subject others to our domination. This is because in such a situation of anarchy, when everyone acts on her own will and when in case of a dispute a competent judge is not at hand, we are not safe from the violence of others (1797/1982, p. 430). After Kant has painted such a bleak picture of the initial stateless situation, it does not come as a surprise that he holds the state in high esteem and underlines that the very first duty of every individual is to ensure that the pre-historic, natural state is left behind and that a strong sanctioning power is established (1797/1982, p. 430). Kant (1797/1982, p. 434) posits that by submitting to the rule of law, humans do not sacrifice any of their freedom as it is by their practical reason that they are led to do so:

> [...] der Mensch [...] hat die wilde gesetzlose Freiheit gänzlich verlassen, um seine Freiheit überhaupt in einer gesetzlichen Abhängigkeit, d.i. in einem rechtlichen Zustande unvermindert wieder zu finden; weil diese Abhängigkeit aus seinem eigenen gesetzgebenden Willen entspringt.

Kant's rejection of democracy is linked to his failure to even recognise the fundamental philosophical and political puzzle created by moral pluralism. Democracy, as a peaceful dialogue and coexistence of competing moral concepts, solves a problem that Kant does not see. This is because Kant views practical reason as a natural gift that is essentially identical in all human beings—reflecting the same divine voice speaking to all humans directly and individually through their conscience. To Kant, society is a place of coexistence of free individuals seeking to equitably balance all interests at stake under one general law, and not a political arena where individuals who have radically diverse moral views and convictions have to, with great difficulties, agree on terms of their peaceful coexistence. While it is obviously Kant's intention to construct morality as enabling autonomous individuals to coexist peacefully, he, ironically, does not consider the most significant source of social rifts and conflict, namely moral disagreement and diversity.

Kant was right in finding that the individual person cannot avoid deciding on the normative basis of her action, and hence is impelled to legislate and thus to create for herself the normative basis of her agency. Yet he was wrong to believe that the problem of coordination and peace is solved by the fact that, in legislating, all listen to the same divine prompter. Without its religious foundation, Kant's ethics takes on a much more radical grounding. It is from this fundamental aporia that, in conditions of modernity, the normative construction and social integration of a polity and the legitimisation of its government have to depart. This requires a conclusive answer to the questions as to what explains and grounds human morality and its powerful forces. What needs to be clarified, first, is how practical reason makes its way into the human brain, and the explanation cannot take recourse to a conscience implanted in humans by a benevolent creator.

In a historical perspective, Kant's assumption that autonomy is anchored in human nature—and a divine will—fostered a gross underestimation of the level of indefiniteness and plasticity of human morality. While it may be reassuring to assume that everyone is guided by her conscience as a reliable source of a close to divine morality, this all too optimistic assumption, is from a political perspective, a dangerous mistake.

In this respect, it makes little difference whether morality is firmly rooted in practical reason and divine guidance or in moral sentiments, as long as morality is viewed as part of a universal and uniform human nature. From his sentimentalist and utilitarian assumptions, which are in radical opposition to the views held by Kant, Hume (2009, p. 56) arrived to conclusions that are very similar to Kant's:

> Mankind are so much the same, in all times and places, that history informs us of nothing new or strange in this particular. Its chief use is only to discover the constant and universal principles of human nature [...].

The concepts of dignity inherent in human nature due to humans' permanent dialogue with God—in Kant's perspective—or due to moral sentiments implanted in their genes—in a reading inspired by Hume—share the confidence in humans' safe possession of their outstanding and distinguishing moral quality. This reassuring belief in the immutability and reliability of human conscience that remains unaffected by societal discourses prompted an undue confidence in the firmness of individuals' moral judgment and a risk of undermining moral alert systems. These consequences showed when collectivist and particularistic moral doctrines denied everything that was dear to Kant or Hume and when the centrifugal political forces of societal and ideological diversity gradually disintegrated the normative fabric of Western societies. One of the many bitter lessons of the twentieth century is that human morality is, to a surprising and disturbing degree, undecided, plastic, malleable and hence prone to manipulation, distortion, misdirection and abuse by political powers capable of large-scale indoctrination and propaganda. Confidence in and reliance upon individuals' natural morality and autonomy rendered liberal democracies defenceless against the formative powers of planfull and systematic nationalist and racist mass indoctrination.

Hence, an appropriate understanding of human dignity cannot take Kantian ethics as its point of departure or any other moral theory that founds human dignity on a capacity inherent in humans, and for two reasons. Firstly that such approaches are, in a political perspective, dangerously oversimplistic and naive. Secondly, from an ethical point of view, because any attempt to construct human dignity as acknowledging an outstanding quality of humans by which they excel compared to all other animals meets difficulties in capturing all humans, including infants, senile dements, or coma patients. This objection must be raised to any concept that grounds dignity in a human ability or capacity. For example, James Griffin founds human dignity on personhood and personhood on agency. "A person is a bearer of human rights in virtue of being a normative agent" (2009, p. 41). The word "human means, roughly, a functioning human agent" (2009, p. 35). But such a concept comes with a risk of excluding all humans that do not-or not yet, or no longer-"function" as human agents. Jean Hampton, arguing along Kantian lines, posits that we are obliged to respect our fellow human beings "insofar as each human being is an autonomous, rational being" (2007, p. 117), which excludes, for instance, infants and certain categories of persons with mental disabilities. Julian Nida-Rümelin suggests to found human dignity on self-respect, but observes himself that infants do not respect themselves, and hence Nida-Rümelin, like many others, ends up with a concept of human dignity for some (2009, p. 255).

If humans are exceptional, then this is in respect of the degree to which they depend on others and in respect of the remarkable fact that they have turned this dependence into a strength by developing unique forms of close sociality and cooperation. In the end, the concept of human dignity does not reflect the grandeur of homo sapiens, but humans' exceptional neediness and reliance on others. This becomes clear as soon as one takes a closer look into what actually constitutes an individual's self-awareness and agency, on which Kantian autonomy is premised.

3.3 Body, Soul and Agency

To allow for clearer differentiations between humans as living organisms and persons as social entities, which underlie Kant's distinction between *homo phaenomenon* and *homo noumenon*, forms of consciousness need to be distinguished. This will also allow an understanding of where and how 'languaging'—the use of symbolic languages—as the basic form of human cooperation comes in.

3.3.1 Orders of Consciousness

Edelman (2004) coined the terms primary and higher-order consciousness. He explores the mechanisms of mappings, concept formation and short-term memory, which allow simple perceptual categorisations, of which many animals are capable. They can carry out plans and react appropriately to situations based on their categorical memory (Edelman 2004, p. 98). Primary consciousness emerges 'as a result of re-entrant interactions between brain areas mediating value-category memory and those mediating perceptual categorization', interactions which enable the construction of a manageable present scene to which the organism responds effectively (Edelman 2004, p. 115). Primary consciousness is "not self-reflective, it is not verbalized, and it lasts only during a present moment that corresponds to 'now'" (Stern 2000, p. xvii).

However, compared to humans, other animals lack what Edelman calls a socially and linguistically defined 'nameable self' and a concept of the past and the future (Edelman 2004, pp. 97–98, 116, 2006, p. 38). Although they exist and act in situations, they do not view themselves as being and acting in situations. Hence, other animals cannot account for their behaviour, as this faculty is premised on the mastery of a symbolic language, which presupposes a community of users. Only persons as members of communities operating propositional languages command an episodic memory and are aware of themselves as identical over time and as situated in natural and social contexts. Only humans possess a narrative or autobiographical self (Stern 2000, pp. xxiii–xxv). "Self-consciousness, awareness, mind—these are phenomena that take place in language. Therefore, as such they take place only in the social domain" (Maturana and Varela 1987/1998, p. 230).

Hence, what marks the difference between humans and other primates is the particular ability of humans to share symbols as conventional representations of the outside world. This ability of brains to link their processes to those occurring in other brains by means of acoustic or visual signals makes language-based communication and cooperation possible.

By their linguistic abilities, persons as social entities become free from 'bondage to the present' (Edelman 2004, p. 118). The concept of a lasting and continuous social identity enables persons to enter into future-oriented commitments—like taking out a credit loan—to accept responsibility for their past conduct—like a criminal offence—and even to foresee that in some future they may be held to account for action which they are just about to engage in.

The point is that, while bodies change constantly, future and past actions are attributable to the same person as a cultural and social identity that is construed as persisting invariably over time. The person as a normative construct—a symbol—is not affected by changes in the empirical world, unless norms so decide. (To give an example, even if Max Frisch's *Stiller* underwent dramatic and traumatic experiences abroad and could rightly claim that he is, in a very significant way, no longer the person he was before, he is nevertheless, from a social and legal point of view, still *'er'*, Stiller, and hence has to meet the obligations into which he allegedly entered a long time ago before leaving Switzerland.)

A crucial aspect of this liberation from the present is the ability of a person to reflect on what she is about to do and why, including her impulses, desires and other motivation. This is the ability to, in a way, step back and look at oneself, and one's present and future behaviour 'from a distance' before taking action. It allows persons to—instead of relatively blindly reacting to stimulating situations—consider and censor in advance their future conduct based on a reflection of reasons in favour and against courses of optional conduct.

In philosophy, agency as the capacity to critically assess one's own conduct has been highlighted as a crucial point of departure when it comes to explaining the particular human faculty of reason. Korsgaard (2008, p. 4) argues that only we humans are aware of the potential grounds of our actions and that this awareness is the source of our reason, as we are compelled to decide on the validity of the grounds militating against or in favour of action.

Neither this particular reflective distance nor the urge to take a decision comes to us from 'deep within'. We learn to reflect as we learn to use a language. Reflection is a language-based process and hence premised on higher-order consciousness. Children start with a limited faculty to resist temptations, but over the period of childhood, while they learn to command the language of their society, their ability to control impulsive behaviours improves continuously and enables them to develop into responsible agents (Haidt 2001, p. 823).

3.3.2 The 'I'

Consciousness is not something that happens to an organism but denotes an activity. Consciousness is thinking (Hofstadter 2008, pp. 275–280). First-order-thinking creates a symbolic representation of the world as an environment. Second-order-thinking—or second-order consciousness—creates within this representation, others and oneself as thinking and acting and the world as the object of our agency. The subject has access to the object only within the sphere, in which the subject exists, in the sphere, that is, of communication. Hence, the subject encounters the object only as a symbolic representation, as the construction of an object constructed as existing not only in communication, but also in an environment that is inferred, not encountered.

One can be held to account for what one considers and for what one ignores. Consciousness is an activity, and higher-order consciousness can even be considered as responsible action. Hence, it makes perfect sense to ask another person to think carefully about something, for instance, what she will do next.

Thinking—consciousness—did not evolve primarily to enable human beings to contemplate their specific situation or the world in general, but to act and to survive based on the ability to construct and, on the basis of this construction, control those parts of the environment on which their survival is premised. To grasp one's situation means to command a model of reality—an interior analogue of the exterior world—that is complex and structurally similar enough to what it models to allow an actor to take appropriate decisions and to survive. While primary consciousness puts organisms in a position to react blindly and inflexibly to their environment, higher consciousness enables fully fledged agency based on a model-based critical reflection on one's situation and on a hypothetical assessment of the consequences of one's own possible action. The categories applied by higher consciousness are symbolic, "our thinking always takes place by means of some sort of symbols" (Mead 1934, p. 146). They developed and improved over many generations, becoming more and more powerful in modelling the environment of humans and enabling them to predict the results of various possible courses of their action. Higher consciousness is the specific form of human cooperation and coexistence and reflects the compelling requirements of human existence; "consciousness can never be anything else than conscious existence, and the existence of men is their actual life-process" (Marx and Engels 1970, p. 47).

Agency is premised on exercising control of one's situation. This becomes most visible in exceptional circumstances when individuals lose this control to overpowering forces. To situations of traumatic stress—e.g. in situations of sexual abuse, car accidents or war experiences—the brain can react by a fragmentation—or compartmentalisation—of the self that is referred to as dissociation. This can—in cases of secondary dissociation—entail that the higher functions of critically observing and reflecting on one's action are separated from routine and largely automated reactions (Fischer and Riedesser 2009; Putnam 1989; van der Kolk et al. 2000, b; Wilson et al. 2001). Splitting into multiple roles—one blindly acting and one observing and contemplating as from a distance—mirrors the fact that, because of perceived loss of control, observations and reflections cannot perform their function of steering a person's conduct. Hence, the observing and reflecting 'I', incapable of exercising control, disintegrates from the 'I' steering one's action (Mead 1934, p. 146).

War reports sadly offer a wealth of examples. For instance, vivid descriptions of such experiences appear in a detailed documentation of the Gallipoli campaign during World War I drawn up by Steel and Hart (1995). In an attempt to capture the Ottoman capital of Constantinople, British troops in April 1915 landed on the peninsula Gallipoli, which led to a particularly fierce battle. The authors quote extensively from diary entries, letters and other written accounts reported by British soldiers, which frequently relate strange experiences of seemingly being detached from their situation and body. As an example in point, the authors report the comments of Lieutenant Leslie Grant who noted down (Steel and Hart 1995, p. 359):

> I can't bring myself to believe in the reality of things here, it is as if you were watching a cinema show or children playing at soldiers. I feel inclined to treat the whole thing as a big joke.

Another young officer concisely describes one situation as follows (Steel and Hart 1995, pp. 282–283):

> My body and soul seemed to be entirely divorced, even to the extent that I felt that I no longer inhabited my body. My shell at the bidding of purely automatic forces, over which I had no control, ran hither and thither collecting men, hacked its way through the scrub with a rifle, directed the fire of my platoon and in short struggled with all the duties which I had

> been taught to perform. But my mind was a distinct and separate entity. I seemed to hover at some height above my own body and observe its doings and the doings of others with a sort of detached interest. I speculated idly on the possibility of my body being hit and thought it probably would be. I wondered if it would be in the head, round which so many bullets seemed to be flying; I felt no fear, only a mild sense of curiosity. Meanwhile my body strove and swore and sweated.

Such an experience of being detached from one's body and its activities is difficult to integrate in one's autobiographical memory as it undermines an individual's trust in the controllability of her world and the confidence of being master of her body and situation, a confidence on which all agency and accountability are premised (Fiedler 2002). A meaningful autobiography presupposes the assumption of agency. Otherwise, what remains is the description of a body reacting instinctively to its environment. Being forced to acknowledge the fact that one's survival can, in any moment, change into a matter that lies completely beyond one's sphere of control discomfortingly challenges an individual's sense of being the master and maker of her life, rather than the plaything of obscure overpowering and determining forces. Such experiences challenge the integration of a self and the sense of being a person with a meaningful and consistent biography, which because of its meaning is worth living.

3.4 Fichte and Human Dignity as the Right to be a Person and to Partake in Human Culture

It was mentioned above that Kant saw practical reason as inherent in human nature and that this even relates to the contents of moral laws, which Kant believed to be fundamentally the same in all humans. Hence, the problem of how society can integrate radically diverse moral concepts does not arise in Kantian ethics. However, Kant's vision of a society based on individuals' autonomy and mutual respect takes a critical turn under conditions of pluralism. The more radically individuals' moral views diverge, the more challenging becomes the political task of a society's normative integration.

For Kant, humans participate in culture from their beginning. The task of parents and teachers is restricted to making children aware of what they already know, at least in principle. Kantian education is about supporting children in awakening to a preformed consciousness and reason. As a plant develops into a certain predetermined shape, individuals develop into moral persons.

Obviously, Kant's views on the matter are not compatible with an updated assessment of cultural diversity and evolution. It is evident that an individual in a tribal society 'awakes' to a consciousness that is fundamentally different from the consciousness that an adult person commands in a diverse Western democracy. If any moral substance was inherent in all humans, the fundamentally different views between, for instance a Chewong, believing that, importantly, you must not laugh in the presence of animals, and modern morality, taking no issue with laughing when animals are around, cannot be explained. In the twenty-first century, the idea of human reason as a universal capacity firmly anchored in the human genome cannot be defended.

Therefore, to preserve essential elements of Kant's philosophy, it is necessary to reconstruct the system of his ethics on an updated and secular basis. The idea of moral laws implanted in human nature by a benevolent creator cannot serve as the founding assumption of a modern society. One must start then from the question of how practical reason makes its way into human brains—if not by God addressing us through our conscience—or, looking at the same issue from the side of individuals, how humans have access to the sphere of culture and normativity.

Such a reconstruction must preserve Kant's plausible intuition of humans existing in two distinct spheres. Humans can be conceived as living organisms, as 'human bodies'. Yet humans can also be meaningfully described as a cultural species and in fact as the only such species. Their behaviour is premised not on their genes alone, but also on the social and cultural norms of their community, which are handed and develop from one generation to the next. To maintain peaceful coexistence and cooperation, humans, living collectively in large groups and societies, depend strongly on guidance and coordination by means of social rules and on shared notions, concepts and assumptions. Through their communication, humans are constantly engaged in constructing a common model of the social and natural world within which they live together, as well as of themselves as persons. They "put a construction upon the events" through which they live, to adopt a phrase of Geertz (1973a, p. 45).

However, if practical reason and moral autonomy are not inherent qualities of human beings, they cannot serve as the foundation of universal human dignity. When it comes to explaining dignity, humans' moral autonomy and their participation in culture would intuitively suggest themselves as relevant aspects. However, once traditional religious accounts are left behind, the empirical source and contingent nature of these qualities becomes an issue.

3.4.1 The Dignity of All Who Carry a Human Face

Fichte's concept of human dignity paves the way towards an understanding of human dignity that reflects, not a quality inherent in human beings, but human being's specific dependency on a human community, marking the particular situation into which the human individual is born.

In 1794, before leaving Zürich to take up his new position as professor at the University in Jena, Fichte gave a brief farewell-lecture titled 'On the Dignity of Man' (*Über die Würde des Menschen*). While this lecture was meant as a conclusion and summary of his teachings on the Science of Knowledge, Fichte warns in advance that it is not part of his dry enquiries, but an expression of the enraptured sentiments that follow his enquiries ("*Ausguss der hingerissensten Empfindung* nach *der Untersuchung*"). It appears that this lecture was of utmost importance to Fichte, as he concludes by emphasising that he would wish to be remembered by this lecture.

Fichte bases his theory of dignity on a notion of man that, on the one hand, serves to denote all individuals who—in a biologic and genetic sense—possess 'a human face'. On the other, being human implies humanity as the very moral quality that allows for human sociality, including such attitudes as kindness, mercifulness, benevolence, compassion, solidarity with, and sympathy for other human beings. By short-circuiting the descriptive and the normative, the notion of man seemingly evades the question as to the worthiness of humans—suggesting that those who are human (*menschlich*)—in a biologic sense—are worthy because it is good to be human (*menschlich*)—now in a moral sense. The more human(e) an individual is, the better. Enthusiastically, Fichte declares (1794a, p. 414, 1794b):

> [...] je mehr einer Mensch ist, desto tiefer und ausgebreiteter wirkt er auf Menschen; und was den wahren Stempel der Menschlichkeit trägt, wird von der Menschheit nie verkannt; jedem reinen Ausflusse der Humanität schließt sich auf jeder menschliche Geist, und jedes menschliche Herz.

> [...] the more a man is a man, the more deeply and extensively does he influence men; whatsoever carries the stamp of pure humanity will never be misapprehended by mankind; every human mind, every human heart opens to each pure outflow of humanity.

In these many usages of *'Mensch'*—*,Menschheit'*, *,Menschlichkeit'*, *,Humanität'*—descriptive and normative meanings flow inseparably into one another. This indicates that in Fichtean ethics, the human being is the point of departure, at least in the sense that it is only the human being who creates the law and recreates the entire universe in culture according to her law. Nature receives from the human being her new, brighter design.

The Ego as the source of practical reason—of 'spirit'—creates the phenomenal world by imposing her order on chaotic, dead and amorphous matter, thus bringing nature to life. What is striking here—like in many other instances of Fichtean philosophy—is his radical normative constructivism. It is the acting and observing Ego that generates order and harmony, as far as her acting and observing reach into a constructed object world (1794a, p. 412, 1794b).

> Erst durch das Ich kommt Ordnung und Harmonie in die tote, formlose Masse. Allein vom Menschen aus verbreitet sich Regelmäßigkeit rund um ihn herum bis an die Grenze seiner Beobachtung, – und wie er dieses weiter vorrückt, wird Ordnung und Harmonie weiter vorgerückt. Seine Beobachtung [...] bringt Einheit in die unendliche Verschiedenheit.

> Only through it [the Ego] is order and harmony brought into the dead, formless matter. From man alone does regularity proceed, and extend around him to the boundary of his perception; and in proportion as he extends this boundary are order and harmony also extended. His observation [...] brings unity into this infinite variety.

Hence, what accounts for dignity is the fact that any human being is a member of the species that *collectively* creates a world in culture, including themselves as selves. *Jointly*, humans build *one spirit in many bodies*. While Kantian reason is the quality of the individual, spirit in Fichtean philosophy is the achievement of an entire species. By the collaboration of the collectivity, the spirit of its members continuously draws closer to the ideal of humanity and of ever-higher moral standards. This ideal forms the centre of the collective project (1794a, p. 414, 1794b).

> Um den höheren Menschen herum schließen die Menschen einen Kreis, in welchem derjenige sich dem Mittelpunkte am meisten nähert, der die größere Humanität hat. Ihre Geister streben und ringen sich zu vereinigen, und nur Einen Geist in mehreren Körpern zu bilden. Alle sind Ein Verstand und Ein Wille, und stehen da als Mitarbeiter an dem großen einzigmöglichen Plane der Menschheit.

> Around the nobler man his fellow-beings form a circle, in which he approaches nearest to the centre who has the greatest humanity. Their souls strive and labour to unite with each other to form but one soul in many bodies. All are one reason and one will, and appear as co-labourers in the great, only possible destination of mankind.

The somewhat opaque formula of humans creating one soul in multiple bodies will be clarified later. However, it is obvious that Fichtean ethics does not focus on the autonomous individual in splendid isolation, but is rather like an ellipse with two strictly interdependent foci, one on human culture as the unique and defining project of humankind, one on the human being as a member of humanity. While the evolution of culture is premised on the contributions of human beings, the latter are valued as members of the species that creates culture and exists—next to its biological lives—in the sphere of culture. Every human being represents the species that creates culture.

Similar to Kant, Fichte's philosophy builds on a strict dualism of the biologic and the phenomenal—cultural or spiritual—sphere. The spirit liberates itself from the body—its needs and drives—and only returns to the body to control and use it as an instrument to its ends (1794a, p. 414). The intellectual—higher—human being is, because of her liberation from her body, entirely self-determined and self-sufficient. "*Er ist schlechthin durch sich selbst [...] und aus eigener Kraft*" (1794a, p. 414). Social norms oppose humans' natural inclinations, including inertia. They prohibit or command. Thus, culture operates as a limiting counterforce to nature, including humans' biological drives, instincts and needs. In Fichte's terms, what defines practical reason is the restraining of natural forces and drives by means of language and culture ("*die Mäßigung der Kraft durch Begriffe*", Fichte 1796a, p. 45).

Fichte's emphasis rests on unrestricted, unconditional universality of human dignity as an entitlement of all who carry 'a human face'; he stresses that all human beings are equals brought by their belonging to the species whose members refer to themselves as 'I'. This unity of humankind spans not only continents, but also times. Fichte maintains that human culture develops gradually, and thus progressively approximates an ideal of pure spirit. However, all stages of this evolution are necessary steps within the same collective project, all rungs of the same ladder. Fichte addresses the indigenous people of Patagonia—visited in the 1760s by John Byron and James Cook—as representing an early phase of the development of human culture and as contributing their share to its development, as later stages build on previous steps of cultural and political development. Thus, Fichte bridges the distance between early—band, tribal, segmentary—and higher developed societies. He declares his solidarity as a human being with slaves growing sugarcane under the whip of their masters, treated like animals, and—what is more remarkable—even with the most corrupt and base villains. (This solidarity with villains has consequential effects on Fichte's theory of punishment, as will be explored in Chap. 4). All humans are united by the bonds of brotherhood (1794a, p. 415, 1794b).

> Das ist der Mensch; das ist jeder, der sich sagen kann: *Ich bin Mensch*. [. . .] Das ist jeder, der mir sagen kann: *Ich bin*. – Wo du auch wohnest, du, der du nur Menschenantlitz trägst; – ob du auch noch so grenzend mit dem Tiere, unter dem Stecken des Treibers Zuckerrohr pflanzest, oder ob du an des Feuerlandes Küsten dich an der nicht durch dich entzündeten Flamme wärmst, [. . .] oder ob du mir der verworfenste, elendste Bösewicht scheinest – du bist darum doch, was ich bin; denn du kannst mir sagen: Ich bin. Du bist darum doch mein Gesell und mein Bruder.

> Such is man; such is everyone who can say to himself: I am man. [. . .] Such is everyone who can say to me: I am. Wherever thou mayest live, thou, who carryest but a human face; whether thou plantest sugar-cane under the rod of the overseer, as yet scarcely distinguishable from the brute creation; or whether thou warmest thyself on the shores of the Fireland at the flame, which thou didst not kindle, [. . .] or whether thou appearest to me the most miserable and degraded villain, thou art, nevertheless, what I am; for thou canst say to me: I am. Thou art, nevertheless, my comrade and my brother.

Hence, it is the gradual creation of culture—of spirit—that distinguishes humankind; and it is all humans' membership of humankind and involvement in the one grand project of creating a truly human culture that unites humanity. From a historical perspective, it is worth noting that the Nazis perceived and quoted Fichte's formula of the fundamental equality of all who carry a human face as the purest expression of the liberalism, universalism and cosmopolitanism that they so fiercely refuted (Stourzh 2009, pp. 138–141).

*3.4.2 Fichte's Theory of Calling (*Aufforderung*)*

In marked contrast to the Kantian self-sufficient autonomous person, Fichte's assumption of humankind as the species creating one spirit in many bodies posits the human being in strong dependency on a human community. To show what Fichte means by this, two aspects need to be emphasised: firstly, the dynamic, evolving character of an individual's personhood and agency, secondly the crucial role performed by society in the development of an individual's personhood. Kant views dignity as a more or less fixed quality of autonomous persons, Fichte as referring to qualities that can, under favourable conditions, develop in interactions with others. In George Herbert Mead's words, Fichte's self is no longer "a soul" that is "born into the world with the body" and "endowed by a divine fiat", but rather "a certain process, something that is going on", and the "first characteristic of this process which Fichte laid stress upon was that it involved a not-self" (Mead 1936, p. 88). In Mead's own theory, this aspect is prominent. "The self is something which has a development; it is not initially there, at birth, but arises in the process of social experience and activity, that is, develops in the given individual as a result of his relations to that process as a whole and to other individuals within that process" (Mead 1934, p. 135).

What, hence, Fichte highlights is an individual's existential—physical and mental—dependence on being initiated and integrated in a community of humans and that, without such a process of assimilation, a human being would never have a chance to develop as a person and to participate in social life. In Fichte's own words (1796/1971, p. 39; 1796/2000, p. 37):

> Der Mensch [...] wird nur unter Menschen ein Mensch; und da er nichts Anderes sein kann, denn ein Mensch, und gar nicht sein würde, wenn er dies nicht wäre - sollen überhaupt Menschen sein, so müssen mehrere sein. [...] Der Begriff des Menschen ist sonach gar nicht Begriff eines Einzelnen, denn ein solcher ist undenkbar, sondern der einer Gattung. The human being [...] becomes a human being only among human beings; and since the human being can be nothing other than a human being and would not exist at all if it were not this - it follows that, if there are to be human beings at all, there must be more than one. [...] Thus the concept of the human being is not the concept of an individual - for an individual human being is unthinkable - but rather the concept of a species.

The reason why Fichte conceives the human being as dependent on a community is that an individual's consciousness is premised on a reflexive view of herself that is by far too complex to be developed by the individual in isolation. In order to arrive at an idea of herself as an accountable and autonomous agent, the individual depends on others who implant in her the seeds of reflexive consciousness and accountable agency by calling on her to act. However, in order to understand that she is called on, the individual has first to grasp that there exist persons outside of her who by calling on her act in a deliberate, purposeful manner. Hence, what we are brought to assume is (Fichte 1796/1971, p. 33; 1796/2000, pp. 31–32).

> [...] ein *Bestimmt-Sein des Subjekts zur Selbstbestimmung*, eine Aufforderung an dasselbe, sich zu einer Wirksamkeit zu entschließen. [...] das Selbstbewusstsein, dessen Möglichkeit erklärt werden soll, [...] kann nicht anders begriffen werden, denn als eine bloße Aufforderung des Subjekts zum Handeln. So gewiss daher das Subjekt dasselbe begreift, so gewiss hat es den Begriff von seiner eigenen Freiheit und Selbsttätigkeit, und zwar als einer von außen gegebenen. Es bekommt den Begriff seiner freien Wirksamkeit, nicht als etwas, das im gegenwärtigen Momente ist, denn das wäre ein wahrer Widerspruch, sondern als etwas, das im künftigen sein soll. [...] the subject's being-determined as *its being-determined to be self-determining*, i.e. as a summons to the subject, calling on it to resolve to exercise its efficacy. [...] it is the possibility of self-consciousness that is supposed to be explained. [...] Thus as surely as the subject comprehends the object, so too does it possess the concept of its own freedom and self-activity, and indeed as a concept given to it from the outside. It acquires the concept of its own free efficacy, not as something that exists in the present moment (for that would be a genuine contradiction), but rather as something that *ought* to exist in the future.

Norbert Elias' sociology offers an elaboration of these aspects of Fichtean philosophy. Elias, like Fichte, departs from the societal formation of individuals. As Elias puts it in an article titled "The society of individuals", concluded in 1939 (1939, p. 20):

> Half consciously, half unconsciously, most people carry about with them even today a peculiar myth of creation. They imagine that in the 'beginning' a single person first appeared on earth and was then joined afterwards by other people. [...] It seems as if

> grown-up people, in thinking about their origins, involuntarily lose sight of the fact that they themselves and all adults came into the world as little children. Over and over again, in the scientific myths of origin no less than in the religious ones, they feel impelled to imagine: In the beginning was a single human being, who was an adult.

Against this myth, Norbert Elias focuses on the fact that the biological and social existence of humans is premised on communicative processes of socialisation and hence on the fact that individuals are born into groups (1939, p. 21):

> Each individual is born into a group of people who were there before him. Not only that: each individual is by nature so constituted that he needs other people who were there before him in order to be able to grow up. One of the basic conditions of human existence is the simultaneous presence of a number of interrelated people. And if, to symbolize one's own self-image, one needs a myth of origin, it seems time to revise the traditional myth: In the beginning, one might say, was not a single person, but several people who lived with each other, who caused each other joy and pain as we do, who came into being through each other and passed away into each other, as we do, a social unit large or small.

Thus Fichte's theory of *Aufforderung* calls our attention to the social preconditions of a person's saying 'I am' and to the complex situation in which this becomes possible. The human being is necessarily affected by this situation before she can say 'I am' and for that reason does not witness this situation, because 'my retrospective position casts doubt on whether or not I can describe this situation at all, since strictly speaking, I was not present for the process, and I myself seem to be one of its various effects' (Butler 2015, p. 2).

Previously, it was believed that a child growing up in solitude would nevertheless command enough words to express her thoughts (Hallpike 2004, p. 54). However, there is a plethora of empirical indications to the contrary, mostly resulting from studies of so-called 'wolf-children', brought up by animals from early infancy. According to Hallpike, such children "do not develop any distinctively human characteristics at all, either of intellect or personality," rather, when they are found as adults, the "general profile that emerges is one of complete absence of speech [...] and the restriction of reasoning to that of a child of about two or three" (Hallpike 2004, p. 55). Hallpike concludes (2004, p. 55):

> Social life is not something which is added on to the life of the individual: without social life there *is* no individual life at all, in a human sense, but only that of a rather ineffectual animal. Human rationality is only a potential that, without an upbringing among people can never materialize, and in this sense the individual is inescapably a social being.

Hence, humans are essentially social beings. They only develop as individual persons within communities. In this vein, Wolff (1969, pp. 28–29) observed:

> The influence of society upon the individual is primarily positive, formative, supportive – indeed, indispensably so. The child who grows to manhood outside a social group becomes an animal, without language, knowledge, the capacity to reason, or even the ability to love and hate as other men do. As the infant is reared, he internalizes the behaviour patterns and evaluative attitudes of that immediate circle of adults whom the sociologists call his primary group. [...] Throughout life, the individual seeks approval from his 'significant others,' willing to submit even to death rather than violate the mores he has learned. [...] Without that inheritance, the individual is exactly nothing – he has no organized core of personality into which his culture has not penetrated. The most thorough radical is the

> merest reflection of the society against which he rebels. So we are all naturally, irremediably, beneficially, bound up with the social groups in which we locate ourselves and live out our lives.

This is precisely what Fichte—at the end of the eighteenth century—as well as George Herbert Mead and Norbert Elias—in the first half of the twentieth—aimed at. In the latter's words (1939, pp. 21–22):

> [...] it is only in society that the small child with its malleable and relatively undifferentiated mental functions is turned into a more complex being. Only in relation to other human beings does the wild, helpless creature which comes into this world become the psychologically developed person with the character of an individual and deserving the name of an adult human being. Cut off from such relations he grows at best into a semi-wild human animal. He may grow up bodily; in his psychological make-up he remains like a small child. Only if he grows up in a group does the small human being learn connected speech. Only in the society of other, older people does he gradually develop a specific kind of far-sightedness and instinct control. And which language he learns, which pattern of instinct control and adult make-up develops in him, depends on the [history and the] structure of the group in which he grows up, and finally on his position in this group and the formative process it entails. (translation corrected, A.D.)

Hence, to develop as a person commanding reflexive self-consciousness, a human being depends on a society of humans, as such reflectivity is premised on linguistic skills. The ability, so dear to Fichte, to say 'I am' is premised on participation in a language community, on a child being taught the use of a language by others who call on her to act and to cooperate and who, by their calling, initiate the child as a member of a community of language users (FRA 2012, p. 21). Without this initiation, a human being would not achieve a level of consciousness exceeding the mental abilities of non-human primates.

Language usage cannot be explained as the accomplishment of a brain or of a number of interacting brains but only—in phylogeny—as the product of long-term cultural evolution and—in ontogeny—as the result of a child's education. It is solely in interaction with culturally competent others that individuation and the experience of an autonomous self and of agency can emerge (Singer 2002, pp. 73–74; Stern 2000). "Consciousness is, therefore, from the very beginning a social product, and remains so as long as men exist at all" (Marx and Engels 1970, p. 51).

The elementary units of culture—its atoms—are processes of communication, in which human individuals construct rules of conduct, societal networks and themselves as their members. What the first calling on the infant initiates is a process of 'formatting', of working out the most basic normative concepts—such as persons, action, an object world on which persons act, decisions, sanctions and accountability—thus creating a 'deep structure' on which the 'surface structure' of concrete social norms can build. The person—or the 'subject', that which emerges when an infant is subjected to human culture—is a normative category that implies agency, and agency implies accountability and a normative order. Hence the person only develops within a normative order as its element. As Judith Butler puts it (2015, p. 5):

> In a theoretical vein, we can, following a general Foucaultion line, simply state that the subject is produced through norms [...]. They condition and form us, and yet they are

> hardly finished with that work once we start to emerge as thinking and speaking beings. Rather, they continue to act according to an iterative logic that ends for any of us only when life ends, though the life of norms, of discourse more generally, continues on with a tenacity that is quite indifferent to our finitude.

Later Butler observes (2015, p. 6):

> I do not arrive in the world separate from a set of norms that are lying in wait for me, already orchestrating my gender, race, and status, working on me, even as a pure potential, prior to my first wail. So norms, conventions, institutional forms of power, are already acting prior to any action I may undertake, prior to there being an "I" who thinks of itself from time to time as the seat or source of its own action.

Both society and the person are established in culture by iterative and recursive processes of communication and discourse. In these processes, normative order emerges as well as persons existing within the normative order that they create and reproduce by their acts of communication. Persons are the source and the result of their actions, which, therefore, can only be conceptualised as recursive loops binding together persons in networks and continuous flows of communication. In an article titled "Cultural Anthropology and Psychiatry", Edward Sapir in 1932 expressed this idea in the following terms (2015, p. 515):

> The true locus, however, of these processes which, when abstracted into a totality, constitute culture is not in a theoretical community of human beings known as society, for the term 'society' is itself a cultural construct which is employed by individuals who stand in significant relations to each other in order to help them in the interpretation of certain aspects of their behaviour. The true locus of culture is in the interactions of specific individuals and, on the subjective side, in the world of meanings which each one of these individuals may unconsciously abstract for himself from his participation in these interactions.

In short: Culture is the use of symbols in concrete processes of communication. As symbols do not exist in isolation, but only in complex systems called languages, culture can also be defined as the entirety of usages of language, as 'languaging'. Awareness, self-consciousness and what we refer to as the 'mind' or 'spirit' are processes that occur in language and hence only in culture, or what Maturana and Varela call 'the social domain' (Maturana and Varela 1987/1998, p. 230). The social domain is distinct from the biological domain, in which human bodies, and human brains, exist. However, the communicative processes creating culture supervene and hence are premised on biological brain processes. While the meaning of shared symbols is processed in the social domain, signifiers are processed in the biological domain. Language, higher-order consciousness, and awareness are, in the Kantian sense, phenomenal properties that are ontologically independent of physical properties, on which they empirically—naturally—supervene (Chalmers 1996, pp. 124–126). In an evolutionary perspective, culture and a specific organisation of a surprisingly indistinct and plastic human brain coevolve as a matter of gene-culture coevolution. The maintenance of culture is therefore premised on trans-generational transfers, based on various mechanisms of social learning (Boyd and Richerson 1985, 2005; Richerson and Boyd 2004).

Persons cannot remember the early interactions that led to their individuation and primary socialisation, because these interactions precede the development of an episodic memory and of a lasting narrative self. This early-childhood amnesia accounts for the particular quality of our reflective consciousness, which we experience as resting deep inside us and as an indisputable matter of course (Singer 2002, pp. 74–75). The powerful and intrusive societal interventions that antecede and induce our higher-order consciousness remain part of our individual and - as Elias (1939) highlighted - the collective unconsciousness, although they necessarily occur in language—in the social domain—as Lacan rightly pointed out (Lacan 1990, pp. 181 and 185).

Fichte was among the first to realise that humans cannot possibly develop as rational beings on their own. What in Fichte's view marks the beginning of the development of self-awareness is the call of others prompting the child to act ('*Aufforderung des Subjekts zum Handeln*', Fichte 1796/1971, p. 33). Unless another subject is understood as calling on the individual, the latter cannot conceive of herself as a person called on to act and to accept accountability. The individual understands that she is being tasked by another person. By facing the task and by making it her own she emerges as a person within a normative 'language game'. In Kantian ethics, the subject and her duty exist independently of one another. In Fichtean theory, the subject develops in rising to the challenges of her society's normative order. In the words of George Herbert Mead (1936, p. 89):

> This Fichte presents as the reality of the moral experience—that one finds before him something to be done and then, in the doing, finds himself identified with it. It is not only a task: it is his task. He is involved in it. And the accomplishment of the task, the doing of the duty, realizes the individual. [...] Selfhood is attained in a process in which the individual identifies himself with his task. The individual realizes himself in that process.

The following sentences are quoted extensively not only because of Mead's precise understanding of Fichte, but also as demonstrating the crucial importance of Fichtean ethics for Mead's own theorizing (1936, pp. 94–95):

> Fichte can [...] point [...] to the very nature of the self. The self is a type of experience which we attain only by becoming, in a certain sense, not-selves. That is, we cannot get the experiences of ourselves as selves except in so far as we take the attitude of another and regard ourselves from that point of view. [...] We have to realize ourselves by taking the role of another, playing the part of another, taking the attitude of the community toward ourselves, continually seeing ourselves as others see us, regarding ourselves from the standpoint of those about us. This is not the self-consciousness that goes with awkwardness and uneasiness. It is the assured recognition of one's own position, one's social relations, that comes from being able to take the attitude of others toward ourselves. We cannot recognize our rights in demanding them of others without being ourselves in their place and recognizing their rights. [...] Here again Fichte can come back to a character of the self which involves a not-self. There must be a not-self in order that the self may exist.

The call of competent language users initiates interactions with a view to establishing the child as—not only a rights-holder, but—an autonomous and responsible agent. That is the meaning of raising children. In Fichte's words:

> Die Aufforderung zur freien Selbsttätigkeit ist das, was man Erziehung nennt. Alle Individuen müssen zu Menschen erzogen werden, außerdem würden sie nicht Menschen (Fichte 1796/1971, p. 39).

> The summons to engage in free self-activity is what we call up-bringing. All individuals must be brought up to be human beings, otherwise they would not be human beings (Fichte 1796/2000, p. 38; what Fichte actually says is "otherwise they would not *become* human beings").

While Kantian dignity highlights an excellent quality of individuals, Fichtean dignity reflects humans' specific existential need for community, without which humans could neither survive biologically nor develop as persons in the cultural sphere. Later, Fichte (1796/2000, p. 132) observes 'that the human being must be educated and must educate himself to the status of morality; for he is not moral by nature, but must make himself so through his own labor'.

Again, it is Elias (1939, p. 26, translation corrected by author) who most precisely and truthfully echoes the Fichtean approach:

> The child is not only malleable or adaptable to a far greater degree than adults. It *needs* to be adapted by others, it *needs* society to become [psychically] adult. [...] In order to become psychically adult, a human individual, the child cannot do without the relation to older and more powerful beings. Without the assimilation of preformed social models, of parts and products of these more powerful beings, without the shaping of his psychical functions which they bring about, the child remains, to repeat the point, little more than an animal.

3.4.3 The Concept of a Human Being is the Concept of Humankind

Unlike Hegel's, Fichte's spirit—or general will—is not meant as a category of metaphysics (Dews 2005, pp. 355–356, 2008, pp. 157–158), but refers to empirical culture existing in language, in *Begriffen*. Reflecting on the individual and her self-consciousness we are, in Fichte's view, induced to accept that any notion of a person is premised on a concept of the individual as a member of a human community and an instance and manifestation of humankind. The person is the instantiation of one spirit existing in many bodies. The history of the individual is woven into the histories of the collectivities in which she exists. As Elias (1939, p. 27) put it:

> The new-born, the small child – no less than the old man – has a socially appointed place shaped by the specific structure of the particular human network. [...] There is not zero-point of the social relatedness of the individual, no 'beginning' or sharp break when he steps into society as if from outside as a being untouched by the network and then begins to link up with other human beings. On the contrary, [...] the individual always exists, on the most fundamental level, in relation to others, and this relation has a particular structure specific to his society. He takes on his individual stamp from the history of these relationships, these dependences, and so, in a broader context, from the history of the whole human network within which he grows up and lives. This history and this human network are present in him and are represented by him [...].

It is sometimes maintained that the parents *acknowledge* the child as a person (the German term is *anerkennen*, e.g. Zaczyk 2014). Yet 'acknowledging' is not the same as 'initiating'. To acknowledge means to accept or recognise the presence or quality of something that already exists. Terms like 'acknowledgment' or 'recognition' (or *'Anerkennung'*) insinuate that adults accept as a *given* the personhood of another subject. However, the person does not exist prior to being named, referred to, called on, and held to account by others and any social existence is premised on the continuation of such processes of communication. "One is called a name or addressed as 'you' prior to any sense of individuation, and that calling, especially as it is repeated and rehearsed in different ways, starts to form a subject who calls itself by those same terms, learning how to shift the 'you' to an 'I' or to a gendered third person, a 'he' or a 'she'" (Butler 2015, p. 12). The term *'Anerkennung'* neglects the creative, but at the same time the formative nature of parents' calling. As generating persons—distinct from acknowledging persons—imposes the social order of those who call on the human individual, the dynamic character of culture is also missed out, which depends on being transferred from one generation to the next and thereby underlies evolutionary drifts.

Because Fichte stresses the dynamic character of culture, it is obvious to him that culture must have been, through the entire history of humankind, passed on from one generation to the other. Consequently, Fichte considers that there must have been first humans, and the question arises of who called on them. As it must have been a rational being, he concludes that this must have been God. Obviously, at the time when Fichte—in 1796—published his '*Grundlage des Naturrechts*', an evolutionary theory was not in sight. Charles Darwin and Alfred Russell Wallace published their groundbreaking theories more than 60 years later.

Yet from today's perspective, Fichte's approach is attractive exactly because it opens up the vista of the development of human culture as connecting to and interacting with humans' biological evolution. It also stresses a bifurcation of the medium in which evolutionary processes take place, without denying the autonomy of culture as a self-sufficient system, existing only in processes of symbolic communication. As it is possible to view higher levels of consciousness as emerging from primary consciousness, it is also possible to link this crucial evolutionary step to the emergence of the specific form of human sociality based on the intergenerational transmission of normative language. A refined concept of culture as emerging in the early evolution of humans from a natural basis has been elaborated extensively by Günter Dux (2000, 2014; see also Niedenzu 2014).

Ontologically, primacy is due not to the soliloquising individual, nor to dyadic relationships, but only to the entire system of human culture, in which languages develop and which generates persons by summoning them as responsible agents. What the term 'culture' refers to is precisely acts of communication permanently generating and reinforcing a body of rules of behaviour transmitted from one generation to the next, including the rules governing this transfer and the adaptation of rules to changing environments. Thus, the notion of culture refers to a dynamic process, which links all existing societies as specific configurations of normative orders to the same evolution of a practice of an intergenerational transmission of rules of behaviour. Human culture as the specific technique of stockpiling, over generations, a body of social norms, enabled those engaging in this technique to fare better than other bands. It is possible that this evolution commenced simultaneously at various places. Yet once the social order achieves a rudimentary level of complexity, it offers advantages that allow a group participating in culture to easily defeat a group that does not. Hence, it is plausible that all human societies can be traced back to one early stage, where culture as the technique of intergenerational instruction and social learning took off. In this sense, humankind is united by all societies sharing in the same project of human culture that constitutes them as living as members of a society under its normative order.

Fichte (1800/1848, p. 195) refers to a general will, which joins an individual's will to itself and to the wills of all others. Therefore, the human being is not conceivable as one individual in isolation but only as a member of humankind.

Through this mysterious union does each individual perceive, understand, and love himself only in another; every soul develops itself only by means of other souls, and there are no longer individual men, but only one humanity; no individual thought or love or hate, but only thought, love, and hate, in and through each other.

3.4.4 *Fichte on the Cosmopolitan Right "to go about freely on the earth"*

If personhood and individual autonomy are not qualities inherent in human beings, but premised on the admission to and inclusion in human society, then for the right to dignity, the most fundamental right is access to a normative community as a person with rights, obligations and accountability. Any social existence—the very status of a person as an accountable agent and rights-holder—is premised on an individual's admission to and participation in a societal configuration mediating participation in culture.

Obviously, this right cannot be premised on citizenship as the membership in a society, which presupposes that a person has already entered into legal relationships—a social contract. Hence, the right to be a person must be a 'natural' right, the right, that is, of a human being who seeks to enter a polity—a normative community—with a view of establishing relationships.

Therefore, Fichte posits that the most basic and original human right is the right to seek membership in a society and to be able to enter into legal relations with other human beings and to acquire rights (1796a, p. 384, 1796b, p. 333):

> *Er hat das ursprüngliche Menschenrecht, das allen Rechtsverträgen vorausgeht, und allein sie möglich macht:* das Recht auf die Voraussetzung aller Menschen, dass sie mit ihm durch Verträge in ein rechtliches Verhältnis kommen können. *Dies allein ist das eigentliche Menschenrecht, das dem Menschen, als Menschen, zukommt: die Möglichkeit sich Rechte zu erwerben. [...] Nämlich derjenige, mit welchem der Staat den Bürgervertrag aufhebt, verliert alle seine dadurch erlangten positiven Rechte; aber nicht nur sie, sondern auch das Recht, sich in dieser Gesellschaft Rechte zu erwerben; [...] Der neue Ankömmling hat*

ebenso wenig positive Rechte, als der erste; aber das Recht hat er, zu fordern, dass man die Möglichkeit annehme, mit ihm in ein rechtliches Verhältnis zu kommen.

Aus diesem Rechte folgt sein Recht, das Gebiet des fremden Staates zu betreten; denn wer das Recht zum Zwecke hat, hat es zu den Mitteln; aber er kann den Versuch, in ein rechtliches Verhältnis mit diesem Staate sich zu versetzen, nicht machen, ohne auf sein Gebiet zu ihm zu kommen, und ihm eine Verbindung anzutragen.

In diesem Rechte, auf dem Erdboden frei herumzugehen, und sich zu einer rechtlichen Verbindung anzutragen, besteht das Recht des bloßen Weltbürgers.

He has that original human right which precedes all rightful contracts and which alone makes them possible: *the right to every other human being's expectation [rather: assumption, A.D.] to be able to enter into a rightful relation with him through contracts.* This alone is the one true human right that belongs to the human being as such: the right to be able to acquire rights. [...] If a state cancels the civil contract it has made with a particular citizen, then that citizen loses all the positive rights he had acquired as a result of that contract. Moreover, he loses not only those rights, but also the right to acquire rights in this society [...] Now the newcomer in the foreign state has just as few positive rights as he does; but the newcomer does have the right to demand that others expect it to be [rather: accept that it is, translation corrected A.D.] possible to enter into a rightful relation with him.

This right entails his right to enter into the territory of the foreign state; for if one has a right to the end he seeks to attain, then one also has a right to the means. But he cannot attempt to enter into a rightful relation with this state if he does not encounter it on its own territory and offer to establish a connection with it.

It is this right to go about freely on the earth and offer to establish rightful connections with others that constitutes the right of a mere *citizen of the world.*

In Fichte's view, human dignity as the right to be accepted into a society of humans cannot be restricted to citizens who are already included in a society as its members. It is therefore necessarily a cosmopolitan right that any human being on earth has against all other human beings on earth, the right, that is, to be a person and to participate in the culture of humankind. As culture takes shape in societal networks as its concrete manifestations, the right to participate in human culture equals the right to be included in a society. For this right to be practically effective, the individual must be given the possibility to establish relations with the members of a community.

In this regard, Fichte's views, expressed in 1796, exactly matched the thinking of Kant who in the same year posited that an individual may claim everywhere on earth "a right of resort, for all men are entitled to present themselves in the society of others by virtue of their right to communal possession of the earth's surface. Since the earth is a globe, they cannot disperse over an infinite area, but must necessarily tolerate one another's company" (Kant 1796/1970, p. 106; on Kant's cosmopolitanism Benhabib 2004, p. 25, 2011, p. 5). Hence Fichte and Kant were among the first political theorists who were led by the notion of human dignity to a concept of humankind as a cosmopolitan legal community (Marcuse 2008, p. 156). Fichte's point that because of a human being's dependency on a normative community, without which she cannot develop as a person, a human's first right must be the entitlement to enter into normative relations—of rights and obligations—was later supported by other philosophers, including Hannah Arendt and Seyla Benhabib (Arendt 1951; Benhabib 2004, 2011). In Fichte's view, this right is consequential to an individual's belonging to the global community of humankind. Thus, Fichte overcomes the narrow perspective of the sovereign nation state as the ultimate political framework of reference. As Margalit (1998, p. 274) highlighted, "the worst problems of humiliation in the modern world are often those of people who are not members of the society they live in—people who do not belong." Fichte's point is that all people belong—to humankind, as citizens of the world. Within a normative framework based on human dignity and the solidarity of humankind, borders preventing individuals from 'going about freely on the earth' can hardly be justified. Lately, Fichte's case for open borders has again received much attention from political theorists highlighting that immigration control plays a crucial role in maintaining global inequalities and in unjustly restricting individual autonomy (Carens 2013; Anderson 2013; Cassee 2016).

Fichte's cosmopolitanism coincided with his appreciation of nation states. However, like with Herder, this appreciation did not lead to particularist ethics. Rather, as Ernst Cassirer (1974, p. 185) put it, their valuing nations 'was not only compatible with a real universalism but presupposed it. To Herder every nation was only an individual voice in a universal, all-embracing harmony'. In fact, the aim of cosmopolitanism has never been to establish a global state, but always to integrate constitutional states in a global structure that enables international institutions to monitor the performance of state authorities and to intervene whenever these authorities significantly fail to meet the standards flowing from human dignity and human rights. Cosmopolitanism does not suggest that individuals should leave their loyalties to local and regional communities behind. An individual's sense of home is anyway organised in concentric circles including her family, her neighbourhood, her local community, her home country, and perhaps increasingly also a larger collective, such as all Africans, Americans or Europeans. However, these many shades and dimensions of homeness do not stand in the way of also developing a common understanding that all these collectives form, in the end, parts and modules of one humanity that unites, in a global normative order, all individuals who carry a human face. Thus, the hostile antagonism and, at times, aggressive competition of nation states gives way to an amicable competition of constitutional states and other communities, all striving to draw closer to the one common objective, inherent in human culture, of creating a societal framework that serves best the peaceful development and cooperation of free, autonomous, caring and responsible persons.

3.4.5 *The Socialised Person*

Article 1 of the Universal Declaration of Human Rights posits:

> "All human beings are born free and equal in dignity and rights. They are endowed with reason and conscience and should act towards one another in a spirit of brotherhood."

While the assumption that all human beings are endowed with reason and conscience is very Kantian, it is—taken at face value—also clearly wrong. If this statement was understood as claiming that all human beings are, due to their genetic endowment, able to make rational or ethical judgments, it would have to face the simple fact that newborn children are neither rational nor moral beings. One could be inclined to argue that children are gifted with reason and conscience and that it is merely a matter of time until these talents develop. Similarly, Kant believed that humans are born with the voice of their conscience as an internal judge; the ability to understand the imperatives of practical reason is innate in humans in principle, although it can be cultivated (Kant 1797/1968, pp. 400–401). However, as Fichte points out, if infants develop a moral sense, it is not by unfolding an innate capacity, but only by learning, embracing and internalising the norms taught by their parents and others and by responding to their calls, claims, and instructions. If humans grow to become rational and moral beings, it is due to their society. In other words: 'Personhood is social in nature and emerges from interaction'. Whenever an individual emerges as a person, she 'responds to the call of others, who challenge us to act, to cooperate and thereby to constitute ourselves as responsible and autonomous persons and as members of a society defined by its norms and culture. [...] Self-constitution is the result of symbolic interaction within a social and normative framework, beginning between a child and their parents or other caretakers' (FRA 2012, p. 21).

Hence, the person is a social construct that evolves within a societal structure; 'the individual is what he is, as a conscious and individual personality, just in as far as he is a member of society, involved in the social process of experience and activity, and thereby controlled in his conduct' (Mead 1934, p. 255).

The concept of a 'person' is essentially normative and dynamic. A person is attributed rights and later, ideally in accordance with her developing capabilities, held to account for her actions. While personhood, in principle, exists from the first moment a human being is granted rights, it gains in substance along with an individual's growth as a responsible and autonomous agent.

Agency is premised on accountability, and accountability presupposes a normative order. When the infant is called upon to act and to take responsibility for her action, this implicitly relates to the concrete symbolic normative order establishing the community into which the child is born.

Socialisation is the process by which the child is imprinted with a deep normative structure and thus created as a person within—and subjected to—a normative order. The latter frames the process of her interpellation and the form of subjectivity into which the child is called. It is the order that calls on the child through other family members, and by hearing that call and internalising the order of the society into which she is born the child develops a basic personality. Again, Mead echoes Fichtean thoughts in positing (Mead 1934, p. 162):

> What goes to make up the organized self is the organization of the attitudes which are common to the group. A person is a personality because he belongs to a community, because he takes over the institutions of that community into his own conduct.

Hence, Althusser (1970, p. 50), who uses the term 'ideology' to refer to and highlight the concrete and idiosyncratic formation of a given societal order and its powerful institutions, is precise in asserting that it is ideology—in this sense of a founding normative code—that summons and recruits human beings as subjects: '*l'idéologie interpelle les individus en sujets*.'

In Fichte's model, the role of the child is not passive, but responsive. It is parents or other experienced members of a language community who initiate an interaction by calling on the child, prompting her to engage in and to contribute to the constitution of herself as an accountable person answering to the calls of others (Vogelmann 2014, pp. 325–337).

The term 'calling' should not be understood as relating to verbal interaction only. The process of initiating the infant in a social and cultural domain starts with any form of interaction between the parents and the infant. As observed by Stern (2000, p. xxix): "In the beginning the paralinguistics carry the cultural enactments. Later, the arbitrary sound symbols do so as well."

The infant is called upon by others to embrace her society's normative order and thus to engage in her own constitution as a person, which is the result of dyadic interactions that relate to and, importantly, are imbedded in her society's symbolic and normative order as the powerful third party. Even the initial mother-child relationship cannot be understood without considering its normative and cultural framework, in which the mother has her part and the child is assigned her role (Althusser 1996; Benjamin 1988). Hence, the interaction of mother and child cannot be reduced to these two actors, as the development of personhood cannot result from dyadic relationships alone. As Jakobs has put it, two individuals constituting one another as subjects in isolation would be like two ships anchoring in one another (2008, p. 36).

The child cannot avoid listening to her parent's calling and gradually grasping its meaning. Hence the call that initiates the child as an agent within certain social configurations of a language community also 'condemns' her to act and to have to account for her actions throughout her life. Thus, the calling inescapably inscribes agency and accountability on a child. Once the child understands that she has a choice, she no longer has: She can no longer avoid taking decisions or having to account for them. She has no choice but to choose, to act on her choice and to face accountability (Korsgaard 2009). Whatever she decides, however she acts, she, in any case, joins in culture and the lasting flows of communication that permanently generate normative orders including herself as a person.

Hence, the first instances of communication in a biography are marked by a radical asymmetry between competent language users and a child. The initial relationship between adults and the infant is, if by anything, marked by an immense power-imbalance placing the latter at the mercy of the former. 'I am affected not just by this one other or a set of others, but by a world in which humans, institutions, and organic and inorganic processes all impress themselves upon this me who is, at the outset, susceptible in ways that are radically involuntary' (Butler 2015, pp. 6–7).

Theories that—in a Hegelian manner—characterise the relations between adults and a child as a matter of mutual recognition are overly static and imply a false symmetry (Müller-Tuckfeld 1997, p. 325). Depicting social relations in analogy to a scene, where two individuals recognise one another as persons, risks overlooking that such a scene is possible only on condition that these two individuals were called on and initiated in culture at an earlier stage of their lives. At the point they were called on, the individuals were not, at first, in a position to grasp what was expected of them, let alone had the capacity to assess and reject these demands. As Müller-Tuckfeld comments, the two individuals who mutually acknowledge and thus constitute one another as persons are adults before they are children (Müller-Tuckfeld 1997, p. 325).

Therefore, notwithstanding the strong position of parents and other carers, it should be noted that their subjectivity is not genuine, but determined by the community on behalf of which they act. Hence, it would be a mistake to view the emerging personhood of the child as the result of a process within which an adult extends her subjectivity to the child. Personhood is not inherent in the parent, but remains premised on the adult person being continuously referred to, and hence reproduced by, communicative acts of others. Personhood does not exist in separate persons, but only in normative orders brought forth in acts of communication.

The term 'person' denotes a cultural construct, a mark on the landscape of a society's normative structure defined by social coordinates. In the case of so-called natural persons, the mark is conceived as relating to a human body. However, the person is not the body. A person is a position, an address in the social domain, to which rights and, according to her abilities, responsible agency are attributed in acts of communication (for a brilliant analysis of the normative basis of subjectivation see Müller-Tuckfeld 1996, 1997). The address refers to and represents the person. By the creation of the address, the person is created as an element of the social system (Stichweh 2016).

Usually this position is marked by a name, to which often a reference to the person's family, ancestors, profession, or local community is added as an additional coordinate specifying her position in society (Althusser 1970, p. 51). Naming a child is an important step towards initiating the child as a person. Hallpike observes that some societies "regard infanticide and abortion as permissible because they do not consider either the foetus or the new born baby as human but as a form of animal life"; a human being "requires a name before it can be regarded as a real member of a society" (2004, p. 88).

Names stress accountability and hence are used when accountability matters, e.g. when parents scold their children or when a person signs a contract and thus acquires rights or enters into obligations. It is precisely what in meaningful acts is ascribed to that position—to that name—that makes up a person. In the terms of systems theory, it is in language that the individual person arises as the singularity defined by the intersection of acts of communication in which the person is distinguished (Maturana and Varela 1998, p. 231).

Norbert Elias stressed that we are not used to understanding persons as symbols applied in communication, but rather view ourselves as identical with our bodies and hence as firm and robust entities and society as built on these entities as its material. People believe that the individual exists in isolation and they "think of individuals as something existing prior to and independently of society" (1939, p. 18):

> It is from individuals, as the 'atoms' and 'smallest particles' of society, so it seems to them, that one's thinking should start, building up a concept of their relations to each other, of society, as something coming later. In a word, they conceive individuals as firm posts between which the line of relationships is strung afterwards.

However, this is a misconception. The individual owes her existence as a person not to her biological life but to her presence and occurrence as a symbol in the universe of acts of communication, including the acts of those who welcome her and call on her to act. Being referred to in acts of communication is the only way to exist as a person.

Another ontological mistake is made, according to Elias, by those who substantialise and hypostasize society as a concrete entity. Those who succumb to this mistake, "can only conceive regularities as the regularities of substances or of substantial forces", hence they "can conceive of society only as something supra-individual" and therefore they invent either a collective mind or a collective organism (1939, p. 17).

To avoid both mistakes and to arrive at a proper understanding of social facts, it is necessary "to give up thinking in terms of single, isolated substances and to start thinking in terms of relationships and functions" (Elias 1939, p. 19). An individual becoming self-aware is the result of interactive processes that start with her being called upon by competent language users to act and to join in the constitution of herself as an agent. The child emerges as a person not in relation to a society as a firm given, but rather in various societal—communicative—configurations and networks of relationships depending on shifting social contexts. Societal networks are the fabric into which she is woven. The only point of departure, available to cultural, social or psychological studies, is neither the individual, nor a formal 'society' as given, but only the concrete processes of communication and the clusters of relationships into which they feed. As Sapir explained (2015, p. 519):

> We have learned that the individual in isolation from society is a psychological fiction. We have not had the courage to face the fact that formally organized groups are equally fictitious in the psychological sense, for geographically contiguous groups are merely a first approximation to the infinitely variable groupings of human beings to whom culture in its various aspects is actually to be credited as a matter of realistic psychology.

The language, norms and standards that parents pass on to their children have developed and accumulated over generations and within rapidly fluctuating societal constellations. They perform an intermediary function which is shaped by societal norms—as the grand and powerful third party in the background—that demand of parents to raise and educate their children, to ensure that their children learn to speak, attend school and take in the vast body of symbols and norms handed over to them by their parents' generation. Parents' duties ensure the continuity of societal structures as particular expressions and configurations of human culture based on an evolving normative code. It is through parents that culture recruits its new members. Parents introduce their children into the normative order and into the cooperation of agents creating normativity as a symbolic order. Parents' calling refers to the normative order within which the parents and the child have their positions. It creates the child within their normative order and calls on the child to call on others as social individuals like her. Castoriadis (1975, p. 450) explains:

> En d'autres termes, il faut et il suffit que l'enfant soit renvoyé à l'institution de la signification et à la signification comme instituée et ne dépendant d'aucune personne particulière. [...] Car, bien entendu, le père n'est pas père s'il ne renvoie pas lui-même à la société et à son institution, s'il n'est pas signifié à l'enfant qu'il est un père parmi d'autres pères, qu'il l'est pour autant qu'il désire être à une place qu'il n'était pas dans son pouvoir de créer, et qu'ainsi il figure et présentifie pour l'enfant ce qui explicitement le dépasse lui-même à un degré infini - une collectivité anonyme et indéfinie d'individus qui coexistent dans et par l'institution et se continuent en amont et en aval du temps. [...] Et cela implique la fabrication 'héréditaire' d'individus comme individus sociaux - ce qui veut dire aussi: d'individus pouvant et désirant continuer la fabrication d'individus sociaux.

From the child's perspective, its parents' calling is a challenging, potentially threatening and overwhelming experience unless it is imbedded in a secure emotional environment of mutual trust and of appreciation of the child as a unique human being. The child's courage and resolve to commit to the dialogue initiated and imposed by her parents, to take the risks involved in this interaction, and to cope with disappointing experiences of failures presuppose her confidence that she is important to others and safe (Tugendhat 2004, p. 44). This basic trust is an essential element of the child's relationship to its parents and a model for later relationships (Bowlby 1988). A basic expectation of mutual trust, concern and sympathy is deeply engrained in our social life.

Thus human societies are established in culture as their medium, where the term 'culture' comprises all acts of human language-based communication. Societies form configurations in the cultural domain that organise their own reproduction.

Those communicative processes that control a societal configuration's normative reproduction control the mechanism of initiating humans as its members. They dictate who is entitled to this membership and on what terms.

All observations occur within societal configurations and hence in culture. There is no escape from culture. Whenever we reflect on societal issues, we are bound to do so using the terms, categories and underlying hidden assumptions about nature and ourselves that we have learned in the course of our primary socialisation. Processes of reflection or communication are moves within the system of culture encompassing as subsystems all 'language games', including criminal justice. There is no external prospect, no view from outside on the basic norms and symbols underlying *all* human culture, such as right and wrong, accountable agency, time, space, causality and choice.

3.4.6 Society's Call Prompts Agency

Let an instruction—or order—be a speech act by which a person claims to direct the conduct of another person. An instruction intends to get an actor to refrain from doing what she could do or to do what she could refrain from doing. In abstract terms, an instruction draws, within a field of options of possible conduct, a distinction between right—compliant—and wrong—non-compliant—conduct.

The only appropriate addressee of an instruction is an agent, a person, that is, who is able to choose to abide or not abide by the order. Any agency implies accountability, and accountability is premised on choice. Hence an instruction that calls on an agent—and thus engages in a normative language game—necessarily accepts that it is, in the end, her decision to comply with the instruction or not. Otherwise, the agent had neither choice nor responsibility for what she decides to do. The child fully appreciates the meaning of her parents' calling when she refuses to obey and thereby acts on her parents' implied suggestion of choice and accountability. She develops as a person by saying yes or no to her parents' commands. She acknowledges that it is 'up to her' (Tugendhat 2004, pp. 62–64, 2005, p. 254). Hence, any accountability is premised on this basic binary choice between compliance and non-compliance. Her parents' calling initiates the child as an agent who can choose—and knows she can—and only due to her being able to choose can be held to account for her decisions. As soon as she understands the meaning of normativity and agency, any—obedient or disobedient—reaction to the call of her parents forms part of the interactions that generate the normative order, like a valid move in a game contributes to generating the game.

If the child fully understands the meaning of her parents' calling, she grasps that it expresses the normative standpoint of her parents, but also that the normative order does not belong to—and is not controlled by—her parents alone (Castoriadis 1975, pp. 448–454). In fact, she is called on to adopt a stance of her own. She has a vote to cast like her parents and by casting it assumes her share of the responsibility for the normative order that emanates from the votes cast by her, by her parents and by all others who share in their status as agents and lawgivers. Her parents' calling opens up to her a room of normativity, within which all members of her society exist, communicate and cooperate in preserving and improving their normative order.

Calling on a child to act generates, at the same time, the person as an actor and actions, i.e. behaviour attributed to her in the horizon of a social order, which demands that an actor must control her behaviour and hence must account for what is attributed to her as her actions. By saying 'I', the child adopts the status of a responsible agent. She accepts—and later on claims as the basis of her personhood—the status of an accountable subject who leads and appropriates a meaningful life as a member of her society. Any Fichtean right to be a person implies a legitimate claim of accountable agency.

Hence, what lies at the core of Fichte's lesson is the mechanism by which the calling of the members of a society on a child has the potential to initiate interactions that constitute the child as a person. The status of personhood opens up a sphere that is protected against violence, coercion, and heteronomy and in which autonomous and accountable agency can develop. Except for children with certain forms of learning disabilities, by being treated as a person, the individual is prompted and learns to choose, to decide and to face accountability. Thus the concept of personhood is dynamic: it designates the right of a human being to be attributed a sphere of potential agency, protected against violence and manipulation, within which the human being can develop as an autonomous and responsible actor.

Society's call on a child does not come upon free choice as a previously existing ability of the child but has a potential to *create* free choice by teaching the child the concepts of choice and responsibility. Society's calling insinuates a 'free will' and a decision and thus constitutes a person as an agent. This is the self-fulfilling prophecy, on which culture is founded, that humans, if—and only if—consistently treated as accountable moral subjects, regularly have the potential to develop as accountable agents. Where there is a newborn human brain, there is a chance that in the society of persons, another person can emerge as a participant in culture.

The term 'I' signifies the location in society of a decision-making power. Learning to say 'I' implies learning to say 'No'. This leads up to various—and sometimes dramatic—revolts when the child insists fiercely and unremittingly on saying no, thereby struggling for an autonomous existence distinct from the potentially overpowering claims and impositions of the adults surrounding her. Even "breaks or ruptures" cannot liberate us from our formations, "I am still being formed as I form myself in the here and now. And my own self-formative activity [...] becomes part of that ongoing formative process" (Butler 2015, p. 6).

To comply with the call of her parents, the child is required to establish control of her body and to exercise this control according to social norms. This ability and the autonomy to exercise control over one's own body remain a cornerstone of what it means to be a person. If we conceive of action as processes, where higher-order consciousness interferes with an object world, then our body is our mind's primary object. All other 'causation' is initiated by body movements. Hence, a person experiences any incident where others subject her body to their control as a particularly serious and deeply irritating abuse of her integrity and personhood and often as severely traumatising. The foundation of any form of autonomy is premised on a person's control of her body and exclusion of all others from taking that control. To the extent that the child learns to answer to the calling of society, she gains an understanding that she has to account for her bodily actions or passivity. Her movements are her responsibility as are her failures to act when she should have acted.

A difficult part of getting a grasp of her body is establishing control of her emotions, impulses and instincts. In psychology, this faculty has been coined the 'cool system': Children start with limited powers to resist temptation, but in childhood, their ability to control impulsive behaviour improves (Haidt 2001, p. 823). Reflection is a language-based process and hence requires higher-order consciousness. By their linguistic abilities, persons become free from their 'bondage to the present' (Edelman 2004, p. 118).

3.4.7 Generating a Normative Order

While the normative order engages in the creation of the child as a person, at the same time the child begins to engage in the formation of the normative order. A normative order has no existence beyond the meaningful acts of communication of subjects who continuously respond to its claims. By calling on the child and by subjecting the child to the normative order of the community into which the child is born, this order at the same time exposes itself and turns itself over to the decisions of the subject who is being initiated. Whatever her reaction to the calling of others, she posits herself in relation to the set of norms governing her interaction with these others. "It may seem to be a molding of the individual by the forces about him, but the society likewise changes in this process, and becomes to some degree a different society. The change may be desirable or it may be undesirable, but it inevitably takes place" (Mead 1934, p. 216; compare Günther 2014).

If a mother tells her daughter to close the door, this implies, firstly, that her daughter has a choice to close the door or to leave it open and, secondly, that she has reason to close it. The daughter rejects her mother's order by answering "But it's closed!"—meaning that what her mother demands is not an option—or by saying "But it is terribly hot in here, I'd rather leave it open!", meaning that she rejects her mother's order as unreasonable.

Any action takes place in both spheres, in nature and in culture. It can be observed and constructed as happening in an object world—as a physical activity or passivity—and can also be interpreted and challenged as a meaningful act of communication expressing that a subject, in a given situation, opts for a certain course of action. 'The line of demarcation between the self and the body is found, then, first of all in the societal organization of the act within which the self arises, in its contrast with the activity of the physiological organism' (Mead 1934, p. 187). The person is accountable to the extent that she can answer the question 'Why did you do that?', which implies the deeper question 'Why did you *choose* to do that?', 'Why did you take this decision and not another?'.

Agency operates at two levels: as an activity impacting on an object world and as an action positing a normative statement. What a person asserts when she acts is a personal maxim: "This is how I choose to act in such a situation!" This statement is made in the horizon of the normative claims made in respect of her agency in the situation in which she acts. An action is a person's vote cast—deliberately or carelessly—in support of or revolting against the set of norms aspiring to govern her situation, perhaps in the case of conflicting laws or values, a choice in favour of the one and against the other. Drawing from their anthropological research, Henrich and Ensminger emphasise that 'internalizing a norm does not make an individual a mindless 'norm executer'. People have plenty of competing internalized goals and motivations that demand choosing among alternative goals' (Henrich and Ensminger 2014, p. 22). Similarly, Butler (2015, p. 9) observes that the 'matrix of relations' that forms the subject is not an integrated and harmonious network, but a field of potential disharmony, antagonism, and contest'. Resistance can develop when, within the normative order, inconsistencies are traced and when the normative order is brought to bear against itself (Schütt 2015).

If an individual's decision passes without being revoked by its author or challenged and rejected by others, it stands as a position and as a potential point of future orientation for other subjects (Günther 2014, p. 36). Thus norms and a normative order emerge within a field of lines of normative force originating from acts of communication. In the words of George Herbert Mead (1934, pp. 385–386):

> It is as social beings that we are moral beings. On the one side stands the society which makes the self possible, and on the other side stands the self that makes a highly organized society possible. The two answer to each other in moral conduct.

A norm gains or maintains authority whenever it is complied with by an addressee or defended against a non-compliant addressee, where defending the norm includes (private) self-defence, enforcement by a competent public authority or the censuring or sanctioning of a non-compliant addressee. A norm is created and maintained *solely* by acts of individuals who invoke it as private actors or in an official function. Thus, the powerful normative order of a society and all concrete acts—including those that constitute actors—form a system of recursive processes of normative communication that is binding on itself.

Hence, to say that a norm is binding—or valid, or authoritative—means that the norm is, at large, being respected within a given society, either by compliance or by being defended in the face of non-compliance. The two reasons why a norm is respected, are that addressees or 'defenders' share the moral stance taken by the norm or, while not having strong feelings in this respect, appreciate the authority of the norm's author as legitimate; and such legitimacy, again, results from the moral quality of the norms generated by the authority in question or from the fairness and procedural justice observed by the authority in creating norms (Tyler 2006, 2013). Therefore, the quality of legal bindingness flows from individuals to authorities, not the other way around. A legal order is a system of those norms that are at large being respected and not the sum total of texts produced by acts of norm generation authorised by another—'higher'—legal norm. A legal order has its basis not in some 'highest' foundational norms, but in the morality of the citizens it addresses and in everyday life. In brief, a norm's legal bindingness is not a matter of a legal order's internal affairs, but a matter of social reality. Law is not a 'one-way projection of authority, originating with government and imposing itself upon the citizen', but 'the product of an interplay of purposive orientations between the citizen and his government' (Fuller 1969, p. 204).

However, only because—and to the extent that—an agent is seen as having a choice to disregard a norm, her norm-abiding conduct can be interpreted as supporting the norm. Hence, any normative order is premised on a polity's willingness to take the risk of individuals not abiding by social norms. Norm violations are necessarily part of any normative order. It is part of the semantics of a normative claim that it is, in the end, up to its addressee to acknowledge or to reject its claim and to take the responsibility for this decision. This is not meant to say that the addressee is free to refute the order. Quite the contrary. If a person rejects a claim inherent in a criminal law provision, she may run a risk of being convicted and punished. However, in the 1960s women deciding to have an abortion did just that: They refuted a claim inherent in a criminal law provision. The consequence was the retreat of the norm. Hence, what is inherent in any normative order is its instability, ephemerality and dynamic nature.

The authority of a normative order rests in the propensity of its members to comply with and support its demands and, alternatively, in the firm resolve of its law enforcement agencies and criminal justice institutions to react to law violations. In a normative order's evolution it is decisions to comply with or to enforce a norm that function as 'selective retention', while it is diversity and pluralism that create the variance required as well as education and various forms of normative advocacy that function as transmitters. In this picture, punishment restrains variance by rejecting decisions not to comply with norms of criminal law.

Searle has suggested to call 'deontic powers' what above has been referred to as a norm's authority or bindingness (2010, pp. 8–9, 123). As a matter of comprehensibility and consistency, the term 'normative power' is preferred here. The notion 'power' in general refers to the capacity of agent X to motivate agent Y to perform an action A. Power is about "getting someone to do something" (Searle 2010, p. 147). There are many ways of getting people to do what we want them to do, including brute force, threats, bribes, or deception, means which have above been referred to as heteronomous. The notion 'normative power' refers to the specific situation, where X is able to motivate—or to contribute to motivating—Y to perform A as a matter of Y's autonomous compliance with a normative order.

A police officer orders that a driver should stop. Who has normative power, the police officer or the driver? Both have. The police officer, to the extent that she is able to motivate the driver to stop as a manner of complying with a legal norm authorising the police officer's order; and the driver has the normative power to, by her reaction, reinforce or undermine the officer's authority (Popitz 2006, p. 136). However, there is a fundamental difference between the normative power of the police officer and the normative power of her addressee. The latter exerts the power of a citizen. The police officer does not act as a citizen, but as a public official. Hence, the deontic power she brings to bear is the legitimate rule of law. Legitimacy is vested in the state and its public authorities by citizens who acknowledge and treat the normative claims of state actors as legitimate and binding. Legitimacy is powerful when citizens widely confide in the ability of state actors to respect individuals' human rights and the rule of law, or it is weak, as was the case in many communist European countries before the fall of the wall that divided not only Berlin, but all of Europe. While the police officer and the citizen interact in creating a norm, the roles they perform in this interaction differ. In order to be able to appreciate the power that agents bring to bear in their acts of communication, what has to be taken into account is the institutional framework within which they act and the history of the institutions involved, forces of which the actors themselves may not be fully aware (Bourdieu and Wacquant 1992, pp. 116–149).

While the first actor, who evaluates, orders or instructs, introduces a distinction between right and wrong conduct, the response of the addressees decides on whether the order and the distinction drawn are acknowledged as authoritative—and part of the normative order—or not. As addressees have a choice, the outcome of this process is necessarily open. While the command aims to motivate addressees to abide by it, it comes with a risk of failure. It is the addressees of the command or instruction who operate the difference between illegitimate claims of authoritativeness, which are refuted or ignored, and norms, which are acknowledged as authoritative and binding and thus are attributed normative power. Y *acknowledges* X's command or instruction as indeed having the implicitly claimed authority, that is, Y attributes normative power to X's instruction. Hence, the norm emerges as the result of the interaction and cooperation of those who participate in normative communication (Rundle 2013, p. 100). However, in order to qualify as a normative interaction, the cooperation must be voluntary, not the consequence of one actor threatening the other with punishment. 'The agent who animates Fuller's conception of the legal subject, therefore, is someone not just capable of following rules laid down for her by a lawgiver, but someone capable of voluntarily and actively conveying the level of support towards the legal order that is necessary for it to exist' (Rundle 2013, p. 100). Therefore, to be successful, the norm must appeal to the moral attitudes and convictions of its addressees. As Lon Fuller put it, even a tyrant is brought to realise that legislation 'is, by its very nature, a cooperative enterprise' (1969, p. 106).

Fuller was right to point out that one mistake of legal positivists lies in overlooking the significance of the interaction between those who intend to authoritatively create norms and their addressees. The positivist, Fuller observes, 'does not see the lawgiver and the citizen in interaction with one another, and by virtue of that failure he fails to see that the creation of an effective interaction between them is an essential ingredient of the law itself' (Fuller 1969, p. 193). The positivist views the law 'not as the product of an interplay of purposive orientations between the citizen and his government but as a one-way projection of authority, originating with government and imposing itself upon the citizen' (1969, 204). Against this misconception, Fuller suggests what he refers to as an 'interactional theory of law', according to which the 'success of law depends on a voluntary collaboration between the citizen and his government, as well as upon a coordination of effort among the various agencies of government concerned with the making and enforcing of law' (1969, p. 220).

A normative order constitutes subjects who comply at large and thus engage both in its and their own constitution. The normative order assimilates individuals and thus qualifies them as autonomous agents who by abiding by the normative order continuously attest to its authority and legitimacy. By accepting their subjection and by internalising their society's normative code, the individual develops as a subject who, by abiding by the normative order, reinforces her subjection. Hence, the normative order forms subjects by making them subject themselves. This metamorphosis of an 'animal' turning into a human being by eagerly subjecting herself to and embracing the symbolic code and the laws of her master—the Evil One—is one of the recurrent themes in Kafka's works, for instance in the following passage of the fragments—the 29th aphorism (Kafka 2012, pp. 190–191):

> The mental reservations with which you take evil to yourself are not your own, they belong to the Evil One. The animal wrests the whip from its master and whips itself so as to become master itself, with no idea that this is only a fantasy produced by a fresh knot in its master's lash.

In this picture, even the 'fantasy' of self-determination is caused by the whip of the master, and from what has been said above, it appears that freedom *from* society is indeed not more than an illusory (Kantian) fantasy. However, self-determination *within* society is not only possible, but the basis of any normative order, which is premised on its voluntary recognition and permanent reproduction by persons constituted as autonomous lawgivers and vested with normative power.

This is where the Hegelian dialectic of *Herr* and *Knecht* (1807, pp. 74–75) comes in: A society's normative order as pure normative power initiates and shapes the coming into existence of persons, and whatever persons do is done by the normative order ("*was der Knecht tut, ist eigentlich Tun des Herrn*"). At the same time, the normative order remains premised on the recognition and permanent reproduction by those it creates. What is more, the normative order depends on the appreciation and deliberate support of those whose creation and formation it has initiated. The existence of the person depends on continuing acts of calling into existence and of recognition based on a normative order that, for its part, remains premised on recurrent processes of referencing and acknowledgement. The social existence of persons and of the normative order to which they owe their existence never reaches the safety of a solid shore, everything that is cultural - 'spiritual' - stays strictly processual, in motion and fluid (in Hegel's words: "*Diese reine allgemeine Bewegung, das absolute Flüssigwerden alles Bestehens ist aber das einfache Wesen des Selbstbewußtseins*").

The concepts and norms that fulfil the function of generating compliant subjects and of sustaining the normative order's existence constitute the general ideology underlying any normative order. Next to many specific and particularistic ideologies that may exist within a normative order and which can have a centrifugal and disruptive potential, the general ideology ensures general acceptance of the sacred and thus maintains the unity and ensures the continuity of the normative system.

One aspect of this basic ideology is what it asks of a human being in relation to herself, in particular about her engaging in her own constitution as a responsible agent abiding by a normative code. The individual is called on to constitute herself as a subject of and in relation to the normative order, as, for instance, a good Christian, a patriot, or an autonomous individual gifted with practical reason. Foucault (2014) refers to

> [...] la manière dont on doit se constituer soi-même comme sujet moral agissant en référence aux éléments prescriptifs qui constituent le code.

An important part of an individual's self-constitution consists in the self-attribution and training of attitudes that initially accompany and reflect her actions, but later solidify and gain the potential to motivate her conduct. Learned attitudes establish a link and correspondence between an individual's actions and her personality and integrate her manners of conduct and repertoires across social contexts and time. The internalisation of norms is corroborated by the construction of attitudes, which allow the individual to interpret her law abiding conduct as an idiosyncratic expression of her personality. In the long run, an individual's attitudes mirror the specific manner in which she has internalised the normative order.

Like any system, a normative order ultimately refers to an initial distinction, an ultimate source of the entire system's legitimacy, a concept that represents what is sacred and inviolable in a polity, what C. Wright Mills refers to as a central conception or a master symbol (1959, p. 36). The supreme good cannot be argued, only continuously postulated, evoked, confirmed and defended against being questioned.

The sacred defines the paradigm of a social order. In the course of a polity's evolution, fundamental paradigm shifts change its normative order. These shifts can be from nature and the cosmic order in segmentary societies, to the country's peace in court societies, to God as the source of the divine rights of a monarch in polities based on monarchic rule and positive legislation, to a collectivity—a nation, race, people or class—in organicist and collectivist societies. The concept of the sacred yokes a descriptive and a normative principle: nature, peace represented by the king, prince or church, God represented by the monarch, *das Volk* represented by the *Führer*, are at once conceived as empiric entities, figures or states *and*, at the same time, definitions of the unquestionable *summum bonum*. The sacred thus anchors the normative code in the conceptualisation of the polity's object world.

It is a core function of criminal justice to preserve the sacred. At all times, violations of the sacred—such as breaches of the king's peace, heresy or lese-majesty—are perceived as challenging the normative identity of the polity and hence range among the most severe crimes.

Now the question is: what functions as the sacred in a humanist global order? The best candidates are notions of the 'human', including 'human dignity', and 'humanity'. As has been observed above in relation to Fichte's recurrent usage of the German terms '*Mensch*', '*Menschheit*', '*menschlich*', and '*Humanität*', these terms fulfil the criterion of combining a descriptive and a normative element, as if human dignity was inherent in humans. Also, their negations—such as inhuman treatment or crimes against humanity—come close to defining the ultimate wrong in modern societies. These terms relate, in a way, to the individual human being, to the entirety of all members of the 'human family' and to a bond of basic solidarity—a 'spirit of brotherhood', in the terms of Article 1 of the Universal Declaration—uniting this 'family'. Hence, these concepts in their entirety are the best approximation to the sacred in contemporary modern societies. The most basic distinction on which the normative order is founded tells subjects from objects, individuals who are to be named and respected from all other entities. In a similar vein, Hans Joas has convincingly elaborated the idea that the concepts of human dignity and human rights result from historical processes of the sacralisation of the human person (2013; compare Moyn 2015).

In reconstructing normativity, there is a danger of overemphasising hierarchy. The idea of a powerful dictator commanding obedient subjects models, if anything, the organisation of a band of apes. The point is that social norms are superior to genetic encoding exactly for the flexibility of their contents. Culture permits and obliges parents to instruct their children how to do things—how to walk in an upright position, how to talk properly, which mushrooms to eat, how to cross a road - and it enables children to decide to do the exact opposite. Compared to genetic evolution, culture as a mechanism allowing for a transgenerational transfer of social knowledge is superior for two reasons. Firstly, it accelerates the accumulation of knowledge. Secondly, it allows for an incomparably faster and indeed permanent revision of the accumulated body of 'knowledge', where 'knowledge' refers to norms guiding the modelling of an object world. After all, what is believed to be the case and important in one generation must not necessarily still be correct or important in following generations. This is particularly true in conditions of rapid climatic change as was the situation in the later Pleistocene, when segmentary human societies first developed (Paul 2015, p. 63). Hence, the appropriate approximation is the vision of members of a normative community agreeing on norms and constantly reinforcing, revising and updating their normative repository in permanent flows of normative communication.

While this may seem rather abstract and theoretic, an example—briefly mentioned above—may help to elucidate its practical relevance. In the late 1960s, criminal law provisions prohibiting abortion were so widely disregarded that state authorities became reluctant to investigate and prosecute abortion cases. Still, the remaining official criminalisation had very considerable adverse consequences. Abortions were carried out in back rooms, often under conditions threatening women's health. What radically changed the situation were feminists who openly challenged the norm and publicised the discrepancy between the traditional norm and its widespread disregard. In early 1970, Dutch feminists ('*Dolle Minnas*') publicly claimed the right to decide whether to abort or not—to be 'master in her own belly' ('*baas in eigen buik*'). This was followed in 1971 by media petitions, in which French and German feminists admitted to having aborted. In April 1971, the manifesto of 343 women (*'Le manifeste des 343'*) was published in *Le Nouvel Observateur*, and a similar confession of 374 women in the magazine *Stern*. What these feminists demonstrated was that the prohibition of abortion could no longer rely on a societal consensus. It had ceased to be part of their societies' *effective* normative code. Once made public, this discrepancy forced legislators to react. Today, European laws, with a few exceptions, respect the dignity of women and recognise, at least during an initial phase of their pregnancy, their autonomous decision to give birth or not, without women having to provide reasons for their decisions in the legal sphere.

Regarding the distribution of autonomy and decision-making power, a particular situation exists in the UK, where—in theory—the Offences Against the Person Act 1861 makes abortion a criminal offence in England, Wales and Northern Ireland (while in Scotland abortion remains an offence at common law). However, the Abortion Act 1967, which applies in England, Wales and Scotland, allows for a therapeutic exception covering the first 24 weeks of pregnancy. Thus the Abortion Act entrusts doctors with an important role "as gatekeepers to abortion services" (Sheldon 2016, p. 343). In practice doctors use the broad discretion accorded to them "to respect patient autonomy in this as in other contexts" (Sheldon 2016, p. 365). What remains is to update the law and to acknowledge the right of women to control their own fertility. Such an update would "recognise that a law is overdue reform when there is no appetite for enforcing it in the context for which it was intended, where it has no impact on abortion rates, where it imposes clinically unnecessary impediments that restrict the provision of a high quality, safe and compassionate service, and where it stigmatises one third of British women and the healthcare professionals who care for them" (Sheldon 2016, p. 365).

The examples of Dutch, French and German women claiming autonomy and challenging outdated criminal law provisions demonstrate that the possibility of open non-compliance is an important factor of a society's normative development. The feminist thus 'appears as the representative of a different social order'. She conceives of herself 'as belonging to another social order which ought to take the place of the old one' (Mead 1934, p. 386).

Any action can be interpreted as revealing an agent's personal maxim, which stands as a candidate to be adopted as a general rule. Whether it develops into a norm depends on the—supportive or negative—reactions of others. Women's admission of having aborted cannot only be interpreted in relation to the traditional prohibition as criminal offences, but also as stating a personal maxim and hence suggesting a new norm that acknowledges the dignity and autonomy of pregnant women. However, it must not be overlooked that women's successful opposition was possible because of diverse moral views on the issue of abortion. The contradiction between 'Pro-life' and 'Pro-choice' arose from a situation of moral pluralism and from a societal climate in the late 1960s that openly challenged the norms of a bourgeois society and advocated individual autonomy, diversity and overall societies' modernisation.

While thus systematic non-compliance destabilises a specific norm or a segment of the normative order—such as patriarchal family structures—many norms cope everyday with 'small-scale' disobedience. Whether a norm is (still) supported by a societal normative consensus shows when its infringement becomes known to the public and the authorities. If the latter firmly reject the norm violation and if their reaction is appreciated by their community and interpreted as a legitimate form of sanctioning an offender, the norm is confirmed or even reinforced. If, on the other hand, a norm is infringed with impunity, because those who witness the infringement do not report to the police or because the police do not react, it deteriorates and eventually disappears (Günther 2014, p. 36). To give an example, the prevailing reluctance of victims of hate crime to report their victimisation to the police can significantly impair the criminal justice response to hate crime, disappoint legitimate expectations of victims, and foster the spread of discriminatory attitudes (FRA 2016, p. 27).

In any case, the effectiveness of a normative order remains premised on the persuasiveness of its norms. This restriction is inbuilt in the very mechanism of normativity and prevents a normative code from deviating excessively, persistently and at large from the views and convictions of the community's members on whose compliance the effectiveness and hence sustainability of the normative order remains premised. A normative order cannot be effective unless it maintains the inherent link between its contents and the moral views and convictions of its individual addressees. What sustains a criminal law provision is not the deterrence effected by its penalty, but the moral agreement and resulting compliance of its addressees. Any normative code relies on a consensus of its addressees and hence on the moral quality of its norms and not on means of coercion, such as deterrent or incapacitating sanctions. The objective of a social order is the normative integration of a society of language users based on convincing—persuasive or dissuasive—norms.

Not only is the normative order created by agents; at the same time, it is the order that calls on individuals and thus creates them as agents. Göran Therborn has rightly pointed out that society's calling on children takes this double form of "subjection-qualification": Society's calling subjects individuals to a normative code, thereby simultaneously creating new members who, due to their capacity of responsible agency, are qualified to acknowledge and thus reproduce or change the normative order (1999, p. 17). Subjection and qualification are two sides of the same coin of the permanent creation of subjects and the normative order in recursive processes of normative communication. Hence the autonomous individual self and society must be seen as generating and reinforcing one another: The self joins in the creation of society, and society initiates, fosters and encourages the creation of autonomous selves (Mead 1934, pp. 385–386).

The loops in which individuals mutually address and constitute one another as persons and simultaneously constitute, reproduce and reform their society and its environment as a symbolic order never come to a halt (Müller-Tuckfeld 1997, p. 327). Such an event would be the moment when persons and society cease to exist. Hence, understanding culture and normativity must start from the fact that "subject and object, self and other, psyche and culture, person and context [...] require each other, and dynamically, dialectically, and jointly make each other up [...] human beings and sociocultural environments interpenetrate each other's identity and cannot be analytically disjoined into independent and dependent variables" (Shweder 1990, p. 1, 1991, p. 74). Persons and their societies are co-constituted by the same permanent and recursive processes of languaging that draw meaning exactly from the cultural context, in the constitution of which they are engaged.

According to a beautifully simple and precise formula, as persons we 'are constituted in language in a continuous becoming that we bring forth with others' (Maturana and Varela 1987/1998, pp. 234–235). If anything, human dignity is an individual's unconditional right to be part of this process of culture as continuous becoming of persons.

Thus, society's calling initiates a development consisting of two vectors with opposing directions, which operate simultaneously. On the one hand, culture demands of a child to act, and the normative order of the society in which she is constituted provides, at that time, the only available framework and orientation. On the other hand, the child learns that it is her decision whether to conform to the demands of these social norms or not. It is when she considers the option of not being 'a good girl' that she understands her role as a person free to choose.

The child is integrated into a system of recursive processes interweaving the formation of societal structures and the creation of persons. This interplay takes the form of a person reflecting on, and becoming aware of society's imperatives, and more and more deliberately deciding to confirm or to challenge these or other norms through her actions, thereby conserving or innovating social order. The normative code owes the entirety of its binding forces to the autonomous decisions of individuals by which they acknowledge the normative order and its authority.

3.4.8 Individuation

Because individuals are free to acknowledge certain normative claims and reject others, the dialectic of the abstract order constituting subjects and their autonomy drives normative development. Given the complexities of modern normative orders, individuals cannot, in the end, avoid decisions on priorities of values and on the resolution of normative conflicts. They eventually find themselves in situations where they have to cast their vote by demonstrating what they, as persons, believe to be the right thing to do. By their very nature, complex normative codes fuel open-ended processes of normative development.

A unique personality emerges as the result of a life-long struggle for the integration of a consistent self within a complex normative structure. This consistent self constitutes the subject of an individual's biography and therefore must be preserved as a respected self under all conditions. 'A man has to keep his self-respect, and it may be that he has to fly in the face of the whole community in preserving this self-respect. But he does it from the point of view of what he considers a higher and better society than that which exists. Both of these are essential to moral conduct: that there should be a social organization and that the individual should maintain himself' (Mead 1934, p. 389).

To develop as an autonomous individual, the child must internalise the normative order of the societal configurations into which she is born, revolt against her subordination, assert her own personality and, in fighting it out, detect the limits and adversaries of her self-determination in society. Therefore, it is only in communities that human beings can develop as individual persons (Elias 1939, p. 22).

While a child's first revolt is about having a choice to comply or not with her parents' rules—about the difference between being a good and a naughty girl—in a modern pluralist society a second 'revolt'—often coinciding with puberty—concerns the contents of her parents' rules compared to other orientations. Under the specific conditions of moral diversity and individual autonomy, an agent must do more than decide whether to abide by the rules and the particular ideology of her parents or not. She must, within the wider horizon of the various normative concepts offered by her society, assess her parents' orientation, to position herself and in the end to choose the laws that she deems appropriate to guide her actions as their own maxims and to express her personality.

Hence, the development of an autonomous person is premised not only on the development of agency as choice—or 'decision-making power'—but, in addition, on a critical reflection on the normative framework, within which decisions are made and on a deliberate identification and appropriation of what is one's own laws. To quote Rorty (1999, pp. 117–118):

> There is no such thing as human nature [. . .]. There is only the shaping of an animal into a human being by a process of socialization, followed (with luck) by the self-individualization and self-creation of that human being through his or her own later revolt against that very process.

It is during this second phase that the person emerges clearly as a unique moral personality. By the specific manner of a person's answers to the summons of her society, she positions herself, within the wider framework of her society, in relation to the norms, claims and suggestions of others. In addition to the biological life of an organism, an agent lives her meaningful social life—her *vita*—which is shaped by the decisions she takes. While others create the person first as a mere address—almost like the address of an unfurnished apartment where no one has yet moved in—the individual person takes shape and gives substance to that form by answering in a specific manner to the calling of her society and by finding her place within her society's complex, diverse, inconsistent, and conflictual normative order. Her story is the story of her relations to an encountered set of societal norms (Butler 2005, p. 8). It is her own choices that substantiate and give meaning and expression to herself as a genuine, idiosyncratic, discrete and consistent person (Korsgaard 2009, p. 19).

A person forms an identity by assessing, appropriating or rejecting the orders, commands and demands she faces from two sides. Firstly, from the normative code to which she is subjected by others calling on her and initiating her constitution as a person, and secondly, from the driving powers of her emotions, instincts and the 'demons' of her past still populating her inner life. It is in this field of strong forces that the individual has to struggle for the development of a unique and autonomous personality.

The normative development of modern societies is fuelled by conflicts over individuals' claims to autonomy (Alexy 2010, p. 235). This can be seen in women demanding to decide autonomously on their sexual sphere and reproduction, adults wishing to have a greater say in issues concerning their parenthood, women protesting heteronomous patriarchal family structures and domestic violence, individuals laying claim to decisions concerning the time and conditions of their death, patients not allowing doctors to tell them what is good for them, migrants claiming the right to decide autonomously where on this small planet they want to live, and so on. In addition, individuals claim the right to self-definition and to fend off the imposition of constraining labels with complex implicit connotations, such as race, nationality, gender roles, or traditional standards of sexual orientation.

However, this broadening of individual autonomy can also be viewed as an increasing challenge for individuals to know who they are and to be able to account for how they lead their lives. Being able to find one's way around in society without losing orientation becomes more and more problematic. Study and career choices, family planning and decisions on life style are less and less constrained, and at the same time become increasingly complex and demanding.

While in Kantian philosophy the autonomous individual is a given, it is in Fichte's view an achievement, the result of successfully integrating one's action under one personality as a consistent rationale. Any action demonstrates a personality, a more or less coherent set of opinions, attitudes and reasons, that is, accounting for an individual being determined to act in this manner and in no other. Therefore, the moral evaluation of our actions amounts to a moral evaluation of ourselves. If we do something right, we are proud of ourselves. Charles Stevenson (1963, p. 59) has pointed out:

> When we act in accordance with a peculiarly moral approval we have a secondary approval, so to speak, which makes us proud to recognize our primary one. And when we yield to what we call 'temptation' - or, in other words, when the strength of this peculiarly moral approval is outweighed by our nonmoral disapproval - we have a strong inclination to conceal our conduct from our introspection.

Hence, an individual has to permanently assess the consistency of her actions, firstly, with the challenges of her object world, and, secondly, with herself as a stable and unswerving personality. It is not sufficient that she does the right thing, it should also be what others could expect of her; and if an action is wrong, the ensuing question is what the wrong action reveals about the actor, who, therefore, may be inclined to feel not only guilty, but also ashamed.

Fichte saw the risk that the integration of an empirical self can fail. He believed that a human being's ultimate challenge was to construct a self that allowed her to explain all her actions as resulting from a rational self or personality defined by a coherent system of one's own laws. Only when the individual can account for her actions by showing that her actions result from her personality, the individual demonstrates her autonomy as the absence of heteronomy and determination by foreign forces. Fichte posits (1794c, p. 149):

> The pure I is always one and the same and is never anything different. [. . .] Man is always supposed to be at one with himself; he should never contradict himself. [. . .] A person ought to determine himself and not permit himself to be determined by something foreign. [. . .] The empirical I ought to be determined in a manner in which it could be eternally determined. Therefore, I would express the principle of morality in the formula [. . .]: 'Act so that you could consider the maxims of your willing to be eternal laws for yourself.' [. . .] The ultimate characteristic feature of all rational beings is, accordingly, absolute unity, constant self-identity, complete agreement with oneself. This absolute identity is the form of the pure I and is its only true form; or rather, in the conceivability of identity we *recognize* the expression of the pure form of the I.

Because a person's personality shows in her action and because her action impacts on her object world a person continuously strives to assimilate her object world—nature and society—to her laws. The objects—physical and social entities—she creates reflect her personality, laws, and order. Fichte believed that humans' struggle for a unique and consistent personality that is objectified in an increasingly rational organisation of humans' natural environment and social order was their ultimate vocation (1794c, p. 152):

> Man's final end is to subordinate to himself all that is irrational, to master it freely and according to his own laws. [. . .] Thus it is not man's vocation to reach this goal. But he can and he should draw nearer to it, and his true vocation qua *man*, that is, insofar as he is a rational but finite, a sensuous but free being, lies in *endless approximation toward this goal.* Now if, as we surely can, we call this total harmony with oneself 'perfection,' in the highest sense of the word, then *perfection* is man's highest and unattainable goal.

Perfection, in the Fichtean reading, lies in the harmony between an individual's consistent autonomous self and the objects that the individual creates in cooperation with others and that express the autonomous individual's self as a unique personality. These objects exist in nature and in society and in both cases retroact on the individual. Therefore, what Fichte describes are recursive processes of subjectification and objectification by which the individual and society progress towards a situation of total harmony of autonomous individuals and the natural and societal framework of their existence.

The individual's approximation to this goal of perfection is, in empirical reality, premised on a social order that fosters the development of autonomous individuals and their productiveness and creativity in expressing and objectivating themselves. In the following such an ideal society will be referred to as a global humanist order.

3.4.9 The Crucial Importance of Fichte's Concept of Human Dignity

Fichte's insight that the subject is created based on and within her society's normative order has not yet become commonplace. This is remarkable, given the immense moral and political relevance of Fichte's discovery, which radically places the person as a reflective conscious subject at the mercy of her community's readiness to call on her and to lay the normative foundations of her development as a moral person.

Throughout our lives, our social existence remains tied to this foundation and premised on recurring processes of communication by which it is continuously reproduced. We lose our personhood when these processes stop. The person exists in communication and is extinguished when the individual is no longer addressed as a person and a member of the society. As Lon Fuller pointed out maintaining the particular quality of a human existence is less about biology and more about preserving certain forms of communication (Fuller 1969, pp. 184–186).

To exemplify the formative power of normative communication, Gerald Stourzh (2009, pp. 140–142) relates a court case, decided by the German Supreme Court (Reichsgericht) in June 1936, between the German film production company UFA and the Jewish author Eric Charell, who had been contracted by the UFA to act as a film director. UFA now maintained that, due to changed societal preconditions, Charell was no longer able to work as a director. First, the Supreme Court, quoting the Fichtean formula, observed that, previously, liberal views on a person's legal capacity had, among those who carry a human face, made no differentiation as to the person's race ('Die frühere liberale Vorstellung vom Rechtsinhalt der Persönlichkeit machte unter den Wesen mit Menschenantlitz keine grundsätzlichen Wertunterschiede nach der Gleichheit oder Verschiedenheit des Bluts'). However, in legal history there are also examples of subjects losing their civil and political rights. Persons entering a convent were, under certain conditions, considered by law as deceased. In this sense, the Supreme Court assumed that, as concerns Eric Charell, his legal status as a person had changed due to racial considerations recognised by the legal order ('eine aus gesetzlich anerkannten rassepolitischen Gesichtspunkten eingetretene Änderung in der rechtlichen Geltung der Persönlichkeit'). Morsink (1999, p. 45) sums it up observing that 'the man's Jewishness made him legally dead'. Two years later, Walter Buch, a leading Nazi judge, published in the official periodical 'Deutsche Justiz' his view that a Jew is not a human being, but a sign of rot ('Der Jude ist kein Mensch. Er ist eine Fäulniserscheinung'.)

Against this historic background, the concept of human dignity insists on the unconditional right of every human being to be a person and to have rights equal to those of all others. In a post Auschwitz world this right to be a person and to have full rights is the core element of human dignity and the basis for the construction of a humanist society.

Lacan suggested that subjects refuse to acknowledge the fact that their personhood is premised on the persistent willingness of others to name, address or refer to them as persons. We prefer, so he indicates, not to realise the fact that our social existence as persons depends on others and their attention and cooperation (Lacan 2005). We avoid the disquieting insight that we are, as conscious human beings, at the mercy of others who include us in or exclude us from humanity.

From here emanates the horror of a person becoming a person because her society so demands and gradually turning into vermin when treated as vermin that finds its pure expression in Kafka's Metamorphosis and later works. This was, in a sense, terribly proven true by the Lagers of the Nazis that, by revoking the call of the community on human beings, systematically and on a large scale transformed persons into the living dead referred to, in the language of the *Lager*, as *Muselmann*, alive in a biological sense, but gradually marginalised, negated and extinguished in social terms.

Hence the crucial twist of the concept of personhood—and of human dignity based on personhood—is its radical reinterpretation in the course of its maturing from Kant to Fichte. For Kant, human dignity denotes the legitimate claim to be accepted, acknowledged and valued as the autonomous person that one is. In Fichte's world, society comes in at a much earlier point, namely in engaging in early processes of subjectivation. Human dignity, in Fichte's reading, captures the unconditional right of the human being to be enabled to develop, and supported in developing into an accountable and autonomous person.

From here it is but a small step to realising that what we owe to one another, more than anything else, is unconditional and irrevocable subjectivation—acts of communication, that is, which continually attest to the personhood of others and thus engage in their irrevocable social and normative constitution and inclusion in human culture. *Arendt*'s—truly *Fichtean*—formula is precise: Human dignity is the "right to have rights", to be initiated and accepted, that is, in "some kind of organized community" and, on that basis, to be attributed responsible agency and to be "judged by one's actions and opinions" (Arendt 1951, pp. 296–297). In one of his early writings, Fichte declares that the only fundamental right of a man, from which all others can be derived, is the right to be an 'I' (Recht zur Ichheit). By the moral law "I ought to be an Ego, an independent being, a person – I have therefore a right to be a person and to will my duty" (quoted by Cassirer, p. 112). In this vein, human dignity—the right to be a person—is indeed the source from which all rights flow. Human dignity is the right to become—and to be supported in becoming—a person who has rights and who can, in accordance with her mental capabilities, claim to be held to account for her action based on her legal community's normative code. As will be elaborated in Chap. 4, criminal justice is the main institution ensuring that offenders are respected as accountable agents and that victims are respected as persons entitled to autonomy and care.

In this sense, the German Constitutional Court has recognised, as inherent in human dignity, the right of a child to *become* a person: "*Das Recht jedes Kindes auf Entwicklung zur Persönlichkeit – auf "Person werden" – [. . .]*". Because human personhood is premised on precarious processes of social formation, the child is entitled to be protected in the private and the public sphere against interferences that have a potential to distort these formation processes (BVerfG, W. GmbH, para. 5).

Thus human dignity, in its Fichtean interpretation, does not focus on an inherent, given quality of humans, but on an existential need of and dependence on a social existence and on the processes of subjectivation that remedy this reliance. This dependence on others is multidimensional. It includes a physical need of care; a social need of subjectivation as an autonomous and accountable agent; and an emotional need of the self-esteem and trust enabling an individual to believe in the relevance of her life as a social existence. Human dignity as the right to become a person spans these various dimensions.

However, the right to be initiated into a polity cannot be premised on a membership of a polity, to which the individual already belongs. Hence human dignity as an entitlement of the human being is necessarily addressed—not to a nation state, but—to humankind in its entirety, politically organised as a community of legal communities. It is, in the end, a right of a human individual against any other human individual to treatment as a person, hence to every other human being's readiness to enter into a normative relation with the claimant. The basic normative relationship is not between a citizen and her (nation) state, but between the human individual and humankind, which is identical with all other human beings. This is why Fichte insisted that the very notion of the human person is the notion of a species.

3.5 The Development of Human Rights

The unfolding of human dignity and human rights is not a development that occurs within an isolated legal sphere. Rather the concepts of human dignity and human rights flowing from human dignity emerge as political categories in history, and they answer to two dramatic failures: firstly the failure, manifested in the 30 Years War and the order of Westphalia, of all attempts to integrate European societies on the basis of a shared religion; secondly, the decline, manifested in two World Wars, of the vision of a peaceful European order of co-existing nation states, a failure that concerns both variants, the authoritarian and the liberal nation state. The notions of human dignity and a humanist society, established on human dignity as its normative foundation, overcome the rigorous and dogmatic morality of medieval societies, on the one hand, and the inherently collectivist and discriminatory concept of the nation state, on the other.

Because of their historical and political significance, human dignity and human rights cannot be explained as the aggregated result of decisions of legislators, judicial or non-judicial bodies, and committees acting at national, regional and international levels. Any attempt to describe and explain the emerging of human rights in terms of a sequence of political decisions and legal texts remains limited to observing the shadows cast by large-scale historic and social developments on an official institutional screen.

It follows that the concepts of human dignity and human rights need to be analysed and interpreted within the sociopolitical framework given at a certain time. In a monarchy, in a liberal nation state, and in a dignity-based humanist society, human rights mean significantly different things. In history, human rights arrive in several waves, and every wave is essentially different from its predecessors, owing to shifting societal and political frameworks and paradigms.

To highlight one significant example, in terms of sovereignty, the development moved from a sovereign monarch exceptionally granting human rights as singular freedoms, to sovereign nations allying with human rights in order to strengthen their legitimacy, to finally sovereign individuals tasking governments with realising and defending human rights and supervising their governments' performance by means of national control mechanisms as well as international law and organisations.

3.5.1 The First Generation: Liberal Constitutionalism and Human Rights as a Subject's Private Freedom

In the phase of constitutionalism—starting at least from the Bill of Rights of 1689 granting "the right of the subjects to petition the king"—rights of individuals emerge as enclaves within the vast domain of the monarch's sovereignty, as individuals' limited freedom within a territory of the Monarch's rule. Within this paradigm, rights establish private spheres of autonomy protected—or at least claiming protection—against state intervention, such as freedom and security of person, due process rights, the privacy of homes and the secrecy of correspondence. These freedoms also serve as a framework of emerging religious pluralism, tolerated as long as the practice of religions does not interfere with public order. Later, additional rights enable the—more or less—unrestricted expression of an individual's opinion, the freedom of press - within limits determined by the monarch - the right to collectively and publicly exercise one's religion, and spheres of - to some extent - free private or public association.

In political terms, constitutionalism and the idea of granting to subjects certain rights as protected spheres of autonomy is a first attempt of a monarchic system to reach a compromise between the principle of state sovereignty and the political claims of powerful groups—encouraged by enlightenment philosophers—challenging absolutist rule. In the end, political concessions soften and undermine the very principle of the divine rights of the king.

Rights of subjects constitute enclaves of individual autonomy in the wider sphere of the sovereignty of the prince. By acknowledging liberties of citizens, a constitution allocates spheres of moral decision-making to autonomous individuals who are, within defined margins, allowed to make decisions for themselves. Into these enclaves, the prince can often interfere only if predominant public interests so require and based on a legal regulation existing at the time of the interference. Hence, the phase of constitutionalism and of individuals' liberties marks not only the first generation of human rights but also the emergence of the rule of law.

In continental Europe, two important examples of codifications are strongly influenced by the theory of natural law and on this basis strive to find a viable balance between the interests of the monarch and the rights of subjects. These are the Prussian *Allgemeines Landrecht* (ALR) of 1794 and the Austrian "*Allgemeine bürgerliche Gesetzbuch für die gesamten deutschen Erblande*" (ABGB), which in preliminary versions was first enacted in East and West Galicia in 1797. While only some provisions of the ALR are still in force today, the ABGB is after more than 200 years still applied in - what today remains of - Austria, despite numerous amendments. Many provisions have survived unaltered.

According to Article 16 of the Austrian Civil Code, every human being is to be considered a person endowed with innate rights that are obvious and reasonable. These inherent rights account for an individual's status as a person, ruling out any form of slavery or servitude.

Angeborne Rechte

§ 16. Jeder Mensch hat angeborne, schon durch die Vernunft einleuchtende Rechte, und ist daher als eine Person zu betrachten. Sklaverei oder Leibeigenschaft, und die Ausübung einer darauf sich beziehenden Macht, wird in diesen Ländern nicht gestattet.

Hence, in this perspective the human being is by nature a person entitled to autonomy and therefore cannot be owned or utilised by another human being, e.g. as a slave. In the perspective of enlightenment such spheres of respected individual freedom - such as liberty and security of person, domiciliary rights, and undisturbed private practice of religion - constitute nuclei from which a generalised concept of individual autonomy gradually develops.

By granting rights to subjects, they are at once integrated as citizens in the structure of the state. Their rights are protected and ensured by the sovereign, who appears as guarantor of the rights of individuals and thus seemingly transcends and overcomes the antagonism of public interests and individuals' liberties.

3.5.2 The Second Generation: Liberal Nation States and Human Rights as the Political Rights of Equal Citizens

After the collapse of monarchies anchored in the divine rights of the crown, the proclamation of human rights serves to ground and legitimise the liberal democratic nation state. In the absence of an opposing force, individual autonomy is no longer limited to an exceptional position and to the private sphere, but extends to the public and political domain - at least in theory. In this phase, human rights leave the appeal and sovereignty of the nation state untouched, or rather add to its legitimacy by demonstrating that individuals and their rights prosper within the political environment of the nation state.

If there is a human right that faithfully captures the ideology of republicanism than it is the belief that autonomy requires political autonomy and that equal autonomy implies equal access to *any* public office, from the police officer to the member of parliament and president. In the words of Richard Dagger, "republicans believe that government is a public concern [...] and public concerns are the province of self-governing citizens who will seek to enjoy liberty under and through the law" (2013, p. 46).

The concept of autonomy-rights, which in the era of constitutionalism had been granted by the monarch as enclaves of private freedoms within the vast land of her rule, is now extended to also cover the polity's public sphere. In addition to the classical liberties, political rights are designed to enable autonomous individuals to take charge of their state, such as rights to vote and to stand as candidates in elections to parliamentary assemblies, rights to have equal access to administrative offices, rights to act as jurors in courts, rights to establish political parties and rights to public assembly. These also include the right to *publicly* engage in religious practices, the right to publicly express one's opinion, as well as the abolition of censorship and the unrestricted freedom of media.

As—in the view of republicans and liberal democrats—all public life and normative development is premised on the unconstrained exchange of differing moral points of view, freedom of thought, of conscience, of religion and whatever belief, freedom of private and public expression, and freedom of assembly are primary values in a democratic republic. The public sphere offers a platform where free and prudent people meet to calmly discuss and sort out public affairs. One important underlying assumption is that, although their moral views may differ, all citizens arrive at the public sphere fully equipped with practical reason and hence all the moral and political expertise required for judicious legislation. A liberal constitutional framework allows individuals' morality and reason to come into its own and to openly compete with other convictions and perspectives in political fora, for the sake of the thriving of the community.

The concept of equal opportunities is the signum of republicanism. However, there is an inbuilt limitation, which follows from the fact that the polity's identity and unity is perceived as a nation and the individuals living within the nation state as forming one people. The nation state is the political form of this people. Human rights, in this phase, do not challenge the collectivity as the most fundamental category, but by assuming that human rights and, more generally, human welfare necessarily flourish in a democratic republic rather add to the prestige of the nation state.

Hence, the republic nation state is founded on the difference in status of citizens who are members of the nation and foreigners who are not (Stichweh 2016). The nation state pledges to protect the rights and happiness of its citizens, but does not necessarily care about others who stand outside. Because of this limitation, human rights of the second generation are inherently the rights of citizens and not—in a Fichtean perspective—equal rights of all human beings. The nation state cares about the happiness and wellbeing of its citizens because this forms part of its legitimation and serves its interests.

3.5.3 The Third Generation: the Welfare State and Social Rights

While welfarism formed an important component of enlightened absolutism, the idea of social *rights* only became politically significant after World War I. The nucleus of social rights can be traced to the Constitution of the International Labour Office (ILO), which forms Part XIII of the treaties signed by the victorious Allies in Versailles (with Germany), in Saint-Germain-en-Laye (with German-Austria) and in Trianon (with the Kingdom of Hungary), as well as Part XII of the Treaties of Neuilly-sur-Seine (Bulgaria) and Sèvres (Ottoman Empire), all signed between June 1919 and August 1920.

The main objective of the ILO Constitution was to work towards consistent standards of decent work implemented in all industrial economies to provide a level playing field for competing industries. Hence the Preamble of Section I observes that "the failure of any nation to adopt humane conditions of labour is an obstacle in the way of other nations which desire to improve the conditions in their own countries." The primary means of achieving this objective was the establishment of the International Labour Organisation and the International Labour Office. However, the Preamble also observes that

> conditions of labour exist involving such injustice, hardship, and privation to large numbers of people as to produce unrest so great that the peace and harmony of the world are imperilled; and an improvement of those conditions is urgently required: as, for example, by the regulation of the hours of work, including the establishment of a maximum working day and week, the regulation of the labour supply, the prevention of unemployment, the provision of an adequate living wage, the protection of the worker against sickness, disease and injury arising out of his employment, the protection of children, young persons and women, provision for old age and injury, protection of the interests of workers when employed in countries other than their own recognition of the principle of freedom of association, the organisation of vocational and technical education and other measures; [. . .]

The Preamble assures that the contracting parties are "moved by sentiments of justice and humanity as well as by the desire to secure the permanent peace of the world". (After World War II, this motive to grant human rights as a means of preserving global peace became a driving force of the development of fourth generation human rights.)

In Article 427 of the ILO Constitution, the contracting states agree on the following principles as a matter of urgency:

> First. The guiding principle above enunciated that labour should not be regarded merely as a commodity or article of commerce.
>
> Second. The right of association for all lawful purposes by the employed as well as by the employers.
>
> Third. The payment to the employed of a wage adequate to maintain a reasonable standard of life as this is understood in their time and country.
>
> Fourth. The adoption of an eight hours day or a forty-eight hours week as the standard to be aimed at where it has not already been attained.
>
> Fifth. The adoption of a weekly rest of at least twenty-four hours, which should include Sunday wherever practicable.

Sixth. The abolition of child labour and the imposition of such limitations on the labour of young persons as shall permit the continuation of their education and assure their proper physical development.

Seventh. The principle that men and women should receive equal remuneration for work of equal value.

Eighth. The standard set by law in each country with respect to the conditions of labour should have due regard to the equitable economic treatment of all workers lawfully resident therein.

Ninth. Each State should make provision for a system of inspection in which women should take part, in order to ensure the enforcement of the laws and regulations for the protection of the employed.

These principles aim to ensure, as a matter of supreme international importance, the physical, moral and intellectual well-being of industrial wage-earners and "confer lasting benefits upon the wage-earners of the world."

Several aspects of this text are worth highlighting. Firstly, because of its economic motivation, Article 427 emphasises the rights of those groups of industrial wage-earners who, because of their weaker position on labour markets, are particularly vulnerable to exploitation, namely children, women, elderly and migrant workers. The rights of these groups are defined in terms—not of liberties, but—of welfare and benefits. This marks a break in the development of human rights. The concept of social rights starts out from the assumption that society is responsible for the basic well-being of all its members (Kaufmann 2003, p. 17).

Secondly, because these rights are granted with a view of protecting international industrial competition, they are guaranteed—in theory—to all "wage-earners of the world." At the same time, these rights are not intended to be binding on states as international law. In marked contrast to the fourth generation rights, that become politically influential after 1965, social rights, while for the first time adopting a global perspective, initially still left the full sovereignty of the nation state untouched.

In the 1940s, welfare policies were boosted by the widespread view that the Great Depression and its societal consequences—unemployment and political discontent—had been one of the root causes of World War II (Kaufmann 2003, p. 25). Hence, the concept of social rights was extended beyond the issue of decent working conditions, importantly by ILO's Philadelphia Declaration of 1944, in which the ILO's General Conference updated the organisation's mandate, aims and policy principles. The Declaration departs from the assumptions that "lasting peace can be established only if it is based on social justice", that "poverty anywhere constitutes a danger to prosperity everywhere" and that hence "the war against want requires to be carried on with unrelenting vigour within each nation, and by continuous and concerted international effort". Therefore, the Declaration maintains that:

> all human beings, irrespective of race, creed or sex, have the right to pursue both their material well-being and their spiritual development in conditions of freedom and dignity, of economic security and equal opportunity; [. . .]

In the following year, the UN Charter was adopted, which addresses International Economic and Social Cooperation in Chapter IX. Article 55 commits the UN to "the creation of conditions of stability and well-being which are necessary for peaceful and friendly relations among nations" and to the objective of promoting "higher standards of living, full employment, and conditions of economic and social progress and development".

Finally, the Universal Declaration (1948) in Articles 22–25 spells out the "war against want" by granting rights to social security, to work—including decent working conditions and "just and favourable remuneration ensuring for himself and his family an existence worthy of human dignity"—and "to a standard of living adequate for the health and well being of himself and of his family, including food, clothing, housing and medical care and necessary social services, and the right to security in the event of unemployment, sickness, disability, widowhood, old age or other lack of livelihood in circumstances beyond his control."

3.5.4 The Fourth Generation: Solidarity of Humankind and Universal Rights in a Global Order

The human rights revolution that followed the Second World War and reacted to Nazi atrocities commenced with two events. Firstly, war crime tribunals in Nuremberg and Tokyo made it clear that individuals have obligations under international law, preventing war criminals from invoking as a defence the fact that they acted in accordance with national law. Secondly, the Universal Declaration demonstrates that individuals have rights under international law. Combining these two aspects, the radically new situation post WWII can be seen as defined by the rights and obligations that individuals have among themselves as subjects of international law (Sohn 1982). In other terms, what commences after WWII is the decline of a global order of coexisting - competing and antagonistic - nation states and the rise of the cosmopolitan individual.

The hallmark of this new phase in the development of a global order is the concept of human dignity. To quote O'Mahony (2012, p. 552), it is 'by now clear that human dignity is the central value underpinning the entirety of international human rights law'. While political and social rights emphasised the equality of citizens, dignity rights—against the backdrop of fascist *Gleichschaltung*—stress the frailty and precariousness of the autonomous individual, diversity, societal pluralism and global 'solidarity in diversity'.

According to David Held and Pietro Maffetone, contemporary political theory has reached what they call a 'cosmopolitan plateau'. By this, the authors mean that what they refer to as 'moral cosmopolitanism' provides a framework for political discussions that is accepted by a majority of those who participate in the conversation of political theory. 'Moral cosmopolitanism has come to articulate the boundaries of reasonable disagreement in global political theory', and the most important implication of this cosmopolitan plateau is 'the commitment to basic human rights' (Held and Maffetone 2016, p. 1). This commitment establishes an overlapping consensus, a shared understanding of the moral status of human beings. Endorsing a definition suggested by Thomas Pogge, Held and Maffetone believe that this moral status is characterised by three elements—individualism, universality and generality, meaning that persons are 'ultimate units of moral concern for everyone – not only for their compatriots, fellow religionists, or suchlike' (Pogge 1992, p. 49). Held and Maffetone conclude (2016, p. 8):

> Basic human rights have come to articulate the normative focal point of global political theory. They constitute the most important benchmark (though of course not the only one) for the evaluation both of internal and external state conduct, for the actions of global governance institutions, for the norms and principles that constitute international and transnational regimes, for the policies of multinational corporations and for the behaviour of political leaders and public officials.

The upshot of this is the 'refusal to accept a background picture in which states are sovereign in the traditional Westphalian sense of the term, and consequently, see their international obligations as only justifiable through voluntariness or consent' (Held and Maffetone 2016, p. 12).

Hence, at the current stage of the development of human rights, which gradually commences after the Second World War and gathers momentum during the second half of the 1960s, human rights, based on strong claims of human dignity and universality, function as a critical—and increasingly also legally binding—yardstick enabling individuals to, at national, regional and international levels, challenge the performance of 'their' governments. While, during the era of the powerful nation state, the principle of national sovereignty had barred an individual's access to protection granted by international law, this barrier is now overcome. For the first time, individuals are recognised as holders of rights under international law, and the plea of national sovereignty would no longer prevent an individual from bringing an action against a state party from within its territory (Hare 2009, p. 63).

Following the independence of the United States and the French revolution, democratic nation states and freedom had become thought of as twins and natural allies. A democratic republic, striving to achieve collective happiness, had been somewhat automatically trusted to secure the welfare and rights of its inhabitants. However, the very fact that the Nazis, in a country regarded as politically and culturally mature, came to power in free and democratic elections forcefully rebutted the presumption that a democratic nation state, based on a multi-party system, independent media and free elections, would inherently and necessarily develop towards continually perfecting the rights of its citizens. The trust in the democratic nation state was replaced by the insight that strong institutions of international supervision are indispensable in protecting human rights, as they are capable of intervening in case of an aggressive regime seizing power and jeopardising peace (Kaufmann 2003, p. 24).

However, while the fuse of this reform was lit at the end of World War II, the cord had to keep burning for some time before the anti-authoritarian movement overcame the moral paralysis of Western democracies, exacerbated by the frozen state of the cold war, and until the political energy accumulated that made profound societal reform possible.

The decline of the nation state and the rise of the concept of human dignity were finally heralded by the New Left of the 1960s with its anti-authoritarian scepticism towards nation state institutions, its rejection of Western imperialism and consumerism and its insistence on the global responsibilities of a cosmopolitan civil society. There was the Helsinki process, which eventually, together with other factors, led to the demise of the Soviet Union; the disaster of the Vietnam War, that lastingly undermined the reputation of the other super-power; and the fall of authoritarian regimes in Latin-America and Africa, which had been supported by the US. If there is a year that marks the end of the old and the beginning of a new era, it is 1968, the year of the My Lai massacre in Vietnam, of the quashing of the hope of socialism with a human face by Warsaw Pact troops in Czechoslovakia and of the student revolts in Paris, Berlin and other cities with their radically anti-authoritarian, anti-nationalist and cosmopolitan orientation.

At the level of international human rights, this political fermentation process is best reflected by the adoption in December 1966 of the two international covenants on human rights and the approval in November 1969 of the American Convention on Human Rights, which in its preamble states very clearly:

> Recognizing that the essential rights of man are not derived from one's being a national of a certain state, but are based upon attributes of the human personality, and that they therefore justify international protection in the form of a convention reinforcing or complementing the protection provided by the domestic law of the American states [. . .]

It is the particular architecture that spans autonomous individual rights-holders, duty-bearing authorities at state levels and supervisory institutions at regional and international levels, that signifies a global humanist society as the, to date, last phase in the development of societies' normative codes.

What, at this latest stage of the development of human rights, is added to the concept is the Fichtean insight into the societal preconditions of all rights. Unless the community, in a spirit of human solidarity, calls on, takes care of and introduces a child to the culture of her community, the individual does not arrive to being free or equal. Without a community, freedom and equality remain entirely out of an individual's reach. Hence, it is the calling of her society that, because it references a political and normative order, shapes the autonomy, liberty and equality of the individual. In a sense, the classical trinity of *liberté*, *égalité* and *fraternité*, which had developed from left to right, must now be read in the inverse order: The solidarity of a human community that initiates the infant as its member is the real point of departure. Both components of human dignity and human rights—mutual care and mutual respect—are rooted in the global solidarity of humanity.

This is the point where the blind spot of traditional liberal concepts becomes evident. The freedom-loving person who promotes the vision of the individual living in a state of splendid independence and self-sufficiency may overlook that an individual's freedom and personhood are, and remain throughout her life, premised on the sympathy, concern and compassion of those fellow-citizens who contribute to the process of her initiation in society and to her development as an autonomous person within a normative framework (Jakobs 2008, p. 38).

Hence, solidarity is not a supplement to freedom, but the founding and overarching principle of the trinity of freedom, equality and 'brotherliness'. Consciously or not, it is in a spirit of human solidarity that adults acknowledge, care for and call on an infant as a member of their societal networks and of humanity at large. Autonomy, equality and compassionate concern are aspects of what every human being is entitled to vis-à-vis the rest of humanity. In the interpretation of the fourth generation, all human rights derive their meaning from how they contribute to the process of an individual becoming a member of a global society based, ultimately, on the solidarity of all human beings.

Therefore, the characteristic rights of the fourth generation relate to the initiation of human beings in culture and societal structures, enabling the individual to develop as an autonomous and self-respecting person and protecting this development against distorting forces. In other words, dignity rights are rights of individuals to formation by enculturation, with emphasis on education. In the Universal Declaration, an understanding of human dignity and human rights as an ideology that is to be promoted and defended in a pro-active manner, already shows in the Preamble according to which "every individual and every organ of society, keeping this Declaration constantly in mind, shall strive by teaching and education to promote respect for these rights and freedoms".

The most basic right to be included in a legal community shows prominently in Article 6 of the Declaration proclaiming: "Everyone has the right to recognition everywhere as a person before the law." In addition, according to Article 15, everyone has the right to a nationality. This anchors the individual in a constitutional state as the main political building block of the global and cosmopolitan order, which the UDHR envisages.

Under Article 22 of the Declaration, everyone is entitled to realisation of the "economic, social and cultural rights indispensable for his dignity and the free development of his personality". As to the contents and objectives of education and culture, the second paragraph of Article 26 posits:

> Education shall be directed to the full development of the human personality and to the strengthening of respect for human rights and fundamental freedoms. It shall promote understanding, tolerance and friendship among all nations, racial or religious groups, and shall further the activities of the United Nations for the maintenance of peace.

As individual autonomy and societal pluralism are premised on a sufficient level of differentiation of the social system and on individuals' access to these institutions, importantly Article 27 grants everyone "the right freely to participate in the cultural life of the community, to enjoy the arts and to share in scientific advancement and its benefits." These rights presuppose a societal organisation that ensures that cultural, artistic and scientific institutions are inclusive and can function unimpeded by interference from outside.

Finally, the new—Fichtean—awareness of an individual's dependence on an appropriate societal framework is prominently reflected in Article 29 of the Declaration, which provides that "everyone has duties to the community in which alone the free and full development of his personality is possible." These duties are not restricted to non-interference with other persons' rights, but include fair contributions to the establishment and maintenance of societal structures on which the effectiveness of human dignity and human rights is premised. The ideal social order designed to promote the development of free - autonomous - and accountable persons is here referred to as a humanist society.

3.6 Human Dignity Overcoming Collectivism and Nationalism

The remainder of this chapter undertakes to demonstrate how a humanist ideology—promoting a global society committed to realising human dignity—is apt to overcome the collectivism inherent in the nation state in its two forms, authoritarian nationalism on the one hand, value-neutral liberal democracy on the other. Despite their very significant differences, the closed state ruled by a party and liberal democracy in the end suffer from one disease common to both. They aim to preserve a nation state that is constituted by the difference between those who belong to a people and those who do not. While in the collectivist variant the unifying element of nationalism is permanently invoked, in liberal democracy it is in the background and moves to the forefront only occasionally, e.g. at international football competitions or when foreigners seeking admittance are excluded.

What accounts for the late and spectacular success of the concept of human dignity—arriving in two waves, at first more tentatively immediately after 1945, then more forcefully in the 1960s—is its ability to provide solutions to the main historic and political plights and challenges of contemporary Western societies. The concept of human dignity offers a basis for constructing a normative order that matches the profound political and ethical complexities of modern societies and in this respect is unrivalled by any other normative concept.

A humanist society is preferable to the concept of a nation state for at least two reasons. Firstly, the notion of universal human dignity is apt to lay the foundation for an, at the same time, individualist and cosmopolitan political order that overcomes the explicit collectivism of authoritarian regimes on the one hand and the implicit collectivism of liberal democracies on the other. Secondly, interpreted as the right of individuals to societal conditions that foster their development as accountable and autonomous agents, a humanist political theory provides a normative programme that outcompetes both the discriminatory policies of an authoritarian nation state and the empty formalism and ethical arbitrariness of a morally neutral liberal democracy reduced to the procedural mechanism of majority decisions. This section will elaborate the individualist aspects of human dignity leading to the next section which highlights how this concept prevails over the idea of an ethically neutral 'laissez-faire' democracy.

The notion of human dignity posits the individual person as the ultimate point of reference. To quote a prominent source, the Vienna Declaration and Programme of

Action adopted by the World Conference on Human Rights in Vienna on 25 June 1993 proclaims in an initial recital:

> Recognizing and affirming that all human rights derive from the dignity and worth inherent in the human person, and that the human person is the central subject of human rights and fundamental freedoms, and consequently should be the principal beneficiary and should participate actively in the realization of these rights and freedoms [...].

Only individuals participate in human dignity and have the obligations and rights that are consequential to human dignity. Hence, the concept of human rights deriving from human dignity is opposed to any ethical concept assuming rights or obligations of states, nations, peoples, religious communities or any other collective entities.

The same holds for the European Union, which according to Article 2 of the Treaty on the European Union, is founded on such values as the respect for human dignity and human rights. Even when referring to minority rights, the Treaty maintains an individualist approach and talks of 'the rights of persons belonging to minorities' and not of the rights of minorities as collectivities.

Much of this section revolves around the opposition of collectivism and individualism. This can be a source of confusion, unless the meaning of this opposition is cleared. Here three denotations are distinguished, which are first defined and afterwards looked into more closely from a political perspective.

The first option interprets this opposition as substantive and relating to the *supreme good* of normativity and hence to the *criteria* allowing to tell right from wrong. As explained above, in any given normative order a supreme good defines what is sacred, e.g. the presence of God and gaining access to heavenly afterlife, the wellbeing of a nation or people, or the rights of individuals. This supreme good can relate either to individuals or to a collectivity. The opposition in question pitches organicist and communitarian against individualist ethics: Either some state of welfare or power of a collectivity, or some benefit to or happiness of individuals, functions as the crucial test of what, in a normative system, ultimately serves to distinguish right from wrong. In this criterial sense, the concept of human dignity - and consequently all humanist ethics - is radically individualist, as it is concerned about an individual human being's status as a person. In this view, collectivities have a solely instrumental status and are seen as functional, constructed, organised and funded to serve individuals.

The second understanding of the antithesis of the collectivity and the individual relates not to the contents, but to the *source of normativity*. It pertains to the *sovereign entity* vested with the particular potency of normative power, of producing, that is, normative decisions that are, within a polity, respected as legitimate and binding. Even when the prospering of a collectivity is the supreme good, the ultimate normative power can still rest with a religious or political leader and hence with an individual who is venerated as endowed with normative power. On the other hand, in democracies a situation can arise where individual welfare is officially acknowledged as the supreme good, but the nation state represented by the collective will of its people is regarded as the only source of normativity.

Against such claims, the concept of human dignity views the sovereign individual as the only source of normative power.

The third interpretation of the contrast of the collectivity and the individual is *empirical* in nature and relates to the *source of personhood*, which can be seen as rooted in the individual or in a collective. This opposition can also be referred to as pitching isolationism against relationism. It should not be overlooked that the question whether a human being can develop as a unique individual and personality in isolation or only in society, is purely empirical. As has been made clear, this book adopts a Fichtean perspective that adheres to relationism, maintaining that in reality the source of culture—normativity, languaging, arts etc.—is, rather than the solitary individual, human collectivities, concrete social configurations of processes of normative communication among a large number of individuals continuously creating a web—or cluster—of discourses.

The distinction between empirical individualism and collectivism is politically consequential as regards the societal preconditions of autonomous personhood. This will be dealt with below under the heading of the need for a principled or 'militant' society that ensures the institutional prerequisites on which a humanist society is premised.

3.6.1 Individualism and Universal Rights

Along with the decline of monarchies, a historic bifurcation pitched collectivist and organicist political views against individualist concepts. Still today, one of the most fundamental coordinates of political discourses distinguishes collectivist from individualist approaches.

Plausibly, one can choose between these two options. A normative order is about peacefully integrating individuals in a comprehensive social order. Therefore, when it comes to constructing a societal order one can either start—in a top-down approach—with a vision of a strong, orderly, harmonious and flourishing community and fit individuals into that framework; or depart—in a bottom-up approach—from individuals and their legitimate interests and create an order by conceptually coordinating, balancing and integrating individuals' potentially conflicting interests and claims.

Both approaches have their advantages and weaknesses. The first approach seems to directly tackle the normative task of creating an orderly community, but encounters difficulties in restricting society's demands on individuals. If the well-being and strength of the collectivity is of primary importance, why should individuals have rights that come with a potential to impede and restrict the community in pursuing its interests? In addition, even if individuals are granted rights, it is not in the interest of the community that rights should be equal. Instead, stronger, more capable, efficient and productive individuals should be awarded a wider radius of action and should have more resources available to them than the feeble and less talented. In addition, those who can be seen as supporting the collectivity deserve to be promoted, while restrictions and deprivations should be imposed on those who do not strictly abide by the collective order and public interests. Hence, collectivism fosters the strong and conforming, while turning against the weak and less aligned individuals.

As in a society constructed based on collectivist assumptions many individuals will come off less favourably than others, the stability of the system is premised on a strong and emphatic belief in the importance of the collectivity—the glorious home country, the nation, the people, the race or the religious community. Such a belief is plausible only if the collectivity is sufficiently homogenous and distinct from other collectivities. Any collective requires the construction of a common denominator of its members, and only the perceived uniqueness of the collectivity provides a basis for designing its superiority. Therefore, collectivism necessarily constructs the people as an ethnicity and comes with discriminatory attitudes towards those who do not fit the features defining the members of the collectivity.

While starting from the side of individuals suggests itself as an ontologically modest and cautious approach, it encounters complexities that mirror the difficulties of the collectivist approach. Once the interests of the individual are enthroned as the foundation of the normative code, the question arises why individuals should give their consent to any limitations of their interests and how the interests of one individual can be weighed against those of another. Taking individuals as the point of departure, in the end, may start with insufficient levels of social binding forces and cohesion.

Hence political discourses in the nineteenth and twentieth century oscillated between the demanding Scylla of collectivism and the overly modest and anaemic Charybdis of individualism.

In the second half of the nineteenth century, intense arguments were exchanged on the continent between those advocating ethics centring on the interests and well-being of the community (the German term is '*Sozialethik*') and those starting from the interests of individuals ('*Individualethik*'). As an important example in case, the legal philosopher Georg Jellinek, then a powerful advocate of sociocentric ethics, critically noted that his opponents viewed society not as something valuable in its own right but only as a precondition of individuals' realisation of their moral objectives (Jellinek 1878/2006, p. 20). In marked contrast, Jellinek conceived moral norms essentially as answering to the requirements of society as an entity clearly standing above individuals (Jellinek 1878/2006, pp. 15, 42). He based his own approach on the imperative that individuals should act in a manner maintaining and promoting their society ('*handle so, dass deine Handlungsweise die Gesellschaft erhält und fördert*', Jellinek 1878/2006, p. 20). In this perspective, individuals' actions are means to the ends of society and only derive moral quality from serving 'society'. Later, the radical subordination of individual to collective interests emerged as the trademark of fascist ideologies. 'The community comes before humankind in fascist values, and respecting individual rights or due process gave way to serving the destiny of the Volk or razza' (Paxton 2004, p. 20).

In France, already two decades before Jellinek, Auguste Comte had elaborated the ideology of normative collectivism to its extreme (1854). Individuals are required to function to the benefit of the Grand Being. In Comte's social system, which according to John Stuart Mill aimed at establishing 'a despotism of society over the individual, surpassing anything contemplated in the political ideal of the most rigid disciplinarian among the ancient philosophers' (1859, p. 73), no room was left for individualism or human rights (Braunstein 2003 provides an illuminating critical assessment of Comte's and his successors' ethics). In Comte's words (1852, pp. 146–147):

> [...] le positivisme ne reconnaît à personne d'autre droit que celui de toujours faire son devoir. En termes plus corrects, notre religion impose à tous l'obligation d'aider chacun à remplir sa propre fonction. La notion de droit doit disparaître du domaine politique [...] Le positivisme n'admet jamais que des devoirs, chez tous envers tous. Car son point de vue toujours social ne peut comporter aucune notion de droit, constamment fondée sur l'individualité. [...] Ce ne serait pourtant qu'après une restitution complète que nous serions dignement autorisés à réclamer la réciprocité des nouveaux services. Tout droit humain est donc absurde autant qu'immoral.

In any case, the decisive move towards collectivism—and against the rights of individuals—consists in proclaiming the existence of a higher organic entity—'society', a country, a nation, a people, or a class—and to relate normative issues not to the rights of human individuals but to the needs and interests of this imagined and hypostasized collective entity, of which the individual is an element and derives her status from being an element of the whole (Stourzh 2009, pp. 134–150).

A currently popular example of such sociocentric ethics is provided by public debates about how to select migrants according to their utility for the 'host' country. The scrupulousness of these debates and the readiness to reduce to commodities those who do not belong to 'us' reflect the racism inherent in nation states (Schultz 2016; jour fixe initiative berlin 2001).

In the recent past, the racialised nature of the modern nation state has received much attention from researchers, stressing that the nation state cannot be separated and isolated from a history of colonialism and imperialism based on racism. Thus David Theo Goldberg has argued that racial categories were crucially important as a means 'for defining and refining internal state homogenization, a homogenized state formation thus ethnoracially and racio-nationally differentiated from external states and conditions' (2002, p. 154). Race was and still is 'integral to the emergence, development, and transformations (conceptually, philosophically, materially) of the modern nation-state' (2002, 4). Constructing and hypostasising 'peoples' entitled to self-determination and 'nations' acting as sovereigns serves to conceal the racism inherent in the global order. States can declare their commitment to fighting racism, while they, by insisting on their right to restrict immigration, vindicate racial discrimination at a global scale. However, in Bridget Anderson's words: 'Race, nationality, and poverty are not independent variables' (2013, p. 43). Rather, the modern nation state 'is a racial project, bound up with the making and maintaining of racial difference, and immigration controls are deeply implicated in this project' (2013, p. 47). As a result, contemporary 'colorblind states are racist states absent race, post-racial but not post-racist, raceless yet racist. [...] Raceless states trade, in other words, on the social, economic, political, legal, and cultural conditions historically inscribing differentiated racial configurations and arrangements for their members and non-members alike' (Goldberg 2002, p. 263).

Canetti (1984) was right to stress the religious undertones of nationalism and the importance of a nation's symbolism, the German oak forest, the Swiss mountains, the waves ruled by Britannia, or the rolling hills and vales of green symbolising the Emerald Isle—a specific natural environment or trait that is attributed deeper significance in the formation of national identity. The nation state inherits from its predecessor the idea of a sacred homeland. The integrity, inviolability and sanctity of the monarch are replaced by the same qualities of the home country in its historical shape. Moreover, it is presumed that those families who have, for some generations, lived within the borders of the territory and on its soil, as a result, belong to the mystic entity called 'people', in contrast to all those living outside these borders. Consequently, the nationalist has only contempt for those who are seen as detached from any country and who, by their international or itinerant lifestyle, challenge the concept of a citizen who exists as a member and within the borders of a nation state. Nationalism manifests itself in claims of uniqueness, difference and superiority in relation to other nations and in concerns about the nation's internal homogeneity—'purity'—and the loyalty and patriotism of its citizens (Terkessidis 1998; Morgenstern 2002).

The more than 50 million human beings killed in the course of World War II demonstrates the risks inherent in an organicist and particularistic ideology based on a fundamental difference in value of variously construed human collectivities and their members.

Organicist societies are inherently discriminatory; and the only means of overcoming this aporia rests in a radically universalist and egalitarian vision of humanity, as endorsed by the concept of human dignity and the ethics of humanism, which emphasise the equally supreme quality of *all individuals* who carry 'a human face'. Hence, one aspect of humanism is 'moral cosmopolitanism', which Thomas Pogge (1992, pp. 48–49) perceives as defined by three elements:

'First, individualism: the ultimate units of moral concern are human beings, or persons – rather than, say, family lines, tribes, ethnic, cultural, or religious communities, nations, or states. The latter may be units of concern only indirectly, in virtue of their individual members or citizens. Second, universality: the status of ultimate unit of moral concern attaches to every living human being equally – not merely to some subset, such as men, aristocrats, Aryans, whites, or Muslims. Third, generality: this special status has global force. Persons are ultimate units of moral concern for everyone – not only for their compatriots, fellow religionists, or suchlike'. These three features - individualism, universality and globalism - ground rights and obligations of all members of the human family against one another.

Individualism and cosmopolitism are two sides of the same coin of a global order based on human dignity and overcoming the threats emanating from the particularistic concept of the nation state. Hence, legal documents, before proclaiming human dignity, often refer to the objective of maintaining peace within societies and at a global scale. Thus, the preamble of the Universal Declaration starts with the words:

> Whereas recognition of the inherent dignity and of the equal and inalienable rights of all members of the human family is the foundation of freedom, justice and peace in the world, [...]

Similarly, the Charter's preamble commences with the sentences:

> The peoples of Europe, in creating an ever closer union among them, are resolved to share a peaceful future based on common values.
>
> Conscious of its spiritual and moral heritage, the Union is founded on the indivisible, universal values of human dignity, freedom, equality and solidarity; [...]

These sentences are echoed in the first Articles of the Treaty on European Union. Article 2 of this Treaty commences with the sentence:

> The Union is founded on the values of respect for human dignity, freedom, democracy, equality, the rule of law and respect for human rights, including the rights of persons belonging to minorities.

Article 3 follows up by highlighting the objective of the Union, putting forward, first:

> The Union's aim is to promote peace, its values and the well-being of its peoples.

3.6.2 The Sovereign Nation

In Europe, the decline of monarchies, founded on the divine rights of kings, witnessed the rise of the more secular nation state. The concept of the nation state answers to the plight of a kingdom left without a king, a people in want of an identity and of some foundation of their inherited polity. The nation state has won its independence, but at a high price. It has lost its connection not only with religion, but also with much of the people's cultural life. 'It stands alone – in an empty space' (Cassirer 1974, p. 140). Thus the fatherland emerges as an imagined and hypostasized collective agent and replaces the monarch as the subject of history (Koselleck 2010, p. 221). 'The people' ascends the throne and fills the blank space left behind by the monarch (Berger 2009, p. 56). It is in the vacuum, produced by secularisation, that in the nineteenth century an aggressive nationalism arises, not as a harmonious global concert of nations united in diversity, as Kant, Fichte and Herder had hoped for, but as the hostile particularism of nations competing and distrusting one another. Hegel was among the first to proclaim that next to the Prussian state 'other nations are absolutely without right' and 'count no longer in universal history' (quoted by Cassirer 1974, p. 274).

Hypostasizing the people or the nation as a supreme being provides a new, seemingly secular rationale for individuals' loyalty and submission. It is the people, imagined as an organic entity and organised in a nation state, that inherits a *partly* secularised sovereignty (Opello and Rosow 2004, p. 193; Olson 2016, pp. 107–108; Stourzh 2009, p. 123). National leaders—monarchs, generals, presidents, party-leaders—replace the divinely appointed king or queen and enter into their status as authorities in their own rights.

The nation state, to sustain its identity and to justify its claims to integrity, remains premised on religious connotations, in the sense that the worth of the people originates, in some mystic way, from the land it occupies, exploits and cultivates and from the history of the people who live there. As long as the territory—the 'home country'—is the defining and sacred element of a polity, the process of democratisation remains ambivalent and reversible. The 'head' of the monarch can 'grow' again taking the form of a new monarch, a national leader or a junta successfully claiming to represent the country.

The king is not definitively beheaded as long as his land is endowed with the aura of the sacred. Hence, Marx interpreted persisting strong tendencies towards religions in the United States as an indication that even a democratic nation state is dependent on religions and not ideologically self-sufficient (1843, p. 41). According to Marx, the nation state is only seemingly emancipated from religion, and hence the citizen of a nation state only seemingly free. In fact, the citizen is only an imaginary building block of the nation state's proclaimed glory and sovereignty; in Marx' view, an individual's imagined collective existence as the patriotic citizen of a nation state prevents her from leading a truly rational and autonomous life (Marx 1843, p. 44).

Hence, what is implied in the sovereignty of the nation state is the power to decide who belongs to the people as its member and who does not. Democracy as a people's self-determination is premised on a 'people'—a demos—; the 'people's', self-determination can only work after the 'people' has been constituted by including some individuals as citizens and excluding all others. The power to confer on a human being the status, rights and obligations of a citizen is the ultimate expression of the nation state's sovereignty. When it comes to documents evidencing the attitudes and inherent racism of the sovereign nation state in their purest form, one of the canonical examples stems from the other side of the Atlantic Ocean. In 1856, the U.S. Supreme Court ruled in the case of *Dred Scott v. John F. A. Sandford*, finding that Dred Scott was a 'plaintiff in error', meaning that he did, actually, not have the right of a plaintiff to sue in a court of the USA, for the reason that he was—in the terms of the Supreme Court—a 'negro' (on the Dred Scott case Stourzh 2009, pp. 112–116). The Court found:

> The question is simply this: Can a negro, whose ancestors were imported into this country, and sold as slaves, become a member of the political community formed and brought into existence by the Constitution of the United States, and as such become entitled to all the rights, and privileges, and immunities, guarantied by that instrument to the citizen? One of which rights is the privilege of suing in a court of the United States in the cases specified in the Constitution. [...] The words 'people of the United States' and 'citizens' are synonymous terms, and mean the same thing. They both describe the political body who, according to our republican institutions, form the sovereignty, and who hold the power and conduct the Government through their representatives. They are what we familiarly call the 'sovereign people,' and every citizen is one of this people, and a constituent member of this sovereignty. The question before us is, whether the class of persons described in the plea in abatement compose a portion of this people, and are constituent members of this

> sovereignty? We think they are not, and that they are not included, and were not intended to be included, under the word 'citizens' in the Constitution, and can therefore claim none of the rights and privileges which that instrument provides for and secures to citizens of the United States. On the contrary, they were at that time considered as a subordinate and inferior class of beings, who had been subjugated by the dominant race, and, whether emancipated or not, yet remained subject to their authority, and had no rights or privileges but such as those who held the power and the Government might choose to grant them.

A nation state is free to award citizenship rights and entitled to deprive of these rights, and, as Seyla Benhabib (2006, p. 35) observes: 'Every democratic demos has disenfranchised some, while recognizing only certain individuals as full citizens'. In fact, the nation state claims a twofold right to exclude from citizenship: Aliens, who are 'by nature'—race or ethnicity—not part of 'the people', have no claim to citizenship rights; and offenders are denied these rights if they do not live up to the standards defined by the nation state and therefore are considered unworthy of (full) membership. Ostracising offenders and expelling aliens are two sides of the same coin of the nation state's right to define conditions of membership and grant citizen rights. On the other hand, once the concept of the sovereign nation state is called into question, both rights of this state—to exclude immigrants and to lock away offenders—become questionable.

Hence, the best way to overcome the nation state is to challenge the habit of hypostasising 'a people' and to insist that the individual is the only sovereign in the precise sense of being a source of normative power.

3.6.3 The Sovereign Individual

The traditional polity, based on the concept of the divine rights of the king, is fully overcome only when sovereign individuals emancipate themselves from collective concepts of the country, the nation, or society as the foundation of their polity and social existence. Fichte executes the monarch's conclusive replacement by the sovereign individual positing (1794a, p. 415, 1794b):

> Das ist der Mensch; das ist jeder, der sich sagen kann: *Ich bin Mensch.* Sollte er nicht eine heilige Ehrfurcht vor sich selbst tragen, und schaudern und erbeben vor seiner eigenen Majestät!
>
> Such is man; such is everyone who can say to himself: I am man. Should he not then carry within himself a holy self-reverence, and shudder and tremble at his own majesty?

However, the concept of the individual replacing the monarch is much older and first became politically relevant in seventeenth-century England, when during the civil wars radically individualist movements challenged traditional authorities, including the Diggers (Berens 2008) and the Levellers. In 1646, John Lilburne posited that 'all and every particular and individual man and woman that ever breathed in the world [...] were by nature all equal and alike in power, dignity, authority, and majesty – none of them having (by nature) any authority, dominion or magisterial power, one over or above another' (1998, p. 31). In the same year, Richard Overton, at the time imprisoned in Newgate, sent to the House of Lords his famous tract titled 'An Arrow Against All Tyrants and Tyranny'. There Overton, in clear terms, expressed the view that the power to legislate rests with the individual, who can delegate this power within limits determined by the individual. Hence the authority to legislate flows from the represented to their selected representers. As all men are born with a 'natural, innate freedom and propriety', 'from this fountain or root all just human powers take their original – not immediately from God (as kings usually plead their prerogative) but mediately by the hand of nature, as from the represented to the representers [. . .] every man by nature being a king, priest and prophet in his own natural circuit and compass, whereof no second may partake but by deputation, commission, and free consent from him whose natural right and freedom it is' (Overton 1998, p. 55). From this basis, Overton challenges the position of the king. As the sovereign power extends no further than from the represented to the representers, and as this power is originally not inherent in the king, the power of the king cannot be legislative but only executive (Overton 1998, p. 63).

In any case, an individualist approach is what remains if a normative order's legitimacy flows neither from a collectivity, nor from nature, nor from a divine will. In this case, the normative order can be legitimised only by taking recourse to the—however imperfect—moral capacity and authorship of individual human beings, an insight that necessarily leads to some form of democratic organisation of society. After the demise of collectivist ethics, the only possible answer for the source of a normative order's legitimacy recognises legislation as premised on the moral autonomy of individuals cooperating within the framework of democratic societies.

If sovereignty denotes the position of a supreme legislator who recognises no moral authority above her, the autonomous individual is the sovereign of a truly democratic cosmopolitan order under conditions defined by human dignity and human rights. The individual replaces the monarch and her divine rights. Thus, a society's normative organisation has the autonomous agency of individuals as its foundation. All political institutions are legitimised by their capacity to realise human dignity and human rights. Public institutions at various—local, 'national', regional, and international—levels serve solely as means to individuals' ends and to the effective organisation of a peaceful coexistence of all human beings.

What is new about normativity under conditions of a secular modernity is individuals' awareness of their status as lawgivers. They now realise that it actually never was external forces that generated laws, but that all normative power all the time rested with individuals' acts of normative communication. Whoever raises normative claims, these claims receive their bindingness from acts of communication that ongoingly and recursively 'observe', reference, acknowledge, support and reinforce norms. Normativity never was anything but individuals binding themselves and one another.

However, there is a pitfall to avoid. It is the mistake of short-circuiting autonomy and dignity, of assuming that the quality of autonomy accounts for human dignity. This comes with a risk of excluding from dignity all individuals who are not, or not yet, or no longer capable of acting autonomously. Recently, Rainer Forst has argued that the 'point and ground of human rights' rests in the Kantian cosmopolitan view of all human beings as equal in their status as lawgivers. In Forst's view, human rights 'are not just rights to be protected in one's status as a legally, politically and socially non-dominated person; they are in a reflexive sense, also basic rights to determine the rights and duties that define that status' (2016, 23). However, while normativity under conditions of a modern secular polity is indeed premised on the normative power of autonomous individuals, to what extent an individual will develop as an autonomous person is not pre-determined by her genes. An individual's subjectivation is a contingent, open ended process. Basing dignity on autonomy, in a Kantian manner, fails to recognise that the human being is not born as an autonomous lawgiver and has a chance to develop as a lawgiver only premised on societal conditions that foster such development. Autonomy is not a quality inherent in all humans but a faculty that, under certain conditions, individuals can develop.

Kant, by identifying autonomy with dignity, fails to construct the latter as a fully universal quality. Fichte, on the other hand, by distancing the two and maintaining their interdependency, constructs human dignity as one focus and culture, resulting from the autonomous agency of many individuals, as the second of an elliptical political order. The distance between these two foci is a necessary consequence of the fact that autonomy is not the precondition, but the possible and contingent result of personhood. What earns Kant's highest esteem is individual autonomy; the ultimate objects of Fichte's appreciation are human culture on the one hand and the person as a member in the project of collectively creating culture on the other.

In humanist reading, human dignity constitutes the unity—and calls for the solidarity—of all beings who carry 'a human face', because they belong to the species that generates culture, including autonomous subjects and normative orders. Humankind stands out as a species because of its capacity to collectively develop culture as what is substantially human. However, human dignity is not premised on an individual's autonomy as her empirical capacity to contribute to culture, but only on her carrying a human face and hence belonging to humanity.

Therefore as a normative principle, human dignity expresses the equal appreciation of all beings who belong to the species that collectively creates and continually advances culture as the product of autonomous and accountable agency.

The Kant/Fichtean concept of human dignity offers a solution to the profound historical plight of modernity, to the aporia, that is, of having to legitimise a highly demanding normative order without being any longer able to take recourse to nature as a wise and pre-stabilised cosmic order or to a ruler's divine vocation. The crucial question is how a society's normative basis can be sustained once a shared belief in the concepts that in former phases of societies' normative development served as the foundation of normativity have lost their convincingness. Such shared notions have included the belief in a grand cosmic design, the sacredness of the king's peace in the country, the trust in a divine lawgiver, or confidence in the chosen nation or people as a supreme value from which all normativity flows. What modern and secular societies inherit from their traditional monarchic predecessors is positivity of their normative order without legislators' divine backing.

The concept of human dignity—already in its Kantian version—emphasises and esteems an individual's moral autonomy as the only remaining source of normativity, even if in the Kantian cosmos an individual's normative power is a heavenly endowment. The concept of the sovereignty of the monarch as a law-giver, founded in the divine rights of the king, is replaced by the sovereignty of the human individual. In the traditional state, the monarch is the head of the polity, endowed by God with the divine rights of a king and hence the power to legislate. The monarch's sovereignty is objectified and quantified by the monarch's territory. If the king is the head of the polity, its territory resembles a body that draws its sanctity from the fact that it constitutes one dimension of the monarch's sovereignty, as do the individuals who populate that territory and because of this fact are subjected to the monarch's rule.

The concept of the nation state emerges in the second half of the 18th and dominates European history throughout the nineteenth and twentieth century. The monarch is replaced by the nation or the people as a collective subject constituted by loyal, patriotic citizens. What develops after World War II as an alternative concept is the vision of a cosmopolitan order based on human dignity and human rights. This vision combines the (Kantian) notion of the individual as the only possible lawgiver with the (Fichtean) idea of a universal equality of and solidarity among human individuals. Thus the individual leaves traditional tutelages behind and gradually frees herself from the clutches and the ideology of the nation state.

This emancipation has far-reaching political consequences.

Firstly, individuals' personhood is no longer anchored in their citizenship and membership in a nation state, but now rests in their cosmopolitan status as human beings and their belonging to humankind. The primary framework of moral responsibilities and claims of rights is not the relationship among citizens, but the relationship of all human beings among themselves: the legitimate claims of every individual against and accountability to all others (regarding the status of the individual in the post-1945 legal system Parlett 2011).

Secondly, political organisation is no longer a matter of constructed ontological categories—the people, the country, the nation—but merely a matter of normative requirements and administrative practicability. Political powers are not claimed as inherent rights of nation states, but are deliberately attributed to authorities organised at the very level that allows them to most effectively act on these powers to the benefit of the rights of individuals. What emerges is therefore a more complex and stratified political organisation, where no level can claim a privileged position, but the individual (hence, what Pogge 1992 describes as "a vertical dispersal of sovereignty" should rather be seen as the result of deliberate organisational decisions of sovereign individuals).

What, under conditions of modernity, remains to orient a polity is human dignity as the epitome of societal conditions that most reliably support the respect for the human person and the development and peaceful coexistence of autonomous individuals. Human dignity is the construction principle of a global humanist—or 'decent'—social order that fosters respect and individual autonomy as the preconditions for its normativity.

Human dignity and a humanist societal order are interdependent: while human dignity is premised on a decent societal order, the latter derives its legitimation from the former. Not all individuals arrive at the same level of autonomous moral reflection, but all are entitled to a social order that protects them against heteronomy in its many guises and supports them in developing as autonomous agents and lawgivers and in leading a self-determined life.

Human dignity answers to the challenge of modernity by turning the law's legitimation upside down and back on its feet. What justifies the normative order is that it has a foundation in the moral autonomy of the very individuals it addresses. The concept of an individual's moral autonomy rescues normativity by entrusting those who are bound by the law with the task of its creation and by demanding that they take the responsibility for the norms they create. Individual moral autonomy resolves the crisis of the law's legitimation by postulating the identity of sovereign governors and the governed. It expresses the deepest respect for the human individual—as another more credible legislator to be chosen, venerated and burdened with the task of the law's creation and innovation does not exist. In light of this political functionality, what best explains the success of the concept of human dignity is the fact that it is left, on the stage of history, without a serious competitor.

Thus humanism as a political theory truly overcomes the plight of the traditional concept of the sovereign king, in contrast to the mere mimicry of various forms of collectivism, which only substitute a national, fascist or communist leader for the retired monarch, as well as in contrast to the liberal democratic nation state, which stops half way in replacing the monarch, but only substitutes a *demos*, a people, a nation or some other reified and hypostasized collective entity for the monarch. Arguably, when it comes to construing a social order under conditions of modernity, the majesty and sovereignty of the individual—of every single member of the species that collectively creates culture—is the only possible point of departure. What remains is basing a "conception of morality on the humanistic assumption that the only justification for morality is human" (Margalit 1998, p. 37).

Modern societies depend on individual autonomy as subjects' potential to engage in the reproduction of their society's normative foundation; human dignity defines the societal preconditions on which the generation of autonomous individuals relies. Hence, the chain of deduction runs from a social order, which under conditions of modernity is premised on the normative capacity of autonomous individuals as its source, whose development is premised on a humanist organisation of society. That is to say, human dignity can be defined as the foundation stone of a liberal and pluralist society that pursues the primary objective of fostering the development and peaceful coexistence of autonomous individuals.

However, a normative order can draw its normative power from individual autonomy only if the human being is valued as a source of normativity. It is not sufficient that individuals learn to act autonomously, they must also be esteemed as lawgivers. A modern society's normative order is premised on processes that treat the individual human being, not only as autonomous, but also as sacred and as deserving of concern and respect.

3.7 The Second Enlightenment: from Liberal Democracy to a Humanist Society

Kantian dignity, which in a way corresponds to the concept of liberal democracy, starts out from individual autonomy as an inherent quality of the human being on which state and society rest. Fichtean dignity—and humanism based on Fichtean insights—considers that personhood is premised on interactive processes of attribution, of claims and of recognition of personhood and is called into question and undermined by reverse processes (including, prominently, hateful, derogatory and discriminatory public speech). According to Kant, individual freedom is the foundation and the point of departure of liberal democracy. In a humanist perspective, individual freedom is the ultimate and ideal objective of culture. Humanism reflects the insight that society must establish and defend the preconditions on which the development of individual autonomy and personhood are premised. Liberal democracy is about organising the rule of a majority of inherently autonomous individuals, a decent society about preserving the preconditions on which the development of autonomous individuals depends in a contingent manner. Hence, what is here referred to as a second enlightenment denotes the processes by which individuals become aware of and critically reflect on their own formation, its societal preconditions, and on the normative order they internalised in the course of their primary formation as subjects.

From these different—Kantian versus Fichtean—assumptions, diverging views emerge concerning the relationship of society and individual morality. In the liberal perspective, individual morality and society are distinct from one another. An individual's morality is the unswerving foundation of her status as an autonomous person and the basis from which she enters into the arena of public discourses. Hence, society is external to individual morality.

In diametrical opposition, humanism acknowledges that it is society that constitutes individual subjectivity and morality. Not only is it society's call on the individual that grants her access to the spiritual universe of communication, but even in those instances where the individual strives to find her own moral views she is bound to rely on the material and concepts she finds within her society. How she perceives herself, others and the social and natural environment is shaped by the concepts constituting her intellectual apparatus. Even the seemingly most intimate traits of an individual's personality and character are to be viewed in terms of her socialisation and hence within the context of the historical societal configuration within which she is constituted (Mills 1959).

However, some profound risks to human autonomy emanate from this fact, which will be looked into in this section; firstly, the threat of normative conformism and uniformity; secondly, the risk of distorting and alienating ideologies and processes of subjectivation that—in a concealed or open manner—impose a particularistic morality.

As a response to these threats, a humanist society is required to take precautions to secure freedom, the complex conditions, that is, on which individuals' formation as autonomous subjects remains premised. It is the awareness of the necessity to gradually establish a social structure granting, enabling, and protecting autonomy that defines a humanist society, which overcomes an ethically strictly agnostic laissez-faire democracy Weimarian style.

3.7.1 The Mistake of Innate Autonomy and Unrestricted Moral Relativism

The concept of a liberal democracy combines two elements, a nation state and autonomous individuals as its citizens. Democracy means that a people rules itself. Liberal democracy views the people as a community of autonomous citizens, legislating jointly. As the moral views of all citizens are entitled to the same respect, a disagreement can only be solved by a majority decision. The majority vote is the hallmark of liberal democracy.

The liberal democracy is conceived as the ideal political form of the cooperation of individuals endowed by a benign god or nature with practical reason. It is a concept rooted in a firm belief in rational and intelligent citizens' ability to discuss and agree on a fair societal and political organisation, an ability that is due to their inherent reason. Liberalism tends to view the state as potentially repressive and a permanent threat to freedom. What a state needs to provide is a parliament where citizens can meet to discuss and decide by a majority vote on public matters. For the rest, liberals do not want the state to overly interfere with their private lives.

The moral sense of a citizen is conceived as a capacity which exists independently of and precedes society. In the world of the philosophers of the social contract, when citizens arrive at the stage of society to agree on a constitution they bring along a fully developed capacity of moral wisdom and practical reason. Thus, liberal democracy is the consequence and political expression of a Kantian reason inherent in all human beings. Even to the present day, interpretations of human rights based on Kantian concepts of freedom and autonomy are popular, and they still lead their followers to an understanding of human rights as the rules underlying liberal democracy (Bielefeldt 1998, p. 170).

If autonomy flows from the conscience of autonomous individuals, all moral concepts and convictions have equal status. There is no external point of view from where the moralities of individuals could be revaluated. Hence, the advocates of liberal democracy are brought to take the position of radical ethical relativism, even assuming that tolerance—often valued by democrats—should respect intolerance, as, from their point of view, there is no objective and reliable reason for tolerance to claim superiority over intolerance. If all moral points of view are equally legitimate, state authorities have no legitimation to prevent people from propagating nationalism, racial supremacy, homophobic views or the abolishing of democracy. In 1933, Kelsen explained the concept of liberal democracy as a polity that does not defend itself against its enemies and even offers to them equal opportunities to develop (1967):

> Sie ist diejenige Staatsform, die sich am wenigsten gegen ihre Gegner wehrt. Es scheint ihr tragisches Schicksal zu sein, daß sie auch ihren ärgsten Feind an ihrer eigenen Brust nähren muss. Bleibt sie sich selbst treu, muss sie auch eine auf Vernichtung der Demokratie gerichtete Bewegung dulden, muss sie ihr wie jeder anderen politischen Überzeugung die gleiche Entwicklungsmöglichkeit gewähren.

This form of political pacifism is consequential to the philosophical view of morality as an innate capacity of individuals that cannot be subjected to any criticism based on objective standards. If it were true that individuals on their own develop as moral subjects whose value judgments are firmly rooted in their innate conscience, unlimited, liberal democracy would be the perfectly appropriate political organisation.

However, this perception of the self-made, self-sufficient human individual is far from realistic. The liberal belief in individuals existing as private persons independent of and prior to their normative community and, from this comfortable and superior position, establishing, controlling and keeping in check the state and its institutions is out of step with reality. Throughout the twentieth century, confidence in inherent human dignity based on innate reason proved not only too optimistic but a dangerous mistake, that radically underestimates the normative order's formative powers and clings to a misguided faith in a stabilised harmony, founded on humans' invariable nature. Castoriadis observes (1975, pp. 452–453):

> À moins de croire [...] que le nouveau-né humain est prédestiné par sa nature [...] à une existence sociale qui mûrit en lui avec les années, comme grandissent ses membres et augmente son poids; à moins de rêver qu'il est, génétiquement ou on ne sait comment, préorganisé pour constituer (ou 'refléter') un réel cohérent avec celui de tout le monde et référé aux mêmes significations, reconnaître spontanément autrui et son autonomie, se reconnaître comme individu, n'avoir jamais que des désirs qu'une harmonie préétablie accorde toujours avec ceux des autres, pouvoir exister dans une collectivité intégralement non instituée, ou pouvoir dès sa naissance (ou plus exactement, dès sa conception) négocier librement son entrée dans une société instituée; bref, à moins d'ignorer intégralement ce qu'est la psyché et ce qu'est la société, il est impossible de méconnaître que l'individu social ne pousse pas comme une plante, mais est créé-fabriqué par la société [...].

If, according to Fichte's insight, reason is not innate in humans but a result of cultural and political formational forces, what the normative order means to the individual is not repression, but her constitution. But this means that the political system—the elite in power—by controlling the society's normative order also controls the normative formation of citizens (for a similar criticism of liberalism see e.g. Honneth 2000, pp. 287–289).

Marx was among the first to criticise the liberal concept of human rights for not considering the social formation of individuals, for separating the private, isolated individual and her rights from the public political sphere, and for assuming that the individual and her freedom are external to and limited by—instead of premised on—her society.

> Keines der sogenannten Menschenrechte geht also über den egoistischen Menschen hinaus, über den Menschen, wie er [...] vom Gemeinwesen abgesondertes Individuum ist (Marx 1843, p. 55).

However, the person does not exist independent of or prior to society. In Althusser's words (1970, p. 50), *'l'idéologie interpelle les individus en sujets'*, where the term 'ideology' refers to the system of concepts, norms and beliefs that frame the initiation of an individual in personhood. It is the normative code of a society that initiates the creation of persons and dictates the language and categories of their formation; and it is an individual's concrete education that, within the margins of available societal discourses, teaches an individual's fundamental lessons.

3.7.2 In Need of a Second Enlightenment

Fichte demonstrated that Kant's concept of enlightenment is naïve and unrealistic. The individual who, against all external normative hegemony, heroically brings her moral autonomy into position is a Don Quichotic figure, fighting an imagined battle that is lost before it started. To be able to oppose her society the individual would need to be in a position to adopt, as an autonomous moral person, a firm stance outside her society. However, this is impossible, as all morality is societal and only exists in society, as does the person. The Kantian free-spirited rebel is unaware of the fact that her morality is, to a large extent, the result, not of her own 'in-house production', but of her socialisation and hence derives from the external sources she wants to critically confront. While Kant took considerable pains to erect autonomy as the fortified bastion protecting the individual against the claims and tutelage of her society, Fichte demonstrated that this bastion is, prior to the arrival of the individual, in enemy hands.

The difference between Fichte's and Kant's notion of human dignity is the direction of causation: from Kantian individuals, endowed with freedom by nature, constituting a polity, to Fichte's polity constituting individuals as subjects; as individuals, that is, subjected to their society's calling, which inscribes normativity and sociality in their bodies and thus enables and initiates dialogic communicative processes generating persons. The question is not how autonomous subjects *maintain* their freedom *in spite* of society, but whether and how *society enables human beings to develop as autonomous persons*. While liberalism views the state as a threat to freedom, humanism conceives the normative order as an enabling structure that allows the individual to develop as an autonomous person (Müller-Tuckfeld 1996).

Human dignity is not simply attributed to an individual by others, where the role of the individual would be passive. Nor is human dignity a quality achieved by commendable acts by individuals, meaning that some deserve, more than others, to be respected as shining examples of superior autonomous agency. Rather human dignity demands a societal organisation that enables and fosters individual subjectivation, the generation, that is, of respected, accountable and autonomous moral subjects.

Kantian ethics equates human dignity with autonomy. Fichtean ethics respects the individual in full awareness of the fact that an individual's autonomy is subject to severe inherent limitations and premised on contingent preconditions. Obviously, a child's capability to make autonomous decisions is restricted. What human dignity demands is not that a child's decisions are taken at face value but that a child is supported in developing as an autonomous agent. To give another example, individuals cannot be expected to make autonomous decisions if they are trapped in a situation of want or entangled in relationships marked by significant power imbalances. Thus, severely exploitative employment contracts violate human dignity, regardless of whether the employee concerned has agreed to her exploitation or not. What an exploitative labour contract demonstrates is not the parties' autonomy, but the readiness of one party to take advantage of the other's plight and lack of autonomy (for many examples of the severe exploitation of migrant workers in the EU see FRA 2015, pp. 38–40). In a situation of social and economic deprivation, an individual's decisions cannot be interpreted as expressing her normative views and as suggesting moral standards to her community. Autonomy is not a given, but contingent and premised on processes of subjectivation and on situational preconditions that are not always met, including balanced powers of those involved in an interaction.

In addition, Kant misjudges the source and, consequently, widely overestimates the originality, and idiosyncrasy of an individual's morality. The individual owes her autonomous morality to society, rather: *she* as a person *is societal*, even her wish to be autonomous and untied from tutelage is—where it exists—societal and must be questioned and analysed as to its sources and societal functions. Therefore, the individual attempting to critically distance herself from her society resembles Gottfried August Bürger's fabulous Baron of Münchhausen who, without further ado, pulled himself and his horse out of the swamp by his own plait.

A disquieting aspect lies in the fact that an individual's critical opposition to her society is premised on the normative code of that very society. Even if the individual develops to maintain a critical distance to her society, the possibility to do so is granted by her society. We cannot escape and leave behind the social structures on which our personality is built. There exists no emergency room deep inside of us to where we can retreat, safely shut the door and leave society outside. Even in the deepest recesses of her soul the individual is societal and, hence, never transcends the cultural framework of her becoming. Any autonomy is owed to society and its open and pluralistic organisation. Therefore, when we use the concept of individual autonomy we have to remember that autonomy is premised on internal and external preconditions (Griffin 2009, p. 151).

Hence, what is needed is a concept of enlightenment that takes the social nature of an individual's personality into account. True enlightenment requires a process of individuals seeking to get to the bottom of their own socialisation and to critically reflect on their internalisation of a social structure. While Kantian enlightenment demands that the person should cast off the chains of imposed laws, Fichte adds the hint that the individual should not look for these laws only outside of herself. A revised concept of Enlightenment asks the individual to critically reflect on the laws that constitute herself as a person, laws that resist this attempt as they primarily serve the function of subjecting her and of ensuring that she accepts the social order within which she has been constituted. "Know yourself!" is the creed and battle-cry of second enlightenment.

3.7.3 The Evolution of the Normative Order

In subsequent sections, it will be maintained that the emergence of the concepts of human dignity and a humanist society responds in a particular manner to the challenges of modernity and marks the latest stage in the evolution of a normative order. However, to make this claim plausible—or at least clear— it is first necessary to briefly consider what, in this claim, the terms 'order', 'normative order' and 'evolution of a normative order' refer to (the following draws inspiration from the systems theory of evolutionary epistemology, in particular from Riedl 1978, 1984).

'Order'—as opposed to 'chaos'—denotes uniformity, regularity, and foreseeability of processes occurring in a system. What is generated and regulated in a 'normative' order are meaningful actions occurring within a social collective. In a collective, order means that actions are foreseeable, and the reason why actions are ordered is to enable a sufficient level of peaceful coordination and effective cooperation within the collective (where the 'collective' is defined by the range and level of compliance with a normative order and hence does not have sharp borders). As has been discussed in Chap. 2, the method of ordering consists, at a society's initial stage, in asserting normative claims and sanctioning defectors.

Thus an element of hierarchy is introduced in the system of normative communication. Asserting rules and censuring defectors are acts of communication that are about other acts; they are meta-acts about acts as their objects, and their purpose is to increase the uniformity, regularity and foreseeability of their objects. A normative order evolves by increases in numbers of levels of hierarchy and, correspondingly, by increases in the level of complexity and flexibility within the normative order and the magnitude of the social collective that it can integrate. Another level of hierarchy is added to a normative order by finding a solution to the main problem of order, namely what can be done to improve the uniformity of acts at the top level of the normative order's hierarchy. For instance: What can be done to increase the regularity and foreseeability of acts? Rules can be asserted, obeyed and enforced by sanctions. What can be done to increase the regularity of sanctioning? Secondary norms about sanctioning defectors can be introduced and underpinned by punitive sentiments. However, this is not a perfect solution to the problem of ordering sanctions, as it leaves the issue of partiality unsolved. A by far superior solution consists in introducing, in the social system, a judge as a specialised role, required to supervise the parties' compliance with relevant procedural rules. This solution achieves sizeable gains in the predictability of judgments, including sanctions. Notably, thus the distinction is drawn—introduced in the system—between a private sphere, constituted by kinship ties, and a public office, detached from such ties (and not premised on personal charisma, Popitz 2006, p. 125). Due to the efficiency and success of this solution, soon more judges are needed and criminal courts develop, creating the problem of how the uniformity, regularity and foreseeability of judgments can be ensured across a number of courts. Apart from the solution of the king as the presiding judge travelling permanently from one court to the next, the problem is, in the end, solved by the development, in the public sphere, of another function: legislation and general criminal law provisions. Finally, the problem arises of how to coordinate and standardise a multitude of legislators and to ensure an appropriate level of legal protection of individuals against impunity, and this is where human rights and the political and legal accountability of state actors comes in. In this perspective, the rise of human dignity is essentially about standards of substantive criminal law provisions overcoming impunity of slavery and slave-trade, forced labour, genocide, racism, torture, organised crime, violence against women and so on.

One of the many aspects left out in this sketch concerns the dark side of order: Any increase in levels of hierarchy is at the expense of the system's variance, flexibility and adaptability to changing demands, both in relation to the system's environment and the system's internal states, including the necessity to look for ways of increasing the level of order. Without flexibility, there is no normative evolution. Hence, the evolution of the normative order includes a history of permanent attempts to maintain a sufficient level of flexibility. The introduction of equity courts is one example, the development of legislation from a tool of strict standardisation to a mechanism of innovation—the invention of law's positivity—another, and the evolution of individuals' autonomous morality and of societal pluralism yet another.

Another fundamental aspect relates to the sacred, to the source, that is, of the normative order's authority. As it is always the latest and supreme level of the order's hierarchy—the council of elders making decisions, the king in his role as judge, the monarch as legislator—that is in need of legitimacy in the particular function it aims to perform, the normative order's evolution is accompanied by gradually shifting foundational myths and grand narratives about nature, ancestors, gods, sacred nations and chosen peoples. Maybe the most remarkable feature of the latest stage of this development is the collapse of these narratives, a twist in the history of the sacred that is reminiscent of The Emperor's New Clothes. What then becomes visible is human individuals creating norms on which their existence and survival is premised.

On the basis of these assumptions, the opposition of closed, in extremis even totalitarian societies on the one hand, and pluralist societies committed to individual autonomy on the other are about the level of flexibility preserved by the normative order. Fichte's insight into the social formation of subjects fundamentally changes the issue of diversity versus conformism. If humans were born with innate moral autonomy and an idiosyncratic personal conscience, these qualities could exert centrifugal forces and challenge a society's integration. On the contrary, if it is society that constitutes subjects, then it is not diversity, but conformism and uniformity, which are the real threats. If a person is generated, primarily, in processes of communication, into which the individual enters by responding to her society's call, it follows that the individual cannot bring an outside perspective into the constitution of herself or of society. Instead the individual is—at least at initial stages of her subjectivation—entirely dependent on the concepts and norms provided by her society's normative order.

Anthropologic evidence supports the view that humans are particularly good at quickly grasping, learning and internalising the rules of the society into which they are born. As has been seen, children are genetically predisposed towards assuming that competent (adult) others are following rules that are to be complied with, towards getting angry with others who deviate from an inferred rule of observed conduct, and on this basis towards even imitating irrelevant behaviour (Henrich 2015, pp. 108–110). Genetically, we are designed to conform to social norms, not to rebel against them. In fact, mechanisms referred to by anthropologists as 'intergroup competition' and 'cultural group selection' account for much of our cultural evolution (Henrich 2015, pp. 166–184; Henrich and Henrich 2007, pp. 66–70), mechanisms, that is, which rely on differences between groups and not on diversity and non-conformism within a polity. Henrich (2015, pp. 167–169) lists five mechanisms that, in our history, propagated norms of one group to the detriment of another, namely violent conflicts, differential group survival (favouring groups who cooperate more effectively), migration, differential reproduction (spreading the norms of groups with more children), and prestige-biased transmission of the norms of a particularly successful group to others (one group learning from another). A community's internal diversity is not on Henrich's list.

From an evolutionary perspective, this interpretation is plausible. Normativity developed as a mechanism to preserve and accumulate culture over generations and to adapt collective human behaviour to rapidly changing natural environments, as well as to the rising internal complexity of social order under conditions of rapidly growing human communities (Shariff et al. 2011). In categories of normative evolution, the differentiation and stratification of pluralist societies with generally binding legislation on the one hand and individual moral autonomy on the other, encouraging all individuals to develop normative concepts in their own private laboratories, occurred only 'yesterday'. This final step creates an impressive stock of proposed solutions to societal and moral issues. While inter-societal competition with mounting size and continuance of societies diminishes in importance, its task is taken over by intra-societal normative competition of ideologies and lifestyles.

The salient point is that cultural evolution is premised on competing distinct moralities. A high level of conformity does not endanger cultural development as long as competition exists among societies. However, the mechanism of intergroup competition—of 'voting with feet' (Gürerk et al. 2009)—would come to a halt if, one day, there existed only one global society. In a peaceful global system, external selection pressure exerted on polities ceases. Thus, there arises an imminent danger of the system fossilising in conformity, unless the global society ensures and safeguards its strong internal diversity. This diversity is to be maintained by competing constitutional states, on the one hand, and by societal pluralism within these states, on the other. Competition between societies must be replaced by a sufficient amount of competition of diverse cultural concepts within a global society. The normative order's emerging globalisation can be viewed as a challenge of integration, but also requires, from the opposite point of view, the preserving and ensuring within this order of an appropriate level of contradiction and diversity.

Evolution is premised on variation, and processes of cultural learning on cultural variation. If this variation is not offered by the stiff competition of significantly divergent societal systems, one possible reaction is the internalisation of variation by allowing a wider leeway to individual creativity in terms of inventing normative concepts and alternative lifestyles. Hence, in a global society, fostering normative development is premised on efforts to promote an intra-societal market place of competing normative models and on organisational precautions ensuring diversity and non-conformism and averting the risk of paralysing uniformity.

The suffragette movement, the ‘hippies’ of the later 1960s, environmentalists and vegetarians all started as groups who were marginalised, mocked and not always taken seriously. Yet within only a few decades, more like-minded spirits and supporters gathered behind them and in the end changed Western societies. Peter Singer recalls that when protesters in December 1999 managed to upset a meeting of the WTO, Thomas Friedman wondered in the New York Times whether there can be ‘anything more ridiculous in the news today than the protests against the World Trade Organisation in Seattle?’ He went on to call the protesters ‘a Noah’s ark of flat-earth advocates, protectionist trade unions and yuppies looking for their 1960’s fix’. Singer remarks that these ‘ridiculous’ protesters ‘succeeded in generating a whole new debate about the impact of world trade and the WTO’ (2004, p. 52). By now, critical views on the WTO’s activities are almost commonplace. Thus, the ethical laboratories inherent in pluralist societies have the potential to encourage opposition and dissent, which fuel reform. The differentiation of a pluralist society’s normative organisation allows individuals to engage in designing and living radically diverse normative concepts. Compared to normative development based on inter-group competition, diversity of competing moral concepts relying on individual autonomy has a potential to accelerate society’s normative development by orders of magnitude.

However, if human dignity is premised on individual autonomy, it is premised on a humanist society, a social structure, that is, which protects the societal preconditions of diversity and pluralism, on which individual autonomy draws. Rights of individuals to freedoms of expression, of religion and of association, as well as institutional guarantees of independent media, of academia and of arts foster diversity and pluralism. In establishing a humanist society, the rights of individuals to autonomy and to protection against discrimination are of crucial importance, as is the necessity to ban intolerance and destructive or particularistic ideologies, including effective measures adopted to protect immigrants and their descendants against racist and xenophobic discrimination. Recently, Latcheva and Herzog-Punzenberger (2016) have drawn attention to the exclusionary effects of discriminatory treatment and to its negative impact on subjects’ self-esteem and feelings of belonging to a societal community.

3.7.4 Alienating Socialisation

In what he called the sociology of knowledge, Karl Mannheim was among the first to not only pinpoint the social foundation of an individual’s thoughts and beliefs, but to also stress the political implications of this (on Mannheim see Srubar 2010).

The entire system of Mannheim's sociology of knowledge served to highlight the extent at which all discourses are founded on categories predetermined by the society in which they occur. In his ground breaking analysis of Ideology and Utopia, Mannheim (1929, pp. 2–3) explained:

> The principal thesis of the sociology of knowledge is that there are modes of thought which cannot be adequately understood as long as their social origins are obscured. It is indeed true that only the individual is capable of thinking. There is no such metaphysical entity as a group mind which thinks over and above the heads of individuals, or whose ideas the individual merely reproduces. Nevertheless, it would be false to deduce from this that all the ideas and sentiments which motivate an individual have their origin in him alone, and can be adequately explained solely on the basis of his own life-experience. [. . .] Only in a quite limited sense does the single individual create out of himself the mode of speech and of thought we attribute to him. He speaks the language of his group; he thinks in the manner in which his group thinks. He finds at his disposal only certain words and their meanings. These not only determine to a large extent the avenues of approach to the surrounding world, but they also show at the same time from which angle and in which context of activity objects have hitherto been perceptible and accessible to the group or the individual. [. . .] Strictly speaking it is incorrect to say that the single individual thinks. Rather it is more correct to insist that he participates in thinking further what other men have thought before him.

Thus Mannheim, in a pragmatist manner, embeds the thinking of the individual in the context of her group's cooperation and joint efforts to master its everyday life. The communication occurring in a group reacts to the situations in which it finds itself. Mannheim refutes the prevailing approach that not only separates thinking from doing, but also isolates the thinking of the individual from the context of her group's collective activities.

However, Mannheim's political intention was not to demonstrate the futility of an individual's struggle for autonomy, but rather to support self-reflection, which Mannheim saw as premised on a revised—and less naïve—understanding of the counterforces that an individual's autonomy has to match, as well as the limits set on, an individual's intellectual self-sufficiency. In Mannheim's words (1929, pp. 4–5):

> But this is not to say that in those domains where attachment to the group and orientation towards action seem to be an essential element in the situation, every possibility of intellectual, critical self-control is futile. Perhaps it is precisely when the hitherto concealed dependence of thought on group existence and its rootedness in action becomes visible that it really becomes possible for the first time, through becoming aware of them, to attain a new mode of control over previously uncontrolled factors in thought.

Mannheim's emphasis on the social formation of an individual's concepts and thoughts draws attention to the necessity to defend an individual's subjectification against repressive, distorting, or alienating moralities, whether they worship a nation, a race, a class, a religion, or competition and private property.

However, any criticism of a social order as dysfunctional—as distorting or alienating human beings—is premised on the possibility of defining a social order that functions properly and hence on pinning down a genuine function of human culture. Only if it is possible to identify a genuine purpose fulfilled by normativity, is it possible to assess to what extent a given order serves or deviates from this purpose.

Over previous sections, some elements of the functions of normativity have surfaced. Firstly, culture has been identified as a mechanism of collective social learning, rapidly improving the adaption of the behaviour of a community's members to their natural environment. Secondly, it appears that social norms enable large-scale peaceful cooperation, even with complete strangers. Thirdly, it has been shown that social norms influence the behaviour of a legal community's members, not by means of force or threat, but by the much subtler method of normative power, which builds on moral persuasion and the establishment and reinforcing of a normative consensus. A normative order can perform its functions only as long as individuals communicate within a space that is reserved for arguments and reasons and protected against heteronomy, including violence, threats, deception, want etc.

At the level of modern societies, the best approximation to defining the task of normativity is human dignity, the concept that cherishes the respected autonomous and accountable individual and demands a humanist society, a society, that is, which, in the best possible way, fosters the development of autonomous subjects. A humanist society is premised on a pluralist societal organisation that differentiates and protects relatively autonomous societal subsystems, such as a diverse civil society, politics, economy, mass media, academia and arts.

In contrast, a society is alienating to the extent that it effectively prevents the development of autonomous and accountable subjects, in particular by diverting them from realising or by discouraging them from claiming their full potential as agents. In other words, what is equivalent to the absence of alienation is a decent society, which is defined as the social structure that, in an ideal manner, fosters the development of accountable and autonomous individuals.

If enlightenment is the result of an individual's critical and unbiased reflection on the foundations of her morality, subjects, rather than relying all too readily on their moral capacities as autonomous individuals, are called on to reflect on how they are brought to unconsciously accept as a given a social order that falls short of meeting the standards of a humanist society. The best way of detecting internalised barriers is to sceptically scrutinise one's society's structure in terms of distribution of power, respect and autonomy and to analyse the mechanisms—the ideological concepts, discourses and myths—that motivate people to take their society's deficiencies as given and necessary. Hence, the second enlightenment is the process of individuals overcoming their unfreedom by becoming aware of the norms, concepts, discourses and myths which they have internalised as part of their society's normative order and which prevent them from developing their full potential as accountable and autonomous agents; institutions, norms, concepts, discourses and myths that they, themselves, support and reproduce, as long as they don't see through and protest against them. By their socialisation, individuals are enticed into complicity with—and engage in the maintenance of—norms, etc. that constrain and oppress them as well as others. Hence, Bourdieu has referred to these norms, etc. as symbolic violence (Bourdieu and Wacquant 1992, pp. 142–143):

> La violence symbolique est, pour parler aussi simplement que possible, cette forme de violence qui s'exerce sur un agent social avec sa complicité. [. . .] Et c'est presque toujours dans les ajustements entre les déterminants et les catégories de perception qui les constituent comme tels que l'effet de domination surgit. [. . .] J'appelle méconnaissance le fait de reconnaître une violence qui s'exerce précisément dans la mesure où on la méconnaît comme violence; c'est le fait d'accepter cet ensemble de présupposés fondamentaux, pré-réflexifs, que les agents sociaux engagent par le simple fait de prendre le monde comme allant de soi, c'est-à-dire comme il est, et de le trouver naturel parce qu'ils lui appliquent des structures cognitives qui sont issues des structures mêmes de ce monde. [. . .] De toutes les formes de 'persuasion clandestine', la plus implacable est celle qui est exercée tout simplement par l'ordre des choses.

The fight against false consciousness replicating oppressive social structures has an early predecessor in radical enlightenment philosophers' criticism of clerical concepts and ideologies infiltrating French education (Larrain 1979). However, with Fichte this infiltration mutates from an exception to the principle. What Fichte renders visible is the eminent risk that the social order, in creating subjects, distorts human beings and alienates them from their vocation and ideal existence as autonomous and accountable persons. Because of the overwhelmingly powerful impact of the social order on the formation of subjects, the issue of alienation is less a problem of individual biographies, but rather a matter of the entire social order's capacity to conceal its debilitating, discouraging and deforming traits and involve individuals in reproducing the order that subjects them.

From a historical perspective, Fichte's views had a significant influence on the philosophy and political theory of Karl Marx, who—partly directly, partly mediated by Hegel—adopts many of Fichte's basic concepts (Bloch 1985, pp. 248–253). In particular, Fichte drew Marx' attention to the crucial role of the social order in constructing its subjects. Like Fichte, Marx emphasises that the human individual can only be comprehended universally as the species of communicating and cooperating individuals. Accordingly, Marx contrasts the biological existence of the individual human being with the phenomenal, meaningful, and productive life of the entire species and posits that the biological life of individuals is only a means of enabling the cultural life of the species (1844, pp. 82–83):

> Der Mensch ist ein Gattungswesen [. . .] indem er sich zu sich selbst als der gegenwärtigen, lebendigen Gattung verhält, indem er sich zu sich als einem *universellen*, darum freien Wesen verhält. [. . .] Das produktive Leben ist aber das Gattungsleben. Es ist das Leben erzeugende Leben. In der Art der Lebenstätigkeit liegt der ganze Charakter einer species, ihr Gattungscharakter, und die freie bewusste Tätigkeit ist der Gattungscharakter des Menschen. Das Leben selbst erscheint nur als *Lebensmittel*.

Alienation (*Entfremdung*) is a key concept in Marxian theory. The truly Fichtean vision of humankind as the species of free and autonomous individuals who, by their productive objectivation create culture and make sense of their existence, Marx juxtaposes with a capitalist society and its dominant ideology forcing workers to sell themselves together with their humanity (1844, p. 42; on Marx and ideology Larrain 1979, 1983). Because the worker is coerced into a relationship of contractual employment within which she does not decide herself what and how to produce, she is reduced to a machine (1844, p. 41). Her work is not productive in the Fichtean sense of establishing harmony of herself as a subject and an object world that she creates as her mirror, but alienating. Work that serves only to produce more wealth distorts the worker (1844, p. 43). The wealth of society implies and is premised on systematic social deprivation of workers (1844, p. 44).

In the views of Fichte and Marx, the processes of deformation and alienation do not affect individuals in a state when they are adult persons, but are already inbuilt in the formation, socialisation and subjectification of children and adolescents. What distorts and alienates the individual are not external forces, in the sense that she would first develop into a free human being and later be distorted by her work. Instead, it is the internalised social structure of a capitalist society that is learned from an individual's first calling, as compared to a society's normative order that is decent in the sense that it fosters the development of humans as genuine autonomous and productive persons. The subject is constituted as an instantiation of her society's ideology and normative order. Hence, it is, according to Marx, the ideology of capitalism that calls humans into a distorted social existence and hence dictates the formation of self-alienated individuals. Only when the logic inherent in capitalism is transcended through a historic and cross-cultural perspective can the fundamental deficiency of capitalism as an ideology become visible. To the extent that socialism enables individuals to see through the alienating functions of capitalism and market economy, it entails an element of enlightenment.

How enlightenment can function is best explained by exemplifying key movements in history. During the 1960s, the emerging discourse of human dignity and human rights was fuelled by several social movements that, by revealing and confronting repressive elements of dominant ideologies, pursued a liberating and enlightening objective.

The approach adopted by Martin Luther King can serve as a case in point. King in his later views—as expressed in the 1960s—highlighted the "slave chains" inbuilt in an ideology operating to persuade subjects to accept their lower social status. He called on Afro-Americans to recognise that their "personality is corroded by a sense of inferiority, generated by this degraded status." King—here quoted by Baker-Fletcher (1993, p. 139)—claimed:

> The imposition of inferiority externally and internally are the slave chains of today. What the Emancipation Declaration proscribed in a legal and formal sense has never been eliminated in human terms. By burning in the consciousness of white Americans a conviction that Negroes are by nature subnormal, much of the myth was absorbed by the Negro himself, stultifying his energy, his ambition, and self-respect.

In an article, titled "True dignity", King analyses the images and narratives implanted in American culture as elements of a repressive ideology, including the "ideological distortion of history", all to the effect that the Afro-American "was brainwashed to honor his exploiter and dishonor himself" (Baker-Fletcher 1993, p. 143). These internalised self-restraints King counters with the concept of "assertive selfhood" (Baker-Fletcher 1993, pp. 141–142):

> The Negro will only be truly free when he reaches down to the inner depths of his own being and signs with the pen and ink of assertive selfhood his own emancipation proclamation.

Thus enlightenment requires and encourages a struggle to 'reach down to the depths of one's own being' to uncover in one's own personality the internalised structure of a suppressive society, as well as the—cultural, historical, religious—narratives, traditions, concepts and myths that conceal, stabilise and immunise external and internal unfreedom.

Similarly, feminism in the 1960s—in the course of the second feminist movement—raised awareness of how, by the permanent reproduction of gender roles and stereotypes, men and women are brought to accept as a given the social and economic power-imbalance structuring their relationships, as well as their unequal opportunities to lead an autonomous and meaningful life. One of the canonical texts, Betty Friedan's "The Feminine Mystique", reveals how the dominant ideology assigned women the role of housewife and mother and how women, by accepting this role, were prevented from leading a meaningful and fulfilling life (on Friedan, Simone de Beauvoir and false consciousness see Meinhof 1980, pp. 125–131). Much of Friedan's text revolves around the classical Fichtean concepts, such as humanness, identity, or 'the I'. By submitting to their role as housewives, American women are, in Friedan's view, "suffering a slow death of mind and spirit" (1963, p. 248).

One of the central chapters of The Feminine Mystique is titled "Progressive Dehumanization: The Comfortable Concentration Camp". It uses the example of a concentration camp to shed light on how individuals, confronted with the ideology of an overpowering institution, are brought to adjust to and internalise its order, even up to the point of accepting their nothingness and the denial of their right to exist. Friedan puts forward (1963, p. 247):

> In fact, there is an uncanny, uncomfortable insight into why a woman can so easily lose her sense of self as a housewife in certain psychological observations made of the behaviour of prisoners in Nazi concentration camps. In these settings, purposely contrived for the dehumanization of man, the prisoners literally became 'walking corpses'. Those who 'adjusted' to the conditions of the camps surrendered their human identity and went almost indifferently to their deaths. Strangely enough, the conditions which destroyed the human identity of so many prisoners were not the torture and the brutality, but conditions similar to those which destroy the identity of the American housewife.
>
> In the concentration camps the prisoners were forced to adopt childlike behaviour, forced to give up their individuality and merge themselves into an amorphous mass. Their capacity for self-determination, their ability to predict the future and to prepare for it, was systematically destroyed. It was a gradual process which occurred in virtually imperceptible stages – but at the end, with the destruction of adult self-respect, of an adult frame of reference, the dehumanizing process was complete. [...] It was said, finally, that not the SS but the prisoners themselves became their own worst enemy. Because they could not bear to see their situation as it really was – because they denied the very reality of their problem, and finally 'adjusted' to the camp itself as if it were the only reality – they were caught in the prison of their own mind.

Humanism aims at enabling the individual to see through internalised degradation, dehumanisation and unfreedom; the internal chains, the prison of one's own mind. By drawing our attention to the normative order underlying our formation, human dignity as full and undistorted development of a self within a societal framework fostering accountability and autonomy has a potential to conceptually grasp the threat of alienating ideologies.

The writings of Fichte and Marx inspired another important line of criticism made up of philosophers and social scientists like Georg Simmel, Antonio Gramsci, Theodor W. Adorno, Herbert Marcuse, Erich Fromm, Robert Paul Wolff, C. Wright Mills, Jürgen Habermas, Michael Theunissen, Hartmut Rosa and many others. These scholars, in the course of a century, joined in the analysis of how the formation of economic subjects assimilates them to the logic, technical rationality and needs of large-scale organisations and markets. This assimilation creates subjects who fit smoothly and flexibly into the complex machinery of depersonalised institutions with their ideals of frictionless uniformity, constantly increasing efficiency and endless acceleration, all in the interest of productivity. The 'modern', disciplined, aligned and adaptable individual, called on and formed by the ideology of capitalism and free markets, renounces her dignity to perceive herself—in terms of the underlying logic of commodities—as essentially useful and attractive to productive organisations. As early as 1844, Karl Marx—in his Economic and Philosophical Manuscripts—deplored what he referred to as estranged labour and observed:

> 'The devaluation of the world of men is in direct proportion to the increasing value of the world of things. Labour produces not only commodities; it produces itself and the worker as a commodity – and this at the same rate at which it produces commodities in general'.

Thus the individual engages in her self-rationalisation, the result of which has been described by Marcuse as the One-Dimensional Man (1964) and by Mills as the Cheerful Robot (1959, p. 171). In terms of the latter, the rational organisation is an alienating organisation (1959, p. 170).

> There is then rationality without reason. Such rationality is not commensurate with freedom but the destroyer of it.

The ideology of free markets replaces the concept of free individuals. Again, it is argued that a repressive ideology causes dehumanisation and prevents individuals from claiming their right to a decent society. While individuals, truthful to enlightenment ethics, claim human dignity and the principle that no human being must ever be treated as a commodity and a means to the ends of others, the same individuals establish and maintain an economy that is founded on their 'self-commodification'. In the logic dictated by the ideology of free markets, individuals are, 'simultaneously, promoters of commodities and the commodities they promote. [...] The test they need to pass in order to be admitted to the social prizes they covet demands them to recast themselves as commodities: that is, as products capable of catching the attention and attracting demand and customers' (Bauman, 2007, p. 6). This is a perfect example of how an ideology creates and shapes its subjects and becomes part of the very foundation of their subjectivation. In the words of Zygmunt Bauman (2007, p. 12):

> In the society of consumers no one can become a subject without first turning into a commodity, and no one can keep his or her subjectness secure without perpetually resuscitating, resurrecting and replenishing the capacities expected and required of a sellable commodity. [...] The most prominent feature of the society of consumers - however carefully concealed and most thoroughly covered up - is the transformation of consumers into commodities; or rather their dissolution into the sea of commodities [...].

Thus individuals are brought to internalise social structures and categories Afro-Americans, women, workers—that serve to legitimise degradations. The individual learns both the general ideal of the autonomous and free individual as well as all the differentiations that serve to explain why the general ideal does not apply to her personally—because she belongs to a particular group (of Afro-Americans, of women, of people with a disability, of employees, of non-citizens, of children or the elderly).

If individuals, in the course of their socialisation, internalise a social order that prevents them from perceiving and understanding their unfreedom, people end up with opaque problems that have no names—to use an expression coined by Friedan (1963; compare Litowitz 2000). With feelings of discontent and unhappiness, such individuals have a nagging suspicion that they are being manipulated and deceived without, however, being able to easily pin down and express what it is that keeps them in a situation of unfreedom and prevents them from fully developing their potential. Enlightenment is the process of coming to understand how one's personal troubles have their roots in public issues of an internalised social structure and hence can only be addressed effectively at that level (Mills 1959). The individual, who attempts to critically reflect on distorting traits of culture, is aware of the fact that she herself is subject to these distorting forces and can reflect on her own situation only in terms of the culture that distorts. However, the manipulation effected by ideology must be taken into account; or how else is one to explain that individuals who value and praise democracy opt to spend their lives working in organisations that are far from democratic; that subjects who are committed to equality opt for a form of economy that—within national borders and at global levels—systematically produces mounting inequality (Stiglitz 2013); or that individuals who oppose discrimination support a normative order that is inherently nationalist and racist (Goldberg 2002). These individuals *really are* devoted to democracy, to equality and to human dignity and they, arguably, *really are* engaged in reproducing autocratic organisations, societal inequality, global racism, and their own commodification. Of course, this is not how they view their situation—otherwise it would not persist. The coexistence of noble values and a societal reality that mocks all principles of fairness or dignity can be explained only by factoring in powerful ideologies that constitute a thick layer of false and misleading concepts as well as ceaselessly repeated half-truths, which serve the purpose of blurring the vision of individuals' societal reality. A theory of ideology can support individuals in overcoming destructive political processes (Eagleton 2007).

The autonomous individual who is aware of her own best interests and has at her command all the information allowing her to make rational choices is an ideal market player, but not a realistic assumption. As Akerlof and Shiller—the authors of Phishing for Phools: The Economics of Manipulation & Deception—have explained at some length, what is closer to reality is people having 'informational or psychological weaknesses that can be profitably exploited' (2015, p. 170). How people act in markets is motivated by the stories they are brought to tell themselves, and this is what 'phishing for phools' is about (p. 173):

> The phish is a way to get someone to make a decision that is to the benefit of the phisher, but not to the benefit of the phool. [...] It also brings into economics a new variable. That variable is the story that people are telling themselves. Furthermore, it makes natural the idea that people make decisions that can be quite far from maximizing their own welfare, and that these stories are quite manipulable. Just change people's focus and one can change the decisions they make.

According to the authors, 'the ability of free markets to engender phishing for phools of many different varieties is not an externality. Rather, it is inherent in the workings of competitive markets' (p. 166), which 'by their very nature spawn deception and trickery' (p. 165). However, 'economists (including those in finance) systematically ignore or downplay the role of trickery and deception in the working of markets' (p. 165). It is blind spots like this one that reveal the effects of ideology and prevent individuals from asking why they accept rules governing their economic lives that systematically foster 'deception and trickery'.

This in mind, a humanist approach avoids relying too quickly on the autonomy of individuals without questioning the societal conditions of their subjectivation. Of course, every subject is socialised on the basis of some ideology, otherwise she could not be constituted. Obviously, there is no such thing as education isolated from societal concepts and norms. All that can be asked is that an individual is encouraged and educated to critically assess the norms and cultural concepts imposed on her by her society and to reject those that are not constitutive for the project of humanity as a specifically normative enterprise.

However, Fichte's attitude of emphatically embracing all of mankind and insistence on the solidarity of all human beings points the way to an understanding of human dignity as the basis of an ethical principle. Realising a fully autonomous human identity is tantamount to being nothing but human—in Fichtean terms: nothing but the *Gattungswesen Mensch*. Loyal to the motto of humanism that my being human means that nothing that is human is alien to me (homo sum, humani nihil a me alienum puto), human dignity embraces in a normative sense all of humanity. As a moral ideal, human dignity demands that the individual assimilates humanity in her personality by taking in all that is universally human and rejecting all particularities, specificities and peculiarities that distinguish, separate, and distance her from others. Fichte gives an example by claiming that both sexes should be educated in the same way and together, as a separation would run counter to the principles of 'education to perfect humanity. [...] The smaller society in which they are formed into human beings must [...] consist in a union of both sexes. Each must first recognise and learn to love in the other their common humanity' (Fichte 1808/2008, p. 136). Thus the subject must orient her life towards the universality, generality and commonality that includes all individuals as equal subjects (Theunissen 1982).

Hence, human dignity requires that the individual takes to her heart all norms on which the existence of humanity is premised—where 'humanity' denotes the community of all individuals who cooperate and coexist peacefully on the basis of normative language—and rejects, at the same time, all other norms. The individual human being strives to grow into the universal human being, 'imbued with a spirit not narrow-minded and exclusive, but universal and cosmopolitan' (Fichte 1808/2008, p. 91). This implies that the individual should support all norms that safeguard normativity and autonomy and rule out heteronomy in its many forms. To this end the individual must critically assess the norms she has learned and internalised as part of the social structure into which she was born and assimilated; and the measure of this assessment is whether these norms foster or impede human dignity and a global humanist society as the conditions of individuals who care for and respect one another as autonomous and accountable persons.

The second enlightenment is not like stepping from darkness into bright daylight, but a Sisyphean task. Still, it is only by bringing to light how the mechanisms of alienation work that an individual is enabled to detect distorting elements of the order forming subjects and herself. It is in this vein that the concept of the sovereign state's right to the punishment of the offender and the myth of the vindictive victim are to be challenged as ideological in the sense that they protect the status quo against criticism and prevent from emerging a criminal justice system that fosters human dignity, human rights and a global humanist society.

3.7.5 *Particularistic Morality and Totalitarianism*

The utmost threat to an open and pluralist society is totalitarianism, defined as a powerful political group's imposition of their particular morality on an entire society and the denial of individual autonomy.

The twentieth century marks—and should be recognised as marking—a break in moral and political thinking. The Armenian genocide, Holodomor, dekulakization and the Gulag, Auschwitz, the Killing fields, the Rwandan Genocide, Srebrenica and East Timor are among those experiences that consistently demonstrate that a particularistic and discriminatory—nationalist, racist, religious, class-based—doctrine of superiority and salvation, combined with political power, means of mass communication and large-scale political propaganda, as well as a general culture of discipline and submissiveness to authority, have a destructive potential compared to which most catastrophes of previous ages shrink to fairly modest size.

What is less recognised is the crucial role that morality—destructive, particularistic morality—has in staging genocide and large-scale atrocities. In view of our current knowledge of the high level of plasticity of human morality and of the impact of public discourses - and of "emotional contagion" (Hatfield et al. 1994) -

on mass consciousness and generally held moral beliefs, the confidence in individuals' conscience of former times proves a fatal mistake. If political leaders control the media and the machineries of political propaganda, if they, in short, control public language, they control the mind-sets of individuals to an extent that enables them, to an alarming degree, to mobilise allegiance to their politics. The possibility of enforced conformity—*Gleichschaltung*—of public opinion and of the moral views of wide sections of the population makes totalitarian rule possible, including mass atrocities supported or at least condoned by a majority of the population. None of the large-scale slaughters of the twentieth century would have been possible without a collectivist ideology, neutralising humans' innate dispositions to compassion and empathy. With the means of mass-communication, the possibilities of moral standardisation, indoctrination and rigid, inescapable societal conformity and hence the threat of totalitarian ideologies has reached a new dimension.

It is the shock of this discovery of the radical plasticity and large-scale formability of persons as moral subjects and of the possibility of governments controlling the rational mind of those governed that in the first half of the twentieth century found expression in novels like Yevgeny Zamyatin's *We*, published in 1924, Aldous Huxley's *Brave New World* of 1932 or George Orwell's *1984*. It also accounts for much of the horror transpiring from *Kafka's* works circling around individuals who are manipulated and brought to appreciate and contribute to their own destruction. Kafka's *Verwandlung* demonstrates how a human being ceases to be a person when others in communicative interactions stop treating him as a person and thus revoke his initial constitution as a member of the human family. It anticipates the reality of the *Muselmann*, the term coined in *Lagerszpracha* to refer to those living dead who had been brought to accept this revocation (Agamben 1998).

What lies at the heart of Nazi ideology is a particularistic, essentially discriminatory morality, which deliberately rejects the claims of universal ethics—including the concepts of human dignity and human rights—and the vision of an open, pluralist, and potentially global society. By inventing the new German race and, for this purpose, drawing various distinctions, Nazi ideology premised the status of the German citizen on certain characteristics, which were used to radically discriminate against those who were different. Thus, Nazi ideology is fundamentally based on the concept that the status of citizenship is reserved to those who satisfy these characteristics, while all others are human beings of a lower quality.

In other terms, one crucial lesson of the twentieth century is that morality must not be trusted at face value. Historians and philosophers have assembled overwhelming evidence demonstrating that what made Auschwitz possible was not the unchecked immorality of the SS but their disciplined destructive morality (a summary of the state of research is provided by Gross 2010). Indoctrination and propaganda, as developed by the Nazis to some perfection, included the creation of new language, a new symbolism, and new rituals of an idiosyncratic Pagan religion. The language of Nazi Germany was literally invented in radical opposition to the spirit of liberal democracy and as the basis of a counter-morality to the ideals of individual freedom and universal human rights denounced as Jewish.

The ultimate consequence of particularistic morality is the exclusion of individuals from personhood. The denial of rights and extermination of the Armenians in Anatolia, based on the deportation laws of May 1915 and systematically and scrupulously 'administered' within only a few months, as well as Auschwitz and the Gulag stand as archetypes of ideologies, administered and enforced, denying personhood, of desubjectivation and extinction of individuals perceived as intolerably different.

Particularistic ideologies react to what is perceived as the burden of liberalism and pluralism. They offer a means of reducing the complexity of society by designing a narrow identity and by depersonalising and eliminating those who do not fit in the model. It was Armenian families who had been living in Anatolia for centuries who were eradicated in Van, Sivas, Bitlis and Erzurum. In Auschwitz, Germans, Austrians, and Poles were killed for being perceived as unbearably different from what was modulated as the future Arian race. Gulags and Stasi prisons gathered citizens who were singled out and redefined as the class enemy. The Lager is the expression of a society's inability to cope with the challenges of universalist humanism and societal pluralism and of the resolve to violently reduce the internal complexity of social reality by denying personhood to those who do not fit in a new tight definition and construction of the proper member of the nation state. This is not about an issue that a polity has with external enemies, but about a social structure deliberately reducing its complexity and inclusiveness, because it is unable to cope with the level of complexity of its internal environment.

While a radically relativist and liberal concept of democracy trusts in the natural moral competence and conscience of individuals, responsible political thought post Auschwitz lacks this confidence. The ability to reflect in moral terms is not part of human nature but premised on a child's initiation in language and society and, concretely, on an education enabling the individual to make autonomous, reasonable decisions, which at best respect the equal autonomy of others. Thus, the understanding of humans' moral plasticity and the individuals' resulting exposure and vulnerability to manipulation, seduction and indoctrination takes on a radically new and alarming quality. It is likely that a child raised by parents fervently supporting the Nazi regime and later by *Hitlerjugend* or *Bund Deutscher Mädchen* will emerge as a deeply convinced Nazi, and his or her genes cannot be relied on to prevent this outcome. This subject will not be without morality; it is, to the contrary, very probable that she or he will have strong moral convictions. However, we cannot but feel that these convictions are wrong.

The mass-murder of human beings perceived as Jewish cannot be detached from decades of antisemitic propaganda. Among those convicted and executed in Nuremberg was Julius Streicher, founding editor of *Der Stürmer*, the weekly magazine that had been the voice of antisemitism since it was founded in 1923, ironically in Nuremberg. The Judgment of the International Military Tribunal observed (quoted by Hare 2009, p. 75):

> For his 25 years of speaking, writing, and preaching hatred of the Jews, Streicher was widely known as 'Jew-Baiter Number One'. In his speeches and articles, week after week, month after month, he infected the German mind with the virus of anti-Semitism, and incited the German people to active persecution [...] Streicher's incitement to murder and extermination [...] constitutes a crime against humanity.

However, the Nazis' antisemitism and racism would not have fallen on fertile ground without the racism and the cult of sedentariness inherent in the nation state in combination with the anemic ideology of value-neutral liberal democracy that undermined the defences of the Weimarian Republic.

Human dignity is fragile and constantly in peril exactly because it is not innate or inherent in the human individual but, at times, contained in and promoted by social norms and culture. Because the views and behaviour of humans are a function of their concrete societal formation and culture, the essence of human uniqueness and the potential warrant for humans' peaceful coexistence, comes with a risk that vast parts of a society are misdirected by an ideology offering simple and comforting orientation.

Ethics today is ethics after Auschwitz; and, unless one avoids the sight of Auschwitz, the main tasks of ethics are to the precise and scrupulous analysis of the societal preconditions of Auschwitz and how a society can be imagined and created that is, to the extent possible, immune to the virus of particularistic and suppressive morality. Humanism is the attempt to answer this question by radicalising the claims of enlightenment philosophy and by insisting that individual conscience must not be trusted unless it has developed under conditions of a fairly decent society, a society, that is, which overcomes and rejects all particularism and distorting differentiations, including the inherent nationalism, on which the construction of nation states is premised.

The nation state is conceptualised as state sovereignty controlling a territory and its borders. It operates a distinction between those on the one side of the border and those on the other, where those who are within the borders of a territory have, in principle, a right to be there, while those who are outside, in principle have not. The only appropriate answer to Auschwitz is a global order that overcomes the concept of the nation state and sets to work constructing a cosmopolitan order based on an individual's right to decide how and where to live and to travel freely.

3.7.6 Defending the Preconditions of a Humanist Society

The rise of fascist parties and their capacity to shape public opinions by a mixture of mass-propaganda, indoctrination, intimidation, and the silencing of their political opponents demonstrated the necessity to ensure the societal preconditions of individual autonomy based on a plurality of opinions and an unimpeded exchange of views.

This is where the flip-side of the Fichtean coin of the individual created, in normative terms, by the call of her society shows. In The Anatomy of Fascism,

Robert Paxton analyses in some detail the rise of fascist movements in Europe. He highlights how fascism 'rested not upon the truth of its doctrine but upon the leader's mystical union with the historic destiny of his people' (2004, p. 17), 'sought to appeal mainly to the emotions by the use of ritual, carefully stage-managed ceremonies, and intensely charged rhetoric' (2004, p. 16), and 'changed the practice of citizenship from the enjoyment of constitutional rights and duties to participation in mass ceremonies of affirmation and conformity' (2004, pp. 11 and 79). However, what Paxton emphasises in particular is how fascist regimes 'set out to make the new man and the new woman (each in his or her proper sphere). It was the challenging task of fascist educational systems to manufacture 'new' men and women who were simultaneously fighters and obedient subjects' (2004, p. 143). To this end, fascist regimes 'contained multiple agencies for shaping and molding the citizenry into an integrated community of disciplined, hardened fighters. The fascist state was particularly attentive to the formation of youth, jealously attempting to retain a monopoly of this function' (2004, p. 143). As Hitler explained to the Reichstag in December 1938, German boys 'join our organization at the age of ten and get a breath of fresh air for the first time; then, four years later, they move from the Jungvolk to the Hitler Youth and there we keep them for another four years. And then we are even less prepared to give them back into the hands of those who create our class and status barriers, rather we take them immediately into the Party, into the Labor Front, into the SA or the SS . . . and so on' (quoted by Paxton 2004, pp. 143–144).

The sole objective of education, indoctrination and mass propaganda was Gleichschaltung—the unification, standardisation and conformity of a people's mindsets and morality. The results of Nazi propaganda and indoctrination are explored in great detail in Christopher Browning's research on the men forming the Reserve Police Battalion 101, which was extensively involved in executing the Final Solution in Poland. Browning demonstrates the 'insidious effects of constant proaganda and indoctrination. Pervasive racism and the resulting exclusion of the Jewish victims from any common ground with the perpetrators made it all the easier for the majority of the policemen to conform to the norms of their immediate community (the battalion) and their society at large (Nazi Germany)' (Browning 1992, p. 186). The point is that Browning is right to assume that these policemen, engaged in the most horrible atrocities, were, at the same time, conforming to the norms of their society. This bears little resemblance to the Kantean autonomous individual, endowed by nature with an infallible conscience and engaged in a constant dialogue with her Creator. It has everything to do with the Fichtean subject created by the calling of her society and integrated into her society's normative order (compare Neitzel and Welzer 2014, in particular pp. 201–204, 293–299).

In order to achieve their objective of Gleichschaltung, the Nazis not only controlled the education of their people, but also developed a novel use of language designed to fit the purposes of propaganda. Ernst Cassirer has contributed a particularly enlightening analysis of this aspect of Nazi rule. He describes how the Nazis' 'cunning artisans' skilfully fabricated what Cassirer refers to as 'political myths'. According to Cassirer, 'the military rearmament was only the necessary consequence of the mental rearmament brought about by the political myths' (1974, p. 282). What Nazi propaganda amounted to was a fundamental change in the function of language, in that 'words which formerly were used in a descriptive, logical, or semantic sense, are now used as magic words that are destined to produce certain effects and to stir up certain emotions. Our ordinary words are charged with meanings; but these new-fangled words are charged with feelings and violent passions' (Cassirer 1974, p. 283). For these magic words to be fully effective, they are supplemented by the introduction of new rites.

> And since, in the totalitarian state, there is no private sphere, independent of political life, the whole life of man is suddenly inundated by a high tide of new rituals. They are as regular, as rigorous and inexorable as those rituals that we find in primitive societies. Every class, every sex, and every age has a rite of its own. No one could walk in the street, nobody could greet his neighbor or friend without performing a political ritual. And just as in primitive societies the neglect of one of the prescribed rites has meant misery and death. Even in young children this is not regarded as a mere sin of omission. It becomes a crime against the majesty of the leader and the totalitarian state (1974, p. 284).

Cassirer concludes that the effect of these new rites is obvious, as 'nothing is more likely to lull asleep all our active forces, our power of judgment and critical discernment, and to take away our feeling of personality and individual responsibility than the steady, uniform, and monotonous performance of the same rites' (1974, pp. 284–285).

It was emigrants like Ernst Cassirer, Herbert Marcuse (1934), Karl Loewenstein (1937a, b, 1939) and Karl Mannheim (1943) who first and with determination drew the conclusions. Again in the clear words of Ernst Cassirer:

> When we first heard of the political myths we found them so absurd and incongruous, so fantastic and ludicrous that we could hardly be prevailed upon to take them seriously. By now it has become clear to all of us that this was a great mistake. [...] What we have learned in the hard school of our modern political life is the fact that human culture is by no means the firmly established thing that we once supposed it to be (Cassirer 1974, pp. 296–297).

In marked opposition to the views of liberal democracy, these emigrants developed the concept of 'militant' democracy (Flümann 2014; Hoffmann-Riem 2010; Kirshner 2014; Sajo 2004; Thiel 2003, 2009; Tyulkina 2015).

After the consequences of liberal, laissez-faire democracy had proved its underlying assumptions terribly wrong, the lesson was learnt that human dignity and human rights must be protected against their enemies and institutions must be constructed that are apt to preserve the necessary societal and political preconditions of human dignity. It was another émigré, Karl Popper, who in his work on the open society and its enemies, pronounced the creed of the new perspective. In precise opposition to Kelsen's view quoted above, Popper (1945, p. 581) sets out what he calls

> the *paradox of tolerance*: Unlimited tolerance must lead to the disappearance of tolerance. If we extend unlimited tolerance even to those who are intolerant, if we are not prepared to defend a tolerant society against the onslaught of the intolerant, then the tolerant will be destroyed, and tolerance with them. [...] We should therefore claim, in the name of tolerance, the right not to tolerate the intolerant. We should claim that any movement

> preaching intolerance places itself outside the law, and we should consider incitement to intolerance and persecution as criminal, in the same way as we should consider incitement to murder, or to kidnapping, or to the revival of the slave trade, as criminal.

To capture the same message, Herbert Marcuse later coined the notion of 'discriminating tolerance', meaning that tolerance does not extend to the protection of ideologies and movements of an aggressive or destructive character. "To tolerate propaganda for inhumanity vitiates the goals not only of liberalism but of every progressive political philosophy (1969, p. 120). Part of the struggle for a real democracy is "the fight against an ideology of tolerance which, in reality, favors and fortifies the conservation of the status quo of inequality and discrimination" (1969, p. 123).

Hence, the resolve not to tolerate intolerance and to treat "incitement to intolerance and persecution as criminal" is part of the unifying beliefs of those promoting what is referred to as a principled or militant democracy.

Building on previous research (1935), Loewenstein's seminal article on "Militant Democracy and Fundamental Rights", published in 1937, drew public attention to a long list of contemporary authoritarian parties in Europe, unified by "rampant nationalism", the leadership principle, the wish to abolish democracy, and hatred towards communism, Marxism, freemasons, and pacifists (1937a, p. 421). According to Loewenstein, a state is authoritarian to the extent that "the group in power controls public opinion as well as the machinery of government" (1937a, p. 417). This combination of political and public discursive powers enables the government to rule by emotions. In Loewenstein's terms, an authoritarian government is characterised by "a supersession of constitutional government by emotional government" (1937a, p. 418). The "cohesive strength of the dictatorial and authoritarian state is rooted in emotionalism", the combination, that is, of "high-pitched nationalist enthusiasm" and "permanent psychic coercion, at times amounting to intimidation and terrorization scientifically applied" (1937a, p. 418). Hence, what in Loewenstein's view (1937a, p. 423) lies at the core of fascism is a "political technique".

> Colossal propaganda is launched against what appears as the most conspicuously vulnerable targets. A technique of incessant repetition, of over-statements and over-simplifications, is evolved and applied. The different sections of the people are played off against one another. In brief, to arouse, to guide, and to use emotionalism in its crudest and its most refined forms is the essence of the fascist technique for which movement and emotion are not only linguistically identical.

Loewenstein argues that it is the trust in the spirit inherent in human beings and the blind legalistic formalism of liberal democracy that crucially supports the rise of fascism as a political technique (1937a, pp. 423–424).

> This technique could be victorious only under the extraordinary conditions offered by democratic institutions. Its success is based on its perfect adjustment to democracy. Democracy and democratic tolerance have been used for their own destruction. Under cover of fundamental rights and the rule of law, the anti-democratic machine could be built up and set in motion legally. Calculating adroitly that democracy could not, without self-abnegation, deny to any body of public opinion the full use of the free institutions of speech,

> press, assembly, and parliamentary participation, fascist exponents systematically discredit the democratic order and make it unworkable by paralyzing its functions until chaos reigns. They exploit the tolerant confidence of democratic ideology that in the long run truth is stronger than falsehood, that the spirit asserts itself against force. Democracy was unable to forbid the enemies of its very existence the use of democratic instrumentalities. Until very recently, democratic fundamentalism and legalistic blindness were unwilling to realize that the mechanism of democracy is the Trojan horse by which the enemy enters the city. [. . .] It is the exaggerated formalism of the rule of law which under the enchantment of formal equality does not see fit to exclude from the game parties that deny the very existence of its rules.

Loewenstein concludes (1937a, p. 423) that democracy "must fight on its own plane a technique which serves only the purpose of power. Democracy must become militant." He (1937a, pp. 426–427) draws on the German example to demonstrate that

> the lack of militancy of the Weimar Republic against subversive movements, even though clearly recognized as such, stands out in the post-war predicament of democracy both as an illustration and as a warning. [. . .] A survey of the legislative defences of the Republic against the enemies of the democratic order reveals an almost tragicomical picture of half-hearted, laggard, and thoroughly ineffective methods of dealing with the subversive technique. [. . .] Democracy had surrendered to National Socialism long before Hitler was 'legally' appointed Chancellor of the Reich.

From a comparative analysis of legislation enacted in those European countries that took action against the rise of authoritarian ideologies, Loewenstein distils a list of necessary and successful measures. This includes, among others, the proscription of subversive movements (1937b, p. 645), movements, that is, which are prepared to unlawfully usurp state functions (1937b, p. 646); legislation proscribing para-military formations, uniforms and symbols (1937b, p. 648) and legislation protecting parliamentary institutions against their abuse by extremist parties (1937b, p. 650). It also includes criminal law provisions forbidding incitement to violence or hatred against sections of the population and the "agitation against and baiting of particular sections of the people because of their race, political attitude, or religious creed" (1937b, p. 651). In this context, Loewenstein (1937b, p. 651) highlights that "under the Weimar Republic, owing to the ill-advised yet inveterate attitude of the courts in interpreting the criminal code, Jews and Marxists as members of a group were left entirely without protection if they could not prove that the attack was directed personally against the complainant".

From his overview of measures adopted by European states reacting to the challenge of authoritarian extremism, Loewenstein (1937b, p. 656) concludes that "European democracy has overstepped democratic fundamentalism and risen to militancy". He suggests (1937b, p. 658) that democracy must be redefined as the "application of disciplined authority, by liberal-minded men, for the ultimate ends of liberal government: human dignity and freedom".

It is not necessary to follow Loewenstein into all corners of his theory. In principle, his line of reasoning is irrefutable. A societal configuration's political sub-system can be defined as the entirety of those elements of a societal structure that are involved in the reproduction of the normative order, including education, public speech, associations and other civil-society organisations engaged in political activities, as well as the parliamentary and bureaucratic institutions. If it is true that modern means of public and mass-communication, of emotionalism, indoctrination, propaganda and other forms of manipulation can be used by powerful groups to distort the political sub-system and to prevent it from fostering the generation of autonomous individuals, then the latter must be prevented from turning against the system's ultimate end of continually realising human dignity.

Given the powers of modern mass-communication and indoctrination, a notion of democracy defined merely as a rule by majority votes falls short of legitimising a government. As Popper (1945, pp. 118–119, 368) put it, the concept of democracy is "not based upon the principle that the majority should rule", as a majority might "rule in a tyrannical way". Rather, democracy should be seen as an attempt to "create, develop, and protect, political institutions for the avoidance of tyranny" and "always open to improvement".

Popper's observations cast a light on the relationship between human dignity and legislation. In a decent society, human dignity and human rights elaborating human dignity necessarily take precedence over legislation, which, like all other state functions, serves human dignity and human rights. Human dignity and human rights are not up for parliamentary discussion, except as guidelines for legislation. They are not to be touched or interfered with in any way, but serve as a foundation and orientation for parliamentary activities. Kant is right in claiming that 'democracy, in the truest sense of the word, is necessarily a despotism, because it establishes an executive power through which all the citizens may make decisions about (and indeed against) the single individual without his consent, so that decisions are made by all the people and yet not by all the people; and this means that the general will is in contradiction with itself, and thus also with freedom' (Kant 1796/1991, p. 101). However, Kant's criticism targets a system of liberal democracy, not the political system of a humanist society, where parliament cannot dispose of 'freedom', but has to respect the dignity and rights of each and every individual. Human dignity is not law but 'right' and therefore ranks in a hierarchy of norms above any form of legislation.

Whether a societal structure counts as decent is not a matter of regular free parliamentary elections and legislation alone but a matter of its entire organisation. What needs to be taken into account is the political education of individuals as critical autonomous citizens, discourses deconstructing ideological elements of social structure and a society's level of differentiation. Such a society should also feature the formation of subsystems that function unimpeded according to their genuine logic without interference from other parts of society and hence can perform their role as potentially critical of politically powerful actors. In addition, the societal structure must ensure the effective protection of individuals against humiliating, discriminatory, threatening, intrusive, deceptive, or manipulative forms of communication, apt to undermine or distort the formation of individual autonomy. Political analysis often focusses on a few state institutions, such as a government and parliament. However, normative power does not originate from these political institutions, but from individuals. Therefore, power is a pervasive constituent of all social relationships, and a politically aware and sensitive analysis of societal realities must take this into account.

While Kantian dignity translates into an unrestricted liberal democracy in which the general law is the expression of individuals' autonomy and hence, without any limitation, at the disposal of politics, humanism insists on the primacy of human dignity over parliamentary democracy. In a humanist society, the supreme authority rests with constitutional, regional or international courts that cooperate in assessing the performance of state actors in terms of human digntiy and human rights. In a humanist society, 'right'—human dignity—takes precedence over politics and legislation. Ideologies that promote violence, contempt or discrimination are consequently banned from the public sphere and parliament.

Thus the concept of a humanist society aims to overcome the deficiencies and feebleness of an agnostic or relativist Weimarian style democracy. Instead of providing only the procedural framework and, for the rest, relying on individuals' innate morality, a polity that recognises human dignity as its supreme value is tasked with ensuring and contributing actively to the formation of respectful, compassionate, accountable, and autonomous individuals. The primary objective of a polity's design, institutions and procedures is to promote a societal structure that fosters the development of accountable and autonomous subjects.

Hence, the protection of human dignity in a humanist society materialises in institutions that control the human rights conformity of government policies and parliamentary activities. At state level, this includes constitutional courts, strong and independent heads of state, independent human rights institutions and ombudspersons, as well as non-governmental organisations and media advocating human rights and overseeing government and legislation; at transnational levels, courts, the Security Council, treaty bodies etc.

3.7.7 The Primacy of Human Dignity and Human Rights: Humanism Overcoming Unconstrained Majoritarianism

A liberal, value-neutral democracy coordinates autonomous individuals; a humanist society promotes the development of autonomous individuals. In a liberal, value-neutral democracy, the majority's parliamentary rule is unrestricted, and so are public debates shaping political opinion. This follows from the simple fact that in a liberal democracy no moral orientation, ideology or value is backed by a consensus strong enough to allow it to claim precedence over other opinions. In contrast, a humanist society is not only committed to realising, but also gives precedence to human dignity and human rights over parliamentarism and unrestrained public discourses. The respect owed to the individual takes priority over and sets clear limits to public and political debate. It is a core task of any constitution to 'constrain the exercise of democratic self-rule by protecting fundamental individual rights' (Ackerman 2000, p. 718).

Having learned the lessons from more than one totalitarian regime, in Europe there exists today a strong common conviction that the public promotion of intolerance, including advocating totalitarian ideologies, the denial of the Shoah, or 'hate speech'—the public incitement to discrimination, hostility or violence against an individual or a social group—cannot be tolerated and is to be banned unambiguously by effective criminal law provisions.

The underlying principle that human rights do not imply tolerating the intolerant is expressed in Article 30 of the Universal Declaration of Human Rights, which states:

> Nothing in this Declaration may be interpreted as implying for any State, group or person any right to engage in any activity or to perform any act aimed at the destruction of any of the rights and freedoms set forth herein.

A very similar—slightly stricter—provision is to be found—under the heading "Prohibition of abuse of rights"—in Article 17 ECHR, which posits:

> Nothing in this Convention may be interpreted as implying for any State, group or person any right to engage in any activity or perform any act aimed at the destruction of any of the rights and freedoms set forth herein or at their limitation to a greater extent than is provided for in the Convention.

Article 7 of the Universal Declaration recognises everyone's rights to equality before the law and to protection against any incitement to discrimination.

> All are equal before the law and are entitled without any discrimination to equal protection of the law. All are entitled to equal protection against any discrimination in violation of this Declaration and against any incitement to such discrimination.

The entitlement to protection against any incitement to discrimination found its way into the UDHR on the initiative of the USSR delegate Bogomolov who submitted (quoted by Morsink 1999, p. 70):

> Between Hitlerian racial propaganda and any other propaganda designed to stir up racial, national or religious hatred and incitement to war, there was but a short step. Freedom of the press and free speech could not serve as a pretext for propagating views which poisoned public opinion. Propaganda in favor of racial or national exclusiveness or superiority merely served as an ideological mask for imperialistic aggression.

The proposal met with wide support, including A.L. Easterman, representing the World Jewish Congress, and Renè Cassin, who observed that incitement to discrimination 'included organized conspiracies and was extremely dangerous. Even in a democracy citizens should not be allowed liberties which ran counter to the liberties of others' (quoted by Morsink 1999, p. 71), at the global level, the clearest expression of militancy is to be found in Article 4 of the International Convention on the Elimination of All Forms of Racial Discrimination, adopted in 1965, which states:

> States Parties condemn all propaganda and all organizations which are based on ideas or theories of superiority of one race or group of persons of one colour or ethnic origin, or

> which attempt to justify or promote racial hatred and discrimination in any form, and undertake to adopt immediate and positive measures designed to eradicate all incitement to, or acts of, such discrimination and, to this end, with due regard to the principles embodied in the Universal Declaration of Human Rights and the rights expressly set forth in article 5 of this Convention, inter alia:
>
> (a) Shall declare an offence punishable by law all dissemination of ideas based on racial superiority or hatred, incitement to racial discrimination, as well as all acts of violence or incitement to such acts against any race or group of persons of another colour or ethnic origin, and also the provision of any assistance to racist activities, including the financing thereof;
>
> (b) Shall declare illegal and prohibit organizations, and also organized and all other propaganda activities, which promote and incite racial discrimination, and shall recognize participation in such organizations or activities as an offence punishable by law;
>
> (c) Shall not permit public authorities or public institutions, national or local, to promote or incite racial discrimination.

In addition, Article 20 of the International Covenant on Civil and Political Rights, adopted by the UN General Assembly in 1966, shall be quoted here, as it tellingly links together the external and the internal aggressiveness of particularistic ideologies, by stipulating:

> 1. Any propaganda for war shall be prohibited by law.
>
> 2. Any advocacy of national, racial or religious hatred that constitutes incitement to discrimination, hostility or violence shall be prohibited by law.

Recently, in December 2015, the Council of Europe's European Commission against Racism and Intolerance (ECRI) adopted its General Policy Recommendation No. 15 on Combating Hate Speech. This Recommendation denotes as hate speech "the advocacy, promotion or incitement, in any form, of the denigration, hatred or vilification of a person or group of persons, as well as any harassment, insult, negative stereotyping, stigmatization or threat in respect of such a person or group of persons and the justification of all the preceding types of expression," on the ground of any characteristic or status. The Recommendation observes that "hate speech may take the form of the public denial, trivialisation, justification or condonation of crimes of genocide, crimes against humanity or war crimes which have been found by courts to have occurred, and of the glorification of persons convicted for having committed such crimes". It calls on governments to

> take appropriate and effective action against the use, in a public context, of hate speech which is intended or can reasonably be expected to incite acts of violence, intimidation, hostility or discrimination against those targeted by it through the use of the criminal law provided that no other, less restrictive, measure would be effective and the right to freedom of expression and opinion is respected.

This Recommendation states that

> forms of expression that offend, shock or disturb will not on that account alone amount to hate speech and that action against the use of hate speech should serve to protect individuals and groups of persons rather than particular beliefs, ideologies or religions.

This definition is precise. What militancy protects is the dignity and rights of individuals and not traditional views. Insult and discrimination target individuals, not only views. Hence criticising political convictions or any other views is essentially different from acts of communication that directly and deliberately insult, discriminate against, or otherwise violate the dignity of individuals (Hampton 2007, pp. 120–129).

At the level of EU legislation, the normative consensus noted above is reflected by Council Framework Decision 2008/913/JHA of 28 November 2008 on combating certain forms and expressions of racism and xenophobia by means of criminal law (OJ L 328, 6.12.2008, p. 55), which obliges EU Member States to criminalise racist and xenophobic hate speech, as well as acts of publicly condoning, denying or grossly trivialising atrocity crimes.

To demonstrate the meaning of these principles, a telling example is the ECtHR's Decision—of November 2004—as to the admissibility of the application by Mark Anthony Norwood against the United Kingdom, alleging a breach of Article 10 ECHR, which protects everyone's right to freedom of expression. The circumstances of the case, as summarised by the Decision, have it that Mr Norwood was a Regional Organiser for the British National Party (BNP), an extreme right wing political party. Until 9 January 2002, when the poster was removed by the police following a complaint from the public, he displayed in the window of his first-floor flat a large poster, supplied by the BNP, with a photograph of the Twin Towers in flame, the words "Islam out of Britain – Protect the British People" and a symbol of a crescent and star in a prohibition sign. The ECtHR observed that the "general purpose of Article 17 is to prevent individuals or groups with totalitarian aims from exploiting in their own interests the principles enunciated by the Convention." The Court recalled its previous case-law, according to which "the freedom of expression guaranteed under Article 10 of the Convention may not be invoked in a sense contrary to Article 17", and concluded:

> The Court notes and agrees with the assessment made by the domestic courts, namely that the words and images on the poster amounted to a public expression of attack on all Muslims in the United Kingdom. Such a general, vehement attack against a religious group, linking the group as a whole with a grave act of terrorism, is incompatible with the values proclaimed and guaranteed by the Convention, notably tolerance, social peace and non-discrimination. The applicant's display of the poster in his window constituted an act within the meaning of Article 17, which did not, therefore, enjoy the protection of Articles 10 or 14.

Unfortunately, the ECtHR is not always as determined and unswerving as in its judgment in the *Norwood* case. In the judgment on *Perincek v. Switzerland*, it was left to a minority to state the rather obvious that 'racist speech and genocide denial, combined with the intent to insult others or make others suffer, may as such be characterised as an activity aimed at the destruction of any of the rights and freedoms set forth in the Convention, within the meaning of Article 17' (Additional

Dissenting Opinion of Judge Silvis, Joined by Judges Casadevall, Berro and Küris, para. 8).

As demonstrated in the *Norwood* case, a limit to political discourses is necessary, a limit that rules out intolerant, intimidating or degrading public speech and propaganda directed against the rights of any individual or any perceived category of individuals. There is a border beyond which discourses turn against morality itself as a means of enabling individuals to become autonomous persons, and this border must be defended by all means. The indispensable minimum of all legitimate morality accepts that all human beings have a right to personhood and therefore are entitled to the amount of care and respect on which developing as a person is premised. Human dignity requires a decent, humanist society fostering and protecting the constitution of autonomous subjects. This necessitates a militant society. The concept of militancy embraces the necessity to preserve the societal conditions on which a decent society is premised.

Hence the scope of all human rights has to be determined in a manner ensuring that the basic principle is respected that "All human beings are born free and equal in dignity and rights." In other words, no human right can ever be interpreted as conflicting with the underlying rationale of human dignity, from which all rights flow. The entire organisation of a humanist society's normative order has to respect this basic construction principle. In the era defined as post-Auschwitz, a militant society that preserves and defends personhood, which the liberal notion of human rights had mistaken for a natural given, is indispensable; and this mission is not at the disposal of political institutions.

Thus, the relationship between politics and human rights is reversed. In a liberal democracy, the entire normative system is at the political subsystem's disposal, including human rights. In contrast, in a principled society, human dignity and human rights define and delimit the legitimate radius of action of political institutions, including parliaments. By its own rules, liberal democracy is a system of politics' unlimited control of the law. Hence, liberal democracies are unprotected against the rise of authoritarian ideologies and regimes within the parliamentary system. As Bienenfeld, speaking for the World Jewish Congress, pointed out during the initial phase of the drafting of the UDHR, 'under the Nazi regime thousands of people had been deprived of their liberty under laws which were perfectly valid' (quoted by Morsink 1999, p. 39). On the contrary, in the perspective of a militant humanist society, human dignity and its societal preconditions are not at the disposal of state authorities, including parliament and its fluctuating majorities. Human dignity as the corner stone of the revised system of human rights insists that there is a marked limit to the range of acceptable ideologies and to political pluralism and parties. The political subsystem may not overstep the line drawn by every single human individual's entitlement to respect as an esteemed, responsible and autonomous person, as well as to the societal preconditions allowing her to develop as such a person. This respect is owed to the individual by humankind and not premised on the views of any parliamentary majority. As concerns her dignity and human rights, the individual is not subjected to the rule of a majority. To give just one, obvious example: As death penalty violates human dignity, a parliament cannot, in a humanist society, vote on its introduction. Humanism rules out the tyranny of a majority of whatever size.

No other context is more apt to highlight the sharp contrast between liberal democracy and a militant, humanist society than a polity's position on hate speech. For those who believe in the individual's unshakeable moral autonomy and in democracy as the unimpeded, unlimited rule of majorities, Dworkin (2009, p. viii) has formulated the creed: "So in a democracy no one, however powerful or impotent, can have a right not to be insulted or offended." For those who in a humanist perspective perceive the moral individual as the result of formative processes of communication, occurring within a normative framework and public societal climate, the political creed would rather posit that "in a humanist society every one, however powerful or impotent, has a right not to be insulted or discriminated against." In liberal democracy, the rules of unrestricted political and parliamentary debate take precedence over human dignity; in humanist society, human dignity—including an individual's right to be respected as a person—takes precedence and consequently defines the limits of what is to be questioned and at the disposal of public discourses and a parliament's majority votes. Human dignity is not. Liberal democracy is about 'a people'—demos—and its right to self-determination, which takes precedence over the respect owed to the individual. The individual has to bear being insulted because this may serve the interests of the people. On the contrary, humanism is about the individual and her right to self-determination and to a development that enables her progressively to make autonomous decisions. This development is to be protected against the destructive, crippling and distorting forces of contempt, intimidation, discrimination and indoctrination, and this protection is not a matter of political decisions or majorities. Human dignity is not at the state's disposal. A society that allows that an individual is exposed to hateful speech on behalf of her perceived ethnicity, sex, disability or sexual orientation, has given up on human dignity.

3.8 Human Dignity as the Foundation and Guiding Principle of a Global Humanist Society

Although some aspects will only become clearer in what follows, it seems appropriate to, at the outset of this section, briefly define human dignity, as the term is used here, by answering three questions: What is the contents of the notion, who is entitled to human dignity, and why? As concerns the contents and meaning of the concept, the approach adopted here departs from a clear and stable anthropological basis. What defines humans is culture, the particular ability and technique, that is, to coexist peacefully and to cooperate on the basis of shared systems of symbols and communication. What defines humans is their dependence on culture. Answering to this dependency, human dignity denotes the entitlement of a human being to be initiated in culture and to, according to one's abilities, participate in the human project of a rapidly evolving human culture. The notion of human dignity captures the social preconditions of such participation: The right to be named and called on as a respected, accountable and autonomous agent and rights-holder and to be supported in developing as such a person. As an individual's development as a participant in culture is premised on social preconditions, these social preconditions can be referred to, in their entirety, as a 'humanist' society. In this sense, human dignity denotes an individual's right to a humanist—or, synonymously, a 'decent'—society. To answer the second question, every being carrying a human face and born into the complexities of the human condition is entitled to be accepted to the human family as its member. No restriction is made, because no restriction stands the test of reasonable argument. If human dignity reacts to conditions in which all human beings share, there is no plausible reason why human dignity should not equally benefit all. Why are human beings entitled to human dignity? Because they so decide. Within a human dignity paradigm, persons create and address one another as members of a global community.

The Universal Declaration of Human Rights contains several indications of the fact that the real concern of Human Rights is not abstract principles, but a societal reality that brings these principles to life. The initial sentence of the declaration, following the recitals, posits that these Human Rights are proclaimed 'to the end that every individual and every organ of society, keeping this Declaration constantly in mind, shall strive by teaching and education to promote respect for these rights and freedoms and by progressive measures, national and international, to secure their universal and effective recognition and observance'. In addition, Article 28 UDHR puts forward:

> Everyone is entitled to a social and international order in which the rights and freedoms set forth in this Declaration can be fully realized.

Therefore, what the UDHR demands is more than the observance of a list of rights. It aims at a global social order, in which human dignity and human rights are effectively recognised and observed and individuals can fully realise their rights. It is suggested here to use the term 'humanist' to denote a global societal order that respects Article 28 UDHR by progressively creating the optimal conditions for human dignity to flourish and for individuals being able to fully realise their rights. Hence, in the sections to follow, the concept of human dignity serves as the base and guiding principle for constructing a global humanist society as the institutional expression and consequence of the solidarity of all human beings respecting and caring for one another.

Opting for the term 'humanism' has the disadvantage that this notion comes loaded with meaning and history. However, both the term's connotations and its protagonists strongly relate to human dignity and human rights, an anthropological view on humans as fundamentally similar, an emphasis on the solidarity of the human family, a strong accent on individual autonomy, and a focus on education and individual development. Similarly, Julian Nida-Rümelin has recently observed that what humanist approaches have in common is their emphasis on individual autonomy, on reason, and on a cosmopolitan universalism (2016, pp. 218–221), but also on human dignity (2016, pp. 353–356). In fact, if the concept of humanism comes charged with history and meaning, this can also be seen as increasing the leverage of the concept and is not necessarily of disadvantage, as long as its meaning fits the understanding and purpose of how and why the term is used here. In any case, there is the obvious aspect that the notions ‘human dignity’ and ‘human rights’ invoke the ‘human’ individual, as does ‘humanism’. Certainly, all these concepts share their concern with the human being.

As a political concept, humanism differs from all particularistic and collectivist—including nationalist—approaches in that it views humanity as a community of sovereign and autonomous lawgivers who have morally and legally binding claims against one another, claims to solidarity, care and respect. With liberal approaches, humanism shares the understanding that the individual is entitled to personhood and to count as a full member of humanity (Forst 2011, p. 122). However, humanism is markedly different from liberal concepts in that humanism views the truly autonomous person not as the starting point and basis, but as the ultimate objective of a society that is geared towards realising the vision of a society that enables every human being to enjoy human rights and to be the master of her life. Liberalism is about the rights of persons who are inherently autonomous individuals (Forst 2011, p. 132), humanism about the chance to, under the conditions of a humanist society, develop as a person and about an individual’s right to be supported in that development.

What, hence, underlies the concept of a humanist society is a dynamic view of the human personality. In the UDHR this is reflected by the accent on teaching and education. Article 26 UDHR provides that education ‘shall be directed to the full development of the human personality’, and Article 29 stipulates that everyone ‘has duties to the community in which alone the free and full development of his personality is possible’. This clear and strong emphasis on an individual’s dependence on her society—in which alone her personality can develop—is the most significant indication of humanism turning away from and overcoming the liberal view of the self-sufficient and autarkic person. Johannes Morsink, the author of a particularly thorough and informed analysis of the UDHR, commented that the word ‘alone’ in Article 29 UDHR ‘may well be the most important single word in the entire document, for it helps us answer the charge that the rights set forth in the Declaration create egotistic individuals who are not closely tied to their respective communities’.

Without this word ‘the Declaration would have lifted the individual out of his or her social context and the rights declared would have been those of an abstract and unrealistic individual, the kind that does not exist’ (1999, pp. 247–248).

3.8.1 *Human Dignity and Human Rights are Normative Categories*

Article 1 of the Universal Declaration, which was quoted above, claims: 'All human beings are born free and equal in dignity and rights. They are endowed with reason and conscience and should act towards one another in a spirit of brotherhood'. This provision is not to be understood at face value as an anthropological analysis of homosapiens, but in a purely normative sense. What it really means is that all human beings are entitled to dignity and equal rights; they are entitled to be supported in developing as rational and moral persons; and they are entitled to the solidarity of all other human beings. It also means that human beings are obliged to respect others and their equal rights, to support others in developing as rational and moral persons, and to meet all others in a spirit of human solidarity. Dignity and human rights are strictly normative—or prescriptive—and not descriptive terms. They are, from the start, notions expressing what *should* be the case and not what *is* the case. Still, there are philosophers who attempt to place human rights in a factual category, in particular by assuming that human rights reflect needs - e.g. basic needs that all human beings share (Miller 2016, pp. 31–33) - or interests or aim at preventing harm. As a case in point, Shue (1996, p. 18) defines basic rights as:

> social guarantees against actual and threatened deprivations of at least some basic needs. Basic rights are an attempt to give to the powerless a veto over some of the forces that would otherwise harm them the most.

Thus, rights safeguard needs and protect individuals against harm. In consequence, what in the end counts for Shue is not rights, but actual enjoyments, what he calls the substance of a right (1996, p. 16):

> The substance of a right is whatever the right is a right to. A right is not a right to enjoy a right – it is a right to enjoy something else, like food or liberty. [. . .] ordinarily when we say someone is enjoying a right, we mean the person is enjoying the substance of the right.

This understanding brings human rights to the level of things we enjoy, like food, property or health. Shue (1996, p. 20) also provides the following example:

> [. . .] if people have rights to free association, they ought not merely to 'have' the rights to free association but also to enjoy their free association itself.

However, what does it mean that people *ought to enjoy* their free association? What if many prefer not to associate? Does it affect rights of voting or of nomination to parliament if a population's majority does, in fact, not enjoy voting or running as a candidate and chooses not to vote or stand for parliament? Is the right to practice one's religion premised on a certain percentage of the population being religious and wishing to practice their religion? Is the right to found a family dependent on sufficiently many aspiring to do so?

Similar to Shue, Margalit (1998, p. 38) assumes that "rights are interests – interests of a particular kind, but interests nonetheless." More specifically, rights are interests that are "good in and of themselves". Margalit (1998, p. 39) views these inherently good interests as "constituting human dignity". Thus, Margalit designs a bottom-up construction, where rights flow from real interests and human dignity forms the top of the pyramid.

However, understanding rights or human dignity as a kind of interest or need is a simple category mistake. If we say that a person has a right to practice her religion, we assert neither that she is in need of practicing her religion, nor that she is interested in or enjoys doing so. Even the most hardboiled atheist has a right to practice her religion, and the fact that she does not care to do so is not a counterargument, because her rights and her interests are categorically unrelated. However, if the right to practicing one's religion is not an interest, it cannot be an inherently good interest either. Similarly, if we say that someone has a right to marry and to found a family, we are not claiming that individuals—categorically, or regularly—feel an urge to marry and found families, but that everyone should be free to do so if she so prefers. A person who is determined not to found a family still maintains the right to do so. The assumption that having such a right implies that humans are in need of, or interested in, founding families is not only wrong, but, again, a category error that mistakes a purely prescriptive for a descriptive notion, an *ought* for an *is*. It is a confusion of describing and prescribing as two distinct language games.

For a normative order based on human dignity as its supreme principle to have a foundation in empirical interests, there would have to be something like a child's empirical interest to be called on as an autonomous and accountable agent. However, a child cannot have such an interest prior to her constitution as a person. In fact, it is difficult to tell whether life without normativity would be more pleasant or not. In any case, the reason we call on a child as a person, is not that she asked for it or otherwise demonstrates real interest in being constituted as a person, but because it fits our normative order and continues our project of culture. It is culture reproducing culture, nothing else. In fact, culture can be constructed as a strictly autopoietic—self-reproducing—system of meaningful acts of communication, possibly next to only one other such system, namely the cell, which accounts for the reproduction of all biological organisms, including our bodies. While the nation state often comes with a promise of happiness, a normative order based on human dignity pledges solidarity, respect as well as autonomous and accountable agency, all of which are normative categories.

A humanist society does not claim to know for people what they need, enjoy or are interested in. It only claims that marrying, founding a family, voting for a political party and practicing a religion mark spheres of individual autonomy and hence are necessarily part of the vision of a humanist society. This autonomy enables a person to lead a self-determined life. The concept of human dignity is not premised on the empirical assumption that most individuals prefer to be free—as such a preference would already presuppose freedom—but departs from the normative presupposition that people *should* be free to, in accordance with their abilities, make their choices and lead a self-determined life.

Any attempt to base rights on a factual category—like enjoyments, desires, happiness, interests, wellbeing, or, negatively, avoidance of harm— meets the objection challenging all empiricist or descriptivist approaches that people radically differ as to their preferences, and that even the same person will, over time, change her preferences and priorities. Even something as basic and simple as food means quite different things to a girl struggling with bulimia, to a single-mother of two small kids living in poverty, or to an overweight person suffering from cardiovascular diseases; and potentially means these different things to the same person experiencing various challenges at different stages of her life. While the health of many individuals is impaired by malnutrition, others die from heart attacks caused by obesity. To think of food simply as something that 'we humans enjoy' misses out on the complexities of human reality.

When reacting to objections of this sort, empiricists tend to be a bit less empirical and to distinguish between interests and good interests, between what a person wants at a given moment and what she *truly* or *really* wants. Yet such a response introduces normative criteria through the back-door to vamp up the empirical evidence. Instead of a neutral account of the desires given at a certain time and place, we are then presented with an anthropological analysis of typical or ideal human needs, which can also be read as an admission of failure to provide a theory of ethics without adding normative ingredients.

However, humans differ not only in their needs and preferences, they also differ as to what their happiness or enjoyments mean to them in principle. It is again too simple to assume that all humans consider their personal joy or happiness as their supreme objective. Many look beyond these categories, which is where normativity—the perspective of humankind as a cultural project 'transcending' biology and nature—comes in. As Law (2011, p. 120) put forward, someone "continuously injected with happiness-inducing drugs might have a pleasurable time, but that wouldn't guarantee a particularly worthwhile or meaningful existence." And Bertrand Russell observed that

> the dignity of which human existence is capable is not attainable by devotion to the mechanism of life, and that unless the contemplation of eternal things is preserved, mankind will become no better than well-fed pigs (Russell 2009, p. 149).

Human dignity entails the challenge of an autonomous person being called on to decide for herself what is important for her as a human being, and possibly the person will struggle her life long to come to terms with and meet the challenge of autonomous and accountable agency. Many activities that are good candidates as examples of what can count as inherently meaningful—such as voting in parliamentary elections or volunteering to work for a victim support service—would be difficult to express in terms of personal enjoyments or happiness, but easily translate into examples of individuals acting on spheres of their autonomy, such as freedom of association or political citizenship.

The concept of human dignity entails a vision of a humanist society in which individuals are able to authentically appropriate their lives in radically different ways and fashions. This openness also reflects the right to experiment, to try and to err, and even to radically change one's mind over night.

3.8.2 *The Structure of a Global Humanist Society*

Human dignity as a normative paradigm aspires to found a global order legitimised by the normative power of individuals' autonomous and accountable agency. Hence, human dignity is a cosmopolitan concept that refers at once to humankind and to the individual. A cosmopolitan humanist order places the primacy of individual human beings as political agents and the accountability of politcal actors at its centre (Held 2002, p. 1).

The primary focus of human dignity is right, not positive law. This means that a person's dignity—and all related claims—are not premised on any acts of legislation. Rather, any legislation can be criticised if it does not acknowledge human dignity and meet the standards flowing from this concept. All provisions pertaining to human dignity—including Article 1 of the Universal Declaration, Article 1 of the Fundamental Rights Charter and Article 1 of the Grundgesetz—are of a merely declaratory, not of a constitutive nature. The reason is that human dignity is constituted, not within a political institution—such as a nation state— but as a normative relationship among individuals who care for and respect one another in a spirit of solidarity. This is what heralds the end of the Westfalian order—reaffirmed at the Congress of Vienna—and the advent of a new era, this is what Seyla Benhabib (2006, p. 16) highlights as the fundamental transition from an international to a cosmopolitan normative order:

> Norms of international justice most commonly arise through treaty obligations and bilateral or multilateral agreements among states [...]. They regulate relations among states [...] Cosmopolitan norms of justice, whatever the conditions of their legal origination, accrue to individuals as moral and legal persons in a worldwide civil society. Even if cosmopolitan norms arise through treaty like obligations, such as the UN Charter can be considered to be for the signatory states, their peculiarity is that they endow individuals rather than states and their agents with certain rights and claims. This is the uniqueness of the many human rights agreements signed since World War II. They signal an eventual transition from a model of international law based on treaties among states to cosmopolitan law understood as international public law that binds and bends the will of sovereign nations.

What generates human dignity as the cornerstone of a cosmopolitan humanist society are individual acts of communication that recognise and accept human dignity as—morally and legally—binding. As Jeremy Waldron (2006, p. 98) put it, norms of cosmopolitan justice 'emerge in the world, they are iterated and transformed in the world, and they apply to the world – all in the lives of ordinary people dealing with one another, with friends and with strangers, without preconceived ideas of who's in or who's out of their circle'.

By postulating human dignity and by acclaiming the human individual as the measure of all things and the sovereign lawgiver, the most basic and foundational recursive loop is established and upheld in continuous flows of communication, the loop, that is, that generates, at the same time, human dignity as the basis of a normative paradigm and the human person as both its source and its main product. In other words, to view human dignity and a humanist society as a normative paradigm is tantamount to positing that the normative universe is created by communicative acts of individuals who are sacred lawgivers because they so will. It is a paradigm because it comprises and organises all elements of the normative order and encompasses all the normative—symbolic—forces that are at work and renders the magic of a normative order possible (Bourdieu and Wacquant 1992, p. 123).

In a humanist perspective, normative power flows from individuals to political institutions established at state level or at a global scale, including the United Nations and the International Criminal Court. Neither the United Nations nor states generate human dignity. Otherwise they would also have the power to abandon it. Sovereignty rests solely with individuals, not with states or global actors.

At the very core of human dignity is the unconditional entitlement of every human being to belong to humankind: to be named and called on and to be initiated in culture as humankind's full member, within a humanist order that realises human dignity as its supreme value and guiding principle. An individual's entitlement to be a person is inherent in a paradigm based on human dignity and has its foundation in the sphere of the right we know from wrong, independent of positive laws. The Universal Declaration of Human Rights commences with the words:

> Whereas recognition of the inherent dignity and of the equal and inalienable rights of all members of the human family is the foundation of freedom, justice and peace in the world, [...]

This is the ideal, the vision. It interrelates the human family and its members. Human dignity, as the term is understood here, is the unconditional right of the human being to be, irrevocably, accepted and included as a person into the "human family", a right that has its foundation in a sphere of justice and right, not only positive legislation.

This sphere of justice and right is also what Article 2 of the Treaty on European Union refers to by stating:

> The Union is founded on the values of respect for human dignity, freedom, democracy, equality, the rule of law and respect for human rights, including the rights of persons belonging to minorities. These values are common to the Member States in a society in which pluralism, non-discrimination, tolerance, justice, solidarity and equality between women and men prevail.

Article 2 TEU does not create these values by stipulating them nor by referring to other acts of legislation, but relates to these 'values' as per se binding; and respect for human dignity is not one value among several others, but the underlying normative ideal, from which all other values and all human rights flow.

Everyone who carries a human face is entitled to be met by all others with an attitude of solidarity, compassion and respect. Hence, the status of a person includes the attribution of equal fundamental rights with others, as well as the status of being held, in accordance with one's capabilities, to account for one's actions.

Dignity and the human rights flowing from dignity are attributed to "all members of the human family", an expression, which, on the one hand, views the individual in relation to all other human beings and, on the other, excludes status differences of birth rights, as all are perceived as belonging to one and the same family. Hence, human dignity establishes a bond of equal rights and mutual responsibilities among all human individuals, it constitutes humankind as a community defined by attitudes of solidarity and sympathy for one another, it turns into a normative and political concept and claims Fichte's intuition of the human subject as the notion of an entire species—a "*Gattungsbegriff*".

The concept of human dignity invokes humanity as a community of solidarity—of 'brothers and sisters'—and thus indicates the appropriate size and the borders of the normative community. It thus concludes a long series of consecutive forms of polities of increasing size and normative complexity, including the band, the tribe, the city-state, the kingdom, and the nation state (the latter comprising states of the size of Russia or China). A global humanist society is the collectivity of all human individuals, and these individuals partake in and represent humankind. For that reason, the collectivity and the individual, endowed with dignity, are the two foci of one emerging global polity, which overcomes monarchies, empires and nation states as its predecessors. The values highlighted by the European Union's primary law assume a clear and firm stance against nationalism and other particularistic ideologies (Roll 2016).

Human dignity is premised on a global, cosmopolitan perspective, which again requires a social theory focussing on flows of communication that continuously organise the internal stratification and structures of one global social system (Stichweh 2016).

Obviously, a decent global order, organised with a view to making human dignity a reality, requires a stratified institutional structure. It is suggested to view the normative functions involved in establishing and reproducing a decent global order as organised at four levels.

Firstly, functions relating to standard setting, monitoring and supervision are located at regional and international levels. This category includes treaties and treaty bodies, the UN Security Council, regional human rights courts, the International Criminal Court, National Human Rights Institutes and so on. To give only one example, since in 2005 states' responsibility to protect their populations from atrocity crimes—genocide, war crimes, ethnic cleansing, and crimes against humanity—has been clarified and emphasised, several UN actors are involved in prevention, early warning and oversight, adding to international human rights supervision.

Secondly, in a system adhering to the rule of law, legislation performs a pivotal role in spelling out and in promoting agreed standards of human rights. Hence, legislation is organised at regional, state and provincial levels, as it is necessarily positioned at levels below international standards and supervision and above levels of implementation.

Implementation—the entirety of public institutions and procedures that realize human rights—is located at many levels, ranging from regional institutions to district and local authorities. These are the levels at which public actors deliver their contributions to making human dignity and human rights a reality. Courts and administrative authorities transform abstract and general human rights standards into the concrete rights and obligations of individuals. Schools and youth welfare authorities provide the framework within which children can develop. Universities preserve and elaborate the global society's knowledge base and ensure its transfer to the next generation.

Fourthly, crucially important functions are performed by morality, ranging from individuals' autonomous decisions, vested with normative power, to instances where citizens jointly act on their moral convictions—including various private associations, trade unions, media, arts, academia, etc.—as well as political advocacy, acting again at various levels. Individuals' morality is the key driver for innovation and pluralism and at the same time the force preserving a stable normative order.

This complex vertical architecture is necessary to bridge the distance between a global community and its individual members. At the same time, the structure sketched above is not far-fetched and in fact not even far from what exists or at least emerges today.

3.8.3 Horizontal Societal Differentiation Fostering Pluralism

A decent social order requires militancy. Criminal codes, in particular, must be deployed as a means of maintaining the societal preconditions on which, in the end, effective protection of human dignity and human rights is premised. To give only one example, the Grand Chamber of the European Court of Human Rights in the *Nachova*-case dealt with the racist killing of two young men by Bulgarian military police. The Court recalled the crucial functions of the criminal justice system in reinforcing human dignity and the vision of a pluralist society, holding (para. 145):

> Racial violence is a particular affront to human dignity and, in view of its perilous consequences, requires from the authorities special vigilance and a vigorous reaction. It is for this reason that the authorities must use all available means to combat racism and racist violence, thereby reinforcing democracy's vision of a society in which diversity is not perceived as a threat but as a source of enrichment.

Thus protecting societal diversity as a reflection of human dignity—which includes the right to self-definition—is an important function of criminal justice.

To safeguard and enhance individual autonomy and diversity, a decent society establishes and preserves a high level of the societal structure's horizontal differentiation, enabling an unimpeded development of various autonomous spheres of communication that follow their own rationale. Thus a decent society provides a framework within which an individuals' autonomy can develop in various cultural dimensions, including universities and other academic institutions, political parties, religious communities, private associations, reasonable market economies, libraries, a sphere of private and family life and institutions where arts can be performed. As societal sub-systems, these institutions require an appropriate organisation and regulations that foster the particular type of communication they are devoted to, as well as protection against distorting interventions from outside threatening to reduce the level of societal differentiation.

To this end, a decent society relies not only on a functional differentiation of its structure, but also on a new separation of powers. While the classical theory of *contrat sociale*, with its focus on the legal and political system, led to the postulate of a separation and equilibrium of *state* powers, an updated concept would stipulate, in addition to the internal differentiation of constitutional state functions, a comprehensive separation of societal subsystems, where politics, economy, media, science, arts, education and institutions of civil society—such as labour unions or religious denominations—are carefully distinguished and separated from one another, institutionalised in mutual independence, and where the relations between these subsystems are transparent, ensuring that all societal subsystems remain sufficiently autonomous and can function truthfully to their own logic and laws and preventing the interference and hegemony of one subsystem over another.

3.9 Human Rights and Obligations

Human dignity materialises firstly as a right that encapsulates the entire system of human rights, secondly as the corresponding obligation to acknowledge and respect equal human dignity and human rights of all others, and, thirdly, as an obligation to contribute one's due to establishing a decent social order.

In a normative order based on the political ideal of human dignity, individuals are morally called on to make a commitment to the protection of human dignity to prevent human rights being merely illusory. To become practically effective, human dignity and human rights are premised on a decent social order. In a societal structure based on the political ideal of human dignity, every individual is introduced to a societal network of various communities by being called on to engage in her constitution based on a normative order and to contribute to its preservation. This call not only implies that the individual is prompted to internalise the vision of communities committed to the political ideal of human dignity, but also that she is requested to contribute to establishing and maintaining a humanist social order. This obligation is part of what it means to be called on as a cosmopolitan citizen and an expression of the solidarity of the 'human family'.

According to Article 28 of the Universal Declaration, "[e]veryone is entitled to a social and international order in which the rights and freedoms set forth in this Declaration can be fully realized." However, such a "social and international" order can only be achieved by a collective commitment, to which everyone is called on to contribute her fair share. Consequently, Article 29, in its first paragraph, determines that everyone is under an obligation to her community. It is striking that Article 29, to justify this obligation, puts forward an argument that brings the Fichtean individual to mind, who, to develop as a person, is reliant on a normative community. Article 29 of the Universal Declaration states:

> Everyone has duties to the community in which alone the free and full development of his personality is possible.

The term "free" development can be read as opposing social orders that restrict or distort an individual's development as a person. In any case, Articles 28 and 29 UDHR lay the foundation to an individual's obligation to engage in establishing and preserving a global humanist society, in which individuals can fully develop as respected, accountable and autonomous persons.

3.9.1 Respect and Care

Because human beings exist in two distinct spheres—in nature and in culture—any concept seeking to capture the entirety of human relations necessarily reflects this duality. An individual develops at two levels, one physiological, one social, and at both levels depends in the beginning on the attention and support of others. If the concept of human dignity is to entirely encapsulate what we as humans existentially rely and what, in a society respecting human dignity, we owe to one another as participating in humanity, it is necessary to split the concept into two dimensions, for which here the terms 'care' and 'respect' are used. Both terms denote forms of attention to and concern for others, but they aim at different dimensions of others' reliance on us. 'Care' concerns the somatic aspects of our relationships, 'respect' relates to the personhood and social status, to qualities, that is, which have their foundation in the normative stratum of culture. Therefore, the concept of human dignity combines rights to be treated with compassion and care, as well as with respect.

Both aspects are profoundly dynamic. Treating an infant with care and respect requires different forms of behaviour compared to such conduct in relation to an adult. Human dignity materialises in interactions that reinforce and further the personhood of another individual; and personhood is in itself the dynamic concept of a person growing while leading a—biological and social—life according to her laws.

It should be stressed that treating a person both with care and respect entails, beyond behavioural aspects, an attitude of appreciation and of attaching importance to the other, supporting her in developing a sense of self-esteem and of her life being significant. The individual's experiences that others care for her as a human being establish the preconditions for later developing cultural capacities (Erikson 1980; Bowlby 1988; Stern 2000). Whereas acknowledging the distinctiveness and autonomy of the other is crucially important for an attitude of respect, care reacts to the dependency and needs of a human being as a biological organism. Both care and respect flow from a fundamental attitude of solidarity that human beings owe to one another. In the case of care, it is the solidarity of "individuals" who know about the others' needs, whilst in the case of respect it is the mutual recognition of persons who, within the framework of a normative order, constitute one another in culture.

In extremis, behaviour lacks compassion and care for another human being when it is cruel, inhuman or barbaric because it causes physical suffering—or fails to end the suffering—of another person, while disrespectful behaviour can amount to degrading, insulting, humiliating or debasing treatment.

Exposing a person to a socially crippling situation of deprivation, poverty or want amounts to an instance of humiliation, as the person concerned is forcefully prevented from leading an autonomous and meaningful life in the sphere of human freedom and culture. She is denied the resources that would allow her to fully participate in social life, and this denial expresses a lack of respect.

It may be noted that the above descriptions of various forms of disrespect would sound peculiar when applied to the treatment of animals. While some farms breed poultry under conditions that are cruel and inhuman, denoting such treatment as humiliating or debasing would require a concept of animals that is not usual in modern societies. While there is nothing strange about granting animals a right not to be subjected to cruel treatment, animals are in modern societies usually not also assigned rights to esteem and respect (while they are in some band and tribal societies, in certain—e.g. Buddhist or Manichean—religions, and in other ideologies).

The quality of treating another person with sympathy and care does not concern the dimension of the other's cultural existence that in modern societies distinguishes humans from other animals. Still, the development of personhood is premised on being cared for, because a person's self-esteem is based on a sense of being important to and appreciated by others. A child's trust in the fundamental friendliness and solidarity of others develops at an early age and provides a foundation for her later development as an autonomous person. Experiences of being cared for establish a physiological, mental and emotional foundation on which autonomous and responsible agency can supervene. Wilkinson and Kleinman explain the concept of 'care' in the following terms (2016, p. 161):

> Particularly through the early and later years of our lives, the realization of our human dignity is dependent upon the quality of care we receive. Through care we are equipped to participate in social life, and in being cared for we are affirmed with recognition and value. In acts of care real things are at stake, including life itself. In relationships of care we are made present to each other and are there for each other. Emotions are invested and worked through and become the grounds of interpersonal solidarity.

Thus, the realisation of human dignity relates to the quality of care that an individual receives during certain phases of her life or at occasions, when she is in need of care because of particular circumstances, such as a disease or in the aftermath of an accident.

However, obviously we cannot constantly worry indiscriminately about all other fellow human beings. There must be a sharing of the burden and rules determining who is expected to take care of whom. Therefore, a society's normative order ties obligations to attend to others to certain roles—parents, professional careers, teachers, doctors—or exceptional situations, for instance when confronted with a severely injured victim of a road accident. Still, these specific obligations are rooted in a general attitude of solidarity that we owe to one another and on which the effective cooperation of the members of a community remains premised.

It should be noted again that agency, more than rights to care and to respectful treatment, depends on a person's capacities. This is particularly the case concerning the amount of responsibility a person can be expected to shoulder. In extreme cases, such as coma-patients, what remains of an individual's 'agency' will only be the element of protection against objectification, against, that is, being used by others—in an instrumental or strategic manner—for their purposes. Such individuals would not be expected to shoulder care responsibilities, or respect responsibilities, over others.

The respect and care discussed in this section are thus a basis for human dignity, certain aspects of which are accentuated by human rights. Four categories of human rights can be distinguished. They will be referred to here as formation rights, care rights, autonomy rights, and resource rights.

3.9.2 Formation Rights and Corresponding Obligations

Human dignity as a right is the entitlement to be continually constituted as a person, to a formation, that is, as a valued and esteemed, in principle autonomous and accountable agent. Human dignity flows from the right to be met by all others in a spirit of solidarity and respect as a member of 'the human family'.

The central provision is the first sentence of Article 1 of the Universal Declaration, stating: "All human beings are born free and equal in dignity and rights." In view, not least, of the relation between the concept of human dignity and the criminal justice system, it should be emphasised that Article 1 creates rights *and obligations*. This sentence expresses the entitlement of every being born with a human face to be treated as a person with care and respect. However, this would remain a hollow promise if all others were not obliged to respect and treat the individual born with a human face as a person and welcome her to the human family. Obviously, the entitlement of one individual to respect is premised on and hence implies obligations on all others to respect.

However, all others can meet this obligation only if they are, to the extent possible, called on and constituted as accountable agents and respond to that call, thus engaging in their own constitution. As part of the obligations consequential to an individual's entitlement to personhood, all others have a duty to, at least in principle and to some extent, engage in constituting one another, as well as themselves, as accountable agents and members of a legal community. Any normative system is premised on the constitution of agents and hence cannot remain indifferent as to whether individuals engage in the constitution of others and themselves as persons or not. Hence, an individual's constitution as a person is both a right and an obligation.

Therefore, the right of one individual to be constituted as a rights-holder implies an obligation on all others to accept and engage in their own constitution as accountable agents, respecting the rights of rights-holders. A decent society is geared to the development of persons as accountable rights-holders, where having rights and having to respect the equal rights of others are the two sides of the same coin of accountable personhood.

On the one hand, personhood only develops in a mode of autonomous and self-determined agency. Hence, self-constitution cannot be enforced. On the other hand, as a moral claim on persons, the imperative to engage in their own formation as members of their polity is conceivable and indeed plausible, as a normative order can only be sustained if individuals engage in its preservation. Therefore, modern societies are premised on attitudes commonly referred to as republicanism, the readiness, that is, of citizens to actively contribute their share to the public life of their polity. Republicanism can include legal duties. Obligations on children to attend schools are an obvious case, as are obligations on adults to pay taxes and to engage as voters or jurors in the normative preservation of their polity.

Hence, Article 1 of the Universal Declaration forms the basis of constitution rights, as well as obligations, to constitute others and to engage in one's own constitution as a person and citizen. By stipulating human dignity, Article 1 founds an entire system of rights and obligations serving to ensure that the individual is called on as a person and encouraged to engage in her own constitution as a person.

From what has just been said, it follows that personhood implies not only rights but also obligations that relate to others and to oneself. The person has a duty to respect others, but also to engage in her own constitution as a respected, autonomous and accountable agent. Human dignity demands that the individual treats herself with self-respect (Hampton 2007, pp. 51–56).

As the human family is organised in polities, the right to be included in the human family is premised on access to polities. According to Article 6 of the Universal Declaration, "Everyone has the right to recognition everywhere as a person before the law". The term "before the law" relates to legal entitlements and obligations. The following Article 7 specifies: "All are equal before the law and are entitled without any discrimination to equal protection of the law." The term "before the law"—used in both provisions—refers to the relationship between an individual and a public authority, representing the polity. The individual is to be recognised as a person on equal terms with all others *everywhere*, hence not only by 'her' state, defined by birth or residence, but by any public authority worldwide. Therefore, Article 6 of the Universal Declaration is to be read as transcending the nation state and as providing the basis of some form of global citizenship within the framework of an international normative order.

Articles 6 and 7 are complemented by Article 10, stipulating: "Everyone is entitled in full equality to a fair and public hearing by an independent and impartial tribunal, in the determination of his rights and obligations and of any criminal charge against him." Hence, an individual's status as a person before the law implies obligations, accountability and the responsibility for criminal acts. These norms—Articles 1, 6, 7 and 10 of the Universal Declaration—form the basis of the victim's right to be respected as a person holding rights, as well as the basis of the obligation of all others to respect the victim and her rights, and to account for their actions as responsible agents.

More specific formation rights flesh out the right of a human being to be constituted as a person and comprise the right to be educated and supported in developing as a respected, accountable and autonomous person, as well as the right to be treated respectfully, including at work, and to be protected against discrimination and other degrading treatment.

The particular thing about formation rights is that they correspond to obligations, which is not the case with other rights. The claim is not that an individual has to respect the formation rights of *others*. While this is true, it is not in any way specific, but the same with all rights. Rather the claim concerns *one's own* personhood; the claim is that an individual is not only entitled, but also obliged to be a person, within the limits of her abilities. The call on a human being heteronomously imposes personhood, including accountability, in accordance with a legal community's normative order. This is necessarily the case, as, without already being a person, no one can opt to be a person. Within a normative system based on human dignity, the obligation to accept the status of an accountable agent follows from the fact that the personhood of others is premised on being respected and hence on the accountable agency of others.

While autonomy rights concern concrete decisions in concrete situations, formation rights are about personhood as the underlying basic status of a respected, autonomous and accountable agent. How an individual decides to act is, within the limits of her autonomy, a matter of her freedom and at her disposition; but her status as an autonomous person is not. Neither did an individual choose to be called on and initiated as a person nor can she later choose to waive the right to be treated as a person. Human beings calling on one another as agents is the indispensable mechanism sustaining human culture under conditions of modernity. Hence, an individual is not free to consent to being treated in an inhuman, degrading or contemptuous manner, nor to live or work under conditions which offend against human dignity. Her participation in human dignity is a status that she can overcome and leave behind only by withdrawing from the company of humans.

3.9.3 Care Rights

Care rights—rights, that is, to be treated in a compassionate and sympathetic manner and in a spirit of human solidarity—acknowledge the biological aspects of human existence. All human beings have a right to live and to be spared physical or emotional pain or impairment of their health, independent of their autonomy. Care rights include an individual's entitlement to a healthy and liveable environment and climate, as well as to consumer protection, as highlighted by Articles 37 and 38 of the Charter.

Care rights are particularly important to persons who are not in a position to autonomously look after themselves. This can include children, elderly people, persons with certain disabilities or health conditions, or individuals who because of particular circumstances—e.g. a road traffic accident—have temporarily lost the ability to act autonomously. However, while care rights become obvious in such conditions, they are not restricted to them. A person is at any time entitled to protection against cruel or inhuman treatment.

Caring for infants and children in terms of their physical and emotional needs and development is a matter of their care rights, while their right to education and to be supported in their intellectual development—to be introduced in human culture—constitutes a formation right.

3.9.4 *Autonomy Rights*

Autonomy rights—or freedoms—define spheres of autonomous agency (Holz 2015, pp. 66–68). There exists one generic right to autonomous agency, namely an individual's right to respect of her private life. In addition, there are numerous specific autonomy rights, e.g. rights to life, to the integrity of the person, not to be subjected to slavery or forced labour, to found a family, to freedom of thought, conscience and religion, to political autonomy, the freedom of the arts and sciences, informational self-determination, and so forth.

The recognition of these spheres of autonomous agency reflects the particular significance of certain fields of action for the individual. This significance is reflected in the individual's entitlement to act freely and to exclude all others from interference with these fields of action. Thus, autonomy rights constitute and attribute various spheres of self-determined existence.

Several of these rights only become effective when they can be exercised within an institutional framework that is protected against external interference. In other words, some freedoms are premised on institutional forms of autonomy, such as autonomous universities, media, trade unions, private associations, or faith communities. One way of protecting a decent society consists in ensuring a society's differentiation and structuring based on strong institutional forms of autonomy.

One important area of action is participation in legal affairs and everyday business life under private and administrative law. An individual's full legal capacity to, in her own name, conclude contracts, acquire and exercise property and personal non-property rights, bear obligations, and be plaintiff or defendant in court are significant aspects of her participation in the economic sphere and of her social status in general. This is part of what it means to be—according to Article 6 UDHR—recognised as a person before the law. A specific aspect of this legal capacity is the possibility to conclude a contract by which a legal person is established. Creating a legal person—e.g. a private company or association—is a means of participating, jointly with others, in a community's economic or civil society activities and an expression of the founders' autonomy rights. According to Article 17 UDHR, everyone has the right to own property 'in association with others', and an association can own property only as a legal person. In addition,

Article 20 UDHR grants a right to association, which is more effective when the association has the status of a legal person.

Does a legal person hold human rights? The obvious answer would be No. Certainly, a legal person does not share in human dignity. However, a legal person may, in a sense, hold the human rights of its founders or owners, at least the autonomy rights which the founders acted on by establishing the legal person that then acts on their behalf. For instance, the legal person holds property rights for those who, through the legal person, are able to hold property rights in association with others.

Autonomy rights create spheres of morally autonomous decisions and, from the perspective of a decent society, function as the gateway to moral diversity and learning. Within a sphere of autonomy, the individual is, although not legally, nevertheless morally accountable. Thus, a right creates a sphere that allows for moral dissent and diversity.

However, autonomy rights are not meant to create amoral spheres and attitudes. A right to self-defence does not promote a morality of normative fixation requiring that the individual should, under all circumstances, resist any unlawful attack. Rather it leaves the decision up to the individual to either back away and avoid a violent conflict or to defend her rights; and arguably it will depend on the circumstances, which of the two is the 'right' way to deal with the situation. However, it remains up to the person, whose rights are in peril, to decide and to take the moral responsibility for her decision, even if her decision cannot be challenged legally. A right to private property is not a right to unscrupulous greed and the reckless exploitation of others, but a right to decide in a morally accountable manner of how to make use of one's property. It includes the possibility to not only pay taxes, in accordance with legal provisions, but, in addition, to donate a large portion of one's fortune to charities or artists. Rights are not intended to encourage their abuse. Gaius' principle (Honsell 2015, p. 56) is still valid that we must not make bad use of our rights: *Male enim nostro iure uti non debemus.*

Over the last third of the twentieth century, some fierce normative disputes arose over questions relating to whether an issue required and justified generally binding legal regulations or should be left to individuals' moral autonomy and choice of life style. The—partial or complete—decriminalisation of vagabondage, begging, gambling, possession and use of drugs, prostitution, pornography, adultery, abortion, homosexuality, or of accompanied suicide all pointed to the direction of individuals successfully claiming moral autonomy and of modern states failing to argue convincingly why the imposition of binding regulations would be legitimate and necessary. Overall, the last decades of the twentieth century witnessed a considerable decline of state paternalism and the rise of individual moral autonomy respected and protected by state laws. However, recently the trend seems to be going in the reverse direction. Provisions are enacted criminalising migration, the concealing of one's face, and, again, begging. Not only are there still countries in Europe where women are denied the right to autonomously decide to terminate their pregnancy—countries with an eminent Catholic tradition, like Malta, Poland and Ireland—there are also countries—including Italy and Portugal—where legislation respects this right, but is implemented in a restrictive manner. In April 2016, the Council of Europe's European Committee of Social Rights published its Decision on a complaint filed by the *Confederazione Generale Italiana del Lavoro* claiming that in Italy many women are, in practice, unable to access abortion services. The Committee unanimously found a violation of women's right to protection of health under Article 11 of the European Social Charter reasoning that "women seeking access to abortion services continue to face substantial difficulties in obtaining access to such services in practice".

3.9.5 Resource Rights

A decent, humanist society is a society constructed to maximise the equal autonomy of individuals (Nida-Rümelin 2006, pp. 144–146). What is meant is not autonomy according to the letter of the law but autonomy that is practically effective in the sense that individuals can actually live a self-determined, dignified and meaningful life. Human dignity is premised on real options of leading a life that is 'one's own' and can be narrated as a sequence of autonomous and responsible decisions.

As one precondition of such effective autonomy, everyone is entitled to a share of society's resources sufficient to enable her to live a dignified, meaningful life. 'Sufficient' means having enough to be able to participate fully in the exercise of rights and liberties and to develop one's talents. Hence, a humanist society is challenged to ensure that everyone has the means to lead life with dignity and to participate in society as full members.

When it comes to determining the resources that allow individuals to live a self-determined and meaningful life, material resources first come to one's mind, such as a basic income and health care. However, just as important are the resources needed for a spiritual development, such as access to cultural goods, a sufficient amount of recognition and esteem, and an environment that enables an individual to live free of fear for her rights.

In its preamble, the Universal Declaration envisages "the advent of a world in which human beings shall enjoy freedom of speech and belief and freedom from fear and want", echoing Franklin Delano Roosevelt's Four Freedoms announced in his State of the Union Address of January 1941. While freedom of speech and belief constitute autonomy rights, the expression "freedom from fear and want" recalls that individual autonomy is premised on available resources. Individuals are entitled to have fair access to vital resources, on which their participation as autonomous subjects in societal contexts is premised. Resource rights concern the material basis and other preconditions of autonomous agency, such as social security, protection against deprivation, a sufficient level of personal security and a right to asylum, as well as access to knowledge systems, including the internet. Ensuring that an individual can live without fear expresses a spirit of mutual solidarity and esteem.

Human dignity is premised on subsistence rights, protecting an individual against the paralysing and humiliating effects of poverty or fear of poverty. Protection against poverty means not having to worry about food or shelter. However, it also implies being in a position to participate in relevant spheres of society, including the labour market, knowledge systems, arts, media or politics and to have access to infrastructures, such as systems of transport and telecommunication. In a humanist society, no one has to live in poverty or in fear of poverty. Particularly in a rich society, everyone has a basic human right to good health care, to decent housing and adequate nutrition.

It is not enough that there is a fair competition for these valued goods; the 'losers' in such competition still deserve a 'fair share' of society's bounty. In a decent society, all individuals have an equal right to autonomy and hence a right to equal autonomy. This rules out a situation in which individuals do not have the resources to fully participate in the life of their community. But it also rules out a situation of inequality, where some individuals have enough resources to exert economic power. Any significant power-imbalance runs counter to the principles of a humanist society and equal autonomy.

Resources are not in themselves forms of agency, nor do they necessarily relate to a specific area of autonomy. Rather they define, in a more cross-cutting manner, general prerequisites of autonomous agency. A person who lives in constant fear of violence, in poverty or insecurity or who is in a situation of illness but does not have access to health care, is prevented from living her life and from developing as an autonomous agent. Thus, resource rights relate to autonomy rights in that they concern the basis on which leading an autonomous life relies.

3.9.6 Rights are to be Practically Effective

The ECtHR constantly reiterates "that the Convention is intended to guarantee not rights that are theoretical or illusory but rights that are practical and effective" (*Al-Dulimi*, para. 127). A right is effective if it is successful in producing a factual situation that allows the rights-holder to practically exercise her right and to trust that others will not hinder her in doing so. If, for instance, an individual has a right to an effective remedy, the effectiveness of her right is enhanced by measures facilitating her access to a court and supporting her in having such access, while undermined by all circumstances that impede such access.

3.9.7 *The Effectivity of Rights is Premised on a Decent Social Order*

All human rights are to be practically effective, and in all instances, this effectiveness is costly and premised on investments in public institutions and procedures, including systems of justice and law enforcement, institutions of education, administration and public services in general, health care systems, environmental and consumer protection, as well as institutions and procedures that enable participation in public and political life, such as a parliament, fair elections, participation of citizens in criminal justice or transparent procedures ensuring equal access of all citizens to public offices. Because human rights materialise in real acts of communication, because, in other words, human rights exist only where they are practically effective in real life, the institutions and procedures, on which the effectiveness of human rights is premised, form an integral part of the system of human rights. In other words, human rights imply decent social structures. All rights are premised on the existence of public or publicly funded institutions and procedures that render these rights effective.

This requires institutions and procedures of good administration and the availability to individuals of effective remedies in situations where they can arguably claim that their rights have been violated, including an independent judiciary.

In addition to these general aspects, there are specific institutional and procedural requirements linked to many rights. An individual's right to personal integrity requires that effective police protection measures are available in a situation of a real and immediate risk. Citizens' political autonomy is premised on a costly parliament and costly electoral procedures. The right to benefit from medical treatment requires investments in the education of doctors and in hospitals.

Thus an individual's human dignity is premised on societal institutions and procedures established by the contributions of others. Human dignity as a right and the source of rights is one side of a coin, to which corresponding obligations to actively contribute to the establishment and preservation of the necessary institutions and procedures form the flipside.

One crucial aspect of constitutional norms governing public institutions is their independence, their protection, that is, against extraneous, potentially distorting interventions. The aim of such protection is to ensure that institutions—subsystems of society—can follow their respective genuine logic.

The differentiation of societal spheres is premised on effective rules of mutual respect and non-intervention. Administration should not be governed by interests of private or family life, which requires safeguards against nepotism. While economy follows its logic, neither courts nor academic institutions should be affected by economic interests. While religious denominations should be protected in the free exercise of their belief, the political system, public institutions, including universities, must reject argumentations that take recourse to the existence of one or more divine beings. While parliaments follow political discourses, public services and museums should not, and so on. A decent society defends the independent existence of a multitude of societal subsystems as distinct spheres of discourses.

3.10 In Conclusion: Why Human Dignity?

In 1982, Douglas Hofstadter, in the Scientific American, presented a game called Nomic. Playing Nomic implies changing the rules of the game you play. When it's a player's turn, she does two things: First she proposes a rule change and the proposal is voted on; then she makes a move within the game, e.g. throws a die and adds the points to her account (Hofstadter 1982, 1985, pp. 70–89; Suber 1990). This game, like any game, is defined by its rules, which, however, include rules about generating rules. Hence, when you play a game of Nomic for some time, you end up playing an entirely different game, which, however, is still the same game of Nomic on which you embarked some time earlier.

What characterises modern societies is the fact that individuals cooperate based on binding social norms that they themselves deliberately create and change; and that they become aware of their situation as law-abiding lawgivers. Thus, in a Kantian spirit, they finally grow up and leave all tutelage behind, including not only their collective reliance on divine or natural authorities, but—having learned their Fichtean lesson—also their naïve trust in the authority of their own individual morality, which they see through as being just one manifestation and expression of norms and values that, for the time being, constitute their normative order and them as persons. Cultural configurations are like nets constantly being weaved, torn, mended and improved in interactive processes without being, at any points, firmly lashed to the ground or ever replaced entirely by another net.

The positive message is that individuals are free to decide themselves on the social norms by which they want to abide and cooperate. The other side of this is that individuals have no choice but to do so, and that they can, in doing so, rely on no external guidance. Nature has fallen silent, gods and their monarchs, charismatic national and religious leaders have either abdicated or are not allowed into parliaments. Hence, in the end, every individual cannot but rely on her own moral judgments. Some may find this message liberating, others discomforting or even frightening.

What may help is a sound analysis of the present situation. It is, firstly, worth remembering that the task of legislation has remained unaltered. It is still about the construction and enacting of a normative framework that fosters effective large-scale cooperation and the maintenance, at various scales, of societal peace.

Secondly, it appears that in our particular situation, the functioning of a good society depends on the autonomous individual and on enabling her to live up to the situation of an individual who realises that she is morally bound only by the norms she and others adopt as binding on themselves. In a sense, the notion of human dignity can be seen as making a virtue of conditions to which there is anyway no alternative. Given our awareness of the weakness and vulnerability of the individual, whose social existence is premised on contingent processes of personalisation controlled, at least at initial stages, by others; given, in addition, our understanding of the extent to which individuals alone are responsible for preserving human culture, it is arguably a wise move to put all of one's eggs into the one remaining basket and to postulate the individual person as sacred. The notion of human dignity emphasises the necessity of preserving societal preconditions which will hopefully enable individuals to collectively perform their role as the masters of culture and history.

Human dignity is the core concept crystallising a wider and complex response to the particular complexity of preserving a society in conditions of sovereign, autonomous and self-defining individuals. These conditions have not been chosen or voted for, but are simply the result of a historical development that has washed away all authorities and left behind only the autonomous individual, who therefore has no choice but to take over the task of—and the responsibility for—preserving, reforming and reinforcing a societal order, on which the existence of all individuals is premised.

However, it is one thing to reconstruct human dignity genealogically as a concept that evolves as the potential basis of a universal culture; it is another to advocate this development and to support and argue for a humanist society based on human dignity. Given the necessarily axiomatic nature of all normativity, if human dignity defines the paradigm of a normative order as its most basic concept, there cannot be a moral argument in favour of human dignity. All that can be done now is to make it plausible that to ensure the normative order of a global society there is no realistic alternative to the concept of human dignity (Kaufmann 2003, pp. 43–44).

This argument necessarily takes the form of, firstly, demonstrating why and in what sense normativity and human culture in general are indispensable, and of, secondly, showing why, if one opts in favour of normativity at all, a normative order based on human dignity is more promising than any other concept.

3.10.1 Why Normativity?

The term 'normativity' here denotes the specific human technique of organising a collectivity by means of social norms and the—'nosist'—willingness of individuals to accept all other members of the collectivity as peers and to recognize that their views, interests and choices are on par with one's own. Any argument in favour of normativity cannot be itself normative, or it would amount to a *petitio principii*, an 'argument' founded on its conclusion. It seems that what remains is personal preferences in favour of maintaining normativity or abandoning it altogether.

However, this choice we do not really have. We have evolved as the cultural species and, by now, as the species entirely dependent on culture (Elias 2014, p. XXIX). As Joseph Henrich puts it, we have crossed the Rubicon and we can't go back (2015, p. 317). Even as hunter-gatherers we could not survive without culture (Henrich 2015, p. 318):

> It's not merely that people in modern societies need culture to survive. Hunter-gatherers, as well as other small-scale societies studied by anthropologists, are massively dependent on large bodies of culturally acquired know-how, related to tracking, food processing, hunting, and tool manufacture. [...] All human societies, whether they live as hunter-gatherers or not, are entirely dependent on culture.

Without culture, humans are momentously incomplete and insufficient. As Clifford Geertz observed, homo sapiens are "not an intrinsically talented but unfulfilled ape, but a wholly mindless and consequently unworkable monstrosity" (1973b, p. 68). According to Geertz (1973a, p. 46), what sets man off most distinctly from other species is "less his sheer ability to learn (great as that is) than how much and what particular sorts of things he *has* to learn before he is able to function at all."

> Undirected by culture patterns – organized systems of significant symbols – man's behaviour would be virtually ungovernable, a mere chaos of pointless acts and exploding emotions, his experience virtually shapeless. Culture, the accumulated totality of such patterns, is not just an ornament of human existence but – the principal basis of its specificity – an essential condition for it.

To survive, we have to preserve culture. Normativity is the defining human social technique, the particular way of human togetherness, which enables humans to transfer skills, norms and concepts from one generation to the next, to cooperate relatively peacefully in very large numbers, and to survive.

3.10.2 The Crucial Challenge: Legitimising Normativity Under Conditions of Modernity

What is particular about modernity is the aporia of how to justify a political order without being any longer in a position to rely on an external authority. The cultural project of humankind under the unique conditions of modernity faces the challenge of how to preserve and to legitimise binding norms, without being able to draw on a natural order or a divine will. This is the paramount challenge of human sociality after the decline of traditional ideologies.

Human dignity spells out the preconditions of maintaining normativity under the conditions of modern secular, pluralist societies. The concept of human dignity focuses on what is needed in order to sustain a normative order under conditions of modernity: on individuals' autonomous and accountable agency; on valuing the human individual as an agent; and on societal preconditions that enable and foster the development of respected, autonomous and accountable persons.

Modern societies have arrived at the point of understanding that the normative order's only source is the normative power inherent in individuals' autonomous agency. The latter is premised on individuals' actions that can be interpreted as the results of autonomous moral decisions and not as the mere consequences of external (or internal) driving forces, such as violence, coercion, deceit, addiction, or situations of deprivation. Norms are preserved whenever they are complied with in circumstances where they, from an individual's egoistic and strategic perspective, could have been violated. Human dignity preserves the societal conditions under which the actions of individuals can be understood as the result of moral decisions and, therefore, as carrying their charge of normative power, on which the preservation of culture is premised.

In a philosophical jargon, the normative order owes its existence entirely to performative acts of communication, which create it. Notoriously, the category of performative speech acts was coined by J. L. Austin, who drew attention to our way of doing things with words in situations where "to *say* something is to *do* something", including, for example, "the utterance 'I do' (take this woman to be my lawful wedded wife), as uttered in the course of a marriage ceremony" (1955, pp. 12–13). As much as utterances of 'I do' create, under certain circumstances, a marriage, acts acknowledging the normative order bring it about.

Thus the concept of human dignity answers to the particular challenges of a culture that is informed of its autopoietic, self-generating nature, that is, in other words, aware of the fact that a normative order's legitimacy rests solely on acts of recognition. The normative system observes itself as generating itself and reacts by preserving the preconditions of these recursive processes. That is to say, the source of a modern normative order's legitimacy is the enacted deliberate decisions of individuals to attribute validity to the normative order, of which these individuals form a part—to acknowledge the normative order as legitimate and binding on those who create the order that creates them.

Therefore, individuals' decision not to comply with the normative order's rules have an unlimited potential to unhinge and annul these rules or the entire order. The moment when a community decides to no longer abide by a political order is the moment when this order ceases to exist.

As long as, in history, normativity is not conceived as man-made, but is viewed as founded on some external—natural or metaphysical—basis, the fact remains hidden that there cannot be a *normative* foundation and legitimation for the entire system of social norms. In other words, the specific trait of modern culture lies in its awareness of the fundamental aporia that any normative system is necessarily axiomatic and cannot be reasoned beyond the basic assumptions on which it is founded. A normative order's claims have no external foundation or justification, and individuals' decisions to abide by this order are the only source of its authority and cannot be reasoned in moral terms, but are consequential only to an individual's existential preference of a normative order enabling the continuance of humans as a species.

Here, the specificity of human dignity as a fundamental normative category shows. On the one hand, establishing and preserving a global normative order can only succeed based on a concept that emphatically cherishes and, with determination, fosters the autonomous and accountable subject. On the other hand, the concept of human dignity strictly contents itself with what is necessary to achieve that end. It denotes the normative minimum, the amount of bindingness on individuals that is indispensable to ensure the maintenance of *any* stable normative order.

In other words, the ban on heteronomy prohibits acts that compromise the preservation of normativity. This is because morally relevant acts stemming from the individual can be interpreted as suggesting general social norms. However, there are acts which, if read as suggesting a general norm, would impair and nullify the normative order. For example, violent behaviour, by its very nature, is not fit to serve as a general maxim, as violence negates autonomy, as much as debasing treatment negates the principle of mutual esteem.

Hence, participation in *any* 'normative language game' is premised on compliance with certain inherent rules that spell out the preconditions of *any* normative language game, most importantly, the recognition of others as free agents. Abiding by these rules enables human beings to engage in normative communication, to call, that is, on one another as moral agents and to join in the collective constitution and preservation of a normative order and the mutual constitution of one another as persons.

If a person wants to participate in culture—as the social form of human existence in which all normative 'language games' are embedded—she must adhere to the rules that constitute culture as the normative communication between esteemed autonomous subjects. She must, in other words, respect and treat others as agents entitled to and capable of moral autonomy. This rules out all forms of disregard or heteronomy, such as violence, deception, or manipulation. Otherwise, she is not playing a normative language game as she is not addressing and calling on other persons *as autonomous moral agents* and thus is not engaged in creating a normative order. By ruling out the objectification of others, human dignity defines the minimal conditions of any normativity. The concept of human dignity essentially captures the very mechanism of normativity, the core processes on which a normative system's maintenance is premised. It defines the demands on an individual that she cannot refute without calling the preconditions into question on which any normativity is premised, including her own personhood and moral capacity to argue. Hence an individual's claim not to accept the duty to respect human dignity would be contradictory in itself, as *any* moral claim is premised on the minimal preconditions of morality represented by the value of human dignity.

What fosters autonomous agency is a societal framework that enables and encourages individuals to perceive and experience their lives as self-determined, meaningful and, therefore, as a source of pride and self-respect. If this is to materialise, the processes of communication establishing a society must be oriented towards enabling individuals to develop as autonomous and responsible agents and to, at the same time, respect the equal dignity of others. In other terms, human dignity is a measure that serves to assess a given societal structure through the extent to which its elements foster the development of responsible moral subjects who are capable of leading a life that they experience as self-determined and fulfilling.

Any normative system is founded on the enforcement of norms that protect and reinforce the agency of autonomous and accountable subjects as the only source of normative power. No one can, without (at least performative) self-contradiction, invoke a right to an autonomous decision to abolish the preconditions of autonomous decisions. Whoever opts in favour of autonomy—as for the concept of human dignity—must be ready to support the preservation of conditions on which autonomy is premised.

This could be understood as positing that a normative order based on human dignity is morally preferable to any other moral and political order. However, such a statement would be phrased in too abstract and too ambitious terms. Moral judgments can exist as meaningful only within a concrete societal and historical context. We—Europeans living in the twenty-first century—can assess various moralities, but only from our own point of view, a normative perspective shaped by the discourses of modern pluralist societies. The question is not which normative order the Chewong in the Indonesian forests or the Netsilik Eskimos should adopt for themselves, but which normative concept is apt, in our concrete political and historic situation, to serve as the foundation of an emerging global moral and political order spanning large, complex and diverse societies on six continents.

3.10.3 Dignity Norms and Conventional Norms

A legal order based on human dignity necessarily operates a distinction that restricts the legitimate scope of legislation. Human dignity functions like an imagined rule in the above mentioned game of Nomic that immunises certain rules against being changed. While, in principle, all rules are at a parliament's free disposition and in this sense based on a polity's agreement and consensus, but open to change, some rules are not, namely the norms spelling out human dignity and human rights. This distinction marks the difference between law and rights in the strong sense highlighted above. A polity committed to human dignity treats law as a matter of political choice, but human dignity and human rights as a given and as withheld from the vicissitudes of public, political and parliamentary debate. All state actors—including legislators—have to respect the universal and equal status of autonomous persons and to protect this status against violations committed by non-state actors.

Conventional laws are generally binding norms. However, their authority is justified only by their necessity and the agreement of those involved in legislation, not by their morally compelling contents as such. The product of such legislation is law, but not necessarily 'right' in an emphatic sense. Someone who does not abide by the decision can be criticised for undermining a norm that is practically necessary, not for what she has done per se. Driving on the wrong side of the road when no other person is around is still not acceptable as it irritates and undermines trust in norm compliance. However, driving on the wrong side of the road is per se not a manifestation of disregard of others as respected and autonomous persons or of their rights (Hampton 2007, p. 120).

Recent history offers a wealth of evidence as to the costs of an illiberal social order founded on nationalism or any other particularistic categorisation. Any differentiation introduced to narrow down the general concept of an autonomous and accountable agent necessarily imports a distinction of status that turns against some parts of societies; and at this level of abstraction, it makes no difference whether the distinction relates to a national, racial, religious, or sexual characteristic. Any distinction, made in a polity's normative order, between 'us' and 'them', if it touches on the societal status of members of a community, runs counter to the genuine task of normativity of fostering peaceful interaction and cooperation and of engaging as many community members as possible in cooperative enterprises and the normative order's preservation.

In addition, a normative order that respects the difference between human dignity and conventional laws ensures a high degree of the normative order's flexibility and adaptability and hence a strong capacity to improve. Normative development is premised on variation and on a diversity of alternative and competing models of morality. If, in a global, all-encompassing order, these alternatives cannot exist *outside* the order—in terms of a multitude of societies competing for the most effective form of peaceful cooperation—diversity must be provided and ensured *inside* the normative order. Spheres of individual moral autonomy create open spaces for moral creativity, diversity, controversy and development. Thus, the normative competition among polities is replaced by spheres of individual autonomy - protected by criminal law - within a global pluralist society.

3.10.4 Making a Virtue of Necessity

What hence defines the present phase in the normative evolution of European societies is a process of individuals gradually realising that it is, whether they like it or not, entirely up to them to reinforce and to reform the social structures of which they—very literally—form parts. What is new at this stage is the level of reflectivity involved in this process. While in preceding phases, individuals saw themselves as confronted with a normative order that originated from nature, a divine will mediated by a chosen monarch or the essence of their nation or faith community put into words by a charismatic leader, individuals now become aware that they, in the end, cannot rely on any external authority but are entirely left to themselves. They can for the first time in history see through the very mechanism of culture that generates themselves as persons, as well as the normative fabric on which their social existence is premised and into which it is intermeshed in continuous recursive processes of communication. For the first time, the unique reflective consciousness of humans allows them to see a fairly unimpeded view of their situation as the species that, at a cultural—essentially normative—level, creates itself.

In this situation, individual autonomy is not the claim of a particular ethical or political orientation, but a simple fact. It is what remains after the resignations of Nature, God, the Crown and the Nation as reliable sources of normativity. As long as one does not opt for the termination of the project of human culture and humankind as a species, the autonomous individual is the only beacon of hope. Hence, *everything* depends on a societal structure's ability to foster and encourage the nurturing and education of proud, self-respecting, self-confident, empathic, critical, sensible and accountable children and adults.

In fact, many of the heirs of Fichte's understanding of the social fabrication of the human person, consequently, shared a strong and genuine interest in education—including Durkheim (1999), Dewey (2008), and Adorno (1970). What enables a citizen to make informed and rational political decisions is nothing but a profound ethical, historical, political and social awareness. Without a thorough education, there is a certain risk that democracy degenerates into a practice where a small, well-educated elite observes a less well-informed majority of voters taking decisions that quite obviously run counter to their own interests, decisions that are, occasionally, driven by a lack of comprehension and the racism inherent in nation states. In contrast, a humanist society emphasises the necessity to establish powerful public institutions of school education and lifelong learning and to organise the economic sphere in a way that individuals are left with sufficient time to engage and develop as persons and citizens. With a vast and rapidly growing stock of knowledge and an increasingly complex societal order, the task of preserving and transferring human culture from one generation to the next becomes more and more challenging and necessarily demands mounting societal investments.

The two and a half decades from 1965 to 1990 witnessed the breathtaking rise of a new paradigm. However, the reaction was not long in coming, and it arrived as Thatcherism, Reaganomics, the Washington Consensus, neo-liberalism, neo-colonialism, and, most of all, neo-nationalism. And yet answers to the challenges of the future are not to be found in past centuries, but in the globalism and cosmopolitanism heralded by human dignity and equal universal rights. Respecting human dignity makes a virtue of necessity. The normative development of European societies has arrived at a point from where only free, autonomous, self-defining individuals can further advance it and where the most important question is how one can construct a society enabling individuals to perform this function. An individual's *entitlement* to freedom, autonomy and self-definition is one side of the coin, the individual being, from these rights, *tasked* with constructing a society, including herself, and *obliged* to take responsibility, the other.

The concept of human dignity offers solutions to problems that to date many societies—such as the Tauade in Papua New-Guinea—do not face. However, with the rapid processes of globalisation, the normative complexities reach a new climax, as previously distinct and essentially unrelated polities now have to relate and to find common normative denominators. When it comes to elaborating an ideology that defeats nationalism and to designing a pluralist and peaceful society at a global level, humanism is without alternative. No other concept is complex and powerful enough to overcome the precarious and conflictual relationships of sovereign nation states and to peacefully integrate a highly diverse global community. 'War remains the decisive human failure' (Galbraith 2005, p. 56), and this failure can only be eradicated by strengthening institutions and procedures of global governance and global justice.

A crucial and particularly difficult step in establishing a cosmopolitan normative order consists in abandoning and eradicating the idea that states are in principle entitled to exclude individuals from their territory. However, recently a consensus gradually emerges among political theorists that within a global order based on human dignity there is no basis for denying a global right to free movement (Cassee 2014, 2016; Cassee and Goppel 2014; Cole 2011; Oberman 2016). In this vein, Peter Singer posited that the twenty-first century faces the task of developing a suitable form of government for one single world. 'It is a daunting moral and intellectual challenge, but one we cannot refuse to take up. The future of the world depends on how well we meet it' (Singer 2004, p. 201). It is the task of political philosophy to not allow us to confuse justice and the will to preserve a given distribution of wealth and power (Ruby 1996, p. 111). A wrong remains a wrong, even when their is no political actor in sight willing to redress it (Cassee 2016, p. 280), except that, in the end, normative power and responsibility lie with autonomous individuals deciding to abide by or to disobey unjust immigration laws (Hidalgo 2015).

References

Ackerman, B. (2000). The new separation of powers. *Harvard Law Review, 113*(3), 633–725.

Adorno, T.W. (1970). *Erziehung zur Mündigkeit: Vorträge und Gespräche mit Hellmut Becker 1959–1969* (G. Kadelbach, Ed.). Frankfurt am Main, Germany: Suhrkamp.

Agamben, G. (1998). *Quel che resta di Auschwitz. L'archivio e il testimone*. Torino, Italy: Bollati Boringhieri.

Akerlof, G. A., & Shiller, R. J. (2015). *Phishing for phools: The economics of manipulation and deception*. Princeton, NJ: Princeton University Press.

Alexy, R. (2010). *A theory of constitutional rights*. Oxford: Oxford University Press.

Althusser, L. (1970). *Idéologie et appareils idéologique d'État*. Chicoutimi, Quebec, Canada: J.-M. Tremblay. Retrieved April 23, 2015, from http://classiques.uqac.ca/contemporains/althusser_louis/ideologie_et_AIE/ideologie_et_AIE.html

Althusser, L. (1996). *Ecrits sur la psychanalyse: Freud et Lacan*. LGF.

Anderson, B. (2013). *Us & them? The dangerous politics of immigration control*. Oxford, England: Oxford University Press.

Arendt, H. (1951). *The origins of totalitarianism*. ... Cleveland, OH: Hardpress Publishing.

Austin, J. L. (1955). *How to do things with words*. Harvard University Press.

Baker-Fletcher, G. (1993). *Somebodyness: Martin Luther King, Jr., and the theory of dignity*. Minneapolis, MN: Trinity Press International.

Bauman, Z. (2007). *Consuming life*. Cambridge, England: Polity.

Benhabib, S. (2004). *The rights of others: Aliens, residents, and citizens*. Cambridge, England: Cambridge University Press.

Benhabib, S. (2006). Another cosmopolitanism. In R. Post (Ed.), *Another cosmopolitanism* (pp. 11–80). Oxford, England: Oxford University Press.

Benhabib, S. (2011). *Dignity in adversity: Human rights in troubled times* (1st ed.). John Wiley & Sons.

Benjamin, J. (1988). *The bonds of love: Psychoanalysis, feminism, & the problem of domination*. New York: Pantheon.

Berens, L. H. (2008). *The Digger Movement: Radical communalism in the English Civil War*. St Petersburg, FL: Red and Black Publishers.

Berger, W. (2009). *Macht*. Wien, Austria: facultas.wuv.

Bielefeldt, H. (1998). *Philosophie der Menschenrechte*. Darmstadt, Germany: Wissenschaftliche Buchgesellschaft.

Bleckmann, A. (1988). Probleme des Grundrechtsverzichts. *Juristenzeitung, 43*(2), 57–62.

Bloch, E. (1985). *Experimentum Mundi: Frage, Kategorien des Herausbringens, Praxis*. Frankfurt am Main: Suhrkamp.

Bourdieu, P., & Wacquant, L. J. D. (1992). *Réponses: Pour une anthropologie réflexive*. Paris: Éditions du Seuil.

Bowlby, J. (1988b). *A secure base: Parent–child attachment and healthy human development*. New York: Basic Books.

Boyd, R., & Richerson, P. J. (1985). *Culture and the evolutionary process*. Chicago: University of Chicago Press.

Boyd, R., & Richerson, P. J. (2005). *The origin and evolution of cultures* (1st ed.). Oxford, England: Oxford University Press.

Braunstein, J.-F. (2003). La religion des morts-vivants: Le culte des morts chez Auguste Comte. *Revue des sciences philosophiques et théologiques, 87*(1), 59–73.

Browning, C. R. (1992). *Ordinary men: Reserve police battalion 101 and the final solution in Poland*. New York: Harper Perennial.

Butler, J. (2005). *Giving an account of oneself* (New.). New York: Fordham University Press.

Butler, J. (2015). *Senses of the subject*. New York: Fordham University Press.

Canetti, E. (1984). *Crowds and power*. (C. Stewart, Trans.). New York: Farrar Straus & Giroux.

Carens, J. H. (2013). *The ethics of immigration*. Oxford, England: Oxford University Press.

Cassee, A. (2014). Das Recht zu bleiben. Irreguläre Migration und die Erfordernisse der Gerechtigkeit. In A. Cassee & A. Goppel (Eds.), *Migration und Ethik* (pp. 211–232). Münster, Germany: Mentis.

Cassee, A. (2016). *Globale Bewegungsfreiheit: Ein philosophisches Plädoyer für offene Grenzen*. Berlin, Germany: Suhrkamp.

Cassee, A., & Goppel, A. (2014). Ein doppeltes Recht auf Ausschluss? Einleitende Gedanken zu Migration und Ethik. In A. Cassee & A. Goppel (Eds.), *Migration und Ethik* (pp. 9–20). Münster, Germany: Mentis.

Cassirer, E. (1974). *The myth of the state*. New Haven/London: Yale University Press.

Cassirer, E. (1979). *Symbol, myth, and culture: Essays and lectures of Ernst Cassirer 1935–1945* (D. P. Verene, Ed.). New Haven, CT: Yale University Press.

Castoriadis, C. (1975). *L'institution imaginaire de la société*. Paris: Éditions du Seuil.

Chalmers, D. J. (1996). *The conscious mind: In search of a fundamental theory* (1st ed.). Oxford University Press.

Cole, P. (2011). Open borders: An ethical defense. In C. H. Wellman & P. Cole (Eds.), *Debating the ethics of immigration: Is there a right to exclude?* (pp. 157–313). Oxford, England: Oxford University Press.

Comte, A. (1852). *Catéchisme positiviste*. (F. Dupin, Ed.). Editions du Sandre.

Comte, A. (1854). Système de politique positive; ou, Traité de sociologie, instituant la religion de l'humanité: Comte, Auguste, 1798–1857: Free Download & Streaming. *Internet Archive*. Retrieved April 23, 2015, from https://archive.org/details/systmedepoliti01comt

Dagger, R. (2013). Republicanism and the foundations of criminal law. In R. A. Duff & S. P. Green (Eds.), *Philosophical foundations of criminal law* (pp. 44–66). Oxford, England: Oxford University Press.

de Schutter, O. (2014). *International human rights law: Cases, materials, commentary* (2nd ed.). Cambridge: Cambridge University Press.
Dewey, J. (2008). *Democracy and education*. Radford, VA: Wilder Publications.
Dews, P. (2005). Intersubjektivität und der "Raum der Gründe": Fichte im Spiegel der postanalytischen Diskussion. In T. Grundmann, F. Hofmann, C. Misselhorn, V. L. Waibel, & V. Zanetti (Eds.), *Anatomie der Subjektivität: Bewußtsein, Selbstbewußtsein und Selbstgefühl* (pp. 325–357). Frankfurt am Main, Germany: Suhrkamp.
Dews, P. (2008). Intersubjectivity and the "Space of Reasons": Fichte in the post-analytic context. *Graduate Faculty Philosophy Journal, 29*(1), 133–159. doi:10.5840/gfpj20082915.
Durkheim, É. (1999). *Éducation et Sociologie*. Paris: Presses universitaires de France (PUF).
Dutton, Y., & Heath, C. (2011). Cultural evolution: Why are some cultural variants more successful than others? In M. Schaller, A. Norenzayan, S. J. Heine, T. Yamagishi, & T. Kameda (Eds.), *Evolution, culture, and the human mind* (pp. 49–70). London: Routledge.
Dux, G. (2000). *Historisch-genetische Theorie der Kultur: Instabile Welten. Zur prozessualen Logik im kulturellen Wandel*. Weilerswist, Germany: Velbrück Wissenschaft.
Dux, G. (2014). Geistesgeschichte als Gattungsgeschichte: Eine Einleitung in den Band. In G. Dux & J. Rüsen (Eds.), *Strukturen des Denkens: Studien zur Geschichte des Geistes* (pp. 17–34). Wiesbaden, Germany: Springer.
Dworkin, R. (2009). Foreword. In I. Hare & J. Weinstein (Eds.), *Extreme speech and democracy* (pp. v–ix). New York: Oxford University Press.
Eagleton, T. (2007). *Ideology: An introduction (New and Updated edition)*. Brooklyn, NY: Verso.
Edelman, G. M. (2004). *Wider than the sky: The phenomenal gift of consciousness*. Yale University Press.
Elias, N. (1939). *The society of individuals* (Reissue.). New York: Continuum.
Elias, N. (2014). *Über die Zeit*. Frankfurt am Main, Germany: Suhrkamp.
Erikson, E. H. (1980). *Identity and the life cycle*. New York: W. W. Norton.
Fichte, J. G. (1793). Zurückforderung der Denkfreiheit von den Fürsten Europens, die sie bisher unterdrückten: Eine Rede. In I. H. Fichte (Ed.), *Zur Politik und Moral. Fichtes Werke VI* (Vols. I-XI, Vol. VI, pp. 1–35). Berlin, Germany: Walter de Gruyter & Co.
Fichte, J. G. (1794a). Über die Würde des Menschen. In *Fichtes Werke I: Zur theoretischen Philosophie I* (pp. 412–416). Berlin, Germany: Walter de Gruyter & Co.
Fichte, J. G. (1794b). *The dignity of man*. (A. E. Kroeger, Trans.). The Perfect Library.
Fichte, J. G. (1794c). Some lectures concerning the scholar's vocation. In *Early philosophical writings* (pp. 144–184). Ithaca, NY: Cornell University Press.
Fichte, J. G. (1796/1971). Grundlage des Naturrechts nach Prinzipien der Wissenschaftslehre. In I. H. Fichte (Ed.), Zur Rechts- und Sittenlehre I. Fichtes Werke (Vols. I–XI, Vol. III, pp. 1–385). Berlin, Germany: Walter de Gruyter & Co.
Fichte, J. G. (1796/2000). *Foundations of natural right*. (M. Baur, Trans., F. Neuhouser, Ed.). Cambridge University Press. Retrieved April 25, 2015, from http://www.cambridge.org/us/academic/subjects/philosophy/philosophy-texts/foundations-natural-right
Fichte, J. G. (1800/1848). *The vocation of man* (W. Smith, Trans.). London: Chapman.
Fichte, J. G. (1808/2008). Addresses to the German Nation. In G. Moore (Ed.), Cambridge texts in the history of political thought. Cambridge: Cambridge University Press.
Fiedler, P. (2002). *Dissoziative Störungen*. Göttingen, Germany: Hogrefe.
Fischer, G., & Riedesser, P. (2009). *Lehrbuch der Psychotraumatologie* (4., aktual. erw. Aufl.). Stuttgart, Germany: UTB.
Flümann, G. (2014). *Streitbare Demokratie in Deutschland und den Vereinigten Staaten: Der staatliche Umgang mit nichtgewalttätigem politischem Extremismus im Vergleich* (2015th ed.). Wiesbaden, Germany: Springer VS.
Forst, R. (2011). *Kritik der Rechtfertigungsverhältnisse: Perspektiven einer kritischen Theorie der Politik*. Frankfurt am Main, Germany: Suhrkamp.
Forst, R. (2016). The point and ground of Human rights: A Kantian constructivist view. In D. Helm & P. Maffettone (Eds.), *Global political theory* (pp. 22–39). Cambridge: Polity.

Foucault, M. (2014). *Histoire de la sexualité (Tome 2) – L'usage des plaisirs*. Editions Gallimard.

FRA. (2012). *Making hate crime visible in the European Union: Acknowledging victims' rights*. Luxembourg: Publications Office of the European Union.

FRA. (2015). *Severe labour exploitation: Workers moving within or into the European Union*. Luxembourg: Publications Office of the European Union.

FRA. (2016). *Ensuring justice for hate crime victims: Professional perspectives*. Luxembourg: Publications Office of the European Union.

Friedan, B. (1963). *The feminine mystique*. Penguin Classics.

Fuller, L. L. (1969). *The morality of law* (Revth ed.). New Haven/London: Yale University Press.

Galbraith, J. K. (2005). *The economics of innocent fraud*. London: Penguin Books.

Geertz, C. (1973a). The impact of the concept of culture on the concept of man. In *The interpretation of cultures* (pp. 33–54). New York: Basic Books.

Geertz, C. (1973b). The growth of culture and the evolution of mind. In *The interpretation of cultures* (pp. 55–83). New York: Basic Books.

Goldberg, D. T. (2002). *The racial state*. Oxford, England: Blackwell Publishers.

Griffin, J. (2009). *On human rights*. New York: Oxford University Press.

Gross, R. (2010). *Anständig geblieben: Nationalsozialistische Moral* (2nd ed.). Frankfurt am Main, Germany: S. Fischer Verlag.

Günther, K. (2014). Zurechnung, Strafe und das Selbstverständnis von Personen. In C. Prittwitz, M. Baurmann, K. Günther, M. Jahn, L. Kuhlen, R. Merkel, et al. (Eds.), *Rationalität und Empathie: Kriminalwissenschaftliches Symposion für Klaus Lüderssen zum 80. Geburtstag* (pp. 9–37). Baden-Baden, Germany: Nomos.

Gürerk, Ö., Irlenbusch, B., & Rockenbach, B. (2009). *Voting with feet: Community choice in social dilemmas*, Discussion No. 4643. Institute for the Study of Labor (IZA).

Haidt, J. (2001). The emotional dog and its rational tail: A social intuitionist approach to moral judgment. *Psychological Review, 108*(4), 814–834.

Hallpike, C. R. (2004). *Evolution of moral understanding*. Alton, England: Ingram International Inc.

Hampton, J. (2007). In D. Farnham (Ed.), *The intrinsic worth of persons: Contractarianism in moral and political philosophy*. Cambridge: Cambridge University Press.

Hare, I. (2009). Extreme speech under international and regional human rights standards. In I. Hare & J. Weinstein (Eds.), *Extreme speech and democracy* (pp. 62–80). New York: Oxford University Press.

Hatfield, E., Cacioppo, J. T., & Rapson, R. L. (1994). *Emotional contagion*. Cambridge: Cambridge University Press.

Hegel, G. W. F. (1807). Phänomenologie des Geistes. (E. Moldenhauer & K. M. Michel, Eds.) (Vols. 1-Werke in 20 Bänden mit Registerband, Vol. 3). Frankfurt am Main, Germany: Suhrkamp.

Held, D. (2002). Law of states, law of peoples: Three models of sovereignty. *Legal Theory, 8*, 1–44.

Held, D., & Maffetone, P. (2016). Introduction: Globalization, global politics and the cosmopolitan plateau. In D. Held & P. Maffetone (Eds.), *Global political theory* (pp. 1–21). Cambridge, England: Polity.

Henrich, J. (2015). *Secret of our success: How culture is driving human evolution, domesticating our species, and making us smarter*. Princeton: Princeton University Press.

Henrich, J., & Henrich, N. (2007). *Why humans cooperate: A cultural and evolutionary explanation*. Oxford, England: Oxford University Press.

Hidalgo, J. (2015). Resistance to unjust immigration restrictions. *Journal of Political Philosophy, 23*(4), 450–470.

Hoffmann-Riem, W. (2010). Versammlungsfreiheit für Rechtsradikale – Kapitulation des Rechtsstaats? In G. F. Schuppert, W. Merkel, G. Nolte, & M. Zürn (Eds.), *Der Rechtsstaat unter Bewährungsdruck* (pp. 87–105). Baden-Baden, Germany: Nomos.

Hofstadter, D. R. (1982). Metamagical themas: About nomic: A heroic game that explores the reflexivity of the law. *Scientific American, 246*(6), 16–28.

Hofstadter, D. R. (1985). *Metamagical themas: Questing for the essence of mind and pattern* (Book Club.). New York: Basic Books.
Hofstadter, D. R. (2008). *I am a strange loop* (Reprint.). Basic Books.
Holz, W. (2007). *Justizgewähranspruch des Verbrechensopfers*. Berlin, Germany: Duncker & Humblot.
Honneth, A. (2000). *Das Andere der Gerechtigkeit: Aufsätze zur praktischen Philosophie* (5th ed.). Frankfurt am Main: Suhrkamp.
Honsell, H. (2015). *Römisches Recht* (8th ed.). Berlin, Germany: Springer.
Hume, D. (2009). *Enquiry concerning human understanding*. Seven Treasures Publications.
Israel, J. I. (2011). *Revolution of the mind: Radical enlightenment and the intellectual origins of modern democracy*. Princeton University Press.
Israel, J. I., & Mulsow, M. (Eds.). (2014). *Radikalaufklärung* (Originalausgabe.). Berlin, Germany: Suhrkamp Verlag.
Jacob, M. C. (2006). *The radical enlightenment - Pantheists, freemasons and republicans* (REV Cornerstone edition.). Lafayette, LA: Cornerstone Book Publishers.
Jakobs, G. (2008). *Norm, Person, Gesellschaft.: Vorüberlegungen zu einer Rechtsphilosophie*. (3., erhebl. veränd. Aufl.). Duncker & Humblot.
Jellinek, G. (1878/2006). *Die socialethische Bedeutung von Recht, Unrecht und Strafe*. Adamant Media Corporation.
Joas, H. (2013). *The sacredness of the person: A new genealogy of human rights*. Washington, DC: Georgetown University Press.
jour fixe initiative berlin (2001). Wie wird man fremd? In jour fixe initiative berlin (Ed.), *Wie wird man fremd?* (pp. 7–12). Münster, Germany: UNRAST.
Kafka, F. (2012). *A hunger artist and other stories*. (J. Crick, Trans.). Oxford, England: Oxford University Press.
Kant, I. (1785/1968). *Grundlegung zur Metaphysik der Sitten*. Akademie-Textausgabe, Vol. 4. Berlin, Germany: Walter de Gruyter.
Kant, I. (1785/2012). *Groundwork of the metaphysics of morals*. (M. Gregor & J. Timmermann, Eds.) (2nd ed.). Cambridge, England: Cambridge University Press.
Kant, I. (1788/1968). *Kritik der praktischen Vernunft*. Akademie-Textausgabe, Vol. 5. Berlin, Germany: Walter de Gruyter.
Kant, I. (1788/2015). *Critique of practical reason*. (M. Gregor, Trans.) (2nd ed.). Cambridge, England: Cambridge University Press.
Kant, I. (1793/1968). *Die Religion innerhalb der Grenzen der bloßen Vernunft. Akademie-Textausgabe* (vol. 6, pp. 1–202). Berlin, Germany: Walter de Gruyter.
Kant, I. (1796/1991). Perpetual peace: A philosophical sketch. In H. S. Reiss (Ed.), Kant: Political writings. Cambridge, England: Cambridge University Press.
Kant, I. (1797/1968). *Die Metaphysik der Sitten*. Akademie-Textausgabe, Vol. 6. Berlin, Germany: Walter de Gruyter.
Kant, I. (1797/1996). *The metaphysics of morals*. (M. Gregor, Ed.) (Cambridge texts in the history of philosophy.). Cambridge, England: Cambridge University Press.
Kant, I. (1798/1968). *Der Streit der Fakultäten*. Akademie-Textausgabe, Vol. 7. Berlin, Germany: Walter de Gruyter & Co.
Kaufmann, F.-X. (2003). *Die Entstehung sozialer Grundrechte und die wohlfahrtsstaatliche Entwicklung*. Paderborn, Germany: Verlag Ferdinand Schöningh. Retrieved June 4, 2016, from https://pub.uni-bielefeld.de/publication/1880704
Kelsen, H. (1967). Staatsform und Weltanschauung. In N. Leser (Ed.), *Demokratie und Sozialismus. Ausgewählte Aufsätze* (Verlag der Wiener Volksbuchhandlung., pp. 40–59). Wien.
Kirshner, A. S. (2014). *Theory of militant democracy*. New Haven, CT: Yale University Press Academic.
Kloppenberg, J. T. (2016). *Toward democracy: The struggle for self-rule in European and American thought*. Oxford: Oxford University Press.

Korsgaard, C. M. (2008). *The constitution of agency: Essays on practical reason and moral psychology*. New York: Oxford University Press.

Korsgaard, C. M. (2009). *Self-constitution: Agency, identity, and integrity*. New York: Oxford University Press.

Koselleck, R. (2010). *Begriffsgeschichten*. Frankfurt am Main, Germany: Suhrkamp.

Lacan, J. (1990). *Les Quatre Concepts fondamentaux de la psychanalyse, 1964*. (J.-A. Miller, Ed.) (Vol. 11). Paris: Seuil.

Lacan, J. (2005). *Mon enseignement*. (J.-A. Miller, Ed.). Paris: Seuil.

Larrain, J. (1979). *The concept of ideology*. London: Hutchinson.

Larrain, J. (1983). *Marxism and ideology*. Atlantic Highlands, NJ: Humanities Press.

Latcheva, R., & Herzog Punzenberger, B. (2016). Perceived discrimination, modes of collective belonging and self-esteem among descendants of immigrants in Austria and Germany. In J. Grimm, L. Huddy, P. Schmidt, & J. Seethaler (Eds.), *Dynamics of national identity: Media and societal factors of what we are* (pp. 141–169). London: Routledge.

Lilburne, J. (1998). The freeman's freedom vindicated: A postscript, containing a general proposition. In A. Sharp (Ed.), *The English Levellers* (pp. 31–32). Cambridge: Cambridge University Press.

Litowitz, D. (2000). Gramsci, hegemony, and the law. *Brigham Young University Law Review, 2*, 515–551.

Loewenstein, K. (1935). Autocracy versus democracy in contemporary Europe. *American Political Science Review, 29*(4), 571–593.

Loewenstein, K. (1937a). Militant democracy and fundamental rights, I. *American Political Science Review, 31*(3), 417–432.

Loewenstein, K. (1937b). Militant democracy and fundamental rights, II. *American Political Science Review, 31*(4), 638–681.

Loewenstein, K. (1939). *Hitler's Germany: The Nazi background to war*. Kessinger Publishing.

Mannheim, K. (1929). *Ideology and Utopia: An introduction to the sociology of knowledge*. Mansfield Centre, CT: Martino Fine Books.

Mannheim, K. (1943). *Diagnosis of our time*. Routledge.

Marcuse, H. (1934). Der Kampf gegen den Liberalismus in der totalitären Staatsauffassung. *Studies in Philosophy and Social Science, 3*, 161–168.

Marcuse, H. (1964). *One-dimensional man: Studies in the ideology of advanced industrial society* (2nd Revised ed.). Routledge.

Marcuse, H. (1969). Repressive tolerance. In R. P. Wolff, B. Moore, & H. Marcuse (Eds.), *A critique of pure tolerance* (pp. 81–123). Boston: Beacon Press.

Marcuse, L. (2008). *Meine Geschichte der Philosophie: Aus den Papieren eines bejahrten Philosophiestudenten* (4th ed.). Diogenes Verlag: Diogenes Verlag.

Margalit, A. (1998). *The decent society*. (N. Goldblum, Trans.) (Revised ed.). Cambridge, MA: Harvard University Press.

Marx, K. (1843). Zur Judenfrage. In I. Fetscher (Ed.), *Karl Marx - Friedrich Engels. Studienausgabe in 5 Bänden: Band I: Philosophie* (1st ed., pp. 36–66). Berlin, Germany: Aufbau Taschenbuch.

Marx, K. (1844). Ökonomisch-philosophische Manuskripte. In I. Fetscher (Ed.), *Karl Marx - Friedrich Engels. Studienausgabe in 5 Bänden: Band II: Politische Ökonomie* (Vols. 1–5, Vol. 2, pp. 38–135). Berlin, Germany: Aufbau Taschenbuch Verlag.

Marx, K., & Engels, F. (1970). In C. J. Arthur (Ed.), *German ideology* (1st ed.). New York: International Publishers.

Maturana, H. R., & Varela, F. J. (1998). *The tree of knowledge: The biological roots of human understanding* (Revised edition.). Boston: Shambhala.

Mead, G. H. (1934). *Mind, self, and society: From the standpoint of a social behaviorist*. Chicago: University of Chicago Press.

Mead, G. H. (1936). *Movements of thought in the nineteenth century*. Chicago: University of Chicago Press.

Meinhof, U. (1980). *Die Würde des Menschen ist antastbar: Aufsätze und Polemiken*. Berlin: Verlag Klaus Wagenbach.

Mill, J. S. (1859). *On liberty and the subjection of women*. London: Penguin Classics.
Miller, D. (2016). *Strangers in our midst: The political philosophy of immigration*. Cambridge, MA/London: Harvard University Press.
Mills, C. W. (1959). *The sociological imagination* (40th Anniversary ed.). Oxford: Oxford University Press, U.S.A.
Morgenstern, C. (2002). *Rassismus - Konturen einer Ideologie: Einwanderung im politischen Diskurs der Bundesrepublik Deutschland*. Hamburg, Germany: Argument Verlag.
Morsink, J. (1999). *The universal declaration of human rights: Origins, drafting, and intent*. Philadelphia: University of Pennsylvania Press.
Moyn, S. (2012). *The last Utopia: Human rights in history*. Cambridge, MA: Harvard University Press.
Moyn, S. (2014). *Human rights and the uses of history*. London: Verso.
Moyn, S. (2015). *Christian human rights*. Philadelphia, Pennsylvania: University of Pennsylvania Press.
Mühlpfordt, G. (2015). *Demokratische Aufklärer II: Radikalaufklärer* (1st ed.). Halle, Germany: Mitteldeutscher Verlag.
Müller-Tuckfeld, J. C. (1996). Strafrecht und die Produktion von Anerkennung: Hypothesen zur normativen Integration durch Strafrecht und zu deren Theoretisierung. In K.-D. Bussmann & R. Kreissl (Eds.), *Kritische Kriminologie in der Diskussion: Theorien, Analysen, Positionen* (pp. 123–169). Opladen, Germany: Westdeutscher Verlag.
Müller-Tuckfeld, J. C. (1997). *Integrationsprävention: Studien zu einer Theorie der gesellschaftlichen Funktion des Strafrechts* (1st ed.). Frankfurt am Main, Germany: Lang, Peter Frankfurt.
Neitzel, S., & Welzer, H. (2014). *Soldaten: Protokolle vom Kämpfen, Töten und Sterben*. Frankfurt am Main: Fischer.
Nickel, J. W. (2007). *Making sense of human rights* (2nd ed.). Malden, MA: Blackwell Publishing.
Nida-Rümelin, J. (2006). *Demokratie und Wahrheit*. München: C. H. Beck.
Nida-Rümelin, J. (2009). *Philosophie und Lebensform*. Berlin: Suhrkamp.
Nida-Rümelin, J. (2016). *Humanistische Reflexionen*. Berlin: Suhrkamp.
Niedenzu, H.-J. (2014). Die Genese der Normativität: Natur und Geist im Bildungsprozess der Normativität. In G. Dux & J. Rüsen (Eds.), *Strukturen des Denkens: Studien zur Geschichte des Geistes* (pp. 35–55). Wiesbaden, Germany: Springer.
Oberman, K. (2016). Immigration as a human right. In S. Fine & L. Ypi (Eds.), *Migration in political theory: The ethics of movement and membership* (pp. 32–56). New York: Oxford University Press.
Olson, K. (2016). Conclusion: Fragile collectivities, imagined sovereignties. In A. Badiou, P. Bourdieu, J. Butler, G. Didi-Huberman, S. Khiari, & J. Rancière (Eds.), *What is a people?* (pp. 107–131). New York: Columbia University Press.
O'Mahony, C. (2012). There is no such thing as a right to dignity. *International Journal of Constitutional Law, 10*(2), 551–574.
Opello, W. C., & Rosow, S. J. (2004). *The nation-state and global order: A historical introduction to contemporary politics* (2nd ed.). Boulder, CO: Lynne Rienner Publishers Inc.
Overton, R. (1998). An arrow against all tyrants (October 1646). In A. Sharp (Ed.), *The English Levellers* (pp. 54–72). Cambridge: Cambridge University Press.
Parlett, K. (2011). *The individual in the international legal system: Continuity and change in international law*. Cambridge: Cambridge University Press.
Paul, R. A. (2015). *Mixed messages: Cultural and genetic inheritance in the constitution of human society*. Chicago: University of Chicago Press.
Paxton, R. O. (2004). *The anatomy of fascism*. New York: Vintage Books.
Pico della Mirandola, G. (1486). Oration on the dignity of man: De hominis dignitate. (C. Wallis, 6457 Trans.). CreateSpace Independent Publishing Platform.
Pogge, T. W. (1992). Cosmopolitanism and Sovereignty. *Ethics, 103*(1), 48–75.
Popitz, H. (2006). *Soziale Normen*. Frankfurt am Main, Germany: Suhrkamp.
Popper, K. (1945). *The open society and its enemies* (Revised ed.). London: Routledge.

Putnam, F. W. (1989). *Diagnosis and treatment of multiple personality disorder* (1st ed.). New York: The Guilford Press.
Rancière, J. (2016). The populism that is not to be found. In A. Badiou, P. Bourdieu, J. Butler, G. Didi-Huberman, S. Khiari, & J. Rancière (Eds.), *What is a people?* (pp. 101–105). New York: Columbia University Press.
Richerson, P. J., & Boyd, R. (2004). *Not by genes alone: How culture transformed human evolution*. Chicago: University of Chicago Press.
Riedl, R. (1978). *Order in living organisms: A systems analysis of evolution*. Chichester, England: Wiley.
Riedl, R. (1984). *Biology of knowledge: The evolutionary basis of reason*. Chichester, England: Wiley.
Roll, E. (2016). *Wir sind Europa! Eine Streitschrift gegen den Nationalismus*. Berlin, Germany: Ullstein.
Rorty, R. (1999). *Philosophy and social hope*. New York: Penguin Books.
Ruby, C. (1996). *Introduction à la philosophie politique*. Paris: Éditions La Découverte.
Rundle, K. (2013). *Forms liberate: Reclaiming the jurisprudence of Lon L Fuller (Reprint.)*. Oxford, England/Portland, OR: Bloomsbury.
Russell, B. (2009). *Autobiography* (1st ed.). London: Taylor & Francis Ltd.
Sajo, A. (2004). *Militant democracy*. Eleven International Publishing.
Salem, O. (2015). *The missing peace: The role of religion in the Arab-Israeli conflict*. New Haven: Averroës Books.
Sapir, E. (2015). *Selected writings of Edward Sapir: In language, culture and personality*. Forgotten Books.
Schütt, M. (2015). *Anrufung und Unterwerfung: Althusser, Lacan, Butler und ŽiŽek*. Wien: Turia + Kant.
Schüttauf, K. (2012). Menschenwürde. Zur Struktur und Geschichte des Begriffs. In G. Brudermüller & K. Seelmann (Eds.), *Menschenwürde. Begründung, Konturen, Geschichte* (pp. 25–41). Würzburg, Germany: Königshausen und Neumann.
Schultz, S. (2016). Die zukünftige Nation: Demografisierung von Migrationspolitik und neue Konjunkturen des Rassismus. *Movements, 2*(1), 117–138.
Searle, J. (2010). *Making the social world. The structure of human civilization*. Oxford, England: Oxford University Press.
Shariff, A. F., Norenzayan, A., & Henrich, J. (2011b). The birth of high gods: How the cultural evolution of supernatural policing influenced the emergence of complex, cooperative human societies, paving the way for civilization. In M. Schaller, A. Norenzayan, S. J. Heine, T. Yamagishi, & T. Kameda (Eds.), *Evolution, culture, and the human mind* (pp. 119–136). London: Routledge.
Sheldon, S. (2016). The decriminalisation of abortion: An argument for modernisation. *Oxford Journal of Legal Studies, 36*(2), 334–365.
Shue, H. (1996). *Basic rights: subsistence, affluence, and U.S. Foreign Policy* (Second with a N.). Princeton, NJ: Princeton University Press.
Shweder, R. A. (1990). Cultural psychology: What is it? In J. W. Stigler, R. A. Shweder, & G. Herdt (Eds.), *Cultural psychology: Essays on comparative human development*. Cambridge, England: Cambridge University Press.
Shweder, R. A. (1991). *Thinking through cultures: Expeditions in cultural psychology*. Cambridge, MA: Harvard University Press.
Singer, P. (2004). *One world: The ethics of globalization*. New Haven/London: Yale University Press.
Singer, W. (2002). *Der Beobachter im Gehirn: Essays zur Hirnforschung* (8th ed.). Frankfurt am Main, Germany: Suhrkamp.
Sohn, L. B. (1982). The new international law: Protection of the rights of individuals rather than states. *The American University Law Review, 32*(1), 1–64.
Srubar, I. (2010). Der Streit um die Wissenssoziologie. In G. Kneer & S. Moebius (Eds.), *Soziologische Kontroversen: Beiträge zu einer anderen Geschichte der Wissenschaft vom Sozialen* (pp. 46–78). Frankfurt am Main, Germany: Suhrkamp.

Steel, N., & Hart, P. (1995). *Defeat at Gallipoli* (New edition). London, England: Papermac.
Stern, D. N. (2000). *The interpersonal world of the infant: A view from psychoanalysis and development psychology* (1st ed.). New York: Basic Books.
Stevenson, C. L. (1963). *Facts and values: Studies in ethical analysis*. Westport, CT: Greenwood Press.
Stichweh, R. (2016). *Inklusion und Exklusion: Studien zur Gesellschaftstheorie* (2nd ed.). Bielefeld, Germany: Transcript Verlag.
Stiglitz, J. E. (2013). *The price of inequality: How today's divided society endangers our future*. New York: Norton.
Stourzh, G. (2009). *Spuren einer intellektuellen Reise: Drei Essays*. Wien: Böhlau.
Suber, P. (1990). *The paradox of self-amendment*. New York: Peter Lang Publishing.
Terkessidis, M. (1998). *Psychologie des Rassismus*. Opladen/Wiesbaden, Germany: Westdeutscher Verlag.
Therborn, G. (1999). *The ideology of power and the power of ideology* (Revised.). London: Verso.
Theunissen, M. (1982). *Selbstverwirklichung and Allgemeinheit: Zur Kritik des gegenwärtigen Bewusstseins*. Berlin, Germany: Walter de Gruyter.
Thiel, M. (2003). *Wehrhafte Demokratie* (1., Aufl.). Tübingen, Germany: Mohr Siebeck.
Thiel, M. (2009). *The "Militant Democracy" principle in modern democracies* (New edition.). Farnham, England: Ashgate.
Tugendhat, E. (2004). *Egozentrizität und Mystik: Eine anthropologische Studie* (2nd ed.). München, Germany: C.H. Beck.
Tugendhat, E. (2005). Über Selbstbewusstsein: Einige Missverständnisse. In T. Grundmann, F. Hofmann, C. Misselhorn, V. L. Waibel, & V. Zanetti (Eds.), *Anatomie der Subjektivität: Bewußtsein, Selbstbewußtsein und Selbstgefühl* (pp. 247–254). Frankfurt am Main, Germany: Suhrkamp.
Tyler, T. R. (2006). *Why people obey the law*. Princeton/Oxford: Princeton University Press.
Tyler, T. R. (2013). *Why people cooperate: The role of social motivations*. Princeton/Oxford: Princeton University Press.
Tyulkina, S. (2015). *Militant democracy: Undemocratic political parties and beyond*. ACPIL.
van der Kolk, B. A., McFarlane, A. C., & van der Hart, O. (2000). Ein allgemeiner Ansatz zur Behandlung der posttraumatischen Belastungsstörung. In B. A. van der Kolk, A. C. McFarlane, & L. Weisaeth (Eds.), *Traumatic stress. Grundlagen und Behandlungsansätze* (pp. 309–330). Paderborn, Germany: Junfermann.
van der Kolk, B. A., van der Hart, O., & Marmar, C. R. (2000). Dissoziation und Informationsverarbeitung beim posttraumatischen Belastungssyndrom. In B. A. van der Kolk, A. C. McFarlane, & L. Weisaeth (Eds.), *Traumatic stress. Grundlagen und Behandlungsansätze* (pp. 241–261). Paderborn, Germany: Junfermann.
Vogelmann, F. (2014). *Im Bann der Verantwortung* (1st ed.). Campus Verlag.
von der Pfordten, D. (2009). *Menschenwürde, Recht und Staat bei Kant: Fünf Untersuchungen*. Paderborn, Germany: mentis.
von der Pfordten, D. (2016). *Menschenwürde* (1st ed.). C.H. Beck.
Waldron, J. (2006). Cosmopolitan norms. In R. Post (Ed.), *Another cosmopolitanism* (pp. 83–101). New York: Oxford University Press.
Waldron, J. (2015). Reply to commentators. In M. Dan-Cohen (Ed.), *Dignity, rank and rights* (pp. 133–148). New York: Oxford University Press.
Wilkinson, I., & Kleinman, A. (2016). *A passion for society: How we think about human suffering*. University of California Press.
Wilson, J. P., Friedman, M. J., & Lindy, J. D. (2001). A holistic, organismic approach to healing trauma and PTSD. In J. P. Wilson, M. J. Friedman, & J. D. Lindy (Eds.), *Treating psychological trauma & PTSD* (pp. 28–56). New York: Guilford.
Wolff, R. P. (1969). Beyond tolerance. In R. P. Wolff, B. Moore, & H. Marcuse (Eds.), *A critique of pure tolerance* (pp. 3–52). Boston: Beacon Press.
Zaczyk, R. (2014). *Selbstsein und Recht: Eine rechtsphilosophische Untersuchung*. Frankfurt am Main: Vittorio Klostermann.

Chapter 4
Criminal Justice Respecting Human Dignity

4.1 What this Chapter is about

Chapter 1 raised the question of how criminal law and criminal justice should be constructed to acknowledge the victim as the person whose primary rights have been violated by the offender. It was suggested that this would require a paradigm shift from criminal law protecting public interests, to criminal law protecting rights of individuals and consequently a shift of criminal justice from enforcing rights of the state to the punishment of offenders to granting secondary rights of victims to justice. It was observed that some courts—including the ECtHR, the IACtHR, and the German Constitutional Court—recognise, within defined limits, fundamental rights of victims to the prosecution, identification, conviction and punishment of offenders.

However, when it came to justifying claims of the victim to the punishment of the offender, the analysis of this novel approach encountered difficulties. These can be summed up as meeting the challenge of Kant's principle, according to which the interference with fundamental rights of one person cannot be justified as serving the rights or interests of others. Thus, within a normative framework based on human dignity, the problem of how to justify punishment vis-à-vis the offender takes on a much more challenging and pressing form, as under such conditions punishing the offender cannot be legitimised by the fact that it benefits others. Human dignity entails the promise that the rights it grants to the individual subject will not be sacrificed for the rights or interests of others, or, in other words, that the person will not be reduced to a means to an ends for others.

Therefore, justifying punishment under conditions of a normative order founded in human dignity requires that punishment reflects the dignity of the punished. In Chap. 1, this Kantian principle of non-instrumentalisation was defined as the watershed distinguishing critical from affirmative theories of criminal law and criminal justice. What must be avoided is the assumption, typical of affirmative theories, that the function of punishment is identical to its justification. Demonstrating that

A. Dearing, *Justice for Victims of Crime*, DOI 10.1007/978-3-319-45048-3_4

punishment is beneficial to a community and fulfils certain functions in the community's interests—such as preserving its normative basis—is one aspect, showing that punishment is legitimate in relation to the offender is quite another.

Hence, these two issues were looked into separately. Chapter 2 focused on the societal functions of punishment as preserving social norms and thus enabling large communities to cooperate peacefully and to prosper.

Chapter 3 served to clarify the specific challenges one meets under conditions of modernity. The primary aim of that chapter was to shed light on human dignity as the principle apt to found and guide the construction of a highly diverse global normative order. It was maintained that Fichtean ethics highlights the societal preconditions of normativity in general and of modern pluralism in particular. Kantian claims of autonomy face inherent restrictions, as they are premised on the belief in individual autonomy and morality as parts of the innate, basic configuration of any human being. In contrast, Fichte stresses the fact that a person can only develop when called on by her legal community. An individual's autonomy is premised on acts of communication that hold her to account. This insight makes it possible to properly view Kant's principle as not precluding norms on which individual personhood and autonomy necessarily rely.

This chapter utilises this insight in constructing a critical theory of crime and punishment built on the foundation of human dignity. Such a humanist theory of punishment revolves around two focal points, which are inherently linked to one another. The first is the principle of guilt of the offender, meaning that the only justification of punishing an offender is that she deserves to be punished. The second is the concept of the victim as a person and rights-holder, entitled to the identification, conviction and, in appropriate cases, also the punishment of the offender as an expression of the solidarity of her legal community.

Hence, as envisaged in Chap. 1, this chapter gives answers to the two questions of, firstly, what legitimately constitutes a crime, and, secondly, what rights individuals consequently have if a crime has been committed. The answer to the first question is that a crime is a violation of a system of human rights founded on human dignity. The response to the second question takes the form of denying any free-standing rights of citizens to the punishment of their fellow-citizens. Instead, it grounds the punishment of offenders in their own fundamental, universal, inalienable and unforfeitable right to be treated as persons and hence to be called on to account for their actions in accordance with their personal—intellectual and physical—abilities on the basis of a normative order respecting their dignity.

However, holding an offender accountable is premised on an understanding of the rights violation the offender has to answer for. The rights in question flow from the same concept of dignity on which the offender's status as a person is based. Hence, the offender's accountability is intrinsically linked to the wrong suffered by her victim. Criminal law is defined as that part of the legal order that protects the norms on which individuals' personhood relies—the rights and dignity of the victim as much as the status of the offender as an accountable person.

4.1.1 Restrictions Inherent in a System of Criminal Justice Founded on Human Digntiy

Founding criminal law and criminal justice on a concept of human dignity and human rights provides them with a solid basis. However, this shift also comes with a number of very significant inherent restrictions. Four of them shall be mentioned at the outset.

Firstly, arguing for criminal justice to be based on the victim's right to justice entails that human dignity is important not only concerning victims, but also offenders. Any theory attempting to advocate the human rights of victims without being prepared to deal with the human rights of offenders on an equal footing would be inconsistent. Victims and offenders have the same dignity. This is the reason why, ironically, Kant's principle forms the crucial challenge to a theory of criminal justice based on victims' right to justice. Unless convicting and punishing the offender can be justified in relation to the offender as an autonomous person, criminal justice and human dignity remain at odds.

It will be shown that Kant's principle does not prevent criminalising conduct that calls the premises of the offender's autonomy into question. Violations of human dignity justify criminalisation, unless they can be dealt with effectively by applying less intrusive means. Hence, secondly, basing criminal law and criminal justice on human dignity comes with a significant restriction of what may legitimately be criminalised. For example, as entering a country without permission does not violate human dignity or its implications, it cannot be legitimately criminalised. While all sanctions preserve norms, punishment restores persons as members of their societies and of humankind at large and thus relates to human dignity and a system of human rights flowing from human dignity. In the terminology introduced above, criminal law protects dignity, while conventional laws serve other purposes on the basis of an agreement of the citizens concerned.

In yet another dimension, human dignity restricts with what criminal justice may legitimately concern itself. Even if an individual nourishes evil thoughts, such thoughts do not legitimise criminal justice unless they result in a violation of the system of human rights. This is not about the significance of the rights protected, but about the quality of acts that have the potential to violate a system of human rights. Conceptualising criminal justice as a means of protecting human dignity and human rights, comes, thirdly, with a restriction of criminal justice to censuring acts of communication that actually violate human dignity and human rights. This rules out extending criminalisation to acts that in themselves do not—or do not yet—amount to infringing the rights of individuals, such as, by mistake, attempting to steal one's own mobile phone or attending a training camp for terrorists, which per se does not (yet) pose a violation or even a concrete threat to the human rights of individuals.

Fourthly, founding criminal justice on human dignity means that prosecuting, convicting and punishing offenders must be carried out in a manner respecting the dignity of the offender and, more generally, the human rights of all individuals concerned, including, for instance, the offender's family. By being convicted—and in appropriate cases even punished—the offender contributes her due to the authority of the victim's primary rights. This must be achieved in a manner respectful of human dignity in everyone, including the offender and her family.

This chapter deals with aspects of substantive, not procedural law. The question is, what rights do individuals—victims, offenders and others—have because of the fact that a crime has been committed, rights that reflect the nature of a crime as a violation of human dignity and the system of human rights. As the historic perspective of the nation state paradigm is replaced by a normative order founded on human dignity and human rights, the question goes to the rights of individuals to the conviction and, in appropriate cases, the punishment of the offender that replace the state's right to the punishment of the disobedient subject.

4.1.2 *Establishing the Truth, Convicting, Sentencing and Punishing Offenders*

The core aspect addressed in this chapter is the victim's right to justice, and the objective is to construct a system of criminal justice that meets this right. To date, victims' rights are mostly dealt with merely as a matter of criminal proceedings or sanctions, but very rarely as a matter of how to define crime in a manner that conceives of the offence as a violation of the rights of an individual or individuals. With a few important exceptions (including Duff 2001; Fletcher 1995; Hörnle 2006, 2011; Lüderssen 2002; Prittwitz 2000; Sautner 2010; Schmidt 2015), current theories of crime and punishment tend to ignore the victim as a holder of human rights.

What lies at the heart of many aspects of criminal justice is the fundamental Kantian distinction and antagonism between a world of norms and a world of instincts, desires and seductions. In dealing with criminal justice what can be confusing is how these two worlds overlap and interweave, such that drafting criminal law provisions as well as prosecuting and convicting offenders constitutes the normative discourse about what is right and wrong, while treating the offender harshly occurs in the sphere of enticements and base motives, including the—powerful—temptation to throw off the yoke of the normative order and responsibility. The victim's sense that what the offender did to her was wrong and demands a response of her legal community, belongs to the cultural world. The victim's fear that, if the offence passes unremarked, others could yield to the temptation to follow the example of the offender pertains to the material world of seductions and countervailing discouragements.

Normative persuasion, on the one hand, and the neutralization and cancelling out of the temptations and attractions of unrestrained, wild and unscrupulous disobedience, on the other, belong to different spheres of human existence, the first to the space of autonomy and normative reasoning, the second to the realm of heteronomous, external incentives. In the interest of a sound analysis of the mechanisms of the criminal justice system, it is important to keep these two spheres apart. By announcing a criminal law definition, the legislator appeals to the moral sense of citizens; by threatening them with punishment, she does not. Rather, what the announcement that offenders will be punished can achieve is to signal to conditional cooperators that committing crimes is not only wrong, but also unattractive, and hence they can have confidence that others will not free ride on their contributions.

This distinction between the wrongfulness and the attractivity of offending is also reflected in the tendency of many legal orders to punish attempted offences more leniently. The difference between attempted and successful crimes is not a difference of wrong, but of appeal to potential imitators. If the offender failed to achieve the advantage she sought to gain, a conditional cooperator's fear that the offender could be the one 'who laughs last' is less pertinent. Still, the offender's action challenges the bindingness of the norm and the respect owed to the victim. By attempting to commit a crime the offender demonstrates her decision to ignore the normative order's authority. Therefore, the offender, in principle, still owes her contribution to supporting the norm and to recognising the victim as a person and rights-holder. But it takes less to render unattractive the offender's failed attempt compared to successful offending.

From the outset it must be stressed that doing justice is not merely—or primarily—about punishment. Rather justice, from the victim's perspective, breaks down into four elements that all matter to the victim and hence have to be considered separately. These four elements of doing justice are the establishing of the facts as well as convicting, sentencing and punishing the offender.

That the court authoritatively establishes the truth, supports the victim in coming to terms with her victimisation. After the court has spoken, no one can deny that the victimisation, with all its consequences, forms part of the victim's life story. The offence is recognised as a significant event in the life of the victim, the offender, and their community.

By the verdict of the court, the offender is formally declared guilty of an offence. If the offence is understood—as is the case in a humanist society—as a violation of the primary rights of the victim, the conviction of the offender, firstly, acknowledges and confirms the rights of the victim and her status as a rights-holder, secondly, determines that the offender's action was wrong as it violated the rights of the victim and disregarded her as a person, and, thirdly, expresses the offender's responsibility and reprimand for the offence, thus potentially disburdening the victim of feelings of her own guilt or shame. The conviction authoritatively declares that what the offender did to the victim no one must do to the victim, due to her rights and status as a person. In this function of restoring the victim as a full member of her society, the conviction of the offender forms the key element of what doing criminal justice can mean to the victim.

What the sentence adds to the conviction is that the wrong, established by the offender's conviction, is measured, quantified, and implicitly compared with other wrongs suffered by other victims or done by other offenders.

The execution of the sentence demonstrates that the offender is made to contribute her due to rendering offending costly and to reassuring conditional cooperators. Thus the offender has to bear her share of the investments involved in preserving the norms that found the rights of the victim as well as the equal rights of all others.

It is a bad habit of many legal theorists to focus on the punishment of the offender and to treat the other elements as minor matters. The only excuse is a certain argumentum a major ad minus, meaning that if punishment can be justified, so can the other elements, simply because punishment presupposes and implies the other elements as they are necessary steps on the path to punishment. However, this bad habit can mislead those who yield to it about the fact that punishment is not necessary in every single case. In minor cases, the offender can contribute sufficiently to the authority of the norm by acknowledging that she wronged the victim, by apologising in a credible manner, by swiftly and fully compensating the victim or by, for instance, donating to a victim support service. In any case, when it comes to doing justice to victims it must not be overlooked that what is of primary significance to the victim is the establishment of the truth and the conviction of the offender, while sentencing and punishing are more relevant in severe cases where the victim must be reassured that her society takes the preservation of her rights and her status as a person very seriously.

4.1.3 Criminal Justice in Transition from a Nation State Paradigm to a Humanist Society

This chapter builds on the historic and evolutionary perspective adopted in previous chapters. It aims to understand the transitional process of a system of criminal justice that gradually leaves the context and framework of the nation state paradigm behind and moves into the new paradigm of human dignity and the vision of an emerging global humanist society. What founds criminal justice is no longer a state's claims to the punishment of disobedient citizens, but the entitlement of individuals to the conviction, sentencing or even punishment of individuals.

One aspect of this transition is the globalisation of criminal justice. At the latest, after the establishment of an International Criminal Court, criminal justice developed as a matter of cooperation of courts established at different scales. More importantly, criminal justice answers to claims that are anchored in human dignity and universal human rights. The basic views and concepts applied by criminal law and criminal justice cease to be a matter of diverse national traditions, as they have a common basis in notions of global reach. This is not a matter of international law, of the legal relationships, that is, between nations, but about the cosmopolitan rights of individuals to be effectively protected against impunity, rights guaranteed by a global community of human beings and put into practice by state institutions.

While this chapter does not focus on the procedural implications of the new paradigm, it is worth noting that one actor, whose function and orientation, in the course of this transition, changes fundamentally is the public prosecutor. Instead of representing the interests of the state or some collective, the prosecutor, in a way, mutates into a human rights advocate. In a criminal justice system based on human dignity, the prosecutor will, in principle, be mindful of the human rights of all individuals concerned. However she will restrain herself to the extent that the offender and the victim are willing and apt to assert their rights and concerns themselves. In any case, as criminal justice is not only about the victim and the offender, but indirectly about the equal rights of all others, it is these rights that the prosecutor has to represent in all circumstances.

4.2 The Nation State: Criminal Law Unleashed

Traditional criminal law has its roots in the belief in a strong nation state, which, starting with the era of revolutions, was fully developed in the second half of the nineteenth century and still exists today.

At the end of the 19th century, the appreciation of the nation state was a common denominator. It underlined schools of thought that, for the rest, departed from very different assumptions, some naturalist, hypostasising society as a living organism, others idealistic and legalistic, emphasising the state as representing the will of 'the people'. However, in their results, both schools concurred in cherishing the collectivity and in radically devaluing the (rights of the) individual.

The first naturalist or 'positivist' approach was supported in Italy by the *scuola positiva* around Cesare Lombroso, Raffaele Garofalo, and Enrico Ferri, as well as by Emil Wahlberg, Franz von Liszt and Georg Jellinek in Austria, Adolphe Prins in Belgium and Gerardus Antonius van Hamel in the Netherlands, all united in a quasi-biologistic view of criminal justice as defending society against dangerous offenders, often perceived in anthropologic categories. The second approach was mainly taken by the *scuola classica*—e.g. Francesco Carrara and Giovanni Carmignani—and by German legal theorists, including Karl Binding, Karl von Birkmeyer, Ernst Beling, and Johannes Nagler, who all emphasised the authority of a state's law and the role of criminal justice in preserving this authority. As examples, in the following the views of Franz von Liszt and Ernst Beling shall be briefly presented.

4.2.1 Franz von Liszt

In Liszt's theory, the point of departure is society organised as a state. Society and state coincide; Liszt refers to the "state society" ("*staatliche Gesellschaft*", 1883, p. 126). The offender is situated outside and in opposition to the community, personified by the state. Without hesitation, Liszt refers to the offender as a sacrilegious person ("*Frevler*"), against whom the state defends the legal order, armed with the sword of justice (1883, p. 150):

> Die Staatsgewalt hat das Schwert der Gerechtigkeit in die Hand genommen, um die Rechtsordnung zu schützen gegen den Frevler, der an ihr sich vergreift.

Thus the purpose of criminal law is to prevent conduct that harms common interests of the community ("*Hintanhaltung gemeinschädlicher Handlungen*", 1883, p. 127). Liszt refers to common interests protected by criminal law as 'legal goods' ("*Rechtsgüter*"); hence the objective of criminal law and criminal justice is the protection of 'legal goods' ("*Rechtsgüterschutz*" 1883, pp. 126, 142; the formula of criminal law as "*Rechtsgüterschutz*" is still popular today with legal doctrine of German tongue).

Liszt stresses the impulsive and instinctive character of punishment; over and over again he refers to punishment as a compulsive act of the state ("*Triebhandlung*", 1883,

p. 142). Thus, Liszt assimilates punishing with a biological reflex against an interference with an organism's vital interests. However, the crucial move is to relate the struggle to survive to a collectivity. The individual organism's self-preservation is merely a function of the survival of the species (1883, pp. 136–137); and Liszt equates the species not to humankind at large, but to society (1883, p. 138). According to Liszt, both animal and primitive human societies know punishment as a compulsive reaction against infringements of their societies' vital living conditions (1883, p. 135).

Liszt, on the one hand, emphasises the objective functionality of punishment and, on the other, insists that punishment is not premised on any subjective purposefulness; Liszt rejects the idea of a strategic purposefulness of punishment ("*Zweckgedanke*") and insists that because punishment, historically, precedes its deliberate employment by state policies, it exists strictly independently of any strategic aims. Hence Liszt rejects all relativist—consequentialist—theories of punishment (1883, pp. 132–134):

> Indem ich die primitive Strafe als blinde, instinktmäßige, triebartige Reaktion, mit einem Worte als Triebhandlung bezeichnete, wollte ich damit zunächst und in allererster Linie eine negative Eigenschaft der primitiven Strafe zum möglichst scharfen Ausdrucke bringen. Die Strafe ist eben nicht, wie die Anhänger der relativen Theorien übereinstimmend annehmen, eine Ausklügelung menschlichen Witzes, ein Ergebnis staatlicher Rechenkunst; sie ist nicht hervorgebracht durch den Zweckgedanken, sondern unabhängig von ihm und ihm vorhergehend in die menschliche Kulturgeschichte eingetreten. [...] Um diese Notwendigkeit der Strafe, ihre Unabhängigkeit von Menschenwitz und staatlicher Klugheit, um die Ablehnung des Zweckgedankens in der primitiven Strafe in klarster und unzweideutigster Weise zum Ausdrucke zu bringen, habe ich sie als Triebhandlung bezeichnet [...].

At the same time, Liszt submits that by state policies, punishment's "blind" functionality is transformed into deliberate purposefulness. Liszt refers to this transformation as objectivisation ("*Objektivierung*") to highlight a process of rationalisation and increasing controllability (1883, p. 132). Thus punishment, in Liszt's theory, is at once genuinely instinctive and *not purposeful,* as well as controlled and domesticated and hence *purposeful.* It remains unclear why Liszt believes that punishment, despite its transformation into a purposeful tool of society, also maintains its original 'blindness' and instinctiveness.

However, by his evolutionary naturalism—or positivism—Liszt seeks to avoid 'philosophical' questions. He sells a collective organism's repulsive reaction against an impairment of its living conditions as simply a matter of necessary, natural self-preservation, not in need of any further justification. Liszt believes that by fading out moral issues he can bypass complex ethical questions, such as those concerning the necessary guilt and blameworthiness of offenders, which Liszt declares irrelevant.

> Die Strafe als repulsive Reaktion gegen Störung der Lebensbedingungen, als Verteidigung durch Angriff, ist nichts der menschlichen Geschichte Eigentümliches. Und wenn dieser Satz auch bezweifelt werden sollte: die in der menschlichen Geschichte auftretende primitive Strafe ist unabhängig von irgend einem sittlichen Urteile über die geschehene Störung der Lebensbedingungen. Sie richtet sich gegen das schädigende Tier, gegen das Kind, gegen den Wahnsinnigen; sie tritt ein, ohne jede Rücksicht auf das Verschulden des Täters [...].

It is because of this naturalism—his biological anthropology—that Liszt believes he can avoid the question of how to legitimise punishment in relation to the offender. In Liszt's theory, the justification of punishment is confounded with its objective necessity in the interest of society, thus sacrificing the individual for the sake of collective benefits. This radical subordination of the individual to the welfare of the 'people' is—at least from today's perspective—reminiscent of subsequent totalitarian criminal policies (e.g. Frommel 2013; Marxen 1975; Naucke 1982; Wetzell 2014).

While in Chap. 1 it was observed that punishing an individual for the sake of others violates the concept of human dignity, it is exactly this offsetting of interests of the offender against the—always prevailing—interests of the community that is characteristic of affirmative constructions of criminal law under conditions of the nation state.

4.2.2 Ernst Beling

In positivist theories of legal norms, the concept of law is radically emptied of any inherent normative content, enabling the law to minister to whatever authority is in a position of power. As long as legislation is passed in accordance with the constitutional rules of procedure, any legislation passes as a legitimate manifestation of the will of the sovereign, be it a monarch or a people.

As to criminal law, this process of rendering the law flexible and functional was achieved by a process of abstraction, reducing the notion of crime to the violation of whatever is passed as a criminal law by a competent authority. While, for a long time, criminal law had been understood as a record and compilation of ancient, well-established types of wrong-doing, deeply rooted in people's moral convictions, at the end of the nineteenth and the beginning of the twentieth century an abstract notion is formed void of any content, but the fact of an infringement of a state's positive law.

One outstanding example is Ernst Beling's "*Die Lehre vom Verbrechen*", published in 1906. For Beling, the essential feature of a crime is that it denotes an action that fits a criminal law definition (an action's *Tatbestandsmäßigkeit*, that is). It is positive criminal law definitions—*"die positivrechtlich angegebenen Tatbestände"*—that decide what constitutes a crime (1906, p. 21). More precisely, it is a *nation state's* definitions that are relevant. With regard to definitions comprised in foreign or international law, Beling emphasises that only 'our' definitions are important for 'us'; whether the criminal laws of other countries are similar or different, is of no import (1906, pp. 113–114):

> Aber Übereinstimmung und Verschiedenheit sind für uns belanglos: die Verbrechenskonstruktion kann sich nur auf den durch unsere Strafgesetze positivierten Tatbeständen aufbauen. Verbrechen kann nur die deutsch-strafgesetzlich-tatbestandliche Handlung und zwar nur auf der Basis des geltenden Rechts sein. [...] auch hier ist es der nationaldeutsche Tatbestand, in dessen Erfüllung das Verbrechen besteht.

This abstract notion of a nation state's criminal law definition operates in two directions. It strengthens national boundaries and at the same time reinforces a nation state's normative power to define whatever it perceives as running counter to public interests as criminal. According to Beling, criminal law definitions determine and shape types of wrong, and while legislators' decisions can be arbitrary, they nevertheless define authoritatively what constitutes a crime. The only difference between violations of criminal law and infringements of other parts of the legal order consists in the fact that an offence fits a criminal law definition and hence corresponds to a type of crime while infringements of other areas of law do not. In Beling's words (1906, p. 147):

> [...] der Unterschied zwischen dem strafbaren und dem straflosen Unrecht liegt [...] vornehmlich im Vorhandensein oder Nichtvorhandensein eines positiv formulierten Typus [...]. Und da die Typen absolut willkürlich vom Gesetz geformt werden, und heute Typus sein kann, was es gestern nicht war, und umgekehrt, so erhellt, dass die Scheidung keine wahrhaft prinzipielle ist.

Hence, criminal law definitions, in Beling's understanding (1906, p. 147), do not imply a value judgment; the assessment of whether a certain behaviour fulfils a criminal law definition or not takes place on strictly neutral territory. Consequently, Beling (1906, p. 137) challenges Liszt's understanding that a criminal offence should be interpreted as the violation of a protected good or interest ("*Rechtsgüterverletzung*"), unless one would conceive of the legal order as the protected legal good. It is the authority of the legal order that criminal law protects.

Hence, the only reasoning and justification that criminal law, in Beling's view, offers its subjects is that, as citizens, they are expected to abide by legal norms, whatever they demand, as they express the will of the state. What crystallises as the essence of crime is nothing but a subject's insubordination and defiance of the legal order. Beling (1906, pp. 127–128) clearly expresses this étatist and authoritarian attitude by defining crime as essentially a contradiction to the normative will of the state and hence a form of disobedience to the legal order (*Ungehorsam gegen die Rechtsordnung*).

> Vor solcher Atomisierung bewahrt uns der Begriff der Norm. [...] sie führt aus der Vielheit der Erscheinungen zu dem in den Rechtssätzen lebenden staatlichen Willen, der Nachachtung heischt, zu der Rechtsordnung als Ganzem in ihrer Verbindungskraft für menschliches Handeln. Sie lehrt, dass das Verbrechen nicht durch Verstoß gegen den einen oder anderen einzelnen Rechtssatz charakterisiert wird, sondern das das Charakteristikum des Verbrechens, der Geist, der in ihm lebt, der Widerspruch gegen den staatlichen normativen Willen ist, also (unter Hinzunahme der subjektiven Seite: der Schuld) ein Ungehorsam gegen die Rechtsordnung.

This is what lies at the heart of Beling's doctrine of crime. What to him is essential is what all offences have in common, namely a subject's insubordination to a nation state's law. Criminal law is not necessarily more than Gessler's hat on a pole, to be saluted and respected by all subjects.

Hence, while Liszt hypostasizes the nation state as an organism defending itself against adversaries, Beling elevates and transfigures the legal order into the expression of the nation's will and thus immunises criminal law against any criticism.

4.2.3 Overcoming the Nation State in Criminal Law

Despite their radically different approaches, in terms of their consequences, the theories of Liszt and Beling concur in at least two crucial aspects.

Firstly, in both theories, the rights of the individual are trumped by the interests of the collectivity. Criminal law expresses the interests of a society or a state, which take precedence over the rights of individuals. What justifies the punishment of the offender is the fact that it is beneficial to others: the community, society etc. This violates Kant's claim that, because of her dignity, an individual must not be treated as a means to an ends for others, but must in all cases be acknowledged as autonomously pursuing her own ends. However, if it is the collectivity that counts in the end and not the individual and if, hence, punishment serves the collectivity, there is no room for Kant's principle.

The classical views have been criticised as overly collectivist and as relying on the vertical relations between state authorities and their relatively obedient subjects. Therefore, it has been observed that classical theories of criminal justice do not fully comply with contemporary political ideas, which emphasise the rights and legitimate interests of individuals. Modern European societies have their foundation in an individualist concept of ethics (Weigend 2010, p. 41).

Secondly, criminal law which preserves public interests is unlimited in scope. Whatever irritates society or the state can justify criminal law provisions. The rights of individuals cannot, within a nation state paradigm, assume a function as limiting criminal law. Hence, there exists no inherent limit to the subjection of individuals to the collectivity. The consequences of this flaw and the resulting unboundedness of criminal law become obvious today. Whatever is perceived as impairing public interests can be criminalised to defend society or the legal order. Meanwhile, various wars have been declared in criminal law terms against unpleasant social phenomena, including on migration, on individuals in irregularised situations of residence, on smugglers supporting migrants in crossing borders, wars on illegalised markets and money laundering involving many sectors of the economy and undermining relationships of trust, a war on a war in Syria and Iraq and on everyone supporting or intending to support the wrong side. Criminal law provisions have made a breath-taking career as, among others, instruments of health policies, migration policies, and foreign policies, but, by criminalising begging or sleeping on a park bench, also as a repressive form of social policies, and—maybe most alarming—by criminalising women wearing certain head scarves—again—as a means of restricting societal pluralism. (It will be remembered that Kemal Atatürk in 1925—after attending military exercises in the French Picardie—had a criminal law provision enacted obliging men in Turkey to wear hats,—as if modern headware would induce a modern mindset. Formally, this law is still in force today).

Therefore, what is needed to contain the inflationary spread of criminal law are criteria enabling a critical assessment of whether an interest warrants protection by means of criminal law or not, as well as criteria allowing for an assessment of whether a particular criminal law definition is an acceptable means of criminalising fellow citizens. Most fundamentally, what needs to be overcome is sociocentric ethics (*Sozialethik*), ethics, that is, based on a hypostasized collectivity—'the society', 'the state', 'the nation', 'the people' or 'the public'—levered against and claiming precedence over the individual and her rights.

It should be stressed again that the development overcoming the traditional paradigm of criminal justice as an issue that the state has with the disobedient offender needs to be contextualised in the much wider framework of the historical emergence of a universal political order ending the era of the nation state. Starting at the time of the Carolingian Empire, concepts of the sacredness and divine rights of kings emerged enabling monarchs to rule by the grace of God. This normative paradigm was overturned when the sovereignty of the king was replaced by the sovereignty of 'the people' and 'the nation', a development that is reflected in the peace of Westphalia and leads up to the revolts of various sovereign peoples, e.g. in 1688, 1776, 1789 and 1848. During this phase, political power is ultimately legitimised by a people's right to national self-determination. In our times, the decline of the nation-state coincides with the rise of a global political order that overcomes the hypostatisation of the collectivity. Nations and peoples are replaced by the vision of a human family, establishing a complex political order, within which regional organisations like the European Union, instead of merely continuing the concept of the nation state at a larger scale, occupy one important level within the complex structure of a diversified and stratified normative order, which spans global organisations, state level institutions, local authorities, and autonomous individuals.

The vision of humankind as the point of departure and the primary community to consider does not introduce yet another hypostasized collectivity. All the concept of 'a human family' expresses is that the global order rests on a basic sense of solidarity of all individual human beings, who agree that every human being has the right to be called on and initiated as a member of the human family and therefore has the right to have rights and responsibilities according to her abilities. Given the level of globalisation and interconnectedness that has been reached today, the vision of a human family only captures the community of fate in which humans actually find themselves. It is no longer an individual's nationality or ethnicity that, in political and legal terms, primarily defines her identity, but her human face accounting for her rights and obligations in relation to all other members of the human family.

This historical narrative emphasises the political and cultural upheaval taking off in the 1960s and impacting heavily on international law and human rights institutions throughout the 1970s and 1980s. In this process of a second renaissance, a more self-confident, self-defining and self-determined individual emerges, who takes a far more critical stance vis-à-vis 'their' nation states—'home countries'—and all authorities. This distantiation implies the establishment of effective control mechanisms at regional and international levels.

In terms of the strengthening of control functions within the framework of the Council of Europe, the year 1990 is remarkable for two innovations, which both reflect subjects' newly felt desire to monitor the performance of governments. It is the year when the Council of Europe's Committee for the Prevention of Torture (CPT; on the CPT Ginther 1990) implemented its first inspection—visiting Austria and publishing a highly critical report about the human rights situation of suspects detained by the police, concluding "that there is a serious risk of detainees being ill-treated while in police custody" (CPT/Inf (91) 10 of 3 October 1991)—; and it is the year when Protocol No. 9 to the ECHR was signed in Rome, enabling citizens to apply directly to the Court to claim that a state violated their rights. It is with this Protocol that individuals, for the first time in history, had the possibility to lodge a complaint against 'their' government with a regional court.

The angle changes significantly if the normative order is established not on dubiously hypostasized collectivities, but on the solid footing of human dignity and human rights. Within this framework, the questions of what is the unique feature and prominent role of criminal law and how criminal justice can be restricted to performing this role can be tackled. Arguably, it is about time that the rights of individuals—victims, offenders and third parties—are introduced back into court rooms, from where they were expelled during the phases of state-centred, étatist, often authoritarian criminal justice systems serving the political interests of monarchs and nation states.

4.3 A Fresh Start: Human Dignity and the Principle of Guilt

4.3.1 The Paradox of Deterrence

Just as criminal law cannot be based on consequentialism, so it is wrong to justify criminal law on the deterrence of potential offenders. One can imagine a situation of perfect deterrence, where, to preserve a norm, those violating the norm are threatened with particularly harsh punishments and, in addition, a sophisticated system of surveillance makes sure that, without exception, any norm violation is detected and punished. While this could, on first sight, seem like the perfect situation of conformity with the norm achieved by deterrence, it is in fact a situation in which a legal norm necessarily erodes.

The reason is simple. A norm owes its authority to acts of recognition, by which normative power is vested in the norm's authority, preserving the norm. However, in a situation where abiding by the norm is practically the only way of avoiding a harsh sanction, obedient behaviour cannot be interpreted as an individual's autonomous vote cast in favour of the norm. Compliance can express a normative decision in support of the norm only under conditions where there exists, from a strategic perspective, a real alternative. As submitting to a threat does not involve a normative evaluation, behaviour that on first sight looks like abiding by the norm, on closer inspection is not. If I am threatened with a gun and forced to hand the money in my possession to a mugger, my conforming my behaviour to my mugger's demand does not lend itself to a moral interpretation: I am not demonstrating my support for her actions or for the maxims she follows. If people, for the only reason of avoiding painful consequences, comply with an order, they are obviously driven by extrinsic motives, but not by the moral appeal of the order. They are bowing to terror, not to the norm.

There is a second aspect to this argument, one that does not focus on acts, but on agents. A normative order is premised on individuals acting as autonomous and accountable agents, as well as on acts constituting human beings as such agents. By not appealing to a person's capability to make normative decisions, but to the fear of sanctions and to the merely strategic avoidance of harm, deterrence treats human beings not as free and autonomous agents, but as organisms avoiding pain and harm. Deterrence does not appeal to a person's sense of fairness or justice, but merely to her instinctive propensity to avoid hardship.

In brief, normativity is premised on freedom. Only in a situation where an individual's decisions are not motivated by threats, deception, want or another form of heteronomy can her decisions be interpreted as autonomous and as expressing her normative views and maxims, thereby contributing to her community's cooperation in creating and maintaining a normative order. Solely acts that represent an agent's intrinsic morality are moves in a normative language game. External incentives crowd out these intrinsic motives.

This argument can be extended to all security strategies, with the only exception of securing interests by acknowledging and promoting norms and by appealing to the morality of addressees. Whenever, to secure a good, a person is brought to act or prevented from acting in a certain manner by means other than moral persuasion, whenever, that is, an individual is not treated as a free, autonomous person, capable of understanding and appreciating moral reasons, the normative order is undermined, even if a good or interest is maintained.

Thus, total security of goods and interests may be equivalent to the end of norms and rights. If there is no chance to disregard a right, an action cannot be interpreted as acknowledging the norm granting the right. Rights depend on norms, and norms on autonomous decisions, which necessarily imply a risk that the agent decides against the norm. Normativity can only exist in spaces of freedom and agency. Hence the normative order is premised on a legal community's readiness to accept the risk of norm violations and to trust that normativity is worth bearing this risk. An attitude or culture of securitism, which treats persons as dangerous and aims to eliminate this danger, eventually undermines all normativity. On the other hand, by treating individuals as responsible and autonomous agents, a legal community expresses its identity as a polity founded on morality and freedom (Günther 2005, p. 88).

Hence the rationale of threatening punishment cannot be deterrence, and the rationale of punishment cannot be reinforcing the threat of punishment with a view to deter. What keeps the norm alive and strong is, firstly, individuals abiding by the norm because they morally support the norm, and, secondly, punishment as a reaction to the wrong suffered by victims, acknowledging the primary rights of the victims and the respect owed to the victims as persons and full members of the legal community. Criminal law provisions proclaiming that those who violate human rights will be prosecuted, convicted, and, at least in particular severe cases, also punished, are not intended as a deterrent, but, firstly, express—and appeal to—a community's moral convictions and, secondly, assure conditional cooperators that, in case of their victimisation, they will not stand alone, but can rely on their community's solidarity (Fletcher 1998, pp. 37–38). What the announcement of punishment promises is not that a norm will not be violated, but that in case of its violation the victim can count on the solidarity of her legal community and that the offender will not be allowed to get away with it with impunity (Lesch 1999).

Deterrence expresses an attitude that sits comfortably with an authoritarian nation state, but is incompatible with a criminal law paradigm based on human dignity and autonomy (Hassemer 2009, p. 107). In fact, there is still little to add to Hegel's brief and precise remarks in para. 99 of his Philosophy of Right (1820) on the matter:

> A threat presupposes that a man is not free, and its aim is to coerce him by the idea of an evil. But right and justice must have their seat in freedom and the will, not in the lack of freedom on which a threat turns. To base a justification of punishment on threat is to liken it to the act of a man who lifts his stick to a dog. It is to treat a man like a dog instead of with the freedom and respect due to him as a man. But a threat [...] discards justice altogether.

Rights are premised on freedom and autonomy, as only acts performed under conditions of freedom can be understood as a vote supporting the right and furnishing normative power. In the end, it is the normative decisions of free and autonomous persons that preserve the norm and the rights it grants, or undermines the norm and calls rights into question. This is what Lon Fuller referred to as the inner morality of law. Whatever conveys the message of indifference to the individual's powers of autonomous self-determination, departs 'from the principles of the law's inner morality' and therefore constitutes 'an affront to man's dignity as a responsible agent' (Fuller 1969, p. 162). The morality—or immorality—of the law is nothing but the morality—or immorality—of those addressees that abide by the law and thus furnish it with normative power. A norm's bindingness emanates from the support it enjoys amongst its addressees. When Napoleon, in 1802, reintroduced the Code Noir he could rely on the racism of the populace he addressed, and the same holds with regard to the Nuremberg Laws of 1935. These laws were effective because they did not speak to slaves or Jews, but executed their exclusion on the firm basis of the particularistic morality widespread among their addressees.

In principle, this also holds for the primary rights of the victim and for the victim as a person. The only thing that can restore the primary rights of the victim, violated by the offender, and the victim as a person, fully entitled to the respect of her rights, are acts of communication siding with and acknowledging the victim and her rights. This can only be achieved by censuring the offender's norm violating conduct and by, consequently, insisting that the offender settles her debts with the victim (or the victims), and ideally bringing the offender to accept her responsibility.

4.3.2 Calling on the Offender

In his seminal book on The Decent Society, Avishai Margalit searches for a human trait that can justify respecting people in general, and even those in particular who live a life of evil (1998, p. 74). Margalit puts forward the following proposal (1998, pp. 70–71):

> The trait I would like to suggest for justifying respect for humans is based on a capacity. The capacity is that of reevaluating one's life at any given moment, as well as the ability to change one's life from this moment on.
>
> What is involved here is the ability of human beings to repent of their sins, in the secular sense of this concept – that is, to abandon their evil ways. The claim is that humans have this ability. Even if there are noticeable differences among people in their ability to change, they are

> deserving of respect for the very possibility of changing. Even the worst criminals are worthy of basic human respect because of the possibility that they may radically reevaluate their past lives and, if they are given the opportunity, may live the rest of their lives in a worthy manner. [. . .] Thus respecting humans means never giving up on anyone, since all people are capable of living dramatically differently from the way they have lived so far.

To this Margalit adds, some pages later (1998, p. 75):

> Now what about the evildoer who lives a wicked life, and who is very likely to continue in this wretched existence? Likelihood must not be confused with presumption. Even though it is likely that she will continue living this way, this likelihood should not be turned into a presumption, because in principle an evildoer has the capacity to change and repent. This capacity implies that she deserves basic respect as a human being who should not be 'given up on', precisely because there is a chance, no matter how small, that she will repent.

This view is open to serious objections. Any attempt to found respect in a human capacity excludes those who do not avail of this capacity. Infants and dementia patients may not be in a position to decide that they want to radically change their way of living. Margalit explicitly states (1998, p. 117):

> Every human being has the radical possibility of starting life anew at any moment irrespective of his life's previous course. This freedom to shape one's life is, in another sense, the only nature humans have, in contrast to other animals and things. Humans have no character, but they do have a nature in this sense.

However, this is not correct. There is no sense in positing that a coma patient has the radical possibility of starting life anew, as that is, unfortunately, simply not the case. However, even more importantly, those who have this capacity do not owe it to their nature as humans, but to the—contingent—fact that they were called on as potentially autonomous and responsible agents by others and thus initiated into a normative order. Margalit's views suffer from the mistake common to all ethics inspired by Kant that they overestimate the moral qualities *inherent* in human beings. Human dignity is not the consequence of capacities inherent in humans, but the right to be constituted as a person and to be introduced to the community of humankind.

Nevertheless, Margalit points to a crucially important fact. The point is not that humans have the ability to radically change their lives any time. The point is that to sustain normativity and culture we must, under certain conditions, assume that humans have this potential, not as part of their nature, but because of their ability to, under normal circumstances, develop as autonomous and accountable persons who, by deciding on their conduct, define who they opt to be. The collective project of human culture can only carry on as long as we continue to presume that human beings have, if called on as autonomous and responsible agents, the potential to develop as such agents. This is a presumption we hold on to until we have reasons to assume in a particular case that an individual in her specific health conditions is not capable of such a response. A normative order can only be sustained under the assumption that, as a rule, an adult person is able to understand the demands made by criminal law and to adjust her behaviour accordingly. In any case, an individual is entitled to be treated as a person and accountable agent, unless particular circumstances indicate that such treatment would ask too much of the individual concerned.

Convicting a person is strictly premised on two—contingent—preconditions. Firstly, that the person is able to understand the normative claims made by criminal law on her behaviour. Secondly, that she was, at the time of her offending, able to not only understand, but also to abide by these claims. If we change our attitudes and practice and start treating offenders based on their dangerousness and of the likelihood that they will, due to their evil inclinations, fail to act in accordance with legal norms, we undermine or give up altogether the human project of normativity and culture on which our existence as humans is premised.

Therefore, a humanist society cannot but adhere to the hypothesis that treating individuals as persons is what constitutes a person and hence operates as a self-fulfilling prophecy. The opposite is also true; that treating someone as dangerous may well prevent that person from developing as an accountable moral agent. Hence, unless there are specific reasons to doubt her accountability, an adult offender is entitled to treatment as a person, as an autonomous and responsible agent, that is, who is capable of deciding any time to abide by the law and who as a moral person can be expected to act according to this ability.

4.3.3 Human Dignity, the Principle of Guilt and Limits of European Integration

It follows that the only legitimate rationale of punishment is that it respects human dignity in victims and offenders as persons. It respects the offender as an accountable person punished only because and to the extent that, in light of the decisions she made, she deserves to be punished, because she disregarded the victim as a person.

In fact, the German Constitutional Court has consistently held that the principle of guilt (*nulla poena sine culpa*, *Schuldgrundsatz*) is enshrined in human dignity (Müller-Dietz 1967; Stratenwerth 1977). In its *Lissabon* judgment of 2009, the Constitutional Court stressed that the concept of human dignity, founding the German Constitution, conceives of the human individual as a free moral person, capable of autonomously determining her behaviour and of choosing between right and wrong. It is this concept of accountability that defines punishment as reflecting the relation between guilt and atonement (the Court says "*Schuld und Sühne*"). Therefore, criminal law must be founded on the principle of guilt, which flows from human dignity, guaranteed by Article 1 of the Basic Law, and hence is not subject to the disposal of a state or a supranational organisation.

> Criminal law is based on the principle of guilt. This principle presupposes a human being's own responsibility, it presupposes human beings who themselves determine their actions and can decide in favour of right or wrong by virtue of their freedom of will. The protection of human dignity is based on the idea of Man as a spiritual and moral being which has the capabilities of defining himself, and of developing, in freedom (see BVerfGE 45, 187 < 227>). In the area of the administration of criminal law, Article 1.1 of the Basic Law determines the idea of the nature of punishment and the relationship between guilt and atonement (BVerfGE 95, 96 < 140>). The principle that any sanction

presupposes guilt thus has its foundation in the guarantee of human dignity under Article 1.1 of the Basic Law (see BVerfGE 57, 250 < 275>; [...]). The principle of guilt forms part of the constitutional identity which is unassailable due to Article 79.3 of the Basic Law and which is also protected against encroachment by supranational public authority.

The German Constitutional Court shares the understanding of punishment as atonement—or expiation—with the German Supreme Court. The latter observed, in a judgment of 1963, that the objective of atonement requires that the offender is allowed the possibility of an autonomous decision to accept her punishment as just (quoted by Schmidhäuser 1971, p. 28):

Der anerkannte Sühnezweck der Strafe beruht gerade darauf, dass der Bestrafte das Strafübel nicht nur gezwungenermaßen erträgt, sondern kraft freien, unerzwingbaren sittlichen Entschlusses als gerecht hinnimmt und seine Tat auf diese Weise sühnt.

More recently, in the case of *R. v. OLG Düsseldorf*, the German Constitutional Court in December 2015 confirmed that the principle of guilt is not only part of the foundation of criminal justice, but also a crucial element of human dignity. This is essential for understanding the limits of European integration brought about by a mechanism of states conferring powers on the Union as a supranational organisation. Because human dignity entails the principle of guilt and because any act delegating state powers to a supranational entity is to be understood as inherently restricted by the limits set by the concept of human dignity, the European Union *cannot possibly* be empowered to any other form of criminal justice but criminal justice founded on the principle of guilt.
The press release, issued by the Constitutional Court explains:

As a rule, sovereign acts of the European Union and acts of German public authority – to the extent that they are determined by Union law – are, due to the precedence of Union law (*Anwendungsvorrang des Unionsrechts*), not to be measured against the standard of the fundamental rights enshrined in the Basic Law. However, precedence only applies insofar as the Basic Law and the Act of Assent permit or provide for the transfer of sovereign rights. Its scope is limited by the Basic Law's constitutional identity that, according to Art. 23 sec. 1 sentence 3 in conjunction with Art. 79 sec. 3 GG, is neither open to constitutional amendments nor to European integration (*verfassungsänderungs- und integrationsfest*).

The Constitutional Court found that the Italian court's decision to extradite the complainant was in violation of his right to dignity under Article 1 of the German Constitution. Under the principle of guilt,

any criminal sanction presupposes that the offence and the offender's guilt are proven in a procedure that complies with the applicable procedural rules. The principle of individual guilt is rooted in the guarantee of human dignity enshrined in Art. 1 sec. 1 GG. It therefore also has to be guaranteed in the context of extraditions pursuant to the Framework Decision on the European arrest warrant if they are meant to ensure the execution of sentences that have been rendered in the absence of the requested person.

It appears that the Court adopts a broad reading of the principle of guilt, which is interpreted as not only determining the subject matter of criminal proceedings and the justification of punishment—as expiation of the offender's guilt—but also as covering procedural guarantees of due process. However, the Court argues that the complainant's rights under Article 1 section 1 Grundgesetz are at stake, because the execution of a sentence rendered in absence enforces, through criminal law, a reaction "that is incompatible with the guarantee of human dignity and the rule of law (*Rechtsstaatsprinzip*) unless the accused's individual blameworthiness (*individuelle Vorwerfbarkeit*) has been determined by the competent court." The Court explains:

> In Germany, criminal law is based on the principle of individual guilt, which is enshrined in the guarantee of human dignity and in the rule of law (Art. 20 sec. 3 GG) and which, due to Art. 79 sec. 3 GG, is part of the inalienable constitutional identity. The effectiveness of the principle of individual guilt is at risk if it is not ensured that the facts of the case are determined. To mete out an appropriate sanction that also constitutes a socio-ethical reproach (*sozial-ethischer Vorwurf*) presupposes that the personality of the accused is taken into account and, therefore, as a rule, that the accused is present at the trial.

It cannot be emphasised too much that, in the—well-argued—reading of the German Constitutional Court, within the legal order of the European Union any criminal law and criminal justice must respect Article 1 of the Fundamental Rights Charter and Article 2 of the Treaty on European Union and hence be founded on the principle of guilt implied in the concept of human dignity.

The German Constitutional Court warrants support in assuming that in light of the principle of guilt, a conviction by a criminal court reproaches the offender and that punishment can be viewed as a means of the offender expiating her guilt. However, when it comes to defining the wrong done by the offender, a wrong that weighs heavily enough to justify such normative language, the Court is remarkably vague and conservative. At one instance, the Court refers to punishment as "a reaction to socio-ethical misconduct" (*Reaktion auf ein sozial-ethisches Fehlverhalten*), a concept that evokes the image of a state disciplining a misbehaving subject and in any case can hardly serve to define the threshold beyond which conduct is deserving of punishment.

This being said, it should be recalled that recent case-law of the German Constitutional Court was referenced in Chap. 1, which, in line with rulings of the ECtHR in Strasbourg, acknowledges the rights of victims of violent crime and of comparable offences to effective investigation aimed at holding offenders to account. The Constitutional Court, so far, has not interrelated these two strands of case-law, by assuming that an offender has to accept being reproached and having to make amends for her guilt *only* in cases of severe human rights violations, nor argued why such a restriction would apply. In fact, this would require that the Constitutional Court accepts the shift of paradigm from sociocentric ethics to criminal law based entirely on human dignity and an individualist ethical framework and, on this basis, would recognise that the offender's obligation to expiate her guilt is only the flip side of the victim's right to justice.

Still, it should be acknowledged that the German Constitutional Court, by highlighting the fundamental importance of the principle of guilt and by recognising rights of victims to the prosecution, conviction and punishment of offenders, who violated the victims' personal interests (*höchstpersönliche Rechtsgüter*), provided the main building blocks of a new criminal justice paradigm. In addition, these two strands of case-law are inherently related to one another by the fact that they both take recourse to human dignity as stipulated by Article 1 section 1 of the Grundgesetz, thereby conferring on these principles and requirements the specific status of immutability.

4.4 The Offender's Right to be Held to Account

Chapter 3 analysed human dignity as a normative concept highlighting the right of every human being to be welcomed into the human family as a person within a normative order. Next to entitlements to care and respect, the concept of a person entails the element of being called on as an accountable agent, where accountability develops in accordance with an individual's mental and moral capacities. It is families, kindergartens and schools that support individuals in developing as accountable agents. However, a societal structure relying on its normative order is premised on the assumption that, under normal conditions, an adult person is able to live up to the normative standards defined by criminal law. Hence, the respect to which an adult person is entitled comprises the right to be treated as an accountable agent able to meet the demands on her behaviour made by her legal community's criminal code. Therefore, if an individual has committed a crime, she is entitled to answer for her behaviour and therefore to be prosecuted, convicted and, under certain conditions, punished.

In short, the individual has a right to be called on and to be respected as an autonomous person, as well as to be held to account for her agency based on a humanist society's normative order. As the offender, because of her dignity, is entitled to such constitution, she has, in case she has committed a crime, a right to be prosecuted, convicted and punished, as well as to, by contributing her fair due to the normative order and the victims' rights, be restored as a respected member of her society. This section will explore this claim through a historical perspective.

Within the—small—group of authors advocating a right of the offender to her conviction and punishment, two lines of argument can be distinguished. The first maintains that the offender, when committing the offence, knew that she would be punished and hence chose to be punished, and that this choice should be respected. This line of argument was developed by Hegel and later supported by others, including prominently Herbert Morris (but see also Gardner 1980, 1989). The second line of reasoning—represented by Fichte and Max Scheler—argues that the offender must accept the societal terms and conditions on which her own dignity and rights are premised as a means of protecting these rights.

4.4.1 Choosing Punishment?

Hegel shared Fichte's understanding that individuals cannot achieve moral personality on their own and independently of others, but only by education and admittance to a society, if, in Hegel's terms, the child is 'fed on the breast of common morality' ('*an der Brust der allgemeinen Sittlichkeit getränkt*', 1802, p. 507).

Hegel (1820, pp. 91–92) derives a right of the offender to be punished from his notion of freedom as reason. The hardship inflicted on the offender reflects her own decision; it is an expression of her freedom and therefore her right (pn Hegel's theory of punishment Seelmann 2011). As Hegel observes, the alternative to punishing the offender in proportion to her action is to treat her as a wild animal. Hence, by being punished, the criminal is respected as an autonomous agent.

> The criminal is honoured as reasonable, because the punishment is regarded as containing his own right. The honour would not be shared by him, if the conception and measure of his punishment were not deduced from his very act. Just as little is he honoured when he is regarded as a hurtful animal, which must be made harmless, or as one who must be [deterred] or reformed. (Translation corrected by A.D.; the German text says "*oder in den Zwecken der Abschreckung und Besserung*".)

Herbert Morris in his seminal article on "Persons and Punishment", first published in 1968, relies on a concept of the person that is very similar to Hegel's ideas. In the introduction to his essay (1968, p. 32), Morris makes an allusion to a tradition of philosophers who "expressed themselves in terms of the criminal's *right to be punished.*" He later (1968, p. 49) remarks that his views are "reminiscent of an era of philosophical thinking about rights that many consider to have been seriously confused", whereby Morris apparently refers to German Idealism. In fact, Morris' central assumption (1968, p. 48) that in the traditional system of criminal justice "a person chooses the punishment that is meted out to him" and that importantly "what happens to a person is conditioned by that person's choice and not that of others", is fairly identical with Hegel's perspective on the matter.

At the outset, Morris (1968, p. 32) states his intention to demonstrate

> first, that we have a right to punishment; second, that this right derives from a fundamental human right to be treated as a person; third, that this fundamental right is a natural, inalienable, and absolute right; and, fourth, that the denial of this right implies the denial of all moral rights and duties.

What Morris describes as a fundamental, inalienable and absolute right to be treated as a person, on which all other rights are premised, is here referred to as human dignity. In fact, much of Morris' essay reads as an analysis of the notion of human dignity in relation to punishment; and yet Morris not once uses this notion, for reasons that are not clear.

To achieve his objectives, Morris contrasts the traditional system of criminal justice with a therapeutic institution (again very similar to Hegel's juxtaposing punishment with humans being conditioned by reform and deterrence). Large parts of Morris' analysis can be read as refuting opinions—quoted in a footnote—that concur in claiming that the institutions of conventional criminal justice should be replaced by a system of medical treatment and that such a system would be more humane. Morris undertakes to show that these assumptions are mistaken. Such systems are ready to give up holding offenders to account, which amounts to abandoning the concept of autonomous and accountable agency, on which personhood is premised. By eliminating the concept of agency, the difference between considered actions and mere events is erased. One human being killing another would have to be "looked upon as a happening with a causal explanation rather than an action for which there were reasons" (1968, p. 37).

However, a criminal justice system that renounces treating offenders as persons is bound to end up in conditions far from humane. Morris' analysis is powerful in describing the consequences of a therapy system, in which an individual's harmful conduct is treated "as a symptom of some pathological condition in the way a running nose is a symptom of a cold" and actions "diverging from some conception of the normal are viewed as manifestations of a disease" (1968, p. 36). Among such consequences available in a therapy system, a principle of proportionality makes no sense as Morris points out that "It is perfectly plausible giving someone who kills a pill and treating for a lifetime within an institution one who has broken a dish and manifested accident proneness" (1968, p. 39). Also, "protests with respect to treatment are likely to be assimilated to the complaints of one whose leg must be amputated in order for him to live, and thus, largely disregarded" (1968, p. 39).

Thus, Morris emphasizes the difference between the unpredictability of a therapy system and the predictability of punishment. Morris highlights "the inestimable value to each of us of having the responses of others to us determined over a wide range of our lives by what we choose rather than what they choose" (1968, p. 41).

Hence, in Morris' perspective, an offender holds a right to foresee her punishment and to be punished in accordance with her legitimate expectations. The measure of the criminal justice system' quality is the reliability of its criminal code as a prediction of punishment. The criminal code not only threatens punishment; its deeds measure up to its words. Individuals can trust that they will be punished in accordance with the criminal code and are safe from being punished as long as they abide by the law.

However, that the criminal code threatens punishment does not amount to a justification. Punishing the offender is not legitimate merely because it was threatened. Rather, it must only be threatened when it is legitimate. Justice and predictability are two different qualities. It is easy to imagine an unjust system of criminal justice operating in a perfectly steady and foreseeable manner. There cannot be a right of the offender to punishment, unless the latter is legitimate. Hence, the demonstration of a right of the offender to her punishment is premised on evidence that the punishment to which the offender is entitled is also justified.

Hegel believes he can overcome this difficulty by assuming that the offender, by her offence, not only chooses to be punished but also chooses the severity of her punishment. She chooses to be punished as she treated the victim. However, this move renders a general weakness of this position even more obvious, namely that it answers a normative question—what legitimates the punishment of the offender—by offering an empirical fact, namely the choice—allegedly—made by the offender. This leads to two objections, which are both able to refute this approach. Firstly, assuming that the offender's choice to be punished would justify her punishment violates Hume's law, meaning, it sells an 'is' for an 'ought'. It is by no means obvious why the empirical fact of an offender's choice would legitimise her punishment. Secondly, premising the legitimacy of punishment on the fact of the offender's choice raises the question: And if not? What if the offender, demonstrably, simply relied that her offence would never be detected and in fact thoroughly dislikes the idea of being punished; what then would justify her punishment?

4.4.2 Fichte's "Expiation Contract" and a Citizen's Right to be Punished

Fichte's theory of punishment has the advantage of departing from an understanding of punishment as an indispensable means of preserving the normative order on which the constitution of norms and persons is premised. Fichte deals with criminal justice in the context of "public security". However, "security" in Fichtean ethics does not advocate a state protecting subjects against various kinds of harms and perils defined as such by the state, but solely means the necessity of preserving the authority of individuals' rights within a societal structure that endorses the rule of law administered by independent courts. The issue is how to enable an individual to "count on the security of his rights in the other's presence" (1796, p. 123), how, in other words, she can trust others to respect her rights.

Fichte departs from the assumption that, if a normative order is premised on a general confidence that others are willing and able to abide by the norms on which the legal community is founded, the plausible reaction to a norm violation is ostracism, the exclusion, that is, of an offender from the community. An individual can be included in a legal community only if she "is fit to live in a community of rational beings" (1796, p. 226). If an individual displays a lack of sense of justice and persistently demonstrates that she cannot be relied on as cooperating in the preservation of her community's normative order, she must be excluded.

However, a normative order can be defended by means that are less costly and drastic than ostracism, while still achieving the objective of stabilising the normative system. To reach that goal, the members of a community can be imagined to have negotiated an addendum to their social contract to renounce ostracism and to replace it by less severe and nevertheless effective means of preserving the general confidence in the authority of their rights. As was usual at the time when Fichte wrote his *Foundations*, this societal consensus is expressed in terms of a public contract (1796, pp. 227–228).

> This can be arranged only through a contract of all with all, which would subsequently become the norm for the executive power. The content of this contract would be as follows: All promise to all others not to exclude them from the state for their offenses (provided that this is consistent with public security), but rather to allow them to expiate their offenses by some other means. We shall refer to this contract as the *expiation contract* [*Abbüßungsvertrag*].
>
> This contract is useful for all (for the state as a whole) as well as for each individual citizen. Under it, the whole obtains both the prospect of preserving citizens whose usefulness outweighs their harmfulness, as well as the *obligation* to accept their expiation; the individual citizen obtains the *perfect right* to demand that some expiation be accepted in place of the more severe punishment that he deserves. The citizen has a right – a very useful and important right – [to be punished] (Translation corrected by A.D.; the German terms are "*abgestraft zu werden*").

Fichte's expiation contract enables the normative order to integrate the case of its violation. By creating, so to say, a Plan B, the normative order anticipates its violation and adopts a mechanism to deal with such cases. By this amendment, the normative order raises its complexity to expect the, in principle, unexpected. The offender is integrated as a figure forecasted and hence controllable.

Instead of, by her offence, placing herself outside of the normative order, the offender now remains within what is envisaged as exceptional and can be handled by the normative order. However, the offender's continued membership of the legal community is premised on her passing through the particular procedure foreseen in cases of significant norm violations, put in place to prevent the norm violation from severely and lastingly damaging the normative order. Without an expiation contract, the offender had turned into an outcast or even enemy of the legal community. With the expiation contract, the offender remains a member of the community, although temporarily in the particular, precarious, and transitional status of a blameworthy debtor who still has to contribute her fair due to the preservation of the order on which her existence as a person is premised; yet remains a member nevertheless.

Hence, Fichte interprets a criminal code as defining the terms and conditions by which offenders are entitled to expiate their guilt and on this basis to come to terms with their legal community and, all the time, to remain its members. In a humanist society, founded on the political ideal of human dignity, the offender, like any other subject, possesses the unconditional right to be a person, to be, that is, called on and treated as a respected and accountable member of the societal formation in which she is constituted and can develop as a person. However, by disregarding the victim as a person, the offender potentially unsettled the victim's and all others' confidence in the authority and reliability of their rights against the offender, as well as in the offender's trustworthiness as cooperating in the constant creation of a normative order generating and protecting their rights. By paying her debt, the offender has the right to settle her debts and come to terms with the victim and with her legal community; and thereafter no one should hold a grudge against her any longer or censure her again for committing the offence. The offender can expect that, once the issue has been dealt with, the subject matter is closed, so that peace is restored—the normative order is preserved—and all can move on.

In other words, the offender has a right to make amends for the wrong done to the victim and, on this basis, to be acknowledged and remembered not as the person who wronged, but as the person who, by making amends, righted the wrong done to the victim. Thus the offender remains a member of her legal community. With Fichte, the focus of punishing is no longer on ostracising offenders, but on the question of how a community manages to restore its normative fabric and to rehabilitate and reintegrate offenders. Punishment 'addresses offenders, not as outlaws who have forfeited their standing as citizens, but as full members of the normative political community; it is inclusionary rather than exclusionary' (Duff 2001, pp. 129–130).

The attitude of solidarity of all members of humankind is a clear thread running through Fichtean philosophy. An individual's right to be treated unconditionally as a full member of her normative community is at the very heart of a Fichtean concept of dignity. As has been extensively discussed in the previous chapter, the concept of human dignity denotes that a human being, because she carries a human face, has a right to be constituted—under the terms and conditions of a humanist societal configuration and in a spirit of compassion and solidarity—as a significant, accountable and autonomous person. In this sense, holding an offender liable for her actions reaffirms her "status as an autonomous and responsible actor", meaning that the offender "is recognised as capable of independently making choices and being held accountable for the actions that result from those choices" (FRA 2012, p. 21).

4.4.3 *Max Scheler: Punishment as Atonement and Reconciliation*

Along with Neo-Kantians in Marburg and Heidelberg, Max Scheler is to be credited with preserving and updating German Enlightenment philosophy in the ethical discourses of the early twentieth century (on Scheler see Srubar 2010). In his seminal book on Formalism in Ethics (the original title is "*Der Formalismus in der Ethik und die materiale Wertethik*") Scheler develops a theory of punishment that emphasises its function as atonement and its significance in restoring the victim and the offender within their social and moral community; "punishment is the form through which the *possibility of a moral relationship between the harmed person and the evildoer is restored*" (1921, p. 365). By highlighting the significant functions of punishment in restoring the victim as a person, Scheler reaches beyond Fichte.

Firstly, and with regard to the victim, the value of "reprisal for a misdeed" consists in the "purification of the soul" of the victim "by affording him the feeling of satisfying a demand for atonement, a feeling of 'satisfaction', and therefore by recreating the basis of truly moral relations" with others, including the offender (1921, p. 364). Secondly, from the offender's perspective punishment is atonement in the sense that the offender makes amends for the wrong done to the victim. Punishment does not rely on repentance, as repentance is premised on voluntariness, but punishment as atonement gives the offender "an *opportunity* to offset his evil morally by an act of repentance" (1921, p. 365). Thus, punishment acknowledges and respects the offender as an accountable person. It renews the basis for social and moral relations between the offender, the victim, and all who side and sympathise with the victim. Scheler postulates (1921, p. 366):

> For the evil-doer or the one who is guilty of any kind of grave crime possesses the *moral right,* insofar as he is mature and of sound mind, to demand *recognition* of his person and his dignity as a moral being. Irrespective of what the positive law may be in any individual case, he also possesses, on the basis of *this* right, a moral right to demand *factual* and *true* punishment [. . .]. Above all, he possesses a right to the power of punishment *as* punishment that can purify him, and a right to its inherent power to restore his relations with the harmed person and with all who participate, through postfeeling and fellow feeling, in his harm and his negative moral tenor with respect to the evil-doer.

Scheler fights a war on two fronts, against the legal positivists—including Binding, Birkmeyer, and Beling—on the one side and, more fiercely, against social positivism on the other, spearheaded by Franz von Liszt and the *défense sociale*.

Scheler insists that an offender's right to punishment shields him from "moral injustice on the part of all who would make him the exclusive object of their protective disciplinary measures" and "an immature object of questionable socio-political experiments" (1921, p. 366). Faithful to Kant's principle, Scheler comments in a footnote:

> Much as the modern positivistic theory of protective punishment with its praxis would like to appear 'humane', 'human', 'social' etc., it rests in fact on a deep and immoral disregard of 'man' as the *person* in man; it degrades the person to the level of a mere means for purposes completely and exclusively outside the person.

The criminal justice system cannot rely on the offender's willingness to repent and to accept her responsibility. It must be prepared to deal with both remorseful and intransigent offenders. However, it is at this point important to stress that these two alternatives are not on a par. A normative order geared to foster the development of autonomous and accountable persons must be ready to make considerable efforts to encourage the offender to take responsibility for the wrong done to the victim and to make the offender a fair and reasonable offer in terms of swift and unbureaucratic proceedings as well as foreseeable and bearable sanctions. Nevertheless, convicting and punishing the offender is ultimately not premised on her cooperation. Under all circumstances, the offender is to be treated as an accountable agent. What justifies punishment is not the offender's repentance or penance, nor our hope that she will come to repent her crime, but solely her right to be treated as a person, her right to a treatment, that is, that respects both her autonomy and her accountability. The right to be constituted as a person is not premised on an individual's wish to be constituted as a person. In fact, the initial and most foundational calling on a child is necessarily an imposition.

In terms of the categories introduced above, the right to be convicted and punished is a formation right. It springs from an individual's right to be treated as belonging to and to be included in the family of humankind. The right to be—in line with one's capabilities—held to account, convicted, and punished according to the normative order of a decent society is an essential part of what it means to be a person. A person does not exist independently of the processes of communication in which she is respected. Within a societal landscape, a person is the address common to all meaningful acts that reference her as having rights or obligations. If others stop attributing rights and obligations to this address, the person ceases to exist, leaving behind only the bare body.

Hence, the offender is entitled to be held to account and to make amends for her criminal behaviour because no other treatment is compatible with her right to be continuously called on and thereby initiated and integrated in culture and society as an accountable agent under the laws of her society. It would be disrespectful to ignore her behaviour or to treat her as dangerous and thereby to deny her the most fundamental right—to be respected and treated as a person.

By being convicted and, in appropriate cases, even punished, the offender regains the right to be acknowledged as a full member of her society. In several cases, the ECtHR has emphasised 'the rehabilitation function of incarceration' and held that it would be incompatible with human dignity if life prisoners were not given 'a real opportunity to rehabilitate themselves'. A life prisoner is entitled to know what she must do to be considered for release (*Harakchiev and Tolumov*, para. 246; *Murray*, para. 103; *Vinter et al.*, para. 122). In other words, every offender must be given a real chance to come to terms with her society and to overcome the status of an offender.

4.4.4 A Right to Hardship?

The argument that human dignity implies an appreciation of accountable agency and that the only way of treating an offender as an accountable person consists in charging, convicting and prosecuting her seems rather straightforward. Hence, one is led to wonder why the offender's right to be held to account is not a common view; and the plausible reason is that many people assume that such a right would be premised on offenders *desiring* to be punished (Sadurski 2010, p. 245).

The right to life corresponds to a general appreciation of one's life, hence one could be led to take for granted that the right to life presupposes the desire to live. However, it does not, as a person who, weary of life, attempts to commit suicide does not thereby forfeit her right to life. The same applies to other rights. The fact that in recent elections to the European Parliament a majority (of some 57 %) of voters preferred not to participate leaves their fundamental right to vote untouched.

While the assumption that human rights are about joy or happiness is widespread, it is nevertheless a misconception and a result of unfortunate consequentialist and utilitarian ethics. Still, when it comes to human dignity, a hedonistic approach seems particularly far-fetched, even if one leaves philosophical doctrine aside. In ordinary language, too, what a dignified life earns is respect—including self-respect—rather than joy and happiness. Certainly, in philosophy, human dignity was from the beginning about the particular freedom of humans to decide for themselves who they opt to be, about autonomy, self-determination and self-definition, about the person rising above and gaining freedom from nature, instincts, needs and drives, as well as freedom from traditional beliefs. The concept of human dignity as developed by Pico, Kant, Fichte and others is about humans' struggle to establish ownership of their biography—as individuals and as members of polities—and to render their lives worthwhile and meaningful.

In addition, maybe those who are convinced that rights are about needs and benefits, should pause for a moment to consider whether being punished, in the long run, is not beneficial to some offenders. After all, it is the offender who has to live and cope with what she has done for the rest of her life. She has to come to terms with the people living in her social environment. In addition, the right to be punished can perhaps be looked at in terms of the 'moral injury' that the offender suffers from her offence.

The concept of 'moral injury' has been explained as resulting from an individual "perpetrating acts that transgress deeply held moral beliefs and expectations" (Steenkamp et al. 2011, p. 100). Examples of potentially morally injurious experiences include "killing or seriously injuring others" and "participating in or witnessing cruel and inhumane actions". "Such experiences may be intrusively re-experienced and lead to shame and social disengagement, as well as self-handicapping, self-harm, and demoralization."

However, as far as can be seen, to date 'moral injury' has been researched only in relation to participants in combat and war veterans (Brock and Lettini 2013; Dombo et al. 2013; Drescher et al. 2011; Frame 2016; Litz et al. 2009, 2015; Maguen and Litz 2012; Nash and Litz 2013; Shay 2014), not as regards criminal offenders. The research on the moral injury suffered by military staff deployed to Vietnam, Iraq or Afghanistan has grown rapidly. This research sheds light on how having committed or contributed to atrocities affects service members, "confronted with numerous moral and ethical challenges" (Litz et al. 2009, p. 696).

It is likely that many perpetrators of severe offences also suffer moral injury, as their offence will in many instances conflict with their own moral beliefs and self-image and hence cause feelings of guilt and shame. Not only the victim, but the offender too has to come to terms with what she has done. Her offence has the potential to call into question her self-respect and feeling of worthiness. The offender has to find an answer to the question of how she can experience her life as worthwhile if it is a life she is not proud of, the life of a person it is difficult to esteem. Arguably, criminal justice offers to her the chance of distancing herself from her offence and of demonstrating to herself and to others that the offence is not typical of her, or at least not typical of the new person she chooses to be and commences to be by taking responsibility and making amends.

In any case, rights are not a matter of needs but of our understanding of what it means to live an autonomous and meaningful life within a community of persons who owe their personhood to the normative order that they jointly establish and preserve. It follows from human dignity that every individual has the inalienable right to be treated as an accountable and autonomous agent, including in a situation where the individual has committed a crime and may or may not prefer to be held to account.

It was explained above that, as a specificity, formation rights correspond to obligations. As part of an individual's duty to contribute her fair due to the preservation of her community's normative order, an individual is, in principle, obliged to engage in her own formation as a person, as the rights of others are premised on the endeavour of all to develop accountable agency. Hence the offender is not only entitled to be treated as a person, but also, in principle, morally obliged to strive to live up to the status of an accountable agent who can be trusted to contribute her share to the normative order's reproduction. In other words, an individual is not free to choose to live in the midst of her community while not taking any responsibility. Hence, in addition to the right to be held to account, the offender also faces a moral obligation to accept responsibility for the crime committed. From the perspective of others, this means that a legal community is not only entitled and obliged to prosecute, convict and punish the offender, but also entitled to expect that the offender makes an effort to engage in normative communication and to acknowledge and answer for the wrong done to her victim.

4.4.5 *Expiation and the Nation State*

As has been shown above, the German Constitutional Court emphasises the principle of guilt and, on this basis, conceptualises punishment as expiation of guilt (*Sühne*). In addition, the mechanism of individual guilt and atonement has its foundation in human dignity. This inevitably suggests the question of how, if punishment as atonement flows from the dignity of the offender, the latter cannot be entitled to such treatment. Does the offender not have a right to be treated based on her participation in human dignity? If so, does she not have a right to answer for her deeds and to expiate her guilt?

In searching for an explanation of the striking reluctance of German legal theory to consider such questions, Eberhard Schmidhäuser's theory of punishment suggests itself, because Schmidhäuser, more than other German legal scholars, conceptualised punishment as expiation. In his treaty on the meaning of punishment (*Vom Sinn der Strafe*), Schmidhäuser interprets criminal justice as offering the offender the opportunity to admit her deed, to accept, in accordance with her community, censure of her behaviour and to take on the burden of her punishment, thereby restoring the order disturbed by her offence (1971, p. 105). Understood in this sense, punishment, according to Schmidhäuser, can have a deep and positive meaning for the offender, who takes responsibility for her community and at the same time restores a moral relationship to the victim (1971, p. 106). Because the offender shoulders her punishment, all can and should be reconciled with her (1971, pp. 106, 117).

From these assumptions, it would be but a little step to developing a theory of punishment interrelating the offender, the victim and all others. Hence, it would appear that Schmidhäuser's premises lend themselves to the construction of a theory of punishment based on the rights of the offender and the victim to be treated with respect. However, the reason why Schmidhäuser's approach cannot develop this potential lies in the fact that his theory is, at the same time, deeply entangled in sociocentric ethics. In his approach, the concept of the community (*Gemeinwesen*) plays a pivotal role. Schmidhäuser justifies punishment by positing that the welfare of the community, as the basis of all culture, is bought with hardship imposed on some (1971, p. 93). The happiness of the individual is sacrificed to the happiness of the entire community (1971, p. 94):

> Hier jedenfalls folgen wir der Glückseligkeitslehre, zwar nicht, dass wir individuell eigenes Glück erstreben, aber eben doch das Glück der Gemeinschaft, dem wir das Glück des Einzelnen opfern. Es ist die schmerzliche Einsicht, dass das Strafen – wie überhaupt alle staatlich Rechtsordnung, die sich faktisch letzten Endes immer auf die Macht zur Strafe stützt – nichts als eine Notmaßnahme ist, nichts als ein Ausdruck unserer menschlichen Unzulänglichkeit, Reflex unserer Egoismen, die die Gewalt notwendig machen, wenn das Ganze gedeihen soll.

Hence, Schmidhäuser's theory regresses to a traditional, utilitarian theory of punishment serving general deterrence. Schmidhäuser sees this weakness and the contradiction to Kant's principle (1971, p. 96). Later, Schmidhäuser expressly rejects Kant's claim and insists that the offender is indeed used as a means to an ends for others, which—according to Schmidhäuser—is justified as long as punishment is restricted to what is indispensable for the sake of general deterrence (1985, p. 20). Apparently, Schmidhäuser is not ready to sacrifice his belief in a higher collective being, which we all serve and in which we are all contained. This belief protects the nation state's right to banish offenders.

In contemporary legal theory, the view that justifying punishment relies on a theory of punishment as atonement or expiation is rare. Jescheck and Weigend, on first sight, quite precisely follow the footsteps of Fichte and Scheler. They put forward that, although repentance is premised on the offender's voluntary decision and cannot be enforced, nevertheless the state must punish to enable the offender to accept her punishment and thus to regain her moral freedom; and in addition, society must be ready to be reconciled with the offender, once she has served her term (1996, pp. 64–67). However, in their theorising this aspect is not in the forefront. Primarily, what, in the view of Jescheck and Weigend, justifies punishment is its indispensability to the preservation of the legal order. Punishment serves the interests of the state ("*staatspolitische Rechtfertigung der Strafe*"). In punishing the legal order proves its authority (1996, pp. 64–65). The law is the law. However, if this is what justifies punishment, recourse to the personhood and rights of the offender is redundant. On the other hand, if one accepts an offender's right to her conviction and punishment, this renders the entire construct of a nation state's entitlement to the punishment of the offender void. In short, a right of the offender to her punishment does not fit in the nation state paradigm, as is the case with the victim's right to the conviction and punishment of the offender.

Therefore, the task remains to construct a system of criminal justice based on a clear concept of human dignity, and hence it is indispensable to take Kant seriously, but also crucially important to understand why and where Kant's principle fails.

4.4.6 The Justification of Punishment

We punish the offender for two coinciding reasons. Firstly, because we owe it to the victim as a person, rights-holder and member of our legal community to confront the offender with the wrong she has done and with her responsibility; secondly, because we owe it to the offender to confront her with her responsibility as a person and to engage in a conversation with her that is based on the assumption that she owes it—and that we expect her to understand that she owes it—to the victim and to her legal community to take responsibility for the wrong done to the victim and to bear the consequences of her wrongdoing. We address the offender, not merely to inform her that she will be punished, but with a view to reaching a consensus with her about what she has done, what it means to the victim and what, consequently, she owes to the victim. In fact, what the offender owes to the victim is primarily—in the cultural domain—recognition as a person and rights-holder and only secondarily—in the material world—her fair contribution to preventing that her example of disregarding the victim's primary rights attracts followers, including among those who are willing to cooperate in maintaining a normative order only as long as shirkers are not allowed to ride free on the investments of others. Von Hirsch claims that it is entirely up to the offender whether she reacts to her conviction and punishment with feelings of guilt or shame (2011, p. 51). However, this overlooks that the offender is obliged to engage in her constitution as an accountable person. Convicting and punishing the offender aims to bring the offender to her moral senses and to make her realize the wrong done to the victim. The purpose of triggering in the offender feelings of guilt and remorse is pursued to the extent that such feelings are appropriate in light of her wrongful action.

What, therefore, can justify punishment is the right of the offender to be treated as a person and to be attributed full responsibility for her offence. Criminal justice renews the call on the offender as an accountable agent, thereby expressing society's respect of the offender as a person who can understand that what she did was wrong and is expected to act accordingly. In the words of Sanford Kadish (1987, p. 77):

> Much of our commitment to democratic values, to human dignity and self-determination, to the value of the individual, turns on the pivot of a view of man as a responsible agent entitled to be praised or blamed depending on his free choice of conduct.

However, an offender's right to be convicted and punished is premised on two conditions, one concerning a conviction's criminal law basis, the other regarding the concrete wrong suffered by the victim. Firstly, an offender's legal community must have sufficient reason to censure her behaviour and a normative justification for doing so. This raises the question—for which the name 'Kant's principle' above was coined—as to the normative basis of censuring an autonomous agent and to the moral foundation of the law on which her conviction and punishment rely. The question goes to the limits of legitimacy of substantive criminal law. The answer will be that the offender must have violated a norm upon which her own personhood and autonomy are predicated.

Secondly, the offender's responsibility is premised on a concrete wrong, for which she must answer. Thus, the conviction and punishment of the offender refer to the wrong suffered by the victim and the violation of her rights. The offender's right to be punished is intrinsically linked to a complementary right of the victim to the conviction—or even punishment—of the offender. Neither can stand alone. The offender is required to contribute not more and not less than her fair due to the preservation of the rights and status of the victim as a person. Hence, what in the end is the decisive measure of the offender's responsibility is the victim's right to justice.

4.5 Defining the Limits of Criminal Law

4.5.1 Kant Does Not Hold the Answer

Recently, Albrecht (2011a, b), Naucke (2015) and Sander (2007) made separate attempts to found a limitative theory of criminal law and criminal justice on Kantian concepts of human dignity, freedom and autonomy. While their liberal intention to draw on Enlightenment philosophy as a means of protesting the excessive use of criminal law and criminal justice for preventive and security purposes merits support, it must be doubted that Kantian ethics offers an apt basis for their endeavours. The reason is that in Kantian philosophy, individual autonomy is inherent in humans and not premised on societal conditions. This endows individual autonomy with an aura of the absolute, unconditional and unlimited. It does not help in a situation where agents have different views of what their autonomy should cover, which is the typical situation of a pluralist society. If a person believes that she has a right to smoke in restaurants, to censure homosexuals, or to the corporal punishment of her children, there is, from a Kantian perspective, little to object to these views. This is so long as she is willing to accept that everyone else should have the same rights, which, so it can be assumed, she gladly will do.

Hence, an individual's possibility to invoke her status as an autonomous individual and the authority of her conscience to reject obligations resulting from criminal law does not, in Kantian ethics, encounter inherent limits. If a person with a patriarchal mind-set is convinced that it is, as the head of the family, his duty to maintain order by enforcing his rule, this would have to be accepted as long as his abusive, threatening and degrading conduct corresponds to his convictions and his inclination to perceive of the rest of the world through the same lenses. If a devout Catholic physically prevents women from entering an abortion clinic, it is not obvious that Kantian ethics provides a basis for censuring her behaviour; and the same holds for a religious Muslim aggressing a woman for having committed adultery or apostasy. Not only may these individuals act in accordance with their conscience, they would strongly welcome it if the maxims that they adopt for themselves would be respected by everyone. Neither a Kantian concept of individual autonomy, nor a categorical imperative offers a basis for criticising their behaviour.

With Fichte, the angle shifts profoundly. For him, the normative order's primary task is not the protection, but the creation of freedom and individual autonomy. The Fichtean insight that an individual's status as a person is owed to her being called on by her parents and others initiating and including her in a societal structure points to very significant prerequisites and inherent limitations of an individual's autonomy and, consequently, of moral relativism. Hence, what changes with Fichte is the fact that we now are able to identify certain norms that are, under all conditions, indispensable elements of any normative order; and these are the norms that make normativity possible by banning violence and heteronomy and by thus creating a space of autonomous interaction, in which alone normative communication becomes possible, on which the existence of the normative order is premised. In this way, a Fichtean perspective legitimises a generally binding ban on violence and on other forms of imposing one's will on others, and this perspective makes it then also possible to determine the limits of legitimate criminalisation.

4.5.2 Criminal Law and Punishment Limited to Preserving Dignity Rights

In September 1995, governments met in Beijing at the United Nations' Fourth World Conference on Women. They adopted the Beijing Declaration and Platform for Action. The latter details a long list of measures, defining what UN Member States are required to do to pay due attention to the rights of women conceived as human rights.

One of these strategic objectives (D.1.) obliges governments to adopt integrated measures to prevent and eliminate violence against women. This paragraph—paragraph 124 of the Platform of Action—commences by providing that governments should:

a. Condemn violence against women and refrain from invoking any custom, tradition or religious consideration to avoid their obligations with respect to its elimination as set out in the Declaration on the Elimination of Violence against Women;
b. Refrain from engaging in violence against women and exercise due diligence to prevent, investigate and, in accordance with national legislation, punish acts of violence against women, whether those acts are perpetrated by the State or by private persons;
c. Enact and/or reinforce penal, civil, labour and administrative sanctions in domestic legislation to punish and redress the wrongs done to women and girls who are subjected to any form of violence, whether in the home, the workplace, the community or society; [...]

This text is interesting for more than one reason. Firstly, it emphasises the obligation of Member States to protect the human rights of women by enacting and enforcing criminal law provisions to "punish and redress the wrongs done to women and girls" subjected to any form of violence. This reflects the shift of paradigm from criminal law as a matter of sovereign nation states enforcing their laws and protecting whatever interests they consider worth protecting, to states obliged to enact and enforce criminal law provisions as an indispensable means of human rights protection.

Secondly, it establishes a certain priority rule, giving precedence to states' obligation to protect women against violence, as states may not rely on traditions, local customs or religious considerations to justify refraining from such protection. Their obligation to protect against violence comes first, above any reference to other normative dimensions of their societies. Hence, an individual's rights to—based on her autonomy—express her opinion or practice her traditions and religion, such as through blocking entry to an abortion clinic, reaches a limit set by the unconditional ban on violence.

In this respect, the Beijing Platform of Action had a predecessor in the Declaration on the Elimination of Violence against Women adopted by the UN General Assembly in December 1993. This Declaration provides in Article 4:

> States should condemn violence against women and should not invoke any custom, tradition or religious consideration to avoid their obligations with respect to its elimination.

These provisions can be generalised as suggesting a hierarchy of values (Holzleithner and Strasser 2010, p. 32). An individual's right not to be subjected to violence or heteronomy of any form cannot conflict with rights of others to practice their religion, freely express their opinions or to live in accordance with their traditional customs. This is because in a system of human rights based on human dignity, rights to freedom of expression and to religious or traditional practice are *inherently* limited to respectful and peaceful forms of expression. Hence, a society's pluralism finds an intrinsic limit in a state's obligation to protect individuals against violence and heteronomy. The ban on violence limits societal openness and pluralism, and, in a decent society, this limit is equally binding on states and individuals.

The reason for giving this priority is that human dignity protects the communicative formation of moral subjects and that violence is the negation of normative communication and moral reasoning. Hence, violence, manipulation, and deception are not acceptable, except, within narrow limits, when violence is exerted as a means to reject unlawful acts, as is the case in certain instances of self-defence, law enforcement or criminal justice.

The important distinction between dignity norms and conventional norms was argued above. A normative order is premised on autonomous and responsible agency and therefore on dignity norms banning violence and other forms of heteronomy which have a potential to destroy the basis of agency. No one can, without self-contradiction, invoke a right to an autonomous decision to abolish the preconditions of any autonomous decisions. Kant's insistence on an individual's right to be respected as an autonomous lawgiver reaches an inherent limitation when it comes to norms on which any personhood is premised. The individual cannot bring her autonomy to bear as an argument against dignity norms which spell out the societal preconditions of personhood. Hence, Kant's principle does not stand in the way of demanding that the offender accept her duties to respect the dignity of all others and to constitute herself as an accountable agent, duties that result from the concept of human dignity as the right to be a person and hence to be treated as an accountable agent.

While, in principle, all rules are at a parliament's free disposition and in this sense based on a polity's agreement and consensus, and open to change, some rules are not, namely the norms spelling out human dignity and human rights. This distinction marks the difference between law and *'right'*. Therefore, violations of human dignity and human rights are wrong independently of whether they are, in addition, also prohibited by a positive criminal law provision. They are *mala in se*, and at the same time all that criminal laws may justifiably criminalise. "The reasons I have to refrain from such actions, reasons that the criminal law presupposes, lie in their pre-legal wrongfulness, and are independent of the legal system under whose jurisdiction I find myself" (Duff 2011, p. 360).

A polity committed to human dignity treats law as a matter of political choice, but human dignity and human rights as a given and as protected from the vicissitudes of public, political and parliamentary debate. While human dignity and autonomy are a matter of human rights protected by criminal law, the rest of a legal order's binding provisions are conventional and merely a matter of public order protected by non-criminal sanctions.

This differentiation between norms banning heteronomous interaction and other standards and norms, falling within the wide domain of public order, public risk management and administration, is essential when it comes to limiting the legitimate scope of criminal law and criminal justice. While norms banning heteronomy are indispensable to any normative order, all other norms are, in the end, a matter of—however convincing or arbitrary—agreements reached among autonomous individuals and open to revision any time.

What, then, about prohibitions of vagabondage, of begging, of illegally residing in European Union territory, of (consensual) bigamy or of the possession of cannabis? An individual's autonomy is not premised on others refraining from wandering about, begging, residing illegally in the EU, being married to more than one person, or possessing cannabis. Hence, some forms of such conduct can be subjected to administrative penalties maintaining public order, but should never be a matter of criminal law and criminal justice.

The point is that punishing subjects for committing offences that are not violations of human dignity cannot be justified in relation to these subjects. As has been seen, there are clear reasons for criminalising conduct that affects human dignity. An individual's participation in moral discourses as an autonomous agent is premised on her being constituted by others as a participant in culture and as a respected and autonomous agent. If she invokes her moral autonomy, she relies on and hence implicitly accepts the norms on which her constitution as an autonomous person is premised. One cannot, without contradiction, claim respect as a moral person and, at the same time, question the normative preconditions that are constitutive of oneself as a moral person—a rudimentary form of human solidarity, respect, autonomy and accountability (where autonomy and accountability depend on an individual's capacity).

On the other hand, conduct which does not affect human dignity, whether I dislike it or not, cannot be subject to criminal law. If a person, as a matter of her moral autonomy, insists that we should bear with her wandering about, begging, residing illegally in the EU, or possessing cannabis, we cannot *blame* her for having these habits. We can, as a majority believing that administrative regulations are necessary, impose on her an administrative penalty that is moderate in relation to her infringement of the rules and financial means. However, we cannot censure her for having idiosyncratic views, as within the paradigm of human dignity it may be clear that her conduct is illegal, but it is not decided that it is wrong. Crimes are wrongs in an emphatic sense in which breaches of administrative regulations are not. Antony Duff stresses this difference as follows (2009, p. 81):

> This is, after all, what distinguishes criminal punishment from other measures. Criminal convictions and punishments do not merely penalise; they condemn. A tax may be intended to discourage the conduct taxed, but it does not condemn that conduct; a fine, by contrast, when imposed as a punishment, condemns the conduct as wrongful. [...] A system of 'administrative regulations' [...] attaches penalties to breaches of the regulations – penalties designed to discourage disobedience. What distinguishes it from a system of criminal law and criminal punishments is that it does not condemn the conduct it penalises as wrongful, or those who engage in such conduct as wrongdoers; they have simply broken the rules and must pay the appropriate penalty.

As always, there are borderline cases. What if burning the national flag of a country is witnessed by a patriot and experienced as a disrespectful, shocking and offensive action? Under normal circumstances, the burning of a flag would be interpreted as expressing criticism or rejection of a country, its policies or political leaders, but not as disrespectful towards a bystander or others who learn of this incident. As the concept of human dignity entails an individual's right to define herself, it is up to the bystander to identify with the country concerned or not, and the burning of a country's flag can be interpreted as asserting that one should not unconditionally identify oneself with that country. In any case, the fact that a person commits herself to loyally, devotedly and faithfully supporting that particular country, does not bar others from criticising it. Offending a person or persons violates human dignity, offending a country or government does not, as countries and governments do not participate in human dignity, but have only instrumental status (as means of promoting human dignity) and hence can—and indeed should—be assessed critically as fulfilling their tasks or not.

In short, certain restrictions on an individual's behaviour are inherent in the concept of human dignity fostering individual autonomy as without these restrictions, individual autonomy would not increase, but vanish. Although it may seem that criminal law provisions prohibiting heteronomous interaction—violence, insult, deceit, manipulation—restrict individual autonomy, in fact individual autonomy is premised on these prohibitions. As long as criminal law provisions are strictly limited to protecting and fostering the development of respected, self-respecting, autonomous and accountable individuals, they contribute in a crucial manner to realising a maximum of autonomy and are therefore not restrictions of freedom.

This is why Kant's principle has in-built limits. Individual autonomy does not provide a basis for justifying acts that are destructive of individual autonomy. Human dignity is premised on a humanist society, which in turn is defined as societal conditions fostering individual autonomy. Hence, Kant's principle cannot serve to criticise criminal law and criminal justice as long as they are restricted to protecting persons by vindicating their dignity and human rights.

4.5.3 Criminalisation: the Message Sent by Criminal Law

What, then, is the message that a criminal law provision conveys? When parliament adopts legislation, criminalising a certain conduct, who speaks to whom, in the first place? Is it the state addressing its subjects threatening punishment in case they do not abide by the state's new law? Or is it us, the citizens, speaking to one another within and through our parliament?

It is, firstly, us agreeing and pledging to respect our rights inherent in the concept of our dignity; and it is, secondly, us agreeing and pledging to, in case of a violation of an individual's rights, stand together in solidarity with the victim and the offender; to demonstrate to the victim that she was right to rely on the norm we agreed on and that we will insist that the offender pays tribute to the victim's rights and the authority of our norms; to demonstrate to the offender that she wronged the victim and that we will not allow this to pass with impunity, that she is acknowledged as an accountable person, expected to make amends, and entitled to, on that basis, remain a full member of our community.

Hence, our agreement and pledge comprises three parts. In the first part, we acknowledge certain rights of individuals as dignity rights, as rights, that is, the respect of which is necessary as a means to promote the development of respected, autonomous and accountable persons. We confide, as cooperating partners, in the ability of all as rational beings and as members of our legal community to respect and abide by our law and thus to contribute, by their example, their share to its authority.

The second part addresses all individuals—and in particular conditional cooperators—as potential victims and contains the promise that they, in case of their victimisation, will not stand alone, rather that we will see to it that the wrong done to the victim is established and acknowledged, that the victim is restored as a person and rights-holder, and that the offender is made to contribute her fair share to the authority of the victim's rights and our laws and that thus the offender's behaviour will not stand and pass as exemplary. The criminal law provision expresses a legal community's solidarity with potential victims. It signals to them that, in case of their victimisation, state authorities will not allow the offender to get away with it with impunity.

The third part contains an expiation contract stipulating the terms and conditions by which an offender will be allowed to make amends for her offence, thus contributing her share to the authority of the victim's rights, and to, on this basis, remain a respected member of our community. It is noteworthy that our model criminal law provision does not address anyone as being unreliable, dangerous, or not trustworthy. Criminal law provisions are the expression of a legal community's condemnation of the criminalised conduct. They alert citizens to the normative standards of their community and appeal to their morality. However, they do not aim to deter offences, but rely on the community's normative consensus and strength as well as on the readiness of individuals to abide by the norms called for by human rights. There is a marked difference between criminal law provisions as expressions of a community's normative consensus and criminal law provisions as deterrence. Normative communication does not encompass menacing or in any other way manipulating the addressee. Thus, the criminal code respects individuals as reasonable and autonomous persons and moral agents, it does "not resort to the language of threats" (Duff 2011, p. 375).

4.5.4 The Scope of Criminal Law Based on Human Dignity

In a humanist world view, there exists an objective truth and that is the faculty of human beings, due to their ability to communicate in normative language, to live together and cooperate peacefully in creating a society that creates free and autonomous individuals as persons. This truth, over the history and evolution of humankind, gradually becomes a reality to the extent that social networks foster the development of autonomous subjects; and it is prevented from materializing whenever a societal structure oppresses, manipulates and indoctrinates individuals and thus impedes their development as autonomous and accountable persons. In other words, the truth of humankind is its dependency on a normative order and hence on societal preconditions that enable human beings to exist in culture as persons and to continuously reproduce and improve their normative order. It is the one and only legitimate objective of criminal law and criminal justice to protect the preconditions of culture and to preserve a space of normative communication, unaffected by heteronomy, violence, and deception in all their guises and shapes, including threatening, humiliating, slandering, and discriminatory public speech, directed against an individual or a constructed group of individuals.

Hence, one of the practically most important questions is how criminal law protecting human dignity relates to criminal law as it stands today. Does human dignity provide a basis for reconstructing our traditional criminal law and, if so, is the result similar to what is criminalised today?

The answer is that within the human rights paradigm there cannot be an offence without a violation of human rights of one—or more than one—individual. The only justifiable parts of a criminal code are those that criminalise a human rights violation that is serious enough to justify a criminal conviction or even punishment.

While all legitimate criminal law provisions protect the system of human rights, the distance between the offence and an individual victim can vary considerably. Not all types of criminal offences require that an identifiable individual is victimised. While, for instance, violent crimes, sexual and property offences all imply the violation of the human rights of at least one individual person, this is not the case for other types of offences. It would appear that in respect of this criterion—the offence's proximity to the rights of an individual—three groups of offences can be distinguished.

The first—and by far largest—group consists of offences targeting persons individually. This group comprises offences which infringe on the rights of an individual, or of individuals, and includes all offences that refer to the violation of an individual's rights to respect or autonomy, including physical integrity, personal freedom, sexual autonomy, freedom from coercion, threat or deception. Therefore, offences requiring that an individual has been wronged constitute the paradigmatic category, including murder and homicide, assault, rape and sexual abuse, coercion, deprivation of liberty, kidnapping, robbery, and so on. In relation to this by far most important group of offences, all other types only form the periphery of the criminal justice system.

The second category relates to offences that, because of the nature of the right in question, necessarily concern a large number and often an imprecisely limited range of individuals. Environmental crimes are a case in point. Offences of environmental pollution, by creating a danger zone of an indeterminate radius, compromise the rights of a multitude of individuals to a healthy environment. So-called atrocity crimes, like genocide, negating or condoning genocide, or other crimes against humanity, are by definition directed against a multitude of individuals. An offence of incitement to discrimination— hate speech—, while not directed against the rights of one particular, identifiable individual, jeopardises the rights of many individuals. Such acts are severely disrespectful of the many victims of the crimes in question, but these victims are numerous and not a group with precise boundaries.

The third category relates to criminal law provisions that protect the functioning of those institutions and procedures that are an indispensable component of any system of human rights, such as provisions targeting corruption, abuse of power, resistance against authorities, tax evasion, contempt of court, perverting the course of justice, or electoral fraud. What, from a human rights point of view, is central to the understanding of these offences is that human rights are not meant to be only theoretical, but practical and effective. Consequently, any system of human rights relies on powerful, well-functioning state institutions designed to protect and to promote human rights standards, as well as on certain procedures by which these institutions perform their functions abiding to the rule of law. Defending a system of human rights implies the resolve to effectively protect those institutions and procedures that are designed and apt to make human rights a social reality and without which an effectively functioning system of human rights is impossible. Offences targeting the effectiveness of such institutions and procedures, by impairing the institutional basis on which an effective system of human rights protection is premised, therefore directly concern all members of the legal community and their human rights.

It is with regard to this group of offences that we feel most inclined to say that they concern 'the public' (Duff 2013, p. 139). Still, these offences can also be seen as affecting the rights of all members of the legal community that relies on the proper functioning of the authorities and procedures affected. It would be a mistake to conceive 'the public' as an entity that is added to the individual members of a legal community.

Various limitations result from the notion that criminal law provisions can be justified only if they react to violations of human rights. Firstly, mere public order offences do not fall within the remit of criminal law. Residing in EU territory without an administrative entitlement may be breaching public order, but does not violate the right of another individual or of individuals, as such behaviour neither expresses disregard nor infringes on the autonomy of others. Also, behaviour that breaches rules of public morality or decency, such as prostitution, sexual intercourse among adult relatives, or adultery, does not violate the human rights of others and hence cannot be of concern to criminal law.

Secondly, to justify criminalisation human rights violations must be of sufficient severity in terms of expressing disregard of the rights of others. For example, compared to intentional or reckless offending, negligence is a by far weaker expression of disregard of another person and hence should be criminalised only in particular momentous cases, if at all. The ECtHR has repeatedly held that if an infringement of the right to life or to physical integrity is not caused intentionally, the obligation on states to establish an effective remedy does not necessarily require the provision of a criminal-law remedy in every case. The obligation may also be satisfied by a remedy in the civil courts or by disciplinary measures (*Branko Tomašić*, para. 64).

Thirdly, criminalisation must not be extended to preparatory acts that may, or may not, eventually lead to rights violations, as long as concrete rights of individuals are not yet jeopardised. Attending a training camp for terrorists is not yet a threat to the rights of others. Criminal law safeguards human rights and hence responds only to actual human rights violations, but is not a universal instrument of crime prevention reacting to perceived risks of various sorts (on criminal law and its misuse for prevention purposes Gierhake 2013).

4.5.5 Criminal Law Relating to Different Categories of Human Rights

In addition to grouping criminal law provisions based on the range of individuals concerned, crimes can also be categorised according to the type of human rights violation they involve. In Chap. 3, four categories of human rights were distinguished—formation, care, autonomy and resource rights. Accordingly, criminal law provisions can be analysed as relating to these categories. For interpreting criminal law definitions, the human right protected by the definition provides the key point of reference.

Violations of formation rights have in common that an individual, or a group of individuals, is disregarded by conduct that is insulting, disrespectful, humiliating or debasing. All discriminatory behaviour violates formation rights as it, by imposing a label, infringes a person's right to define herself (on self-definition and 'social visibility' see FRA 2012, pp. 20–22). Insulting or humiliating expressions must also be prevented as much as the imposition of defining characteristics.

In its publication on Making hate crime visible in the European Union, the European Union Agency for Fundamental Rights addresses this issue in the following terms (FRA 2012, p. 21):

> Human dignity, conceived as the right of individuals to be initiated as persons in society and as protecting the autonomous formation of personal identities, [...] implies the right to be the 'author' of one's own personality and the necessity to protect individuals against alienating or degrading definitions others attribute to them.

Much still remains to be done, e.g. in terms of eliminating the impact of gender-roles or of preventing religious denominations from, forcing irrevocable signs of membership on the bodies of children. Various forms of genital mutilations as the inscription of a religious or cultural affiliation on an infant or child raise concerns. Such practices negate the preliminary and tentative nature of an individual's primary education and deny an individual's right to define herself later on in life, when she is able to make such decisions. Other examples of violations of formation rights are slavery, servitude or particularly exploitative working conditions, which will often violate a worker's autonomy, but in addition and in any case violate human dignity and the respect owed to a person.

A second category of care rights is violated by all forms of cruelty or inhuman treatment of others, but typically also by offences committed by omission, including offences of child neglect or of failures to render assistance in violation of professional duties or in situations of exceptional distress, e.g. caused by a traffic accident.

In the third, and by far the largest, group are offences violating autonomy rights, protecting individuals against physical violence and coercion, threats, and deception. Clearly, reacting to violence is the core competence of any criminal justice system. All forms of violence and domination constitute expressions of disregard for the victim as a person and are hence essentially humiliating. At the same time, the domination over and humiliation of the victim can provoke in the offender feelings of power, control and superiority. Therefore, the reaction of criminal justice to violence must, at the level of normative communication, reject, in no uncertain terms, the offender's arrogant pretension of dominance and confirm and restore the victim as a respected and autonomous person and rights-holder, as well as, at the level of extrinsic incentives, neutralise interfering influences such as the offender's libidinous feelings of omnipotence, supremacy and grandeur.

In addition, some actions, while not per se manipulating the behaviour of another individual, intervene in a sphere that is reserved for an individual's autonomous decisions. The removal of a diseased organ, even if beneficial to a patient's health, constitutes, when performed without the consent of the patient, a severe violation of her autonomy to decide on actions that foreseeably impact on her physical integrity or health. It is this type of offences that Malcolm Thorburn has in mind when he highlights that criminal law allocates "jurisdiction" (2013, pp. 33–35):

> The doctor who performs a blood transfusion against a competent patient's will commits a criminal assault even if it is necessary to save her life and her reasons against it are trivial or even silly. The question of whether or not to accept a blood transfusion is in the patient's jurisdiction, not the doctor's, no matter how morally superior the doctor's view of the matter might be.

Thus, criminal law provisions protect particularly sensitive spheres and contexts of autonomous agency, such as sexuality; private and family life, as well as rights to spheres within which an individual can, unimpeded by others, express her opinion, demonstrate in public or exercise her religion.

Legislation carves out domains of autonomy to which individuals are entitled and protects these claims against invaders. To violate a human right of this category means to usurp on another person's autonomy. The offender imposes his decision on a matter that it was for the victim to decide. By depriving the victim of a sphere of decision to which she was entitled, the offender excessively exerts decision powers and disregards the victim's entitlement to equal autonomy.

Finally, in contrast to the many forms of 'autonomy offences', criminal law provisions protecting resource rights are rare. A pertinent group of offences comprises various forms of impairments of a healthy environment, which have been set out above. In addition, violent partner relationships have crippling effects on victims and therefore must, as well as being construed as violations of formation and autonomy rights, also be seen as depriving victims of essential resources in terms of self-esteem, health and a basic sense of security.

4.6 A Crime Victim's Secondary Rights

A secondary right is a human right of the victim that she has exactly because of a violation of her primary human rights. It is put forward that, in a criminal justice paradigm based on human dignity and human rights, a crime victim has three secondary rights, namely to non-recurrence (or protection against repeat victimisation), to care and respectful treatment in the aftermath of victimisation (or protection against secondary victimisation), and to justice (or to redress).

If the status of a victim of crime and the secondary rights attached to that status have their basis in an individual's primary human rights, can a legal person be a victim? The answer is Yes, but only to the extent that the legal person exerts the autonomy rights of its founders or owners. While the rights of victims under secondary EU legislation—the Framework Decision and the VRD—are restricted to natural persons (CJEU, *Dell'Orto*, para.s 52-59; *Eredics*, para.s 24-31), legal persons still hold human rights to the extent that they are vicarious agents acting on the autonomy rights of the natural persons who through the legal person participate in various spheres of the life of their communities. Legal persons hold human rights on behalf of natural persons and to this extent are to be acknowledged as victims of crime in the case of a violation of these rights. Any other view would deprive the autonomy rights of natural persons of some of their effectivity. By recognising, within the limits determined by the autonomy rights of those who act through the legal person, the rights of the legal person, the normative order acknowledges the human dignity in which the natural persons share who create, task and operate the legal person.

4.6.1 Right to Non-recurrence

The right to non-recurrence is part of an individual's right to the protection of her rights, but reflects the particular aspect that an individual's victimisation obliges the police to consider whether the offence results from a risk that continues to pose a threat to the security of the victim's primary rights.

Under normal conditions, human rights are protected by criminal law provisions, which emphasize the significance of a certain aspect of human rights, appeal to the moral sense and accountability of citizens, and signal to citizens as potential victims that in case of an offence they can count on the solidarity of their legal community and its resolve to insist that offenders acknowledge the authority of the victim's rights and her status as a person. Under normal conditions, this is sufficient protection.

However, state authorities have to take additional, targeted measures in situations where there exist concrete indications that the rights of an individual are in peril. To better determine this requirement, the ECtHR has developed and consistently applied the so-called *Osman*-test, which originates from the Court's judgment in the case of *Osman v. the United Kingdom* (para.s 115–116). Recently, the Court has held as follows (*Olszewscy*, para.s 58–59):

> The Court recalls that the first sentence of Article 2 para. 1 enjoins the State not only to refrain from the intentional and unlawful taking of life, but also to take appropriate steps to safeguard the lives of those within its jurisdiction [. . .]. This involves a primary duty on the State to secure the right to life by putting in place effective criminal-law provisions [. . .]. It also extends in appropriate circumstances to a positive obligation on the authorities to take preventive operational measures to protect an individual whose life is at risk from the criminal acts of another individual (see *Osman v. the United Kingdom* [. . .]). [. . .] Bearing in mind the

> difficulties in policing modern societies, the unpredictability of human conduct and the operational choices which must be made in terms of priorities and resources, the scope of the positive obligation must be interpreted in a way which does not impose an impossible or disproportionate burden on the authorities. Accordingly, not every claimed risk to life can entail for the authorities a Convention requirement to take operational measures to prevent that risk from materialising. For a positive obligation to arise, it must be established that the authorities knew or ought to have known at the time of the existence of a real and immediate risk to the life of an identified individual from the criminal acts of a third party and that they failed to take measures within the scope of their powers which, judged reasonably, might have been expected to avoid that risk (see *Osman*, cited above [...]).

This obligation to take operative measures in situations posing a "real and immediate risk" is not limited to the right to life under Article 2 ECHR, but extends to all risks of victimisation.

An obvious example are violent domestic relationships. If there is reason to suspect that an individual has abused his partner or ex-partner, there is also reason to assess whether the threat persists or not, and, in case it does, to adopt measures that effectively protect the victim's rights. In the recent past, the ECtHR had to deal with several cases where the question arose whether the police and courts had adopted sufficient measures to protect the victim against repeat victimisation (refer to e.g. the ECtHR's judgments in the cases *Valiulienė* and *Eremia*).

Under the European Union's VRD, Member States are obliged to ensure a sufficient level of protection of victims against violence, including "procedures established under national law for the physical protection of victims and their family members" (Article 18 VRD).

4.6.2 Right to be Treated with Care and Respect

Similarly, the victim's right to be treated with care and respect in the aftermath of her victimisation pays due attention to a victim's legitimate expectation to be supported by her community in re-establishing a sense of self-esteem, self-confidence, control, and autonomy.

In this respect, it is crucially important that the victim is not confronted with the offender or the offence at a time or under circumstances where the victim is not or not yet in a position to cope with this confrontation. The victim must be protected against situations that could make the victim re-experience her victimisation or reinforce the victim's feeling of not controlling her situation and being subjected to overpowering forces. The ECtHR has—first in the *S.N. v Sweden* case (para. 47), and thereafter consistently, e.g. recently in the case of *Y. v Slovenia* (para. 103)—based the victim's secondary right to respectful treatment on Article 8 ECHR. In its *Pupino*-judgment, the CJEU emphasised the vulnerability of children as victims and their right to an appropriate level of protection (CJEU, *Pupino*, para. 56).

Further, if an offence is viewed as the frustration of a victim's primary expectation to the recognition of her rights, and if punishment is conceived as a means of confirming a victim's primary expectation in the face of its frustration and is aimed to reduce the negative effects of the offence, then a failure to express such a confirmation corroborates the offence's negative impact on the victim's rights. In this vein, the offence can be seen as the primary victimisation, while a failure to rehabilitate the victim's rights and to reassure the victim of their protection constitutes secondary victimisation. Because the victim is entitled to the legal community's solidarity and recognition of her rights and her status as a person, a lack of acknowledgment constitutes secondary victimisation.

Secondary victimisation reinforces the primary victimisation caused by the offender. The violation of the victim's autonomy and the disrespect of the victim as a person entitled to the acknowledgment of her rights, which represent the essential aspects of a criminal offence, are verified whenever a victim's arguable claim that she has been victimised remains unheard or is not responded to in a respectful manner. They are also corroborated in the investigation and the subsequent proceedings whenever the victim feels that she is not acknowledged as a person, but dealt with as yet another case-file. This happens when decisions are made without her having been consulted; whenever the victim is intimidated by the offender, which can be the case already if the victim is exposed to the presence of the offender without her consent, appropriate preparation and protection; or whenever the victim, again, experiences feelings of helplessness, inferiority, or a loss of control of her situation. This can also result from opaque, bureaucratic proceedings, a lack of transparency or of information and explanations provided to the victim; in short, whenever the victim's autonomy is again undermined.

The victim's protection against secondary victimisation is one of the objectives pursued by the VRD (Rafaraci 2015). According to Article 18 VRD, Member States have to ensure "that measures are available to protect victims and their family members from secondary [...] victimisation". To this end, victims have a right to access victim support services (Articles 8 and 9 VRD) and a right to be protected in the context of restorative justice services (Article 12 VRD). In addition, Member States are obliged to individually assess a victim's protection needs (Article 22 VRD) and, in accordance with a victim's needs, protect the victim against secondary victimisation throughout criminal proceedings (Articles 23 and 24 VRD; on support services in particular and victims' rights under the VRD in general see FRA 2014).

4.7 A Killed Victim's Right to the Punishment of Her Murderer

There are many possible answers to the question of why a murderer should be punished which can relate to the victim's family, the offender or to wider society. However, what is of particular interest here is how punishing a murderer relates to the human being who has been killed.

This person had a right to live. She had a right to a respected and protected sphere of autonomy regarding all decisions about the termination of her life. All others were obliged to refrain from any action that entailed a relevant risk of causing her death, unless she had autonomously agreed to that particular action, which we, in this case, would not refer to as 'murder.' How then can the question of why a murderer should be punished, be answered in a way that reflects the victim's primary right to life that the murderer violated?

Many possible responses of the criminal justice system do not answer this question. For example, punishing the offender as a means of deterrence is not a valid response. If the murderer is punished for the purpose of preventing her from killing others or of preventing others from killing third parties, punishment does not relate to the original victim, who cannot be killed again. The only relation between her death and the offender's punishment would be that it was her death that manifested and drew attention to the dangerousness of her murderer and the risk of the murderer's reoffending; or to the risk that others could feel inclined to follow the offender's example. In the perspective of deterrence, the killing of the victim only evidences the necessity to take action for the sake of protecting *others* from being killed. Hence, deterrent punishing of a murderer in no plausible manner serves the rights of her victim.

The same holds with all forms of preventive punishing, such as reforming or incapacitating offenders. A society that punishes murderers to prevent further killings looks into the future and thus turns its back on the dead victim. Such a society not only failed to protect the victim against a violation of her right to life, but, by not remembering the victim when punishing the offender, also attests to the victim's social death and the insignificance of her rights.

If punishing is not about preventing harm in the future, is it about defending the legal order? Clearly, the murderer demonstrated disrespect of the prohibition of killing. By the offender's retributive punishment, the legal norm is vindicated. Punishing the murderer because she disrespected the prohibition of killing settles her debt with this—crucially important—norm. By punishing the offender, the state, impersonating the legal order, ensures that the authority of the norm is preserved. This is the possible meaning of retribution at the stage of a nation state representing the people and the community's abstract public interests or legally protected goods (or *Rechtsgüter*). In this view, the task of criminal justice is to vindicate whatever is adopted as criminal law by a national parliament representing the sovereign people.

Nevertheless, this interpretation must be challenged as again the state convicts and punishes the offender as a matter between these two, and the victim does not enter the picture. She is, again, not remembered as the person whose primary right to life was negated. If retribution means censuring and emphatically rejecting violations of a nation state's criminal code, this form of retribution shares with all preventive interpretations of punishment a profound disregard of the victim.

And yet, can the victim's life serve as the point of departure for constructing criminal justice, once the victim is dead? After all, whatever efforts the state makes to investigate, to prosecute, to convict and to punish, will not return the victim to life.

In the *Tanlı* case, the European Court of Human Rights held that by failing to account for the death of Mahmut Tanlı during his detention at the Uluyol police station and by not conducting an effective investigation into the circumstances of the victim's death, Turkey violated its procedural obligations under Article 2 ECHR, which grants a right to life. However, in his partly dissenting opinion, Judge Gölcüklü challenged this argumentation by denying the causal link between a lack of an effective investigation following the death of Mr Tanlı on the one hand and his death on the other, 'as though the lack of an effective investigation had killed the individual in question, which defies all logic.'

But this argumentation mixes the normative level of a right to life with the biological category of an organism's life. The former belongs to the world of culture, the latter to the sphere of biology. Article 2 ECHR states: 'Everyone's right to life shall be protected by law.' The second paragraph of Article 2 makes it clear that not every instance of taking life—e.g. in self-defence—also violates an individual's right to life. Contrarily, attempted murder, while not ending the victim's life, disrespects her right to life. Therefore, what a person in a case of (completed) murder, is deprived of is her life and not her right to life. A right exists in the sphere of culture, not in nature.

Still, in a sense, Judge Gölcüklü is right. As highlighted above, in the Court's understanding procedural aspects of material Convention articles—such as of Article 2 ECHR—serve to insist that by punishing human rights violations, states are obliged to protect rights by means of deterrence. Thus, the Court in its decision on the case of *Menson v. the United Kingdom* explained:

> The Court [. . .] recalls that by requiring a State to take appropriate steps to safeguard the lives of those within its jurisdiction [. . .], Article 2 para. 1 imposes a duty on that State to secure the right to life by putting in place effective criminal law provisions to deter the commission of offences against the person, backed up by law enforcement machinery for the prevention, suppression and punishment of breaches of such provisions [. . .].
>
> With reference to the facts of the instant case, the Court considers that this obligation requires by implication that there should be some form of effective official investigation when there is reason to believe that an individual has sustained life-threatening injuries in suspicious circumstances. The investigation must be capable of establishing the cause of the injuries and the identification of those responsible with a view to their punishment.

If deterrence is the objective of punishment, Judge Gölcüklü has reason to wonder how punishment serves the rights of the person who has been killed. Why should a dead individual have a right to the identification, conviction and finally punishment of her murderer if this punishment only serves to deter future offences that necessarily matter little to the dead victim? This, in the words of Judge Gölcüklü "defies all logic". Recently, Sachs has raised the identical objection against the decision passed by the German Constitutional Court in the *Gorch Fock* case, that punishing the offender will do nothing to protect the life of the dead victim ("*. . . weil ein Schutz des individuellen Lebensgrundrechts des bereits getöteten Verbrechensopfers durch eine noch so harte und effektive Bestrafung des Täters offensichtlich nicht mehr zu erreichen ist*", 2015, p. 377).

Indeed, as concerns the relationship between life and the right to life, there is reason to assume that the latter ends with the former; the reason being that the right to life constitutes a sphere of an individual's autonomy and that autonomy is premised on agency and agency on life. Once an individual has died, she is prevented from taking any further decisions concerning the ending of her life, and this fact, on first sight, renders her right to life meaningless, once she is dead. There is no sense in protecting the autonomy of a dead person.

It is likely that Mahmut Tanlı was not only killed but also tormented and made to suffer. In this case not only his autonomy rights, but also his care rights were severely violated. However, as care rights reflect the frailty and needs of the human being as a biological organism, there is arguably even less sense in attempting to preserve them once the human being has died.

Yet there still remains a significant distinction between the finding that an individual's life has been taken—implying that a human being is biologically dead—and considering that an individual's right to life has been disregarded—meaning that the victim has been wronged and discounted as a person and rights-holder. As not being subjected to the violence of another person forms a crucial element of human dignity, by negating the victim's right to life the offender implicitly called the victim's status as a person, entitled to respect as a person and of her rights, into question. Treatment as a person means that others attribute and respect personhood. If anything, the respect owed to human beings as persons lies at the heart of the concept of human dignity.

This observation brings the victim's constitution rights into focus, the right, that is, to respectful treatment as a person, which forms the core component of human dignity. While autonomous agency ends with an individual's death, there is no reason why the primary right to respectful treatment should too. It will be remembered that a person is constituted by acts of communication that call on and acknowledge her as a person. As much as the parents' references to their expected child commence the constitution of a person, those living after the victim's death are not prevented from keeping the victim 'alive' as a social person who is remembered in various manners. While the victim's autonomy is premised on actual agency and ends with her biological existence, her right to respectful treatment as a person before the law does not.

Hence, punishing a murderer acknowledges the victim as a person who was, at the time of her death, and still is, entitled to respect of her primary right to life as an implication and expression of her personhood (compare Schmidt 2012, pp. 112–137, who also interprets the offence as disrespect to the victim as a person). By denying this entitlement, the offender disregarded the victim's status as a person and rights-holder and thus incurred a debt to the victim. As long as the legal community identifies as committing to human dignity, it will insist as a matter of solidarity with the victim that the offender pays tribute and settles her debt to the victim as a person.

The victim's enduring right to be treated as a person in conjunction with the offender's right to be held to account justifies the conviction and punishment of the offender.

However, the dead victim's right to be acknowledged as a person has its basis not in Article 2, but in Article 13 ECHR and, respectively, in Article 47 of the Charter, whenever applicable. The objective of Article 13—the right to an effective remedy—is to oblige the courts to deal with the substance of a claimed human rights violation and to, in case a violation is established, grant the victim appropriate relief. Hence, the purpose of Article 13 ECHR is to ensure that a severe violation of a human right does not go unanswered, but is acknowledged and redressed. By establishing and recognising the violation of her rights, the victim is acknowledged as a rights-holder and person.

Thus, the victim's right to criminal justice has its foundation in the victim's sharing in human dignity (the victim's rights are consistently deduced from the victim's dignity and personhood by Schmidt 2015). Cornelius Nestler (2014, p. 195) is right to claim that the victims of the atrocity crimes committed by the Nazis deserve, to the present day, to be acknowledged as persons who had rights and were entitled to expect that their rights would be respected and deserve that those are identified who were responsible for the wrong done to the victims.

> Man durfte sich an dem Massenmord nicht beteiligen—das ist die Antwort, die die Angehörigen von der deutschen Justiz verlangen können. Nicht, weil dies der Selbstverständigung der Deutschen dient, sondern weil die deutsche Gesellschaft, in deren Auftrag die Justiz tätig wird, den Opfern diese Antwort bis auf den heutigen Tag schuldet.

In Transitional Justice processes, the 'social life' of the dead victims and offenders takes on particular significance. In the words of Michelle Veljanovska, the 'dead and the missing are enlivened and permanently linked into the new political order through the anxiety of families and the communities these missing persons belonged to' (2012, p. 196). In a sense, the dead remain 'undead' as long as they still await recognition as rights-holding or accountable persons, deserving of their community's respect. By acknowledging rights and responsibilities, a polity establishes and maintains a normative order and comes to terms with its past. Hence, as concerns the victim of atrocity crimes, "the plot of a life story is never securely in the possession of its subject. It is part of the ongoing moral work of those who live on" (Biehl 2014, p. 118).

Convicting and punishing those responsible for killing him would have been a means of insisting on the respect owed to Mr Tanlı. As a matter of justice, humankind owes it to him, as one of its members, that his personhood is defended against being called into question by the offenders. In prosecuting, convicting and punishing the murderers of Mr Tanlı, the global legal community would have expressed its commitment to human dignity and to the respectful remembrance of a member of the human family. Convicting and punishing offenders acknowledges the wrong done to victims and recognises victims as persons entitled to rights and respect.

Hence, the justification of criminal justice is almost entirely intrinsic; it lies primarily in what identifying, convicting and punishing offenders communicates and not in what it causes in the future. Human dignity demands that murderers are convicted and punished as a means of acknowledging and restoring the personhood of their victims (Schmidt 2015, p. 187).

The call on a human being entails the promise of treatment as a person. Because of this promise, society owes to the victim that her status as a person is respected and defended, even after her death. The victim's right to the truth, as well as to the identification and punishment of her offenders, is an expression of her legal community's loyalty and solidarity. With regard to partner violence, Antony Duff has highlighted this point in the following terms (2009, p. 141):

> What makes domestic abuse a public wrong is that [...] it concerns us all, as a wrong in which we share: we must not leave the victim to pursue her own grievance, but must collectively pursue it with her and for her; her assailant should answer not merely to her, but to us as her, and his, fellow citizens for his attack on her and his violation of the core values by which we define ourselves as a polity.

Hence, a victim's secondary right to justice lives on after her biological death, along with her primary right to be respected as a person. Unless a society ceases to care about what it stands for as part of the project of humankind, as long as it upholds its identity as a community based on human dignity and on the solidarity of the human family, it will insist on punishing those who, in light of the human rights violations they have committed and of what they owe to their victims, deserve to be punished. A decent society will not allow for impunity. Otherwise its members could be seen as betraying the victim and as collaborating in a "public violation of justice" (Kant 1797, p. 106).

It can therefore be seen that killing a person violates her right to life and calls her status as a person into question. However, what about less severe offences? Above it has been claimed that criminal law provisions are necessarily restricted to protecting human dignity and the system of human rights flowing from and spelling out dignity. Therefore, all the elements constituting a decent society and enabling individuals to develop, within the limits of their personal capacities, as autonomous and accountable persons can justifiably be the concern of criminal law provisions. In other words, if human rights are conceptualised as flowing from the one principle of human dignity as the right to be a person, it follows that any human rights violation concerns the victim as a person. For the rest, whether prosecuting, convicting and punishing the offender is appropriate, is a matter of necessity and proportionality that are to be assessed in the light of the circumstances of the individual case. It is worth noting that this approach coincides with positions that suggest restricting criminal justice to offences that are not only wrongful, but, in addition, also "an affront to the victim's value or dignity" (Hampton 2007, p. 115), causing "diminishment" and "moral injury" (Hampton 2007, pp. 122–124). These assumptions, too, lead to a retributivist theory of punishment as vindicating the victim's dignity (Hampton 2007, p. 135).

4.8 The Victim's Right to Justice

Prosecuting, convicting and punishing the offender has been described by Jeffrie Murphy as a social ritual in which, through the symbolism of criminal proceedings, the offender's "message of contempt for the victim—a message that the victim is of less than equal value with the wrongdoer—is emphatically repudiated, and another message—that of the full value of the victim as an equal citizen—is emphatically asserted" (2011, p. 35). This description nicely captures the basic function of the criminal justice system to restore the victim as a person and rights-holder.

As the basis of substantive criminal law, the victim's fundamental right to justice entails three aspects, namely rights to the truth, to the identification and conviction of offenders, as well as, under certain conditions, to their punishment. As this right is not meant to be only theoretical, but to become practically effective, the victim's right to justice also covers the victim's right to access justice, which entails the rights to an effective remedy and to a fair trial. Again, the right to access justice must be practically effective. This requires institutions and procedures that enable and encourage the victim to seek access to justice and support her in doing so. In the end, the victim is entitled to a system of criminal justice that is victim-friendly in the sense that it is designed to respect the victim and her rights.

Generally speaking, the victim's right to justice is only theoretical and illusory unless justice is done in a manner that allows the victim to sense and to experience that justice is done, implying that the facts of the case are acknowledged, that the wrong done to the victim is recognised, that the offender's responsibility is highlighted, and that the offender makes amends for her wrong-doing. It is these experiences that are apt to restore the victim's confidence that her rights are being taken seriously and that she is respected as a person. Hence, the victim must be allowed to feel that she obtains what is due to her in reparation of the injustice suffered. This satisfaction is nothing but what justice in reality can mean to the victim, as much as feeling sorry, making amends and expiating her guilt is what justice can mean from the offender's perspective.

From the standpoint of the victim's right to justice, the offender's conviction is of primary importance rather than her punishment. It is the offender's conviction that establishes the truth, acknowledges the wrong done and implicitly the rights of the victim, and holds the offender liable. Klaus Günther commented on the discussion of the rights of victims that what would enhance the debate is a clear understanding that for the victim the conviction of the offender is of primary importance, not punishment (2014, p. 197):

> Ich denke, dass man die Diskussion erheblich nüchterner führen könnte, wenn man von der Fixierung auf die Strafe als Resultat eines Strafverfahrens wegkäme und wirklich klarmachte, dass das Entscheidende am Strafverfahren die öffentliche Feststellung von Unrecht und Schuld ist und nicht die Strafe. Das Opfer hat von der Unrechts- und Schuldfeststellung mehr, weil die Gesellschaft ihm und dem Täter gegenüber klarstellt, dass die Tat Unrecht (und nicht Unglück) war und dass es für dieses Unrecht einen Verantwortlichen gibt, und zwar weder das Opfer noch die Gesellschaft, sondern den Täter. Das ist entscheidend und nicht die Strafe.

In addition, from the perspective of the offender's status as a respected person, her conviction expresses censure and deals out criticism that the offender has to bear. In other words, the offender's conviction is a reputational sanction, although administered in a controled manner and restricted, essentially, to the criminal proceedings. Whether the offender's conviction is sufficient as a sanction or whether punishment is required in addition to the conviction will depend on various factors, including the damage done to the rights of the victim, whether and how credibly the offender takes responsibility for her wrong-doing and apologises, and to what extent the offender, overall, benefited from committing the offence. If the wrong done is of minor significance, if the offender convincingly accepts her responsibility and apologises, if the offender readily compensates the damage done, punishment will often not be necessary in order to do justice. In extreme cases, offenders are convicted for traffic accidents which caused the death of a family member. In such a case it is pointless to mete out punishment in addition to the offender's conviction. Hence, Wilfried Holz suggests to refer to the conviction of the offender as a primary sanction and to punishment as a secondary sanction (2007, pp. 33–38; Günther 2014).

It has been demonstrated above that where rights of individuals, protected by criminal law provisions, are violated, victims have a right under Article 13 ECHR to an effective remedy, a right, that is, to an investigation and to the prosecution, conviction and punishment of offenders. This right to justice—or to redress—is the backbone of victims' rights under the ECHR.

At its core, the victim's right under Article 13 ECHR has not changed in 20 years of case law from *Aksoy* to very recent judgments. In the *Aksoy* judgment of December 1996, the Court held:

> The nature of the right safeguarded under Article 3 of the Convention (art. 3) has implications for Article 13 (art. 13). Given the fundamental importance of the prohibition of torture (see paragraph 62 above) and the especially vulnerable position of torture victims, Article 13 (art. 13) imposes, without prejudice to any other remedy available under the domestic system, an obligation on States to carry out a thorough and effective investigation of incidents of torture.
>
> Accordingly, as regards Article 13 (art. 13), where an individual has an arguable claim that he has been tortured by agents of the State, the notion of an 'effective remedy' entails, in addition to the payment of compensation where appropriate, a thorough and effective investigation capable of leading to the identification and punishment of those responsible and including effective access for the complainant to the investigatory procedure. It is true that no express provision exists in the Convention such as can be found in Article 12 of the 1984 United Nations Convention against Torture and Other Cruel, Inhuman or Degrading Treatment or Punishment, which imposes a duty to proceed to a 'prompt and impartial' investigation whenever there is a reasonable ground to believe that an act of torture has been committed. However, in the Court's view, such a requirement is implicit in the notion of an 'effective remedy' under Article 13 [...].

The victim has a right to proceedings, capable of leading to the conviction and punishment of offenders, exactly because she has a right to the truth, as well as to the conviction and, in appropriate cases, also to the punishment of offenders, although these rights are premised on the accountability of the offender and hence on her right to be held to account. Thus, Kant's principle is respected.

The victim's right to justice—under Article 13 ECHR and Article 47(1) of the Charter, when applicable—comprises several elements which in their entirety enable a victim to experience that, in response to her victimisation, justice is done to her as a person and to her rights (the European Union Agency for Fundamental Rights—FRA—consistently conducts research into victims' access to justice and the VRD, see e.g. FRA 2014, 2016, p. 14; for a general analysis of an individual's right to an effective remedy refer to Berger 2013, p. 96).

In the case-law of the ECtHR in Strasbourg, the victim's right to an effective remedy under Article 13 ECHR or under the procedural aspect of another Article comprises the following aspects (for an overview of case-law on Article 13 ECHR and Article 47 of the Charter see FRA and Council of Europe 2016, pp. 157–163):

1) Individuals have a right to the protection of their rights by comprehensive criminal law definitions that capture the essence of severe human-rights violation (*M.C.*, para.s 150–152; Söderman, para.s 82–85; *I.C.*, para. 52).
2) The victim has a right to criminal proceedings that are initiated ex officio, independent of her reporting to the police.
3) The victim is entitled to a thorough and effective investigation capable of leading to the establishment of the facts and to the identification and punishment of offenders. This is not an obligation as to the results to be achieved but as to the means to be employed. The authorities must have taken the steps reasonably available to them to secure the evidence concerning the incident, including eyewitness testimony, forensic evidence, etc. (*M.C.* and *A.C.*, para. 111; *Mustafa Tunç*, para. 169; *Sakir*, para. 63; *Armani da Silva*, para.s 229–234).
4) The investigation and the proceedings must be carried out with promptness and reasonable expedition (*M.C.* and *A.C.*, para.s 111–112; *Mesut Deniz*, para. 52; *Sakir*, para. 64; Uğur, para. 101; *Armani da Silva*, para. 237).
5) The investigation and the proceedings must enjoy a sufficient level of independence and impartiality (*Mustafa Tunç*, para. 177; *Armani da Silva*, para. 232).
6) The investigation and the proceedings must be open to public scrutiny (*Mustafa Tunç*, para. 179; *Armani da Silva*, para. 235).
7) The victim—or the deceased victim's family in her stead—must be given effective access to the investigation and the proceedings (*Mustafa Tunç*, para. 179; *Armani da Silva*, para. 235).
8) The victim is entitled to an effective legal remedy against a decision not to prosecute or to discontinue proceedings.
9) There must not be a manifest disproportion between the gravity of the offence and the punishment imposed (*Myumyun*, para.s 67–68; *Uğur*, para. 97; *Armani da Silva*, para. 238).
10) The victim has a right to payment of compensation, where appropriate.
11) Whenever there are indications of possible discriminatory motives, the victim is entitled to investigations conducted with a view to 'unmask' such motives (e.g. *Nachova*, para. 160; *M.C. and A.C.*, para. 113; *Sakir*, para. 64).

The following sections focus on aspects of substantive criminal law—the essence of justice for victims—and neglect the procedural consequences of the victim's right to justice.

4.8.1 Right to the Truth

Once the court has spoken, what until then had been the personal story of the victim transforms into part of her society's official record and narrative. What the offender has done to her is acknowledged by the court representing the legal community, including the fact that this conduct violated her rights and disregarded her as a person. The victim no longer has to fight to make her story heard and recognised. It is transformed into facts that are no longer disputed.

To this end, the competent authorities are required to carry out an investigation and prosecution capable of leading to the determination of the offence and to the identification of those who have violated the victim's rights; all available evidence must be collected and assessed, the truth must be sought and, as far as possible, found and asserted in clear terms. In a normative community, it is the role of the court to find the truth, and to find and state the relevant facts in an authoritative manner, ending disputes in this respect in a binding judgment. The court trial is tasked not only with gathering evidence, but also with, authoritatively, establishing—speaking—the truth. The facts determined by the court count as truth. In a society governed by the rule of law, the court's is the relevant view of the matter. Once the court finds the offender guilty, the victim is entitled to consider the offender guilty and to expect that others will not offhandedly deviate from that view. Hence, the court's assessment at least enjoys a strong presumption of being correct.

If the court would not have this power to determine what has happened, criminal justice could not perform its crucial function of restoring peace, in particular as far as the victim is concerned. For her to come to terms with what has been done to her, it is of crucial importance that this experience is transformed into an account that is authoritatively accepted, pronounced and settled by the court. This limits the damage done by the offender to the status and rights of the victim (Sautner 2014, p. 185).

4.8.2 Right to the Conviction of Offenders

Convicting offenders—placing blame and responsibility—is the core function of criminal justice, not punishment. It is a misconception of criminal justice to view punishment as its central element. Rather, criminal justice should be conceptualised around the conviction of the offender as an expression of censure and the attribution of responsibility for the wrong done to the victim or the victims. The core function of criminal justice is to acknowledge and restore the victim as a person and rights-holder, and the conviction of the offender is the main means to this end.

While in the nation state paradigm the state's right to the punishment of the offender is at the forefront, in the human dignity paradigm it is the right of the victim to be acknowledged and vindicated as a person and rights-holder which comes to the fore. In the human rights paradigm, criminal justice is conceptualised in terms of performative acts of normative communication that restore the victim and the offender by acknowledging them as rights-holders and accountable persons.

In many instances, criminal justice can restore the persons involved as full members of their community and societal peace on that basis without imposing a sanction on the offender. This is particularly true if the offender, in the course of proceedings, accepts that she has wronged, takes full responsibility, compensates the victim and asks for her forgiveness. The offender expressly taking responsibility and regretting what she has done can go a long way towards rehabilitating the victim and the offender as persons.

4.8.3 Right to the Punishment of Offenders and to the Compensation of Damages

For the victim to trust in the binding nature of her rights and the state's resolve to protect them effectively, the conviction of an offender must in many cases—but not always—come with an appropriate sanction.

Along with the offender's conviction, punishment is, firstly, an expression of the legal community's solidarity with the victim as a person holding rights, inasmuch as the offender is made to contribute her fair due to the acknowledgement and authority of the victim's rights and the victim as a person. The legal community, in solidarity with the victim as its member, does not allow the offender to 'get away with it' with impunity, where 'it' refers to an act that disregards the victim by calling her rights and her status as a person into question. Thus, secondly, punishment allows the offender to settle her debt and to come to terms with the victim and her legal community. Thirdly, punishment by accentuating the dignity and the rights of the victim and by restoring her confidence reassures conditional cooperators that they can trust that in case of a violation of their rights they will not stand alone. It is these three functions that account for the participation of the victim, the offender, and the public prosecutor as parties to the criminal proceedings and determine the angle of their participation.

In cases where the victim suffers a loss in terms of damages, it is crucially important that the victim be effectively and swiftly compensated. Criminal courts adjudicating compensation and making sure that their decisions are implemented is an essential part of doing justice to victims of crime. To give an example, in 2016 the NGO La Strada International started a campaign called Justice at last—Access to compensation for trafficked persons. The campaign rightly claims that compensation should be a core element of criminal proceedings and that lawyers, prosecutors and judges should be trained on the importance of compensation. Indeed, if sanctions serve the purpose of demonstrating that offending is not a successful strategy, it follows that neutralising the economic incentives for offending is of paramount importance for the success of criminal proceedings. From the victim's perspective, seeing to it that she is compensated demonstrates her society's resolve to support her in having access to justice. In this vein, the CJEU has, in a number of cases, emphasised victims' entitlement to compensation for damage and the importance of granting victims access to justice (*Cowan; Giovanardi; Comm v Italian Republic*).

On the basis of their extensive comparative analysis of criminal justice systems in Europe, Brienen and Hoegen have stressed the importance of compensation and, at the same time, have arrived at a fairly sobering assessment of the current state of play (2000, p. 1169), suggesting, for instance, that judges' "negative attitude toward compensation as a whole, should be seriously combated and, ultimately, renounced."

In addition, whenever the offender draws profit from the commission of the crime, it is indispensable that the proceeds of crime be confiscated, in order to demonstrate that the criminal offence did not pay for the offender.

In continental trials, sentencing often does not attract much interest and is treated as a mere appendix to the conviction. It is a big advantage of common law proceedings to draw a much clearer distinction between conviction and sentencing. This encourages courts to pay attention to questions that, after all, have a potential to impact on the future course of the lives of the offender, the victim, and their families.

4.8.4 Right to Access Justice

The victim's right to have access to justice, captured in Article 47 of the Charter, combines—in terms of the ECHR—the right to an effective remedy (under Article 13 ECHR) and fair-trial rights (similar to Article 6 ECHR).

Proceedings should be of a quality that allows the victim and everyone else to see that justice is done, which entails a sufficient level of independence of all state institutions involved in the administration of criminal justice, a system of checks and balances establishing an equilibrium among the parties to the proceedings and appropriate means of public scrutiny of all stages of the proceedings.

The victim has a right to actively participate in proceedings and to influence their outcome. Article 1 VRD postulates:

> The purpose of this Directive is to ensure that victims of crime receive appropriate information, support and protection and are able to participate in criminal proceedings.

As to the objective to foster victims' participation in proceedings, the VDR provides a wide range of information rights (Articles 4–6 VRD), supports the victim in communicating in the proceedings (Articles 3 and 7 VRD), and recognises rights of victims to be heard and to provide evidence (Article 10 VRD). Still, the main objective of the VRD is to ensure that victims are acknowledged and granted an appropriate role in criminal proceedings.

4.9 The Relation Between the Victim's and the Offender's Rights

Traditionally, a criminal offence is conceived of as comprising two components, wrong and guilt (or responsibility, or liability). In a human rights paradigm, it is plain to see that what constitutes the wrong of an offence is the violation of the victim's—or the victims'—primary rights, while the category of guilt relates to the right of the offender to be treated as an accountable person within the margins set by her personal capabilities. The wrong done to the victim combines an objective and a subjective component. Firstly, the offender's act compromises what the victim's primary human rights warrant. Secondly, the offender acts in defiance of the victim's primary human rights protected by criminal law.

However, while it is the rights abuses suffered by the victim that establish the wrong of the offence and found the victim's right to justice, this right remains premised on the liability of the offender and, consequently, on her right to be held to account, convicted and punished. In other terms, the offender's guilt is the wrong done to the victim viewed through the lens of the offender's accountability.

The victim has a right to the conviction and, in appropriate cases, the punishment of the offender. However, this is only to the extent that the offender has such a right to be convicted and punished. To do otherwise would subject the offender to the rights of the victim and thus violate Kant's principle and human dignity. Hence, the victim's right to justice is necessarily premised on and corresponds to a right of the offender to be convicted and punished; and the offender's right to be punished is premised on a violation of dignity rights and hence on a secondary right of the victim to the punishment of the offender. The offender's guilt comprises, as one factor, the wrong done to the victim; and the victim's right to be acknowledged as wronged is premised on the guilt and right to expiation of the offender. Thus the rights of the victim and the offender are intertwined and mutually referential (Schmidt 2015).

The victim's secondary right to justice—to the prosecution, identification, conviction and punishment of the offender—belongs to the same category of constitution rights as does the offender's right to be held to account and punished. Prosecuting, convicting and punishing the offender as a means of her coming to terms with what she owes to her normative community in general, and the victim in particular, respects the same status as a person of the offender and the victim. The offender's right to account for what she owes to the victim and the victim's right to the offender being held to account for the wrong done to the victim are the two sides of the same coin. In a nutshell, the purpose of criminal justice is to restore persons equally entitled to respect—to restore the victim as a person and rights-holder and to restore the offender as a person, accountable agent and duty-bearer.

However, the notion of what in substance constitutes punishment has yet to be defined: what does the term 'punishment' mean in practice? What could it mean to fit a theory of criminal justice based on human dignity?

4.10 Restoring the Offender's Full Status as a Member of Her Legal Community

What justifies punishment is the fact that the offender has wronged the victim. This justifies punishment in two respects. Firstly, it accounts for the symbolic aspect of punishment. The reason we must—and are entitled to—censure the offender is that she has violated the dignity and rights of the victim. At the level of normative communication, not only convicting, but also sentencing and punishing the offender contribute to conveying the message that a humanist society refutes the maxim propagated by the offender and, thereby, reconfirms the status of the victim as a person and rights-holder entitled to the respect of all others.

Secondly, the wrong done to the victim accounts for the fact that we choose to convey our message of censure by depriving the offender of some social resources, such as financial means or freedom. Punishment is unique in this respect. It is difficult to think of any other message that we insist on conveying by means of harsh treatment. However, by being treated harshly, the offender is made to contribute her share to discouraging potential shirkers who may, otherwise, be tempted to follow the example of the offender and to also disregard the dignity and rights of the victim. The more important the rights violated by the offender, the larger the contribution she owes to preventing that others draw inspiration from her example.

As all offences—that are justifiably criminalised—violate the one human dignity in which all human beings share all criminal offences concern everyone, and all state authorities engaged in identifying offenders and administering criminal justice share in the performance of a function that is essentially of concern to the global community. That a case of robbery or burglary is dealt with by a district rather than by an international court is a matter of proportionality, economy and effectiveness. But the reason is not that such a crime is in principle of concern only to a local community. Punishment is necessarily hardship; otherwise, it could not perform its function of neutralising external, selfish incentives and of ensuring that the offender's example does not seduce followers. However, in a humanist society, punishment is also part of the formation of the offender as an accountable agent, and this, too, must be reflected in the design of criminal sanctions, not as a constitutive, but as a regulatory aspect, ensuring that punishment respects the dignity of the offender, the right, that is, to be supported in developing as an accountable agent.

4.10.1 Punishment as Hardship

The author of a popular textbook on Austrian criminal law explains to his students the indispensability of criminal law by pointing to the function of sanctions as preserving the law. If the state would not intervene, an offence could have a negative role model effect or provoke retaliation, as Fuchs observes (Fuchs 2016, p. 14). Those of his students who are convinced that they would never feel inclined to follow the example of an offender, Fuchs invites to imagine how they feel when they are stuck in a traffic jam and observe that some drivers overtake them on the service lane. Fuchs imagines that their wellbeing improves when they finally see that the police stop and fine these drivers; without punishment, so Fuchs concludes, shirkers could look smart ("*wird der Rücksichtslose zum Klugen*"), and, so one could add, those abiding by the norm could feel stupid. Fuchs joins the observation by noting that it is hardly a coincidence that in 1495 finally an end was set—more or less—successfully to practices of traditional feuding (by the *Ewige Landfriede*) the same year when the Imperial Chamber Court (*Reichskammergericht*) was established and able 'to take over' (2016, p. 15).

In the same vein, Chap. 2 suggested that punishment is a means of preserving social norms by making offenders endure hardship and thus contribute their share of necessary investments in the norms' authority; in this way, punishment enables large communities to cooperate peacefully. Punishment insists that an offender must settle her debt to a social norm and its beneficiaries, before everyone can return to life as normal.

The social norm is a public good. Because all benefit from the norm, all are expected to cooperate in its preservation. Those who abide by the norm by their example invest in its authority. Inversely, those who flout the norm undermine its prestige and normative power. They therefore owe something to the norm and to their community as the norm's beneficiary. By making the offender sacrifice a good that is generally viewed as desirable, it is demonstrated that the norm is binding on everyone and that offences can have unpleasant consequences. Thus, the offender is held to contribute and settle her debt to the norm's normative power and the authority of the victim's rights. In addition, Chap. 2 highlighted that this mechanism is driven by a bundle of strong and mutually reinforcing social emotions.

It was also emphasised above that criminal law and criminal justice cannot depart from the assumption that persons are dangerous and likely to infringe criminal law provisions, but are bound to trust in an adult person's ability to understand and abide by criminal law standards. However, this does not mean that criminal law and criminal justice should turn a blind eye on offences when they happen. Rather, it is crucially important that the criminal justice system does not allow offenders to get away with it without having to balance their account. Only a sufficiently effective sanctioning mechanism will enable conditional cooperators to trust that if their legitimate expectations are disappointed, the offender at least runs a significant risk of having to make amends to the victim. This is not meant to say that, in the example sketched out by Fuchs, the police have to be there in every instance. However, offenders should face a real risk of being held to account. Convicting and sentencing offenders demonstrates that depriving others of their rights, while at the same time enjoying the respect paid by others to these rights, is not a strategy that the legal community will crown with success and allow offenders to get away with.

Following his explanation of the law's indispensability, quoted above, Fuchs comments that this functionality does not justify punishing offenders. It is not an open-and-shut case that the individual must always be subordinated to the interests of her community, as this would surrender the individual entirely to a state's criminal policies, reducing the individual to a mere means to the purposes of others, in violation of Kant's principle (2016, p. 15).

The point is that, while all sanctions highlight norm-violating behaviour, only with punishment do things 'become personal'. Punishment is the only sanction that not only criticises behaviour but also censures the offender for her behaviour and for the attitude it expresses. Charging a person with a criminal offence affects her reputation, while accusing her of irregular parking habits does not. Such habits are unfair play—not playing by the rules—but not dishonourable; they do not bring shame and disgrace on the offender. However, a criminal offence does, because of the attitude it manifests, which is an attitude of disregard of others as persons entitled to rights and to the respect of their rights. A criminal offence is an action manifesting disregard—not only of a rule of decent cooperation—but of another person or others entitled to the solidarity and mutual respect that humans owe to one another.

Hence, criminal law operates at two levels, at the level of conduct and norms regulating conduct, but in addition, at the level of persons being respectful or disrespectful and respected or disregarded. An individual's personhood is constituted by concrete acts that call on her and address her as an autonomous and responsible person entitled to the consideration of her fellow citizens. Her personhood—her participation in human dignity—is premised on acts of others attributing personhood to her. By grossly violating this status, by treating her, that is, in a manner that is disrespectful, ruthless, inhuman, degrading, deceitful, manipulative, careless or otherwise in disregard of her personhood, an offender undermines the victim's status as a person. She thus incurs a debt to her, as well as to others who sympathise with the victim and who cooperate in establishing a society based on the respect of all citizens. They too may be concerned and unsettled by the offender's behaviour, as it calls into question the authority and reliability of the norms constituting the personhood of all.

4.10.2 *Criminal Justice Serves the Offender's Formation*

Above it has been argued that human dignity as the right to be treated as a person is premised on a humanist society, which furthers the development of autonomous and accountable agents. Hence, human dignity entails the right of an individual to be supported in developing as a person able to abide by the norms of her community. Punishing offenders forms a part of this wider mechanism of enabling individuals to live in accordance with the basic norms of their society. Hence, convicting and punishing offenders inherently and necessarily serves the purpose of constituting offenders as norm-abiding citizens. It calls on their moral ability to recognise the wrong they have done and to act in accordance with this recognition of the rights of the victim and the equal rights of others. If criminal justice is fashioned in line with the political ideal of human dignity, it is designed to call on the offender to acknowledge that she has wronged the victim and to take responsibility for her action. This general orientation sets inherent limits on how punishment can be designed and implemented.

The offender's morality is not a natural given, but something that develops because of interactions between the offender and her community. Knowing this, it is not possible to burden the offender with responsibility and leave her alone with it. The legal community owes it to the offender to ensure that she is supported in developing as an autonomous and accountable agent. Hence, punishment will necessarily take the form of cooperation based on a spirit of mutual respect and solidarity, with the aim of educating and empowering the offender as a moral person and of allowing her to autonomously lead a life—her life—within the normative framework of her society.

This is not meant to say that convicting and punishing the offender is justified by its beneficial consequences. It is not. What alone justifies punishment is the offender's right to be treated as an accountable person, which is the flip-side of the victim's right to be restored as a full person entitled to respect. However, it is the very rationale of a humanist society that it supports individuals in developing as accountable agents. Treating human beings as persons implies integrating them in a legal community and disposing them to abide by a normative order. Criminal justice is part of a wider range of educational institutions that constitute persons within human culture in general and a legal order in particular. Criminal justice partakes in the underlying objective of a humanist society, which is to support individuals in developing as autonomous and accountable agents, who are in a position to understand and abide by the norms of their legal community.

Criminal justice continues and specifies society's call that initiates a subject's constitution as a person and enables her to become a full member of a community based on social norms and the rule of law. Through punishment, this formative and pedagogic process, aiming to initiate and integrate the individual as a member of a normative community, is extended into adulthood. While the severity of punishment has to reflect the seriousness of the violation of rights suffered by the victim, the specific design of punishment must strive to support normative learning and the formation of autonomous agency. In this sense, the German Constitutional Court has held that only a penitentiary system aimed to integrate the offender in society and to enable her to lead a life in accordance with her society's legal order respects the dignity of the offender (Laubenthal 2015, pp. 99–100).

4.10.3 Punishment: Exclusion or Inclusion?

Discussing incarceration as a form of punishment, Lynn Stout puts forward the following (2011, p. 211):

> Prison, as we have seen, is an expensive punishment. At least one thing can be accomplished by throwing offenders into jail, however, that can't be accomplished by fining them, flogging them, or cutting off their ears. Jail removes offenders from society. Prison 'incapacitates' inmates, making it impossible for them to harm those outside the prison walls.

One is left to wonder what it means that offenders are removed from society. Is there no social life in a prison? The inmates playing on the football team of the prison wards, family members visiting, the social worker interacting with the prisoners—is that not social life? However, if it is, it is not part of the social life with which the nation state has concern. It is much like the social life on another continent, which is also not the concern of the nation state. What happens in prison, happens outside the nation state. Prisoners are not locked in, they are locked out. By imprisoning offenders, the nation state exercises its right to exclude, to ostracise. Later Stout (2011, p. 214) rightly wonders

> why many people seem indifferent to the horrific conditions convicts often endure in jail, including overcrowding, lack of medical care, and physical and sexual abuse by guards and other prisoners. This indifference may reflect a belief that convicts are no longer members of the in-group known as civilized society. Just as a criminal may perceive strangers as out-group members whose interests do not deserve consideration, law-abiding citizens may view convicts as out-group members whose interests are of no concern. The underlying attitude seems to be something like 'if you won't play nicely with us and act like an in-group member, then we won't treat you like an in-group member either: go play with the other criminals.'

This is indeed the nation state's message: If you don't abide by my laws, you are no longer a citizen. Go play with other non-citizens. It does not occur to Stout that she herself, three pages earlier, removed offenders from society. Outside the nation state, offenders no longer have the right to have rights in the nation state. They lack the status of citizens.

Contrary to the nation state scenario, in a humanist society, the state does not hold rights and, in particular, is not entitled to ostracise offenders. Interpreting criminal law provisions as expiation contracts among citizens implies that offenders, while incurring censure and having to settle their debts to victims, remain within their society. In a decent society, criminal law provisions serve the purpose of preserving, not of calling into question the offender's status as a person and member of society. Hence punishment must take the form of including, not of excluding offenders.

The construction of criminal sanctions should pursue the strategy of, within the limits of proportionality relating the severity of sanctions to the offender's guilt, achieve as much as possible in terms of supporting the offender in developing as an autonomous and accountable agent. The wrong suffered by the victim and the offender's guilt determine the amount of hardship owed to the authority of the victim's rights and to the victim as a person; but they do not determine the currency in which this amount is to be paid. The choice of sorts of punishment must reflect the regulatory aspect of punishment as serving the dignity of the offender. It should burden the offender with measures that support her in developing as a person and avoid meaningless sanctions—such as paying an amount of money to the state or wasting time in detention. The state must attempt to establish a dialogue and cooperation with the offender, based on an understanding of society's solidarity with the offender and of the shared responsibility for the offender's conduct (Stratenwerth 1977, pp. 41, 48).

Hence, the first question must be: which measures support the offender in developing as an accountable agent able to respect others as persons and their rights? Various forms of anti-aggression and anti-violence training have been implemented and some of them evaluated (Brückner 1998; Egger et al. 1995; Flood 2015; Logar et al. 2002; Morran and Wilson 1997; Zimmermann et al. 2001). The basic objective of such programmes is to confront offenders with their deeds, to allow them to understand what their behaviour meant from the victim's perspective, to encourage them to accept responsibility for the wrong done to victims and to learn social techniques of dealing, in a respectful manner, with situations of conflict. To the extent that such programmes make offenders imagine the feelings that their actions caused others, such programmes are retributive, however, at the same time a meaningful way of supporting offenders in developing as responsible persons (Hampton 2007, p. 138).

Probation services are significant means of supporting offenders in learning how to live a life that is self-determined and in accordance with human dignity. Importantly, Duff has argued that probation should be understood as a constructive form of punishment that aims to encourage offenders to face up to the implications of their crimes, to rehabilitate them and to restore and reconcile moral and social relations (2003). Duff observes that not only probation, but also Community Service Orders and criminal mediation and reparation programs 'are appropriate punishments because they are suited to the aim of persuading offenders to face up to and to repent their crimes, to begin to reform themselves, and to make apologetic reparation to those whom they wronged' (2001, p. 145).

To the widest extent possible, offenders should stay in their homes and with their families, keep their jobs, and hence remain in the environment within which they will, in the future, have to master their lives in accordance with the legal framework of their societies. If issues of the security of the rights of others make a certain amount of supervision indispensable, this can be achieved by electronic monitoring in combination with the services of a probation officer, or the offender can be placed in a residential community organised and controlled by a probation service. If the offender does not have a job, meaningful community services can be a second-best solution to enable the offender to spend her time in a constructive, sensible and dignified manner.

In this context, attention should be devoted to the fundamental rights of the offender's family members to the respect of their family life. How the conviction and punishment of the offender affects the rights of her family has to date not aroused much interest. One very noteworthy exception is Susan Sharp's research on the effects of the death penalty on the families of offenders (2005). Sharp concludes that the families of those sentenced to death suffer much like the families of the victims, except that they are targeted by negative reactions from others, including shaming and 'ostracism' (2005, p. 180).

However, children, partners and parents are entitled to maintain their relationships with the offender as their family member. As they have not offended, there is hardly a basis for justifying that they are prevented from preserving family links to the offender. From a fundamental rights perspective, the effect of punishment on minor children of offenders is an important issue that is currently hardly considered (Huigens 2003, p. 45). In a way, a parallel can be drawn between the two exclusionary rights claimed by nation states. When immigration policies are discussed, it must not be overlooked that restricting residence of one individual can impact on the rights of others, e.g. on the rights of individuals who consider the foreigner a member of their family, their football team, or their city council, in which case excluding the individual from residence in the country affects citizens' rights to respect of their private and family life, their right of association, or their political right to elect as member of their city council who they deem able to perform that function. Excluding a person from being present in a community concerns those who wish to maintain or enter into social relationships to which they are in principle entitled. As soon as exclusion is no longer conceived as a matter solely between a state and an individual, but as restricting relationships among individuals, things become more complex, because the collateral damage done to the rights of third parties enters into the equation and can upset the balance.

In case and to the extent that prisons are in the future still needed to deal with particularly severe cases, they should be restricted to what is absolutely indispensable both in terms of the length of the sentence and the regime preventing the offender from leading a life under normal social conditions. Given that inflicting hardship on the offender serves neither to incapacitate her nor to deter others, but merely to underline the bindingness of the victim's dignity and rights as well as to render the offender's criminal conduct unattractive to potential followers, there cannot be a justification for imposing long prison sentences, not to mention life sentences, which obviously violate the offender's dignity and right to, under all conditions, remain a member of her society.

4.10.4 The Offender's Right to Her Full Rehabilitation

Once the sanctions, imposed by the court, have been executed, there is no basis for further reproaching the offender. As much as criminal justice aims to allow the victim to leave the status of a victim behind and to move on, so criminal justice allows the offender to overcome being censured for her offending. The offender has a right not to be reproached for an offence for which she has made amends and, under the relevant terms of the criminal law, settled her debt to the social norm's prestige and leverage and thus to the beneficiaries of this norm, primarily the victim, but indirectly also to all others. Once the offender has 'redressed her balance', upset by her offence, she recovers the right to be treated as a fully respectable citizen and not to be blamed for the offence any longer.

The task of criminal justice is to absorb the irritation created by the offence and to restore societal peace based on mutual respect and a general confidence in the rule of law. This can only be achieved if all are required to, once the courts have spoken and sanctions have been administered, treat the matter as closed and refrain from further reproaching the offender for the offence. The offender has a right to have access to criminal justice as a safe, transitional process that enables her to come to terms with her community and to, once the case is closed, leave the past behind, a right, that is, to be censured as long and only as long as she has not made appropriate amends for her criminal conduct.

After that point, the offender must not be treated in consideration of her offence. Article 113 of the Austrian Criminal Code (titled '*Vorwurf einer schon abgetanen gerichtlich strafbaren Handlung*') serves as a case in point. This provision threatens with imprisonment up to 3 months whoever censures another for an offence for which punishment has been executed. This provision conveys the powerful message that the offender, by making amends for her offence, acquires the right to overcome being treated as an offender. This reflects the fact that criminal justice serves to settle a matter and end it. Thereafter, the offence no longer stands in the way of the offender who thus restores her status as a fully respected member of her society.

Thus, a crucial function of criminal justice lies in limiting the offence's negative effects on the social status of the offender. Criminal justice serves the purpose of pacifying and integrating a society. As far as possible, the consequences of an offence are to be dealt with and contained by the criminal justice system. Once the offender has made amends and repaired the rights of the victim and the legitimate interests of all others, the offender is entitled to 'forgiveness' strictly in the sense of no longer being censured, reproached or resented for having committed the offence.

Thus, the offender's rehabilitation complements the victim's right to the truth, which entitles the victim to be acknowledged as the person against whom an offence has been committed. The victim's right to the truth protects the victim's status as the person who has been wronged and who is therefore entitled to justice and to the community's sympathy and support. While there may be limits to that entitlement, it is not the task of criminal justice to define them. However, it is the task of the criminal court to, by sentencing the offender, define the limits of the reproach and sanctions levelled against the offender.

4.11 Everyone's Right to the Security of Their Rights

Criminal justice is a public matter in the sense that it concerns not only the victim and the offender, but all members of the community, firstly, because of their solidarity with victims and offenders, secondly, because the offence, directly or indirectly, affects their rights.

Criminal justice is about all citizens because of their solidarity with victims and offenders. Even if offences, first, affect their direct victims, "our concern for the victim as our fellow citizen makes them our business. So does our recognition of the wrongdoer as a fellow citizen: what is done by one of us, when it impinges on our shared values, is our business" (Duff 2013, p. 139).

How criminal justice treats victims and offenders is exemplary and allows all others, who by definition hold equal rights with victims and offenders, to see what their rights mean in practice. Hence, the violation of the primary rights of one individual—the victim—also concerns others, who also have a right to the punishment of the offender, not only as a matter of sympathy for the victim but because of their own legitimate interests in the preservation of the norm's authority.

The victim's right to the punishment of the offender is a public, not a private affair. It is a matter of constitutional and criminal law, not of civil law. In the ECtHR's *Perez case*, the applicant challenged the authorities' decision not to launch an investigation, which prevented her from being joined in the proceedings as a civil party. Thus, so she claimed, she was 'deprived of a form of 'private revenge'.' However, a victim's right to the punishment of the offender is not a right to 'private revenge' and therefore not a civil right in the sense of Article 6 of the Convention. This is also what the ECtHR found (para. 70; see also the Court's *Gorou* judgment, para. 24). Clearly, a victim's right to justice is a matter of human rights and hence of Article 13 ECHR, and not of merely private rights and Article 6 ECHR.

In criminal proceedings, all members of the legal community are represented by the public prosecutor, who no longer appears for the state, but for the public in the sense of all individuals forming the legal community and their rights.

Norms granting rights to identifiable individuals—by far the majority of criminal law provisions—cannot be violated but by the violation of the rights of a concrete individual or of several concrete individuals. Only by reacting to such violations is the norm defended in the common interest of all members of the community. Thus, the rights of individual victims and the legitimate interests of all in the maintenance of a system of human rights coincide and are inextricably interrelated. Often, the concern of others is mediated by the violation of a victim's primary rights, and others are only indirectly affected. However, that is not necessarily the case. In corruption cases, where the functioning of public authorities is in question, all are directly concerned.

All hold equal rights with the offender to be held to account and by undergoing criminal proceedings, conviction and punishment, to restore their status as fully respected members of their society. Again, from the manner in which the offender is dealt with, others can tell what their right to be treated as an accountable person and a member of their legal community is worth, and what it means in practice to be entitled to a procedure that enables an offender to come to terms with victims and their community and thus to overcome the diminished status of an offender.

The only public security that criminal justice should be concerned about is the security of the rights of all that results from the authority and bindingness of the norms granting these rights and calling on the members of the legal community to respect them (Lesch 1999, p. 96).

References

Albrecht, P.-A. (2011a). *Die vergessene Freiheit: Strafrechtsprinzipien in der europäischen Sicherheitsdebatte* (3rd ed.). Berlin, Germany: Berliner Wissenschafts-Verlag.

Albrecht, P.-A. (2011b). *Securitized societies: The rule of law: History of a free fall* (1st ed.). Berlin, Germany: Bwv Berliner-Wissenschaft.

Berger, M. (2013). *Organisation und Verfahren der ordentlichen Gerichtsbarkeit im Lichte der Rechtsprechung des Gerichtshofes der Europäischen Union*. Wien, Austria: MANZ Verlag Wien.

Biehl, J. (2014). Ethnography in the way of theory. In V. Das, M. Jackson, A. Kleinman, & B. Singh (Eds.), *The ground between: Anthropologists engage philosophy* (pp. 94–118). Durham, NC: Duke University Press.

Brienen, M. E. I., & Hoegen, E. H. (2000). *Victims of crime in 22 European criminal justice systems*. Nijmegen, The Netherlands: Wolf Legal Productions.
Brock, R. N., & Lettini, G. (2013). *Soul repair: Recovering from moral injury after war*. Beacon Press.
Brückner, M. (1998). *Wege aus der Gewalt gegen Frauen und Mädchen: Eine Einführung*. Frankfurt am Main, Germany: Fachhochschulverlag.
Dombo, E. A., Gray, C., & Early, B. P. (2013). The trauma of moral injury: Beyond the battlefield. *Journal of Religion & Spirituality in Social Work: Social Thought, 32*(3), 197–210. doi:10.1080/15426432.2013.801732.
Drescher, K. D., Foy, D. W., Kelly, C., Leshner, A., Schutz, K., & Litz, B. (2011). An exploration of the viability and usefulness of the construct of moral injury in war veterans. *Traumatology, 17*(1), 8–13. doi:10.1177/1534765610395615.
Duff, R. A. (2001). *Punishment, communication, and community*. Oxford University Press USA.
Duff, R. A. (2003). Probation, punishment and restorative justice: Should Al Turism be engaged in punishment? *Howard Journal of Criminal Justice, 42*(2), 181–197.
Duff, R. A. (2009). *Answering for crime: Responsibility and liability in the criminal law*. Oxford, England: Hart Publishing.
Duff, R. A. (2011). In response. In R. Cruft, M. H. Kramer, & M. R. Reiff (Eds.), *Crime, punishment, and responsibility: The Jurisprudence of Antony Duff* (pp. 351–379). Oxford, England: Oxford University Press.
Duff, R. A. (2013). Responsibility, citizenship, and criminal law. In R. A. Duff & S. P. Green (Eds.), *Philosophical foundations of criminal law* (pp. 125–148). Oxford, England: Oxford University Press.
Egger, R., Fröschl, E., Lercher, L., Logar, R., & Sieder, H. (1995). *Gewalt gegen Frauen in der Familie*. Wien, Austria: Verlag für Gesellschaftskritik.
Fichte, J. G. (1796, 2000). *Foundations of natural right*. (M. Baur, Trans.). Cambridge University Press. Retrieved April 25, 2015, from http://www.cambridge.org/us/academic/subjects/philosophy/philosophy-texts/foundations-natural-right
Fletcher, G. P. (1995). *With justice for some: Protecting victims' rights in criminal trials*. Reading, MA: Basic Books.
Fletcher, G. P. (1998). *Basic concepts of criminal law*. New York: Oxford University Press.
Flood, M. (2015). Work with men to end violence against women: A critical stocktake. *Culture, Health & Sexuality, 17*(sup2), 159–176.
FRA. (2012). *Making hate crime visible in the European Union: Acknowledging victims' rights*. Luxembourg: Publications Office of the European Union.
FRA. (2014). *Victims of crime in the EU: The extent and nature of support for victims*. Luxembourg: Publications Office of the European Union.
FRA. (2016). *Ensuring justice for hate crime victims: Professional perspectives*. Luxembourg: Publications Office of the European Union.
FRA. and Council of Europe (Ed.). (2016). *Handbook on European law relating to access to justice*. Luxembourg: Publications Office of the European Union.
Frame, T. (2016). *Moral injury: Unseen wounds in an age of barbarism*. Sydney, NSW: University of New South Wales Press.
Frommel, M. (2013). Was bedeutet uns heute noch Franz von Liszt? *Journal der Juristischen Zeitgeschichte, 14*(1), 291–311.
Fuchs, H. (2016). *Strafrecht Allgemeiner Teil I: Grundlagen und Lehre von der Straftat* (9th ed.). Verlag Österreich.
Fuller, L. L. (1969). *The morality of law* (Revth ed.). New Haven/London: Yale University Press.
Gardner, M. R. (1980). The right to be punished – A suggested constitutional theory. *Rutgers Law Review, 33*, 838.
Gardner, M. R. (1989). The right of juvenile offenders to be punished: Some implications of treating kids as persons. *Nebraska Law Review, 68*(1), 182–215.

Gierhake, K. (2013). *Der Zusammenhang von Freiheit, Sicherheit und Strafe im Recht: Eine Untersuchung zu den Grundlagen und Kriterien legitimer Terrorismusprävention*. Berlin: Duncker & Humblot.

Ginther, K. (1990). The European Convention for the prevention of torture and inhuman or degrading treatment or punishment. *European Journal of International Law, 2*, 123–130.

Günther, K. (2005). *Schuld und kommunikative Freiheit. Studien zur personellen Zurechnung strafbaren Unrechts im demokratischen Rechtsstaat* (1st ed.). Frankfurt am Main, Germany: Klostermann, Vittorio.

Günther, K. (2014). In C. Prittwitz, M. Baurmann, K. Günther, M. Jahn, L. Kuhlen, R. Merkel, et al. (Eds.), *Rationalität und Empathie: Kriminalwissenschaftliches Symposion für Klaus Lüderssen zum 80. Geburtstag* (p. 197). Baden-Baden, Germany: Nomos.

Hampton, J. (2007). In D. Farnham (Ed.), *The intrinsic worth of persons: Contractarianism in moral and political philosophy*. Cambridge: Cambridge University Press.

Hassemer, W. (2009). *Warum Strafe sein muss: Ein Plädoyer*. Berlin, Germany: Ullstein Hardcover.

Hegel, G. W. F. (1802). Über die wissenschaftlichen Behandlungsarten des Naturrechts, seine Stelle in der praktischen Philosophie und sein Verhältnis zu den positiven Rechtswissenschaften. In E. Moldenhauer & K. M. Michels (Eds.), *Werke in 20 Bänden mit Registerband: Jenaer Schriften 1801–1807* (Vol. 1 & 2, pp. 434–530). Frankfurt am Main: Suhrkamp.

Hegel, G. W. F. (1820). *Philosophy of right*. Kitchener, Ontario, Canada: Batoche Books.

Hörnle, T. (2006). Die Rolle des Opfers in der Straftheorie und im materiellen Strafrecht. *JuristenZeitung, 61*(19), 950–958.

Hörnle, T. (2011). *Straftheorien* (1st ed.). Tübingen, Germany: Mohr Siebeck.

Holz, W. (2007). *Justizgewähranspruch des Verbrechensopfers*. Berlin, Germany: Duncker & Humblot.

Holzleithner, E., & Strasser, S. (2010). Multikulturalismus im Widerstreit: Debatten über kulturelle Diversität, Geschlechtergleichheit und sexuelle Autonomie. In S. Strasser & E. Holzleithner (Eds.), *Multikulturalismus queer gelesen: Zwangsheirat und gleichgeschlectliche Ehe in pluralen Gesellschaften* (pp. 27–46). Frankfurt am Main, Germany: Campus Verlag.

Huigens, K. (2003). Dignity and desert in punishment theory. *Harvard Journal of Law & Public Policy, 27*(1), 33–50.

Jescheck, H.-H., & Weigend, T. (1996). *Lehrbuch des Strafrechts.: Allgemeiner Teil* (5th ed.). Berlin, Germany: Duncker & Humblot.

Kadish, S. H. (1987). *Blame and punishment: Essays in the criminal law*. New York: Macmillan Publishing Company.

Kant, I. (1797/1996). *The metaphysics of morals*. (M. Gregor, Ed.) (Cambridge texts in the history of philosophy.). Cambridge, England: Cambridge University Press.

Laubenthal, K. (2015). *Strafvollzug* (7. Aufl. 2015.). Berlin, Germany: Springer.

Lesch, H. H. (1999). *Der Verbrechensbegriff. Grundlinien einer funktionalen Revision*. Köln, Germany: Heymanns, Carl.

Litz, B. T., Lebowitz, L., & Gray, M. J. (2015). *Adaptive disclosure: A new treatment for military trauma, loss, and moral injury*. New York: Guilford Publication.

Litz, B. T., Stein, N., Delaney, E., Lebowitz, L., Nash, W. P., Silva, C., et al. (2009). Moral injury and moral repair in war veterans: A preliminary model and intervention strategy. *Clinical Psychology Review, 29*(8), 695–706. doi:10.1016/j.cpr.2009.07.003.

Logar, R., Roesemann, U., & Zuercher, U. (2002). *Gewalttätige Männer ändern (sich): Rahmenbedingungen und Handbuch für ein soziales Trainingsprogramm* (1., Aufl.). Bern, Germany: Haupt Verlag.

Lüderssen, K. (2002). Historische Erkenntnisinteressen moderner Kriminalpolitik. In K. Lüderssen (Ed.), *Die Durchsetzung des öffentlichen Strafanspruchs* (pp. 21–37). Köln, Germany: Böhlau.

Maguen, S., & Litz, B. T. (2012). Moral injury in veterans of war. *PTSD Rearch Quarterly, 23*(1), 1–6.
Margalit, A. (1998). *The decent society*. (N. Goldblum, Trans.) (Revised ed.). Cambridge, MA: Harvard University Press.
Marxen, K. (1975). *Der Kampf gegen das liberale Strafrecht.: Eine Studie zum Antiliberalismus in der Strafrechtswissenschaft der zwanziger und dreißiger Jahre* (1st ed.). Berlin, Germany: Duncker & Humblot.
Morran, D., & Wilson, M. (1997). *Men who are violent to women: A groupwork practice manual* (Spi.). Lyme Regis, England: Russell House Publishing Ltd.
Morris, H. (1968). Persons and punishment. *The Monist, 52*(4), 475–501. doi:10.5840/monist196852436.
Müller-Dietz, H. (1967). *Grenzen des Schuldgedankens im Strafrecht*. Karlsruhe, Germany: C. F. Müller.
Murphy, J. G. (2011). Repentance, mercy, and communicative punishment. In R. Cruft, M. H. Kramer, & M. R. Reiff (Eds.), *Crime, punishment, and responsibility: The Jurisprudence of Antony Duff* (pp. 27–36). New York: Oxford University Press.
Nash, W. P., & Litz, B. T. (2013). Moral injury: A mechanism for war-related psychological trauma in military family members. *Clinical Child and Family Psychology Review, 16*, 365–375.
Naucke, W. (1982). Die Kriminalpolitik des Marburger Programms 1882. *Zeitschrift für die gesamte Strafrechtswissenschaft, 94*(3), 525–564.
Naucke, W. (2015). Abhandlung über das Strafrecht als Machtbegrenzung. In *Negatives Strafrecht: 4 Ansätze* (pp. 69–132). Berlin, Germany: LIT Verlag.
Nestler, C. (2014). Sind die heute noch möglichen Strafverfahren wegen NS-Verbrechen noch legitim? In C. Prittwitz, M. Baurmann, K. Günther, M. Jahn, L. Kuhlen, R. Merkel, et al. (Eds.), *Rationalität und Empathie: Kriminalwissenschaftliches Symposion für Klaus Lüderssen zum 80. Geburtstag* (pp. 182–196). Baden-Baden, Germany: Nomos.
Prittwitz, C. (2000). Opferlose Straftheorien? In B. Schünemann & M. D. Dubber (Eds.), *Die Stellung des Opfers im Strafrechtssystem: Neue Entwicklungen in Deutschland und in den USA* (pp. 51–73). Köln, Germany: Heymanns.
Rafaraci, T. (2015). New perspectives for the protection of the victims in the EU. In S. Ruggeri (Ed.), *Human rights in European criminal law: New developments in European legislation and case law after the Lisbon Treaty* (pp. 215–225). Cham, Switzerland: Springer.
Sachs, M. (2015). Grundrechte: Anspruch des Opfers auf Strafverfolgung des Täters. *JuS, 2015*, 376–378.
Sadurski, W. (2010). *Giving desert its due: Social justice and legal theory* (Softcover reprint of hardcover 1st ed. 1985 edition.). Dordrecht, the Netherlands: Springer.
Sander, L. K. (2007). *Grenzen instrumenteller Vernunft im Strafrecht: Eine Kritik der Präventionsdoktrin aus strafrechtsgeschichtlicher und empirischer Perspektive*. Frankfurt am Main, Germany: Lang, Peter Frankfurt.
Sautner, L. (2010). *Opferinteressen und Strafrechtstheorien: Zugleich ein Beitrag zum restorativen Umgang mit Straftaten*. Innsbruck, Austria: StudienVerlag.
Sautner, L. (2014). *Viktimologie: Die Lehre von Verbrechensopfern*. Wien, Austria: Verlag Österreich.
Scheler, M. (1921). *Formalism in ethics and non-formal ethics of values: A new attempt toward the foundation of an ethical personalism* (5th ed.). Evanston, IL: Northwestern University Press.
Schmidhäuser, E. (1971). *Vom Sinn der Strafe*. (E. Hilgendorf, Ed.). Berlin, Germany: Logos Berlin.
Schmidhäuser, E. (1985). *Strafrecht. Allgemeiner Teil. Lehrbuch.*. Tübingen, Germany: Mohr Siebeck GmbH & Co. K.
Schmidt, A. (2012). *Strafe und Versöhnung: Eine moral- und rechtsphilosophische Analyse von Strafe und Täter-Opfer-Ausgleich als Formen unserer Praxis*. Berlin, Germany: Duncker & Humblot.

Schmidt, A. (2015). Täter-Opfer-Staat: Zur Stellung des Opfers im Strafrecht. In M. Asholt et al. (Eds.), *Grundlagen und Grenzen des Strafrechts* (pp. 175–200). Baden-Baden: Nomos.

Seelmann, K. (2011). Hegels Straftheorien. In A. von Hirsch, U. Neumann, & K. Seelmann (Eds.), *Strafe – Warum? Gegenwärtige Strafbegründungen im Lichte von Hegels Straftheorie* (pp. 31–41). Baden-Baden, Germany: Nomos.

Sharp, S. (2005). *Hidden victims: The effects of the death penalty on families of the accused*. New Brunswick, NJ: Rutgers University Press.

Shay, J. (2014). Moral injury. *Psychoanalytic Psychology, 31*(2), 182–191. doi:10.1037/a0036090.

Srubar, I. (2010). Der Streit um die Wissenssoziologie. In G. Kneer & S. Moebius (Eds.), *Soziologische Kontroversen: Beiträge zu einer anderen Geschichte der Wissenschaft vom Sozialen* (pp. 46–78). Frankfurt am Main, Germany: Suhrkamp.

Steenkamp, M. M., Litz, B. T., Gray, M. J., Lebowitz, L., Nash, W. P., Conoscenti, L., et al. (2011). A brief exposure-based intervention for service members with PTSD. *Cognitive and Behavioral Practice, 18*, 98–107.

Stout, L. (2011). *Cultivating conscience: How good laws make good people*. Princeton/Oxford: Princeton University Press.

Stratenwerth, G. (1977). *Die Zukunft des strafrechtlichen Schuldprinzips*. Heidelberg, Germany: Müller, C F.

Thorburn, M. (2013). Criminal law as public law. In R. A. Duff & S. P. Green (Eds.), *Philosophical foundations of criminal law* (pp. 21–43). Oxford, England: Oxford University Press.

Veljanovska, M. (2012). The consequences of judicial obligations as a politics of transition in post-war Serbia, Bosnia and Herzegovina, and Croatia. *Temida, 15*(1), 179–204.

von Beling, E. L. (1906). *Die Lehre vom Verbrechen*. Aalen, Germany: Scientia.

von Hirsch, A. (2011). Warum soll die Strafsanktion existieren? – Tadel und Prävention als Elemente einer Rechtfertigung. In A. von Hirsch, U. Neumann, & K. Seelmann (Eds.), *Strafe – Warum? Gegenwärtige Strafbegründungen im Lichte von Hegels Straftheorie* (pp. 11–30). Baden-Baden, Germany: Nomos.

von Liszt, F. (1883). Der Zweckgedanke im Strafrecht. In *Strafrechtliche Aufsätze und Vorträge. Band 1: 1875 bis 1891* (Vols. 1–2, Vol. 1, pp. 126–155). Berlin, Germany: De Gruyter.

Weigend, T. (2010). "Die Strafe für das Opfer"? Zur Renaissance des Genugtuungsgedankens im Straf- und Strafverfahrensrecht. *RW, 1*, 39–57.

Wetzell, R. F. (2014). *Inventing the criminal: A history of German criminology, 1880–1945* (1st New edition.). Chapel Hill, NC: The University of North Carolina Press.

Zimmermann, S., Hinz, W., & Frommel, M. (2001). *Täterarbeit. Programm zur Arbeit mit gewalttätigen Männern*. Berlin, Germany: wvb Wissenschaftlicher Verlag.

Chapter 5
Differences Between Traditional Criminal Justice and a Human Dignity Based Approach

5.1 Justice for Victims, Offenders and All Others: the Line of Argument

Arguably, contemporary criminal justice systems are situated in an uncomfortable transitional zone between the fading era of the nation state still causing social convulsions and the dawning age of a cosmopolitan individualism based on human dignity and human rights. From the perspective of political anthropology, Ted Lewellen (2003, p. 220) observed that '[m]any anthropologists see, as a primary aspect of globalization, the decline or demise of the current state-centric system, in which dominant power is vested in national governments. The idea of the nation-state is a recent invention, dating back only a few hundred years, and in a very real sense it was always a myth'.

This chapter resumes the discussion of emerging new concepts of state and crime, which place human dignity and human rights at the heart of the normative order and the criminal justice system. To this end, it recapitulates the main theses of this book and, in addition, highlights some characteristic differences between the old and the new paradigms.

5.1.1 The Incompatibility Between the Traditional Concept of Criminal Justice and Victims' Participation in Proceedings

In their comparative analysis of "Human Dignity and Victims' Rights in the German and Israeli Criminal Process", Anat Horovitz and Thomas Weigend observe that in both countries "human dignity plays a relatively minor role in the context of victims' procedural rights" (2011, p. 266). The authors comment that "the participation of the victim in the criminal process raises similar concerns and

A. Dearing, *Justice for Victims of Crime*, DOI 10.1007/978-3-319-45048-3_5

difficulties in both countries, which may explain why the basic concept of human dignity does not go far in shaping the legal arrangements in these countries" (2011, p. 266). While they acknowledge that "a claim can be made for the victim's legal option to play a more active role", Horovitz and Weigend conclude (2011, pp. 297–298):

> That claim can be based on the premise that the victim's human dignity gives him a right to be treated as a 'subject' in the criminal process. The critical issue for that argument is whether the criminal process against the suspect/offender is (also) the victim's process. If that is the case, the victim may have a right not only to address the court and to present his views, but to also co-determine the outcome. If, on the other hand, the criminal process is primarily a matter between the state and the accused, the victim has not claim to allocution rights or to an even more active role. In such a case, the victim is, structurally, a mere by-stander. [...] However great the individual victim's interest in the conviction and sentencing of 'his' offender may be, it remains true that the criminal process, regardless of its adversarial or inquisitorial structure, is about the defendant's responsibility toward the state. It is the state that imposes, through its courts, criminal sanctions, and it is the state that enforces them.

This is precisely the crux of the matter. As long as it is "true" that criminal justice is about the state convicting and punishing the offender, the victim remains "structurally, a mere by-stander", and hence there is, within this traditional paradigm, little sense in attempting to introduce the victim in proceedings that have nothing to do with her. What therefore is decisive is not procedural, but substantive criminal law, as it is in substantive law that the offence is conceptualised and that it is determined whom it concerns. If the offence is a violation of a nation state's laws, it is the state that is entitled to the punishment of the offender. If the offence is conceptualised as the violation of an individual's rights, it is the victim—the person whose rights have been infringed—who can legitimately expect to have a position at the centre stage of criminal justice, allowing her to claim that the offender be convicted and punished.

However, from a methodological point of view, it may be questioned whether "it remains true that the criminal process [...] is about the defendant's responsibility toward the state". What is the basis of such "truth"? Is criminal justice a natural given that can only be observed and described, or is it an institution shaped by political decision? In fact, the authors proceed to observe that there is no basis "for regarding the victim as a 'natural' party in the criminal process." Against such naturalism, it may be remembered that for some two thirds of European history of criminal justice—from the sixth to the sixteenth century—victims and their families were the main force and actors driving the conviction and punishment of offenders. It was only monarchs, advocating the divine right of kings, who replaced the victim in this role, and that even at times of the fiercest absolutist rule some personal and 'private' issues—such as insult or trespass on the victim's home—remained for the victim to prosecute. In fact, the conceptualisation of a crime as a confrontation between the state and the offender is a characteristic of the nation state, while it does not fit the complex stratification of a feudal society. Still, private prosecution survived the high tide of nationalism. Hence, the perception that criminal justice is exclusively a matter between the state and the offender was at no time of the development of criminal justice in Europe entirely 'true', even if the domain of private prosecution at times shrank to a modest size (Weigend 1989, pp. 86–88).

What Horovitz and Weigend offer as evidence is the fact, that it "is the state that imposes, through its courts, criminal sanctions, and it is the state that enforces them." This seems to suggest that as long as it is state authorities that convict and punish, criminal justice can only be conceived as enforcing the state's right to the punishment of the offender. However, this is not necessarily the case. A criminal justice system is conceivable where the state is not entitled, but obliged to convict and punish offenders to avert the impunity of severe human rights violations and to ensure that the victims of such violations command an effective remedy. Moreover, since 1985, a growing number of courts at various levels in a plethora of cases have been saying just that: victims of severe human rights violation are entitled to an effective investigation and to prosecution capable of leading to the identification, conviction and punishment of offenders. Hence, the paradigm shift in criminal justice from states entitled to the punishment of offenders to states obliged to investigate, prosecute, convict and punish has now been under way for more than three decades and cannot be ignored.

Arguably, it is about time to start thinking more comprehensively, systematically and carefully through a new paradigm of criminal justice that takes human dignity and the rights of individuals seriously. In this paradigm the state is—expressed in human rights jargon—not a rights-holder, but a duty-bearer, obliged to respect and protect human rights and to provide effective remedies in cases of severe human rights violations.

5.1.2 *A New Paradigm and Start-Up Difficulties*

However, in constructing a consistent theoretical basis for the new paradigm, the most fundamental requirement is that it should respect both the victim and the offender as persons sharing in human dignity. If the purpose of punishing is to deter future offenders, criminal justice would fail on both counts. Punishing would treat the offender as a mere means of protecting others and would, at the same time, detach punishing from the actual victim, as deterring future offenders fails to relate punishment to the concrete victim. Deterrent punishing violates human dignity in relation to both the victim and the offender.

Hence what is needed is a theory of punishment that meets two requirements. Firstly, punishing must be conceptualised as a means of acknowledging the victim as a person and rights-holder and of redressing the wrong done to the victim. Secondly, convicting and punishing the offender must not reduce the offender to a means used to the ends of others (including the victim), but respect the dignity of the offender. In Chapter 1, the term 'Kant's principle' was coined to underline this crucial challenge that any theory, claiming to respect human dignity, must face.

In Chapter 1 it was also decided to strictly distinguish between the functions and the justification of punishment, as a criminal justice system that achieves its aims must not necessarily also be justified in terms of a normative order respecting human dignity and human rights. While Chapter 2 proposes and elaborates a theory of the societal functions of punishment, Chapters 3 and 4 aspire to answer the complex question of how convicting and punishing fellow citizens can be justified within a normative framework based on human dignity and human rights.

5.1.3 The Animal That Punishes

Chapter 2 enquires into the benefits of punishing, starting out from the fact that punishment comes close to a human universal. The reason is simply that societies that are too large to rely on bilateral relationships based on mutual reciprocating and personal trust are premised on generally binding social norms and on mechanisms ensuring that norm violations are sanctioned. Abiding by the rules is burdensome, and the readiness of citizens to accept this burden is premised on their confidence that others too will contribute their fair due. However, that is not always the case, and witnessing that others freeride on the efforts of loyal cooperators seriously damages the morale of those who, in principle, would be willing to contribute their share to the society's cooperation in establishing and preserving a normative order. To be precise, offending can be attractive in two respects. Firstly, the offender rids herself of the burden of the normative order and helps herself to a portion of unrestrained freedom to which she is not entitled. Secondly, she draws profit from her offending. While the first benefit is inherent in norm violations, the second is contingent on the circumstances of the offence. However, in both respects punishment counteracts and neutralizes the pleasure gained by offending. Hence, sanctions react to norm violations, vindicating the norm by confirming the legitimate expectations of cooperators and rendering defecting unattractive. The basic function of punishment is therefore to respond to a norm violation by signalling to those who feel exploited and taken for fools that they were right to cooperate and that the shirker is not the one who laughs last.

Still, what calls for an explanation is the fact that this semantics of retributive punishment is understood across so many cultures and times. The reason is, as elaborated in Chapter 2, that the meaning of punishment is genetically encoded in an entire network of powerful punitive sentiments which drive retributive punishment and thus preserve and vindicate a society's normative order. These emotions are not threats to justice, but a crucial part of its basis, as they motivate third parties' costly investments in criminal justice.

5.1.4 Human Dignity as the Right to be a Person

Analysing the functions of punishment in abstract terms is one thing; answering the question of how and to what extent punishing can be justified within a concrete normative framework based on human dignity and human rights quite another. In developing a concept of human dignity, Chapter 3 relies on a broad consensus that this concept expresses an appreciation of the human individual and her entitlement to be free and to live a self-determined life.

Certainly, freedom and autonomy are key terms in the ethics of Kant, who is often credited with crucially contributing to the conceptualisation of human dignity. However, the problem with Kant's notion of autonomy is that it refers to an innate quality of humans who are called on by their Creator as moral beings. Fichte, on the other hand, believed that only the first humans were called on by God, which set in motion a chain of cultural development within which a mounting body of cultural achievements is passed on from one generation to the next.

Hence, it is the calling of her parents that initiates the process of the formation of a child as a person and a member of the human family. Human dignity has its foundation not—as Kant would have it—in a particular quality inherent in humans, but in an unconditional entitlement, namely the right to be—and to be respected as—a person and to be supported in developing as a person. Because of her being genetically human, the individual is entitled to being constituted as a person and a member in the cultural project of humankind. The Fichtean reading of human dignity thus anticipates Arendt's fundamental right to have rights and to belong to a legal community.

It should, however, not be overlooked that the right of one individual to be constituted as a rights-holder implies an obligation on all others to accept their constitution as accountable agents who respect the rights of rights-holders. In a polity committed to the ideal of human dignity, individuals have both a right and an obligation to develop as persons, as the preservation of a normative order can only be achieved by the cooperation of both autonomous and accountable persons.

The political implications of Fichte's views cannot be overstated. The primary task of society is not to respect and protect individual autonomy, but to generate persons. While liberal ideology claims that the state should withdraw from the public arena as much as possible to allow individual freedom to prosper in a democracy founded on individuals' innate autonomy, the state's principal function is, in a Fichtean perspective, to establish, guarantee and protect the societal preconditions on which the formation of autonomous and accountable persons is premised and to guard processes of subject formation against distorting or crippling ideological forces.

What hence corresponds to and reflects the ideal of human dignity at a political level is a decent society constructed with a view to optimise the societal preconditions of individuals' development as respected, accountable and autonomous agents. This vision entails the concept of a principled—or militant—society that is ready to confront discourses that have a potential to deform the generation of persons, e.g. because they are discriminatory or discourage groups of individuals—women, persons with disabilities, Roma—from claiming their right to develop their full potential as autonomous persons.

5.1.5 Criminal Justice Supporting the Formation of Persons

If the political ideal of human dignity is about supporting and protecting individuals in their development as persons, what does that imply in terms of reconstructing criminal justice based on human dignity?

From the victim's perspective, the offence violates her rights and disregards her as a person, thus challenging her status as a respected full member of the human family. What justifies the conviction and, in appropriate cases, also the punishment of the offender is the fact that by her offending she has incurred a debt to the collective formation of the victim as a respected person and rights-holder. She owes to the victim her fair contribution to the collective endeavour of preserving the norms that found the victim's rights and of generating the victim as a full member of the human family. Convicting and, if necessary, also punishing the offender expresses the community's solidarity with the victim and determination to insist that the offender settles her debt to the authority of the victim's rights and status as a person.

From the offender's perspective, the community's reaction to her offending must stand the test of respecting the—adult and healthy—offender as an accountable agent. Hence, the offender is entitled to be called on to take responsibility for the wrong done to the victim and, accordingly, to be convicted and punished. Obviously, a normative order based on human dignity is premised on a practice of holding agents to account for the wrong done to others. In this respect too, criminal justice is a corner stone of a humanist normative order.

However, the offender's right to her conviction and punishment is premised on two conditions, which together represent Kant's principle. Firstly, the offender's right not to be used as a means to the ends of others is inherently restricted. It does not provide an argument against the enforcement of norms on which the offender's own constitution as a person is premised. The offender's autonomy does not justify opposition against its own preconditions. In other terms, Kant's principle does not stand in the way of the enforcement of the rights and obligations that flow from the concept of human dignity.

Secondly, throughout the investigation, the proceedings and the execution of sanctions, the offender must be treated in conformity with her dignity and her community's solidarity. All acts addressing the offender must express the endeavour to support the offender in developing as an accountable person, who is able to understand the normative claims of her legal community and to respect others as fellow citizens. In fact, as much as the offender owes to the formation of the victim as a respected and autonomous person, as much is owed to her own formation as an accountable person and reliable cooperator. Therefore, it is in the end exactly and only the interplay of the human rights violation suffered by the victim and the right of the offender to be held to account for the wrong done to the victim that together justify the offender's punishment.

Knowing this, the question can be answered as to what functions a criminal law provision fulfils. It can be read from two different perspectives, firstly as expressing a strong public disapproval of the criminalised conduct, a firm and binding societal consensus in this regard, and as the state's commitment to supporting this consensus by safeguarding the rights of victims; but secondly also as defining what it will cost the offender as a citizen to restore her full membership rights; and these costs reflect the significance of the wrong done to the victim. The objective of criminal law is not to deter, but, firstly, to appeal to a normative consensus that exists or is developing in a legal community, secondly, to reassure and encourage conditional cooperators, and, thirdly, to ascertain the price to be paid by offenders as a condition for their remaining respected members of their community.

5.2 The Deep Roots of the Traditional State-Centred Paradigm

The traditional state-centred paradigm is premised on collectively binding decisions on what is to be considered abstract legal goods (*Rechtsgüter*) or public interests, which, when violated, result in 'harm' or 'public wrong'. These assumptions are, firstly, collectivist, secondly, consequentialist, and, thirdly, mistaken. What defines an open, pluralist society is exactly the unavailability of a binding consensus of what is to be considered as 'good' or 'a good' or an interest in which all share. If the traditional paradigm is to be overcome, it must be eradicated with its deep roots in nationalism and consequentialism.

How a normative order founded on human dignity overcomes collectivism and nationalism has been explored above and need not be repeated here. However, what must be reconsidered is the crucial importance of leaving consequential ethics behind, which manifests itself in seemingly descriptive terms such as harm, goods, and interests.

5.2.1 Deontological Versus Consequentialist Ethics

To demonstrate the difference between deontological and consequentialist ethics one can imagine a doctor in a hospital carrying out complicated surgery on a young man who has been severely injured in a road accident. The outcome is on the razor's edge and the doctor is almost tempted to give up, when it crosses her mind that, if this young man dies, with his organs the lives of three other patients could be saved who are desperately in need of organ donation and otherwise likely not to survive (Law 2011, p. 87). May the doctor, in this situation, give up on one patient, whose life might be doomed to end anyway to save the lives of three others?

Similarly, if four terrorists have hijacked a plane with seven passengers and five crew members on board and now steer the plane, loaded with explosives, towards a crowded football stadium, are the armed forces allowed or even obliged to destroy the plane and the lives of the 16 persons on board to save the lives of hundreds of people?

In consequentialist ethics the moral assessment of an action considers the positive and negative effects it is likely to bring about. The results would be that it is commendable to sacrifice the life of one patient to save the lives of three others or to kill 16 people in favour of rescuing the lives of hundreds.

A deontological approach must be entirely different, because this approach, firstly, does not see goods as having an invariable value and, secondly, does not see ethics as a means of safeguarding goods in the first place. Normativity is less about saving lives and more about respecting individuals as autonomous and responsible persons, who follow their own, idiosyncratic path of life. Individuals' autonomy means that it is up to them to decide what for them is, at a certain time, good or important. This is not for others—including the state—to decide.

It is true that life is the basis of all agency. However, in the first example, one of the patients waiting for organ donation may be the mother of the young man and may not want to live at the cost of her son's death. As an autonomous agent she may prefer dying to living at this price. In any case, it is not for anyone but her to know and to decide. In terms of an individual's autobiography, actions shortening the time span of her life are too important to be taken by others in her stead. In an ethics based on human dignity and valuing individual autonomy, a subject may decide to sacrifice her life for the benefit of others, but no one else is entitled to make such a decision in her place. Human dignity protects the individual from being sacrificed for the sake of others. It forbids any action that disrespects human dignity in any one individual. Within narrow margins, such an ethics may also demand that action is taken for the sake of human dignity in another person—e.g. parents obliged to raise and look after their children or a legal community punishing an offender—but the aim of such action must be to enable and foster personhood, not to disrespect human dignity in any one person.

Hence, in the two examples sketched above, the doctor may not decide to sacrifice the life of her patient to the lives of others, nor may a military commander decide to kill passengers or crew members to save the lives of hundreds. In a way, when it comes to human beings, human dignity is blind to numbers. Human dignity is not a count noun. There is only one human dignity that shows in every single human being and her claim to respectful treatment. In consequentialist ethics, lives are counted and pitched against one another. In ethics departing from human dignity, all human beings are viewed as united in the common project of human culture. The assessment of any action is based on the question of whether it respects human dignity in all persons—every single person, that is,—or not.

However, what about the hijackers? If no other passengers or crew members were on board, would it be lawful to destroy the plane and thus kill the terrorists to save the lives of the people in the football stadium? What about human dignity in the terrorists? The answer should be that it is permissible to kill terrorists if it is the only means of saving the lives of others. This is premised on demonstrating that killing the terrorists is not disrespectful of human dignity in the terrorists. It is not, because in being killed they are respected as accountable agents in view of the wrong they are about to inflict on others. The victims' right to self-defense is premised on the aggressors' right to be treated as accountable agents.

5.2.2 *Consequentialism in Ethics and Legal Theory*

It has been demonstrated numerous times the extent to which criminal law based on consequentialism runs counter to the moral intuitions that—as the result of the coevolution of culture and genes—are deeply ingrained in our convictions and sentiments. A particularly conclusive criticism of consequentialist ethics has been put forward by Philippa Foot (2002), who demonstrates that consequentialism encounters difficulties in answering relatively simple questions, such as: Why would attempted murder be punishable, although no harm has been done? Or: why would killing a person by accident be significantly less blameworthy compared to killing her intentionally? Kyron Huigens offers the following objection to consequentialism (2003, pp. 33–34):

> The scapegoating objection points out that if punishment is justified by deterrence, or by any other beneficial consequences, then a net gain in good consequences should be pursued regardless of traditional notions of guilt and desert. If a quick conviction and hanging will avoid mob violence in a town upset by a heinous crime, then the authorities should quickly convict and hang someone. Anyone will do, provided that the person hanged can plausibly be portrayed as the perpetrator. Neither finding the true perpetrator nor determining an appropriate sentence should matter if this 'punishment' is justified by a net gain in social welfare.

If one leaves out the normative dimension, victimisation shrinks from a rights violation to harm, and punishment translates from an expression of censure into the intentional causation of more harm, which, however, can be outweighed by beneficial effects. When Shue (1996, p. 58) compares a case of intentional assault or murder to another situation, where similar harm is caused unintentionally, he finds that

> for the two victims the difference between intended physical harm and unintended physical harm may matter little, since the harmfulness of the action taken may be the same in both cases and may be even greater where unintended.

Yet this will probably be true only if the victim is a hard-boiled consequentialist philosopher. Otherwise, it is likely that intentional assault or murder will be experienced by the victim as a blatant disregard of her right to physical integrity and as a failure to acknowledge her as a person. This will not be the case if the bodily injury is caused unintentionally. Whether the act of another person expresses respect or disregard matters to persons because they have been constituted by acts of recognition and have internalised a sense of self-respect. Therefore, they experience intentional violations of their rights as disparaging, while natural catastrophes do not cause such feelings. This is what marks the difference between a 'goods/harm-approach' and a 'right/wrong-approach' to criminal justice. For the latter, severe human rights violations touch, in addition to what damage may have been caused, on the victim's legitimate claim that others respect her rights, as in respecting her rights they respect her as a person and confirm her social existence.

However, if consequentialism has been refuted so many times in perfectly convincing manners, the question remains, why it is that consequentialism rises and resurfaces over and again like an undead creature of ethics?

Arguably, what is attractive about consequentialism as the basis for ethical decision-making is that it entails two promises, firstly, to overcome relativism, and, secondly, to exclude emotions. Consequentialism fails on both promises, because it cannot possibly deliver on either.

5.2.3 Empiricism and Objectivity

By relying on descriptive categories, instrumental reasoning and rational procedures—such as preference optimisation and making up the balance of beneficial and harmful effects—consequentialism minimises "the ratio of normative to empirical claims" (Huigens 2003, p. 41). The aim is to achieve objective assessments and to avoid subjective evaluations. However, this endeavour of consequentialism to base moral assessments in general—and criminal law in particular—on objective, empirical categories, such as harm or damage, is premised on a false hope as to the potential gains of such a manoeuvre. Consequentialism is motivated by the belief in the objectivity, reliability, and stability of empirical categories. However, this is a premature assumption. In fact, there is reason to question what is referred to as the 'correspondence theory of truth', the idea, that is, that we command means of assessing objectively whether assumptions about empirical reality are true in the sense that they correspond—and can be shown to correspond—to reality.

The construction of an environment is a function of the interaction and cooperation that allows us to, collectively, sustain our existence. Humans are highly social and cooperative animals, and their interactions are based on 'shared' models and assumptions about their environment, which provide a common interpretation and orientation and enable cooperation and a joint struggle for survival. The models processed by our brains fulfil a practical function and are not construed as a matter of theoretical contemplation. Already Fichte saw clearly that our knowledge of the external world is a consequence of the necessity of joint action (1800/1848, p. 131):

> From this necessity of action proceeds the consciousness of the actual world; and not the reverse way, from the consciousness of the actual world the necessity of action. [...] We do not act because we know, but we know because we are called upon to act: - the practical reason is the root of all reason.

If humans would not closely and permanently cooperate, they would not be in need of a highly sophisticated shared interpretation of their environment. Initially, the concept of a crocodile does not serve the purpose of biological research but of communicating why it is about time to get out of the water. Empirical cognition is a function of acting and acting a function of collective survival. In other words—those of Geoge Herbert Mead (1936, p. 345)—,

> the intelligence of the human form is one which has arisen through its ability to analyze this world by discrimination, and, through significant symbols, to indicate to other forms with which it works and to the form itself what the elements are that are of importance to it. It is able to set up such a structure of symbols, images, which stand for the object that it needs. Thinking is an elaborate process of selecting, an elaborate process of presenting the world so that it will be favorable for conduct. [. . .] That is, the test of intelligence is found in action.

Empirical assessments are a function of practical reason, and not the other way around; and because of the functional priority of the normative over the empirical, the idea of premising normative evaluations on empirical categories—such as interests, goods, or harm—amounts to putting the cart before the horse.

The rejection of the correspondence theory of truth is inextricably linked to the name of Richard Rorty. To give a fresh perspective, a statement shall be quoted that comes from a very different corner of academia. Humberto Maturana, in his lecture on Fundamental Relativity posits as follows (2013, p. 92):

> In these circumstances, what are we talking about when we speak of Reality? The word "Reality" comes from the Latin word "Res", which means "thing", or "entity", and we use this word to refer to a domain of entities and processes that are thought to exist independently of what we do as human beings as we distinguish them. But as we know now that we cannot say anything about anything that we think exists by itself independently of what we do when we distinguish it, we know that the notion of Reality is an invented explanatory proposition that, if it does what we think it does, would permit us to claim that what we say is universally valid. From all that I have said already, it should be apparent that I think that it is not so, and that I think that knowledge, explanations, behaviours, scientific theories and so on are not related to an independent Reality, but are related to our operation in the worlds that we generate in the realization of our living as languaging molecular autopoietic systems.

Not only is consequentialism wrong to believe that norms can be conceived as a function of empirical categories. On the contrary, our empirical—descriptive—categories and notions are a function of practical—or pragmatic—reason. We construe an objective world to allow subjects to, individually and collectively, act and take responsibility. The basic categories of our perception—such as nature following laws of causation, while we as agents are free from causation—only make sense in a world of accountable agents living and generating one another within culture as a profoundly normative order.

5.2.4 Is There an Escape from Consequentialism?

Three forms or levels of consequentialism can be distinguished. Act-consequentialism morally evaluates an act based on the beneficial or harmful effects it causes. An act-consequentialist theory of punishment would assume that punishment is justified by its beneficial consequences, e.g. by deterring future offenders or by incapacitating the actual offender. Clearly, this view has not been supported in the preceding chapters.

There also exist more sophisticated versions of consequentialism, including rule-consequentialism. A rule-consequentialist account of punishment would posit that, while the function of punishment is to preserve the norm that has been violated by the offender, what justifies the norm—and hence indirectly also justifies punishment—is the beneficial consequences of the norm. Such a theory would maintain that punishment is justified as a means of vindicating legal norms (the common German term is '*Rechtsbewährungsfunktion der Strafe*'). This is indeed how the function of punishment was explained in Chapter 2: as a means of preserving norms of fair cooperation.

However, this is not how Chapter 4 justifies punishment, the reason being that such a 'justification' would not pass the test of Kant's principle. Whatever norm a parliamentary majority would deem beneficial and desirable could be legislated and enforced against norm violators. Such punishment would serve the interests of the majority but not respect the autonomy and dignity of the offender. What justifies punishment is exactly that it respects human dignity in the offender, in the victim and in all other members of the human family who have equal dignity rights. Punishment serves human dignity and the normative order founded on this political ideal. It is an indispensable means of preserving a decent society and of vindicating its norms.

Do we then end up with a sort of system-consequentialism, where, what in the end justifies punishment is its function of preserving normativity and where the normative order based on human dignity is justified by its beneficial effects? It is true that above it was maintained that without a normative order humankind cannot survive, and that a normative order based on human dignity is the most promising candidate when it comes to designing a global political order. At least, this is what those who drafted and voted the Universal Declaration of Human Rights believed.

However, if a normative paradigm comprises all elements of a normative order, there cannot exist yet another and even more profound norm justifying the entire system. Even if the survival and evolution of humankind are premised on a global normative order based on human dignity—as may well be the case -, survival and evolution are not moral categories. The decision to answer to the call of others and to engage in the project of humankind is therefore not a moral decision. If anything, it can be seen as existentialist or aesthetic, meaning that it is, in any case, entirely up to the individual to decide and by her decision to demonstrate who she is.

5.3 From Technical Rationality to Lively Communication

5.3.1 Criminal Justice as a System of Acts of Communication

Others have, for some time, highlighted the expressive (Feinberg, Hampton, von Hirsch) or communicative (Duff) functions of the criminal justice system and emphasised that punishment is a means of censuring offenders for their behaviour and, as the flip-side of the same coin, of acknowledging the rights of and the wrong suffered by victims (Hampton 2007; for the German discussion compare Bussmann 1996; Hörnle 2006).

This places punishment at the level of communication and suggests that the offence and the punishment of the offender are 'moves in a language game'. The term 'game' is not meant to overlook or belittle in any way the serious nature of what is communicated and at stake for the victim, the offender and all other members of the polity. Instead, it emphasises that the meaning of an action cannot be understood by analysing this action in isolation but only by viewing it and understanding its position within the wider framework of the social reality of criminal law and criminal justice, including all forms of everyday communication that use their language.

In this perspective, criminal justice is an institution that serves as a stage for those who claim that their rights or the rights of others have been violated and for those who are called to answer to such charges.

Rights, then, are not solely or primarily a matter of laws. They only become a reality when they are attributed, acknowledged and acted on. They are a matter of communication, of concrete symbolic interactions of individuals who share a normative language. Individuals are awarded rights, which are confirmed and strengthened whenever they are respected and are challenged and called into question when they are ignored and infringed upon. As long as they only exist in law books, rights are theoretical, uncertain and faint, if not illusory. However, they become practical, robust and reliable when they are claimed and recognised in daily life or when they are announced, officially and publicly, by a legitimate public institution.

Criminal justice is a complex organisation of communicative acts, and in this sense a 'language game'. It starts with a legislator acknowledging rights and assuring all individuals of the protection of their rights by criminal sanctions. This is followed by a crime, negating the rights of a victim and thereby calling into doubt the reliability of equal rights of others. From the victim's perspective, the reaction of others to her victimisation and the following course of procedural interactions negotiate and determine the meaning and the significance of the offence to her as a person. The role of the police is to define and acknowledge the wrong of the suspect's conduct as calling the victim's rights into question. The defendant is charged by the prosecutor with having infringed on the victim's rights. This can lead to the defendant acknowledging her conduct and taking responsibility for it or to the formalised dispute of a public hearing. Finally a court is tasked with the authoritative jurisdiction, with the 'speaking of the law', *Rechtsprechung*—with a view to confirm the rights and social status of the victim as much as the equal rights of all others.

The court's verdict is the last word, although not necessarily the end of the story, not yet for the offender who might face the execution of a sentence, and not for many victims who may still struggle to fully grasp and to come to terms with their victimisation. However, that the violation of her rights was ascertained, that the offender's conduct was censured, that the offender is made to bear the consequences of her conduct, that thereby the victim's rights and her status as a full member of society are acknowledged, all this is meaningful and makes it easier for the victim to formulate an account of her victimisation in which the offence figures as a wrong of the offender and not a mistake of the victim, as an incidence where the victim was right in not expecting the offender's conduct. By singling out the offender's behaviour as a norm violation and unacceptable, the victim and others can maintain their confidence that others will respect their rights. In short: The rules stay in place. This eases the integration of the potentially highly unsettling experience of a victimisation in the autobiography of victims and enables them, on this basis, to come to terms with what they have encountered and to move on in their lives.

5.3.2 From Manipulation to Conviviality: Making Criminal Justice a Participatory Institution

Ivan Illich has called our attention to the opposition between what he refers to as "manipulative" and "convivial" institutions. Participation in manipulative institutions is "achieved in two ways, both coercive: by forced commitment or by selective service", and this includes "treatment-institutions", even when they assume a therapeutic or compassionate image. Convivial institutions, on the contrary, are used voluntarily and spontaneously, without people having to be convinced that it is to their advantage to do so. While the rules establishing manipulative institutions "call for unwilling consumption or participation", the rules regulating and restricting the use of convivial institutions in no way impair the autonomy of their clients as free agents. Convivial institutions "support personal growth rather than addiction" (1970, pp. 52–57, 1973).

This spectrum is helpful, as it serves to highlight that the criminal justice system has developed from a convivial institution, which could be used by victims and their families to express their anger and indignation and to demand that the offender should make amends for her wrongdoing, to—at the other extreme—the courts of Inquisition from the fourteenth to eighteenth century. Such courts abused individuals, including victims and offenders, as witnesses in supporting roles in proceedings that were staged for the sole purpose of demonstrating the power and the glory of the Roman Catholic Church and of the crowns supported by this church. Since the nineteenth century, significant improvements have been achieved in moving the criminal justice system gradually back again in the other direction.

A criminal justice system that adheres to the value of human dignity aims to restore, as far as possible, the parties to the offence as autonomous and accountable agents. To fulfil their objective, institutions of criminal justice should be easily accessible, transparent and practically useful for citizens who want to engage in and contribute to criminal proceedings. They must allow individuals to perform an appropriate role within the criminal justice system and support them in doing so: as a victim claiming justice, as a defendant accepting or denying accountability, or as a witness contributing her share, as a citizen, to the determination of the truth. Whenever the institutions of criminal justice become inhibiting, overly complex, bureaucratic, time-consuming, opaque, manipulative, disconcerting or even intimidating they defeat their purpose of fostering the development of persons and of peace among them, based on a normative order.

In a criminal justice system embracing human dignity, the functions of accusing and convicting an offender aim at making the offender understand and accept that what she did was wrong. This is not an unreasonable imposition as long as criminal justice remains confined to protecting human dignity and its implications. Convicting an offender is premised on her guilt, which implies her ability to understand and abide by the norm she has infringed. Criminal proceedings should attempt to realise this potential and to enable the offender to understand the wrong she has done to the victim and the legal community.

Penalties are not just because they are dissuasive but dissuasive because they are just and correspond to citizens' moral convictions. By notifying its citizens of its resolve to react to the commission of a severe human rights violation, a state not only does justice to the principle of *nullum crimen sine lege* but also acknowledges and underlines the seriousness of a certain human rights violation and thus confirms and reinforces the moral intuitions and convictions of its citizens.

One important institutional aspect relates to the potential incapacitation of victims and offenders by their lawyers. Lawyers should advise and accompany the parties, not replace them, as is often the case today. The rights of defendants and victims to actively participate in criminal proceedings mutate into 'rights' of lawyers acting on their behalf. As Caplan (1977, pp. 103–194) has put it:

> Most litigants are required to surrender complete control of their case to the lawyers on the ground that they do not know what is best for them, and meekly accept relegation to the position of observer in a drama which could radically alter their lives. Although lawyers claim to act only on instructions, that is only the literal truth and not the reality.

Instead of empowering the parties, lawyers incapacitate and replace them in proceedings, taking over and seizing possession of the case. Christie (1977, p. 3) described the first impression of an observer entering a European courtroom.

> Here again, the periphery of the parties is the striking observation. The parties are represented, and it is these representatives and the judge or judges who express the little activity that is activated within these rooms. [...] the symbol of the whole system is the Supreme Court where the directly involved parties do not even attend their own court cases.

Christie (1977, pp. 3–4) refers—in his markedly contoured style—to lawyers as professional thieves, because they "are particularly good at stealing conflicts. They are trained for it. [...] Conflicts become the property of lawyers."

A criminal justice system aspiring to respect human dignity treats all individuals involved as autonomous lawgivers and accountable persons. Firstly, the offender has a right to be taken seriously. If she admits to her criminal conduct and is ready to make amends this must not be ignored. In this respect, much can be learned from the common law tradition. The guilty plea of the accused to the charges laid against her impacts on the following procedure and on sentencing for good reasons. On the continent, often much of the offenders' and victims' time and taxpayers' money is wasted on complex and costly efforts to prove that what the offender has been admitting from the beginning is true.

In Italy, on the other hand, the defendant has the right to ask for an abbreviated proceeding (*giudizio abbreviato*). In this case, no formal court trial is carried out. At the request of the prosecutor or the defendant, the Judge of the Preliminary Hearing (*Giudice per l'Udienza Preliminare*, 'GUP') decides on conviction and sentencing from the evidence gathered in the course of the investigation. The offender is rewarded with a reduction of the sentence by one third.

Secondly, the victim, as a party to the proceedings, has the right to be heard and to be taken seriously by the court, even in summary proceedings. This is a fundamental right of any party that must be respected in all circumstances, under various conditions, including cases where the defendant pleas guilty. Listening to the victim's account will, in any case, help the court to assess whether the defendant admits to all violations of the victim's rights that are at stake. However, if the views of the public prosecutor, the victim and the offender coincide in all essential aspects, there is no point in the court carrying out tedious proceedings for the taking of evidence.

In a criminal trial, the victim must have rights to request that evidence be taken, to be present at all hearings, to ask questions to witnesses and the defendant, in short, to act as a full party to the proceedings. And these parties should be referred to as 'defendant' and 'victim', not as 'presumed victim' or 'potential victim'. It is sometimes maintained that the presumption of innocence requires that the victim be referred to in such vague terms (e.g. Holz 2007, p. 26). But that is not the case. If a person is found dead with a knife in her back, the presumption of innocence means that we may not assume, before her conviction, that X is the offender; it does not mean that we may not assume that an offence has been committed at all. The presumption of innocence relates to the question of a particular individual's guilt, not to the question of whether or not an offence has occurred. If a person can arguably claim that her rights have been violated by the commission of an offence, this person is to be treated as a victim holding all the rights attached to this position in the investigation and the ensuing proceedings.

The inclusion of both the defendant and the victim as parties is a more convivial means of conducting criminal justice proceedings. Not only substantive criminal law, but criminal proceedings too must be constructed in a manner fitting a humanist society.

5.3.3 The Promise of Objectivity and the Myth of the Vindictive Victim

Those who hold traditional views of criminal justice often prefer that court rooms should have an atmosphere of cool, distant, dispassionate objectivity. They distrust emotions in general and the emotions of victims in particular. This is why they wish that criminal proceedings be conducted, to the widest extent possible, by legal professionals with their trained legal rationality.

Distrust in emotions can be traced back to Kant. Kant distills respect for the law as the quintessential moral sentiment (1785, p. 17) and, at the same time, the only entirely trustworthy moral motive, as long as it remains a "pure sense-free interest of practical reason alone" (1788, p. 66). On one occasion, Kant first admits that benevolence can strongly corroborate the effectiveness of moral laws, but then considers that even sympathy as a motive is annoying as it can confuse the moral principles of an intellectual person. Kant concludes (1788, p. 96):

> Inclination is blind and servile, whether it is kindly or not; and when morality is in question, reason must not play the part of mere guardian to inclination but, disregarding it altogether, must attend solely to its own interest as pure practical reason.

While Kant is right to insist on the primacy of practical reason, he tends to sweepingly distrust all sentiments and underestimates how significantly moral sentiments corroborate practical reason. While Kant convincingly stresses that morality shows when an individual resists sweet temptations, his generally skeptical view on emotions leads Kant to underestimate the positive role of social sentiments. There is no reason to look down on what Damasio (2012, p. 134) refers to as social emotions, such as pride, self-esteem, compassion, sympathy, shame or guilt. Rather, social emotions are one of two pillars on which human morality rests. In practice, these two pillars of social, moral sentiments and respect for the law are not opponents, but fight side by side as powerful allies. In fact, morality and prosocial sentiments in most instances sit so well with one another that it is difficult to imagine that they should have developed independently of one another. What is needed is a theoretical concept of the relation of practical reason and prosocial emotions in humans, such as the concept of Gene-culture coevolution and a theory of structural coupling of practical reason and moral sentiments.

One obstacle that all attempts to improve the situation of victims as rights-holders meet is the myth that banning victims from court rooms protects the criminal justice system against the victim's emotionality in general and her irrational desire for rampant vengeance in particular.

This is not very plausible, firstly, because what would, from this point of view, need to be explained is why victims who in the traditional system usually know how to behave when called on to testify as witnesses, would forget all their good manners and mutate into avengers, beside themselves, when allowed to act as parties to the proceedings. In addition, if victims would be driven by blind forces towards ruthless payback and would for that reason need to be banned from court rooms, it is unclear why victims' violent predispositions do not result in a plethora of devastating atrocities outside of court rooms.

Shapland has stressed "that, in England and Wales, as successive British Crime Surveys have shown, the vindictive victim is a rarity" (Shapland 2000, p. 163). Along the same lines, Reneé Zauberman (2000, p. 38) has explained that in France "the conventional legal view has traditionally been suspicious of victims as party to the criminal justice process". Victims' presence in criminal proceedings was considered "some kind of surviving relic of a still barbarian state of law, close to a system of vengeance. The concept of vengeance, believed to be primitive and endless, therefore tending towards the death of society, was perceived to lie in direct opposition to regular, institutionalized justice whose exclusion of the victim seemed to be a major victory of civilization in a society pacified at long last." Zauberman confronts this myth with historical facts and concludes (2000, p. 39) that the

> doctrinal use of barbarism as a mythical foil was accepted unconditionally for a long time, despite important anthropological studies showing that vengeance is by no means anarchic and uncontrolled, but rather an infinitely regulated, precise mechanism. It is based on exchange, aims at redress and includes procedures for appeasement and reconciliation [...] the jurists' 'evolutionist' narrative of a mythical changeover from immediate, excessive, blind personal vengeance to mediated, measured, personalized public justice can no longer be seen as a historical view of law, but rather as an ideology of law within the context of the construction of a state intent on appropriating a monopoly on force and punishment.

Zauberman also commented that "the crux of the victims-criminal justice relationship resides in the concept of the state" and that history has more to teach us about that relationship than legal discourse, "which has often been no more than a rationalization reflecting political practices." These observations concur with the approach taken here, which views criminal justice and punishing as reflecting the normative order they defend and vindicate. Within the political framework of a nation state, the state is viewed as entitled to the punishment of the offender. Consequently, the rights of victims to criminal justice are denied, and this denial is underpinned by an ideology that serves the purpose of rendering the victim's claims illegitimate and dubious. Popular myths about the vindictive and irrational victim who cannot be trusted stabilise the normative order of the nation state.

However, this issue points to a much broader question, namely whether our ideal of criminal justice should require that emotions are kept out of court buildings. Such a claim is neither reasonable nor realistic. Arguably, what must be feared is not social sentiments but the cold, impersonal logic and technical rationality that, according to Adorno, made Auschwitz possible (Adorno 1970, p. 5). The mechanism of criminal justice can work and drive a society's normative reproduction and development only because it is fuelled by powerful moral sentiments that motivate victims to report their victimisation to the police and others to testify as witnesses. What lies at the core of all these emotions is a shared understanding that the offender has wronged the victim. The various sentiments relate to this fact from different perspectives. However, they all serve to motivate a reaction that appropriately answers to the wrong done to the victim and, to the extent possible, reverses or mitigates the negative impact of the offence on the victim's rights, on the victim's status as a moral person, on the normative order and indirectly on social cohesion and peace mediated by this order.

Therefore, regarding the second promise of consequentialism, to keep emotions out of the court room, the ideology of criminal proceedings as a matter of cool functionality and rational social engineering, premised on the victim's banishment from the court room, is not reasonable. In line with a long tradition of ethical intuitionism and sentimentalism—spanning from Anthony Ashley Cooper, Third Earl of Shaftesbury (1683), David Hume (1751), Francis Hutcheson (1755) and Adam Smith (1759) to contemporary philosophers including Peter Frederick Strawson (1974), Ernst Tugendhat (2006) and Raphael Gross (2010)—this analysis views the institutions of criminal justice as, on the one hand, driven by and, on the other, controlling and modulating strong emotions of resentment and anger of victims, by others' emotions of sympathy for victims and indignation towards offenders, as well as the latter's sentiments of shame and guilt and the desire to restore a good reputation and to regain the respect of her community. Not only is there nothing wrong with social sentiments, it is likely that normativity could not be sustained without them (Huigens 2003, pp. 43–44).

In conclusion, the objective of criminal justice is not to protect subjects against harm or hazards, but to protect persons and their rights against violations, where both the person and her rights are constructed in acts of normative communication. Hence, the purpose of criminal justice is to vindicate persons and their rights, not to protect goods or interests (*Rechtsgüter*).

The only security which the criminal justice system should be concerned about is the security of individuals' personhood and rights and the method of protecting them is not by deterring violations, but only by reacting to their violations as a means of demonstrating solidarity with the victim and confirming that the victim was right to expect that her rights would be acknowledged and that she would be respected as a person partaking in human dignity.

5.3.4 Criminal Justice as Restoration of the Normative Order and the Persons Concerned

As a mechanism aimed at maintaining social peace in the sense of the integration of a society based on a generally respected normative code, criminal proceedings allow the offender, the victim and all others to put the offence behind them in a formal procedure. In this view, the process of addressing the offence, of identifying those responsible and of convicting and punishing them is a rite of passage, allowing a society to find a way to deal with and to get over the offence in a manner minimising its negative impact on a society's normative fabric and the irritation of the peaceful cooperation of its members, caused by the offence. In this sense, criminal justice isolates and contains violations of a society's basic normative code and enables them to refute and leave the offence behind. Convicting the offender restores the victim and the offender as persons and allows them and their legal community to live on as persons equally entitled to respect (Schmidt 2015, p. 186).

To this end, punishment reassures victims, in the face of the wrong they have suffered, of the validity of the normative code, of the authority of their rights, and of their reliable and robust status as members of a legal community. Convicting and punishing offenders demonstrates that the victim was entitled to expect that the offender would abide by the law, that the offender was wrong to violate the law and, as he does not get away with it, that the legal community sides with the victim in solidarity and makes sure that she is compensated as regards her material and immaterial losses.

Punishment allows the offender to make amends for her offending and on that basis to remain—or to be restored as—a member of her society. Criminal justice defines the terms and conditions under which the offender remains included in her society. The offender is offered a chance to distance herself from her offending. In any case, by holding the offender to account, criminal justice renews society's call on the offender as a fully respected person.

To all, criminal justice sends a signal of condemnation of the offence, thus making it unattractive to follow the example set by the offender. It is also a signal of reassurance that their rights are protected and that, in case of their victimisation, they will not stand alone.

The concept of criminal justice serving human dignity has a strong focus on normative categories—on norms protecting rights—and thus differs significantly from the traditional approach of 'restorative justice'.

The glossary supplementing the Handbook of Victims and Victimology defines restorative justice as a "catch-all term that encompasses a range of different interventions, all concerned to ensure the more active involvement and participation of the victim in dealings with the offender. One underlying principle of restorative justice is to reintegrate both the victim and the offender into the community with a focus on ways of making amends for what has happened" (Walklate 2007, p. 499). Karmen (2012, p. 439) identifies as the aims of restorative justice processes "victim recovery, offender sensitization to the harm caused, a cessation of mutual hostilities and a sense of closure, in which both parties put the incident behind them and rebuild their lives."

However, Dignan (in Walklate 2007, p. 312) assesses all "inspirational strands" that have merged into the restorative justice movement as "profoundly ambivalent in their attitudes towards victims." The reason is the inextricable link between the restorative justice movement and a harm-based approach. For instance, McCarney (2002, p. 3) defines restorative justice in the following terms:

> Restorative Justice begins with value statements about the primary goal of intervention and the process itself. Specifically, because crime is viewed first as harm to victims and victimised communities, the justice intervention must focus on repairing this harm, or healing the wound crime causes. The process necessarily elevates the role of the victim and focuses on victim needs, while allowing for victim, offender, and community input and involvement in a process that seeks to find common ground and attend to the mutual needs of each co-participant. [...] In Restorative Justice three [...] questions receive primary emphasis: What is the nature of the harm resulting from the crime? What needs to be done to make it right or repair the harm? Who is responsible for making it right or repairing the harm?

This model's scepticism towards the criminal justice system provides fertile ground for suggestions to divert criminal proceedings away from the traditional institutions and to look out for 'less formal' alternative solutions. Overall, these innovations have a certain potential to produce a sort of creative chaos, at the cost of weakening the rule of law and of causing inequality and systemic contradictions, such as offenders emphatically taking responsibility for crimes for which they are legally and officially still presumed innocent.

On the one hand, this exodus from formal proceedings at every available opportunity does little to reform the traditional system of criminal justice, which is so much in need of reform. On the other hand, imagining and creating better alternatives to the formal system was, in the past, a way of drawing attention to deficiencies of the traditional model. What was appreciated as advantages of alternative ways of conflict resolution corresponds to what a human-rights based model defines as necessary reforms of the traditional system. It is, for instance, praised that enabling victims to participate in restorative justice initiatives could be "very liberating in that it allows victims of crime to confront the offender and to have their say" (Reeves and Mulley 2000, p. 173). It is assumed that this marks an inherent difference between restorative justice and the formal criminal justice system. However, there is no reason to believe that criminal justice systems cannot be changed to allow victims to "confront the offender and to have their say" *within* the setting of a formal court hearing.

While an approach founded in human dignity and human rights views the objective of criminal justice as restoring the victim and the offender as persons, as well as the peace of the legal community based on the preservation of its normative order, this model radically deviates from conventional 'restorative justice' approaches, because both the individual person and society are interpreted as normative and not as naturalistic categories, as is the case in a harm-based model.

In other words, criminal justice serves the integration of societies by redressing injustices and restoring justice based on a vision of human dignity and human rights. In this view, punishment and the reparative functions of criminal justice are not in opposition to one another. Rather the conviction and, in appropriate cases, also the punishment of offenders, as well as the recognition of victims, are means of 'repairing' justice and restoring social peace. However, in a human dignity paradigm, social peace is seen as rooted in just and effective social norms. The offence has caused a fissure in the normative fabric of society and has irritated the social equilibrium in terms of a fair and equal distribution of autonomy and rights; hence the equilibrium must be restored, the fissure mended. However, only after the victim is acknowledged as an individual whose rights have been violated and the offender has redressed the wrong inflicted on the victim can the offender be rehabilitated and ultimately reintegrated in society and can offender and victim be reconciled. In this paradigm, social peace is premised on justice.

A legally binding court decision convicting the offender in a public hearing sends clear and powerful messages to the offender, to the victim and to the public. In the terms of Article 48 of the Charter, the offender is proved guilty according to the law and hence no longer presumed innocent. It is thereby publicly acknowledged that the offender has violated the rights of the victim and hence has to make amends. This is the beginning of justice being done and of overcoming the offence. None of these functions can be properly—or should be—performed outside a criminal court. Victim-offender mediation, when implemented outside a criminal court, is not a substitute for criminal justice and not a means of redressing human rights violations. Victim-offender-conferencing as a means of restorative justice merits strong support as long as it happens in court rooms or at least controlled by a court and is not moved onto an informal side-track. While a human rights approach to criminal justice shares much of the criticism passed by advocates of restorative justice on the fixation of traditional criminal justice systems on the relations of states and offenders and on neglecting the victim, leaving criminal courts behind is not an option, at least not from a human rights perspective.

5.4 In Conclusion

To wrap up the essential contents of this book, a humanist theory of criminal law and criminal justice is best defined as the sequence of the following five assumptions:

1. The survival of humanity is premised on a normative order.
2. A normative order is premised on persons who exert normative power and cooperate in creating a normative order and in mutually creating themselves as respected lawgivers within this order.
3. Individuals can exert normative power only under conditions that open and protect a space of respect and autonomy, within which normative communication can occur.
4. Such a space of respect and autonomy is premised on social norms - including prominently criminal law provisions - banning disregard, contempt, violence, threats, or manipulation and fostering respect, accountability and autonomy.
5. As social norms are public goods, their collective generation is premised on sanctions that render freeriding unattractive and assure conditional cooperators that in case of their exploitation they will not stand alone. By defending social norms and by contributing to the recognition of victims as persons who hold rights and of offenders as persons who are accountable, criminal justice minimises the negative impact of offences on a society's normative fabric.

In a nutshell: The continued existence of humanity is premised on the preservation of a normative order. The continued existence of a normative order is premised on human dignity, criminal justice and a humanist society, which spell out the minimal requirements for the continued existence of a space of normative communication under the conditions of modernity, a space, that is, within which the normative order persists and evolves, including the reproduction of persons endowed with normative power. Criminal justice contributes to preserving these preconditions of normativity by protecting the personhood and accountability of offenders, the personhood and rights of victims, and indirectly the equal personhood of all others.

The theory of a global humanist society rests on the insight in the interdependency between normativity and the (normative power of) autonomous—law-giving—persons. What preserves normativity is only the normative power of moral agents. Hence, the sustainability of a normative order is premised on continuous processes of formation of autonomous subjects, processes, that is, that call on individuals asking them to join in their constitution as persons.

The 'person' is a highly aggregated and abstract concept. As has been argued in Chapter 3, it can best be conceived as the right to have rights. As rights—or, more precisely, those rights that above are referred to as 'freedoms'—are much about access to participation in social life, the 'person' is an attributed status encompassing many potential specific statuses in various social contexts. Thus to be a person includes the right to education and, hence, to attend schools; the right to marry, to found a family and, hence, to participate in a protected sphere called family life; the right to vote and to have access to public offices as a citizen in a political sphere; rights to property, to conclude contracts and to freely choose one's occupation within an economic subsystem; the right to practice one's religion within a community of believers; the right to participate in academia or to publicly express one's opinion in media, and so on. To be a person—ideally—means to be a full member of society and, therefore, to have participation rights—as a holder of rights and obligations—in all these various social spheres and some more.

What lies at the heart of the concept of 'sovereignty' is the attributed power to create a normative order; and the most basic aspect of this power rests in the entitlement to control access to the normative order by deciding who will—and who will not—be initiated within the normative order as a person and a member of the legal community. As much as being a person is about having access to participation in various social spheres, as much sovereignty is about granting access to this fundamental status of a person within a normative order, about including—and excluding—human beings in—respectively from—personhood. Hence, the notion of the sovereign individual lies at the heart of a humanist theory.

The nation state's sovereignty finds its purest expression in the right to initiate human beings as citizens and in two fundamental rights of the nation state to exclude from this status, namely the right to exclude foreigners from immigration, from entering, that is, into a legal order and from becoming citizens, as well as the right to exclude offenders from participation in social life. In the nation state paradigm, the offence is an act of defiance and insubordination, by which the offender forfeits her status as a full citizen. In this paradigm, any punishment takes the form of ostracism, of exclusion, that is, from full participation in social life. This is clearly the case with capital punishment, incarceration and the loss of civic or political rights, and monetary sanctions, too, can be understood as reducing an individual's means of participation in social life.

It is, within this paradigm, difficult to challenge the right of the state to punish and exclude those who fail to meet the normative standards defined by the sovereign nation state.

However, in a historic perspective, the decline of the nation state is evident, and it is long overdue at least for two reasons: For the inability of nation states to secure peace, solidarity and equality at a global scale and for their inability to protect the equal rights of individuals against excessive claims of 'public interests' within nation state societies.

In a normative order based on human dignity, the offender still has to accept that she is censured and that her reputation and social standing are compromised. However, there are two fundamental differences compared to the nation state paradigm. Firstly, human dignity means that the offender's right to be a person is unconditional and irrevocable. Secondly, it follows that, if her social status is subject to qualifications, these can only be of a temporary kind. The offender has the right to come to terms with her society and to then be fully restored as a respected member of her society. What alone justifies the conviction and under certain conditions even the punishment of the offender, is her right to be respected and to be treated in accordance with her dignity. She has a right to be treated as an accountable agent and to assume responsibility for her offending. By being convicted, the offender gains the right to be restored as a person and fully respected member of humankind. What within the nation state paradigm is in the forefront of criminal justice, is the punishment of the offender as the subject who is made to suffer for the sake of the nation state's self-preservation. What within the paradigm of a humanist society takes centre state is the conviction of the offender as an act of public communication that addresses the offender as an accountable person and the victim as entitled to respect and rights.

The human rights abuse—the wrong—suffered by the victim call her status as a person into question. In this situation, the victim is entitled to the solidarity of her legal community representing, in a cosmopolitan perspective, the entirety of humankind. By demanding that the offender contributes her fair due to the preservation of the victim's primary rights, the normative community restores the victim's status as a person entitled to rights and to the respect of all others.

By insisting on the respect owed to the offender and the victim, criminal justice preserves the identity of a normative order based on human dignity and human rights.

References

Adorno, T. W. (1970). *Negative Dialektik*. Frankfurt am Main: Suhrkamp.

Bussmann, K. (1996). Kritische Kriminologie und Systemtheorie: Zur Bedeutung von Strafrecht aus systemtheoretischer Sicht. In K. Bussmann & R. Kreissl (Eds.), *Kritische Kriminologie in der Diskussion: Theorien, Analysen, Positionen* (pp. 73–122). Opladen, Germany: Westdeutscher Verlag.

Caplan, J. (1977). Lawyers and litigants: A cult reviewed. In I. Illich, I. K. Zola, J. McKnight, J. Caplan, & H. Shaiken (Eds.), *Disabling professions* (pp. 93–109). London: Marion Boyars.

Christie, N. (1977). Conflicts as property. *British Journal of Criminology, 17*(1), 1–15.

Damasio, A. (2012). *Self comes to mind: Constructing the conscious brain*. London: Vintage.

Fichte, J. G. (1800/1848). *The vocation of man* (W. Smith, Trans.). London: Chapman.

Foot, P. (2002). Morality, action, and outcome. In *Moral dilemmas* (pp. 88–104). Oxford, England: Oxford University Press.

Gross, R. (2010). *Anständig geblieben: Nationalsozialistische Moral* (2nd ed.). Frankfurt am Main, Germany: S. Fischer Verlag.

Hampton, J. (2007). In D. Farnham (Ed.), *The intrinsic worth of persons: Contractarianism in moral and political philosophy*. Cambridge: Cambridge University Press.

Hörnle, T. (2006). Die Rolle des Opfers in der Straftheorie und im materiellen Strafrecht. *JuristenZeitung, 61*(19), 950–958.
Holz, W. (2007). *Justizgewähranspruch des Verbrechensopfers*. Berlin, Germany: Duncker & Humblot.
Horovitz, A., & Weigend, T. (2011). Human dignity and victims' rights in the German and Israeli criminal process. *Israeli Law Review, 44*, 262–300.
Huigens, K. (2003). Dignity and desert in punishment theory. *Harvard Journal of Law & Public Policy, 27*(1), 33–50.
Hume, D. (1751). *Enquiry concerning the principles of morals*. (J. B. Schneewind, Ed.) (New Ed.). Indianapolis, IN: Hackett.
Hutcheson, F. (1755). *A system of moral philosophy* (Reprint.). Cambridge, England: Cambridge University Press.
Illich, I. (1970). *Deschooling society* (New edition.). London: Marion Boyars.
Illich, I. (1973). *Tools for conviviality*. London: Marion Boyars.
Kant, I. (1785). *Groundwork of the metaphysics of morals*. (M. Gregor & J. Timmermann, Eds.) (2nd ed.). Cambridge, England: Cambridge University Press.
Kant, I. (1788). *Critique of practical reason*. (M. Gregor, Trans.) (2nd ed.). Cambridge, England: Cambridge University Press.
Karmen, A. (2012). *Crime victims: An introduction to victimology* (8th ed.). Wadsworth, OH: Cengage Learning.
Law, S. (2011). *Humanism: A very short introduction*. Oxford: Oxford University Press.
Lewellen, T. C. (2003). *Political anthropology: An introduction* (3rd ed.). Westport, CT: Praeger.
Maturana, H. R. (2013). *Fundamentale Relativität: Reflexionen über Erkenntnis und Wirklichkeit (Fundamental relativity: Reflections on cognition and reality)* (1st ed.). Berlin, Germany: Deutscher Kunstverlag.
McCarney, W. (2002). *Restorative justice: International approaches*. ERA-Forum I-2002, 2–13.
Mead, G. H. (1936). *Movements of thought in the nineteenth century*. Chicago: University of Chicago Press.
Reeves, H., & Mulley, K. (2000). The new status of victims in the UK: Opportunities and threats. In A. Crawford & J. Goodey (Eds.), *Integrating a victim perspective within criminal justice* (pp. 125–145). Dartmouth, NH: Ashgate.
Schmidt, A. (2015). Täter-Opfer-Staat: Zur Stellung des Opfers im Strafrecht. In M. Asholt et al. (Eds.), *Grundlagen und Grenzen des Strafrechts* (pp. 175–200). Baden-Baden, Germany: Nomos.
Shaftesbury, A. A. C., Third Earl of. (1683). *Inquiry concerning virtue, or merit*. (D. E. Walford, Ed.). Manchester, NH: Manchester University Press.
Shapland, J. (2000). Victims and criminal justice: Creating responsible criminal justice agencies. In A. Crawford & J. Goodey (Eds.), *Integrating a victim perspective within criminal justice* (pp. 147–164). Dartmouth, NH: Ashgate.
Shue, H. (1996). *Basic rights: subsistence, affluence, and U.S. Foreign Policy* (Second with a N.). Princeton, NJ: Princeton University Press.
Smith, A. (1759). *The theory of moral sentiments*. CreateSpace Independent Publishing Platform.
Strawson, P. F. (1974). *Freedom and resentment and other essays* (1st ed.). London: Routledge.
Tugendhat, E. (2006). Das Problem einer autonomen Moral. In N. Scarano & M. Suárez (Eds.), *Ernst Tugendhats Ethik: Einwände und Erwiderungen* (pp. 13–30). München, Germany: C.H. Beck.
Walklate, S. (Ed.). (2007). *Handbook of victims and victimology* (1st ed.). Cullompton, England: Taylor & Francis Ltd.
Weigend, T. (1989). *Deliktsopfer und Strafverfahren* (1st ed.). Berlin, Germany: Duncker & Humblot.
Zauberman, R. (2000). Victims as consumers of the criminal justice system? In A. Crawford & J. Goodey (Eds.), *Integrating a victim perspective within criminal justice* (pp. 37–53). Dartmouth: Ashgate.

Table of Cases

UN Committee Against Torture

Halimi-Nedzibi v. Austria No. 8/1991, A/49/44

Judgments of the European Court of Human Rights (ECtHR)

A. v Croatia, No. 55164/08, 14 Oct. 2010

A. v the UK, No. 25599/94, 23 Sept. 1998

Acquaviva v France, No. 19248/91, 21 Nov. 1995

Adalı v Turkey, No. 38187/97, 31 March 2005

Adnaralov v Ukraine, No. 10493/12, 27 Nov. 2014

Airey v Ireland, No. 6289/73, 9 Oct. 1979

Akdivar et al. v Turkey, No. 21893/93, 16 Sept. 1996 (Grand Chamber)

Aksoy v Turkey, No. 21987/93, 18 Dec. 1996

Al-Dulimi and Montana Management Inc. v Switzerland, No. 5809/08, 21 June 2016 (Grand Chamber)

Armani da Silva v the United Kingdom, No. 5878/08, 30 March 2016 (Grand Chamber)

Assanidze v Georgia, No. 71503/01, 8. April 2004 (Grand Chamber)

Aydın v Turkey, No. 23178/94, 25 Sept. 1997 (Grand Chamber)

A. Dearing, *Justice for Victims of Crime*, DOI 10.1007/978-3-319-45048-3

B. v Moldova, No. 61382/09, 16 July 2013

Bouyid v Belgium, No. 23380/09, 28 Sept. 2015 (Grand Chamber)

Branko Tomašić et al. v Croatia, No. 46598/06, 15 January 2009

CLR - Centre for Legal Resources on behalf of Valentin Campeanu v. Romania, No. 47848/08, 17 July 2014 (Grand Chamber)

Costello-Roberts v the UK, No. 13134/87, 25 March 1993

De Cubber v. Belgium, No. 9186/80, 26 October 1984

E. et al. v the UK, No. 33218/96, 26 Nov. 2002

Eremia v Moldova, No. 3564/11, 28 May 2013

Gäfgen v Germany, No. 22978/05, 1 June 2010 (Grand Chamber)

Gorou v Greece (No. 2), No. 12686/03, 20 March 2009 (Grand Chamber)

Guerra et al. v Italy, No. 14967/89, 19 February 1998

Habimi et al. v Serbia, No. 19072/08, 3 Sept. 2014

Harakchiev and Tolumov v Bulgaria, No. 15018/11, 61199/12, 8 July 2014

H.L.R. v France, No. 24573/94, 29 April 1997 (Grand Chamber)

Husayn (Abu Zubaydah) v Poland, No. 7511/13, 24 July 2014

I.C. v Romania, No. 36934/08, 24 May 2016

I.P. v the Republic of Moldova, No. 33708/12, 28 April 2015

İlhan v Turkey, No. 22277/93, 27 June 2000 (Grand Chamber)

İpek v Turkey, No. 25760/94, 17 Feb. 2004

Ireland v the UK, No. 5310/71, 18 Jan. 1978 (Plenary)

Jalloh v Germany, No. 54810/00, 11 July 2006 (Grand Chamber)

K.U. v Finland, No. 2872/02, 2 December 2008

Kaya v Turkey, No. 22729/93, 19 Feb. 1998

Kudła v Poland, No. 30210/96, 26 Oct. 2000 (Grand Chamber)

Külah and Kuyuncu v Turkey, No. 24827/05, 23. April 2013

L.C.B. v UK, No. 23413/94, 9 June 1998

Lakatoš et al. v Serbia, No. 3363/08, 7. Jan. 2014

M.C. v Bulgaria, No. 39272/98, 4 Dec. 2003

M.C. and A.C. v Romania, No. 12060/12, 12 April 2016

Marckx v Belgium, No. 6833/7413, June 1979 (Plenary)

Mastromatteo v Italy, No. 37703/97, 24 Oct. 2002 (Grand Chamber)

McCann et al. v UK, No. 18984/91, 27 Sept. 1995

Menson et al. v UK, No. 47916/99, 6. May 2003 (Decision on admissibility)

Menteş et al. v Turkey, No. 23186/94, 28 Nov. 1997 (Grand Chamber)

Mesut Deniz v Turkey, No. 36716/07, 5 Nov. 2013

Mudric v Moldova, No. 74839/10, 16 July 2013

Murray v the Netherlands, No. 10511/10, 26 April 2016

Mustafa Tunç and Fecire Tunç v. Turkey, No. 24014/05, 14 April 2015 (Grand Chamber)

Myumyun v Bulgaria, No. 67258/13, 3 Nov. 2015

Nachova et al. v Bulgaria, No. 43577/98, 43579/98, 6 July 2005 (Grand Chamber)

Nada v Switzerland, No. 10593/08, 12 Sept. 2012 (Grand Chamber)

Nicolay Dimitrov v Bulgaria, No. 72663/01, 27 Sept. 2007

Nikolova and Velichkova v Bulgaria, No. 7888/03, 20 Dec. 2007

Norwood v UK, No. 23131/03, 16 Nov. 2004 (Decision on admissibility)

Öneryildiz v Turkey, No. 48939/99, 30 Nov. 2004

Olszewscy v Poland, No. 99/12, 3 Nov. 2015

Opuz v Turkey, No. 33401/02, 9. June 2009

Osman v UK, No. 23452/94, 28 Oct. 1998

Perez v France, No. 47287/99, 12 Feb. 2004 (Grand Chamber)

Perinçek v Switzerland, No. 27510/08, 15 Oct. 2015 (Grand Chamber)

Plattform Ärzte für das Leben v Austria, No. 10126/82, 21 June 1988

Pretty v UK, No. 2346/02, 29 April 2002

S.N. v Sweden, No. 34209/96, 2 July 2002

Sadık Önder, No. 28520/95, 8 Jan. 2004

Sakir v Greece, No. 48475/09, 24 March 2016

Salman v Turkey, No. 21986/93, 27 June 2000 (Grand Chamber)

Semse Önen v Turkey, No. 22876/93, 14 May 2002

Söderman v Sweden, No. 5786/08, 12 Nov. 2013 (Grand Chamber)

Soering v UK, No. 14038/88, 7 July 1989 (Plenary)

Stubbings et al. v UK, No. 22083/93, 22095/93, 22 Oct. 1996

T. v UK, No. 24724/94, 16 Dec. 1999 (Grand Chamber)

Tanlı v Turkey, No. 26129/95, 10 April 2001

Tekdağ v Turkey, No. 27699/95, 15 Jan. 2004

Tomašić and Others v. Croatia, No. 46598/06, 15 Jan. 2009

Ülkü Ekinci v Turkey, No. 27602/95, 16 July 2002

Uğur v Turkey, No. 37308/05, 13 Jan. 2015

V. v UK, No. 24888/94, 16 Dec. 1999 (Grand Chamber)

Valiulienė v Lithuania, No. 33234/07, 26. March 2013

Vinter et al. v UK, No. 66069/09, 130/10, 3896/10, 9 July 2013

Virabyan v Armenia, No. 40094/05, 2 Oct. 2012

X and Y v the Netherlands, No. 8978/80, 26 March 1985

Y. v Slovenia, No. 41107/10, 28 May 2015

Yaşa v Turkey, No. 22495/93, 2 Sept. 1998

Yöyler v Turkey, No. 26973/95, 24 July 2003

Z et al. v UK, No. 29392/95, 10 May 2001

Decisions of the European Commission of Human Rights

Association of Parents v the United Kingdom, No. 7154/75, 12 July 1978

Plattform 'Ärzte für das Leben' v Austria, No. 10126/82, 17 October 1985

N. v Sweden, No. 11366/85, 16 October 1986

Costello-Roberts v the United Kingdom, No. 13134/87, 8 October 1991

Judgments of the Inter-American Court of Human Rights (IACtHR)

Rodríguez Vera et al. (the Disappeared from the Palace of Justice) v Colombia, 14 Nov. 2014

Judgments of the Court of Justice of the European Union (CJEU)

Comm v Italian Republic, C-601/14, 11 October 2016

Cowan v Trésor public, C-186/87, 6 Dec. 1988

Dell'Orto, C-467/05, 28 June 2007

Eredics, C-205/09, 21 Oct. 2010

Giovanardi and Others, C-79/11, 12 July 2012

Gueye and Salmerón Sánchez, C-483/09 and C-1/10, 15 Sept. 2011

Katz, C-404/07, 9 Oct. 2008

Pupino, C-105/03, 16 June 2005

X, C-507/10, 21 Dec. 2011

Bundesverfassungsgericht (BVerfG)

Lokalderby, 2 BvR 1304/12, 23 March 2015

Gorch Fock, 2 BvR 1568/12, 6 Oct. 2014

Kunduz, 2 BvR 987/11, 19 May 2015

Lissabon, 2 BvE 2/08, 30 June 2009

Polit-Sekte, 2 BvR 2307/06, 4 Feb. 2010

R., 2 BvR 2735/14, 15 Dec. 2015 (Press Release No. 4/2016 of 26 January 2016)

Tennessee Eisenberg, 2 BvR 2699/10, 26 June 2014

W. GmbH, 1 BvR 1454/97, 31 March 2000

Court of Appeal

DSD/NBV, B2/2014/1643, A2/2014/2662 and A2/2014/2731, [2015] EWCA CIV 646, 30 June 2015

Index

A. Dearing, *Justice for Victims of Crime*, DOI 10.1007/978-3-319-45048-3

The manufacturer's authorised representative in the EU is Springer Nature Customer Service Centre GmbH, Europaplatz 3, 69115 Heidelberg, Germany. If you have any concerns regarding our products, please contact ProductSafety@springernature.com

Printed and bound by CPI Group (UK) Ltd, Croydon, CR0 4YY
01/10/2026
02225865-0014